Development, Duality, and the
International Economic Regime

*S*ÍE *Studies in International Economics* includes works dealing with the theory; empirical analysis; political, economic, and legal aspects; and evaluation of international policies and institutions.

General Editor: Robert M. Stern

Editorial Board: Alan Deardorff
Kathryn Dominguez
Barry Eichengreen
John H. Jackson
Robert Pahre
Robert Staiger
Gary Saxonhouse
Linda Tesar

Development, Duality, and the International Economic Regime

Essays in Honor of Gustav Ranis

Gary R. Saxonhouse
and T. N. Srinivasan, Editors

Ann Arbor

THE UNIVERSITY OF MICHIGAN PRESS

HD
73
.D466
1999

2002   2001   2000   1999   4   3   2   1

*A CIP catalog record for this book is available
from the British Library.*

Library of Congress Cataloging-in-Publication Data

Development, duality, and the international economic regime : essays
   in honor of Gustav Ranis / edited by Gary R. Saxonhouse and T. N.
   Srinivasan.
         p.   cm.
   Based on the proceedings of a conference hosted by Yale's Economic
Growth Center, held in May 1996.
   Includes bibliographical references and index.
   ISBN 0-472-10982-0 (cloth : alk. paper)
   1. Economic development — Congresses.   2. Income distribution —
Developing countries — Congresses.   3. Labor market — Developing
countries — Congresses.   4. Technology transfer — Developing
countries — Congresses.   5. Economic development — Effect of education
on — Developing countries — Congresses.   6. International economic
relations — Congresses.   7. East Asia — Economic policy — Case studies —
Congresses.   8. Ranis, Gustav — Congresses.   I. Ranis, Gustav.
II. Saxonhouse, Gary R.   III. Srinivasan, T. N., 1933–   .
HD73.D466   1999
338.9 — dc21   98-45155
                                                                   CIP

Gustav Ranis

Contents

Introduction

Gary R. Saxonhouse and T. N. Srinivasan

When Gustav Ranis began his scholarly career, the global economy presented a landscape of widely contrasting conditions for its participants. Notwithstanding a few spires of immense prosperity, almost two-thirds of the global population was ill fed, ill housed, illiterate, and lacking in access to proper medical care. Today, four decades later, while standards of living have generally improved and some areas of Asia, Latin America, and the Middle East have joined Western Europe and areas of Western European settlement as highly productive economies, the gap between the few wealthy economies and the rest of the world has widened. Very significant areas of the globe remain desperately poor.

To assess the current issues facing developing economies and development economics and to honor Gustav Ranis, Yale's Economic Growth Center hosted his former students, his present and past colleagues at Yale, and his fellow development economists in a conference in May 1996. From the proceedings at this lively conference, sixteen chapters have been culled and revised for this volume. With the exception of the review essay by Albert Berry and Frances Stewart, these chapters are grouped under four headings: (1) duality and the evolution of labor markets in developing economies; (2) trade, technological transfer, and economic development; (3) the international economic regime and economic development; and (4) finance and economic development. Each of these headings is related to major themes in the study of the process of economic development. Taken together, their scope includes much, though inevitably not all, of what is interesting about the study of economic development today. The topics covered by these four headings are tied together by Ranis's conception of the process of economic development.

The evolution of Ranis's view of how economic development proceeds is outlined in the review essay by Berry and Stewart, the first chapter in this volume. Their essay is as much of review of the evolution of development economics as it is on Gustav Ranis's scholarship — after all, there are few areas of development economics to which he has not made seminal contributions and fewer still that failed to attract his interest throughout his distinguished career. Berry and Stewart show how the concerns of policymakers have interacted with more general changes in economic thinking to produce what they regard as the distinctive field of development economics. At almost every step of the way in this process Ranis has made a significant contribution.

Ranis first made his mark as a major figure in development economics by showing that dualism in labor markets can play a decisive role in shaping the process and patterns of economic development. As Joseph Stiglitz, now the chief economist at the World Bank, notes in the lead chapter in the first section of this volume, duality has long been a challenge to neoclassical economics. In particular, wage differentials within a single economy have been viewed as a particular problem. A combination of labor and capital mobility and trade in goods and services should be sufficient to remove such differentials. Indeed, no one of these factors should be necessary for the removal of wage differentials. Any one of them might be sufficient by itself.

Given that what, in theory, should hardly exist remains in practice, Stiglitz asks how can duality be reduced. He argues that growth strategies will be different whether or not duality is taken as a permanent fact of economic life. In this connection, he notes that a major lesson from the success of the East Asian economies is that there need not be a trade-off between equity and growth. Indeed, policies that ensure equity may enhance growth. Stiglitz presents a series of models that depict several sources of the vicious cycles that allow poverty to perpetuate itself, but that may be broken with selective government intervention. Increasing access to education provides the clearest example of such an intervention; others include assistance in the diffusion of improvements in capital markets, actions designed to reduce the force of discrimination, and programs affecting fertility rates.

How rural labor markets operate is clearly central to an understanding of duality in developing economies. In his essay, Yujiro Hayami examines the Lewis-Ranis-Fei conjecture that wages of labor in agriculture are dictated by community norms and not by marginal productivity. Following T. W. Schultz, Hayami does find that wages in agriculture are linked to marginal productivity, but that this linkage occurs within a framework of community norms that minimizes costly transactions and stimulates employment. Hayami calls this the community-based wage.

While the community-based wage regime virtually excludes the possibility of Lewis-Ranis-Fei-style labor surplus at the onset of industrialization, as Ranis and Fei themselves observe, increases in agricultural productivity can insure the ready availability of labor for the industrial sector. Unfortunately, in Hayami's view, developing economies today have prematurely encouraged the establishment of advanced-economy institutions such as labor unions and have enacted minimum-wage laws. These factors have created dualism in developing-economy labor markets by artificially constricting access to employment in the modern industrial sector. In the Ranis tradition, Hayami recommends the promotion of rurally based small and medium enterprises as an antidote to this problem. This recommendation is in the spirit of the policy proposals outlined by Stiglitz in the concluding section of his chapter.

Stiglitz's chapter outlines how investment in education can help break down duality in labor markets. Mark Rosenzweig, in his essay, seeks to assess education's role in contributing to the overall process of economic growth. To date, the testing of alternative views and theories about the determinants of economic growth has relied on aggregate data that describe different economies at different points in time. Such aggregate cross-country data must be used because micro or household survey data typically depict a single economy at a point in time or over a time period in which there is little growth. As tests of growth theories require variations in levels of development across observations, such data are not very helpful.

Making use of newly available household data from India that cover a long time interval and different regions with differing growth experiences (driven by the differential impact of the green revolution) makes it possible for Rosenzweig to examine systematically competing hypotheses about the role of education in economic growth. Rosenzweig is able to show that the use of aggregate data can provide a very misleading picture of the role of schooling in growth. Aggregate data hides the very real and significant role that increased schooling has played in promoting economic growth in India.

Stiglitz's observation that there be no trade-off between increasing income equality and increasing economic growth is based, at least, in part on the research undertaken by Ranis, the late John Fei, and Shirley Kuo on Taiwan's experience prior to 1972. In their essay, Gary Fields and Jennifer O'Hara Mitchell find, however, that this relationship reverses after 1980. Increases in earnings differentials by gender and educational attainment between 1980 and 1993 appear to play a disproportionate role in accounting for this reversal. This is true despite educational attainment becoming more equitably distributed over this period. Perhaps only the boldest of policy interventions aimed at radically increasing access to higher education could have prevented the observed decline in income equality as the Taiwanese economy's demands for labor became ever more skill-intensive.

In their review essay, Berry and Stewart note the changing role the external sector has played in the thinking of development economists. In the 1950s and early 1960s, the latent potential of surplus labor and the key position of industrialization were stressed, while the role of the external sector was neglected. By the 1970s, as the open economy versions of the Ranis-Fei theory of economic development gained widespread acceptance, the external sector came to be seen as the critical facilitator of growth and development. More recently, it has been argued that economists have oversold the benefits of trade liberalization to developing economies. Indeed, it has been argued that trade liberalization will have no more than a onetime impact on national economic performance. T. N. Srinivasan, however, in the chapter that opens the section of the volume devoted to trade, technological transfer, and economic growth, demonstrates, using many of the traditional models of economic growth, that this view is in error. Trade liberalization can increase the long-run rate of economic growth. An examination of more recently developed models of endogenous growth in which technological transfer through trade plays a major role just reinforces this conclusion.

Srinivasan also finds that analysis of the East Asian economies' success in achieving rapid growth supports the conclusion that far from being the result of a wise government picking industrial winners and actively promoting them so as to create an investment boom, "it is their emphasis on education, enabling government intervention," as Ranis noted, "in fashioning the appropriate organizational and institutional infrastructure, reducing transaction costs and, above all, their outward orientation that are more likely to have been the driving forces."

Richard Nelson and Howard Pack also use their essay to argue strenuously against the view that the capacity for technological transfer is not an important determinant of an economy's potential for growth and development. In particular, they argue that growth accounting inevitably begs all the important questions. Complementing Srinivasan's analysis, Nelson and Pack find that in order to understand East Asian economic success, it is important to look behind their rapid rate of capital accumulation and focus on the nature of the firms there and their decision-making processes, the economic capabilities lent by the presence of a well-educated labor force, and the role of exports.

Like the Srinivasan and Nelson-Pack essays that precede it, Keijiro Otsuka's essay analyzes critical strands in the relationship between technological adaptation and East Asian economic development. Otsuka's analysis has been aided by the collection of a unique dataset that allows him to probe the sources of total factor productivity change in township and village enterprises (TVEs) in China. TVEs are generally recognized to be the major force in China's economic transformation. Surprisingly, Otsuka finds that technological transfer from the much-maligned state-owned and state-subsidized enterprises (SOEs) have played a critical role in the TVEs' success.

It is generally observed that part of the capacity to successfully use imported technology is proper maintenance. In his essay, Mark Gersovitz shows that, in fact, poor maintenance may be a rational strategy in a developing-economy environment of capital scarcity. The higher interest rates that are the result of capital scarcity can paradoxically lead to poorer maintenance of capital because maintenance, by incurring expenses in exchange for future benefits, is similar to investment, which, in turn, is generally discouraged by higher interest rates. This seemingly counterintuitive result is quite consistent with Ranis's earliest work on capital-saving technological change.

While Srinivasan demonstrates the benefits to long-run growth of trade liberalization, his analysis takes the international economic regime as given. In contrast, Koichi Hamada's essay, which introduces the third section of this volume, emphasizes the changing character of the international regime and the consequences of this change for developing economies. Hamada examines the dual role a hegemon plays as a provider of international public goods and as an extractor of economic rents through the use of its global market power. He finds the logic for these two roles quite different. As American hegemonic status has declined, it has become less interested in providing public goods and more interested in exploiting its market power.

Hamada concludes that only by introducing the element of domestic conflict into the analysis of international economic negotiations, as the theory of the two-level game suggests, can one fully account for the present state of international political economy. The domestic political structure in the United States does not seem to allow the first best solution for the United States as a nation. Similarly, other countries are bound by internal domestic conflicts. As American hegemonic power has declined, it is no longer fully capable of mitigating the impasse created by domestic economic conflicts. It is no longer fully capable of widening the "win-set" by reducing uncertainty, by changing the perception of pressure groups, and/or by creating credible threats. In this environment developing economies are the losers.

Jonathan Eaton, Robert Evenson, and their associates in their essay deal with one important element of the international economic regime as it has operated over the past century. They find a very strong home bias in the use of technology. Contrary to widespread belief, most patents have relatively little impact beyond their country of production. While, as Srinivasan and Nelson-Pack note, technological transfer has been the major force driving economic development, this transfer has taken place outside the international patent system. The originators of internationally transferred technology are receiving relatively little in the way of rents. This view is at variance with the conventional wisdom in many developing countries, which holds that economically advanced countries use their monopoly of superior technologies to exploit their poorer trading partners. Eaton, Evenson, and their associates have not yet found evidence in this area of international economic transactions that would support Hamada's conjectures.

While there is little evidence that economically advanced countries have exploited their monopoly of superior technologies, concerns that they might in the future have helped spawn proposals that poorer countries use their own near-monopoly over the world's agricultural genetic resources to bargain for a larger share of global income. In his chapter, Brian Wright examines whether the need for proper feeding of a rapidly expanding global population will actually confer this kind of market power on poorer countries. Wright finds that a rapid increase in global food supply can only come from increases in yields. Expanded cultivation and irrigation will account for very little in the way of increased supply. Increases in yields means having better breeds, but Wright finds that breeders of major crops are not highly dependent on new flows of germplasm from poorer countries. For example, there have been continuing advances in the yields of hybrid corn and soybeans despite an extremely narrow genetic base. Wright concludes that the real danger is that the attempt to capture the meager rents from the flow of new germplasm to breeders will severely compromise a worldwide enterprise that has enjoyed unprecedented success in increasing food supplies to the benefit of all consumers.

Hamada's analysis suggests that the political economy of developing countries often makes it difficult for them to remove protective barriers on their own. Gary Saxonhouse's chapter shows why Hamada is correct in arguing that the imposition of voluntary import expansions (VIEs) is outside of the "win-set." VIEs, while lowering prices in the developing countries adopting them, may still entail a loss in welfare. The benefits to developing-country consumers from a decline in prices can be outweighed by the decline in profits to developing-country firms. Surprisingly, this is likely to be the case when the hegemon's initial market share in the developing country is very small.

While the second and third preceding sections of this volume discuss international technology and trade flows, the final section is devoted to the highly topical issue of international capital flows and financial policy in developing economies. Many of the regime issues that Hamada treats in his analysis of the international trading system reemerge when the international financial system is examined. There are certainly many in developing economies who believe that as American hegemonic status has declined it has become less interested in providing public goods for the international financial system and more interested in exploiting its market power.

In the face of such an international financial environment, domestic financial stability is an issue of continuing concern to policymakers in developing economies. For policymakers confronted with crisis situations involving triple-digit rates of inflation, inability to maintain voluntary debt service, and high protectionist trade regimes, a frequent policy prescription has been to adjust the underlying fiscal imbalance and to undertake a once-and-for-all devaluation; thereafter the exchange rate should be used as a "nominal anchor for slowing down the rate of inflation."

In her chapter Anne Krueger finds that the use of the nominal exchange rate anchor is fraught with difficulties. Foremost among them is the inevitability of the collapse of the regime when reserves are sufficiently reduced so that agents are no longer willing to bet on the continuation of the regime. Even if exit from the nominal anchor can be managed prior to the breakdown of the regime, the realignment of production toward the international economy will be retarded, if not entirely postponed during the period when a nominal anchor holds sway. In addition, as long as the policy is in effect, it is equivalent to a subsidy on foreign investment in local assets, in that foreigners are assured a real return above that in domestic currency.

Krueger concludes that in societies where the costs of inflation are sufficiently high and the domestic currency has lost all credibility, however, it is possible that the very large benefits of controlling inflation outweigh the very high costs of a nominal-anchor exchange rate policy. In her view, unless circumstances are truly exceptional, however, it is doubtful whether a nominal-anchor exchange rate policy is warranted.

The underlying fiscal imbalances that provoke the crises that lead policymakers in developing economies to adopt the exchange rate as a nominal anchor are typically a set of inconsistent and known to be unsustainable policies that are being pursued for domestic reasons. To better understand the unfolding of this process, Willem Buiter provides in his chapter an examination of such medium-term and longer-term issues as government solvency and a government's fiscal, financial, and monetary policies. The empirical background for Buiter's analysis is provided by twelve former Soviet-bloc economies that have been under International Monetary Fund surveillance programs for at least some of the time since they initiated their transitions from plan to market.

One element in the adjustment process that both Krueger and Buiter discuss is foreign aid. In the final chapter of this volume, Howard Pack and Janet Rothenberg Pack analyze the long-held belief, based on a priori grounds, that foreign aid is fungible, that is, aid designated for individual sectors will be reallocated among them. Using data from Sri Lanka during the period 1960–86, they find that categorical aid was indeed fungible. Aid intended by the donor for development was converted into unconstrained income used for purposes more consistent with Sri Lanka's policymakers' preferences ignoring donor intentions. Aid was diverted not only among development categories but from development spending to current spending, revenue reduction, and deficit finance. This suggests that a government's fiscal needs can frustrate the intentions of foreign donors. For example, the many economic interventions suggested by Stiglitz in the second chapter of this volume will likely fail if they are the objective of the foreign donor alone.

The editors have had considerable help in both organizing and bringing this project to a successful conclusion. In particular they would like to thank Louise Danishevsky and the late Dorothy Nitschke of the Economic Growth Center at Yale and Irita Grierson of the Department of Economics at the University of Michigan. This project would have never come to fruition without the continuing guidance of Ellen McCarthy at the University of Michigan Press. Financial support for the conference out of which this publication grew was provided by the Department of Economics and the Economic Growth Center at Yale University and by the Committee on Comparative and Historical Research on Market Economies (CCHROME) at the University of Michigan. Much of the organization of this project took place while one of the editors (Gary R. Saxonhouse) was on a fellowship provided by the Center for Advanced Study in the Behavioral Sciences. He is grateful for their support of his work.

The editors would also like to thank Michael Boozer, William Cline, Ricardo Paes de Barros, Richard Eckaus, Robert Evenson, Albert Fishlow, Philip Levy, William Nordhaus, Dwight Perkins, Richard Porter, T. Paul Schultz, Jaime Serra, Nirola Spatafora, and John Strauss, who served as discussants of the essays that appear in this volume. Their thoughtful comments are greatly appreciated.

CHAPTER 1

The Evolution of Development Economics and Gustav Ranis's Role

Albert Berry and Frances Stewart

I Introduction

Gustav Ranis (GR)'s first publication was in 1955. The forty years that have passed since then span almost the entire history of modern development economics. They have seen considerable changes in the way economists approach the problems of developing countries and in the policies advocated. GR has made an impressive contribution to most of the successive waves of thought, while maintaining a remarkable consistency of objectives and approach. In this essay we place GR's work into the context of the evolution of thought over these years.

The premise of the essay, which also determines its structure, is that there is an underlying logic connecting the real world, thinking, and policies that explains the evolution of thought, challenging the view that development thinking, as is sometimes suggested, is subject to fashion, with changes being adopted as a matter of faddishness and as a means of profiting the purveyors and marketers of these views.[1] We trace through this underlying logic, attempting to explain the changes observed. At almost every stage of the evolution, we find that GR has made an important contribution. The next section of the essay considers the underlying framework adopted, while section III looks at developments over the past forty years in this light. The concluding section considers GR's contribution to development economics taken as whole, focusing both on his methodological approach and his overarching vision.

II The Logic of the Evolution of Development Thought

Examination of developments in thought over the last forty years suggests that the view that the changes have been arbitrary and lacking in

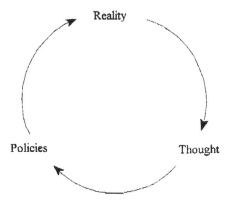

Fig. 1.1.   Thinking and reality — a simple depiction

logic is quite unjustified. It is possible to detect a complex, organic, and cumulative process involving an interaction between reality (or events in the world), thinking, policymaking, and the consequences of those policies on events in the real world that in turn affect the way the world is perceived, leading to a new cycle of thought/policy/events. This somewhat simplistic view is depicted in figure 1.1.

The view is simplistic for the following reasons: first, while our focus is on thought about developing countries, this is inevitably influenced by a parallel process of change going on with respect to economics as applied to developed countries. Because of the dominant position of developed countries and the fact that much development economics takes place in university departments whose main interest is developed countries — often by the same people — changing thought in developed countries has a very strong influence on thinking about developing countries. Thus although our main focus is on the evolution of development thought, it is also necessary to take into account a parallel process of evolution of economic thought in and about the advanced countries.

Second, the causal nexus described omits developments arising from the scientific process, which would occur irrespective of changing events. The empirical testing of hypotheses and the development of new theoretical tools generates its own process of evolution. This undoubtedly occurs — indeed, much of the work of development economists consists of this type of work, with elucidation and elaboration of existing theories in the light of analytic developments and empirical testing. This sort of advance, which we term "scientific" advance, generally occurs within particular topics rather than in the changing focus relating to "the grand issues of the subject," as Stern describes them (1989, 598). We shall focus mainly on the grand issues but will also discuss some areas of scientific advance. As we shall see, GR has contributed both to the grand sweep of changing paradigms and to scientific progress within these paradigms.

Third, thought is affected not only by objective developments leading to a revision in the way the world is perceived, but may also change as a result of the way the interests of different groups are affected by events, especially powerful groups that may influence thinking in their own favor, whether consciously or unconsciously. Moreover, changing power of particular groups can also affect which approach is dominant. We may describe the "interest group" influence as the Marxist source of the evolution of thought.

Fourth, a complication that arises in exploring the cyclical view about the development of thought presented above is that there is never a unique and universally held view of development; it is usually possible to detect a dominant strand of thought, but given the multitude of views and uneven pace at which one view gives way to another, the dominant view at any particular time is often a matter of controversy.[2] In the discussion below, for the sake of clarity of exposition, we describe the process of changing views in rather simpler and more clear-cut terms than was the reality. Figure 1.2 presents a somewhat more realistic view of how thought evolves, taking the points just made into account.

The aim of this essay is to explore the changes in approaches to the grand issues of development over the past forty years, taking as our

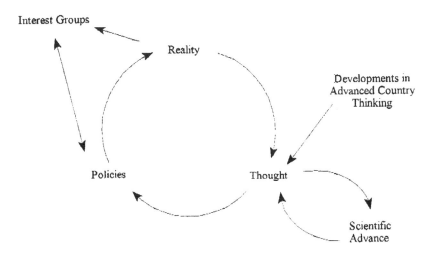

Fig. 1.2. Thinking and reality — a more complex version

basic guide to this exploration the cyclical interaction between events, thought, and policies as depicted in figure 1.1. We will discuss the contribution GR made to each stage. The major shifts in dominant thought in developed countries will be brought into consideration; but we shall generally neglect the other complications discussed above.

A summary of the developments to be considered is presented in headline form in table 1.1. We have categorized changing views into decades for convenience, although it is also true that changes seem to occur (or perhaps more accurately are perceived to occur) more often at the change of the decade than at other times.

III Reality, Development Economics, and Policy, 1950–95

1950s and 1960s

Reality/Events
For developing countries at the beginning of the 1950s the overriding reality was the situation of underdevelopment, characterized by low incomes, a predominantly agrarian structure with a large subsistence subsector, and heavy dependence on the advanced countries for all modern inputs, including goods, technology, and management. With the exception of Latin America, most countries were still colonies. The

TABLE 1.1. Changing Themes in Development Economics

Years	Dominant Strands in Developed Country Thinking	Dominant Themes in Development Economics
1950s	Keynesianism in macro-policies	Growth, planning, and industrialization
1960s	Neo-classical trade theory	
1970s	A. Keynesianism	Employment; redist. with growth; basic needs
	B. Marxism	Dependency
	C. Neo-classical revival	The role of prices and the market in resource alloc.
1980s	Monetarism and neo-classical econ.; rational expectations	Pro-market and anti-state; monetarism in macro-policy; new pol. econ.
Late 1980s to 1995	New theories of growth and trade; informational asymmetries; alternative motivations; institutions	New focus on poverty role of the state as complementary to the market; role of NGOS and communities.

important event for many developing countries during the 1950s and 1960s was the achievement of political independence, which made it possible for them to begin to determine their objectives and explore policies for achieving them for the first time. The intellectual climate in developed countries was Keynesian, favoring fiscal policies, with a strong economic role for government. This climate was a reaction both to the massive unemployment of the 1930s and the successful, planned war economies of the 1940s.

On gaining independence developing countries had two related objectives: to become economically as well as politically independent and to raise their incomes to the levels of the developed countries.

Development Thinking
The initiation of the subject "development economics" was a direct response to these objectives — indeed many of the early development economists' writings were undertaken at the request of governments of developing countries. The advice given, in general, had three prongs:

- that industrialization was an essential element in what Ranis and Fei, following Kuznets, termed the transition to modern growth;
- that surplus labor in agriculture provided a major potential resource;
- and that government intervention of various kinds was needed to tap this potential and promote industrialization.

Not all economists placed equal emphasis on each of these elements. For example, Prebisch and Singer were strong proponents of the need for industrialization to counter the deteriorating terms of trade for primary products; Rosenstein-Rodan particularly emphasized the need for government intervention to overcome externalities, while Mahalanobis stressed the need to develop capital-goods production capacity to permit accelerated investment. Nurkse stressed the potential of unused labor in agriculture.

The most important models developed at that time that incorporated the two key ideas mentioned above — the latent potential of surplus labor and the key role of industrialization in development — were those of Lewis and subsequently Ranis and Fei.[3] Lewis's model has an attractive simplicity while embodying some fundamental truths, which will, perhaps, ensure its permanent position as the first article anyone should read about the economics of development. Yet its simplicity came at the expense of both major theoretical and practical deficiencies — it dealt weakly or not at all with agriculture and the external sector. When translated into policy, the neglect of either can ensure the downfall of economies that are apparently pursuing the Lewis model of growth, as for example many African economies in the 1960s and 1970s.

The Fei-Ranis model of development is much more complex and complete. Agricultural development is a key element: they emphasize the need for "a balanced expansion of agricultural and industrial sectors," arguing that this may be achieved "via the market mechanism and the responsive dualistic landlord (Japan), via total government intervention and allocation (China) or via some intermediate 'mix' " (Fei and Ranis 1964, 215), and they show diagrammatically and algebraically that the process of economic growth may be brought to a halt through deteriorating intersectoral terms of trade if such a balance is not achieved. They also "open up" their model, allowing for trade as a "facilitator of growth" (306), but maintain that the domestic economy is paramount because of "the need to motivate and assure the participation in economic activity of the preponderant mass of economic agents which happen to reside in the subsistence agricultural sector" (306–7). A later article presented an open-economy version of the original model, identifying the need for an initial phase of import substitution to be followed by export substitution (Fei and Ranis 1975).

Technology played an important part in the model. They proposed a formal decomposition of factors responsible for changes in labor absorption in the modern sector into three elements, Hicks-neutral technical advance, changes in factor proportions, and capital accumulation (see also Fei and Ranis 1963). The proposed decomposition depends on the constant elasticity of a well-behaved neoclassical production function and is thus useful only if this view of the production function and technology change is accepted — this, of course, represents one of the central debates in relation to technology and investment.[4]

The Fei-Ranis model incorporates two types of dualism: an organizational dualism, between the traditional and modern sectors, with the former sharing output among its members and the latter obeying the principles of profit maximizing, equating marginal product and wages; and a functional dualism between agriculture and industry.

Although the policy prescriptions advocated by Fei and Ranis were not as strongly interventionist as many of the writings of the time, they did see an important role for government to ensure an adequate agricultural surplus and its transfer to support industry, to promote balanced growth between the sectors, and to lay the groundwork for the better functioning of markets. While they pointed to "limited executive capacity" (an early recognition of the importance of "governance," in modern parlance) as a reason for opposing detailed interventions, they accepted that the "need for development planning is well recognised" (1964, 199).

Criticism of the Fei-Ranis (FR) and other "labor surplus" models has centered on the meaning, existence, and quantification of surplus labor. What can one conclude, with hindsight, as to the accuracy of the perception that there was a substantial body of surplus labor in many less developed countries (LDCs) that could be harnessed in the growth process?

An important component of the Lewis-Ranis-Fei (LRF) interpretation of the labor market was the existence of an institutionally set wage in the traditional sector, involving income sharing, leading to labor market segmentation with its potential for output gain through labor reallocation. Subsequent testing of this hypothesized segmentation and its latent growth potential has generated much disagreement — partly because some of the tests related to an overly restricted version of the model, and partly because they were in any case difficult to carry out in a definitive way. Evidence comes from attempts to measure labor surplus directly, from attempts to test for predictions derived from the model, like the horizontal supply curve of labor to the modern sector, and from ex post evidence on whether economies that seem to fit the contours of the model in fact did well on the growth front. These methodological distinctions are important. The "labor surplus" concept is ultimately important because of the implication that labor of low social cost (i.e., low productivity in the traditional sector) can be reallocated with a resulting gain in overall productivity. Whether zero or even very low productivity input of labor is observed or whether the supply curve of labor from the traditional sector is horizontal or not are peripheral issues, which have too often been confused with the central policy-relevant aspect of labor surplus. For RF, it was not the existence of labor with zero marginal product in the traditional sector but rather the different institutional structure of wage determination in the two sectors that led to a potential for increasing output by reallocation of labor.

As research focused on the labor surplus hypothesis, it became clear that some of the earlier views on the extent of disguised unemployment exaggerated the reality. Berry and Sabot 1978, drawing inter alia on Kao, Anschel, and Eicher 1964, concluded that, even among the more likely candidates for harboring labor surplus, the amount of under-utilization that could be traced to the income-sharing phenomenon was more likely to fall in the range of 5–15 percent of the labor force rather than the 20–40 percent sometimes talked of earlier. The question of whether the marginal product of labor (MPL) in agriculture was zero or very low (relative to average incomes) for a high share of the labor force in such countries was hard to test and by and large not very successfully answered. Cross-section regression analyses (e.g., Desai and Mazumdar 1970 for the case of India) faced methodological complexities that left their conclusions unpersuasive. Most time-use studies (conducted more recently) revealed high levels of work effort even in those sectors of the economy where one might have expected to see a low MPL. The neoclassical school, represented most ably by Rosenzweig, has rejected the intrinsic arbitrariness of income sharing and claims that econometric evidence based on Beckerian economics contradicts both that assumption and more generally the degree of labor market segmentation (see Rosenzweig 1989). The African literature concluded that the low recorded hours-of-work figures were misleading and that land was more evidently in surplus than labor in many African countries (Helleiner 1966; Kao, Anschel, and Eicher 1964).

Empirical tests directed to ascertain whether the supply curve of labor from the traditional to the modern sector was horizontal, as portrayed in the FR model, were often viewed as tests of the validity of the model as a whole (see Staatz and Eicher 1984). Hansen (1969) argued that seasonal fluctuations in wage rates (in the context of Egyptian agriculture) demonstrated that the supply of labor was not unlimited at an institutionally fixed level, although this conclusion was questioned by Hanson (1971), using the same Egyptian data and adjusting for length of working day and seasonality. Some argued that if the labor supply elasticity is not infinite, then the labor surplus condition is not fulfilled (for example, Rosenzweig 1988). In fact, however, there need be no inconsistency between labor surplus (in the most relevant sense of the concept) and a positively sloped supply curve. FR are concerned with the dynamics of intersectoral labor supply at the aggregate level and with the social opportunity cost of labor transferred out of the traditional sector, while many critics have focused on the comparative static response of households to changes in wage rates. Some more careful students have recognized this distinction (e.g., Minami 1970, 27). What labor surplus does is to affect the position and meaning of the supply curve — that is, the supply price can no longer be interpreted as representing the social opportunity cost of labor. Though the existence of labor surplus would lead one to expect a flatter supply curve and a more stable wage than otherwise, this is a matter of degree, not of kind. Hence this body of research was not conclusive on the question of whether or what sort of labor surplus existed; because it was too often construed as a test of that proposition, it became something of a red herring.

In retrospect, it appears that neither the question of whether the supply curve of labor to the modern sector was horizontal (though it may essentially have been in a number of cases), nor the measurement of "surplus" that was econometrically attainable, provided the most useful evidence on the basis of which to judge the central implication of the model that there was potential growth to be reaped from reallocating labor from the traditional to the modern sector, especially in the context of rising agricultural productivity. Some estimates clearly exaggerated the extent of underutilized labor, and some observers underestimated the difficulty of reallocating some of the surplus which did exist. But the other sort of test, and perhaps ultimately the only valid one, is whether growth in countries or regions that appear to have had the conditions suggestive of labor surplus has in some recognizable sense benefited by those conditions.

Evidence from countries like Japan and Taiwan, which experienced rapid modern-sector employment growth without significant rise in real wages, suggests that they did draw successfully on the growth potential of the labor surplus. In so doing they were aided both by the dynamism present in the rural areas and by the absence of a policy-based gap (arising from high minimum wages, strong unions, etc.) between the supply price of labor to the modern sector and the wage paid. Moreover, it is clear that many other countries at an early stage of development have been able to expand their industrial sectors at a rapid rate without hitting a bottleneck in the form of major shortages of unskilled labor, even if wages may rise somewhat. Even less contentious is the conclusion that in many developing countries the inadequate level of productive modern-sector employment has come to be recognized as a major political problem and a challenge to the satisfaction of human needs, as we shall see in the discussion below.

To summarize, while the growth potential of labor surplus may not have been as easily and generally accessible as some optimists expected in the 1960s, a good case can be made for its having been substantial in developing countries meeting certain conditions. While the labor surplus element of FR's thinking is, undoubtedly, of less relevance to Africa than Asia, the agriculture/nonagriculture linkages in the model remain highly pertinent. One of the main errors in the early development strategies of many countries was the relative disregard for agriculture and the importance of raising productivity in that sector. Both India and China underwent forced reassessments that belatedly corrected for this mistake. One too seldom recognized contribution of a healthy agricultural sector was the expansion of its linkages with nonagriculture. The importance of such linkages, especially those located in rural areas, if a country is to achieve growth with equity, is strongly suggested by the contrast between the success of Indonesia — which has had strong agricultural growth and good rural linkages — in poverty alleviation and the slower advance in such Latin American countries as Brazil.

The accumulation of capital is a central aspect of the Lewis and Fei-

Ranis models, as it was of much of the early development literature. Capital accumulation and the financing of Japanese economic development formed the topic of GR's dissertation and were further developed in a number of subsequent works. His first publication, "The Community-Centered Entrepreneur in Japanese Development" (1955), focused, inter alia, on the fact that the both the savings and the technological-innovation proclivities of entrepreneurs and landlords are key determinants of economic progress. He contrasted the Japanese landlord of the Meiji era to Ricardo's "wastrel" type; the former "devoted himself to improvements, promoted societies for the discussion of agricultural techniques, introduced winter drainage and helped sponsor the growth of superior rice strains" (1969, 45). In Japan the main forms of "reserves of productivity" that provided the initial scope for capital accumulation were underused labor and potential productivity increases on the land (Ranis 1969, 37). Small investments in simple tools and machinery, improved irrigation, and better techniques and farm organization allowed output increases with very small additions to capital. At a subsequent stage of development, when these reserves of untapped productivity had been exploited, he suggested it was possible to finance investment without a cut in consumption by drawing on the income growth that had been achieved.

GR was aware of the limitations of capital markets in the early stages of development, when perhaps as much as three-quarters of household savings take the form of tangible assets. The limited confidence of potential savers in investors unknown to them or in intermediaries who had not established their reliability points to the need to have good investment outlets "close enough to home" so that the saver has effective control of the funds and does not have to worry about someone else's reliability. In late-nineteenth-century Japan the bulk of voluntary savings was retained rather than transferred. Investments in sericulture and cotton weaving by small landlords were adjuncts to the agricultural household and economy, accounting for about two-thirds of Japanese industrial investment at the turn of the century. (This contrasted to the South Asian preference for dowries, feasts, and gold and the Latin American preference for luxury housing—Ranis 1969, 1971a). A first step away from own control is collaboration within the family, and a second step is participation in a local cooperative venture (like the Taiwanese farmers' associations). When an economy has evolved to the stage when direct investment is no longer the preponderant method of mobilizing savings, the government needs to assist in the creation and development of an adequate institutional structure of financial intermediation. Postal savings institutions were one such contribution in nineteen-century Japan.

Today, some thirty years after it was first published, the Fei-Ranis model remains the most illuminating comprehensive model of the economy of developing countries. Its key ideas are still valid and relevant, especially for less developed countries at an early stage of development — including the need for balanced growth between agriculture and industry; the key role of savings and investment; the potential for growth via the reallocation of labor across sectors; and the idea that there are phases of development and turning points as each phase ends, and that appropriate policy may differ according to the phase. Those who give advice about the early stages of economic development could benefit greatly from an improved understanding of the ideas contained in this model.

Policies
In general, governments of developing countries accepted much of the advice that emanated from development economists: in particular, they agreed that there was an overriding need to industrialize, harnessing the surplus labor in agriculture, and that this required the promotion of savings and investment (including through state investment especially in basic infrastructure, and the encouragement of foreign investment); import-substituting industrialization was adopted with high tariffs or other restrictions on imports; the state was given a major role in determining economic priorities via price and import controls, in investment planning, and sometimes as a producer. In these respects most governments followed the more interventionist recommendations of the early development economists, rather than the milder government role supported by Fei and Ranis. Despite its neglect in some of the strategies/ models, policymakers did not entirely disregard agriculture; terms of trade were frequently adverse to the sector, but government investment in irrigation and extension, subsidization of fertilizer, and the development and dissemination of new seeds at least partially compensated for the adverse terms of trade.

Consequences
The policies adopted were in some ways remarkably successful. Savings and investment rates rose, sometimes dramatically, and growth accelerated. However, growth was uneven; in most countries it was considerably higher than before; some, notably in East Asia, began to experience spectacular growth rates, while some did less well. Social indicators, such as infant mortality and literacy rates improved substantially in nearly all countries (see table 1.2). But other developments were less welcome. Unemployment and underemployment emerged as serious problems; poverty remained very high as a percentage of the population of many

TABLE 1.2.   Developing Country Progress, 1950s and 1960s

	Life Expectancy at Birth		Percentage 5–14 at Primary School		Annual Growth per Capita Income
	1955–60	1965–70	1950	1970	1950–75
Africa	45	52	17	48	2.4
South Asia	41	49	25	59	1.7
East Asia	52	60			3.9
China	48	60	38	78	2.6
All LDCs	42	49	na	na	3.4
Developed	65	70	na	na	3.2

	Gross Domestic Savings (% GDP)		Gross Domestic Investment (% GDP)		Industry Value Added (% GDP)	
	1960	1977	1960	1977	1960	1977
Low-income	11	18	14	21	17	25
Mid-income	21	25	20	24	32	36
Developed	22	21	21	22	40	37

Source: Morawetz 1977; World Bank, *World Development Reports* (various).

countries and grew in absolute terms. The International Labor Organization (ILO) summarized the position: "it has become increasingly evident, particularly from the experience of the developing countries, that rapid growth at the national level does not automatically reduce poverty or inequality or provide sufficient productive employment" (ILO 1976, 15). Moreover, the economic independence sought was elusive, as dependence on developed countries for capital and technology increased.

1970s

The events of the 1950s and 1960s led to new thinking about development. Three distinct strands may be detected, each a reaction to different aspects of the development experience over the previous twenty years.

The principal concern of one group was the lack of economic independence achieved. The dependency school of thought developed in reaction to this; it included such writers as Frank, Furtado, Sunkel, Amin — predominantly though not exclusively from the South. They focused on the problems — including rising poverty — that they attributed to the heavy dependence of peripheral economies. For the most part, they advocated reduced links between rich and poor countries. Some took a Marxist view, others a structuralist one. While the former believed there was little that could be achieved in the context of a capitalist system, especially since the government of peripheral countries itself was typically co-opted into the system and would not attempt serious reform (see, e.g., Leys 1975), structuralists such as Prebisch, Singer, Vaitsos, Wionczek, Girvan, and Maizels attempted to identify reforms that would reduce dependency and improve the terms of North-South relations.

A second reaction was to the rising social problems that had become evident in the 1960s. It was argued that countries had been pursuing the wrong objective: Seers pointed to the need to "dethrone GNP."[5] Candidates for replacing gross national product (GNP) as the objective were successive employment, redistribution with growth, and basic needs. Seers advocated employment as the major objective of development, leading an ILO employment mission to Colombia that made full employment its central objective and did not even include GNP projections in the main body of the report, though ironically an appendix showed that achievement of the full-employment objective involved a substantial acceleration in growth of GNP.[6]

Further thought along these lines reflected the fact that employment was often not desired for itself (indeed economics has typically assumed that employment implies disutility rather than utility), but rather for the income and other benefits it confers. But much employment fails to generate a subsistence level of income. The fact that other activities (e.g., self-employment) that generate incomes would not be formally classified as "employment" in a Western sense pointed to the need for careful definition of the concept. Another major ILO employment mission — to Kenya, led by Singer and Jolly — focused on productive employment and the problem of low incomes. In proposing policies to raise the productivity and incomes of those already working (often in the informal sector) it shifted attention to that group rather than the openly unemployed. The report emphasized the need for continued expansion of the economy, advocating "redistribution from growth." This theme was taken up and developed by Chenery and others as *Redistribution with Growth* (Chenery et al. 1974). Briefly, the redistribution-with-growth strategy involved syphoning off the fruits of growth in the form of investment resources for the poor, thereby permitting continued growth while gradually increasing the incomes of the poor as they acquired assets. The strategy was never applied in the degree contemplated in this report, perhaps because of a basic political flaw in its reasoning — namely, the optimistic assumption that once elites have secured large benefits from growth they will allow a significant share even of the benefits from current growth to be channeled to the less well off.

The process of deconstructing objectives continued; incomes, it was argued, were not wanted for themselves but for the way of life they made possible. The poor had basic needs that should be met; income was a means rather than an end, and often not a very efficient means since some of the basic needs were for goods or services that were best provided by the public sector. Hence a basic-needs approach to development emerged, first in the ILO, then taken up by the World Bank. The basic-needs approach was not intended to downplay the need for economic growth, but rather to focus attention on the nature of the growth and of its distribution, so that the poor participated more in income generation and consumption. It was suggested, with considerable empirical backing, that such a strategy would tend to increase rather than reduce growth, among other reasons because healthier, better-educated people would also be more productive (Hicks 1979).

The third strand of thought dating from the 1970s and becoming dominant in the 1980s was a reaction to the differential growth performance across countries; "lessons" were derived from the successful East Asian experience in contrast to the capital-intensive and elite-dominated pattern of growth observed in many countries. It was argued that in the latter countries (which included most developing economies) the incentive system had been distorted by government interventions: the government had too large a role in the economy and the market too small a role. A pioneering work in this strand was Little, Scitovsky, and Scott 1970; others came to much the same conclusions simultaneously, for example, Cohen and Ranis 1971; Balassa 1971; Ranis 1971b; and Krueger 1974.

GR was unusual in that he made a number of important contributions to both the latter two strands and also in seeing them as inextricably connected. He contributed to each stage of the evolving focus on employment/income distribution/basic needs, and was in the forefront of those recommending undistorted (namely, market determined) prices, partly on the basis of what he had learned from the Taiwanese development experience.

Employment and Output
In two consequential papers, GR acknowledged the failure of growth to deliver in terms of employment in many countries but argued forcefully against the proposition that this meant that there was an inevitable conflict between growth and employment, or that growth should be "dethroned"; rather he suggested that growth should be given a "sturdier throne" (Ranis 1971b, 1973). The throne he proposed had two legs. The most important one was the adoption of policies that would permit

the changing factor endowment to be "heard" over time, so that the correct signals would "be transmitted to the decision-making units in a society" (Ranis 1971b, reprinted in Jolly et al. 1973, 144). He argued that distortions in prices, with artificially overvalued exchange rates, low interest rates, and biased internal terms of trade, discouraged agriculture, encouraged capital intensity, and worsened income distribution as a result of the limited employment generated and the creation of windfall profits for civil servants and others. While these conclusions were similar to those of Little, Scitovsky, and Scott (1970), Balassa (1971), and others, GR alone provided them with powerful microfoundations — the second leg of the sturdy throne. A series of industrial case studies drawn from the historical experience of Japan and the contemporaneous experiences of Korea and Taiwan provided numerous examples of labor-intensive technology choices and local capital-stretching innovations, which, it was argued, were a response to the endowment-driven factor prices prevalent in these economies. The 1973 article not only made an important contribution to the debate about whether factor proportions in developing countries were rigid (suggested, among others, by Eckaus 1955), strongly supporting the view that there existed significant technological choices; it also identified the potential for local adaptations, in what GR termed *innovational assimilations* (1973, 395). In this he anticipated the work of Katz, Westphal, and Lall a decade or more later. In the theoretical and empirical discussion of the concept of innovational assimilations, one can detect the origins of the large and burgeoning literature about the existence, significance, and determinants of "technological capability" (or "mastery").

The need for and feasibility of labor-intensive technology choices to facilitate the achievement of growth with equity in a labor-abundant country has been one of GR's recurring themes, going back to the original FR model. He has consistently been a proponent of (1) the existence of technological alternatives; (2) the importance of ensuring that firms have the right (derived from an undistorted market) incentives to use appropriate technology (AT); and (3) the proposition that rural industry is an important component of a balanced and equitable development strategy, that it almost invariably adopts AT, and that linkages with agriculture represent the key to its successful development (see below). While part of the recipe to achieve adoption of AT is a competitive setting in which firms are discouraged from simply satisficing and pushed toward the lowest-cost options, getting the most out of the small-scale and substantially rural nonagricultural sector involves something more. A market solution needs to be complemented by institutional reform to ensure that the small-scale activities get an adequate share of credit and foreign exchange (Ranis and Stewart 1990, 37). Further, "An effective AT policy usually requires a more egalitarian distribution of income and assets, both to secure markets for appropriate products and to increase rural linkages."

Employment in the Philippines
In 1973, GR led an international team of thirty-one in one of the ILO's major employment missions (ILO 1974). Like its predecessors, this mission made a substantial contribution to the debate about growth and employment. For the Philippines it became a landmark report against which reforms, even today, are judged.

The report starts by summarizing a Philippine development process very similar to the general LDC experience recorded above: a proindustrialization phase after independence was based on import-substitution brought about through an overvalued currency, protection, low interest rates, and fiscal incentives. The result was a satisfactory rate of growth (6 percent per annum, 1950–70), but an economy that "provides a striking example of the inadequacy of conventional aggregate criteria (sic) of economic growth . . . to judge past development performance" (ILO 1974, 5). Persistent high underemployment and high and worsening income inequality had accompanied the growth.

Both diagnosis and prescriptions focused on two issues that had been treated lightly, if at all, in the previous ILO employment reports — the central issue of rural development and the need for expansion of labor-intensive industrial exports. While the Philippines' agricultural growth had been better than average by international standards, at 4 percent per annum, a weak performance by rural nonagriculture and a deteriorating income distribution prevented the rural sector from absorbing enough of the growing population — contributing to rapid urban migration, which the sluggish growth of employment in the rather capital-intensive industrial sector failed to absorb. Industrial labor-intensive exports, a potential alternative source of foreign exchange and employment, failed to grow, it was argued, largely because of the protectionist macropolicies.

The policies the report proposed to correct these problems contained a balance of government action and reform of incentives. "Rural mobilisation requires the fiscal and organisational energy and imagination of the Government" (ILO 1974, 29). Action recommended included land reform, investment in appropriate infrastructure, and technical assistance for small- and medium-scale industry. For the industrial sector, the main emphasis was on policy reform, with a more realistic exchange rate, reduced protection, fiscal incentives, and higher interest rates. It was also argued that "wage policies must try to protect the working class against further erosion of their real incomes, so that the consumption levels of the lowest income groups are protected" (46).

Income Distribution
Considerations of income distribution were central to GR's thinking from the start. When he and Fei were working on their model, the main hypothesis on the table with respect to the dynamics of distribution in developing countries was that of Kuznets. Lewis had seen his labor surplus framework as an updating of the classical model of Ricardo: as such it had implications for the functional distribution of income, but the household distribution was not introduced directly. Kuznets (1955) postulated that typically the inequality of household income distribution over time first increases (as differentiated incomes in the high-income modern sector rise above the relatively homogenously low incomes of the traditional economy), then decreases as the modern sector comes to encompass most of the economy.

The FR 1964 model incorporates many of the factors most likely to influence distribution in the early and middle stages of development, when labor is not yet very heterogeneous, the tax-and-transfer system is little developed, and income sharing among the large extended family helps to protect family members from unemployment or other misfortune. These factors included the rate of capital accumulation, the factor intensity of technological change, and population growth; special attention is directed to the "turning point" when all of the surplus labor has been absorbed and the urban wage rate starts to rise. At this point, FR argued, the functional distribution of income is likely to begin to improve and with it the household distribution. FR thus accepted the Kuznets hypothesis as generally applicable to the early-stage developing countries, arguing that the Kuznets's distribution turning point would occur when labor surplus was exhausted.

But GR did not consider this outcome inevitable. Drawing on his important and detailed study of the path of income distribution over time in Taiwan with Fei and Kuo (Fei, Ranis, and Kuo 1979; Kuo, Fei, and Ranis 1981), GR concluded that the Kuznets effect was "apparently avoided in Taiwan during a period of unusually rapid growth, and it is undoubtedly this fact, running counter to the generally prevailing evidence, which renders the Taiwanese case of such particular interest" (1978, 397). He viewed the presence of one thoroughly documented counterexample as important in confronting the dominant school of "trade-off" pessimists.

To facilitate their analysis of the *sources* of changing income distribution in Taiwan over several decades, Fei, Ranis, and Kuo (1978, 1979) developed a new method of decomposing changes in the Gini coefficient.

Although data for the pre–1964 period are much less reliable than those from that date, they suggest a sharp decline in inequality, the most obvious interpretation of which is the land reforms carried out in the immediate postwar years. After this effect had been felt but before the economy's turning point, which they date at 1968, distribution improved further, with the dominant factor being the reallocation of rural workers from agriculture to nonagriculture. After 1968, the latter factor was complemented by an improved functional distribution among urban households. Such an impressively detailed analysis of the sources of changing household distribution over time has rarely been reproduced, though the methodology has been applied in both Colombia and Pakistan (Ayub 1977; Ranis 1980); where data permit, replication of the Fei, Ranis, and Kuo (FRK) approach across a series of different types of countries would be enormously instructive.

Basic Needs

GR also contributed, with Fei and Stewart, to the evolution of the basic-needs (BN) approach, helping to develop a macroframework, relating the degree of satisfaction of such needs to the level, growth, and distribution of national income, the sectoral allocation of this income, and organizational features within the major sets of actors, government, private sector, and households (see Fei, Ranis, and Stewart 1985; Ranis 1984). A particular contribution of the work was to identify the objective of a BN approach as being improvements in people's lives (described as "the full life objective"), defined by such characteristics as longevity, health, nutrition, and educational attainments. A certain set of goods and services — for example, health services, food, schools, and sanitation — were then identified as means to achieve the BN objective — not as the BN objective in themselves. Attention was thus focused on the critical empirical relationship between the means (or BN goods and services) and the objective; this relationship, which obtains at many levels — for example, the macroeconomy, the region, the household, or even the individual — was termed the "meta-production function." More empirical information about this key relationship was regarded as essential for the identification of appropriate policies for BN.

The distinction between means (the BN goods and services) and ends (the full life), and the positioning of BN in a macrocontext, were significant departures from previous BN approaches, which had mostly identified the objective in terms of an often somewhat arbitrarily defined set of BN goods and services, such as health services, water supplies, and so forth. This tendency often led to an excessive focus on public-sector delivery of the set of BN goods and too little attention to the need for the economy to grow and the poor to earn incomes to sustain BN fulfillment. The goods-centered approaches were thus subject to the criticism, advanced by Sen and others, of "commodity fetishism."[7]

Policies

Among the major international institutions the ILO was the initiator first of the employment focus and subsequently of the basic-needs approach (ILO 1976).[8] The latter was taken up by the World Bank under McNamara as well as by major bilateral aid agencies, who made basic-needs promotion a major element in their dialogue with governments of developing countries. The United Nations special agencies also adopted a series of BN-style targets in the 1970s, such as universal primary health care and universal primary education. Unfortunately, few developing countries put BN at the center of their development strategy or pursued serious redistributive policies, and in the majority of countries the share of the budget going to the social sectors decreased over the decade. Still, absolute expenditure per capita on health and education did increase in most countries, many made considerable strides toward universal primary education and health care, and some adopted food subsidies and rations and employment schemes. For the most part, those countries that did give a significant role to the satisfaction of BN were those that had already decided to do so for their own reasons, the origin of their policies predating the international advocacy of BN—for example, Sri Lanka, Costa Rica, and several states of India.[9]

In general, it seems, developing-country governments were more impressed by the conclusions of the dependency school, particularly its milder "structuralist" version, and regarded the BN approach recommended by the advanced countries with suspicion, as an excuse to avoid the demands of the New International Economic Order (NIEO). The underlying belief of the dependency school was of the unfairness in the world's economy: this formed the background to OPEC and its successful efforts to raise oil prices and the NIEO put forward by the G77 in 1974. Other policy manifestations of the dependency approach were the restrictions on direct foreign investment and controls over technology transfer that were introduced most comprehensively by the Andean Pact countries and India, although elements were adopted in many other countries.

Formally, the two approaches were not inconsistent—achieving NIEO would have assisted in promoting basic needs and vice versa. But politically they were, as Galtung put it, "two philosophies on a collision course" (see also Stewart 1982). It is noteworthy that the majority of the thinkers associated with the employment/income redistribution/basic-needs school were from the North, and the official institutions that took it up — including some aid ministries as well as the ILO and World Bank — were Northern dominated. This was also true of the promarket school of thought. In both cases, of course, there were also significant contributions from prominent economists from the South, working in Northern institutions. In contrast, the members of the dependency school were largely Southern, and their message was taken up by Third World governments, and also, to an extent, by the United Nations Conference on Trade and Development (UNCTAD), whose creation was itself a response to pressure from developing countries.

As far as general economic policies were concerned, most countries sustained the previous inward-looking macroeconomic and interventionist policies, which were supported in many cases by heavy borrowing abroad (see below). The challenge to these policies, noted above, had little impact at this stage.

Consequences

The employment/basic-needs strand of thought had some effect in altering aid priorities (fig. 1.3). It is less clear that it had much effect on developing-country policies; although there continued to be progress in meeting basic needs over these years (fig. 1.4), there was no evidence of acceleration, taking developing countries as a whole. In fact, it is easy to argue that structuralists from the dependency school, in a context in which Keynesian policies were being followed in developed countries, had a much more substantial effect on the world economy. In the sellers' market created by high world demand, the belligerent attitude of the oil producers led to the oil price rise of 1972–73, which created massive imbalances in the world economy and inflationary pressures in developed countries. Moreover, suspicion of and restrictions on direct foreign investment inspired by the dependency school endorsed the switch to direct borrowing by LDC governments and public enterprises from the commercial banks that occurred in the recycling of the oil surpluses. Keynesian views of economic policy also lent respectability to the policy of borrowing to sustain economic growth that most oil-importing developing countries adopted over the decade of the 1970s.

The accumulation of debt, budgetary, and trade imbalances that were associated with these policies in developing countries were made worse by a further increase in oil prices in 1978–79. In developed countries, inflation rates accelerated. These changes were responsible for a massive turnaround in thinking in both developed and developing countries.

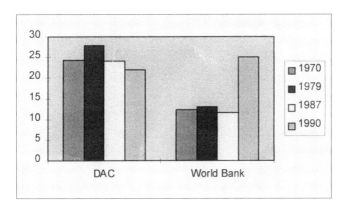

a. Social infrastructure as a percentage of aid, 1970–90

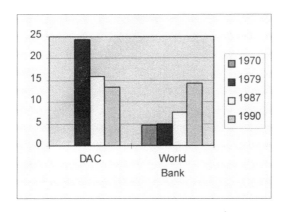

b. Health and education as a percentage of total aid, 1970–90

Fig. 1.3.   Aid priorities and basic needs. (From DAC Reports, various [Paris: OECD].)

1980s

The first and most important revolution occurred in developed countries, Thatcher (from 1979) and Reagan (1981) espousing monetary policies, in principle, if not always in practice.[10] This had the immediate effect of raising world interest rates, ushering in world recession and a downward movement in commodity prices. It also — although

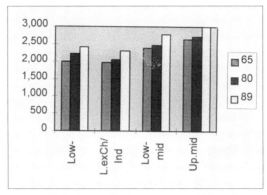

a. Calories available per capita, 1965–89

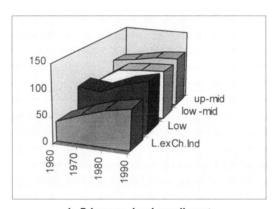

b. Primary school enrollment

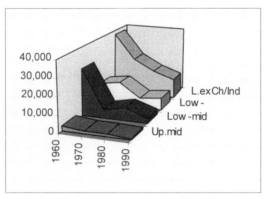

c. Population per doctor, 1960–90

Fig. 1.4.   Progress in meeting basic needs, 1960–90. (From World Bank, *World Development Reports,* various.)

this took longer—imparted a new monetarist, antigovernment, pro-market, laissez-faire philosophy that permeated the international finan-cial institutions (IFIs), bilateral aid administrations, educational estab-lishments in developed countries, and eventually the "technocrats" in developing countries who had been educated in these establishments. The view that the state in developing countries had overreached itself had already been powerfully espoused in the early 1970s by a succes-sion of promarket observers—as noted above. Essentially, they pointed to the inefficiencies associated with government interventions in most areas of policy, including trade, prices, and production, arguing for a smaller role for governments and a greatly enhanced role for the mar-ket. Discrediting of what came to be termed *dirigisme,* with the view that government failures almost invariably outweighed market failures, was carried further in the early 1980s by Lal 1983, Bhagwati 1982, and Little 1982.

The "new political economy" (NPE) took the virtues of an all-embracing market for granted and focused on explaining why govern-ments were almost universally prone to "failure," including failing to "liberalize" (i.e., extend the realm of the market) despite the recommen-dations of neoclassical economists. Krueger's rent-seeking hypothesis provided a starting point, while Bates, a political scientist, pointed to the underlying political economy of African states, which, he argued, tended to be captured by urban elites, to explain why governments chose suboptimal policies.[11] The normal neoclassical assumption of indi-vidual maximizing behavior was subsequently applied to political and bureaucratic behavior by economists (such as Lal 1984; Conybeare 1982; Bhagwati 1982; Srinivasan 1991), drawing on the work of Buchanan and Tullock.[12] This replaced "the image of the benign state with its mirror opposite, the negative state" (Grindle 1991, 43). The actions of self-seeking individuals (bureaucrats and politicians), or groups of individu-als, led to individual rent-seeking, group short-termism, and state preda-tions, arguing for a minimalist state that would do least damage to social welfare.

GR made a different and original contribution to the political-economy debate. He started at the same point: that the promotion of liberalization is desirable and its rejection is welfare-reducing for society as a whole. But whereas the bulk of NPE essentially did little more than apply to developing countries the conceptual approach of Buchanan and Tullock, Ranis and Fei 1988 (and subsequently Ranis and Mahmood 1992) looked to a country's resource endowment as the fundamental source of differential government performance toward liberalization. The hypothesis was that in economies with relatively abundant natural resources, wrong (i.e., import-substituting, monetary expansionist, etc.) policies were affordable and were therefore readily reverted to, whereas in natural-resource-poor countries they could be maintained only at very high cost (i.e., low incomes). Moreover, natural-resource-rich countries earned rents that facilitated under-the-table payments, involving corrupt practices and distorted resource allocation, while natural-resource-poor countries had no such ready source of patronage and were therefore forced to rely on taxation and aboveboard payments, which led to better and more transparent resource allocation. The changing economic cycle faced by natural-resource-rich countries (as the international terms of trade swung) were, it was suggested, reflected in a policy cycle. Thus when primary-product prices were high, there was little immediate incentive for reform; as the prices fell, incentives grew to encourage diversification and efficiency and control inflation; but at the nadir of the cycle, acute shortage of foreign exchange led to a reimposition of controls. Paired-country comparisons provided evidence for both parts of the hypothesis: namely, that natural-resource-rich economies were less inclined to liberalize altogether and more prone to a policy cycle. The large amount of evidence Ranis and Mahmood produced in general supported both hypotheses, but — as is unavoidable with such pairs — the choice of pairs may be partly responsible for the conclusions. For example, a comparison of natural-resource-rich Indonesia with the Philippines might lead to different conclusions from the Thailand/Philippines comparison provided. Despite such qualifications, the work points us in important directions — on the one hand, producing convincing evidence that there is some sort of "Dutch disease" that applies to policymaking as well as to economic variables; on the other, in making the exploration of the determinants of policymaking a subject for careful empirical investigation across countries, and not simply a matter of a priori reasoning.

Policies

By 1980, the antistate, promarket philosophy had been adopted by the World Bank, whose power over policymaking in developing countries enormously increased with the onset of an acute debt crisis and the initiation of structural-adjustment loans. While the World Bank emphasized deregulation, advocated reduced price controls, subsidies, and tariffs, and pushed for the elimination of restrictions against direct foreign investment, the International Monetary Fund (IMF) promoted the monetarist view — that the prime objective of macroeconomic policy should be to eliminate budgetary and trade imbalances through tight control over the budget and money supply.[13] Considerations of poverty reduction or basic needs virtually disappeared from the policy views of these institutions. The IFIs' growing control over policymaking in developing countries was one reason why monetarism and deregulation were adopted, in part at least, in the majority of developing countries over the course of the 1980s.[14] Some countries adopted the policies on their own, suggesting that some of the NPE theorists were excessively determinist about policymaking.

Consequences
For the regions most subject to Washington tutelage — Africa and Latin America — the stabilization and adjustment policies were accompanied by falling GDP per capita for much of the 1980s, worsening income distribution in many cases, falling real expenditure per head on social services, and rising private and social poverty. In many African countries there was evidence of rising malnutrition. In a number of Latin American and African countries, educational enrollments and achievements fell off. Investment rates fell. Despite strong efforts, the imbalances were often not eliminated, as falling commodity prices and continued accumulation of debt made the situation more difficult. Although it does not appear that economic or social performance was systematically worse in "adjusting" than "nonadjusting" countries — and may have been marginally better — the large and widespread rise in poverty led many to question the apparent elimination of human concerns from the development agenda.[15]

Late 1980s–1995

Thinking
The stabilization and adjustment policies of the 1980s were criticized from two perspectives — for their failures with respect to poverty and for the simplistic economic (and political) model that underlay them.

Institutional concern with the rising poverty associated with the policies was initiated in the mid-1980s by UNICEF and rapidly gained support (Cornia, Jolly, and Stewart 1987). From 1987, the World Bank's staff guidelines required policy framework papers for low-income countries to include "a brief description and assessment . . . of the social impact of the government's intended adjustment program." However, the centrality of the Bank's concern with poverty began in 1990 when the *World Development Report* focused on poverty. This was followed in 1992 by the World Bank's *Handbook of Poverty Reduction.* The president, Lewis Preston, declared that "poverty is the benchmark against which we must be judged." There were also changes at the IMF. In 1990 Camdessus, managing director of the Fund, acknowledged that "macroeconomic policies can have strong effects on the distribution of income and on social equity and welfare. A responsible adjustment program must take these effects into account, particularly as they impinge on the most vulnerable or disadvantaged groups in society" (Camdessus 1990). Subsequently, each IMF country mission was required to report on the poverty implications of country programs. A similar concern was exhibited by United Nations Development Program (UNDP), which published its first *Human Development Report* in 1990, focusing on the human dimensions of development. "People are the real wealth of a nation. The basic objective of development is to create an enabling environment for people to live long, healthy, and creative lives" (UNDP 1990, 9). The quality of human lives, both as the central objective of development and as a critical development resource, has been a central theme of development thinking in the 1990s.

Intellectually, these views have their antecedents in the poverty and basic-needs concerns of the 1970s, with many of the same people involved.[16] Their ideas were enriched by A. K. Sen's work on capabilities, which comes to very similar conclusions, and was especially influential in the UNDP (e.g., Sen 1985; Dreze and Sen 1990). The ideas, for the most part, were not new; the change lay in the fact that they were taken up in a serious way by significant actors. This was partly due to the severe consequences of neglecting poverty, not only in terms of unacceptable levels of misery but also of the economically costly destruction of human resources.

In parallel with the focus on the neglect of poverty, the economic model underlying the adjustment philosophy was also reviewed critically. One source of criticism was the relatively weak economic performance of many of the "adjusting" countries, especially the falling investment rates. Another was the failure of the model to capture essential elements of the successful East Asian cases (Wade 1990; Amsden 1989; Lall 1994; Pack and Westphal 1986). In both Taiwan and Korea, the government was shown to have played a much more active role than allowed for in the market model; high savings and investment levels, good human resources, and well-developed institutions (private, public, and community) were also important features of their experience.

Theoretical critiques of the model also gained ground: these included the key role of institutions in development and the importance of history in determining a country's institutions (initiated in the historic studies by North); the assumptions about individual motivation (led by Sen, Bowles, and Gintis, and socioeconomists such as Etzioni);[17] assumptions about information (with a series of important articles on the implications of asymmetric information by Stiglitz and others); new developments in growth and trade theories emphasizing the importance of learning, economies of scale, oligopoly, and externalities (Lucas, Roemer, Krugman, and others); deficiencies in the assumptions in the pure market model about technology and the role of technological capability (following the work of Katz, Westphal, Pack and Westphal, and Lall); and critiques of the views of the new political economists (Bates, Grindle, Toye). Such work is, of course, ongoing.

As a consequence of these criticisms, the views of Killick that the exclusively promarket stance of the early 1980s was "a reaction too far" came to be widely shared. While the economic critique taken as a whole did not gain dominance in such institutions as the World Bank and the IMF, two aspects have been accepted — the importance of human resources and the need to raise investment rates (see, e.g., World Bank 1993).

GR has made significant contributions to the revisionist agenda, while retaining a strong belief in markets as the most effective allocator of resources, and a suspicion of the predatory propensities of governments.

The Role of Institutions
GR's interpretation of the East Asian experience emphasizes the role of institutional development and appropriate government action to facilitate the efficient and equitable operation of markets (e.g., Ranis 1992a, 1992b, 1995). In so doing it reflects also his lifetime philosophy:

> This paper rejects both the claims of those who see the East Asian story as one of the application of pure laisser-faire and the more recent revisionist view that it all resulted from a highly intrusive government. Instead, the paper emphasises the role of institutional/ organisational changes orchestrated by a government which was both sensitive to these systems' initial conditions and to the importance of setting the stage for the fullest participation, through markets, of large numbers of dispersed private actors. (Ranis 1989, 1443)

> Early in the transition, there is likely to be a greater need for the organizational and investment contributions of government: later on, given the increased complexities of the development process, lower transactions costs of markets will begin to carry more weight — but in a context of a changed, not a diminished role for government. (Ranis 1992a, 100)

The Role of Trade Policy

By the early 1980s, advocacy of an almost unadulterated free-trade policy was the dominant perspective. Adherents based their conclusions partly on static trade theory, latterly also giving much attention to the dynamic advantages of freer trade in terms of faster productivity growth (Pack 1989).

As noted above, GR was an early critic of the inefficiencies of ISI, and a supporter of the moderate sort of outward orientation broadly followed by Korea and Taiwan (Ranis 1971a). But like his former Yale colleague, he has been wary of what Diaz-Alejandro (1980) referred to as the "mischievous revisionism" of the harder-line supporters of outward-oriented policies. He notes that the ISI phase in Korea and Taiwan was qualitatively similar (overvaluation, etc.) to those in other LDCs, but generally milder (e.g., lower effective protection) and more flexible (Ranis 1985a, 254). When the primary import substitution phase in these countries — lasting about ten to fifteen years — came to an end with the slowdown in growth of domestic demand for nondurable consumer goods, the countries had to choose between a deeper phase of ISI or a switch to the export of nondurables. After some hesitation they opted for the latter, in the process putting an end to overvalued exchange rates, reducing protection, and bringing interest rates closer to equilibrium rates. A primary export substitution phase followed, which reached its limits when the unskilled labor supply tightened in the early 1970s (Ranis 1985a, 258), at which time the two countries moved into production of capital goods, consumer durables, and so on for domestic and international markets.

Though it was clearly important, GR did not consider trade policy to be the crucial factor in successful development. In Taiwan the mobilization of the rural economy, before the labor-intensive export phase got under way, was the key (Ranis 1990b, 141). Agricultural productivity increase provided the main initial motor of growth, and rural industry played a significant complementary role, absorbing agricultural labor and savings and contributing to the rapid increase in rural incomes, which in turn fueled the demand for locally produced consumer goods. This successful mobilization reflected an unusual degree of policy attention to raising agricultural productivity, to a relatively equal distribution of assets, especially land (thanks to reforms in the earlier Japanese period and then after the war), and to good levels of literacy and general education.

GR has been a strong advocate of the general relevance of the "East Asian model," arguing that the key policy instruments can and should be put into play in other countries (e.g., Latin America) and that its value is not significantly constrained by the "fallacy of composition" argument put forward by Cline (1982). GR's refutation of that argument relied on the fact that since at any given time different LDCs are at different stages of their development processes, not all would be entering the same markets at that time, and that the increasing share of LDC-manufactured exports that go to other countries of the South significantly improves export prospects (Ranis 1985b, 544). It would appear from the fast growth of the second wave of East Asian exporters that events have thus far supported GR's view, although the entry of China and India simultaneously into light-manufacturing markets may test the proposition in a more severe way.

Although growth rates during the primary ISI subphase were generally as high in Latin America as in East Asia (Ranis 1985a, 265), Latin American development strategies suffered weaknesses whose effects were costly later, including paying too little attention to food-producing agriculture. These countries opted for the second stage of ISI after the first one petered out, and increased their levels of protection accordingly. When, more recently, the Latin American newly industrialized countries (NICs) started to export manufactured products, a smaller share than in East Asia fell in the labor-intensive light-manufactures category and more in high-tech areas like cars and aircraft, often related to government's willingness to subsidize. Unlike the cases of Korea and Taiwan, this phase was not preceded by a change in the overall policy package; rather, particular industries or firms were selected for encouragement by tax subsidies and other assurances of windfall profits.

Although he puts less weight on trade issues than many others, GR agrees with the dominant view that ISI has been damaging to the growth performance of many LDCs and has also contributed to negative distributional outcomes, as in Latin America. Though there can be no quibbling with the success of a Taiwan or a Korea, it is clear we need to probe more deeply into the growth and distribution outcomes associated with trade and related policy packages. While there were many problems in Latin America during the ISI phase prior to the debt crisis, it should not be forgotten that the regional growth performance was good. GDP grew at or above 5.5 percent over a thirty-year period, enough to let incomes per capita rise by 3 percent per year over that time. The once reasonable belief, shared by the majority of economists who have studied the Latin economies in detail, that ISI contributed to the high observed levels of inequality, must now be questioned in light of new insights into trade-distribution links and the fact that the last twenty years have seen widespread increases in inequality, simultaneously with the introduction of trade and other policy reforms (Berry 1997). There are, of course, competing interpretations; Morley (1995) places much of the blame on the economic crisis of the 1980s, and others focus on technological change. (Even the view that ISI was systematically damaging to growth in Latin America will appear less evident if the region's still anemic growth rate does not soon accelerate.) If the evidence ultimately implicates the reforms in the increase in inequality, one of the hoped-for pluses from their introduction will have turned into a minus, and there will be an urgent need for correctives. Possibly the error of those who predicted the opposite will have been an excessive focus on the trade variable to the neglect of the surrounding context. The range of experiences under both ISI and outward orientation calls for the richness of analysis and the capacity to construct useful typologies that have been the hallmarks of GR's career.

Human Development
In the 1990s GR made major contributions to the ideas contained in successive *Human Development Reports*. The premise of these reports, as noted above, is that human development (HD) is both end and means of development. In the first report he was largely responsible for categorizing country performance and government policies toward HD according to success in achieving and sustaining HD.

Rural and Urban Linkages
The rather elusive concept of linkages has had a prominent place in development economics at least since the work of Hirschman (1958). GR's emphasis on the importance of intersectoral linkages dates back at least to the 1964 model. While consistently emphasizing the importance of rural and agricultural mobilization as the first requirement of successful development,[18] an integrally related aspect of GR's work has been the emphasis on the importance of rural nonagriculture and the linkages between the two sectors.[19] He noted with satisfaction in the late 1980s that most policymakers and economists had by now given up the idea that "a rapid drive toward industrialization could be counted on to drag the agricultural sector along with it" (Ranis 1990a, 139) but also noted the continued failure to recognize that "what needs to be focused on in most LDCs is rural development rather than simply agricultural development, as part of a domestic balanced growth strategy" (140).

In GR's recent work he has explored linkages in greater depth, focusing first on agriculture-nonagriculture linkages in rural areas (Ranis 1990b; Ranis and Stewart 1993) and subsequently on linkages between the urban formal and informal sectors. The various rural linkages were differentiated, their strength explored in different contexts, and policy measures that might promote a virtuous cycle of agricultural/nonagricultural development assessed. Ranis and Stewart (RS) adapted the Hymer-Resnick model to modern conditions, showing that with a dynamic agriculture and new investment and technologies in rural nonagriculture the decline of Z-goods predicted by Hymer-Resnick need not occur. A similar approach to urban linkages has distinguished a modernizing component of the urban informal sector, with strong linkages to the urban formal sector, which, under favorable conditions, can be expected to generate growing incomes and employment, and a traditional component that has few linkages to the formal sector, where incomes are very low and stagnant, and that can do little more than provide minimal subsistence to that part of the urban labor force which cannot find employment elsewhere.

Consequences
Doubts must remain about how seriously the newly popular poverty agenda is being taken. The World Bank has made relatively minor amendments to its policy stance, and the IMF almost none. The record of World Bank–inspired programs to reduce poverty—for example, the social funds and the attempts to redirect public expenditure and target benefits—have generally been poor. The UNDP's human-development initiative has been widely welcomed by governments of developing countries, and a number of specific plans have been drawn up to accelerate progress in this area. However, the largest recent impact on both poverty and human development has probably occurred through the resumption of growth, following the alleviation of the debt problem and renewed private-resource flows to developing countries. "Trickle-down" has been vindicated by observing how much worse the situation is when average incomes are falling (see Fields 1989). In those few cases where growth has favored the poor (e.g., focused on agriculture and labor-using manufactured exports, as in Indonesia [see Ravallion and Huppi 1989]) poverty reduction effects have been much more marked.

The critical reaction to the cruder versions of the proliberalization and antigovernment philosophy have not yet been translated into policy in any obvious way. But the role of government in providing physical infrastructure and developing human resources has been much more widely acknowledged. It also seems likely that a more interventionist government stance may receive increasing attention under the growing influence of Japan in international institutions.

Conclusions

This review has aimed to present a broad sweep of the "grand issues" of development, highlighting the sequence from events to analysis, from analysis to policies, and from policies to events. In doing so, we may have oversimplified the chronology of ideas — in fact, elements of thinking on each of the grand issues can be found both before and after the decade with which they are identified here. Moreover, many would dispute whether a particular strand of thinking has been "dominant" at a particular time, since typically many strands were present simultaneously. The discussion has also failed to allow adequately for either the scientific or the Marxist interpretation of the evolution of thought as defined in the introduction.

On the former count, though it would be an exaggeration to describe the bulk of research in development economics as systematically scientific, the progress made through careful development and testing of hypotheses in the areas reviewed above has certainly been substantial. It reflects the increasing research effort and availability of relevant information, the advance of econometric techniques, the opportunity to use computers, and so on. General-equilibrium models made their entry into the arena. So, rather belatedly, has a healthy suspicion of the excessive dedication to the idea of equilibrium in economic analysis. The professional contribution of researchers notwithstanding, the Marxist interpretation (that the conclusions toward which the subdiscipline's consensus moves are determined a good deal by the influence of interest groups) cannot be discounted, since it is clear that the institutional location and the sources of finance for research have affected the face of the literature. Expectations and presumptions weigh heavily on the conclusions reached; too often the best predictor of the results of a piece of research is the researcher's views before doing it. It is unavoidable and probably essential for efficiency in research that one start with a set of "priors," but they are also the biggest source of bias and error in the results. Meanwhile, the clear differences between Northern- and Southern-dominated schools of thought is an indication of the relevance of the Marxist interpretation. In a postmodern spirit we would suggest that big-issue logic, scientific progress, and Marxist-type influences have each played a role in the evolution of thought.

Even in the absence of biases in the research process, it would be impossible to reach rigorous scientific answers to many of the great questions in development economics. For this reason, among others, the astute conceptualizer and analyst must have the ability to use the scientific method complemented by a feel for where it falls short of being very scientific, where the results are biased by the questions asked, the countries chosen and so on, to put the results in policy perspective. As the discussion above has indicated, GR has been able to contribute so greatly over his career because of his impressive skills in each of these dimensions. A good feel for which issues are more important and which types of evidence put forward by which researchers are the most useful has remained key to reaching wise conclusions.

The careers of GR and his contemporaries have spanned a methodological flowering within development economics and a change in the relative roles of the "big-question generalists" who dominated the ranks of the subdiscipline's pioneers and the more specialized and econometrically oriented people who have played an increasing role with time. GR is the coauthor of one of the major models of the development process and has continued over his career to be a generalist in the sense of focusing on the economy as a whole and on the big issues. A key element of his methodological approach has been in-depth historical analysis of country experiences that offer lessons of a general character. Sorting out the secrets of their success usually involves both country-specific probing and small-group comparisons, for example, those among the East Asian countries and other labor-abundant countries. Assessing replicability involves small-group comparisons between types of countries, such as the East Asian tigers and the Latin American nations. There are many differences between the experiences being compared, and limited gains to be had from the use of statistical procedures to sort out the factors responsible for the differing outcomes, and the absence of clear methodological norms make such analysis subtle and challenging. GR has made many fruitful comparisons of this sort—see, for example, Ranis 1985a, 1992b. Part of his expertise comes from being one of the few people in the subdiscipline who has lived and researched for a matter of years in East Asia, South Asia, and Latin America, an invaluable source of both insight and defense against simplistic interpretation.

Put another way, GR's methodology has been to find development patterns that work, assess the factors that were central to their working well (usually through an in-depth historical look), and judge their potential for more general applicability. It has been a productive approach. His (and his collaborators) continuing valuable insights over the years exemplify the importance of a strong inductive, innovative, and analytical capacity coupled with a broad base of knowledge of the historical evolution of countries, sectors, and processes. This has been the dominant methodology of that part of development economics that has focused on broad policy issues. The Chenery-style cross-section patterns-of-development approach and more econometric-based analyses have thus far failed to play a comparable role.

GR is a generalist (in the sense of dealing with all aspects of development and all parts and mechanisms of the economy) since this is a prerequisite to effective analysis of the relative performance of economies that differ from each other in a variety of related ways. When GR opines on the trade role in development, it is not so much as a trade economist, though he knows enough of that, but as someone who is equally familiar with the theories and facts relating to agriculture, industry, distribution, and so on. Unlike some more-specialized researchers, he always frames the question in terms of how that sector or mechanism fits into the economy of the country.

He is also one of the great recent practitioners of the two-way flow of ideas involved in inductive and deductive science. Success with the first depends of course on a strong body of factual information and a good feel for the probable veracity of information; much of the weakness in our subdiscipline of late has involved the lack of that base of information. He has straddled a middle road over the years in the sense of chafing a little both at the lack of a theoretical guiding structure in the Chenery et al. "statistical patterns of development" approach (while of course recognizing its value) and also at the application of theory too little encumbered by an understanding of LDC structure of the kind for which he criticized Myint's trade-based interpretation (Ranis 1987).

GR has been one of the most influential development economists over the past forty years. Not only has he made important creative contributions to each stage of the evolution of thought, but, as becomes clear when one views the work as a whole, these have been built around a coherent and comprehensive vision of the functioning of developing economies. Each new piece of work fits in with this overarching view, illuminating a particular area while adding to the total picture. The constant overarching vision has two key features. First, it constitutes a *general* equilibrium system, each element being connected with the others and the interactions between the various elements being critical to the path followed. Second, the key interactions—agriculture/industry, traditional/modern, formal sector/informal sector, and external/domestic—depend on the *structure* and stage of development of the economy. It is thus not a Walrasian CGE-type general-equilibrium model, but may best be termed a *structuralist general equilibrium* approach, where the structure of the economy matters to the outcome, at least until countries have passed through the transition and entered the period of "modern growth." This vision was already present in the original FR model. GR's work since then has enriched and elaborated on the initial conception, without basically departing from it.

NOTES

We are grateful to G. K. Helleiner for helpful comments on an earlier draft.

1. This is not to deny the presence of such forces, especially in the short run, but rather to suggest that their influence is modest over the longer run.

2. The range of views reflects not only articulated differences of interpretation among writers who are in touch with each other but also the fact that thinking naturally proceeds along somewhat different paths within the various partially or wholly separate groups of thinkers, who may be divided by ideology, logistics, or both. Though some of the central themes of development economics can be traced to India (e.g., Mahalanobis on the role of the capital-goods industry), other lines of thought seem to have evolved more or less in parallel inside and outside that country, with limited contact between the strands, as in the case of the dependency-type thinking in Latin America (e.g., Sunkel 1969) and in India (Nehru, as quoted in Nayar 1972, 131–32). This point is emphasized by Srinivasan (1994).

3. The underlying ideas were, not surprisingly, widely held among social scientists and policymakers. What distinguished Lewis and Ranis-Fei were the models they constructed around them and the deductions they drew from the models.

4. See Scott 1990 for a review. He himself rejects the approach.

5. Srinivasan has argued that GNP did not need to be dethroned, since it was never the exclusive object of development — poverty reduction, employment, quality of life, etc. were also objectives, as shown, for example, by analysis of early Indian plans as enunciated by Nehru, and the works of economists such as Tinbergen (1958) and Buchanan and Ellis (1955). See Srinivasan 1994.

6. Stewart and Streeten 1971 pointed out that in many circumstances the output and employment objectives were in fact consistent.

7. See Sen 1988. Despite this important shift in interpretation, which made the BN approach very similar to the *functioning* of Sen's own capability approach, Sen has continued to advance the charge of commodity fetishism at BN approaches generally.

8. Though, as noted above, such ideas were of course present and sometimes well established among the policy objectives of national governments, the attention they received at this time both raised their profile relative to other objectives and led to a more explicit consideration of how they overlapped or did not overlap with the pursuit of GDP growth.

9. As Srinivasan (1977) has pointed out, India "discovered" a BN approach to development long before it became internationally fashionable.

10. Thatcher did succeed in slowing down the growth in the money supply

and securing a budgetary balance. Reagan pursued monetary policies to the point of generating high interest rates. But budgetary and trade imbalances exploded in a most Keynesian way.

11. Bates 1981 and Lipton 1977 had come to very similar conclusions, while Stewart 1975 had attempted to disentangle class interests as they affected government preferences.

12. The underlying assumption was that "agents behave rationally; that is, they have a consistent set of preferences over the outcome of their actions, and they choose an action whose outcome is preferable given the constraints within which they act" (Srinivasan 1991, 126).

13. Williamson 1990b conveniently labeled this set of policies as representing the "Washington consensus."

14. See, e.g., Williamson 1990a, World Bank and UNDP 1989, and Dean, Desai, and Riedel 1994 for evidence of the advance of these policies in Latin America and Africa.

15. There have been numerous studies of the macroeffects of stabilization and adjustment policies, both by the IFIs themselves and by academics. The assessments of the IMF tend to suggest somewhat negative effects on growth, while those of World Bank slight positive effects compared with an estimated "counterfactual." Effects on investment were negative. See, e.g., Khan and Knight 1986; Khan 1990; Killick et al. 1991; World Bank 1990; Mosley, Harrigan, and Toye 1991; Elbadawi 1992. However, most studies have been unable to find significant positive effects in Africa.

16. In the 1970s Jolly, Singer, and Stewart participated in the Kenya mission; ul Haq, Streeten, Ranis, and Stewart in the World Bank basic-needs work; Griffin, Emmerij, and Ghai with the ILO. All have been involved, in one way or another, with the new focus on poverty and human development.

17. Sen has been exploring the implications of the motivational assumptions for many years. He summarized some of his conclusions by asserting that "the purely rational individual comes close to being a social moron" (1982, 99).

18. As noted above, the ILO Philippine mission report (ILO 1973) had this as its single most important message.

19. See also the work of Mellor (1976) and IFPRI in this area, including, e.g., Hazell and Roell 1983.

REFERENCES

Amin, S. 1974. "Accumulation and Development: A Theoretical Model." *Journal of African Political Economy* 1:9–26.
Amsden, A. 1989. *Asia's Next Giant: South Korea and Late Industrialisation.* New York: Oxford University Press.
Ayub, M. A. 1977. "Income Inequality in a Growth-Theoretic Context: The Case of Pakistan." Ph.D. diss., Yale University.

Balassa, B. 1971. *The Structure of Protection in Developing Countries.* Baltimore: John Hopkins University Press.

Bates, R. H. 1981. *Markets and States in Tropical Africa: The Political Basis of Agricultural Policies.* Berkeley and Los Angeles: University of California Press.

———. 1991. "A Critique by Political Scientists." In *Redistribution and Growth,* ed. H. Chenery et al. Oxford: Oxford University Press.

Berry, A. 1997. "The Income Distribution Threat in Latin America." *Latin American Research Review* 32, no. 2:3–40.

Berry, R. A., and R. Sabot. 1978. "Labour Market Performance in Developing Countries: A Survey." *World Development* 6, nos. 11–12:1199–1242.

Bhagwati, J. N. 1978. *Foreign Trade Regimes and Economic Development: Anatomy and Consequences of Exchange Control Regimes.* Cambridge, Mass.: Ballinger.

———. 1982. "Directly Unproductive, Profit-Seeking Activities." *Journal of Political Economy* 90:988–1002.

Bowles, S., and H. Gintis. 1993. "The Revenge of Homo Economicus: Contested Exchange and the Revival of Political Economy." *Journal of Economic Perspectives* 7:83–102.

Buchanan, J. M., and H. S. Ellis. 1955. *Approaches to Economic Development.* New York: Twentieth Century Fund.

Buchanan, J. M., R. D. Tollison, and G. Tullock, eds. 1980. *Toward a Theory of the Rent-Seeking Society.* College Station: University of Texas Press.

Buchanan, J. M., and G. Tullock. 1962. *The Calculus of Consent: Logical Foundations of Constitutional Democracy.* Ann Arbor: University of Michigan Press.

Camdessus, M. Speech to the U.S. Chamber of Commerce, March 26, 1990.

Chenery, H., et al., eds. 1974. *Redistribution with Growth.* Oxford: Oxford University Press.

Cline, W. 1982. "Can the East Asian Model of Development Be Generalised?" *World Development* 10:81–90.

Cohen, B. J., and G. Ranis. 1971. "The Second Postwar Restructuring." In *Government and Economic Development,* ed. G. Ranis. New Haven: Yale University Press.

Conybeare, J. 1982. "The Rent-Seeking State and Revenue Diversification." *World Politics* 35:25–42.

Cornia, G. A., R. Jolly, and F. Stewart. 1987. *Adjustment with a Human Face.* Oxford: Oxford University Press.

Dean, J., S. Desai, and J. Riedel. 1994. "Trade Policy Reform in Developing Countries since 1985: A Review of the Evidence." World Bank Discussion Papers, 267.

Desai, M., and D. Mazumdar. 1970. "A Test of the Disguised Unemployment Hypothesis." *Economica,* xxii.

Diaz-Alejandro, C. F. 1980. "Changing Trade Shares and Economic Growth: Discussion." *American Economic Review* 70, no. 2 (May).

Dreze, J., and A. K. Sen. 1990. *Hunger and Public Action.* Oxford: Oxford University Press.

Eckaus, R. S. 1955. "The Factor Proportions Problem in Underdeveloped Areas." *American Economic Review* 45.

Elbadawi, L. A. 1992. "Why Structural Adjustment Has Not Succeeded in Sub-Saharan Africa." World Bank Working Paper Series, WPS 1000.

Etzioni, A. 1991. "Liberals, Communitarians, and Choices." In *Socio-economics: Towards a New Synthesis,* ed. A. Etzioni and P. Lawrence. Armonk, N.Y.: M. E. Sharpe.

Etzioni, A., and P. Lawrence. 1991. *Socio-economics: Towards a New Synthesis.* Armonk, N.Y.: M. E. Sharpe.

Fei, J., and G. Ranis. 1963. "Innovation, Capital Accumulation, and Economic Development." *American Economic Review* 53.

―――. 1964. *Development of the Labor Surplus Economy.* New York: Richard Irwin.

―――. 1975. "A Model of Growth and Employment in the Open Dualistic Economy: The Cases of Korea and Taiwan." *Journal of Development Studies* 11, no. 2:32–63.

Fei, J., G. Ranis, and S. Kuo. 1978. "Growth and Family Distribution of Income by Factor Components." *Quarterly Journal of Economics* 92:17–53.

―――. 1979. *Growth with Equity: The Taiwan Case.* Oxford: Oxford University Press.

Fei, J., G. Ranis, and F. Stewart. 1985. "A Macroeconomic Framework for Basic Needs." In *Planning to Meet Basic Needs,* ed. F. Stewart. London: Macmillan.

Fields, G. 1989. "Poverty, Inequality, and Growth." Processed, World Bank.

Frank, A. G. 1969. *Capitalism and Underdevelopment in Latin America: Historical Studies of Chile and Brazil.* New York: Monthly Review Press.

Furtado, C. 1967. *Development and Underdevelopment.* Berkeley and Los Angeles: University of California Press.

Galtung, J., P. O'Brien, and R. Preiswerk, eds. 1980. *Self-Reliance: A Strategy for Development.* London: Bogle Ouverture Publications.

Girvan, N. 1971. *Foreign Capital and Economic Underdevelopment in Jamaica.* Kingston, Jamaica: Institute of Social and Economic Research, University of the West Indies.

Grindle, M. S. 1991. "The New Political Economy: Its Explanatory Power for LDCs." In *Politics and Policy Making in Developing Countries,* ed. G. M. Meier. San Francisco: International Center for Economic Growth.

Hansen, B. 1969. "Employment and Wages in Rural Egypt." *American Economic Review* 59.

Hanson, J. 1971. "Employment and Rural Wages in Egypt: A Reinterpretation." *American Economic Review* 61.

Hazell, P., and A. Roell. 1983. *Rural Growth Linkages: Household Expenditure Patterns in Malaysia and Nigeria.* Washington, D.C.: International Food Policy Research Institute.

Helleiner, G. K. 1966. "Typology in Development Theory: The Land Surplus Economy (Nigeria)." *Food Research Institute Studies* 30:181–94.

Hicks, N. 1979. "Growth versus Basic Needs: Is There a Trade-Off." *World Development* 7, no. 11:985–94.

Hirschman, A. O. 1958. *The Strategy of Economic Growth.* New Haven: Yale University Press.

International Labor Organization. 1970. *Towards Full Employment: A Programme for Colombia.* Geneva: ILO.

———. 1972. *Employment, Incomes, and Equality, a Strategy for Increasing Productive Employment in Kenya.* Geneva: ILO.

———. 1973. *Sharing in Development: A Programme of Employment, Equity, and Growth for the Philippines.* Geneva: ILO.

———. 1976. *Employment, Growth, and Basic Needs: A One-World Problem.* Geneva: ILO.

Jolly, R. J., et al. 1973. *Third World Employment: Problems and Strategy.* London: Penguin.

Kao, C., K. Anschel, and C. Eicher. 1964. "Disguised Unemployment in Agriculture: A Survey." In *Agriculture in Economic Development,* ed. C. Eicher and L. Witt. New York: McGraw Hill.

Katz, J. 1984. "Dynamic Technological Innovation and Dynamic Comparative Advantage: Further Reflections on a Comparative Case Study Program." *Journal of Development Economics* 16:13–38.

Khan, M. 1990. "The Macro-economic effects of Fund-Supported Adjustment Programs." *IMF Staff Papers* 37.

Khan, M., and M. Knight. 1985. "Fund-Supported Adjustment Programs and Economic Growth." IMF Occasional Paper 41.

Killick, T. 1988. "Reaction Too Far: Contemporary Thinking about the Role of the State with Special Reference to Developing Countries." Processed, Overseas Development Institute.

Killick, T., et al. 1991. "What Can We Know about the Effects of the IMF Programmes?" Overseas Development Institute Working Paper 47.

Krueger, A. 1974. "The Political Economy of the Rent-Seeking Society." *American Economic Review* 64:291–303.

Krugman, P. 1984. "Import Protection as Export Promotion: International Competition in the Presence of Oligopoly and Economies of Scale." In *Monopolistic Competition and International Trade,* ed. H. Kierskowski. Oxford: Oxford University Press.

Kuo, S., J. Fei, and G. Ranis. 1981. *The Taiwan Success Story: Rapid Growth with Improved Distribution in the Republic of China, 1952–1979.* Boulder, Colo.: Westview.

Kuznets, S. 1955. "Economic Growth and Income Inequality." *American Economic Review* 45.

Lal, D. 1983. *The Poverty of "Development Economics."* London: Institute of Economic Affairs.

———. 1984. "The Political Economy of the Predatory State." Discussion Paper DRD 105, Development Research Department, World Bank.

Lall, S. 1987. *Learning to Industrialise*. London: Macmillan.

———. 1994. "The East Asia Miracle Study: Does the Bell Toll for Industrial Strategy?" *World Development* 22:645–54.

Lewis, A. 1954. "Economic Development with Unlimited Supplies of Labour." *Manchester School* 22, no. 2:139–91.

Leys, C. 1975. *Underdevelopment in Kenya: The Political Economy of Neocolonialism*. London: Heinemann.

Lipton, M. 1977. *Why Poor People Stay Poor: Urban Bias in World Development*. London: Temple Smith.

Little, I. M. D. 1982. *Economic Development: Theory, Policy, and International Relations*. New York: Basic Books.

Little, I. M. D., T. Scitovsky, and M. Fg. Scott. 1970. *Industry and Trade in Some Developing Countries: A Comparative Study*. Oxford: Oxford University Press.

Lucas, R. E. 1988. "On the Mechanics of Economic Development." *Journal of Monetary Economics* 22.

Mahalanobis, P. C. 1953. "Some Observations on the Process of Growth in National Income." *Sankhya* 14, no. 4.

Maizels, A. 1970. *Industrial Growth and World Trade*. Cambridge: Cambridge University Press.

Meier, G. M., ed. 1991. *Politics and Policy Making in Developing Countries*. San Francisco: International Center for Economic Growth.

Mellor, J. 1976. *The New Economics of Growth: A Strategy for India and the Developing World*. Ithaca: Cornell University Press.

Minami, R. 1970. "Further Considerations on the Turning Point in the Japanese Economy, Parts 1 and 2." *Hitotsubashi Journal of Economics* 10:18–60.

Morawetz, D. 1977. *Twenty-five Years of Economic Development: 1950 to 1975*. Washington, D.C.: World Bank.

Morley, S. A. 1995. *Poverty and Inequality in Latin America: The Impact of Adjustment and Recovery in the 1980s*. Baltimore: Johns Hopkins University Press.

Mosley, P., J. Harrigan, and J. Toye. 1991. *Aid and Power*. London: Routledge.

Myrdal, G. 1957. *Economic Theory and Underdeveloped Regions*. London: Duckworth.

Nayar, B. 1972. *The Modernization Imperative and Indian Planning*. Delhi: Vikas Publications.

Nehru, J. 1946. *The Discovery of India*. New York: John Day.

North, P. 1990. *Institutions, Institutional Change, and Economic Performance*. Cambridge: Cambridge University Press.

Nurkse, R. 1955. *Problems of Capital Formation in Developing Countries*. Oxford: Blackwell.

Pack, H. 1989. "Industrialization and Trade." In *Handbook of Development Economics*. Vol. 1, ed. H. Chenery and T. N. Srinivasan. Amsterdam: Elsevier Science Publishing.

Pack, H, and L. Westphal. 1985. "Industrial Strategy and Technological Change." *Journal of Development Economics* 22:87–128.

Persson, T., and G. Tabellini. 1994. "Is Inequality Harmful for Growth?" *American Economic Review* 84:600–621.

Prebisch, R. 1950. *The Economic Development of Latin America and Its Principal Problems.* New York: United Nations.

———. 1964. *Towards a New Trade Policy for Development.* Report by the Secretary General of UNCTAD. New York: United Nations.

Ranis, G. 1955. "The Community-Centred Entrepreneur in Japanese Development." *Explorations in Entrepreneurial History.*

———. 1969. "The Financing of Japanese Economic Development." In *Agriculture and Economic Growth: Japan's Experience.* Tokyo: University of Tokyo Press.

———. 1971a. "Financial Intermediation in Regional Economic Growth." *Revista Española de Econmia,* January–April.

———. 1971b. "Output and Employment in the '70s: Conflicts or Complements?" In *Employment and Unemployment Problems of the Near East and South Asia,* ed. R. Ridker and H. Lubell, vol. 1. Delhi: Vikas Publications.

———. 1973. "Industrial Sector Labor Absorption." *Economic Development and Cultural Change.*

———. 1978. "Equity and Growth in Taiwan: How 'Special' is the 'Special Case?' " *World Development* 6:397–409.

———. 1980. "Distribución del ingreso y crecimiento en Colombia." *Desarollo y Sociedad* (CEDE, University of the Andes, Bogota), 3:9.

———. 1984. "Basic Needs, Distribution, and Growth: The Beginnings of a Framework." In *Trade, Stability, Technology, and Equity in Latin America,* ed. M. Syrquin and S. Teitel. New York: Academic Press.

———. 1985a. "Adjustment in East Asia: Lessons for Latin America." In *External Debt and Development Strategy in Latin America,* ed. A. Jorge, J. Salazar-Carrillo, and F. Diaz-Pou. New York: Pergamon.

———. 1985b. "Can the East Asian Model Be Generalised?" *World Development* 13:543–45.

———. 1987. "Comment on Hla Myint's 'The Neo-classical Resurgence in Development Economics': Its Strength and Limitations." In *Pioneers in Development,* ed. G. M. Meier. Washington, D.C.: World Bank.

———. 1989. "The Role of Institutions in Transition Growth: The East Asian Newly Industrialising Countries." *World Development* 17:1317–498.

———. 1990a. "Asian and Latin American Experience: Lessons for Africa. *Journal of International Development* 2.

———. 1990b. "A View of Rural Development — 1980s Vintage (or Why Some of the Emperor's Clothes — and His Rice — Should Be Made at Home)." In *Trade, Planning, and Rural Development: Essays in Honour of Nurul Islam.* London: Macmillan.

———. 1992a. "The Role of Government and Markets: Comparative Development Experience." In *State and Market in Development: Synergy or Rivalry,* ed. L. Putterman and D. Rueschemeyer. Boulder, Colo.: Lynne Rienner.

————, ed. 1992b. *Taiwan: From Developing to Mature Economy.* Boulder, Colo.: Westview.

————. 1995. "Another Look at the East Asian Miracle." *World Bank Economic Review* 9.

Ranis, G., and J. Fei. 1988. "Development Economics: What Next?" In *The State of Development Economics: Progress and Prospects,* ed. G. Ranis and T. P. Schulz. Oxford: Blackwell.

Ranis, G., and S. Mahmood. 1992. *The Political Economy of Development Policy Change.* Oxford: Blackwell.

Ranis, G., and F. Stewart. 1990. "Macro-policies for Appropriate Technology: A Synthesis of Findings." In *The Other Policy,* ed. F. Stewart, H. Thomas, and T. de Wilde. London: IT Publications.

————. 1993. "Rural Non-agricultural Activities in Development: Theory and Application." *Journal of Development Economics* 40:75–101.

Ravillion, M., and M. Huppi. 1989. "Poverty and Undernutrition in Indonesia during the 1980s." Policy, Planning, and Research Papers, World Bank.

Roemer, P. M. 1986. "Increasing Returns and Long-Run Growth." *Journal of Political Economy* 94, no. 5:1002–37.

Rosenstein-Rodan, P. 1943. "Problems of Industrialisation of Eastern and South-Eastern Europe." *Economic Journal* 53:202–11.

Rosenzweig, M. 1989. "Labor Markets in Low Income Countries." In *Handbook of Development Economics,* ed. H. Chenery and T. N. Srinivasan, vol. 1. Amsterdam: North Holland.

Scott, M. Fg. 1990. *A New View of Economic Growth.* Oxford: Oxford University Press.

Seers, D. 1991. In *Prospects for Employment in the Nineteen Seventies,* ed. R. Robinson and O. Johnston. London: Her Majesty's Stationery Office.

Sen, A. K. 1977. "Rational Fools: A Critique of the Behavioural Foundations of Economic Theory." *Philosophy and Public Affairs* 6:317–44.

————. 1982. *Choice, Welfare and Measurement.* Oxford: Basil Blackwell.

————. 1985. *Commodities and Capabilities.* Amsterdam: Elsevier Science Publishing.

————. 1988. "Development and Capabilities." Processed.

Singer, H. W. 1950. "The Distribution of Gains between Investing and Borrowing Countries." *American Economic Review* 40:473–85.

Srinivasan, T. N. 1977. "Development, Poverty, and Basic Human Needs: Some Issues." *Food Research Institute Studies* 16:11–28.

————. 1991. "Foreign Trade Regimes." In *Politics and Policy Making in Developing Countries,* ed. G. M. Meier. San Francisco: International Center for Economic Growth.

————. 1994. "Development Economics: Then and Now." In *Trade, Aid and Development: Essays in Honour of Hans Linnemann,* ed. H. Kox, W. Tims, and Y. de Wit. New York: St. Martin's Press.

Stern, N. 1989. "The Economics of Development: A Survey." *Economic Journal* 99:597–686.

Stewart, F. 1975. "A Note on Social Cost Benefit Analysis and Class Conflict in LDCs." *World Development* 3:1.

———. 1982. "The New International Economic Order and Basic Needs: Conflicts and Complementarities." In *Development Strategies and Basic Needs in Latin America,* ed. C. Brundenius and M. Lundahl. Boulder, Colo.: Westview.

———, ed. 1985. *Planning to Meet Basic Needs.* London: Macmillan.

Stewart, F., and P. Streeten. 1971. "Conflicts between Output and Employment Objectives in Developing Countries." *Oxford Economic Papers* 23, no. 2: 145–68.

Stiglitz, J. E., and A. Weiss. 1981. "Credit Rationing in Markets with Imperfect Information." *American Economic Review* 71:393–410.

Streeten, P., et al. 1981. *First Things First: Meeting Basic Human Needs in Developing Countries.* New York: Oxford University Press.

Sunkel, O. 1969. "National Development Policy and External Dependence in Latin America." *Journal of Development Studies* 6.

Tinbergen, J. 1958. *The Design of Development.* Baltimore: Johns Hopkins University Press.

Toye, J. 1992. "Interest Group Politics and the Implementation of Adjustment Policies in Sub-Saharan Africa." *Journal of International Development* 4:183–98.

United Nations Development Program. 1990. *The Human Development Report, 1990.* New York: Oxford University Press.

Vaitsos, C. V. 1974. *Intercountry Income Distribution and Transnational Corporations.* Oxford: Oxford University Press.

Wade, R. 1990. *Governing the Market.* Princeton: Princeton University Press.

Westphal, L., Y. Rhee, and G. Pursell. 1981. "Korean Industrial Competence: Where It Came From." World Bank Staff Working Paper 469.

Williamson, J., ed. 1990a. *Latin American Adjustment: How Much Has Happened.* Washington, D.C.: Institute for International Economics.

———. 1990b. "What Washington Means by Policy Reform." In *Latin American Adjustment: How Much Has Happened,* ed. J. Williamson. Washington, D.C.: Institute for International Economics.

Wionczek, M., ed. 1966. *Latin American Economic Integration: Experiences and Prospects.* New York: Praeger.

Wood, A. 1994. "Skill, Land, and Trade: A Simple Analytic Framework." Institute of Development Studies Working Paper 1.

World Bank. 1990. *Report on Adjustment Lending II: Policies for the Recovery of Growth.* Washington, D.C.: World Bank.

———. 1991. *Adjustment Lending Policies for Sustainable Growth.* Policy and Research Series, 14. Washington, D.C.: World Bank.

———. 1993. *The East Asian Miracle: Economic Growth and Public Policy.* New York: Oxford University Press.

World Bank and UNDP. 1989. *Africa's Adjustment and Growth in the 1980s.* Washington, D.C.: World Bank.

Part 1. Duality and the Evolution of Labor Markets in Developing Economies

CHAPTER 2

Duality and Development: Some Reflections on Economic Policy

Joseph E. Stiglitz

It is a pleasure to have this occasion to honor Gus Ranis, a scholar whose work has vastly expanded our understanding of the development process, and whose commitment to raising the fortunes of the less developed economies led him out of academia to put into practice not only the ideas but also the wisdom that he accumulated over the years. I had the good fortune to have been his colleague for seven years in the late 1960s and early 1970s.

But even before that, as I began my studies of development, I became in effect his student. Few ideas have captured the economics profession as did the concept of the dual economy. It was one of those instances — of which there were to be several in subsequent years — in which development economics became a net exporter of intellectual property.

According to traditional neoclassical doctrines,[1] free flows of capital, labor, goods, and knowledge equalized wages and the returns to other factors. To be sure, barriers to the flow of labor and capital *between* countries may exist, but — *by assumption* — no such barriers exist *within* countries. And even if labor did not flow freely, wages still would be equalized across regions so long as capital flows were unimpeded. And even with some barriers to factor flows, the flow of goods would equalize returns (the factor price equalization theorem).

Duality exists whenever there are marked differences in living standards that are greater than can be accounted for by differences in the ownership of physical or human capital — that is, whenever there exist persistent differences in wages that appear larger than can be accounted for by differences in abilities or endowments more generally.[2] (There is a broader sense of duality that will also be explored in this essay: if abilities ["raw talent"] are similar, eventually we would expect [with perfect capital markets] similar investments in human capital, and if preferences are similar, similar amounts of physical capital.[3] In this broader sense, duality exists if there are persistent differences in human and physical capital that cannot be explained by persistent differences in inherited "raw" ability.)

Today we think of problems of duality not only in the context of developing economies, but also within developed economies — such as dual labor markets, pockets of persistent urban and rural poverty in the United States and the southern part of Italy. In some cases, duality exists within the urban sector of the same country — witness ghettos in the United States or the markedly different levels of productivity in manufacturing and service sectors in some Asian economies. In short, sizable wage discrepancies, including huge regional disparities — for workers of approximately similar abilities and skills — exist within countries. The seeming ubiquity of duality represents a fundamental challenge to neoclassical doctrines.

In this essay, I want to reflect on some of the sources of those discrepancies and some of the possible policy responses. Earlier work, including the pathbreaking work of Professor Ranis, took duality as an exogenous factor and investigated its consequences, including the consequences for policy. I want to push the discussion back a step: Can we reduce the extent of duality? If so, how? In other words, I view duality as an endogenous variable that *may* be affected by policy, as opposed to an exogenous variable, to which policy must accommodate itself.

Let me at the onset set forth my answers to these questions: I believe there are forces in our society that serve to perpetuate duality — so that the economic life prospects of individuals do depend markedly on where they are born and who their parents are. I also believe that governments can take actions to reduce persistent disparities between life prospects of those in different groups. In particular, steps can be taken that will go a long way toward equalizing economic opportunity and life prospects. (The latter goal is, of course, a far more ambitious one than the former and will take longer to achieve.)[4]

In many ways, growth strategies based on duality's elimination differ fundamentally from those taking it as given. In the latter, for instance, differences in savings propensities in rural and urban areas, or between peasants, workers, and capitalists, are thought to be fixed, so that there is a trade-off between equality and growth: redistributing income to the rich will yield higher aggregate savings rates and hence faster economic growth. In the former approach, these differences in savings are not taken as given; the rural sector may be induced to save more, for instance through postal savings accounts providing a convenient and safe vehicle for savings. Similarly, universal education can reduce differences in behavioral patterns, including fertility rates.

A major lesson from the success of the East Asian countries is that equality may enhance economic growth: there need not be a trade-off. Such a trade-off was, of course, a fundamental tenet of the older dual-economy models, based on Arthur Lewis's postulates that the primary determinant of economic growth was the pace of capital accumulation, the pace of capital accumulation depended on domestic savings, and savings rates by urban capitalists were substantially higher than either those of rural peasants or urban workers.[5] One of the implications of the models presented below is that a reduction in inequality can be growth enhancing.[6]

In the models below, we shall depict several sources of vicious cycles that allow poverty to perpetuate itself but that may be broken with selective government intervention. Educational access provides the clearest example of such a cycle: With imperfect capital markets, poor families can invest only limited amounts in their children, so their children have low incomes and can invest little in *their* children. There are simple interventions, such as improved access to education, that can ameliorate the effects, if not eliminate the poverty trap itself; but there may be other effective interventions, including programs that affect early childhood education and those affecting fertility rates. Discrimination can give rise to a vicious cycle of poverty; and actions to reduce the force of discrimination may eliminate or reduce duality arising from this source. There are still other sources of vicious cycles: for example, environmental degradation can lead to lower living standards, forcing more extensive use of commons, in turn leading to further degradation (see Dasgupta 1993). All of these models have a similar mathematical structure. It is therefore useful to explore the nature of these vicious cycles in the context of the simplest, and perhaps most studied, version, that associated with efficiency wage theory.

Wage Differentials and Simple Efficiency Wage Theories

The earliest and simplest rationale for the wage differentials associated with dual labor markets was provided by efficiency wage theory. While efficiency wage theory has become a standard part of modern labor economies, it is often forgotten that the theory was developed in the 1960s and 1970s to help provide the theoretical foundations of dual economies. My own work was influenced both by the Ranis-Fei models

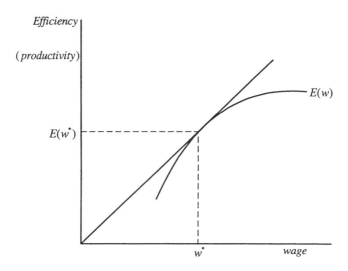

Fig. 2.1. The wage productivity curve. If productivity increases with wages, firm's labor costs may be minimized at a wage, *w** (the efficiency wage), that exceeds worker's opportunity cost.

of the dual economy and my experience in Kenya from 1969 through 1971, where even a casual observer could see huge wage differences not being equalized by market forces.

In subsistence economies, the idea that productivity might depend on nutrition seemed natural, and it was an easy step from here to the idea that paying workers more than their opportunity cost could be a profit-maximizing strategy (fig. 2.1). (The equilibrium wage is referred to as the *efficiency wage.*)[7] While antithetical to neoclassical doctrine, this idea nonetheless has a long and distinguished history in economics, having been discussed or alluded to by Smith, Mills, and Marshall, among others.[8] But despite its potential importance, the idea somehow dropped out of the mainstream of economics — perhaps because, as Marshall suggested, it greatly complicated the analysis.

But in Kenya and some other LDCs, wages paid in manufacturing seemed far above subsistence, and we had to look for other explanations. Four suggested themselves: higher wages reduce turnover, enable firms to select a better-quality labor force, improve incentives (by increasing the cost of being fired), and lastly, improve morale, leading to increased effort. In the more than twenty-five years since I formulated these ideas in Nairobi in 1969, a vast literature has developed, exploring each of these explanations.[9] For now, I simply want to note that these ideas have succeeded in providing a rigorous basis for the assumption that wages in different parts of the economy might be *markedly* differ-ent, *even for workers having identical or similar skills.* This contrasts with standard theory, where slight differences in skills should lead to only slight differences in wages.

The dual-economy hypothesis suggests not only that some workers would receive higher wages than others, but that particular workers persistently would receive higher wages, thus producing a segmented economy. I want to show that slight variations of the standard theory help explain both why slight differences in ability can lead to large differences in wages, and why there may be segmentation.

Nutrition: A General Equilibrium Model

In the simplest version of the efficiency wage model, productivity in one sector of the economy depends on wages. For simplicity, assume there are two sectors, in the second of which productivity does not depend on wages. We thus have

$$Q_1 = g(E(w,p)L_1)$$

$$Q_2 = L_2$$

where Q_i = output in ith sector and L_i = labor input into the ith sector, where, for simplicity, we have assumed constant returns to scale in the second sector and chosen our units so that one unit of labor generates one unit of output in the second sector, and where E is the efficiency of a worker in the first sector, which depends on the wage and the price, p. (We let output in the second sector be the numeraire, so the price is unity.)

In this version of the model, we assume full employment, so that if L is the total labor supply,

$$L_1 + L_2 = L.$$

For simplicity, we assume all consumers have homothetic prefer-ences, so

$$Q_1/Q_2 = d(p)$$

or

$$g(E(w,p)L_1)/[L - L_1] = d(p). \tag{1}$$

In competitive equilibrium, workers in the second sector get a wage of unity, while firms in the efficiency wage sector choose labor input and wages to maximize profits, taking price as given:

$$\max_{\{w, L_1\}} pg - wL_1$$

leading to the two first-order conditions

$$pg'E = w \tag{2}$$

$$pg'E_w = 1. \tag{3}$$

Dividing (3) by (2), we get the standard efficiency wage condition, that the elasticity of productivity with respect to the wage should be unity:

$$h(w,p) = E_w w/E = 1. \tag{4}$$

Equations (1), (2), and (4) provide three equations in the three unknowns $\{w, p, L_1\}$. *In general, the wage in the first sector may exceed the wage in the second sector (unity): identical workers receive different wages depending on the sector in which they work.*

To see the nature of the solution, it is useful to simplify still further, and assume that there are constant returns to scale in the first sector and choose units so $g' = 1$. Moreover, assume that while workers choose to consume both commodities, only consumption of the second commodity affects productivity. Let E' = derivative of efficiency with respect to consumption of that commodity. Let us simplify further and assume unitary price elasticity, so that $S(p) = S^*$, a constant, where $S(p)$ is the share of income spent on the second commodity. Then (4) can be solved for the efficiency wage, w^*, independent of p.[10]

$$S^*E'(S^*w)w/E(S^*w) = 1, \tag{5}$$

while (2) can be solved for p^*:[11]

$$p^* = w^*/E(S^*w^*). \tag{6}$$

Then (1) can be solved for the fraction of the population that work in the first sector:

$$EL_1^*/L - L_1^* = d(p^*).$$

Wage gaps.   A slight modification of this model explains why slight differences in ability can give rise to large differences in wages. Assume that all workers have the same ability in the second sector, but some are slightly more productive in the first sector; that is, there is a very narrow range of abilities, denoted by A, and that efficiency in the first sector depends on ability, wages, and prices,

$$E = AE(w,p).$$ (7)

For simplicity, we normalize the labor supply at unity. Assume that a fraction $L_1(\hat{A})$ has an ability equal to or greater than $\hat{A}$. (For simplicity, we assume L_1 is differentiable, with $L_1 \geqq l_1(A)$, where $l_1(A) = \partial L_1(A)/\partial A$.)

We assume A is observable. It is clear that in this version, the *efficiency* wage does not depend on A. Since all workers would prefer to work in the first sector at the wage $w > 1$, the firms in the first sector can have their "pick" of the labor force. But competition among firms in the first sector ensures that those who are more productive get a commensurately higher wage. We solve (5) as before, but now w^* is the wage paid to the *marginal* person hired into the first sector; more productive workers receive a wage of

$$w(A) = Aw^*/\hat{A},$$

where $\hat{A}$ is the ability of the marginal worker in the first sector. Now, instead of (6) we obtain

$$p^*\hat{A}E(w^*S^*) = w^*,$$ (6′)

and instead of (4) we obtain

$$E\tilde{A}L_1(\hat{A})/1 - L_1(\hat{A}) = d(w^*/\hat{A}E(w^*S^*)),$$ (4′)

$$\text{where } \tilde{A}(\hat{A}) = \frac{\int_{\hat{A}}^{\infty} Al_1(A)A}{L_1(\hat{A})},$$

the mean ability of those with ability in excess of $\hat{A}$. Equation (4′) can be solved for $\hat{A}$, and then (6′) can be solved for p^*. *All workers with an ability equal to or above $\hat{A}$ work in the first sector, receiving a wage of $Aw^*/\hat{A}$. All those with an ability less than $\hat{A}$ work in the second sector, receiving a wage of unity. Those with ability $\hat{A} + e$ receive a wage markedly higher than those with an ability $\hat{A} - e$. Wages are not a continuous function of ability.* See figure 2.2.

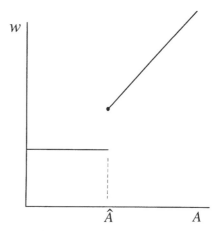

Fig. 2.2. Wages depend discontinuously on ability. The most able are hired into the "efficiency wage" sector. Thus, those with an ability of $\hat{A}$ receive much higher wages than those with ability just below $\hat{A}$.

Segmentation. These wage differences will persist. But even if all workers have exactly the same abilities, there can be segmentation, that is, those who are lucky enough to land a job in the first sector paying a high wage remain there. This will be the case, for instance, if there are even arbitrarily small fixed training costs in the first sector, or in the Shapiro-Stiglitz incentives model of efficiency wages.

Health and Productivity

It has been plausibly argued that productivity depends on health status as well as on current income, and health status depends on cumulative past consumption. Figure 2.3 shows productivity as a function of income for individuals of different health status. (I assume that in the "advanced sector," where productivity is sensitive to wages, individuals are paid daily and that their output cannot be monitored directly, so piece-rate payment is not feasible. However, health status is assumed observable, and I assume there is enough statistical evidence for employers to know the relationship between nutritional status, wages, and output.) Clearly, on a spot market with no long-term contracts, it pays employers to hire individuals with higher nutritional status at higher wages, while individuals with low nutritional status will be rationed out of the market. (In figure 2.3, workers with health status below H^* are not hired; the individual with health status $H_1 > H^*$ receives wage $w_1 > w^*$.)[12] Individuals

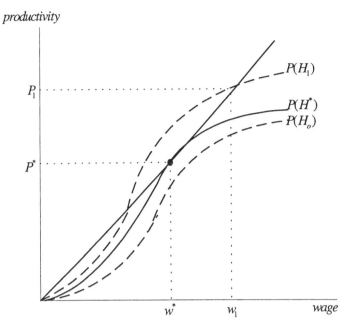

Fig. 2.3. Slight difference in wage productivity curves can result in markedly different outcomes. Those with wage productivity curves below the threshold level do not get hired in the advanced sector of the economy and face discretely lower incomes.

born with better health status or to wealthier parents more able to feed them well will have higher health status. Thus they will be hired at relatively high wages when they enter the labor force, and the high wages will enable them to sustain and improve their health status, so their wages will rise over time (figs. 2.4 and 2.5).[13] On the other hand, low health status workers may be condemned to jobs paying piece-rates, eking out a living at wages that leave them barely able to maintain their health status.[14]

Indeed, workers may begin life with identical health status. Those lucky enough to land a job in the high-wage sector will see their health status improve gradually over time, while those who are unlucky will see it deteriorate over time. In such a world, *even small differences in initial health status can result in large differences in wage profiles, as illustrated in figure 2.5.*[15] In this model, there is also strong segmentation: once workers get hired in the advanced sector, they remain there, because the health status of these workers is higher than that of workers in the other sector.

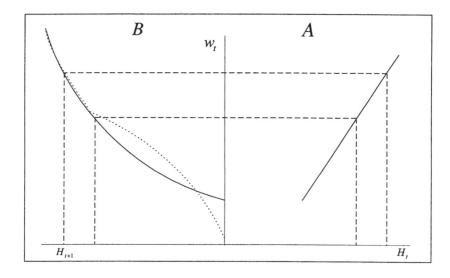

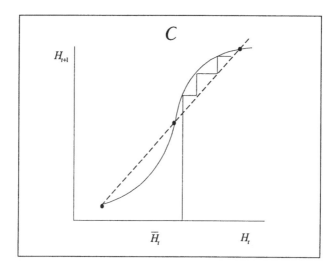

Fig. 2.4. Health dynamics. Higher health status leads to higher wages which leads to improved health status in later years. Panel C shows the "reduced form," with health status improving over time for those with high enough initial health status.

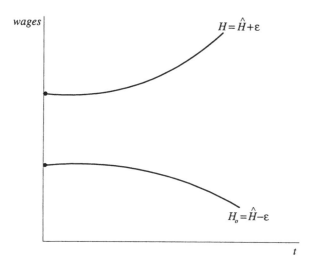

wages

$$H = \hat{H} + \varepsilon$$

$$H_o = \hat{H} - \varepsilon$$

t

Fig. 2.5.   Wages depend discontinuously on health status. The healthiest workers are hired into the efficiency wage sector. As a result of their higher wage, their health status improves over time, leading to still higher wages. By contrast, those in the other sector may experience deteriorating health and declining wages.

It is easy to show that these results can be extended to cases in which employers develop long-term relationships with their employees. The major difference is that it may pay employers to pay even higher wages to workers earlier in their career, since they recognize the benefits of future productivity increases that result from higher current wages.[16]

Limiting cases.   There is one limiting case: if productivity does not depend at all on current wages, but only on health, and if there are no long-term relationships, then wages would simply be proportional to health, and firms would not pay higher wages to increase productivity. There may still be duality: those who begin life with a health status above a critical level receive wages that are high enough to allow their health status (and wage) to improve over time, while those whose health status is below the critical level experience a continual deterioration in their health status.

But in such a situation, there are strong incentives to create long-term relationships. An individual would sign a long-term contract that would allow the firm to increase its profits, and the worker to increase his or her lifetime utility.[17]

Welfare. The analysis so far has been simply descriptive: it has not asked whether the market equilibrium is or is not optimal. Wage differences (for individuals of identical abilities) may be part of a utilitarian solution whenever there are nonconvexities, as there clearly are with the stipulated wage-productivity curve (see Stiglitz 1982b). Ex ante expected utility may be maximized even with wage differentials.

However, there are a number of reasons that *in general* market equilibrium in efficiency wage models is not (constrained) Pareto efficient (that is, taking into account the limitations of information and contracting; see for instance Shapiro and Stiglitz 1984).[18] When there are borrowing constraints (which can be justified in terms of problems of enforcement of loan contracts) and there are not long-term contracts, then wage subsidies for the young may be welfare enhancing; the gain in productivity over the individuals' lives more than offsets any distortionary effect from a small tax. When there are multiple equilibria, under some circumstances these multiple equilibria can be Pareto ranked. The economy (or some group within the economy) may be "stuck" in a Pareto-dominated equilibrium.

Intergenerational mobility. It is also easy to see that similar dynamics occur across generations. Since families with higher health status get to participate in the advanced sector, they earn higher incomes. These higher incomes allow them to provide their children better health status, which in turn allows the children to participate in the advanced sector. By thinking of the subscripts in figure 2.4 as representing generations rather than time periods, we see that intergenerational health and wage dynamics mirror their intertemporal counterparts in our earlier example.[19] The figure illustrates the existence of a vicious cycle of poverty in which one part of the population is condemned to participation in the low-productivity piece-rate jobs, with the associated low wages and health status.

While nutrition and health status may not be the explanation for efficiency wages in more industrialized countries, other "state" variables may serve similar functions.

Other Sources of Productivity Differentials

Differences in wage-productivity functions can be generated in a variety of ways.

Network externalities. For instance, those currently working may transmit to their relatives and friends "inside" information about their jobs, increasing friends' and relatives' productivity. Alternatively, current workers may provide a screening service to their employers (differentiating with some degree of accuracy those applicants likely to be more productive), so that the mean wage productivity curve for the "recommended" is slightly higher than for other, unscreened groups.

Human capital.   The same process used to describe the perpetuation of poverty through health dynamics can occur with human capital. The problem arises from capital-market imperfections: individuals cannot borrow against future earnings to fund their educations. Even if parents care about and are willing to invest in their children's education — whether out of altruism or because they expect to receive part of the return from their children's education — poorer families may have a greater average shadow price of capital. (There is evidence for this assertion: poorer individuals are willing to borrow at higher interest rates, even after accounting for higher default rates.)

Then a simple intergenerational dynamic can be set up: poor families invest little in their children, who then wind up poor, so that poverty perpetuates itself. Figure 2.6, panel A illustrates this process. The relationship between the tth generation's education, E_t, and its income, Y_t, is given by the standard "returns to education" function:

$$Y_t = f(E_t).$$

Panel B of figure 2.6 plots the level of education of generation $t + 1$ as a function of the income of generation t: $E_{t+1} = g(Y_t)$. It reflects the hypothesis that richer families invest more in children's education. Panel C combines the previous results, showing education (or income) of generation $t + 1$ as a function of education (or income) of generation t. The point where this curve crosses the 45-degree line represents a dynamic equilibrium: parents give their children exactly the same level of education they themselves received.

Formally, the dynamics are given by the equation

$$E_{t+1} = g(f(E_t)),$$

and equilibria are given by solutions to

$$E^* = g(f(E^*)).$$

Multiple equilibria can exist so long as for some values of E we have

$$g'f' > 1.$$

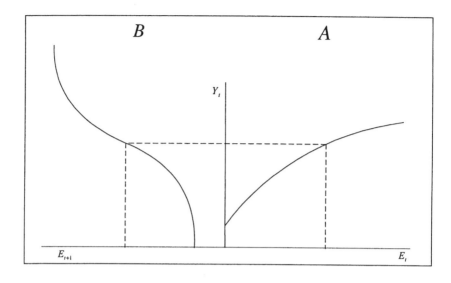

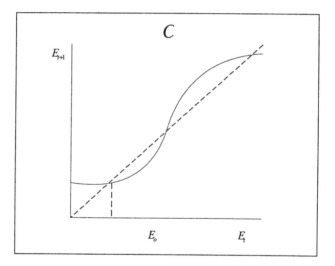

Fig. 2.6. Intergenerational transmission of inequality. Panel A. Those with more education obtain a higher income. Panel B. Families with higher incomes invest more in their children. Panel C. As a result, the higher the education of the parents, the higher the education of the child.

With multiple equilibria, the lowest one, E_o, will be stable, representing a poverty trap. For any generation, low education leads to low income, which leads to low education and hence low income in the next generation. In other words, there can be a dual economy.

A Closer Look at the Family Choice Problem

The preceding analysis assumes that richer families invested more in their children's education. Though there is a strong presumption that this is true, it is useful to look at some special cases where it may not be. Panel A of figure 2.6 depicts the standard education production function, with more investment in education leading to higher incomes. With "perfect" capital markets, investments will occur until the rate of return is equal to the cost of capital: there would be no differences in investment. But capital markets for investments in education are notoriously imperfect, partly because of the noncollaterizable nature of the investments.

With altruistic parents, but imperfect capital markets, investments will occur until the rate of return on education is equal to the opportunity cost of capital; since this is likely to be higher for poor families, they will invest less in education.

These effects may be reinforced by two other considerations: First, parental education affects the returns to "purchased" education. Parents' and children's educations are widely believed to be complements, so that children of more educated parents not only enjoy a higher level of income at each level of formal education, but actually enjoy a higher *marginal* return, as illustrated in figure 2.7. Even with perfect capital markets, parents with higher education will choose higher levels of education for their children under these circumstances.

Secondly, in many LDCs, parents must rely on children for old-age support; then, if parents are risk averse, or if there is significant probability that they will die while their children still need their support, as a large demographic literature has established, poor families actually may choose to have larger families, reducing each child's effective education and thus further increasing the likelihood of a poverty trap.

Discrimination.   Further variants of this model rely on racial or ethnic statistical discrimination. Suppose that employers cannot identify the abilities of a particular individual and must rely on a crude signal, such as ethnicity, gender, or whether the individual has a high school education. With statistical discrimination, an individual's equilibrium wage reflects the average marginal product of other workers of the same ethnicity, gender, and education.

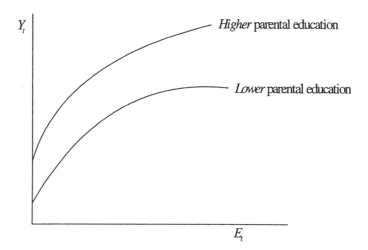

Fig. 2.7. Effects of parental education on returns to education

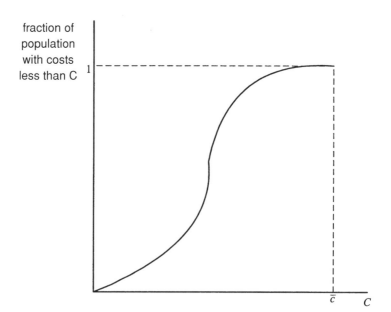

Fig. 2.8. Costs of obtaining a high school education

The *return* to education depends on the difference between wages for those workers who have high school diplomas and those who do not. Assume that individual educational costs differ (e.g., because of varied ability, which can be offset by effort and tutoring). Figure 2.8 presents a cumulative distribution function of individual educational costs.

People having low costs obtain a high school diploma, with the marginal person obtaining a high school diploma being the one for whom returns just equal costs. Let w_e represent the wage (or more accurately, the present discounted value of wage payments) of an educated worker, and let w_u be the present discounted value of wages of an uneducated worker. Then the threshold educational cost is given by

$$\hat{c} = w_e - w_u,$$

so that no one with cost $c > \hat{c}$ will obtain an education, while everyone with cost $c < \hat{c}$ will.

Letting $P(E,c)$ be the (average) marginal product of workers with education level E and educational costs equal to c, and letting $f(c)$ be the density function of c, we have

$$w_e = \frac{\int_0^{\hat{c}} P(E,c)f(c)dc}{\int_0^{\hat{c}} f(c)dc}$$

and

$$w_0 = \frac{\int_{\hat{c}}^{\infty} P(0,c)f(c)dc}{\int_{\hat{c}}^{\infty} f(c)dc}.$$

Thus the return to education is

$$R(\hat{c}) \equiv \frac{\int_0^{\hat{c}} P(E,c)f(c)dc}{\int_0^{\hat{c}} f(c)dc} - \frac{\int_{\hat{c}}^{\infty} P(0,c)f(c)dc}{\int_{\hat{c}}^{\infty} f(c)dc}.$$

It is clear that this function can increase with $\hat{c}$. When few people become educated, the average productivity of those who do not may be quite high. As a result, w_u will fall as $\hat{c}$ increases, increasing the returns to education. While w_e will also fall, it may decrease less quickly than w_0. (This fact is easily seen by differentiating $R(\hat{c})$.) Figure 2.9 shows an example of the returns to education function, with equilibrium occurring when the return equals the cost of the marginal individual, that is, $R(\hat{c}) = \hat{c}$.

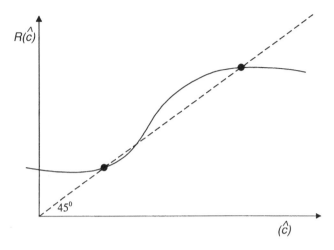

Fig. 2.9. Equilibrium education with imperfect information. The return to education may increase with $\hat{c}$. Equilibrium entails $R(\hat{c}) = \hat{c}$. There may be multiple equilibria; bold marks indicate locally stable equilibria.

It is apparent that different groups may be in different equilibria, with few members of one group obtaining an education. Given the small proportion of the group becoming educated, the returns to obtaining an education will be low, so that no other members of the group can benefit from education. Again we have duality, with differences persisting side by side.

Policy Prescriptions

The ease with which we may combat duality — and thus put a stop to poverty-perpetuating cycles — depends on the sources of the duality. At the very least, we should in practice expect all of the forces described in this essay to operate.

In *theory* — in our oversimplified model, that is — the simplest intervention is that associated with statistical discrimination. Provided those in the low equilibrium trap represent a small enough fraction of the total population, we could simply outlaw discrimination on whatever grounds are at issue, for example, race or gender. For if employers cannot condition wages on ethnicity or gender, only education (or related variables, like experience) will determine wages.[20] As a result, groups originally caught in low-level equilibrium traps will effectively merge into upper groups.

Improving access to education (e.g., through student loan pro-grams) will weaken if not break the link between parents' income and children's education, since perfect capital markets lead all agents to invest until educational returns equal the cost of capital. But so long as parental education affects the returns to purchased education, even re-moving capital-market imperfections entirely, it is possible for equal access to leave the lower-level equilibrium in place. But even so, those trapped at the low-level equilibrium will have higher incomes than be-fore, an unambiguous improvement. And there remains the possibility that only a single equilibrium survives after the granting of equal access. Note, however, that non-means-tested subsidized loans may increase inequality, as the interest sensitivity of those in the "upper" equilibrium may be greater than in the lower equilibrium.

Other policies can affect the intergenerational transmission of in-equality. For example, fertility policies may affect the educational-transmission function.

While I have focused on only some aspects of duality, others may play an important role in the perpetuation of regional disparities. A region may lack the localized nontradable intermediate goods needed to sustain production of complex products generating high incomes, pos-sibly because of inadequate final demand for these products.

Moreover, disparities in access to capital may exacerbate the conse-quences of similar disparities with respect to human capital and techno-logical know-how. In some cases, government policies can strengthen the financial sector in ways that facilitate the flow of capital. Certainly, governments can and have in a variety of contexts facilitated capital flows to agents facing high barriers to access.

And political and economic forces may complement each other. For example, businesses that are attracted to and demand noncorrupt and nonbureaucratic governments help sustain them, while the converse is true for those firms that thrive on political connections.

Cross-industry dualities are no less important than cross-regional ones. In some countries, manufacturing may be competitive and ad-vanced even as other sectors—like retailing—are not. Such discrepan-cies typically survive only in the absence of competitive pressures: while diffusion of knowledge about best business practices may not be instanta-neous, it does occur. This diffusion is all the more relevant given the trend toward "globalization": in any country, entrepreneurs who have developed successful business practices stand ready to try those practices in countries where change has been resisted.

As important as it is to recognize and implement policies that will mitigate dualities, we must also realize that vested interests always are ready to resist change. Moreover, there are always poorer individuals who depend on those interests and therefore will suffer when change comes. Thus while the end of duality may raise average living standards, we cannot forget that there will be losers, many of whom will be ill prepared to bear the burden. Thus it is not enough for a program attacking duality to be based only on creating *opportunity* for the disadvantaged and on fostering *competition* aimed at eroding vestigial rents and privileges, as undeniably vital as these tasks are. Such a program also must incorporate other elements — help, if not total compensation — for those who suffer in the transition.

Appendix: Health Dynamics and Utility Maximization

In this appendix, we establish conditions under which borrowing constraint is binding throughout the individual's life. The individual seeks to maximize

$$\int_0^T U(C)\bar{e}^{vt}dt \tag{A.1}$$

subject to the lifetime budget constraint

$$\int_0^T (C - w)e^{-rt}dt = 0 \tag{A.2}$$

where r is the interest rate and

$$w = kH \tag{A.3}$$

and where H is described by the health dynamic equation

$$dH/dt = h(H,C), \tag{A.4}$$

where $h_c > 0$, $h_{cc} < 0$ with initial conditions H_0, and where the individual faces the borrowing constraint

$$\int_0^\tau (w - C)e^{-rt}dt \geq 0 \tag{A.5}$$

$$0 \leq \tau \leq T$$

for all τ, that is, the present discounted value of consumption up to that point must be less than the present discounted value of wages. It is more convenient if we define $W(t)$ as the individual's wealth at time t; then the wealth dynamic equation is

$$dW/dt = rW - (C - w) \qquad (A.6)$$

and the no-borrowing constraint can be simply written as

$$W \geq 0. \qquad (A.7)$$

We focus on the special case where $r = v$, so that in the standard intertemporal maximization problem, with constant H (wages), consumption is constant (and equal to the wage) throughout the individual's life. (If there is a retirement period, individuals will still have constant consumption, but will save an amount $(w - C)$ while working to finance retirement.)

Assume we can ignore the borrowing constraint. Then the Hamiltonian can be written

$$h = U(C) + q[rW - (C - kH)] + \mu h (H,C) \qquad (A.8)$$

leading to the first-order condition

$$U' = q - \mu h_c \qquad (A.9)$$

with

$$dq/dt = (v - r)q \qquad (A.10)$$

and

$$d\mu/dt = \mu(v - h_H) - qk. \qquad (A.11)$$

When $v = r$, q is constant. Then we can differentiate the first-order condition for consumption to obtain

$$(U'' + \mu h_{cc}) \, dC/dt = -h_c \, d\mu/dt. \qquad (A.12)$$

The sign of $d\ln C/dt$ is the same as the sign of $d\ln \mu/dt$: in the absence of borrowing constraints, the shadow price on health and the level of consumption move together. Substituting (A.11) into (A.12), we obtain

$$(U'' + \mu H_{cc})dC/dt = -h_c[\mu(v - h_H) - qk]. \qquad (A.12')$$

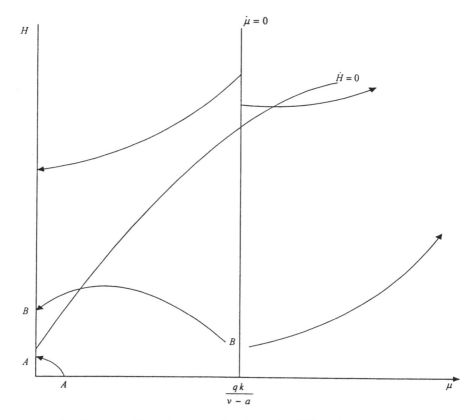

**Fig. 2.A1.   Health and consumption dynamics. With no borrowing con-
straints, the shadow price on consumption declines monotonically over
time, and so does consumption. Under curve *AA*, the individual's health
is improving throughout his life. With wages increasing and consumption declining, and with consumption less than or equal to wages initially, lifetime consumption is less than lifetime income; *AA* cannot be
part of an optimal trajectory. In *BB*, in the latter part of the individual's
life, health deteriorates. (Note: Curve *BB* should be flat when it crosses
line $\dot{H} = 0$.)**

The full dynamics can be described by the phase diagram illustrated
in figure 2.A1:

$$d\mu/dt = 0 \quad \text{when} \quad \mu = qk/(v - h_H). \tag{A.13}$$

If[21] $h = -aH + b(C)$, then

$$d\mu/dt = 0 \quad \text{when} \quad \mu = \mu^* = qk/(v + a). \tag{A.14}$$

$dH/dt = 0$ when $h(H,C) = 0$. Under the additive formulation,

$$H = b(C)/a. \tag{A.15}$$

The boundary conditions are

$$H(0) = H_0 \tag{A.16a}$$

and

$$\mu(T) = 0. \tag{A.16b}$$

Figure 2.A1 shows that μ must decrease monotonically, so that C must decrease monotonically. There are two possible configurations. In the curve labeled AA, consumption is always high enough that health status is always improving. In this case, wages are always increasing. But, under the hypothesis that initially the budget constraint is not binding,[22] C must initially be less or equal to w, so that C must always be below w; but then the borrowing constraint would never be binding and the budget constraint is not binding. Thus, the curve AA cannot be part of an equilibrium. *The only possible configuration is that in which in the final phase of the individual's life, health status is deteriorating*—deteriorating so fast that the wage eventually falls below consumption (see fig. 2.A2). This result can be put another way: *If the individual's lifetime income is high enough so that health status is always increasing, then the budget constraint is always binding, and $w = C$ throughout the individual's life.*

NOTES

The views expressed here are solely those of the author, and do not necessarily represent those of any organization with which he has been or is affiliated. I would like to thank Roderick Duncan, Nikola Spatafora, and T. N. Srinivasan for helpful comments.

1. Some economists have argued that these are *equilibrium* theories, and that neoclassical theory has little to say about the speed with which equilibrium is attained. I am concerned here about situations where wage disparities are persistent; either these wage disparities are part of a (presumably nonneoclassical) equilibrium or the neoclassical equilibrium is of little direct relevance—it only obtains in a far distant future. Moreover, a full equilibrium analysis must include an analysis of the dynamics of adjustment; plausible models of these costs of adjustment cannot account for the extent of persistence of wage differences nor their patterns.

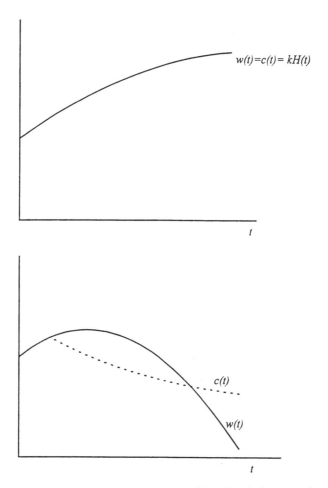

Fig. 2.A2. Wage and consumption profiles. Panel A: normal case, where borrowing constraint is always binding. Panel B: case where borrowing constraint is not binding at the end of the individual's life.

2. In this definition, discrimination can give rise to duality. In this essay, I will not explore this set of explanations. Traditional neoclassical theory has had a hard time accounting for discrimination, other than as a reflection of "preferences" (see Becker 1957). But more recently, a number of alternative theories of discrimination have been put forward (see Stiglitz 1973, 1974b).

3. See Stiglitz 1969, which analyzes the distribution of income and wealth among individuals under assumptions of identical abilities and shows that if preferences are identical, there should be (under fairly general conditions) convergence of wealth. Bevan and Stiglitz (1979) show that if ability is described by a stochastic process exhibiting regression toward the mean, then while there will

be an equilibrium wealth and income distribution, there will not be "duality" in the sense that there is one group of individuals that are permanently of higher income and wealth than another.

4. That is, there may be systematic differences in the extent to which individuals in different groups, facing similar opportunities, avail themselves of those opportunities. There is a deep philosophical issue concerning whether preference should, in this sense, be treated as part of an individual's endowment.

5. All three of these postulates have subsequently been questioned: While capital accumulation is important, there has been increasing emphasis on human capital and knowledge diffusion. Moreover, the large increases of private-capital flows to the developing countries imply that developing countries do not have to rely on their own savings (see World Bank 1997). And the East Asia experience shows that large amounts of savings can be mobilized from both rural peasants and urban workers.

6. A variety of reasons that equality may have been growth enhancing have been posited in the context of the East Asia miracle (see Stiglitz 1996). This paper touches on only some of these, in particular those relating to human capital.

7. If $E(C)$ is the efficiency wage function, giving workers' efficiency as a function of their current consumption, C, if w = wage rate and $f(EL)$ gives output as a function of labor efficiency units, the static problem of employers (ignoring savings, so $w = C$) is to

$$\max_{\{w, L\}} F(E(w)L) - wL$$

such that $w \geq w'$, where w' is the minimum wage at which the firm can hire workers. The efficiency wage is the solution to

$$E'(w^*) = E(w^*)/w^*.$$

If w^* exceeds w', there will be a dual labor structure.

8. For references to this early literature, as well as a general discussion of the causes and consequences of the dependence of productivity on wages (quality on prices), see Stiglitz 1987a.

9. For surveys, see Akerlof and Yellen 1986 and Stiglitz 1986, 1987b. My own work explored each of these possible explanations; e.g., for discussions of the nutritional model, see Stiglitz 1976; Mirrlees 1975; Dasgupta and Ray 1987a and 1987b; and Sah and Stiglitz 1992; of the "effort" model, see Shapiro and Stiglitz 1984; of the "selection model," see Stiglitz 1982a; for the morale model, see Stiglitz 1974a and Akerlof and Yellen 1990; for the labor turnover model in the context of LDCs, see Stiglitz 1974a.

Though each of these explanations provides a slightly different structure, there are striking similarities, as should be evident from a perusal of the above articles (especially the cited surveys). The results derived below for the nutritional model hold more generally.

10. If it should turn out that w^* is less than unity, it would mean that employers

would have to pay a wage of unity to attract workers to that sector; then all workers would receive the same wage.

11. If S depends on p, then we solve the pair of equations

$$S(p)E'(S(p)w)w/E(S(p)w) = 1$$

and

$$p = w/E(S(p)w)$$

simultaneously for p and w, substituting the results into equation (1) as below. (There may, of course, exist more than one solution.)

12. While I assume that individuals consume all of their income, it is easy to extend the model to the situation where individuals maximize utility of lifetime consumption, taking into account the effect of consumption (health) on future wages. In this case, higher consumption leads to higher wages, so that consumption acts like an investment good.

Assume health status and age, H_t, are observable. In equilibrium, wages will be a function of H_t:

$$w = Z(H_t).$$

If health dynamics are described by

$$H_{t+1} = a(C_t)H_t$$

and

$$U_t = u_t(C_t, H_t),$$

then individuals will choose a consumption profile $\{C_o, C_1, \ldots, C_T\}$ to

$$\max \Sigma U_t \delta^t$$

where δ is the pure rate of time discount, subject to

$$\sum_{t=0}^{T} Z(H_t)/(1 + r)^t = \sum_{t=0}^{T} C_t/(1 + r)^t$$

and subject to the health dynamics equation.

In most LDCs, there are borrowing constraints, implying that

$$\sum_{t=0}^{\tau} Z(H_t)/(1 + r)^t \geq \sum_{t=0}^{\tau} C_t/(1 + r)^t \text{ for all } \tau.$$

If these constraints are binding for all t, then in fact $C_t = w_t$ for all t. But even if these constraints are not binding for all t, they are likely to be binding early in life.

13. The simplest version of this dynamic can be represented as follows. $H_{t+1} = H(w_t, H_t)$, where H represents health status. For simplicity, assume it takes on the multiplicative form $H_{t+1} = a(w_t)H_t$, with $a' > 0$. Assume the wage productivity curve takes the form $P = HE(w)$. Denote the efficiency wage by w^*. Then for those hired, the wage is proportional to H, just as in our earlier analysis, the wage was proportional to ability A. For now, we write this as $w = kH$ (where we will solve for k later.) Thus, $H_{t+1} = a(kH_t)H_t$, and

$$\frac{dH_{t+1}}{dH_t} = a + a'kH = a(1 + j) > 0$$

where $v = (d\ln a)/(d\ln w)$. Thus $H_{t+1} > (<) H_t$ as $a > (<) 1$, i.e., as $w_t > (<) \hat{w}$, or as $H_t > (<) \hat{w}/k$, where $\hat{w} = a^{-1}(1)$.

H^* is the "marginal" health status hired, so $w(H^*) = kH^* = pgH^*$ where w^* is the efficiency wage. (Similar results hold if the health function takes on the additive form $H_{t+1} = H_t + a(w_t)$, where $a(w) > $ or < 0 as $w > $ or $< \hat{w}$. Health status improves if $w > \hat{w}$ where $a(\hat{w}) = 0$.)

14. Assume that those who do not get jobs in the "advanced sector" get paid by piece-rate and that they work at full capacity, receiving an income of $Y = b(H)$. For these workers, health dynamics are given by (assuming they consume their full income)

$$H_{t+1} = a(b(H_t))H_t.$$

Assume there is a number x^* such that $a(x^*) = 1$, $a' > 0$, $b' > 0$. Then for all $H_o < b^{-1}(x^*)$, health status and income will decrease continuously.

15. The easiest context in which to see this result is that where individuals face borrowing constraints, using a continuous time version of the model given in note 13. Efficiency is a function of current consumption and health status: $E = E(w,H)$, while health status is a function of past consumption: $dH/dt = h(H,C)$. With wages proportional to health status

$$w = kH,$$

and C equal to w (because of the borrowing constraint) the wage/health dynamics are fully described by

$$dH/dt = h(H,kH) = Z(H)$$

where $Z' = h_1 + h_2k > 0$, so there exists an H^* such that, if H_o, initial health, is below H^*, then H decreases monotonically, and if $H_o > H^*$, it increases monotonically.

Showing that the borrowing constraint is binding is somewhat more difficult. It is easy to establish conditions under which it is binding in the initial phases of an individual's life, as well as in the final phase. Under somewhat more restrictive conditions, it can be shown to be binding throughout the individual's life.

In the absence of borrowing constraints, the solution to the problem of maximizing intertemporal utility, subject to the health dynamic equation involves steadily decreasing consumption, so long as the interest rate is not too much larger than the individual's discount rate; and so long as w_o, the wage associated with the initial health status, H_o, is high enough so productivity, and hence wage, would increase over time if individuals consumed their wages. In the absence of health-consumption effects, individuals would, in a situation with a low interest rate, have steadily declining consumption; but with health-consumption effects, there is a further rationale for early consumption—it increases one's lifetime budget constraint more than later consumption. The improvement in health status has a longer time in which to earn a return. Thus, the shadow price associated with the health consumption effect falls over time, eventually reaching zero. But if individuals cannot borrow, then consumption is limited to the wage; so long as the wage is high enough that that wage supports an increase in productivity over time, the wage will increase over time, thus supporting an increase in consumption over time. Toward the end of the individual's life, the shadow price on health becomes sufficiently small that it can be ignored. "Desired consumption"—what individuals would consume if they could borrow freely—may eventually decline enough that it falls below the wage. In the final part of the individual's life there may then be a phase in which he or she is consuming less than his or her wage (saving). But at the end of the individual's life, consumption must be equal to or greater than the wage. If consumption is high enough, that productivity is nondecreasing; this implies that at the end of an individual's life, the borrowing constraint must be binding. In the appendix, we show that *if the health dynamic equation is additive (that is $h(H,C) = -a(H) + b(C)$, if the borrowing constraint is binding initially, it is always binding.*

16. We use the dynamic model described in the previous note.

To simplify the problem, we assume that the output per efficiency unit of a worker is fixed, so $g(EL) = EL$, and we switch to a continuous time formulation. Then the firm's problem is to maximize

$$\int_0^\infty [E(w(t), H(t)) - w(t)]e^{-rt}dt$$

such that

$$w(t) \geq w'$$

$$\frac{dH}{dt} = h(H(t), w(t)).$$

This problem can be solved using standard intertemporal maximization techniques. If the worker faces a borrowing constraint, then the firm knows that if early in his or her life the worker increases the wage, productivity will be increased. Since the employer captures this return to future productivity (which the employer does not capture when there is no long-term relationship), wages will be higher (provided the wage productivity effect is large enough), especially early in life.

17. There has to be an effective legal system to enforce such contracts, since individuals cannot post a bond; for to post a bond, individuals would have to reduce consumption below their wage, thus reducing their productivity.

18. More generally, whenever there are imperfections of information or incompleteness of markets, equilibrium will not be constrained Pareto efficient. See Greenwald and Stiglitz 1986.

19. We assume that the health status of generation $t + 1$ depends on the wage of generation t, which in turn depends on its health status: $H_{t+1} = G(w_t(H_t))$.

Any solution to the equation $H^* = G(w(H^*))$ is a steady-state equilibrium, and there may well be multiple solutions. A solution with low health status yields a lower steady-state wage, and thus constitutes a vicious cycle of poverty.

These results are quite robust, and they do not depend critically on how families decide to divide income among working adults and children.

20. In practice, matters are more complicated, since employers may look for other observable surrogates for gender and ethnicity. See Rothschild and Stiglitz 1982.

21. The results described below depend only on separability.

22. The same argument holds if it is hypothesized that there is any point at where the budget constraint is not binding.

REFERENCES

Akerlof, G., and J. Yellen. 1986. *Efficiency Wage Models of the Labor Market.* New York: Cambridge University Press.

———. 1990. "The Fair Wage-Effort Hypothesis and Unemployment." *Quarterly Journal of Economics* 105, no. 2:255–83.

Becker, G. 1957. *Economics of Discrimination.* Chicago: University of Chicago Press.

Bevan, D., and J. E. Stiglitz. 1979. "Intergenerational Transfers and Inequality." *Greek Economic Review* 1, no. 1:8–26.

Dasgupta, P. 1993. *An Inquiry into Well-Being and Destitution.* Oxford: Clarendon Press.

Dasgupta, P., and D. Ray. 1987a. "Inequality as a Determinant of Malnutrition and Unemployment: Policy." *Economic Journal* 97:177–88.

———. 1987b. "Inequality as a Determinant of Malnutrition and Unemployment: Theory." *Economic Journal* 97 (March): 177–89.

Greenwald, B., and J. E. Stiglitz. 1986. "Externalities in Economies with Imperfect Information and Incomplete Markets." *Quarterly Journal of Economics* 101, no. 1:229–64.

Mirrlees, J. A. 1975. "A Pure Theory of Underdeveloped Economies." In *Agriculture in Development Theories,* ed. L. G. Reynolds. New Haven: Yale University Press.

Rothschild, M., and J. E. Stiglitz. 1982. "A Model of Employment Outcomes Illustrating the Effects of the Structure of Information on the Level and Distribution of Income." *Economic Letters* 10:231–36.

Sah, R., and J. E. Stiglitz. 1992. *Peasants versus City-Dwellers.* Oxford: Clarendon Press.

Shapiro, C., and J. E. Stiglitz. 1984. "Equilibrium Unemployment as a Worker Discipline Device." *American Economic Review* 74, no. 3:433–44. Reprinted in *New Keynesian Economics,* ed. N. G. Mankiw and D. Romer, vol. 2 (Cambridge: MIT Press, 1991), and in *Implicit Contract Theory,* ed. S. Rosen, E. German, and B. Bergman (Edward Elgar, 1993).

Stiglitz, J. E. 1969. "Distribution of Income and Wealth among Individuals." *Econometrica* 37, no. 3:382–97.

———. 1973. "Approaches to the Economics of Discrimination." *American Economic Review* 62, no. 2:287–95.

———. 1974a. "Alternative Theories of Wage Determination and Unemployment in L.D.C.s: The Labor Turnover Model." *Quarterly Journal of Economics* 87:194–227. Reprinted in *Development Economics,* ed. D. Lal (Edward Elgar, 1991).

———. 1974b. "Theories of Discrimination and Economic Policy." In *Patterns of Racial Discrimination,* ed. G. von Furstenberg et al. Lexington, Mass.: Lexington Books.

———. 1976. "The Efficiency Wage Hypothesis, Surplus Labor, and the Distribution of Income in L.D.C.s." *Oxford Economic Papers* 18, no. 2:185–207.

———. 1982a. "Alternative Theories of Wage Determination and Unemployment: The Efficiency Wage Model." In *The Theory and Experience of Economic Development: Essays in Honor of Sir Arthur W. Lewis,* ed. M. Gersovitz et al. London: George Allen and Unwin.

———. 1982b. "Utilitarianism and Horizontal Equity: The Case for Random Taxation." *Journal of Public Economics* 18:1–33.

———. 1986. "Theories of Wage Rigidities." In *Keynes' Economic Legacy: Contemporary Economic Theories,* ed. J. L. Butkiewicz et al. New York: Praeger.

———. 1987a. "The Causes and Consequences of the Dependence of Quality on Prices." *Journal of Economic Literature* 25 (March): 1–48. Reprinted in *Impresa, Instituzione e Informatzione,* ed. M. Franzini and M. Messori (Bologna: Cooperative Libraria Universitaria, 1991).

———. 1987b. "The Wage-Productivity Hypothesis: Its Economic Consequences and Policy Implications." In *Modern Developments in Public Finance,* ed. Michael J. Boskin. Oxford: Basil Blackwell.

———. 1996. "Some Lessons from the Asian Miracle." *World Bank Observer* 11, no. 2 (August): 151–77.

World Bank. 1993. *East Asian Miracle: Economic Growth and Public Policy.* New York: Oxford University Press for the World Bank.

———. 1997. *Private Capital Flows to Developing Countries: The Road to Financial Integration.* New York: Oxford University Press for the World Bank.

CHAPTER 3

Community Mechanism of Employment and Wage Determination: Classical or Neoclassical?

Yujiro Hayami

A major controversy in development economics in the 1960s surrounded the question whether labor employment and wage determination in Third World agriculture follows the neoclassical principle of marginalism or the classical principle of "total employment" under the institutionally determined wage rate. This controversy reflected the opposing perspectives of two Nobel Prize laureates, W. Arthur Lewis (1954) and Theodore W. Schultz (1964). In the formal theorizing of the two-sector development model, John Fei and Gustav Ranis (Ranis and Fei 1961; Fei and Ranis 1964) were the major contenders for the classical camp, and Dale W. Jorgenson (1961, 1969) represented the neoclassical camp.

The key assumption for the classical dual-economy model of the Lewis-Fei-Ranis variety is the existence of a horizontal labor supply curve to the modern sector (industry) based on "surplus labor" in the traditional sector (agriculture), given the latter's lower marginal productivity as compared with the institutional wage rate. Underlying this assumption is the mechanism by which social norms operate in rural communities, that is, compelling employment of all community members ("total employment") at an institutional wage rate, even if they contribute less to output than the wage rate. This institutional wage rate is itself considered a norm established as an equal share of the community's output (or average product) before industrialization begins.

This assumption is consistent with the traditional image of "community" in sociology, from Karl Marx (1953) to Ferdinand Tönnies (1926) and Max Weber (1924). The traditional view has been to assume a small group of people bounded by blood and locational ties, in which economic principles operate that are different from those of the capitalist market economy. In this view, while the prime motivation in the capitalist economy is private profit-seeking by individuals, the principle of community existence is the provision of mutual help to ensure the subsistence of all its members. Economic rationality in terms of individual profit and utility maximization does not operate in the community that is thus defined.

If the community principle is, in fact, based on mutual help and income sharing instead of profit or utility maximization by individuals, community organizations should fail to achieve efficient resource allocations according to the neoclassical criteria. However, many empirical studies following the lead of Schultz indicate that the wage rates in the rural sectors of developing economies are not significantly different from the marginal value product of labor, implying efficient resource allocation resulting from profit maximization by individuals (Schultz 1964; Hopper 1965; Paglin 1965; Massell 1967; Yotopoulos 1968). Does this mean that a community principle of mutual help and income sharing is an illusion or a mere spoken moral code having no tangible power to control economic activities? Or have traditional communities already been destroyed by the introduction of the market economy into rural villages in developing economies?

This essay aims to shed light on this question based on the results of my village studies in Southeast Asia (Hayami and Kikuchi 1981), as compared with the situation in Japan. It was found that in the study villages the principle of work and income sharing was operating as a social norm with significant power to bind villagers' behavior. Yet, according to our estimates, the rates of compensation to labor under this community principle were not significantly different from those of neoclassical marginalism. Despite this equivalence, adherence to the community principle is considered to have the merit of saving labor transaction costs and hence increasing employment. In the final section of this essay, the possibility of rural industrialization based on this community mechanism shall be discussed in comparison with the historical experience in Meiji Japan, with a focus on the applicability of the Fei-Ranis model to the development of low-income economies.

1 The Different Modes of Peasant Farming

When people familiar with agriculture in Northeast Asia, including China, Korea, and Japan, would visit rural villages in Southeast Asia, such as the Philippines and Indonesia, they were intrigued by the observation that peasants and family members worked relatively little time on their own farms, leaving many of the tasks to hired labor. In recent years in Japan, reliance on hired labor for farm operations has increased as a result of increased off-farm employment opportunities. Before then, farm tasks were predominantly shouldered by family members, with hired and exchange labor used as a minor supplement in peak seasons. According to a nationwide survey by the Japan Ministry of Agriculture for 1934–36, when the traditional pattern prevailed, the ratio of hired labor (including exchange labor) in the total number of workdays used for rice production was less than 10 percent for owner farms and less than 8 percent for tenant farms (top two rows in table 3.1).

In contrast, according to our survey of two rice villages in the Laguna Province, Philippines, the ratio of hired labor amounted to as much as 70 percent, despite the fact that the average operational size of Philippine farms wasn't significantly different from the Japanese farms (middle two rows in table 3.1). Farms dependent on hired labor for more than two-thirds of total labor input are not consistent with the traditional image of "peasants"—small, subsistence-oriented farms mainly dependent on family labor—since Alexander Chayanov (1966). This high dependency on hired labor is not unique to these two surveyed villages but rather universal in the rice-farming areas of the Philippines.

How is such a large amount of external labor employed in small farms? Almost all the external labor is hired for casual work on a daily contract basis. Hired labor is used mainly for peak-season activities such as rice transplanting and harvesting. Both activities demand large quantities of labor in short periods and are visible in terms of work effort outcomes (i.e., transplanted areas and harvested quantities). In con-

TABLE 3.1.   Labor Inputs per Hectare of Rice Crop Area in Japan, the Philippines, and Indonesia

	Workdays per Hectare			Percentage of Hired Labor	Operational Holding per Farm (hectare)
	Total	Family	Hired		
Japan (1934–36 average)					
Tenant	198	183	15	7.6	1.4
Owner	200	181	19	9.5	1.6
Philippines					
Village E (1976 wet season)	105	31	74	70.5	2.0
Village W (1977 dry season)	105	37	68	64.8	1.4
Indonesia					
Village S (1978 wet season)	208	70	138	66.3	0.30
Village N (1978 dry season)	159	35	124	78.0	0.87

Source: Japan: Japan Ministry of Agriculture and Forestry 1974. Philippines: Hayami and Kikuchi 1981, 118 and 137. Indonesia: Calculated from Hayami and Kikuchi 1981, 183 and 202, by assuming six-hour workday.

trast, family labor is used mainly for the tasks that require care and judgment without immediately visible outcomes, for which physical labor requirements are not so large, such as water and pest controls, fertilizer application, and seedbed preparations. Land preparation with the use of water buffalo (carabao) is traditionally the task of family labor. However, in recent years it has increasingly been contracted out to tractor custom services.

This division of labor between family and hired labor is understandable in view of seasonal fluctuations in labor demand as well as the relative ease of monitoring work efforts. It is the common practice in Japan and elsewhere. A unique aspect of this arrangement is that family members rarely work in transplanting and harvesting. Seedlings are prepared and brought to fields by family members, but transplanting itself is performed by a labor crew organized by a contractor called *kabisilya.* More intriguing is the system of harvesting, which requires nearly 40 percent of total labor input in rice production. The traditional system is called *hunusan* ("sharing" in Tagalog), a form of contract by which, when a farmer specifies a day of harvesting in his field, anyone can participate in harvesting and threshing, and the harvesters receive a certain share (traditionally one-sixth) of the output. By custom, the farmer can deny no one the opportunity of harvesting his crop. Neither he nor other family members may go to the harvesting field, even to monitor the work being performed.

2 Origins of Income and Work Sharing

Why do poor peasants employ external labor without fully utilizing family labor on their own farms? This behavior is inconsistent with the Chayanovian concept of peasants as farmers who try to maximize the utilization of family labor even up to the point of zero marginal productivity (Chayanov 1966).

Akira Takahashi (1969) developed a theory to explain this apparent anomaly by absentee landlordism prevailing in the Philippines since the Spanish colonial rule. A common form of land tenancy contract in rice areas was a sharecropping contract by which both output and input costs (including hired wage cost) were shared fifty-fifty between tenants and landlords. Under this contract the larger the payment to hired labor, the smaller was the landlords' share of output. The tenants' share also became smaller with the larger payment to hired labor. However, this reduction in tenants' income could be recovered by receipt of output shares from neighbors. Namely, mutual employment among tenants would maximize their output share at the expense of landlords.

This hypothesis of "tenants' collusion" is apparently plausible in terms of the agrarian history of the Philippines. However, when a similar survey was conducted in West Java, Indonesia, where most farmers were owner-operators instead of tenants, it was found that dependency on hired labor was equally high, despite an average farm size significantly smaller than in the Philippines (bottom two rows in table 3.1).

An alternative hypothesis may be that a social norm of income and work sharing prevails in the rural sector of Southeast Asia. This norm dictates that well-to-do members in a village community should provide income-earning opportunities to poor neighbors by retreating themselves from work. It is a kind of community principle of mutual help to guarantee minimum subsistence to the poor.

The rural community characterized by the principle of income and work sharing may sound like an altruistic utopia. However, this principle is not necessarily inconsistent with economic rationality based on egoism. A condition for original establishment of the sharing principle could have been a low level of agricultural productivity with high risk. Until rather recently, Southeast Asia had been characterized by sparse population relative to available land for cultivation. Before diffusion of modern high-yielding varieties since the late 1960s (the so-called green revolution), rice farming was typically extensive with little fertilizer application and weeding practice, so that yield differences between diligent and idle farmers were much less pronounced than in Japan. Therefore, whether a farmer himself worked hard on his field or left the work to hired laborers did not much affect the level of yield.

On the other hand, production risk was high, especially in the absence of irrigation and drainage systems. During drought, crops in elevated locations may be destroyed, whereas bumper crops may be harvested from lower-lying marshy fields. The reverse is likely to be the case during a season of heavy rain and flooding. Similarly, an outbreak of pests may eliminate crops in a certain area, while other areas might be little damaged. In other words, it is hazardous to rely on production from a single plot for subsistence. Therefore, it is common for a peasant to hold his land in small parcels scattered over a wide area. Similarly, it greatly reduces risk if he allows other villagers to share work and output in his farm, while he is allowed to share work and output in others' farms. This insurance mechanism of work and income sharing would be especially valuable in economies where the market is underdeveloped, providing villagers with no other means of insuring against risk in farm production, such as off-farm employment opportunities or formal insurance and credit systems. This is one of many insurance mechanisms in traditional societies, which generally involve diversifying family members' economic activities widely across different locations (Rosenzweig 1988a, 1988b; Stark and Lucas 1988).

Thus, it is hypothesized that the sharing principle observable in Southeast Asian villages did emerge from people's need to secure subsistence at the low level of land productivity, which is little response to work efforts of cultivators. It was established because it was mutually beneficial to sharing parties. As such, egoists should have found it profitable to observe this principle in terms of their rational economic calculations. However, the sharing system would not have been elevated to a social norm and maintained as such unless violations from this norm (e.g., receiving shares from neighbors without reciprocating to them) could be expected to receive social sanctions such as social opprobrium (which may eventually escalate to ostracism) in the small village community characterized by intensive personal interactions (Becker 1974; Akerlof 1976).

3 Institutional Adjustments under the Sharing System

If the community principle of work and income sharing originated in rational choice under certain economic and technological conditions, its practice would have changed corresponding to changes in these conditions.

In the traditional *hunusan* system, every villager could participate in harvesting and normally receive one-sixth of harvested paddy. In the past, when rice farming was associated with low yields, one-sixth of output could well be close to harvesting labor's contribution (or labor's marginal productivity) to output. However, as the use of modern rice varieties and chemical fertilizers has been promoted, yields per hectare have risen sharply with parallel increases in harvesters' receipts. On the other hand, the market wage rates have remained largely stable under the pressure of labor force growth. As a result, the rate of return to labor under the traditional *hunusan* contract has risen cumulatively above the market wage rate.

Such a tendency can be observed in table 3.2, which summarizes the data from a survey village (village E in table 3.1). This village is located in a marshy lowland area characterized by rice monoculture. From 1966 to 1976, population in this village increased from 393 to 644 persons, while cultivated areas remained virtually constant, resulting in a sharp increase in the man/land ratio from less than four persons per hectare to

TABLE 3.2. Changes in Population, Cultivated Land Area, Rice Yield, and Wage Rate in a Survey Village (Village E) in the Philippines, 1956–76

	1956	1966	1976
Population (no.)		393	644
Cultivated land area (ha)		104	108
Man/land ratio (no./ha)		3.8	6.0
Paddy yield (ton/ha)			
Wet season	2.2	2.4	3.2
Dry season	—	3.1	3.6
TOTAL	2.2	5.5	6.8
Nominal wage rate (peso/day)[a]		3.6	9.8
Paddy price (peso/kg)		0.4	1.0
Real wage rate (kg/day)		9.0	9.8

Source: Hayami and Kikuchi 1981, 103–8.
[a]Average of land preparation, transplanting, and weeding wage rates.

six persons. Meanwhile, major gains in agricultural productivity also occurred. In the absence of irrigation systems, rice was traditionally grown only in the wet season. The extension of a national irrigation system in 1958 made double-cropping in all paddy fields in this village possible, resulting in the doubling of average rice yields per hectare during the 1956 to 1976 period. (Rice yield is usually higher in the dry season under higher solar energy.) The rice yields in both wet and dry seasons increased significantly from 1966 to 1976 owing to propagation of modern high-yielding varieties with increased fertilizer application. These improvements in rice production technology and irrigation infrastructure were combined to triple average rice yield per hectare of paddy field area within the two decades from 1956 to 1976.

The irrigation development that enabled rice planting in the dry season nearly doubled the intensity of land use for rice production. In addition, significant increases in labor demand were a result of the introduction of modern rice technology for weeding, fertilizer application, pest control, and water management. However, under the pressure of both high natural population growth and labor immigration from surrounding mountain areas, the real wage rate for casual farm work remained largely constant at about nine kilograms per paddy per day.

Under the *hunusan* contract of output sharing at a fixed rate (usually one-sixth), increases in rice yield automatically resulted in parallel increases in the real cost of harvesting labor for employers. Thus, this community-type employment contract became a disadvantageous system for employer farmers relative to the market-type daily wage contract, since the market wage rate remained constant in real terms (table 3.2). Moreover, unlike the old days when *hunusan* harvesters had largely been neighboring farmers, a majority of them had now become landless agricultural laborers, many of whom were migrants from outside the village. Therefore, it became difficult for an employer farmer to recover his high payment to harvesting laborers above the market wage rates from reciprocal employment.

Corresponding to these changes, a new system called *gama* ("weeding" in Tagalog) emerged. *Gama* is an output-sharing contract similar to *hunusan,* except that employment for harvesting is limited to workers who worked on the weeding of the field without receiving wages. In other words, in the *gama* system, weeding labor is a free service provided by workers to establish a right to participate in harvesting and to receive one-sixth of output. To the extent that weeding labor is additionally required for receiving the same share of output, the implied wage rate is lower in *gama* than in *hunusan.* Although this adjustment reduced the rate of compensation to labor per hour, it was accepted by villagers because it maintained the traditional sharing arrangement as well as the sharing rate, thereby remaining consonant with the norm of the village community.

With the adoption of the *gama* system the gap between harvesters' share and labor's marginal productivity under the traditional *hunusan* system was closed as illustrated by calculations in table 3.3. First, labor inputs per hectare per crop season are measured in workdays for both harvesting and weeding per hectare (rows 1 and 2). Dividing the market value of harvesters' output share (row 4) by the number of workdays for harvesting (row 1) produces the imputed wage rate of harvesting labor under the *hunusan* contract (row 5). The imputed wage rate under the *gama* contract (row 6) can be obtained by dividing the market value of harvesters' share by the number of workdays for both harvesting and weeding (sums of rows 1 and 2). The results show that if *hunusan* had been used in 1976 when modern rice technology was widely diffused, the rate of compensation to harvesting labor would have been about 60 percent higher than its market wage rate. This gap was eliminated almost completely with adoption of the *gama* system.

These results are consistent with the hypothesis that the *gama* contract represents an institutional innovation designed to reduce disequilibrium between labor's remuneration rate and marginal productiv-

TABLE 3.3. Imputation of Wage Rates for Rice Harvesting Work under Different Contracts in a Survey Village (Village E) in the Philippines, 1976 Wet Season[a]

Number of workdays per hectare		
(1) Harvesting	33.6	
(2) Weeding	19.6	
Actual share of harvester		
(3) Quantity in paddy (kg/ha)	526.5	
(4) Imputed value of paddy (kg/ha)[b]	526.5	
Inputed wage rate (peso/day)		
(5) *Hunusan* = (4)/(1)	15.7	(157)[c]
(6) *Gama* = (4)/[(1) + (2)]	9.9	(99)
Market wage rate (peso/day)	10.0[d]	(100)

Source: Hayami and Kikuchi 1981, 121.
[a]Averages of data collected from employers and employees.
[b]One peso per kg for the market price of paddy.
[c]Index with the market wage rate set equal to 100 in parentheses.
[d]Weighted average of daily contract wage rates for harvesting (11 pesos) and weeding (8 pesos).

TABLE 3.4. Percentage of Rice Farmers Adopting *Gama* Contract in the Laguna Province, Philippines

	Survey Village (E)	Laguna Province
1960	3	n.a.
1965	22	n.a.
1970	45	28
1975	80	85
1978	85	77
1981	85	90

Source: Kikuchi and Hayami 1983, 252.

ity within the framework of work and income sharing in the community. In fact, as shown in table 3.4, the emergence and diffusion of the *gama* contract paralleled the rice yield increases due to irrigation improvements and diffusion of modern rice technology, not only in this study village but also over the wider province of Laguna, where this village is located. These observations seem to indicate that villagers in the Philippines were applying the community principle of sharing based on rational economic calculations. This institutional innovation was not specific to Laguna, but also observed in other rice-producing areas in the Philippines (Hayami and Kikuchi 1981, 84–87).

4 The Indonesia Case of Cumulative Adjustments

Moreover, a similar institutional adjustment was observed in a study village in Indonesia (village S in table 3.1). This village, located in a mountain valley in West Java, is characterized by the practice of rice monoculture. As is typical of Java, population density is high and farm size small in this village. By the time of our survey (1978), this village had not experienced successful introduction of modern rice varieties. For a long time the village had maintained a relatively well designed communal irrigation system, but no significant improvement had been undertaken for many years. As a result, demand for labor increased slower than supply, resulting in about a 10 percent decline in the real wage rate in the 1970s. Correspondingly, a shift was observed from animal (carabao) plowing to hand hoeing, reflecting a desperate effort by landless workers to compensate for decreased wage rates.

The traditional harvesting system in Java was called *bawon,* which was essentially the same as *hunusan* in the Philippines except that *hunusan* was done by sickles, whereas *bawon* harvesting usually used small hand knives for cutting panicles. In the study village and its surroundings, the traditional *bawon* system underwent cumulative changes. Initially, to prevent too many harvesters from stampeding and destroying crops in rush competition, several measures were installed in the *bawon* system to restrict participation.

The traditional "purely open" (PO) *bawon* system was replaced successively, first by a system in which harvesting is open only to members in the same village (OV); second by a system in which only people who come to harvesting before a designated maximum number is reached are allowed to harvest (OM); and third, by limiting participants to only those who received specific invitations. In all the modified systems the traditional one-sixth share for harvesting work was maintained.

Later, the system changed to a new contract called *ceblokan,* in which additional work is requested of those employed in harvesting, similar to *gama* in the Philippines. However, unlike the Philippine case, the *ceblokan* system evolved over a spectrum of arrangements in terms of harvesters' share and obligatory work. Originally, *ceblokan* harvesters received a traditional share of one-sixth for the additional service of rice transplanting without pay (usually meals were served even though cash wages were not paid). Later, their share was reduced to one-seventh, and weeding and harrowing were added to the list of obligatory work required to establish the harvesting right. The harvesting systems in this village shows successive shifts from more open and more generous arrangements to more restrictive and less generous arrangements as shown in table 3.5. Underlying this process was a decline in the return to labor relative to the return to land due to the growth of the labor force against limited land resources under stagnant technology.

Despite its apparent complexity in the process of contract evolution, the shift from *bawon* to *ceblokan* was driven by the same motivation of employer farmers as in the shift from *hunusan* to *gama* in the Philippines. Namely, employer-farmer motivation was to reduce the harvesting labor cost to a level consistent to the market wage rates while maintaining the basic framework of work and income sharing. Table 3.6 imputes the wage rates implicit in various harvesting arrangements, using the same procedures as for table 3.3. Even though *ceblokan* workers did not receive wages for obligatory work such as transplanting and weeding, they were provided with meals that had insignificant values in the village context (meals were not served for harvesting work itself). The imputation in table 3.6 assumes that these meals had the value of one-half the market values of the obligatory jobs. The results of imputation indicate that the rate of compensation to labor under the *bawon* system with the one-seventh share was 40 percent higher than the market wage rate; a shift to the *ceblokan* system with the obligation of transplanting alone reduced the gap to 20 percent. With the further addition of weeding to the obligation the gap was completely eliminated.

TABLE 3.5. Changes in Rice Harvesting System in the South Subang Village (% of farmer adoptors)

| | *Bawon*[a] | | | | *Ceblokan*[b] | | | | | |
	PO	OV	OM	LI	1/6(T)	1/7(T)	1/7(T+W)	1/7(H+T)	1/7(H+T+W)	Total
1950s	35	29	18	18						100
1960–61	29	31	21	19						100
1962–63	16	34	33	17						100
1964–65	9	16	16	32	27					100
1966–67	3	10	8	27	52					100
1968–69	1	4	6	19	44	24	2			100
1970–71			2	10	33	51	4			100
1972–73				8	17	67	8			100
1974–75				7	15	67	10	1		100
1976–77				4	7	67	18	2	2	100
1978				4		72	19	1	4	100

Source: Hayami and Kikuchi 1981, 184.

[a]*Bawon* system: PO — purely open, OV — open for villagers only, OM — open with maximum limit, LI — limited to invitees.

[b]*Ceblokan* system: 1/6, 1/7 — harvesters' share; T, W, H — obligatory work to establish the harvesting right (T — transplanting, W — weeding, H — harrowing).

TABLE 3.6. Imputation of Wage Rates for Rice Harvesting Work under Different Contracts in a Survey Village (Village S) in Indonesia, 1978 Dry Season

Number of work hours (hour/ha)	
(1) Harvesting	324
(2) Transplanting	111
(3) Weeding	147
Actual share of harvester (1/7)	
(4) Quantity in paddy (kg/ha)	421
(5) Imputed value of paddy (rupiah/ha)[a]	27,365
Imputed wage rate (rupiah/hour)	
(6) *Bawon* 1/7 = (4)/(1)	84 (140)[c]
(7) *Ceblokan* 1/7 (T) = (4)/[1 + 0.5(2)][b]	72 (120)
(8) *Ceblokan* 1/7 (T + W) = (4)/[1 + 0.5(2) + 0.5(3)][b]	60 (100)
Market wage rate (rupiah/hour)	60 (100)

Source: Hayami and Kikuchi 1981, 188.
[a]65 rupiah per kg for the market price.
[b]Assume the cost of meals served for transplanting and weeding to be one-half of the wage rate for those tasks.
[c]Index with the market wage rate set equal to 100.

5 The Role of Community Norm

The preceding analysis of harvesting systems in Indonesia and the Philippines indicates a strong tendency in rural villages in developing economies to maintain the institutional framework of sharing work and income. By virtue of this trait, these villages are considered to retain the "community mechanism" of resource allocation that can be distinguished from the capitalist market mechanism, as assumed by classic sociologists, such as Marx, Tönnies, and Weber, whose perspective was incorporated by Lewis, Fei, and Ranis into their dual-economy model. However, the analysis also shows that this community mechanism is sufficiently flexible to make institutional adjustments in response to economic incentives, so that the outcomes of this resource allocation are largely equivalent to those of neoclassical equilibrium resulting from the market mechanism.

Does this mean that the community principle of sharing is a superficial moral code with no substantive impact on people's economic behavior? That is not likely the case. What was not included in our quantitative analysis was transaction costs involved in labor employment. When disequilibrium emerged between the market wage rate and the rate of compensation to labor in the sharing contract like *hunusan*, the sharing contract was maintained instead of being replaced by the time-rate contract. Moreover, the strong force seems to be operating for maintaining the traditional share rate (one-sixth).

It is likely that such an institutional response is based on the interest of employer farmers in saving transaction costs. The daily employment contract at the fixed wage rate is a typical form of market exchange between labor and money. By nature, it is an impersonal spot transaction. Under such a contract, little incentive operates for employees to work properly and conscientiously. Therefore, employers must rely on supervision and command to enforce employees' work, resulting in high labor transaction costs as well as social confrontation between employers and employees.

In contrast, the community-type contracts like *gama* in the Philippines and *ceblokan* in Indonesia encompass several tasks, such as weeding and harvesting, over a season, and it usually continues to be renewed seasonally. Wages are not paid at the time of weeding. In the minds of villagers, weeding with no direct payment is considered to be not a part of a contract based on economic calculations, but an expression of gratitude by laborers for the goodwill of a farmer patron who provides them the opportunity of participating in harvesting and receiving the output share. Such a personal relationship is further strengthened through exchanges of gifts, credits, and personal services. Both the sense of moral obligation and the fear of losing the patron-client relationship would motivate laborers to exert conscientious work efforts. Relative to the replacement of the community-type sharing contract by the market-type fixed-wage contract, the adjustment of the sharing contract by adding extra-work obligations, such as *gama,* would reduce labor transaction costs. To that extent, labor employment would increase for the same wage rate, as it would prevent farm mechanization, which is often strongly motivated by the prospect of saving transaction costs rather than direct wage costs (Hayami and Kikuchi 1981, chap. 3; Hayami, Quisumbing, and Adriano 1990, chap. 6). Thus, adherence to the community principle is effective in raising both economic efficiency and social stability.

It seems reasonable to hypothesize that the general moral principle calling for mutual help through work and income sharing in village communities was instrumental in guiding institutional innovation toward adjustments within the sharing system instead of shifting to the fixed-wage contract. The likelihood of significant psychological and social resistance against violations of an established social norm was demonstrated by one episode in a survey village in the Philippines. When a large farmer announced his intention to reduce harvesters' share from the traditional one-sixth to one-seventh under the *hunusan* system, his standing crop was burned during the night. Thus, the shift from the *hunusan* to the *gama* represents a case in which the social norms and moral codes long nurtured in village communities in the premodern period guided institutional change toward economic efficiency and social stability as modernization forces (such as population explosion, modern agricultural technology, and commercialization) demanded institutional change.

However, it does not follow that the community-type of sharing arrangement is always preserved. In the Indonesia province of West Java, the institutional adjustment in the rice harvesting system took place as diffusion of the *ceblokan* system. In Central Java, however, a different system called *tebasan* did emerge, replacing the traditional *bawon* system. *Tebasan* is a market-type contract in which farmers sell their standing crops immediately before harvest to a middleman, who harvests the crops by laborers employed daily at the fixed market wage rates (Collier, Wiradi, and Soentoro 1977; Hayami and Kikuchi 1981, 155–70). Because farmers, as members of a village community, were bound by the community obligation of sharing, they passed on to middlemen outside the community the task of executing the market-type labor contract. This example adds to the evidence of efforts by rural people in developing economies to achieve efficient resource allocations under the constraint of traditional community norms.

These episodes also indicate that the evolution of community institutions involves the possibility of arriving at multiple equilibrium depending both on the social and cultural traditions that determine people's preference for observing community norms as well as on the strength of social sanctions against violators (Akerlof 1976, 1980). For example, the case in which a large farmer dared to reduce *hunusan*'s share to one-seventh, as previously mentioned, was reported in a village of relatively recent settlement, where cohesive community relationships had not been well established. In our context, however, it is important to recognize that, unlike Akerlof's prediction, adherence to the traditional norm does not necessarily result in inefficiency, as illustrated by the analysis on the shift to the *gama* system in the long-settled village endowed with cohesive community relationships.

6 Toward Community-Based Industrialization

If the rate of compensation to labor under the community mechanism turns out to be equivalent to that of neoclassical equilibrium, the building block of the classical dual-economy model—infinitely elastic labor supply to industry based on surplus labor in agriculture — does not stand. This does not deny, however, the high heuristic value of the Fei-Ranis model applicable to a wide range of low-income economies.

Low-income economies have been under the pressure of explosive population growth ranging from 2 to 3 percent per year. Unlike the assumption of Jorgenson's neoclassical model, this population explosion was not induced by increased income or increased food availability, but was largely exogenous, arising from the importation of medical and public health technology from advanced economies. This pattern is evident from the observation that significant increases in life expectancy and decreases in infant mortality rates in sub-Saharan Africa have been associated with reductions in the level of nutrition intake per capita (Thorbecke 1995). Meanwhile, cultivation frontiers had largely been closed by the 1960s. The rural sector, unable to absorb increased population, pushed its labor force out to the urban sector. Given the rural sector's dominant share of labor in the early development stage, even a small percentage transfer of rural labor force is more than sufficient to prevent labor supply to industry from sloping upwardly, provided that arrival of the "shortage point" can be avoided with the effort of raising agricultural productivity, as Fei and Ranis rightly pointed out.

Applicability of Fei and Ranis's model structure to the strategy of Third World development is thus limited less by the absence of large surplus labor at the onset of industrialization than by the segmentation of the labor market as formulated by Harris and Todaro (1970). Developing economies today have imported the institutions to protect labor, such as labor unions and minimum-wage laws, starting from the early stage of their development. Application of these labor codes has been limited to the "formal sector," consisting of government agencies and large-scale modern enterprises. While workers employed in the formal sector enjoy stable employment at high wages, entry to this sector is closed to laborers in the "informal sector." Such institutional dualism is said to be especially serious in Africa and Latin America relative to Asia (Fields and Wan 1989; World Bank 1993, 266–73).

Under this labor market segmentation, migrant laborers from agriculture cannot become a source of low-cost labor to modern industry but instead become a source of growth in the lumpen proletariat in urban slums with no possibility of serving as the Marxist industrial reserve army. The high wage rates in the formal sector induce adoption of labor-saving technologies, which results in capital deepening instead of becoming more shallow, even in labor-abundant economies, unlike the prediction by the Fei-Ranis model.

One possible way out of this inefficient and inequitable course of industrialization is to develop small- and medium-scale industries, especially in rural areas (Ranis and Stewart 1993). Indeed, industrialization in Japan in its early development phase was heavily dependent on activities of rural-based small manufacturers (Smith 1956, 1988; Rosovsky and Ohkawa 1961; Tussing 1966). A large share of these rural industrial activities was undertaken by entrepreneurial peasants. Their contributions were no less significant than those of large modern corporations developed by urban entrepreneurs who emerged from the preindustrial merchant class (such as Mitsui and Sumitomo) and ex-warrior class (such as Mitsubishi). This development of rural-based enterprises prepared the way for the process of Japan's industrialization to be less capital-intensive than other latecomers to modern economic growth (Smith 1988).

In the past, development and diffusion of appropriate technology with respect to the factor market conditions have traditionally been discussed as a central issue in the promotion of small and medium industries in developing economies (Stewart 1977; Pack and Westphal 1986; Ranis and Stewart 1993). However, a critical condition for rural-based industrialization that has not received due attention so far is the development of a marketing system that can organize a large number of small producers in rural areas for production to meet national and international demands. This condition must be met with development of *relational contract*—the term meaning a long-term contract relation for which accumulated personal ties and mutual trust act as a major means of contract enforcement (Hayami 1998). In the relational contracting system various contracts tend to be interlinked. A typical example is the so-called putting-out contract in which a principal (e.g., trader) advances materials (yarn) for processing to his agent (cottage weaver) and later to collect the finished product (cloth) at a piece-rate payment. Thus, this system combines the contracts on material supply and product purchases with the credit contract for financing a part of the agent's working capital and, also, fixed capital of the processing machine if the loom is lent. Even in a simpler "advance-order" contract in which the principal guarantees the purchase of the finished products but does not advance the materials, the provision of some extra services—such as credit guarantee and technical guidance—usually involved in the contract is to be called "relational." Thus, the relational contract is the mechanism by which not only the products of rural-based industries are delivered to wide markets, but also new technology, credit, and inputs are channeled to rural entrepreneurs.

Relational contracting and vertical integration can be considered two alternatives for an efficient market. If the market is efficient with no transaction costs and no risk, impersonal spot transactions in the market based solely on prices are sufficient to coordinate economy-wide division of labor; neither the vertically integrated firm nor interfirm cooperation by means of relational contracting is therefore needed.

However, in the real world of incomplete information, transaction costs are significant and risk is high. This is especially true of the rural sector in developing economies, where the market is small and segmented, institutions for supplying needed market information (such as product standards, grading, and brand names) are not well established, and insurance and credit institutions are too underdeveloped to cope with market risk. Thus, a trader who finds a large demand for a commodity in an urban or foreign market will face the difficulty of procuring from the spot market a sufficient amount at a sufficient quality in due time. In order to exploit the profit opportunity, he may have to install under his own management a factory for the mass production of standardized commodities. In this way he vertically integrates the manufacturing with the trading activities. Alternatively, he may organize a relational contract with autonomous producers for the assured supply of needed commodities of the right quantity, quality, and timing.

If the vertical integration is commonly chosen, the resulting industrial structure will be such that enterprises are small in number and large in size, which are likely located in urban-industrial centers. This structure will inevitably create segmentation between the formal and the informal sectors. There is little doubt that industrial and commercial activities can spread widely over the rural sector only with the development of the relational contracting system.

Transaction costs for monitoring the work effort of hired laborers in the vertically integrated factory system are known to be very high. Indeed, how to promote work morale and prevent shirking of employees by such incentives as promotions and bonuses has been a central issue in theories of industrial management and organization. The cost of monitoring the work effort of hired labor is nonexistent for the principal in the work contract-out system and relatively modest for the agents whose employees are typically small in number and easy to monitor. The monitoring cost is especially small where the work is performed by the labor of family members, relatives, and friends, as usually is the case with rural-based enterprises.

However, the relational contracting system is subject to high transaction costs with respect to quality and delivery time of products. For example, a trader who organizes the putting-out contract with weavers may be severely damaged by the weavers' "embezzlement" in using consigned yarn less intensively than a specified standard, so that the trader collecting inferior cloth receives low prices or develops a bad reputation among his customers. A similar problem may arise from the weavers' late delivery of their cloth. On the other hand, weavers are also not free from opportunism of the principal trader. It can happen that the trader refuses to accept delivered cloth or requests a price reduction from the weaver on the false charge of quality deficiency. Such mutual distrust may culminate in the prisoner's dilemma solution, ending in the demise of the mutually beneficial contract.

Thus, the success of relational contracting as the basis for rural-based industrialization hinges critically on how much mutual trust and cooperation can be developed so that the exercise of opportunism can be curbed. Sustainability of the two-party cooperative relationship is greatly increased by the community mechanism, which sanctions those who deviate from the norms of community (Kreps and Wilson 1982; Fudenberg and Maskin 1986; Abreu 1988).

In this respect, the community mechanism of sharing, as exemplified by harvesting systems in the Philippines and Indonesia, can be a basis on which effective relational contracting for rural industry and commerce can be built. Indeed, the putting-out contract using the piece-rate payment scheme is a kind of output-sharing contract akin to the harvesting systems. The fact that in the practice of share harvesting farmer-employers seldom go to their fields for monitoring indicates that possible embezzlement is effectively curbed by the community mechanism. Applicability of this mechanism not only to the organization of agricultural production but also to the organization of commercial and industrial activities in rural areas was demonstrated by a study of peasant entrepreneurship in Indonesia (Hayami and Kawagoe 1993).

The community mechanism nurtured in Asian villages through intensive personal interactions under high population density and a strong need for collaboration in rice farming could thus be a unique asset for rural industrialization based on relational contracting. This hypothesis may be supported by historical comparison in the use of the putting-out system between Europe and Japan. In Europe, the putting-out system commonly practiced in the protoindustrialization stage was largely replaced by the factory system when modern industrialization began, presumably because of the difficulty in controlling product quality due to embezzlement (Landes 1969, 118–19; Randall 1990). In contrast, the putting-out system has continued to be used commonly in Japan, presumably because of the strong community mechanism of contract enforcement (Itoh and Tanimoto 1998).

In fact, there is evidence that the practice of putting-out expanded with economic modernization in Japan during the Meiji period. A case study of the Saitama Prefecture shows that before the Meiji Restoration (1868) farmers wove cloth from yarn that they spun themselves from their own harvested cotton crop. The woven cloth was procured at spot prices by guild merchants *(kabu nakama)* in town and shipped to Edo (Tokyo). The opening of international trade and subsequent national unification resulted in a large increase in domestic demand for cotton clothes, partly because of general increases in farm product prices and incomes and partly because of declines in the prices of cotton products due to import competition. This opportunity was exploited by rural-based traders outside the guild (many of them from the upper peasantry class), who leased out looms to farm households and advanced them imported foreign-made yarn on a piece-rate, service-fee contract basis; the woven cloth collected by these traders was transshipped widely across the nation beyond the traditional Edo market (Kandachi 1975; Tanimoto 1986). This example seems to indicate that the putting-out contract is not an archaic system bound to demise with modernization. Instead, it is an efficient mechanism for meeting dynamic demand expansion in a modern market economy by means of mobilizing the labor of low-opportunity costs, especially farm family labor standing idle between farm tasks and household chores, at a minimum labor-monitoring cost, in addition to other merits such as risk sharing and low capital cost.

If rural-based industrialization can be promoted with effective organization of small manufacturers across rural villages and local towns in low-income economies, their economic development pattern will stimulate the Fei-Ranis dual-economy model. It is a common observation that a significant amount of rural labor stands idle or grossly underutilized in the slack seasons for agricultural production. This "surplus labor" can be tapped for industrial production with flexible use of putting-out and other forms of relational contract. Interindustry transfers of labor and food in rural-based industrialization involve much smaller costs than in urban-based industrialization. In fact, much of the commercial and industrial activities including the practice of the putting-out system in the early development phase of Japan was organized by wealthy peasants *(gono),* who cultivated a part of their holdings by themselves and rented out the rest while engaging in nonfarm activities — "dualistic landlords" in the terminology of Fei and Ranis (1964, 164–71).

Japan followed this model in its early development phase, utilizing the traditional community relationship for the effective enforcement of relational contracts. The community mechanism, as illustrated by the evolution of rice-harvesting systems in the Philippines and Indonesia in this essay, suggests that such possibilities are latent in the rural sector of the developing economies.

NOTE

Useful comments from Gary Saxonhouse and John Strauss are gratefully acknowledged.

REFERENCES

Abreu, Dilip. 1988. "On the Theory of Infinitely Repeated Games with Discounting." *Econometrica* 56 (March): 383–96.

Akerlof, George A. 1976. "The Economics of Caste and of the Rat Race and Other Woeful Tales." *Quarterly Journal of Economics* 90 (November): 599–617.

———. 1980. "A Theory of Social Custom, of Which Unemployment May Be One Consequence." *Quarterly Journal of Economics* 94 (June): 749–75.

Becker, Gary S. 1974. "A Theory of Social Interactions." *Journal of Political Economy* 82 (November–December): 1063–93.

Chayanov, Alexander V. 1966. *Theory of Peasant Economy.* Ed. D. Thorner et al. Homewood, Ill.: Richard D. Irwin.

Collier, William, Gunawan Wiradi, and Soentoro. 1977. "Recent Changes in Rice Harvesting Methods." *Bulletin of Indonesian Economic Studies* 19 (July): 36–45.

Fei, John C. H., and Gustav Ranis. 1964. *Development of the Labor Surplus Economy.* Homewood, Ill.: Richard D. Irwin.

Fields, Gary S., and Henry Wan, Jr. 1989. "Wage Setting Institutions and Economic Growth." *World Development* 17 (September): 1471–83.

Fudenberg, Drew, and Eric Maskin. 1986. "The Folk Theorem in Repeated Games with Discounting or with Incomplete Information." *Econometrica* 54 (May): 533–54.

Harris, John R., and Michael P. Todaro. 1970. "Migration, Employment, and Development: A Two-Sector Analysis." *American Economic Review* 60 (March): 126–42.

Hayami, Yujiro. 1998. "Toward an Alternative Path of Economic Development: An Introduction." In *Toward the Rural-Based Development of Commerce and Industry: Selected Experiences from East Asia,* ed. Yujiro Hayami, 1–20. Washington, D.C.: World Bank.

Hayami, Yujiro, and Toshihiko Kawagoe. 1993. *The Agrarian Origins of Commerce and Industry: A Study of Peasant Marketing in Indonesia.* New York: St. Martin's Press.

Hayami, Yujiro, and Masao Kikuchi. 1981. *Asian Village Economy at the Crossroads: An Economic Approach to Institutional Change.* Tokyo: University of Tokyo Press.

Hayami, Yujiro, Ma. Agnes R. Quisumbing, and Lourdes S. Adriano. 1990. *Toward an Alternative Land Reform Paradigm: A Philippine Perspective.* Quezon City: Ateneo de Manila University Press.

Hopper, David. 1965. "Allocation Efficiency in a Traditional Indian Agriculture." *Journal of Farm Economics* 47 (August): 611–24.

Itoh, Motoshige, and Masayuki Tanimoto. 1998. "Rural Entrepreneurs in the Cotton Weaving Industry in Japan." In *Toward the Rural-Based Development of Commerce and Industry: Selected Experiences from East Asia,* ed. Yujiro Hayami, 47–68. Washington, D.C.: World Bank.

Jorgenson, Dale W. 1961. "The Development of a Dual Economy." *Economic Journal* 71 (June): 309–34.

———. 1969. "The Role of Agriculture in Economic Development: Classical versus Neoclassical Models of Growth." In *Subsistence Agriculture and Economic Development,* ed. Clifton R. Wharton, Jr. Chicago: Aldine.

Kandachi, Haruki, 1975. *Meijiki Noson Orimonogyo no Tenkai* (Development of rural textile industry in the Meiji period). 2d ed. Tokyo: Ochanomizu Shobo.

Kikuchi, Masao, and Yujiro Hayami. 1983. "New Rice Technology, Intrarural Migration, and Institutional Innovation in the Philippines." *Population and Development Review* 9, no. 2:2417–57.

Kreps, David D., and Robert Wilson. 1982. "Reputation and Imperfect Information." *Journal of Economic Theory* 27 (August): 253–79.

Landes, David S. 1969. *The Unbound Prometheus: Technological Change and Industrial Development in Western Europe from 1750 to the Present.* Cambridge: Cambridge University Press.

Lewis, W. Arthur. 1954. "Economic Development with Unlimited Supplies of Labor." *Manchester School of Economic and Social Studies* 22 (May): 139–91.

Massell, Benton F. 1967. "Farm Management in Peasant Agriculture: An Empirical Study." *Food Research Institute Studies* 7, no. 2:205–15.

Marx, Karl. 1953. *Grundrisse der Kritik der politischen Ökonomie: (Rohentwurf), 1857–1858.* Berlin: Dietz.

Pack, Howard, and Larry E. Westphal. 1986. "Industrial Strategy and Technological Change: Theory versus Reality." *Journal of Development Economics* 22 (June): 87–128.

Paglin, Morton. 1965. "Surplus Agricultural Labor and Development: Facts and Theories." *American Economic Review* 55 (September): 815–34.

Randall, Adrian J. 1990. "Peculiar Perquisites and Pernicious Practices: Embezzlement in the West of England Woolen Industry: 1750–1840." *International Review of Social History* 35, no. 2:193–219.

Ranis, Gustav, and John C. H. Fei. 1961. "A Theory of Economic Development." *American Economic Review* 51 (September): 533–64.

Ranis, Gustav, and Frances Stewart. 1993. "Rural Nonagricultural Activities in Development: Theory and Application." *Journal of Development Economics* 40 (February): 75–101.

Rosenzweig, Mark R. 1988a. "Risk, Implicit Contracts, and the Family in Rural Areas of Low Income Countries." *Economic Journal* 98 (December): 1148–70.

———. (1988b), "Risk, Private Information, and the Family." *American Economic Review* 78 (May): 245–50.

Rosovsky, Henry, and Kazushi Ohkawa. 1961. "The Indigenous Components in the Modern Economy." *Economic Development and Cultural Change* 9, no. 3:476–501.

Schultz, Theodore W. 1964. *Transforming Traditional Agriculture.* New Haven: Yale University Press.

Smith, Thomas C. 1956. "Landlords and Rural Capitalists in the Modernization of Japan." *Journal of Economic History* 16, no. 2:165–68.

———. 1988. *Native Sources of Japanese Industrialization.* Berkeley and Los Angeles: University of California Press.

Stark, Oded, and Robert E. B. Lucas. 1988. "Migration, Remittance, and the Family." *Economic Development and Cultural Change* 36 (April): 465–81.

Stewart, Frances. 1977. *Technology and Underdevelopment.* Boulder, Colo.: Westview Press.

Takahashi, Akira. 1969. *Land and Peasants in Central Luzon.* Tokyo: Institute of Developing Economies.

Takahashi, Kamekichi. 1930. *Kabushiki Kaisha Bokokuron* [Joint Stock Company Ruins the Nation]. Tokyo: Banrikaku Shobo.

Tanimoto, Masahiro. 1986. "Bakumatsu-Meiji Zenki Menorimonogyo no Tenaki: Saitama-ken Irumagun o Chushin to shite" (Development of cotton Textile Industry in the Late Tokugawa and Early Meiji Period: Centering on the Iruma County in the Saitama Prefecture). *Shakai Kezai Shigaku* 52, no. 2:151–84.

Thorbecke, Erik. 1995. "Health, Nutritional, and Demographic Trends with Particular Emphasis on Sub-Saharan Africa." In Advisory Committee on Health Research, *The Impact of Scientific Advances on Future Health.* Geneva: World Health Organization.

Tönnies, Ferdinand. 1926. *Gemeinschaft und Gesellschaft: Grundbegriffe der reinen Soziologie.* Berlin: K. Curtius.

Tussing, Arlon, R. 1966. "The Labor Force in Meiji Economic Growth: A Quantitative Study of Yamanashi Prefecture." *Journal of Economic History* 26, no. 1:59–62.

Weber, Max. 1924. "Agrarverhältnisse im Altertum." In *Gesammelte Aufsätze sur Sozial- und Wirtschaftsgeschichte.* Tübingen: J. C. B. Mohr.

World Bank. 1993. *The East Asian Miracle: Economic Growth and Public Policy.* Oxford: Oxford University Press.

Yotopoulos, Pan A. 1968. "On the Efficiency of Resource Utilization in Subsistence Agriculture." *Food Research Institute Studies* 8, no. 2:125–35.

CHAPTER 4

Schooling, Economic Growth, and Aggregate Data

Mark R. Rosenzweig

One of the most important issues in the field of economic development is the identification of the factors that promote economic growth. The testing of alternative views and theories about growth determinants has primarily relied on aggregate data, data that describe different economies at a point in time or over time. This dependence on cross-country data is in part due to the fact that micro or household survey data typically describe a single economy at a point in time or over a time period in which there is little growth and hence would appear to have little to say about growth processes. Tests of growth theories would appear to require data that describe variations in levels of development or growth across observations, which certainly is true of data describing countries of the world.

One important set of inquiries about the determinants of growth concerns the role of human capital. The principal evidence that is used to support the view that human capital in the form of schooling augments productivity, and hence growth in the static or neoclassical sense, is based on (1) "earnings function" relations based on wage and schooling data, particularly in World Bank publications, and (2) growth accounting regressions from cross-country data that incorporate schooling as one production factor (e.g., Mankiw, Romer, and Weil 1992). Another perspective on the relationship between human capital and growth emphasizes the importance of schooling in the development process through enabling individuals to exploit new alternatives to increase their productivity (e.g., Nelson and Phelps 1966; Schultz 1975). In this view, schooling net of its contribution to productivity in a static world, which may be small, plays an enhanced role in a world of growth or potential growth. The data required to examine this view must measure growth or change directly, and it is cross-country or cross-economy data that appear to provide the most promising base for testing such dynamic hypotheses, as in Lau et al. 1994 and Benhabib and Spiegel 1994.[1]

In this essay I examine the question of whether the principal methods and specifications that have been used to assess the contribution of schooling to growth based on aggregated, cross-economy data — earnings functions estimates and growth accounting regressions — provide an accurate picture of the true growth-inducing effects of schooling. If the experience of the world's countries over the past forty years is the only database for identifying the determinants of growth, it is clear that our ability to discriminate among competing hypotheses is limited. Without some basis for knowing what is really going on, it is difficult to assess the validity of the different claims that have been made about what these data show. The robustness of results to assumptions can be checked with these data, but little can be said about which assumptions are more correct.

Newly available household data from India that describe over a long time interval the differential spatial growth experiences of India during its "green revolution," however, permit a new exploration of the power of analyses based on cross-economy data. In this case, an aggregate time-series, cross-economy database, which exploits the immobility of labor and other production factors in rural India, can be constructed from panel survey data, and estimates based on the aggregate data that mimic the available cross-country data and those that can be obtained from a rich variety of micro databases can be compared. The main purpose of this exercise is to illuminate how aggregate data can prevent the identification, or provide a misleading picture, of the roles of schooling in growth even if, as is certainly not the case for the existing well-mined cross-country database, the aggregate cross-economy data are spatially and temporally consistent in variable definitions and construction (Srinivasan 1994).

In part 1 of the essay I describe the household data that is used to construct the cross-economy database used to test hypotheses that schooling plays a unique role in the growth process and the India setting described by the data. In part 2, I discuss how earnings functions estimated from cross-economy data can yield quite misleading results and then show how in the case of agricultural wage workers, a large segment of the rural workforce, aggregated data indicate a strong productivity-enhancing role of schooling, in contradiction to the dynamic hypothesis about schooling, that is absent when disaggregated data are used. Section 3 of the essay discusses problems of the identification of the roles of schooling using cross-economy data based on various specifications that have been used in the growth regression literature. Estimates based on these specifications obtained from the aggregated data are shown to completely obscure what appears to be the true contribution of schooling to Indian agricultural growth that is revealed by less aggregated but multilevel time-series and panel data.

1 The Data and the Setting: Rural India, 1968–82

The principal household data used in this study are from data files produced by the National Council of Applied Economic Research (NCAER) from their Additional Rural Incomes Survey (ARIS) and from their follow-up survey, the Rural Economic and Demographic Survey (REDS). The ARIS is based on a stratified random sample of 5,115 households interviewed in the crop year 1968–69 meant to be representative of households residing in all rural areas of India in that year excluding Andaman and Nicobar and Lakshadwip Islands. These households were reinterviewed in the crop years 1969–70 and 1970–71. Two data sets are available from the ARIS survey data: (*a*) a merged panel file providing information for each crop year at the household level for the 4,118 households that were successfully interviewed in all three rounds including information for each individual in the sampled households on time worked in the labor market and wages earned and (*b*) a file describing the household characteristics for the 4,756 households interviewed in 1970–71.

REDS was a resurvey in the crop year 1981–82 of a subset of the 4,756 households responding in the 1970–71 round of ARIS — those households for whom the household head remained the same in the crop year 1981–82 and those households in which the head had died but the rest of immediate male relatives of the head had remained together — plus a random sample of households in 1981–82 not falling into these categories, with the state of Assam excluded (for political reasons).[2] The two subsamples together are meant to be representative of all rural households in 1981 not in Assam.

Important features of the ARIS and REDS are that the names of the villages in which the households reside are identified, there is information on village infrastructural and program variables, and there are approximately twenty households per village due to the cluster sample design. Thus it is possible to construct from the multilevel ARIS and REDS household data not only a household-level panel dataset but also an aggregate, village-based dataset (from the two representative samples) of about 250 observations spanning the interval 1970–71 through 1981–82. In India, each village is plausibly a distinct economy — intervillage, rural labor migration is small, except that by women at marriage, and there are persistent differentials in wages.[3] Yet, the spatial mobility of many commodities, including foods, is relatively high. The constructed Indian village-level dataset thus corresponds in many ways to a cross-country dataset in characterizing variation between distinct economies, except that the aggregate Indian village data are definitionally consistent across the observational units, and the aggregate variables can be constructed from the rich array of survey data so as to more closely correspond to the theoretically appropriate concepts.

The time period described by the data is particularly important. It covers the experience of the Indian green revolution from its beginning in the mid-1960s, and this experience has the potential for providing insights into the effects of technical change on growth and the role of production factors, including schooling. Three characteristics of the Indian green revolution in particular facilitate the study of the role of schooling in economic growth. First, the source of technical change — the flow of new, high-yielding seed varieties — originated outside of India. Human capital within India, at least in the early stages of the revolution, was irrelevant to the technical innovation. The potential contribution of schooling to growth in this setting is confined to its role in augmenting skills in learning new tasks and adopting new technologies efficiently. A second characteristic of the green revolution is that the new seeds were considerably more sensitive to input levels. Thus, the returns to mastering the new technologies of the green revolution were high — mistakes were costly and learning had high payoffs. Finally, because the new seeds required particular soil and water conditions, not all areas of India could benefit equally from the innovations even if mastered perfectly. This spatial variation in the growth potential of the high-yielding seed varieties provides a source of identification of the role of schooling, as discussed below.[4]

The ARIS data indicate that a large fraction of the rural workforce in a low-income rural area, such as pre-green-revolution India, is composed of agricultural laborers, whose work consists of such operations as planting, plowing, weeding, and harvesting — physical operations with little scope for significant error or innovation for which schooling should therefore play a limited role in productivity augmentation.[5] Figure 4.1 provides the percentage distribution of men aged fifteen and over in the rural labor force based on the 1970–71 round of the ARIS. As can be seen, over 40 percent of adult men worked predominantly as agricultural wage workers, hired on a daily basis. Moreover, the data indicate that schooled men shun agricultural wage work. Table 4.1 provides multinomial logit estimates of the determinants of the log-odds of choosing self-employment, nonagricultural wage or salary work, or nonemployment relative to agricultural wage work based on the activities of 8,124

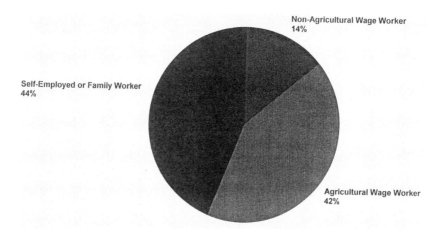

Fig. 4.1.   Types of workers in rural India in 1970–71: Men aged 15+

TABLE 4.1.   Multinomial Logit Estimates from Micro Data: Log-Odds of Being Self-Employed, Working for Nonagricultural Wages, Not Working Relative to Working for Agricultural Wages (8,124 men aged 15–70 in 1970–71)

	Self-Employed	Nonagricultural Wage or Salary	Not Working
Schooling years	.0459	.197	.200
	(5.98)[a]	(15.3)	(21.2)
Land owned (acres)	.0237	−.0337	.00281
	(4.77)	(2.26)	(0.37)
Other assets (Rs.)	.00159	.00010	.000386
	(2.76)	(0.62)	(5.52)
Age	−.0315	−.0481	−.341
	(2.29)	(2.19)	(2.46)
Age squared	−.000472	.000125	.00384
	(2.50)	(0.41)	(19.9)

[a]Absolute values of asymptotic *t*-ratios in parentheses

adult men in the 1970–71 ARIS. These estimates indicate that, for given wealth, the more schooled are most likely to be in the rural non-agricultural sector or not employed, and the least educated are employed as agricultural wage laborers.[6]

Estimates of the returns to schooling based on the relationship between schooling and wages for a sample of the farming wage workers will not only miss a large part of the contribution of schooling to growth, but if estimated correctly, provide an underestimate of its role. Yet, much of the evidence used by the World Bank is based on earnings-function relationships estimated from samples of wage workers. In some cases, the estimates are from nonagricultural wage workers, who make up a relatively small part of the rural labor force, 14 percent in India, and a larger fraction of the urban workforce, but still a highly select sample. Moreover, estimates of the returns to schooling based on data describing aggregate agricultural output and aggregates of the rural workforce and its average education mix together the effects of schooling on productivity for self-employed entrepreneurial decision-makers (farm technology adopters) and for physical laborers. Such estimates may also hide the particular role of schooling in augmenting growth through adoption and efficient learning. To explore hypotheses about the contribution of schooling to growth in the agricultural sector it is thus necessary to examine the distinct effects of schooling in different occupations—in wage employment and in agricultural production. But aggregate, cross-economy data may obscure the roles of schooling in these sectors.

2 Earnings Functions and the Returns to Schooling

a Theory and Identification

If the hypothesis is true that schooling contributes most importantly to productivity and its growth in circumstances in which there are new techniques to master or through innovation, then it should not be the case that schooling and productivity will be strongly related for workers engaged in simple, repetitive operations. I now show that it is possible to find, based on aggregate data, that schooling levels and wage rates in agricultural operations are positively correlated even though schooling does not increase productivity in such tasks. And this is so even without resort to ad hoc notions of institutional wage setting or other constraints placed on competition and the operation of supply and demand. That is, aggregation across economies can lead to an erroneous inference about the role of schooling in productivity augmentation based on the standard technique of earnings function estimation.

A classic model of wage and labor allocation is the Roy (1951) model in which labor is expressed in units of human capital each of which is paid a rental price that is determined competitively and workers sort themselves among jobs or occupations according to where they earn the highest earnings. Consider a simple two-job world in which there is a skilled occupation in which schooling or human capital has worth and an unskilled occupation in which schooling does nothing to increase productivity. As in the Roy model, the wage rate earned by a worker j in economy i in job-type k is given by

$$W_{ijk} = \pi_{ik} \exp(\beta_k E_{ijk}), \qquad i = 1, \ldots, n; j = 1, \ldots, N;$$

$$k = \text{skilled, unskilled} \qquad (1)$$

where E_{ijk} is the number of years of schooling, β_k is the effect of schooling on the number of units of human capital, and π_{ik} is the rental price for human capital. Log wages in the two occupations are thus

$$\ln W_{ijs} = \ln \pi_{is} + \beta_s E_{ijs} \qquad (2)$$

$$\ln W_{iju} = \ln \pi_{iu} \qquad (3)$$

with $\beta_k = 0$ in the unskilled task and $\beta_k > 0$ in the skilled task by assumption.

It is easy to show that wages will vary across economies because of variation in both the rental prices and schooling in both occupations, so that a wage regression (earnings function) estimated on aggregate data that seeks to identify β_k from variation in wages and schooling across economies can lead to any relationship between wages and schooling. That is, the aggregate earnings function estimated for the unskilled workers identifies the derivative

$$\delta \ln W_{iu} / \delta E_i = \delta \ln \pi_{iu} / \delta E_i, \qquad (4)$$

which expresses how schooling and job-specific rental prices are related but not β_u.

Why might the aggregate earnings function relation (4) be positive? Consider the choice that workers make of which job to take, with free movement of workers across jobs. The estimates in table 4.1 suggest that, for given wealth, more schooled individuals choose not to take agricultural (unskilled) wage jobs. Let us assume, for example, that this is simply because more schooled workers just prefer to avoid working for others in agricultural tasks. Figure 4.2 displays wage and job equilibria in two economies, one of which is characterized by a higher overall level of schooling. The solid lines express the relationships, as in equations (2) and (3), between schooling and ln wages in the skilled and unskilled occupations—in the unskilled occupation the line is perfectly flat while in the skilled occupation the line is positively sloped. The ln rental price for each job type in the economy is the intercept of each line with the y-axis (at the minimum level of human capital normalized at

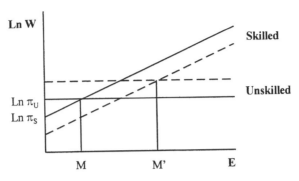

Fig. 4.2.   Wage and job equilibria of skilled versus unskilled occupations

one). In this economy, in which both tasks are performed, workers with schooling below M choose the unskilled job, and those with schooling above the level M choose the skilled job—even workers with some schooling will work in the job that does not reward schooling because the rental price is higher in that job, but on average workers in the skilled job will have higher levels of schooling than workers in the unskilled job, as we observe in the India data.

Now suppose that the overall level of schooling is increased in this economy. If schooling increases workers' distaste for the unskilled job, then more workers will attempt to shift to the skilled job. Given unchanged demand for both types of jobs, this will lower the rental price for the skilled job and increase it for the unskilled job, as depicted by the dashed lines in figure 4.2. In the dashed-line, higher-schooling economy, the average level of schooling is higher in both the unskilled and skilled jobs, and the rental price for unskilled jobs is higher compared to the continuous-line, lower-schooling economy. Thus, an earnings function estimated from data that aggregated economies with different job-specific rental prices and with these characteristics would reveal a positive relationship between ln wages in the unskilled jobs and the schooling of workers in those jobs even though the true effect of schooling on productivity in those jobs is zero.[7]

How might such a spurious relationship be detected? In this case by estimating the relationship between the schooling level of all workers (or just skilled workers) and wages in the unskilled job, controlling for the schooling of the workers in the unskilled job. If the aggregate earnings function relationship between schooling and ln wages for unskilled jobs is due solely to variations in human-capital rental prices because of shifts in the overall supply of schooling, then the average schooling of all workers will explain more of the variation in unskilled wages across economies than the variation in the schooling of the workers who choose the unskilled job.

This example just illustrates the point that to identify the true relationship between wages and schooling it is necessary to control for the equilibrium rental prices, and if there is a one-to-one correspondence between observations and rental prices, as for cross-economy aggregated data, then this is not possible — aggregation precludes identification. Data from one economy in which there is individual variation in schooling across workers in that economy will reveal β_k; that is, only nonaggregated data can identify structural schooling effects on productivity without information on the rental prices.

b "True" and Aggregate Estimates of Schooling Effects on Agricultural-Worker Productivity

What is the "true" relationship between productivity in agricultural tasks and schooling? The best direct information on the productivity of agricultural wage workers I know of comes from data on piece-rate wages earned by Filipino harvest workers, as described in Foster and Rosenzweig 1996a. The dataset provides the daily wages earned by harvesters working for piece rates in identifiable time periods and barrios. Thus, the data describe actual productivity (in harvesting), and there is considerable individual variation in schooling and in productivity within barrios and time periods, that is for given rental prices (the piece rates in this case), as shown in Foster and Rosenzweig 1996a. Note that the productivity effects of individual worker characteristics can be identified based on piece-rate wages from this individual-level data without the necessity of assuming anything about how piece rates are set except that the rates paid per ear of corn picked or per basket of rice harvested are the same for everyone working in the same barrio at a point in time.

Figure 4.3 depicts the partial relationships between harvest productivity and worker height, in the right panel, and worker schooling, in the left panel, based on within-season and barrio regressions of piece-rate wages on worker schooling, age, and height for over four hundred Filipino harvest workers. As can be seen in the right panel, taller workers, for given age and schooling level, are more productive in harvesting, with productivity increasing by about 10 percent for every two inches of additional height. In contrast, for given height, more schooled workers are not more productive harvesters — increasing schooling from zero to fourteen years, the full sample range, increases harvest productivity by

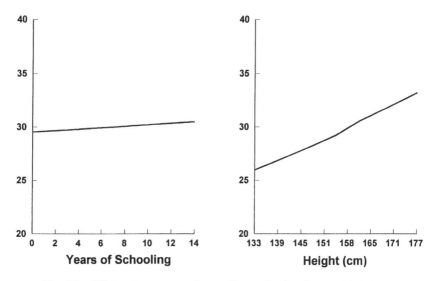

Fig. 4.3. Filipino harvest workers: effects of schooling and height on piece-rate wages (in pesos)

only an insignificant 3 percent. As in rural India, a large proportion of workers work in harvest activities, so it is unlikely that the relationships depicted in figure 4.2 are due to selection based on unobservables.

What does the aggregated India data indicate about the relationship between agricultural wage rates and the schooling of agricultural workers? Table 4.2 reports estimates of earnings (wage) functions for such workers based on two forms of aggregate data — village-level data based on averages of village variables and individual-level (micro) data that are aggregated in the sense that individuals come from possibly different economies, in this case from 204 different villages. The first column of table 4.2 reports the standard wage function specification based on variation across 218 villages in averages of ln wages and schooling years and experience (and its square) for agricultural wage workers. The estimate of the "rate of return to schooling" is almost 6 percent and is precise and significantly different from zero. This would be another supporting row or column in a table in a World Bank report indicating the desirability of schooling investment in low-income rural economies! However, a simple experiment suggests that there may be a problem, as suggested by the framework above. When the average schooling level of all men in the village is also included in the specification, the "own" schooling effect is cut by more than 65 percent. The average schooling level of men in the village has a stronger relationship with male agricultural wages than does the average schooling of male agricultural workers, who make up less than 50 percent of all male workers.

As the estimates in columns 3 through 5 indicate, obtaining individual-level data is not necessarily the cure for problems of identification due to aggregation across economies. The estimates of a standard microlevel earnings function for agricultural wage workers, reported in column 3, not surprisingly provide a similar result as the standard village-level ln wage regression based on data aggregated from the same micro data — the rate of return to schooling for agricultural wage workers is significantly different from zero. The estimate is lower than that obtained using the village averages, but this may be due to errors in measurement in schooling that, under classical assumptions about measurement errors, are reduced by averaging.[8]

When the average level of schooling of all men in the village is entered in the micro earnings function specification, in column 4, we see a result similar to the village-level estimates — the own-schooling effect is greatly reduced (to essentially nothing), and the average schooling level in the village has a greater impact on agricultural wages. It is possible that this is due to the fact that aggregate village-level schooling of all workers measures own agricultural worker schooling better than does the measure of own schooling because of measurement error.[9] As

TABLE 4.2. Estimates of Schooling Returns from Aggregate and Micro Earnings Functions: Male Agricultural Wage Workers, 1970–71

Variable	Aggregate Data		Micro Data		
	(1)	(2)	(1)	(2)	(3)
Years of schooling (own)	.0575	.0240	.0200	.00015	.00586
	(5.11)[a]	(1.60)	(4.29)	(0.027)	(1.81)
Experience	.0295	.0277	.00826	.01156	.00818
	(1.94)	(1.86)	(2.63)	(2.83)	(3.27)
Experience squared	−.000337	−.000348	−.000125	−.000179	−.000109
	(1.50)	(1.58)	(2.79)	(3.124)	(3.58)
Average schooling in village (all men)	—	0.554	—	.0941	—
		(3.27)		(7.06)	
R^2	.12	.16	.04	.19	.77
N	218	218	1,636	1,636	1,636
Village fixed effects?	No	No	No	No	Yes
H_0: No village effect $F(203, 1,405)$	—	—	—	—	4,486
					$p = .0001$

[a]Absolute values of t-ratios in parentheses are corrected for the existence of village and household cluster effects.

noted, the best way to see if individual-schooling variation is associated with individual wages for agricultural workers, for given rental prices, is to estimate the relationship within villages, to control perfectly for village-level occupation rental prices by including village dummy variables.[10] These estimates are presented in the last column. As for the estimates based on actual worker productivity in harvesting operations in the Philippines, within villages in India there does not appear to be any relationship between a worker's schooling level and his wage. Most of the variation across India in agricultural wages is evidently due to variation in equilibrium human-capital rental prices — the explanatory power of the individual-level earnings equation increases by almost fourfold when the village dummy variables are included, with the set of dummy variables explaining more than 57 percent of the variation in individual agricultural wages. Note that this is not because all workers within a village earn the same wage — age (experience) variation, for example, explains a statistically significant proportion of the within-village variability in wages. Within-village schooling variation does not.

3 Production Function Estimates, Aggregation, and the Contribution of Schooling to Growth

a Technology Specification, Schooling, and Growth Accounting

Estimates of the relationship between schooling and wage rates in most low-income and developing economies, even if correct, do not provide a complete indication of the role of schooling in augmenting productivity because, as seen in the rural Indian data, a large proportion of the population is self-employed and does not work for wages or salaries. To estimate the full contribution of schooling an alternative approach is to estimate production functions. In this approach, the role of schooling can be depicted as measuring the skill level of labor, one factor of production, or as playing a special role related to technological change.

To fix ideas about these alternative roles of schooling, I follow the literature in specifying the production technology as Cobb-Douglas. Output Y_{ijt} for an individual enterprise (farm) j located in economy i at time t is determined from a production process described by

$$Y_{ijt} = \theta_{it} K_{ijt}^{\alpha} L_{ijt}^{\zeta} E_{ijt} \mu_i \varepsilon_{ijt}, \tag{5}$$

where K_{ijt} is the capital stock for j in i at t, L_{ijt} is the labor input, E_{ijt} is the schooling level of the labor input, μ_i is a productivity-augmenting factor in economy i that is time invariant, ε_{ijt} is a time-varying, individual production shock, and θ_{it} is the technology level (total factor productivity) in economy i at time t. In this specification, the contribution of (ln) schooling to (ln) output is given by the parameter γ, which is assumed to be the same across all farms and economies. This is the basic technology used to estimate the determinants of growth from aggregate cross-country data by Mankiw, Romer, and Weil. In this specification, schooling plays no special role in determining growth relative to other factors of production.

To identify whether schooling directly affects growth through augmenting total factor productivity or by augmenting productivity when technology is changing, as is implied by Nelson and Phelps 1966 and Schultz 1975, it is necessary to specify the relationship between the level of schooling and the change in technology θ_{it}. In Foster and Rosenzweig 1996b, it is assumed that the productivity of schooling is higher the greater the pace of technical change. In particular it is assumed that

$$\gamma_{it} = \gamma_0 + a\tau_i, \tag{6}$$

where $\tau_i = \ln_{it} - \ln_{i0}$ with a > 0. Thus, the productivity effects of schooling vary across economies depending on their rates of technical change, but vary the same way in each economy. The growth equation, based on (5), is thus

$$\ln Y_{ijt} - \ln Y_{ij0} = \tau_i + \alpha (\ln K_{ijt} - \ln K_{ij0}) + \zeta (\ln L_{ijt} - \ln L_{ij0})$$

$$+ \gamma_0(\ln E_{ijt} - \ln E_{ij0}) + a\tau_i \ln E_{ijt} + \ln \varepsilon_{ijt} - \ln \varepsilon_{ij0} \tag{7}$$

If it is assumed that the level of technology θ is the same for all economies in the initial period (but not overall productivity, which varies with μ_i, all of the parameters in (7) are identified from data describing variation in inputs and in schooling within economies and by the assumption that rates of potential total factor productivity growth across economies are exogenously varying, an assumption that appears to be realistic for green-revolution India, as noted. For example, by including economy- (district-) level dummy variables in (7) and interactions of these with second-period individual schooling, both the set of economy-level changes in technology (the τ_i), the static effect of schooling on productivity in the absence of technical change γ_0 (from the change in schooling) and a, the effect of technical change on the contribution of schooling to output (from the last-period level of schooling), are identified.

If the only data available are aggregated within each economy (defined by its unique experience of technical change), then it is obviously not possible to identify the τ_i or a. It is still possible to identify from such cross-economy (aggregated) data the effect of average technical change across all of the economies on the contribution of schooling, as in

$$\ln Y_{it} - \ln Y_{i0} = \tau + \alpha \,(\ln K_{it} - \ln K_{i0}) + \zeta \,(\ln L_{ij} - \ln L_{ij})$$

$$+ \gamma_0(\ln E_{it} - \ln E_{i0}) + a'\tau \ln E_{it} + \ln \varepsilon_{it} - \ln \varepsilon_{i0} \qquad (8)$$

but it is obvious that this average effect a' will underestimate the true a because what is identified is the average of technical change across economies and the true a. Specification (8) was estimated by Lau et al. (1993) from cross-state data from Brazil. They found that a' was not statistically different from zero.

Benhabib and Spiegel (1994) endogenize τ_i by assuming that schooling directly effects τ_i and that it does so more for economies that are less technologically advanced. They thus assume that

$$\tau_i = b + cE_i + dE_i(\theta_{max0}/\theta_{i0}). \qquad (9)$$

The parameter c is the direct contribution of schooling to technical change through innovation and invention; the d parameter captures the idea that in more "backward economies," economies whose initial-period level of technology θ_{i0} is low relative to that in the most advanced economy, θ_{max0}, growth is accomplished by adopting the technologies of the more advanced countries, with schooling augmenting this adoption. With initial-period measures of the economy-specific levels of technology, the b, c, and d parameters are identified even from aggregated cross-economy data. The problem is where to obtain the θ_i. Benhabib and Spiegel, who base their estimates on aggregate cross-country data, use as a proxy the initial-period per capita income levels of the countries. Thus their growth equation is

$$\ln Y_{it} - \ln Y_{i0} = b + cE_i + dE_i(Y'_{max0}/Y'_{i0}) + \alpha(\ln K_{it} - \ln K_{i0})$$

$$+ \zeta(\ln L_{ij} - \ln L_{ij}) + \ln \varepsilon_{it} - \ln \varepsilon_{i0}, \qquad (10)$$

where Y_i' is country-specific per capita income.

There are two problems with specification (10). The first is that, even if we ignore the contributions of the variable factors to Y_i' in the initial period, variation in Y_i' is confounded with variation in μ_i, the component of economy-specific productivity that is permanent. In pre-green-revolution India, variations in agricultural output per capita Y_i' across areas were likely dominated by variations in inherent and fixed conditions of the soil and of weather as well as by capital, not by variation in technology. The ratio of the most productive area's per capita income to any area's productivity in that period thus would only by coincidence measure that area's potential gains from the technical advances of the green revolution. Thus, this specification applied to data on Indian districts or states over time would unlikely measure the contribution of schooling to growth via technology adoption.

The second problem with the specification (10) is that part of the dependent variable $(-\ln Y_{i0})$ appears directly on the right-hand side as a denominator in a term that is interacted with schooling (Y_{i0}'). Any measurement error in initial income or output will thus result in an upward bias on the coefficient d — a possible false positive for the hypothesis that schooling aids in technology catch-up. And Benhabib and Spiegel find, based on cross-country data, a positive and statistically significant d coefficient, while c is not statistically different from zero. The potential spurious correlation due to the use of the dependent variable as a regressor is an estimation problem, not directly a problem of aggregation. But aggregation may reduce options for instruments that could be used to remedy this problem. And Benhabib and Spiegel do not use instruments to estimate (10).

There is another potentially serious estimation problem in identifying the parameters in (8) or (10). This problem arises from the likely response of schooling investment to technical change. If the hypothesis is correct that the contribution of schooling to productivity growth rises in the presence of technical change, then schooling investment would be expected to increase in a higher-growth environment. This means that the change in schooling from 0 to t in any economy i, or schooling at time t in i (or its average during the period, as used by Benhabib and Spiegel) will be correlated with the economy-specific error term in the growth equation. In particular when $\ln \varepsilon_{it} - \ln \varepsilon_{i0}$ is high, both E_i and $\ln E_{it} - \ln E_{i0}$ will be high. This will also lead to upward biases in the estimated contributions of schooling to growth.

b The Green Revolution, the Contribution of Schooling to Growth, and Growth Convergence in India: Evidence from Multilevel Data

Foster and Rosenzweig (1996b) estimated a variant of the growth equation (7) based on the household-level panel data from ARIS-REDS describing farm households over the period 1971–82, with Indian districts

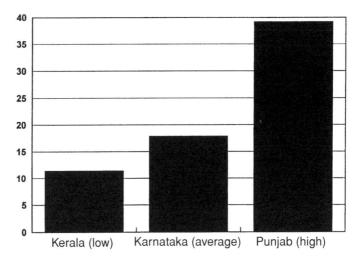

Fig. 4.4 Percent differential in farm profits between schooled and un-schooled Indian farmers in 1982, for low, average, and highest technical change states

used as the relevant technology areas (the i). The specification differed from that in (7) in two ways. First, a linear profit was estimated. Second, all asset (and variable factor price) coefficients were allowed to change with technology growth, not just schooling. In addition, to deal with the potential problem that capital investments including schooling were responsive to shocks to profits and profit growth, instruments were used in estimation.

The estimates indicated that the returns to schooling rose significantly in areas of India where technical change τ_i associated with the new seed varieties was most rapid—evidence that schooling plays an important growth-enhancing role given technical change. Figure 4.4 illustrates the quantitative importance of the growth effect on schooling returns. The estimation of (7) provides estimates of the τ_i and thus permits identification of high-growth areas net of investments. The estimates indicated that among Indian states, Kerala could least take advantage of new seed varieties associated with the green revolution—its growth potential was low. In contrast, in the Punjab, according to the estimates, growth potential was high, with Karnataka state somewhere in the middle. Figure 4.4 displays the differential in profits between farms in which at least one household member had primary schooling and those in which no one had any schooling (a typical household in 1982) for these three states based on the Foster-Rosenzweig estimates. As can be seen, the differential in farm profits by schooling was only 11 percent in the low-growth state Kerala but was almost 40 percent in the highest-growth state Punjab, with the differential 18 percent in Karnataka. On average, the return in terms of the increased yearly profits from obtaining primary schooling rose from less than 10 percent prior to the green revolution to, on average, 18 percent, and to as high as 40 percent.

The estimates of the area-specific rates of growth were also used in Foster and Rosenzweig 1996b to test if schooling investment responded to the changes in rates of return to schooling as indicated by the differential growth rates τ_i. They found that schooling investment did increase significantly, particularly in farm households, in those rural areas experiencing the largest changes in farm productivity net of the wealth effects of those changes (which were weak). This suggests that estimates of the contributions to growth from growth equations such as (7), (8), or (10) will be biased upward unless account is taken of the effects of technical change itself on investments.

The multilevel Indian data also indicate that the pattern of growth was not one of convergence over the green-revolution period. It is possible, using the Foster and Rosenzweig 1995 estimates of a profit function incorporating the use of new seed varieties by farmers, based on the 1968–71 ARIS panel, to construct estimates of area-specific levels of farm profitability prior to the green revolution (the μ_i in (5)). These are simply the farm-level fixed effects, averaged over areas (say, districts), from the profit function estimates obtained from the panel data. Figure 4.5 presents a scatterplot of these district-specific fixed effects and the subsequent growth in 1971 through 1982 in the yields (per acre) for four crops for which there was technical innovation (corn, sorghum, rice, wheat) based on a Laspeyres-weighted yield index. As can be seen, the relationship between pre-green-revolution, area-specific farm productivity and subsequent area-specific yield growth was not very strong, and in fact was weakly positive. The new high-yielding seed varieties associated with the green revolution could evidently be most successfully applied in areas that tended to be slightly more productive to begin with. These results are plausible, given what we know about the external origin of green revolution technical change and its determinants — exogenously given soil and water conditions. Thus, in India there was no catch-up of low-productivity areas to high-productivity areas — the pre-growth, area-specific productivity differentials do not predict growth potential. The Benhabib-Spiegel measure of growth potential used in (10) should not therefore provide any indication of the subsequent contribution of schooling to growth in the Indian context.

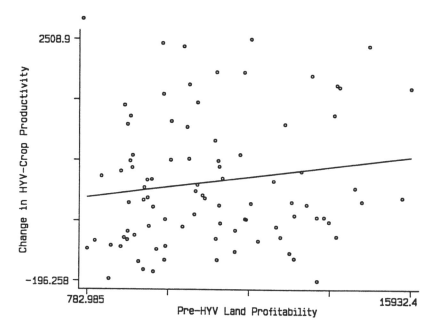

Fig. 4.5. Increases in crop yield after district-specific fixed effects,
1971–82

c Estimates from Aggregate Growth
Accounting Regressions

Table 4.3 reports estimates of the growth-accounting specifications applied to aggregate data constructed from the ARIS and REDS survey data. In particular, sample-weighted averages of the values of farm output, the value of farm capital including land, the number of adults employed in agriculture, and the average schooling level of those workers along with village-level indicators of adverse weather for each of the 241 matched villages in 1970–71 and 1981–82 were constructed and used to estimate the log differenced form of (5), corresponding to the main specification of Mankiw, Romer, and Weil 1992 and Lau et al. 1994, in which schooling is treated as a factor of production. The data were also used to estimate the augmented specification of Lau et al. 1994 corresponding to (8), and the Benhabib-Spiegel specification (10). These estimates are reported in the first three columns of table 4.3, respectively.

The estimates of each specification replicate the findings in the studies in which they were used, based on completely different aggregate data. The estimates from the basic specification incorporating edu-

TABLE 4.3. Cobb-Douglas Agricultural-Sector Growth Regressions: 241 Rural Villages, 1971–82

	No Instruments			Instruments[b]		
Specification	Lau et al.	Augmented Lau et al.	Benhabib-Spiegel	Lau et al.	Augmented Lau et al.	Benhabib-Spiegel
DLcapital	.423	.427	.372	.458	.448	.258
	(9.62)[a]	(9.61)	(8.80)	(2.13)	(1.98)	(1.35)
DLlabor	.310	.305	.422	.704	.709	.629
	(4.81)	(4.69)	(6.81)	(2.07)	(2.09)	(2.73)
DLedyears	0.94	0.98	–	.0304	.0287	–
	(2.80)	(2.87)		(1.64)	(1.25)	
Ledyears	–	.0366	–	–	.0329	–
		(0.65)			(0.12)	
Edyears	–	–	−.0399	–	–	−.0114
			(1.36)			(0.97)
Ed*Y_{max0}/Y_{i0}	–	–	.0066	–	–	.000829
			(6.14)			(0.11)
Dadverse	−.105	−.105	−.0797	−.114	−.115	−.103
weather	(1.08)	(1.08)	(0.87)	(0.90)	(0.92)	(0.91)
R^2	.49	.50	.55	.30	.31	.43

[a]Absolute values of *t*-ratios in parentheses.
[b]Instruments are: adverse weather in 1969–70 and 1968–69; school in village in 1971, small-scale industry in village in 1971; factory in village in 1971; agricultural extension agent in village in 1971; village population in 1971; distances of village to bank, coop, market *(mandi).*

cation as a factor of production indicates that schooling only makes a significant contribution to growth in the classical sense, with schooling returns not being related to the speed of overall growth (the coefficient on the average level of schooling in the second period is not statistically different from zero), just as found by Lau et al. for Brazilian states. But the Benhabib-Spiegel specification suggests, as did their cross-country estimates, that schooling plays an important growth-enhancing role in facilitating the adoption of growth leaders' advanced technology, as the coefficient on the interaction between the average level of schooling in the interval and the first-period ratio of the maximum per capita output and the area's output is positive and statistically significant. Of course, if the Foster-Rosenzweig estimates from the multilevel data are correct, none of these findings are consistent with the reality of the agricultural growth experience in India in this time period.

It is not surprising that the Lau et al. augmented specification cannot pick up the growth-enhancing role of schooling — there is no relationship between the overall growth rate in India and returns to schooling; the effects of technical change were localized. What is surprising are the findings that the static returns to schooling are high and that schooling enhanced catch-up growth, given that more than half of the agricultural labor force are working as laborers in tasks in which schooling has little to do with productivity and there was no convergence in growth potential, as seen above. These results, however, may be due to (i) the fact that schooling change over the period, as indicated in figure 4.4, was positively correlated with area-specific growth and thus with the residuals of the aggregate growth-accounting regressions, and (ii) a correlation between the initial-period income variable with the residuals due to measurement error. To check this, I reran the regressions using instruments for all of the right-hand-side variables except for the change in weather. The ARIS dataset provides some potentially good instruments for predicting the changes in capital stocks, labor, and schooling from 1971 to 1982, and initial per capita output in 1971. The variables that were used as instruments are the village-level estimated fixed effects for profitability for 1969, from the Foster and Rosenzweig (1995) profit estimates from the 1968–71 period, indicators of adverse weather in the villages in 1969 and 1968, village population size in 1970, whether there was a school in the village in 1970, the distances of the village from the nearest bank, credit cooperative, or market *(mandi)*, and whether there was a factory or any small-scale industry in the village, rural non-agricultural factors that importantly affect income in agriculture (Ranis and Stewart 1993).

The last three columns of table 4.3 report these instrumented estimates for each of the three specifications of the growth equations. These results confirm that the positive education effects seen in the first three columns are mostly spurious—the classical static output coefficient for schooling decreases from .09 to .03 when instruments are used, and the catch-up enhancing effect of schooling, in the last column, disappears. Hausman-Wu tests indicate that the set of right-hand-side variables is correlated with the residuals. The output coefficients for farm capital remain the same when instruments are used, while that for labor actually increases. In the fourth-column specification in which the statistically insignificant variables do not enter, the instrumented coefficient estimates for capital and labor are statistically significant at the .05 level.[11]

The estimates of the aggregated growth accounting regressions, when estimated correctly, thus almost completely hide the evident contribution of schooling to growth in India during the green-revolution period. They do so because of aggregation, which makes it impossible to estimate the localized growth-enhancing schooling effects during the green revolution, which can only be identified from the interactions between area-specific growth rates and *within-area* schooling differences among farmer decision-makers. Whether these specifications when applied to cross-country data reveal anything about the contribution of schooling to growth remains an open question, given the absence of better data describing these processes around the world. The results from the India experience, while not necessarily generalizable to all aggregate datasets, do suggest caution in interpreting estimates from cross-economy aggregate data, whether based on earnings functions regressions or estimates of production technologies.

NOTES

The research in this essay was supported in part by grants from NSF, SBR93-08405, and NIH, HD30907. I am grateful to Gary Saxonhouse and to Ricardo Barros for helpful comments.

1. A third perspective, not discussed here, emphasizes externalities from human capital, some of which may be in the form of schooling, as an important engine of growth (Lucas 1988). For evidence on learning externalities based on the data that are used in this paper, see Foster and Rosenzweig 1995.

2. Only 4.8 percent of these eligible households were not resurveyed. The number of panel households providing information is 3,139. For a complete description of the REDS, see Vashishtha 1989.

3. For example, note the title of a well-known article, "Risk and Insurance in Village India" (Townsend 1994). Note also that another important production factor in the context of rural India, land, is also immobile.

4. The principal limitation of the new seeds is that they require an environment with a reliable or controllable supply of water (as well as a high level of fertilizer). Thus, many areas are still unable to exploit the new technologies. The "imported" nature of the technology is indicated in the first rounds of the data. In 1971, the three most-used rice seeds have Asian origins — Taichung-65, Taiwan-3, I.R.-8 (a rice variety from the Philippines International Rice Research Institute) — while the top three wheat varieties have Spanish names — Sonora-64, Lerma Rojo, Sharbati Sonora. No seed variety information is provided in the 1982 round.

5. One possible alternative role of schooling is in disciplining young individuals to perform repetitive tasks under the supervision of nonfamily adults.

6. Average schooling years in the rural population is low — 3.67 years.

7. Note that in this economy in which schooling may affect preferences, increases in schooling among those who are wealthy benefit poor, low-schooled workers.

8. The estimates do not appear to be afflicted by selectivity bias. Based on the multinomial sector choice estimates reported in table 4.1, tests of selectivity, following Lee 1983, were carried out. The null hypothesis of no selection could not be rejected. These tests may not be valid, however, as the estimates do not take into account significant wage differences across villages not accounted for

by schooling and experience, as discussed below. Moreover, the identifying wealth variables are not likely to be exogenous to differences in wage levels. This precludes as well the use of wealth variables as instruments to deal with potential measurement errors in the schooling variable.

9. One alternative explanation is that the productivity of agricultural wage workers is augmented when the schooling of farm operators, whose schooling levels are included in the overall village averages of schooling, is high — that unskilled labor and the human capital of owner-operators are production complements. However, the average schooling of nonfarm workers also has a positive and statistically significant relationship with individual farmworker wages.

10. Another advantage of estimating within-village schooling relationships is that the quality of schooling is not likely to differ among individuals residing in the same village (given immobility). Quality of schooling may differ across villages, which would be another source of bias in the aggregated data.

11. Because the technology estimates are overidentified, it is possible to perform some assessments of the sensitivity of results to the set of instruments. Experiments in which ten combinations of random subsets of the instruments were excluded (up to exact identification) revealed that the results are generally robust to instrument choice. In particular, the absence of any substantial relationship between the lagged output interaction with schooling and growth is never rejected in all experiments, while the coefficients on both labor force and capital stock were statistically significant in eight of the ten experiments. The coefficient on schooling also does not appear sensitive to instrument choice among the set of instruments used.

REFERENCES

Benhabib, Jess, and Spiegel, Mark. 1994. "The Role of Human Capital in Economic Development: Evidence from Aggregate Cross-Country Data." *Journal of Monetary Economics* 34 (May): 143–73.

Foster, Andrew D., and Mark R. Rosenzweig. 1995. "Learning by Doing and Learning from Others: Human Capital and Technical Change in Agriculture." *Journal of Political Economy* 103, no. 6:1176–1209.

———. 1996a. "Comparative Advantage, Information, and the Allocation of Workers to Tasks: Evidence from an Agricultural Labor Market," *Review of Economic Studies* 63, no. 3:347–74.

———. 1996b. "Technical Change and Human Capital Returns and Investments: Evidence from the Green Revolution." *American Economic Review* 86, no. 4:931–53.

Lau, Lawrence J., Dean T. Jamison, Shu-Cheng Liu, and Steven Rivkin. 1993. "Education and Economic Growth: Some Cross-Sectional Evidence from Brazil." *Journal of Development Economics* 41 (June): 45–70.

Lee, Lung-Fei. 1983. "Generalized Econometric Models with Selectivity." *Econometrica* 51, no. 2:507–12.

Lucas, Robert E. 1988. "On the Mechanics of Economic Development." *Journal of Monetary Economics* 22 (July): 3–42.

Mankiw, N. Gregory, David Romer, and David N. Weil. 1992. "A Contribution to the Empirics of Economic Growth." *Quarterly Journal of Economics* 107, no. 2:407–37.

Nelson, Richard, and Edmund Phelps. 1966. "Investment in Humans, Technological Diffusion, and Economic Growth." *American Economic Review, Papers and Proceedings* 61 (May): 69–75.

Psacharopoulos, George. 1988. "Education and Development: A Review." *World Bank Research Observer* 3, no. 1:99–116.

Ranis, Gustav, and Frances Stewart. 1993. "Rural Nonagricultural Activities in Development: Theory and Application." *Journal of Development Economics* 40 (February): 75–101.

Rosenzweig, Mark R. 1995. "Why Are There Returns to Schooling? *American Economic Review, Papers and Proceedings* 85 (May): 153–58.

Roy, A. D. 1951. "Some Thoughts on the Distribution of Earnings." *Oxford Economic Papers* 3 (March): 135–46.

Schultz, T. W. 1975. "The Value of the Ability to Deal with Disequilibria." *Journal of Economic Literature* 13:872–76.

Srinivasan, T. N. 1994. "Data Base for Development Analysis: An Overview." *Journal of Development Economics* 44 (June): 3–27.

Townsend, Robert. 1994. "Risk and Insurance in Village India." *Econometrica* 62, no. 3:539–91.

Vashishtha, Prem S. 1989. "Changes in Structure of Investment of Rural Households: 1970–1 — 1981–2." *Journal of Income and Wealth* 10, no. 2:207–21.

CHAPTER 5

Changing Income Inequality in Taiwan: A Decomposition Analysis

Gary S. Fields and Jennifer C. O'Hara Mitchell

1 Introduction

Gustav Ranis has made some fundamental contributions to the analysis of income inequality in Taiwan. His joint work with John Fei and Shirley Kuo (1978, 1979) assessed the causes of Taiwan's remarkable record of growth with equity. The method they derived for decomposing total income inequality into components due to each factor income source has been used in studies of a wide variety of countries around the world, reviewed below.

This research begins where the Fei-Ranis-Kuo work left off, both chronologically and methodologically. Chronologically, their work sought to explain why family income inequality had *fallen* in the course of Taiwan's rapid economic growth up to 1972 (the latest year for which they had data). But although economic growth has remained rapid (between 1980 and 1993, real per capita GDP grew by 121 percent, or 6.1 percent annually), the inequality trend has reversed, and Taiwan has experienced a slow but steady *increase* in family income inequality since 1980 (Republic of China 1993).

In decomposing the sources of family income inequality in Taiwan, Fei, Ranis, and Kuo (1978, 1979) found that a primary cause of the fall in the inequality of total household income was the decline in *labor* income inequality. When the decomposition methodology of Fei, Ranis, and Kuo (1978, 1979) and Pyatt, Chen, and Fei (1980) has been applied to other countries, including the United States (Shorrocks 1983; Karoly and Burtless 1995), Pakistan (Ayub 1977), and Colombia (Fields 1979), the preeminence of labor income inequality in total income inequality has also been found.

These previous findings led us to hypothesize that the principal source of rising family income inequality in Taiwan was rising *labor* income inequality, and we set out to explain why labor income inequality rose in the course of Taiwan's economic growth since 1980.[1] In doing so, we make use of a newly devised methodology for decomposing income inequality into a number of income-determining factors (Fields 1996). This methodology is being applied for the first time in this work and in a companion study of Korea (Fields and Yoo, forthcoming).

The first surprise was that for the sample of employees analyzed in the empirical work below, the Gini coefficient of *labor earnings* fell by a trivial amount and the underlying Lorenz curve of labor earnings was essentially unchanged. The rest of the paper then seeks to explain why the inequality of labor earnings was unchanged. We assess the quantitative importance of various factors, some of which contributed to rising earnings inequality and some to falling earnings inequality, so as to offset one another.

The plan of the rest of the essay is as follows. Section 2 reviews the major contributions to the literature on income inequality in Taiwan and presents our own calculations. Section 3 outlines the decomposition methodology used, while section 4 contains the empirical results. The findings are summarized in section 5.

2 Review of the Literature on Income Inequality in Taiwan

The early record on family income inequality in Taiwan, though sketchy, reveals a sharp *decline* in inequality: from a Gini coefficient of .558 in 1953 to .440 in 1959 to .328 in 1964 (Fei, Ranis, and Kuo 1979, table 2.16). By the 1960s, Taiwan had one of the most equal distributions of income in the world (Fei, Ranis, and Kuo 1979; Paukert 1973). Reasons for the attainment of low levels of inequality include Taiwan's decentralized development, balanced rural-development strategy, outward-oriented industrial and trade strategies, and high level of human-resource development (Ranis 1978).

Official data from Taiwan's Survey of Family Income and Expenditure from 1964 to the present reveal two clear phases: a phase of *falling* inequality of household disposable income from 1964 to 1980 (the Gini coefficient falling from .321 to .277 during this period) followed by a phase of *rising* household income inequality since 1980. In this latter phase, a Lorenz-worsening took place (fig. 5.1), producing an increase in the Gini coefficient of family income inequality from .277 in 1980 to .316 in 1993 (Republic of China 1993, table 4). The Taiwan government attributes the increasing family income inequality since 1980 to transfor-

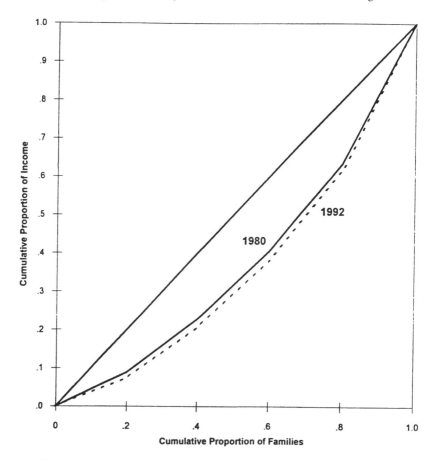

Fig. 5.1.   Taiwan: Lorenz Curves of Family Income, 1980 and 1992. (From Chiou 1995).

mation of the industrial structure toward more labor-intensive industries, change in the pattern of family composition in the direction of
smaller households, faster decline in the size of low-income families, and
growth of the highly educated population (Republic of China 1993, 2–
4). Despite this increase, Taiwan's income inequality remains as low as
that in any country in the world (Deininger and Squire 1995).

A decomposition method devised by Pyatt, Chen, and Fei 1980,
based on work by Rao 1969 and Fei, Ranis, and Kuo 1978, 1979, was
used in empirical studies of Taiwan. These studies by Fei, Ranis, and
Kuo 1978, 1979 and Pyatt, Chen, and Fei 1980 showed that labor income
inequality was the most important source of total income inequality in

Taiwan, at least up to 1972.[2] Subsequently, Chu (1989) found that labor income inequality in 1980 and 1986 was explained principally by the residual in an earnings equation in which education, age, employment status, industry, and occupation were included as explanatory variables and, secondarily, by the number of earners in the household. In view of these previous findings, we hypothesized that the increasing family income inequality since 1980 was attributable in large part to rising labor income inequality and sought to understand what changes in the labor market produced this increase.

Because we do not yet have micro data from the Family Income and Expenditure Survey, we used micro data from Taiwan's Manpower Utilization Survey for all years from 1980 through 1993. Each survey contained more than eighteen thousand households including approximately fifty-eight thousand persons aged fifteen and over. For 1980 and 1993 and all years in between, we calculated the Gini coefficient of labor earnings for everyone with earnings and for all paid employees (excluding the self-employed and employers).

The results came as a considerable surprise: earnings inequality *fell slightly* for both of these groups (table 5.1), and the Lorenz curve was as close to unchanged as one could possibly expect (fig. 5.2).[3] These findings indicate two things. First, *all* of the increase in family income inequality in Taiwan since 1980 is due to nonlabor income. Second, the effects of various changes in the labor market had exactly offsetting effects on the inequality of labor earnings. In what follows, we examine

TABLE 5.1. Taiwan: Gini Coefficients Calculated from Earnings Data

	Everyone with Earnings	All Paid Employees
1980	.313	.249
1981	.297	.247
1982	.300	.254
1983	.305	.261
1984	.304	.253
1985	.298	.250
1986	.306	.261
1987	.301	.259
1988	.299	.251
1989	.292	.247
1990	.294	.248
1991	.296	.244
1992	.294	.240
1993	.298	.246

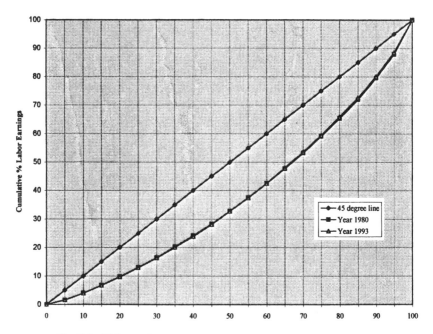

Fig. 5.2.   Taiwan: Lorenz Curves of Labor Earnings, 1980 and 1993

these offsetting effects within the earnings function framework, the method most used by labor economists to study the determinants of labor earnings.

3 Methodology

Fields (1996) has developed a method for decomposing changes over time in earnings inequality. Start with a standard earnings function in which the logarithm of the labor market earnings of worker i at time t is regressed on a number of explanatory variables (indexed by j):

$$\ln(\text{EARNINGS}_{it}) = \alpha_t + \sum_j \beta_{jt} x_{ijt} + \varepsilon_t. \tag{1}$$

This can be rewritten as

$$Y = \sum_j a_{jt} z_{ijt} = a' Z, \tag{2.a}$$

where

$$Y = \ln(\text{EARNINGS}_{it}), \tag{2.b}$$

$$a = [\alpha \; \beta_1 \; \beta_2 \; \ldots \; \beta_J 1] \tag{2.c}$$

and

$$Z = [1x_1 \; x_2 \; \ldots \; x_J \varepsilon]. \tag{2.d}$$

The strategy for deriving a useful decomposition equation is to decompose the log-variance of earnings and then show that the same decomposition applies to other inequality measures as well.

Starting with the earnings functions (2.a–d) for different time periods, take the variance of both sides. On the left-hand side is a simple measure of inequality, the log-variance. The variance of the right-hand side can be manipulated to obtain the following result:

Result 1. The log-variance of earnings is decomposable as

$$s_j = \mathrm{cov}\,[a_j Z_j, Y]/\sigma^2(Y) = \frac{a_j * \sigma(Z_j) * \mathrm{cor}\,[Z_j, Y]}{\sigma(Y)} \tag{3.a}$$

and

$$100\% = \sum_j s_j. \tag{3.b}$$

It would be nice to be able to decompose other inequality measures besides the log-variance. This proves to be quite possible. To show this, a result can be borrowed from the literature on decomposition of inequality by factor components. In this literature, the ith recipient unit's total income Y_i is expressed as the sum of its income from each of several factor components, for example, labor income, capital income, transfer income, and so forth:

$$Y_i = \sum_k Y_{ik}. \tag{4}$$

Letting n denote the total number of income recipients, the question asked in this literature is what fraction of total income inequality, gauged by an inequality measure $I(Y_1, \ldots, Y_n)$, is accounted for by labor income, by capital income, by transfer income, and so on?

Define a "relative factor inequality weight" s_k to be the percentage of income inequality that is accounted for by the kth factor. An important theorem on decomposition by factor components is due to Shorrocks (1982). He shows:

Result 2. Under the six axioms enumerated in the appendix, the relative factor inequality weights s_k are given by

$$s_k = \text{cov } (Y_k, Y)/\sigma^2(Y) \qquad (5.\text{a})$$

such that

$$\sum_k s_k = 1 \qquad (5.\text{b})$$

for *any* inequality index $I(\cdot)$ which is continuous and symmetric and for which $I(Y/N \ Y/N \ldots Y/N) = 0$.

Virtually all inequality indices satisfy these conditions, including the Gini coefficient, the Atkinson index, the generalized entropy family, the log-variance, and various centile measures.

Shorrocks's theorem is directly applicable to the question dealt with in this paper, namely, accounting for differences in labor income inequality using earnings functions. The standard earnings function (2.a) may be rewritten as

$$Y_i = \Sigma_k Y_{ik}. \qquad (2.\text{e})$$

In (2.e), Y_i is (the logarithm of) individual i's earnings and $Y_{ik} = a_k Z_{ik}$, where a_k and Z_{ik} are the kth components of the a and Z vectors given by (2.c) and (2.d) respectively. Using this notation, (3.a) may be rewritten as

$$s_k = \text{cov } [Y_k, Y]/\sigma^2(Y). \qquad (3.\text{c})$$

Note first that the earnings function (2.e) has exactly the same form as the equation expressing total income as the sum of the income from each component (4). Secondly, note that when the inequality of (4) is decomposed, Shorrocks obtains

$$s_k = \text{cov } (Y_k, Y)/\sigma^2(Y) \quad \text{such that} \quad \sum_k s_k = 1,$$

which is exactly the same as (3.b,c). Now, taking advantage of this homeomorphism and applying Shorrocks's theorem, we get the following key result:

Result 3. Under the six axioms enumerated in the appendix, the decomposition of income inequality given by

$$s_j = \text{cov } [a_j Z_j, Y]/\sigma^2(Y) = \frac{a_j * \sigma(Z_j) * \text{cor } [Z_j, Y]}{\sigma(Y)}$$ (3.a)

and

$$100\% = \sum_j s_j$$ (3.b)

holds not only for the log variance but for *any* inequality index that is continuous and symmetric and for which $I(Y/N \ Y/N \ldots Y/N) = 0$, including the Gini coefficient, the Atkinson index, the generalized entropy family, and various centile measures.

This is an extremely powerful result. It says that as long as we agree on the decomposition rules, we do not need to agree on the particular inequality measure to decompose, because virtually *all* inequality measures give the *same* percentage effect for the jth explanatory factor.

Is it also the case that each explanatory factor's contribution to *changes* in income inequality is independent of how inequality is measured? The answer is readily seen to be no: the amount by which inequality rose or fell — and perhaps even *whether* inequality rose or fell — depends on how inequality is measured.

In the empirical work that follows, we proceed parametrically. By choosing a particular inequality measure, we can determine not only whether inequality increased or decreased but also by how much. For this particular inequality measure, we may then calculate how much of the change in inequality is attributable to each income determinant, thereby gauging which is relatively more important: differences in education, in tenure and experience, in unionization, etc.? This is achieved by noting that

$$I_T - I_0 = \sum_j [s_{j,T} * I_T - s_{j,0} * I_0],$$ (6.a)

defining the contribution of factor j to the change in inequality for an arbitrary inequality measure $I(\cdot)$ as

$$\Pi_j(I(\cdot)) \equiv [s_{j,T} * I(\cdot)_T - s_{j,0} * I(\cdot)_0]/[I(\cdot)_T - I(\cdot)_0],$$ (6.b)

and then observing that

$$100\% = \frac{\sum_j [s_{j,T} * I_T - s_{j,0} * I_0]}{I_T - I_0} = \sum_j \Pi_j(\cdot).$$ (6.c)

This gives:

Result 4. The contribution of the jth factor to the change in inequality between time 0 and time T using an arbitrary inequality measure is given by

$$\Pi_j(I(\cdot)) = [s_{j,T}*I(\cdot)_T - s_{j,0}*I(\cdot)_0]/[I(\cdot)_T - I(\cdot)_0]. \qquad (6.b)$$

The same calculations can then be repeated for as many different inequality measures as the analyst is interested in using.

Finally, having run the same earnings function for two separate years, we may ask why the s_j's given by (3) differ. To what extent is the change in any given s_j due to differences between the regression coefficients in the two years? To differences in the inequality of the explanatory variable? To differences in the correlation between the explanatory variable and income? An exact decomposition of the difference in any given s_j can be obtained by logarithmically differentiating (3.a) to obtain

$$\hat{s}_j = \hat{a}_j + \sigma(\hat{Z}_j) + \widehat{\text{cor}\,[\hat{Z}_j,Y]} - \sigma(\hat{Y}), \qquad (3.d)$$

the ^ over the variable indicating a percentage rate of growth.

In real-world applications, the changes in each component are noninfinitesimal. The decomposition of the percentage change in s_j may then be approximated by

$$\text{pctchng}(s_j) \approx \text{pctchng}(a_j) + \text{pctchng}[\sigma(Z_j)] + \text{pctchng}[\text{cor}[Z_j,Y]]$$

$$- \text{pctchng}[\sigma(Y)]. \qquad (3.e)$$

Expressing each of these terms as fractions of the total, we then have:

Result 5. The percentage of the change in relative factor inequality weights accounted for by each explanatory factor can be expressed as:

$$1 \approx \text{pctchng}(a_j)/\text{pctchng}(s_j) + \text{pctchng}[\sigma(Z_j)])/\text{pctchng}(s_j)$$

$$+ \text{pctchng}[\text{cor}[Z_j,Y]])/\text{pctchng}(s_j) - \text{pctchng}[\sigma(Y)])/\text{pctchng}(s_j). \qquad (3.f)$$

In practice, this approximation proves to be quite close. See section 4 for an illustration.

The reader may be wondering how this decomposition procedure differs from the method used by Fei, Ranis, and Kuo (1978) and Pyatt, Chen, and Fei (1980) to decompose total inequality into components attributable to each factor component (e.g., labor income, capital income, land income). Fei, Ranis, and Kuo showed that the Gini coefficient of total income can be decomposed into a weighted sum of "pseudo-Ginis," the weights being given by the corresponding factor shares:

$$G(Y) = \sum_k \phi_k \mathcal{G}(Y_k), \tag{7.a}$$

where Y = total income,

Y_k = income from the kth factor component,

$\phi_k \equiv \sum_i Y_{ik} / \sum_k \sum_i Y_{ik}$ is the share of income from factor k in total income, and

$\mathcal{G}(Y_k)$ is the "pseudo-Gini coefficient" of income from factor k.[4]

Pyatt, Chen, and Fei, building on Rao, showed that the pseudo-Gini coefficient (which they call the "concentration ratio") is in turn the product of the ordinary factor Gini $G(Y_k)$ and a "rank correlation ratio"

$$\begin{aligned} R_k &= \frac{\text{cov}(Y_k, \rho)}{\text{cov}(Y_k, \rho_k)} \\ &= \frac{\text{covariance between factor income amount and total income rank}}{\text{covariance between factor income amount and factor income rank}} \end{aligned} \tag{7.b}$$

and therefore:

$$G(Y) = \sum_k \phi_k G(Y_k) R_k. \tag{7.c}$$

Dividing (7.c) by $G(Y)$, one obtains

$$100\% = \sum_k \phi_k G(Y_k) R_k / G(Y) \approx \sum_k \mathcal{I}_k, \tag{7.d}$$

the sum of the Pyatt et al. relative factor inequality weights. It should be noted that these weights (the $\mathcal{I}_k$ in equation (7.d)) are not the same as the Shorrocks factor inequality weights (the s_j in equation (3.a)), the difference being due to the different decomposition rules used by the different authors.

Let us now see how this decomposition explains inequality in the case of Taiwan.

4 Empirical Findings

What were the proximate reasons for the very slight increase in earnings inequality in Taiwan between 1980 and 1993? In this section, we apply the method described in section 3, taking the Gini coefficient of labor earnings as our measure of inequality.

In the first stage of the analysis, for government and private-sector employees who worked last week and had positive earnings, we regressed the logarithm of labor market earnings per month in current NT\$ (LOGINC) on the following variables: years of education (YRSEDU), years of (potential) experience entered linearly and quadratically (EXP and EXPSQ), years of tenure at the current employer entered linearly and quadratically (TEN and TENSQ), hours of paid labor last week (HOURSP), and indicator variables for gender (GENDER), marital status (MARRIED), and whether the individual changed jobs within the last year (CHJOB). Regression results are reported in table 5.2.

The most striking change in earnings determination between 1980 and 1993 was the increase in the gender effect: whereas females earned 25 percent less than males ceteris paribus in 1980, the gender differential had increased to 35 percent by 1993. Given the large magnitudes of these effects in both periods and the large change between years, it is reasonable to expect that gender was a primary contributor to an increase in earnings inequality.

Another factor that appears to have contributed to rising earnings inequality is education. The coefficient on this variable increased from 5.0 percent in 1980 to 5.7 percent in 1993. Since both the levels and the changes in this variable are less than for the gender variable, it is expected that education would be found to have played a smaller role in explaining inequality change than did gender.

For earnings inequality to have fallen slightly, other factors must have more than offset the effects of gender and education. Earnings function analysis suggests that one such equalizing factor was marital status, the coefficient on which decreased between 1980 and 1993 from 9.1 percent to 4.5 percent. Another is years of experience, the effect of which became flatter over time.[5]

TABLE 5.2. Taiwan: Determinants of Log-Earnings, 1980 and 1993

Variable	1980	1993
YRSEDU	.0501	.0570
	(55.1)	(63.5)
EXP	.0330	.0262
	(34.4)	(34.2)
EXPSQR	−.0006	−.0005
	(−31.9)	(−32.6)
TEN	.0239	.0213
	(16.5)	(19.3)
TENSQR	−.0006	−.0004
	(−13.5)	(−9.9)
HOURSP	.0038	.0066
	(9.9)	(18.0)
GENDER	−.2523	−.3455
	(−40.6)	(−69.6)
MARRIED	.0914	.0460
	(11.9)	(7.6)
CHJOB	−.0031	−.0770
	(−.40)	(−11.3)
CONSTANT	7.880	8.963
	(314.0)	(380.8)
Observations	17,003	21,840
R^2	.4209	.4499
Adjusted R^2	.4206	.4497

Note: t-statistics are in parentheses.
Variable Definitions
 Dependent Variable:
  LOGEARN: Logarithm of labor market earnings per
   month
 Explanatory Variables:
  YRSEDU: Years of education entered psuedo-
   continuously
  EXP: Years of potential experience (AGE-YRSEDU-6)
  EXPSQR: EXP-squared
  TEN: Years of tenure at current employer
  TENSQR: TEN-squared
  HOURSP: Hours of paid work last week
  GENDER: Indicator variable. GENDER = 1 if the
   worker is female.
  MARRIED: Indicator variable. MARITAL = 1 if the
   worker is married.
  CHJOB: Indicator variable. CHJOB = 1 if the worker
   changed jobs within the last year.

In order to quantify and compare the magnitudes of these and other effects, we advanced to the second phase of the analysis. Variables from the regression were included in the decomposition analysis in two ways: some as simple factors (YRSEDU, HOURSP, GENDER, MARRIED, CHJOB) and some as composite factors (EXPERIENCE, TENURE).[6] Equation (3) was used to obtain nonparametric estimates of the relative factor inequality weights s_j for each factor in 1980 and 1993; the levels are shown in columns 1 and 2 of table 5.3 and the changes (Δs_j) in column 3. Those explanatory factors with the largest *levels* of explanatory power (s_j) were gender, years of education, and years of experience, while those with the largest *changes* in explanatory power (Δs_j) were gender and years of education (in the positive direction) and years of experience and marital status (in the negative direction). Other things equal, those factors with larger s_j and larger $|\Delta s_j|$ are the ones that would be expected to have raised or lowered inequality the most.

This is as far as nonparametric analysis can take us. In order to go

TABLE 5.3. Taiwan: Relative Factor Inequality Weights, Levels, and Changes (by percentages)

Factor	(1) $s_{j,1980}$	(2) $s_{j,1993}$	(3) $s_{j,1993} - s_{j,1980}$	(4) Π(Gini)
YRSEDU	10.3	13.2	3.0	+321
EXPERIENCE[a]	12.9	7.1	−5.8	−666
TENURE[b]	5.3	6.1	0.8	+84
HOURSP	−0.2	0.6	0.7	+80
CHJOB	0.0	1.5	1.5	+163
GENDER	10.1	15.5	5.4	+590
MARRIED	3.7	1.1	−2.6	−289
RESIDUAL	57.9	55.0	−2.9	−382
Total	100.0	100.0		100

Column 1: Percentage of monthly earnings inequality in 1980 accounted for by the factor in question.

Column 2: Percentage of monthly earnings inequality in 1993 accounted for by the factor in question.

Column 3: Change in the relative factor inequality weights between 1980 and 1993 = Column 2 − Column 1.

Column 4: Percentage of the change in earnings inequality (measured by the Gini coefficient) between 1980 and 1993 accounted for by the factor in question. (Equation (6.b) in the text). Changes that contribute to an increase in inequality are positive, while those that contribute to a decrease in inequality are negative.

[a]Includes EXPERIENCE entered linearly and quadratically.

[b]Includes TENURE entered linearly and quadratically.

further, an inequality measure must be chosen. For this purpose, we chose the Gini coefficient, because of the prominent role that measure plays in the literature on income inequality in Taiwan. In order to quantify the relative magnitudes of each factor in explaining the Gini coefficient, we used equation (6.b). The results are reported in table 5.3, column 4. Expressed as a percentage of the very modest decrease in the Gini coefficient of earnings, gender and years of education accounted for +590 percent and +321 percent of the change respectively, while experience and marital status worked in the opposite direction (−666 percent and −289 percent respectively.) This shows us that the reason that the Gini coefficient of earnings barely changed in Taiwan is *not* that the underlying earnings determinants remained constant; it is, rather, that some of the underlying factors changed in the direction of increasing inequality, some in the direction of decreasing inequality, and these two sets of factors almost exactly offset one another.

The final step is to understand why each factor had the effect it did. Using equation (3.f), we decomposed the change in each s_j into subcomponents corresponding to (i) the change in the coefficient of that variable in the earnings equation, (ii) the change in the standard deviation of that variable, and (iii) the change in the correlation coefficient between that variable and log-earnings.[7] Results of the decomposition of the s_j's are reported in table 5.4, which is divided into two sections: those that contributed to rising inequality on the left and those that contributed to falling inequality on the right.

Consider gender, which contributed the largest percentage to increasing earnings inequality. According to the decomposition, 74 percent of the increase in the contribution of gender to inequality was due to the widening male-female earnings differential. The second most important reason that gender contributed as much as it did was that gender became more highly (negatively) correlated with earnings; this accounted for 18 percent of the change.[8]

Turning next to years of education, the primary reasons that this variable's contribution to earnings inequality increased were an increase in the correlation between education and earnings (+72 percent of the increased effect of education) and an increase in the return to education (+51 percent).[9] In contrast, the standard deviation of years of education fell from 3.65 to 3.42 between 1980 and 1993, accounting for −26 percent of the change in education's effect. Thus, the more equal distribution of education moderated the potentially large effect of the increase in the return to education on earnings inequality.

Having considered the factors that contributed the most to rising inequality, let us now consider those that contributed the most to falling

TABLE 5.4. Taiwan: Decomposing the Changes in Relative Factor Inequality Weights

Factors Contributing to Rising Inequality in Order of Importance

GENDER	(percentage contribution to inequality change = +590%)			
	1980	1993	%CHANGE	WEIGHT
Contribution (s)	0.101	0.155		
actual change				42.0
estimated change				42.4
Coefficient	−0.252	−0.346	31.2	74.3
Std. Dev. (X)	0.475	0.487	2.5	6.0
Cor (LOGEARN, X)	−0.399	−0.431	7.8	18.5
Std. Dev. (LOGEARN)	0.474	0.470	−0.9	2.1
Total				100.9

YRSEDU	(percentage contribution to inequality change = +321%)			
	1980	1993	%CHANGE	WEIGHT
Contribution (s)	0.103	0.132		
actual change				25.2
estimated change				25.3
Coefficient	0.050	0.057	12.9	51.2
Std. Dev. (X)	3.654	3.421	−6.6	−26.2
Cor (LOGEARN, X)	0.266	0.319	18.0	71.6
Std. Dev. (LOGEARN)	0.474	0.470	−0.9	3.6
Total				100.3

Factors Contributing to Falling Inequality, in Order of Importance

EXPERIENCE	(percentage contribution to inequality change = −666%)		
	1980	1993	%CHANGE
Contribution (s)	0.129	0.070	−59.3
Std. Dev. (X)	13.673	12.881	−6.0
Correlation Effect			
R-Squared	0.172	0.111	−43.7
Coefficient Effect	Let $D(t)$ be the derivative of log-earnings with respect to years of experience (X) in year t.		
	$D(1980) < D(1993)$ for all $X > 29$		
	$D(1980) > D(1993)$ for all $X < 29$		

RESIDUALS	(percentage contribution to inequality change = −383%)			
	1980	1993	%CHANGE	WEIGHT
Contribution (s)	0.579	0.550		
actual change				−5.1
estimated change				−5.1
Coefficient	1.000	1.000	0.0	0.0
Std. Dev. (X)	0.361	0.348	−3.5	67.4
Cor (LOGEARN, X)	0.761	0.742	−2.6	50.0
Std. Dev. (LOGEARN)	0.474	0.470	−0.9	−17.4
Total				100.0

CHJOB

	(percentage contribution to inequality change = +163%)			
	1980	1993	%CHANGE	WEIGHT
Contribution (s)	0.000	0.015		
actual change			193.4	
estimated change			270.3	
Coefficient	−0.003	−0.077	184.3	95.3
Std. Dev. (X)	0.353	0.409	14.6	7.6
Cor (LOGEARN, X)	−0.106	−0.221	70.4	36.4
Std. Dev. (LOGEARN)	0.474	0.470	−0.9	0.5
Total				139.7

MARRIED

	(percentage contribution to inequality change = −289%)			
	1980	1993	%CHANGE	WEIGHT
Contribution (s)	0.037	0.011		
actual change			−106.3	
estimated change			−115.0	
Coefficient	0.091	0.046	−66.2	62.3
Std. Dev. (X)	0.500	0.493	−1.4	1.4
Cor (LOGEARN, X)	0.381	0.233	−48.2	45.3
Std. Dev. (LOGEARN)	0.474	0.470	−0.9	−0.8
Total				108.1

TENURE

	(percentage contribution to inequality change = +85%)		
	1980	1993	%CHANGE
Contribution (s)	0.053	0.061	14.0
Std. Dev. (X)	6.606	6.663	0.9
Correlation Effect			
R-squared	0.143	0.116	−21.0
Coefficient Effect	Let $D(t)$ be the derivative of log-earnings with respect to years of tenure (X) in year t. $D(1980) < D(1993)$ for all $X > 4.6$ $D(1980) > D(1993)$ for all $X < 4.6$		

(continued)

TABLE 5.4. — Continued

Factors Contributing to Rising Inequality in Order of Importance

HOURSP	1980	1993	%CHANGE	WEIGHT
			(percentage contribution to inequality change = +80%)	
Contribution (s)				
actual change	-0.002	0.006		
estimated change			346.8	521.2
Coefficient	0.004	0.007	52.9	15.3
Std. Dev. (X)	7.407	6.551	-12.3	-3.5
Cor (LOGEARN, X)	-0.025	0.061	479.7	138.3
Std. Dev. (LOGEARN)	0.474	0.470	-0.9	0.3
Total				150.3

Note: %CHANGE is the percentage change in the factor with the mean of the 1980 and 1993 values as the base. Actual change is the %CHANGE of the contribution of the given factor. Estimated change (s) = %CHANGE (coeff) + %CHANGE(stddev(X)) + %CHANGE(cor (LOGEARN, X)) − %CHANGE(stddev(LOGEARN)). WEIGHT is the percentage of the change in the relative factor share attributable to each of the four factors.

inequality, years of experience being the most important. This factor enters the earnings function as a quadratic, implying the need for a modification of the standard breakdown.[10] The s_j for the factor EXPERI-ENCE shown in table 5.3 is the sum of the separate s_j's for EXP and EXPSQ. This contribution fell, contributing to falling inequality of earnings. Secondly, the standard deviation of years of experience also fell; this too contributed to falling earnings inequality. Finally, as an analogue to the coefficient effect, recall that the increase in earnings associated with an additional year of experience was lower in 1993 than in 1980 for all years of experience up to 29 — that is, for all but the oldest workers in Taiwan. The smaller experience effect is a third reason that experience contributed to falling earnings inequality between 1980 and 1993.

Besides experience, the other important factor contributing to falling inequality was marital status. This change was driven by a halving of the earnings increment associated with being married, which accounted for 62 percent of the change in the contribution of marital status. The correlation effect was also important, accounting for 45 percent of the reduction.

To sum up, some changes in regression coefficients contributed to rising earnings inequality in Taiwan and some to falling inequality. Likewise, some changes in inequality of the explanatory factors and in correlations between the explanatory factors and log-earnings contributed to rising inequality and some to falling inequality. The advantage of the decomposition approach is that these latter effects are also taken into account.

5 Conclusion

Figures published by the Taiwan government show rising *family income* inequality: the Gini coefficient of family income has risen slowly but steadily since 1980, producing a four-Gini-point increase from 1980 to 1993. The question posed in this research was: What caused the inequality of *labor earnings* to change as it did since 1980?

The first surprising finding was that the inequality of labor earnings fell very slightly in Taiwan during this period of time. This means that *all* of the increase in family income inequality in Taiwan since 1980 is due to nonlabor sources and that various changes in Taiwan's labor market had almost exactly offsetting effects on labor earnings inequality.

Exploring which factors contributed to rising inequality of labor earnings and which to falling inequality of labor earnings between 1980 and 1993, we found:

The factor that contributed most to increasing earnings inequality is gender. This large contribution is due primarily to an increase in the male-female earnings differential.

The next most important factor contributing to increasing earnings inequality is education. Education's contribution increased for two reasons: education came to be more highly correlated with earnings than before, and the returns to education increased from 1980 to 1993. (On the other hand, years of education became more equally distributed between 1980 and 1993, which contributed to decreasing inequality of labor earnings.)

Factors that contributed to increasing earnings inequality but that are small in magnitude are job moving (i.e., whether the individual changed jobs in the last year), job tenure (i.e., years in current job), and hours worked.

Several factors contributed to decreasing earnings inequality, the most important of which is (potential) experience. Experience contributed to falling inequality for three reasons — years of experience became more equal, the gain in earnings for an extra year of experience fell at most experience levels, and experience came to be less correlated with earnings than before.

Marital status also contributed to falling earnings inequality, most importantly because the earnings differential between married and unmarried workers fell and, secondarily, because marital status became less correlated with earnings than previously.

Overall, these specific results show the additional value of moving beyond a regression framework and also analyzing changing income inequality using a decomposition approach — a field in which the name of Gustav Ranis will surely retain a distinguished place for years to come.

Appendix: Conditions on the Decomposition

In the text, Shorrocks's theorem makes reference to six conditions on the decomposition itself. Let Y^{ik} denote the income of the ith income recipient from factor k,

$$Y^i = \sum_j Y^{ik}$$

be the ith recipient's total income,

$$Y^k = \sum_i Y^{ik}$$

be the total income from the kth factor, N be the total number of income recipients, and K be the total number of factor income components. Let $I(Y)$ be an inequality measure defined on the space of total incomes $Y = (Y^1 Y^2 \ldots Y^N)$ and let $S_k = S_k(Y^1, \ldots, Y^K; K)$ be the amount of inequality accounted for by each of the K components. Using this notation, Shorrocks's six conditions may be expressed thus:

Condition 1. (Number of Components) The inequality measure $I(Y)$ is to be divided into K components, one for each income factor, denoted $S_k(Y^1, \ldots, Y^K; K)$.

Condition 2. (a) (Continuity) Each S_k is continuous in Y^k. (b) (Symmetric Treatment of Factors) If $\pi 1, \ldots, \pi k$ is any permutation of $1, \ldots, K$, $S_k(Y^1, \ldots, Y^K; K) = S_{\pi k}(Y^{\pi 1}, \ldots, Y^{\pi k}; K)$.

Condition 3. (Independence of the Level of Disaggregation) The amount of inequality accounted for by any one factor S_k does not depend on how the other factors are grouped.

Condition 4. (Consistent Decomposition) The contributions S_k sum to the overall amount of inequality, namely,

$$\sum_k S_k(Y^1, \ldots, Y^K; K) = I(Y).$$

Condition 5. (a) (Population Symmetry) If P is any $n \times n$ permutation matrix, $S(Y^k P, Y P) = S(Y^k, Y)$; (b) (Normalization for Equal Factor Distribution) If all income recipients have the same value for the kth factor, then the share of inequality accounted for by that factor $S(\mu_k e, Y) = 0$ for all μ_k.

Condition 6. (Two-Factor Symmetry) Suppose the distribution of factor 2 incomes Y^2 is simply a permutation of that for factor 1, Y^1. Then if those were the only two sources of income, Y^1 and Y^2 should receive the same value in the decomposition. Thus, for all permutation matrices P, $S(Y^1, Y^1 + Y^1 P) = S(Y^1 P, Y^1 + Y^1 P)$.

These six conditions generate the factor inequality weights s_k given in the text by $s_k = \text{cov}(Y_k, Y)/\sigma^2(Y)$ such that

$$\sum_k s_k = 1.$$

NOTES

1. For surveys of Taiwan's labor market, see Kuo 1983, chap. 4; Fields and Wan 1989; Lee 1994; Galenson 1996.

2. This decomposition expressed the Gini coefficient of total income as a weighted sum of Gini coefficients of each income component.

3. It is impossible to tell with these data whether the difference between our findings and earlier ones is due to difference in database (Manpower Utilization Survey vs. Family Income and Expenditure Survey), income concept (total income vs. labor earnings), or recipient unit (family vs. individual). If possible, it would be interesting to do calculations of the inequality of labor earnings using micro data from the Survey of Income and Expenditures, but currently we do not have this data source.

4. The pseudo-Gini coefficient of a factor component is the Gini coefficient that would be obtained if income recipients are arrayed in increasing order of total income rather than in increasing order of income from that factor.

5. This may be seen by partially differentiating the earnings equations in table 5.2 with respect to EXP and observing that the 1993 derivative is smaller than the 1980 derivative until EXP reaches 29.0 years and is greater thereafter. Similar calculations can be made for other composite factors such as TENURE.

6. EXPERIENCE consists of EXP and EXPSQ. TENURE consists of TEN and TENSQ.

7. This is for the simple factors. Effects of the composite factors are similar but not identical. See the discussion of experience below in the text.

8. For gender and the other indicator variables, changes in the standard deviation convey no useful economic information because the standard deviation necessarily increases until half the sample is in one category and half in the other and decreases thereafter.

9. For an analysis of the returns to different levels of education in Taiwan year-by-year from 1978 to 1991, see Gindling, Goldfarb, and Chang 1995.

10. The same modification applies to the breakdown of the tenure variable, the other composite variable used in our analysis. Although the effects of composite factors consisting of polynomials or strings of dummy variables are conceptually decomposable into a coefficients effect, a standard deviation effect, and a correlation effect, the total effect is not expressable (even approximately) as a simple sum similar to equation (3.f).

REFERENCES

Ayub, Mahmood. 1977. "Income Inequality in a Growth-Theoretic Context: The Case of Pakistan." Ph.D. diss., Yale University.

Bhattacharya, N., and B. Mahalanobis. 1967. "Regional Disparities in Household Consumption in India." *Journal of the American Statistical Association* (March): 143–61.

Chiou, Jong-Rong. 1995. "A Dominance Evaluation of Taiwan's Official Income Distribution Statistics, 1976–1992." Tamkang University, 1995.

Chu, Y. P. 1989. "Changes in Taiwan's Income Distribution between 1980 and 1986." *Journal of Social Science and Philosophy,* 437–75.

Deininger, Klaus, and Lyn Squire. 1995. "Measuring Income Inequality: A New Data-Base." World Bank, December, processed.

Fei, John C. H., Gustav Ranis, and Shirley W. Y. Kuo. 1978. "Growth and Family Distribution of Income by Factor Components." *Quarterly Journal of Economics* 92:17–53.

———. 1979. *Growth with Equity: The Taiwan Case.* Oxford: Oxford University Press for the World Bank.

Fields, Gary S. 1979. "Income Inequality in Urban Colombia: A Decomposition Analysis." *Review of Income and Wealth* 25, no. 3:327–41.

———. 1996. "Accounting for Differences in Income Inequality." Cornell University, January, processed.

Fields, Gary S., and Henry Wan, Jr. 1989. "Wage Setting Institutions and Economic Development." *World Development* 17, no. 9:147–83.

Fields, Gary S., and Gyeongjoon Yoo. Forthcoming. "Changing Labor Income Inequality in Korea." Cornell University.

Galenson, Walter. 1996. "The Labor Market in Taiwan: Manpower, Earnings, and Market Institutions." Paper prepared for the T. C. Liu–S. C. Tsiang Memorial Conference, Cornell University, May.

Gindling, T. H., Marsha Goldfarb, and Chun-Chig Chang. 1995. "Changing Returns to Education in Taiwan: 1978–91." *World Development* 23, no. 2:343–56.

Karoly, Lynn A., and Gary Burtless. 1995. "The Effects of Rising Earnings Inequality on the Distribution of U.S. Income." *Demography* (August): 379–405.

Kuo, Shirley W. Y. 1983. *The Taiwan Economy in Transition.* Boulder, Colo.: Westview.

Lee, Joseph S. 1994. "Is There a Bona Fide Labor Movement in Taiwan?" Chung-Hua Institution for Economic Research, Discussion Paper No. 9403, April.

Paukert, Felix. 1973. "Income Distribution at Different Levels of Development: A Survey of Evidence." *International Labor Review,* August–September, 97–125.

Pyatt, Graham, Chau-Nan Chen, and John Fei. 1980. "The Distribution of Income by Factor Components." *Quarterly Journal of Economics,* 451–73.

Ranis, Gustav. 1978. "Equity with Growth in Taiwan: How 'Special' Is the 'Special Case?' " *World Development* 6:397–409.

Rao, V. M. 1969. "Two Decompositions of Concentration Ratio." *Journal of Royal Statistical Societies,* series A, 82:418–25.

Republic of China. Various years. *Report on the Survey of Personal Income Distribution in Taiwan Area of the Republic of China.*

Shorrocks, Anthony F. 1982. "Inequality Decomposition by Factor Components." *Econometrica* 50:193–211.

———. 1983. "The Impact of Income Components on the Distribution of Family Incomes." *Quarterly Journal of Economics* 98:311–31.

Part 2. Trade, Technological Transfer, and Economic Development

CHAPTER 6

Trade Orientation, Trade Liberalization, and Economic Growth

T. N. Srinivasan

1 Introduction

The debate on the role of openness to international flows of goods, technology, and capital in the development and growth processes is as old as economics.[1] After all, Adam Smith inveighed against the mercantilists and praised the virtues of openness and competition two centuries ago in *The Wealth of Nations.* Sachs and Warner (1995, 3) point out, "As Smith's followers have stressed for generations, trade promotes growth through a myriad of channels: increased specialization, efficient resource allocation according to comparative advantage, diffusion of international knowledge through trade, and heightened domestic competition as a result of international competition." Whether trading opportunities represent an exogenous "engine of growth" (Robertson 1940) or expansion of trade is simply an endogenous response to growth, in other words, its "handmaiden" (Kravis 1970), was also debated early on.

Gustav Ranis has written extensively on trade and development. As a development economist and an economic historian heavily influenced by Simon Kuznets, Ranis approaches the development process (including the role of trade in it) from the perspective of economic history, particularly the modern growth phase of contemporary developed countries. Thus, in his view,

In long-run perspective, the evolution of the LDCs in the direction of modern economic growth tends to repeat the historical experience of the DCs in terms of statistically measurable structural change. As emphasized earlier, this is equally true in the organizational sense, i.e., there is a general evolutionary trend from heavy direct-market interference to a greater reliance on the market mechanism, complemented by the type of government interference characteristic of the DC. This long-run trend of "liberalization" is, however, not a smooth process and is usually marked by short-run policy oscillations as liberalization packages are adopted and experimented with for a time, only to be abandoned once again under the impact of external shocks. (Ranis and Mahmood 1992, 23)

In summary, our findings suggest that the determinants of the long-run pattern of policy evolution are intimately linked to economic systems' initial conditions. These conditions, given partly by nature and partly by the legacy of history, affect not only their initial level of income and welfare, but also their policy responsiveness and flexibility over time, i.e., the extent to which policy is likely to be accommodative or obstructive of some basic time-phased evolutionary change. (223)

In the mid-1980s, many developing countries initiated reforms of their policy regimes that had been, for several decades earlier, inward oriented, anti-export, and anti-private enterprise by liberalizing their foreign trade and allowing a greater role for the private sector and market forces. Although one can be reasonably confident that a return to dirigisme and extreme inward orientation is very unlikely, the possibility of policy oscillation that Ranis mentions cannot be ruled out altogether. Besides, even as the reforms are under way, some argue that liberalizing restrictions on trade or more generally adopting an outward-oriented development strategy cannot influence the long-run growth rate of the economy but can only have *level* effects, at least as per "traditional or standard" economic theory. Rodrik (1996, 14n. 6), for example, claims,

In traditional economic theory, trade restrictions have *level* effects, but no growth effects. That is, a 20 percent tariff may reduce real income by, say, 0.5 percent of GDP (permanently), but it will not affect the economy's long run growth rate.

Rodrik recognizes that "Empirical work on growth has often claimed to discover a negative relationship between trade protection and growth," but he summarily dismisses this entire literature as "marred by severe analytical and conceptual confusions, with macroeconomic policies often confused for trade restrictions and the endogeneity of trade policy not fully accounted for." If Rodrik is right in his theory and in his critique of empirical work, no general conclusion can be drawn about the role of trade in growth or development! Fortunately, as I argue below, the situation is not that hopeless!

There is a related, but somewhat distinct, debate about what has been called the East Asian miracle, that is, the sustained and rapid growth of the East Asian economies (Hong Kong, Korea, Singapore, and Tai-wan) since the mid-1960s, a growth record matched by few other developing countries. Perhaps the dominant view (Bhagwati 1996; Krueger 1987, 1990; and Little 1996) is that the emphasis on international competitiveness through free trade as in Hong Kong or through an export-oriented strategy as in Korea has a lot to do with their stellar economic performance. A minority view, vigorously expounded by Amsden 1989 and Wade 1990, and endorsed by Rodrik 1997, 1995a, is that Korean success at any rate is largely due to active and consistent industrial policy interventions that "shaped future comparative advantage." Some recent empirical research (Lau and Kim 1994; Young 1995) that showed that, in accounting for East Asian growth, total factor productivity (TFP) growth made only a modest contribution and that most of the growth was due to high rates of factor accumulation has led some (Krugman 1994) to argue that East Asian rapid growth is as unsustainable as in the failed Soviet system, in which high rates of investment led to rapid growth for a time.

Gustav Ranis, a longtime student of East Asian countries (particularly Japan and Taiwan), has written extensively on their development, most recently in Ranis 1992, 1995. Characteristically, he interprets East Asian performance from a historical perspective and comes to a balanced and nuanced view:

There are those who wax eloquent about what they perceive as the unique application in East Asia of pure neo-classical mono-economics combined with laissez faire and those who claim that these situations really represent examples of fairly active and intrusive but somehow wise governments. But the "why" [i.e., why there is a marked divergence in performance between East Asian and South-east Asian], while admittedly difficult, is not often addressed. (Ranis 1992, 76).

We should remind ourselves that all the elements of a typical import substitution policy mix, including protectionism, import controls, multiple exchange rates, government deficits, substantial inflation, emphasis on public enterprises and a pronounced dedication to the idea of government planning were present in East Asia in the 1950's. However, it was a substantially milder version than its South-East Asian counterpart. (1992, 83)

Facing a decline in the rate of industrial growth and the threat of competitive price wars or cartelization at the end of the primary import substitution phase, policymakers in the East Asian NIE's made flexibly pragmatic choices accommodating changes in the economic environment. The so frequently encountered entrenched habits and strong vested interests of hot-house industrialization as found more prominently in South-East Asia had less of a chance to flourish.

In the Toynbee sense of challenge/response the East Asian NIE's had an easier problem. There was no real alternative for them but to build institutions that would tend to mobilize their human resources over time, first unskilled, then skilled, on behalf of the transition growth effort. This included not only the provision of infra-structure and, most importantly, its equitable allocation between urban and rural claimants but also the creation of special facilities such as export processing zones.

The East Asian NIE's recognized that a strong government was essential but that its willingness to exercise self-restraint in selecting the areas in which it could effectively intervene and where it could not represent the key to maintaining an accommodating policy structure.

Any consideration of the lessons of comparative development experience therefore requires not just an examination of the different policy packages deployed, but also, along with these purely technical issues, an understanding of the more subtle political economy-tinged processes. This has led us to examining the political economy context of policy-making for achieving a successful transition to modern growth. It is our contention that an economic system's initial conditions, including its natural resource endowment and the strength of its organic nationalism, affect not only the initial levels of income and welfare but also the policy responsiveness and flexibility which follow, i.e. the extent to which development policies can be counted on to be more or less accommodating rather than obstructive over time. (1992, 87–88)

In honoring Gustav Ranis, it is appropriate to take yet another look at two issues that he himself had analyzed, namely, the effects of openness to foreign trade on growth, and in particular, the evidence from the experience of East Asia. In what follows, in section 2, I demonstrate that the assertion of Rodrik (1996) that, in traditional theory, trade liberalization does not have a long-run growth effect is wrong unless he means by "traditional theory" any theory that yields that result! I do this first by incorporating trade in the popular closed-economy models of early development literature (e.g., Harrod-Domar and Fel'dman-Mahalanobis models). I then show that the same result holds in appropriate versions of the neoclassical growth model. In both sets of models in which constant returns to scale prevail, trade liberalization has a long-run growth effect because the marginal product of capital is either constant, as in Harrod-Domar type models, or, even though it diminishes as the capital-labor ratio increases, it remains above a positive lower bound. Indeed, the widely held but mistaken belief that in all neoclassical growth models long-run growth in output per worker is *necessarily* zero without exogenous technical progress of a labor-augmenting kind, and hence trade liberalization can have only level effects, arises from the failure to recognize that it is driven solely by the assumption that the marginal product inexorably declines to zero as the capital-labor ratio increases without bound. Having said this, I should hasten to add that a production function with a positive lower bound on the marginal product of capital unfortunately implies that labor becomes inessential as a factor of production as capital-labor ratio increases without bound.

The distinction between production of capital goods and that of consumer goods in the two-sector Fel'dman-Mahalanobis model enables me to compare liberalization of trade in capital goods with that in consumer goods. I show that while both are welfare enhancing, the former increases the long-run growth rate of the economy and the latter does not. Since very high (if not prohibitive) tariffs on consumer goods are often the first to be imposed and the last to be lowered in developing countries, this comparison is of some interest. In section 2, I also show that even in models with no long-run growth effect of trade liberalization, there are growth effects along the transition path to a new steady state. In section 3, I briefly review recent empirical studies on openness and growth. In section 4, I comment on the debate over East Asian growth and also show that having access to foreign capital goods of newer vintages at a cost below their domestic marginal product could influence income-based, though not production-based, measures of TFP growth. Section 5 concludes the essay.

2 Growth Effects of Openness in Traditional Theory

2.1 Harrod-Domar Model

Consider the simplest version of the workhorse of early development planning, namely, the Harrod-Domar (Domar 1957) model in which capital is the sole factor of production.[2] Output Y_t at any time t is the product of capital stock K_t in existence at that time and a constant output-capital ratio β. The economy is assumed to be closed to foreign trade. A constant proportion s of output is assumed to be saved and invested so that, given a constant proportional rate of depreciation at the rate δ per unit of time of capital stock, the growth rate g of the economy is $s\beta - \delta$. As long as s is exogenous, so is the growth rate g.

Let me introduce foreign trade into the model in a very simple way by supposing that the economy can trade with the rest of the world at a constant terms of trade of $\Pi(\pi > 1)$ units of investment per unit of output in contrast with domestic terms of trade of unity under autarky. In other words, while under autarky, the economy can transform each unit of output into one unit of consumption or one unit of investment, with trade it gets the same consumption but more (i.e., $\Pi > 1$) investment per unit of output. Implicit in this way of introducing trade is that the economy is too small to influence the world relative price (in terms of home output) of investment good and that it has a comparative advantage in its home output or equivalently, consumption good. Thus with capital as its sole factor of production this Ricardian economy specializes in producing consumption good under free trade.

Let me make savings (equivalently consumption c_t) endogenous (and thus growth endogenous) through the maximization of intertemporal welfare

$$W \equiv \int_0^\infty e^{-\rho t} u(c_t) dt, \tag{1}$$

where, for simplicity of analysis, I assume that the instantaneous felicity function $u(c_t)$ is $(c^{1-\sigma} - 1)/(1 - \sigma)$ (with $\sigma > 0$). I assume, again for simplicity, that international lending or borrowing is infeasible, so that trade has to be balanced at each t. Thus W is to be maximized subject to the constraint investment goods imports equals the value of exports or

$$\dot{K}_t + \delta K_t = \Pi[\beta K_t - c_t] \tag{2}$$

and the non-negativity constraints $c_t \geq 0$, $\dot{K}_t + \delta K_t \geq 0$.

An optimal solution to this problem exists, and is unique as long as $\rho + (\sigma - 1)(\Pi\beta - \delta) > 0$. It is given by

$$K_t = K_o e^{gt} \quad \text{and} \quad c_t = \left[\frac{\rho + (\sigma - 1)(\Pi\beta - \delta)}{\Pi\sigma} \right] K_o e^{gt}, \tag{3}$$

where

$$g = \left(\frac{\Pi\beta - \delta - \rho}{\sigma} \right). \tag{4}$$

The *short and long-run growth rate g* of consumption and capital stock will be positive as long as $\Pi\beta - \delta - \rho > 0$. Now

$$\frac{\partial g}{\partial \Pi} = \frac{\beta}{\sigma} > 0.$$

Since opening the economy to trade involves an increase in the relative price of the consumption good in which the economy has comparative advantage from its value of 1 under autarky to $\Pi > 1$ under free trade, it follows from $\partial g/\partial\Pi > 0$ that the short- and long-run growth rate of the economy, namely, *g*, is increased by such opening. *Thus contrary to the assertion of Rodrik (1996), trade liberalization (which in this case is moving to free trade from autarky) has positive growth effects.*

Now the gross domestic product (GDP) valued in terms of *investment goods* is

$$(\dot{K}_t + \delta K_t) + \Pi c_t = \beta\Pi K_o e^{gt}.$$

Clearly as Π under free trade is raised above its autarky value of unity, there is a *positive level effect* (through $\beta\Pi$) *and a positive* growth effect (through *g*) on GDP (from the move to free trade). The value of GDP in terms of *consumption goods* (or equivalent output) is $\beta K_o e^{gt}$. As such, moving to free trade has only a growth effect but no level effect on GDP.

It is seen from (3) that moving to free trade has a positive growth effect, but an ambiguous level effect (it is positive, zero, or negative according as $(\sigma - 1)\delta - \rho$ is positive, zero, or negative), on consumption in physical units. This reflects the conflict between a *positive* income effect and a *negative* substitution effect as the economy moves to freer trade, arising from the rise in relative price of consumption good in which the economy has comparative advantage. The *value* of consumption, in terms of investment goods, is

$$\Pi c_t = \left[\frac{\rho + (\sigma - 1)(\Pi\beta - \delta)}{\sigma} \right] K_o e^{gt}. \tag{5}$$

Hence, moving to free trade has a *positive growth effect* on it as well. The *level effect* is *positive if and only if* the intertemporal elasticity of substitution $1/\sigma < 1$. However, whether or not the level effect on consumption is positive (either in value or in physical units), it can be shown that intertemporal welfare W increases under free trade relative to autarky, the reason being that even if the *level effect* on consumption of a move to free trade is negative, the positive *growth effect* is more than enough to raise W under free trade above its autarky level.

2.2 Fel'dman-Mahalanobis Model

One of the influential development models was formulated independently by Fel'dman (1928) for the Soviet Union and the physicist-statistician Mahalanobis (1955), who was the author of India's Second Five Year Plan (1956–61).[3] It is a model of a closed economy in which there are two sectors, one of which produces a consumption good, and the other, a capital good. Capital is the only factor of production, and the output of each sector is the product of the stock of capital in existence in that sector and its output-capital ratio. While the *flow* of output of the investment goods sector can be allocated in any fashion to augment the *stock* of capital in either sector, capital, once installed in that sector, cannot be shifted to the other sector.

Fel'dman and Mahalanobis show that the *long-run growth* rate of output in *both sectors* is a monotone increasing function of the proportion of the output of investment goods that is invested in the *capital goods* sector. Mahalanobis used this result to argue that India should invest in heavy industries for achieving rapid long-run growth of *both* consumption and investment.

Erutna (1972) and Ünsal (1990) introduce foreign trade into the Fel'dman-Mahalanobis model.[4] Ünsal points out that Erutna assumes that investment equals the output of the domestic goods sector and, at the same time, that some proportion of capital goods are imported. Thus, a part of the output of capital goods must be exported to pay for the import of capital goods of equal value. This in turn means that the rate of growth of the domestic capital-goods sector determines the long-run rate of growth of the economy as in the closed-economy Fel'dman model. Opening to trade does not alter the basic conclusion of the model.

Ünsal (1990), on the other hand, introduces a third export sector in addition to the capital and consumption goods sectors of the Fel'dman model. The entire output of the third sector is exported, and investment goods of equal value are imported in return. Domestic investment thus equals the sum of the output of the domestic capital-goods sector and imports of capital goods. Investment is allocated among the three sectors, and once capital is installed in a sector, it is not shiftable to any other sector. Although Ünsal views the export sector as exporting consumer goods, formally, adding an *export* sector is equivalent to having two *domestic* sectors producing investment goods, since the entire output of the export sector is exchanged for investment goods one for one. As such, the long-run rate of growth of the economy depends on the shares of investment allocated to the two investment-goods-producing sectors. However, with capital as the only factor of production, as long as the productivity of capital differs between the two investment-goods-producing sectors (that is, the export and domestic capital-goods sectors), the share of investment devoted to the sector with lower productivity will always be zero if investment is allocated efficiently. As such, opening to trade will raise the long-run rate of growth of the economy (given the share of investment devoted to the nontraded consumption goods sector) as long as capital is more efficient in the export rather than the domestic capital-goods sector. Although Ünsal does not do so, one could interpret this result in terms of comparative advantage: with two traded goods (namely, an investment good and an export good) exchanging one for one in world markets, the greater productivity of capital (the sole factor of production) in exports implies that the economy will specialize in it (within the traded-goods sector) once trade opens up. Of course, nontraded consumer goods will continue to be produced.

Ünsal's (1990) model is adequate to demonstrate the possible growth-augmenting effect of opening to trade. However, since it neither allows for domestic consumption of the exportable nor allows consumption goods to be imported, it cannot be used to examine the possibly different growth implications of opening the consumption goods sector to trade in contrast to opening the capital-goods sector.

An alternative version of the Fel'dman-Mahalanobis model (see appendix A) enables such an analysis. Let there be two consumer goods as well as two investment goods (instead of one each) with the marginal product of capital being constant in the production of each good. Let the utility function, and the aggregation function that transforms the output of the two investment goods into aggregate investment, be Cobb-Douglas. Let capital stock be freely shiftable *within* each sector, but with no intersectoral shiftability. Let me assume, for simplicity only, that the share of investment devoted to the accumulation of capital stock in the capital-goods sector is exogenously fixed rather than endogenously determined through intertemporal welfare maximization.

It is easily seen that, under autarky, all four goods will be produced in positive amounts. Suppose now this economy is opened to free trade in consumer goods, with the relative price of the two consumer goods being fixed in world markets. Then the economy will specialize in producing one of the two consumer goods in which it has a comparative advantage, and trade some of it for the other. However, as long as the share of investment devoted to the capital-goods sector is unchanged and that sector is closed to foreign trade, even though the welfare of the economy will rise relative to autarky, *the long-run growth rate of the economy would be unchanged.* In contrast, if the capital-goods sector is opened to free trade (again at fixed world-relative prices) while the consumer goods sector is kept closed, there will be a *positive long-run growth effect and a welfare effect relative to autarky.* The implication is that, from a growth perspective, keeping the growth-inducing sector (which is the capital-goods sector in this model) closed to international competition is costlier than closing the consumer goods sector. But, of course, keeping neither closed would be even better since, for this small economy, there is no market power to be exploited through a tariff policy or any dynamic externalities due to learning effects to be internalized in the model. I make no apologies for assuming away all these. I do not believe that the factors that lead to rewarding strategic interventions in foreign trade in models of New Trade Theory are present in developing countries. Nor do I think dynamic learning effects, even if potentially large, are automatic and independent of the policy environment. For example, in the Indian automobile industry, there was very little evidence of learning, in spite of (I should say because of!) its completely sheltered existence for over four decades.

2.3 Neoclassical (Cass-Koopmans) Model with Foreign Trade

I consider now a simple version of the classic model of optimal growth (Cass 1965; Koopmans 1965) for a closed economy and modify it, as I did with the Harrod-Domar model, by assuming the economy to have a comparative advantage in consumption goods as it opens to trade. Under free trade, it exchanges what it saves out of its output for imported investment goods at a constant relative price of Π ($\Pi > 1$, the autarky price) of consumption good (or output) in terms of investment good. Once again, for simplicity, let there be no foreign lending or borrowing. Let me assume that the labor force grows exponentially at a constant exogenous rate n, and the production function for output is Cobb-Douglas with constant returns to scale in capital and labor.

The social planner[5] maximizes the discounted present value of the sum of felicities of a representative agent. Thus she maximizes

$$W = \int_0^\infty e^{-\rho t} \left[\frac{c_t^{1-\sigma} - 1}{1 - \sigma} \right] dt \qquad (6)$$

subject to

$$\dot{k}_t = \Pi[k_t^\alpha - c_t] - (n + \delta)k_t \qquad (7)$$

where k_t is the capital-labor ratio at time t and δ is the depreciation rate of capital.

It can be easily shown that the optimal path of k_t in this model converges to its steady state value k^* given by

$$k^* = \left(\frac{\alpha \Pi}{n + \delta + \rho} \right)^{1/1-\alpha}. \qquad (8)$$

The steady-state consumption per worker c^* is given by

$$c^* = \frac{k^*}{\Pi} \left[\frac{(n + \delta)(1 - \alpha) + \rho}{\alpha} \right]. \qquad (9)$$

It can be verified that

$$\frac{dk^*}{d\Pi} = \frac{k^*}{(1 - \alpha)\Pi} > 0$$

and

$$\frac{dc^*}{d\Pi} = \left[\frac{(n + \delta)(1 - \alpha) + \rho}{\alpha} \right] \left[-\frac{k^*}{\Pi^2} + \frac{1}{\Pi} \frac{dk^*}{d\Pi} \right]$$

$$= \left[\frac{(n + \delta)(1 - \alpha) + \rho}{\alpha} \right] \frac{\alpha k^*}{(1 - \alpha)\Pi^2} > 0.$$

Thus moving from autarky with $\Pi = 1$ to free trade with $\Pi > 1$ leads to an increase in the steady-state values of *consumption per worker* and *capital per worker*. These are *positive level effects* of trade liberalization. Since, in the steady state, c^* and k^* are constant while the number of workers grows at the rate n, aggregate consumption and capital stock also grow at the *exogenous* rate n as in autarky. Thus, there is no *long-run growth effect* of the move to free trade.

Along the transition path to the steady state, the growth rate of consumption at any given capital-labor ratio k_t increases with Π. This is seen by noting that, given k_t, optimal c_t maximizes the Hamiltonian

$$H = \left(\frac{c_t^{1-\sigma} - 1}{1 - \sigma} \right) + \lambda[\Pi(k_t^\alpha - c) - (n + \delta)k_t], \tag{10}$$

where λ is the costate variable whose time path is given by $\dot{\lambda} = \lambda\rho - \partial H/\partial k_t$. The first-order condition for a maximum of H with respect to c_t is

$$c_t^{-\sigma} = \lambda\Pi \tag{11}$$

so that

$$\frac{\dot{c}_t}{c_t} = -\frac{1}{\sigma}\frac{\dot{\lambda}}{\lambda} = \frac{1}{\sigma}[\alpha\Pi k_t^{\alpha-1} - (n + \delta + \rho)]. \tag{12}$$

Thus,

$$\frac{\partial}{\partial\Pi}\left(\frac{\dot{c}_t}{c_t} \right) = \frac{\alpha}{\sigma} k_t^{\alpha-1} > 0.$$

Thus, given any k_t, moving to free trade from autarky (i.e., raising Π above 1) raises the growth rate of consumption. In appendix 2, the dynamics near the steady state are analyzed to show the positive growth effect of moving to trade on output and capital stock along the transition to the steady state.

It is also easy to obtain a positive *long-run growth effect* of trade liberalization in the Cass-Koopmans model. All one has to do is to specify a production function in which the marginal product of capital is bounded below by a sufficiently high positive value as capital-labor ratio goes to infinity. For example, consider the production function, output $= K^\alpha L^{1-\alpha} + \beta K$. For this function, the marginal product of capital is $\alpha k^{\alpha-1} + \beta$ which has the limit $\beta > 0$ as $k \rightarrow \infty$. Thus, for large capital-labor ratios, the Cass-Koopmans model with this production function behaves like the Harrod-Domar model discussed earlier. As such, positive long-run growth effects of opening to trade are possible. Having said this, I should add that while the simple Harrod-Domar model assumed away any other factor of production besides capital, in the modified production function, even though both labor and capital are factors of production, as I noted earlier, asymptotically labor becomes inessential. Obviously, this is not a desirable feature.

3 Trade and Growth: Recent Empirical Research

The relationship between openness to foreign trade in goods and services, technology, and investment has attracted a good deal of theoretical and empirical attention recently. This was stimulated by two strands of research. The first strand consisted of theoretical advances in endogenizing the processes of growth and technical change, as well as in modeling international trade in differentiated products under increasing returns and imperfect competition. The second strand was empirical research on convergence, which tested variations of the proposition that regardless of initial conditions, all economies with access to the same technology, with the same intertemporal preferences, and experiencing the same rate of growth of labor force will converge to the same steady state. Surveys of earlier empirical literature by Edwards (1993) and recent literature on trade and development by Harrison (1996) are available.

Rodrik (1995b) provides a critical evaluation of the empirical research on trade and growth. Many of his criticisms, to which I made a reference earlier, are certainly well taken. He is indeed right in pointing to severe problems with data, econometric methodology, not to mention conceptual confusions in some of the studies that cast doubt on their findings. Indeed, unless the specification of estimating equations is not arbitrary and, in fact, consistent with a well-articulated theory, the resulting estimates are difficult to interpret in a meaningful way. However, not all these problems are insurmountable, nor is it inevitable that the findings of all the growth-openness studies would be reversed once the problems are addressed. As such, it would be too hasty to dismiss all the studies as worthless if, despite all their faults, *several* of them reach the *same* qualitative conclusions that are *also* consistent with *a priori reasoning*. Such conclusions deserve serious consideration, with due allowances being made for their conceptual and statistical deficiencies.

Before turning to some of these studies, let me note that, since 1950, the world economy, and in particular the developing economies, have enjoyed a remarkable growth of output, not only in contrast to the disastrous period between the two world wars, but also in comparison to the period prior to the First World War. Growth in the volume of trade outpaced that in the volume of output, which is an indication of increasing global integration (fig. 6.1). In 1997, world exports grew by 9.5

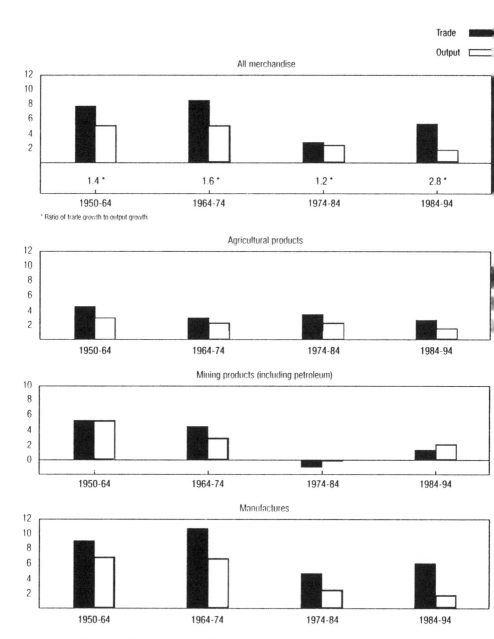

Fig. 6.1. Growth of world merchandise trade and output: 1950–94.
(From WTO 1995, chart 1.6, p. 16.)

percent and output by 3 percent. (WTO 1998, 2). Although in the decade since the first oil shock in 1973, both trade and output grew at a considerably slower pace than in the previous two and a half decades, since the mid-1980s there seems to be a significant recovery, if not a return, to the pre-1973 rates of growth. It is not altogether implausible to suggest that the signing of the General Agreement of Tariffs on Trade (GATT) in 1947, its assuming some of the roles envisaged for the International Trade Organization that failed to get established, and, above all, the successive rounds of trade liberalization negotiated under the auspices of GATT have contributed significantly to the growth in world trade and output. Now that the World Trade Organization has replaced GATT with a membership of 128 countries at the end of 1996 in comparison to the 23 countries that signed the GATT in 1947, it can be expected that the process of global integration will be further strengthened.

Let me turn to recent empirical studies on trade and growth. Sachs and Warner make an ambitious attempt

> to document the process of global integration and to assess its effects on economic growth in the reforming countries. Using cross-country indicators of trade openness as the measures of each country's orientation to the world economy, we examine the timing of trade liberalization, and the implications of trade liberalization for subsequent growth and for the onset or avoidance of economic crises. (1995, 2)

They point out that "in recent decades, there has been no overall tendency for the poorer countries to catch up, or converge, with the richer countries" (3), contrary to the expectation that, in a world of access to common technology and similar tastes and so forth, "poorer countries should tend to grow more rapidly than richer countries and therefore should close the proportionate income gap over time" (2). They conclude that

> this problem is readily explained by the trade regime: open economies tend to converge, but closed economies do not. The lack of convergence in recent decades results from the fact that the poorer countries have been closed to the world. This is now changing with the spread of trade liberalization programs, so that presumably the tendencies toward convergence will be markedly strengthened. (3)

Sachs and Warner define an open economy as one with *none* of five characteristics: tariffs exceeding 40 percent, nontariff barriers covering more than 40 percent of trade, a black market premium of more than 20 percent relative to the official exchange rate on an average during the 1970s or 1980s, a socialist economic system as defined by Kornai (1992), or a state monopoly on major exports.[6] By definition, a closed economy is one that has at least one of the five characteristics. Three of their many empirical findings are of interest: strong association between openness and growth, dependence of income convergence or catch-up among economies on their being open, and lower probability of the occurrence of severe macroeconomic crises in open economies.

They find

> a strong association between openness and growth, both within the group of developing and the group of developed countries. Within the group of developing countries, the open economies grew at 4.49 percent per year, and the closed economies grew at 0.69 percent per year. Within the group of developed economies, the open economies grew at 2.29 percent per year, and the closed economies grew at 0.74 percent per year. (35–36)

By cross-classifying developing countries according to growth and openness, they reject "the null hypothesis of no difference in growth rates between closed and open economies" (36). This finding should be viewed as no more than suggestive, since, strictly speaking, their conventional statistical test (χ^2 test) of independence is not applicable since trade policy as well as growth are endogenous variables.

Their regressions of growth between 1970 and 1989 on initial income in 1970 for 117 countries showed no evidence of convergence. Indeed, there was some evidence of divergence, the coefficient of the variable logarithm of GDP in 1970 was *positive* (instead of being negative were there to be convergence) and close to being statistically significant. However, once trade policy and other relevant explanatory variables are introduced, the coefficient becomes not only negative, but significant as well, indicating convergence. The variables with statistically significant (at 5 percent or better level) effects on growth are given in table 6.1. The variables that turned out to be statistically insignificant were population density, primary and secondary school enrollment rates, and the political variables, namely average number of revolutions and coups per year and average number of assassinations per million of population, both during 1970–85. While it is comforting that all the statistically significant variables have coefficients with expected signs, since some of the explanatory variables (e.g., investment rate, relative price of investment goods) including the all-important dummy variable

OPEN are endogenous, the estimated coefficients are certainly biased, though it is impossible to assess the seriousness of the bias.

Sachs and Warner also relate openness and the occurrence of severe macroeconomic crises (defined as occurrence of any one of rescheduling of debt by official or private donors, arrears of external payments as reported by the International Monetary Fund and an inflation rate in excess of 100 percent). They offer several plausible reasons (greater dependence on debt, greater orientation of investment towards non-traded goods, and higher level of state involvement in the economy) as why closed economies are more likely to experience severe macro-economic crises. Out of seventeen (resp. seventy-three) economies that they classify as open (resp. closed) in the 1970s, as few as one (resp. as many as fifty-nine) experienced macroeconomic crises in the 1980s. Once again, because of endogeneity, their statistical test of independence between openness and crisis-proneness is not valid. As such, the results are to be treated as suggestive and no more.

Sachs and Warner are aware of the pitfalls in their analysis and properly cautious in distinguishing between various components of economic policy and their growth effects. They are certainly right in viewing

TABLE 6.1.   Regression Explaining Economic Growth

Variable	Coefficient	t-value
logGDP70[1]	−1.396	−4.122
OPEN[2]	2.203	4.721
POL[3]	−0.882	1.972
GVXDXE[4]	−6.669	−2.079
PPI70DEV[5]	−0.964	−2.537
INV7089[6]	6.302	1.896
$\bar{R}^2$		0.550
Number of countries		79

Source: Sachs and Warner 1995, table 11, pp. 48–49.

Note: The dependent variable is G7089, the real annual per capita growth in GDP over 1970–89.

[1]LGDP70 is the natural log of real GDP per capita in 1970.

[2]OPEN is a dummy variable set equal to one for open economies.

[3]POL is a composite dummy variable indicating extreme political repression and unrest.

[4]GVXDXE is the ratio of real government consumption spending (net of spending on the military and education) to real GDP.

[5]PPI70DEV measures the relative price of investment goods. It is the deviation of the log of the price level of investment from the cross-country sample mean in 1970.

[6]INV7089 is the ratio of real gross domestic investment (public plus private) to real GDP, averaged over the period 1970–89.

their "measure of trade policy [as serving] as a proxy for an entire array of policy actions" and asserting that

> open trade has tended to be correlated with other features of a healthy economy, such as macroeconomic balance and reliance on the private sector as the main engine of growth. To some extent, opening the economy has helped to promote governmental responsibility in other areas. To that extent, trade policy should be viewed as the primary instrument of reform. (1995, 63)

The Sachs-Warner result that there is "tendency convergence among economies once their trade regime is controlled for" is also shown by Ben-David (1996). He analyzes twenty-five countries that had per capita incomes in 1960 above an admittedly ad hoc cutoff point of 25 percent of the U.S. per capita income that year and were neither primarily oil producers nor former Communists. These included the following developing countries: Argentina, Bolivia, Chile, Mexico, and Uruguay. For each of the twenty-five countries, he forms an *export* group consisting of those countries to which it exported more than 4 percent of total exports in 1985 and an *import* group consisting of those countries from which it imported over 4 percent of its total imports. Both groups ranged in size from a minimum of three to a maximum of nine. Within the trade groups, seven countries (Bolivia, Brazil, Congo, Ethiopia, Ghana, Guyana, and South Korea) that did not satisfy the 25 percent income cutoff point were included as well. He finds that in the export-based (resp. import-based) group, twenty-four (resp. twenty-two) showed income convergence of which sixteen (resp. seventeen) were statistically significant.

Ben-David tests the robustness of his results by examining whether the convergence is just as likely within a *random group* of three to nine countries drawn from the twenty-five as within *trade* groups. Since the number of all possible random groups are large for group sizes exceeding five, he chose random samples of five thousand such groups for sizes six to nine. He found that the probability of observing in random groups a convergence coefficient as high as was estimated from actual trading groups was very low.

Ben-David and Rahman (1996) use the same countries and trade groups as in Ben-David 1996 to examine convergence in income *per worker* (rather than income *per capita* as in Ben-David 1996) and capital per worker. They find that the evidence for convergence in income per worker is even stronger than for income per capita, while there is no evidence at all for convergence in capital per worker. This leads them to conclude that the primary source of trade-related income convergence is convergence in technologies rather than convergence in capital-labor ratios. Baldwin and Seghezza (1996) estimate two basic relationships: the first, between trade barriers and income and growth, and the second, between trade barriers and investment, a channel through which trade affects growth. Various data samples and various measures of trade barriers and so on are used to test the robustness of the conclusions. For their preferred sample of thirty-nine countries that exported manufactures in 1989, their findings (based on three-stage least squares estimation) are given in table 6.2.

The results for the growth equation suggests that the technology catch-up factor is important (as is evident from the significant negative coefficient of initial income per worker). Initial human capital stock (though not subsequent investment in it) is a significant factor as well. Of course, investment in physical capital is, as expected, significant. Turning now to a channel through which trade affects growth, namely, investment, their finding that domestic *and* foreign trade barriers significantly depress investment is very interesting. Clearly domestic trade barriers on the one hand raise domestic rental rate on capital, but on the other, they raise the cost of capital goods by raising the price of imported inputs used in their production. The latter effect, which makes investment less attractive, dominates the former effect, which makes investment more attractive. Their result on the deleterious effect of foreign

TABLE 6.2. Results for Preferred Sample and Specification (sample is manufactures exporters in 1989, number of observations = 39)

	Growth Equation			Investment Equation	
	Coefficient	t-stat		Coefficient	t-stat
Constant	-0.02	-1.5	Constant	0.49	3.4
Initial (1960) real per capita income (Y/L)	$-4e-06$	-3.4	log Y/L	-0.02	-1.1
Population growth	0.29	0.9	log population growth	$-4e-03$	-0.3
Human capital investment (H)	-0.01	-0.8	log H	0.08	4.9
Initial stock of H	$4e-04$	1.8	log initial stock of H	$-2e-03$	-0.2
Physical capital investment	0.24	6.2	Domestic barriers	-1.05	-3.8
			Foreign barriers	-0.82	-2.0
$R**2$		0.54	$R**2$		0.74

Source: Baldwin and Seghezza 1996, table 2.

barriers is apparently new — however, foreign barriers turn out to be less deleterious than domestic barriers.[7]

Coe and Helpman (1995) test the impact of openness on the transmission of technical knowledge and hence on TFP growth. The basic idea is that imports convey information on the state of technological knowledge in the exporting country so that a country that has a larger share of its imports originating in more advanced countries with higher technical knowledge will experience faster TFP growth than one that imports more from less technically advanced countries. Their basic specification is

$$\log F_i = \alpha_{oi} + \alpha_1 \log S_i^d + \alpha_2 \log S_i^f + u_i, \tag{13}$$

where $F_i = $ *level* of total factor productivity in country i

$s_i^d = $ domestic knowledge stock of country i[8]

$s_i^f = $ foreign knowledge stock relevant for country i defined as the sum of import-share weighted domestic knowledge stock of countries from which i imports

$u_i = $ random disturbance.

Their sample includes twenty-one OECD countries and Israel for the years 1971–90. In a second specification, they interact S^d with a dummy for the group of seven (G7) and in a third, they replace $\log s_i^f$ by $s_i \log s_1^f$ where s_i is the share of imports in GDP of country i. Their estimate of the basic specification (others yield similar results) is (omitting the country-specific constant, standard errors of coefficients in parenthesis)

$$\log F = \frac{0.097}{(0.009)} \log S^d + \frac{0.092}{(0.016)} \log S^f, R^2 = 0.558.$$

These results indicate the significant and similar quantitative impact of domestic and foreign knowledge stocks on TFP growth.

Keller (forthcoming) applies the same test as Ben-David (1996) did in his analysis by asking whether the findings of Coe and Helpman will disappear if the foreign knowledge stock variable for any country is constructed based on a *random* import share weighted, rather than an actual import share weighted, of the knowledge stock of its trading partners. He derives his random shares for the twenty-two countries by first constructing a 22×22 matrix of random elements independently drawn from a uniform distribution with support $[0,1]$ and rescaling the off-diagonal elements in each row to sum to unity after setting the diagonal element to zero. By averaging 1,000 such matrices, he gets random shares to be used as weights.

Keller's results are very interesting. His estimate of the basic Coe-Helpman specification using random trade shares is

$$\log F = \frac{0.029}{(0.002)} \log S^d + \frac{0.156}{(0.003)} \log S^f \, R^2 = .702.$$

Surprisingly, replacing actual import share weighted foreign knowledge stocks by random share weighted ones reduces the impact of domestic stock and increases that of foreign stock in explaining TFP! Since the rationale for using actual import weights is that through trading more with a country having a large knowledge stock, a country can augment its productivity by importing a variety of intermediate and capital goods embodying that knowledge. Keller's results based on random, rather than actual, import weights could be interpreted either as raising doubts about trade as a mechanism through which knowledge spillovers occur or alternatively that the growth of knowledge stocks of different industrial countries was very highly correlated so that alternative weighing schemes yield highly correlated values for S^f.

Coe, Helpman, and Hoffmaister (1997) apply the analysis of Coe and Helpman 1995 to a set of seventy-seven developing countries for the period 1971–90. Since few developing countries undertake R&D, the variable S^d of equation (13) is not relevant. In addition to $\log S^f$, they include the secondary school enrollment rate E, *the share of imports from industrial countries M, dummies for time periods 1971–75, 1975–80, 1980–85, and 1985–90,* and the interaction (i.e., product) of S^f with each of M and E. *Since several of the variables turned out to be nonstationary as per unit root tests, they estimate the first difference form of the extended version of equation (13).* It turned out that the coefficient of the first difference of $\log S^f$, that is, the estimated elasticity of TFP with respect to S^f, in equations that did not include country-specific time trends was much too high to be credible on a priori grounds. But when such trends were included, the elasticity estimate became negative. They attribute this to the offsetting interaction of the change in $\log S^f$ and the time dummies. When they drop the time dummies, they find the variable $\log S^f$ no longer has a statistically significant coefficient! Instead of this specification, they prefer to keep the time effects but drop the variable $\log S^f$ (as well as the insignificant interaction of E and $\log S^f$).

Their preferred specification (Coe, Helpman, and Hoffmaister, 1997, table 2, column x) leads to:

$$\Delta \log F = - \frac{9.853}{(3.043)} \Delta M + \frac{0.837}{(0.252)} \Delta (M \log S^f)$$

$$+ \frac{0.247}{(0.096)} \Delta \log E, \text{ Adjusted } R^2 = 0.208.$$

Using this equation, *they estimate R&D spillovers from the industrial countries to the developing countries. These estimates suggest that such spillovers from North to South are substantial and in 1990 "may have boosted output in the developing countries by about 22 billion U.S. dollars.* To put this figure in perspective, total official development aid from multilateral and bilateral sources in 1990 amounted to about 50 billion U.S. dollars" (Coe, Helpman, and Hoffmaister 1997, 148, emphasis added). I am not entirely persuaded by their explanation of the incredibly high elasticity of log S^f or by their reasoning in favor of keeping time effects while dropping log S^f from the preferred specification. Besides, whether their findings are robust to Ben-David-Keller type tests remains to be seen.

Bayoumi, Coe, and Helpman (1996) embed the R&D spillover equation of Coe, Helpman, and Hoffmaister et al. 1997 in the MULTIMOD econometric model of Bayoumi, Hewitt, and Symansky 1995. It is a multicountry model that has short-run dynamics arising from the interaction of sticky prices and forward-looking expectations that make actual output temporarily deviate from its potential level. It also incorporates rational expectations of participants in the markets for goods, finance, and labor. Although, given diminishing marginal returns to reproducible factors of production in the model, *a permanent increase in R&D expenditure has only a level effect and no growth effect in the long run, the convergence to the long-run steady state is rather slow and hence the impact on transitional growth is long-lived.* Thus the simulations of Bayoumi, Hewitt, and Symansky 1996 with the extended MULTIMOD model suggest that if all industrial countries were to *increase their R&D investment permanently by 0.5 percent of GDP, their output would rise after eighty years by almost 20 percent and the output of developing countries by almost 15 percent.* What is more, a further expansion of trade by developing countries by 5 percent of their GDP would raise their output by about 9 percent after eighty years. *These results show the importance for developing countries of productivity improvements stemming from foreign R&D spillovers through trade.*

4 Rapid East Asian Growth: Blood, Sweat, and Tears or a Miracle?

In one of his many celebrated papers, Robert Lucas, after contrasting the economic performance of Korea with an average per capita income growth of 6.2 percent per year from 1960 to 1988 with that of the Philippines with its paltry 1.8 percent per year growth in its per capita income during the same period, concluded,

> I do not think it is in any way an exaggeration to refer to this continuing transformation of Korean society as a miracle, or to apply this term to the very similar transformations that are occurring in Taiwan, Hong Kong, and Singapore. (1993, 251)

Apparently the World Bank agrees with his characterization since it titled its own study (World Bank 1993b) of East Asia as *The East Asian Miracle.*[9] It is almost certain that Lucas was using the word *miracle* not in its meaning as "an act exhibiting control over the laws of nature, and serving as evidence that the agent is either divine or is specially favoured by God" but only in its hyperbolic meaning as "an unusual achievement or event" (*Oxford Universal Dictionary*, 3d ed., 1955). Otherwise, he would be either attributing divinity to the policymakers and bureaucrats in East Asia or claiming that East Asians are the chosen people! Since few, if any, developing countries had as sustained and as rapid a growth as East Asia during this period, the achievement of East Asia is certainly unusual. But given that Lucas himself offers an "economic theory" of the possibility of rapid growth à la East Asia, he certainly was not looking for a "divine intervention" as a possible theory!

Be that as it may, in Lucas's theory

> The main engine of growth is the accumulation of human capital — of knowledge — and the main source of differences in living standards among nations is differences in human capital. Physical capital accumulation plays an essential but decidedly subsidiary role. Human capital accumulation takes place in schools, in research organizations, and in the course of producing goods and engaging in trade. Little is known about the relative importance of these different modes of accumulation, but for understanding periods of very rapid growth in a single economy, learning on the job seems to be by far the most central. For such learning to occur on a sustained basis, it is necessary that workers and managers continue to take on

tasks that are new to them, to continue to move up what Grossman and Helpman call the "quality ladder." For this to be done on a large scale, the economy must be a large scale exporter. This picture has the virtue of being consistent with the recent experience of both the Philippines and Korea. It would be equally consistent with post-1960 history with the roles of these two economies switched. It is a picture that is consistent with any individual small economy following the East Asian example, producing a very different mix of goods from the mix it consumes. (1993, 270–71)

It is certainly true that export promotion has been a characteristic feature of East Asian development strategy. However, if human-capital accumulation is proxied by school enrollment at various levels, as table 6.3 shows, there is little to distinguish Philippines from Korea except to a limited extent in secondary education.[10] This leaves learning and technology spillover effects as the sources of Korean and East Asian growth. It is reasonable to presume that the contribution of these two factors should be reflected in the importance of total factor productivity growth in total growth.

The work of Lau and Kim (1994) and Young (1995) suggests that the widely shared premise

that productivity growth, particularly in manufacturing sectors has been extraordinarily high . . . is largely incorrect. Over the past two and a half decades, productivity growth in the aggregate non-agricultural economy . . . ranges from a low of 0.2 percent in Singapore to a high of 2.3 percent in Hong Kong, whereas in manufacturing productivity growth ranges from a low of -1.0 percent in Singapore to a high of 30 percent in South Korea. (Young 1995, 671)

TABLE 6.3. Education: Percentage Enrolled in Relevant Age Group

| | Philippines | | | Korea | | |
	Primary	Secondary	Tertiary	Primary	Secondary	Tertiary
1960	95	26	13	94	27	5
1970	108	46	28	103	42	16
1980	110	63	26	107	85	18
1990	111	73	27	108	99	29

Source: World Bank 1978, 1983, 1984, 1993.

The calculations of Young reproduced in table 6.4 also show that the share of TFP growth in growth of total output of the economy ranged from a low of 2.3 percent in Singapore to 32 percent in Hong Kong, whereas, in growth of manufacturing, the share (leaving aside Singapore with a negative TFP growth) ranged from 16 percent in Taiwan to 21 percent in Korea. None of these shares is particularly high.[11]

It is well known that East Asian economies have rapidly achieved extraordinarily high domestic savings and investment rates of 30 percent of GDP or higher (table 6.5). Young (1995) calculates (an appropriately weighted) annual average rates of growth of capital stock of 8 percent in Hong Kong during 1966–91, and 11.5 percent, 13.7 percent, and 12.3 percent during 1966–90 in Singapore, South Korea, and Taiwan. Jagdish Bhagwati persuasively argues that this fundamental fact of high rates of growth of capital (largely in the private sector)

TABLE 6.4. Average Annual Rates of Growth of Output and Total Factor Productivity (TFP)

	Hong Kong (1966–91)		Singapore (1966–90)		South Korea (1966–90)		Taiwan[a] (1966–90)	
	Output	TFP	Output	TFP	Output	TFP	Output	TFP
Economy[b]	7.3	2.3	8.7	0.2	10.3	1.7	8.9	2.1
Manufacturing[c]	n.a.	n.a.	8.5	−1.0	14.1	3.0	10.8	1.7
Other industry	n.a.	n.a.	n.a.	n.a.	11.5	1.9	8.8	1.4
Services	n.a.	n.a.	n.a.	n.a.	8.8	1.7	8.2	2.6
Public sector	n.a.	n.a.	n.a.	n.a.			10.0	2.3

Source: Young 1995, tables V, VI, VII, VIII, and IX.
[a]National Accounts measure of public sector output of services has been adjusted to conform to the more standard zero deflation techniques.
[b]In the case of Korea and Taiwan, agriculture is excluded.
[c]In the case of Singapore, the years are 1970–94.

TABLE 6.5. Gross Domestic Savings and Investment (as a percentage of GDP)

	Savings		Investment	
	1970	1991	1970	1992
Hong Kong	25	32	21	29
Korea	15	36	25	39
Singapore	18	47	39	37
Taiwan	26	30[a]	—	—

Source: World Bank 1993 for Hong Kong, Korea, and Singapore; and Ranis 1995 for Taiwan.
[a]1988

cannot but be explained without assigning a major explanatory role to the region's outward orientation . . . . the growth of export earnings [enabled] increasing imports of newer-vintage capital equipment which embodied significant technical change. . . . the excess of the social contribution by newer-vintage-capital-goods over their international cost was the larger because of the phenomenally high levels of literacy and education that characterized East Asian countries — direct foreign investment, like trade, was equally productive in East Asia, reflecting the high returns to the EP [export promotion] strategy. (1996, 2)

The basic argument of Bhagwati, namely that "since East Asian investment rates increased in the *private* sector, whereas similar rises in investment rates occurred in the postwar period in the *public* sector in the former socialist countries, the latter resulting in blood, sweat, and tears but not in growth, the real miracle that requires explanation is that of the phenomenal rise in private investment on a sustained basis to high levels" (5) is well taken. It is easily seen that if the marginal capital-output ratio does not rise significantly as investment rates are sustained at high levels, rates of income growth will also be sustained at high levels. There is considerable evidence that in East Asia, unlike, for example in India, marginal capital-output ratios did not rise primarily because they did not devote a major share of manufacturing investment to capital-intensive sectors.[12] Even in interventionist Korea, the incentive structure did not exhibit chaotic and widely varying returns to investment in different activities so characteristic of many developing countries. Further, not only was labor supply response substantial in the aggregate but, in the absence of significant labor market distortions, labor mobility away from slower-growing (and less productive) agriculture to faster-growing (and more productive) sectors was relatively smooth.

Before turning to possible explanations of sustained high levels of investment and efficient use of capital and other factors in East Asia, a digression on measurement of TFP growth is appropriate. I demonstrate below that even as an economy imports and efficiently utilizes newer-vintage capital, as the East Asians apparently did,[13] any excess social returns of such capital over its cost will not affect growth in TFP as measured from *production* or gross *domestic* product (GDP) accounts, but it will certainly raise that measured from *income* or gross *national* product (GNP) accounts. This is seen, most simply, in an aggregate model of an economy in which all the capital in use is "rented" from foreigners at a rental cost r^* that is lower than its domestic marginal product.

Suppose that the stock of capital, say K^*, at which its domestic marginal product will equal r^* cannot be rented all at once, so that the capital stock in use grows over time to that level. In such a case in the time span in which the amount of capital rented K_t is less than K^*, its domestic marginal product will exceed r^*. Thus

$$\text{GDP} \equiv Y^G(t) = A(t)F(K_t, L_t) \tag{14}$$

$$\text{GNP} \equiv Y^N(t) = A(t)F(K_t, L_t) - r^*K_t. \tag{15}$$

Suppose F is homogeneous of degree one in K and L, that is, returns to scale are constant. Clearly growth in $A(t)$, that is, $\dot{A}/A$ measures TFP growth from a production perspective. Assuming the labor market to be competitive, the prevailing wage rate will be

$$w_t = A(t)\frac{\partial F}{\partial L_t}. \tag{16}$$

$$\text{Labor share in GDP} = \frac{w_t L_t}{Y^G(t)} = \frac{L_t \dfrac{\partial F}{\partial L_t}}{F} \equiv \alpha_t. \tag{17}$$

$$\text{Capital share in GDP} = 1 - \alpha_t = 1 - \frac{A(t)\dfrac{\partial F}{\partial K_t}K_t}{Y^G}$$

(given constant returns to scale). If TFP is calculated *from GDP* using the conventional approach,

$$\text{Growth rate of TFP} = \frac{\dot{Y}_G}{Y_G} - \alpha_t \frac{\dot{L}_t}{L_t} - (1 - \alpha_t)\frac{\dot{K}_t}{K_t} = \frac{\dot{A}}{A} \tag{18}$$

since

$$\frac{\dot{Y}_G}{Y_G} = \frac{\dot{A}}{A} + \alpha_t \frac{\dot{L}_t}{L_t} + (1 - \alpha_t)\frac{\dot{K}_t}{K_t}. \tag{19}$$

Now the excess of domestic marginal product of capital $A_t(\partial F_t/\partial K_t)$ over its rental cost r^* accrues to domestic renters of capital. It is seen that

$$Y^N(t) = A(t) \frac{\partial F}{\partial L_t} L_t + (A(t) \frac{\partial F}{\partial K_t} - r^*) K_t. \qquad (20)$$

Hence, labor share in GNP is

$$\hat{\alpha}_t = \frac{w_t L_t}{Y^N} .$$

The share of capital in GNP is the income share accruing to renters of capital, which equals

$$\frac{(A(t) \dfrac{\partial F}{\partial K_t} - r^*)K_t}{Y^N} = 1 - \hat{\alpha}_t.$$

If TFP is calculated from GNP, then

$$\text{Growth rate of TFP} = \frac{\dot{Y}_N}{Y_N} - \hat{\alpha}_t \frac{\dot{L}}{L} - (1 - \hat{\alpha}_t) \frac{\dot{K}_t}{K_t} . \qquad (21)$$

Now,

$$\dot{Y}^N = \dot{Y}^G - r^* \dot{K} = \dot{A}(t)F + A(t) \frac{\partial F}{\partial L_t} \dot{L}_t + (A(t) \frac{\partial F}{\partial K_t} - r^*) \dot{K}_t$$

$$= \dot{A}F + (w_t L_t) \frac{\dot{L}_t}{L_t} + \{(A(t) \frac{\partial F}{\partial K_t} - r^*)K_t\} \frac{\dot{K}_t}{K_t}$$

$$= \dot{A}F + \hat{\alpha}_t Y^N \frac{\dot{L}_t}{L_t} + (1 - \hat{\alpha}_t) Y^N \frac{\dot{K}_t}{K_t}.$$

Thus,

$$Y^N \left[\frac{\dot{Y}^N}{Y^N} - \hat{\alpha}_t \frac{\dot{L}}{L} - (1 - \hat{\alpha}_t) \frac{\dot{K}_t}{K_t} \right] = \frac{\dot{A}}{A} AF = \frac{\dot{A}}{A} Y^G. \qquad (22)$$

Hence, growth rate of TFP (from income perspective) equals

$$\left[\frac{\dot{Y}^N}{Y^N} - \hat{\alpha}_t \frac{\dot{L}}{L} - (1 - \hat{\alpha}_t) \frac{\dot{K}_t}{K_t} \right] = \frac{\dot{A}}{A} \frac{Y^G}{Y^N} \qquad (23)$$

$$> \frac{\dot{A}}{A}. \qquad (24)$$

Thus TFP growth rate, as calculated from GNP accounts that take into account that excess returns on rented foreign capital accrues to the home economy, is higher than that from GDP accounts by the factor GDP/GNP, which is larger than one. Of course if $\dot{A}/A = 0$, then both GDP-based and GNP-based TFP growth rates will be zero. It can be verified that as long as $\dot{A}/A$, $\dot{Y}^G/Y^G$, and $\dot{K}_t/K_t$ are all positive, then the share of *GDP-based* TFP growth in GDP growth will be less than the share of *GNP-based* TFP growth in GNP growth. It would seem that TFP growth estimates of Young (1995) are GDP based. To the extent the East Asian economies acquired capital at a cost below domestic marginal productivity, then a GNP-based TFP estimate will be higher than his. However, it could be argued that TFP should be related to production and hence to GDP and not to *domestic* factor incomes, that is, to GNP. Besides, the difference between GNP and GDP is unlikely to be high enough to raise TFP estimates by very much.

The facts that the East Asian countries of Korea, Hong Kong, Singapore, and Taiwan succeeded in achieving rapid growth in their exports so that their share in world exports rose from 1.5 percent in 1960 to 7.9 percent in 1990 (World Bank 1993b) and that they achieved high investment rates cannot be disputed.[14] But there is controversy on the explanations of this success. Rodrik describes as "conventional wisdom" that the export boom in South Korea and Taiwan was "in large part due to the change in relative prices in favour of exportables" (1997, 2) and claims that this is incorrect since "the actual increase in relative profitability of exports in the 1960s is small in both countries in relation to the phenomenal increase in exports" (2). He notes that in "both South Korea and Taiwan, the export booms were accompanied by investment booms that are equally impressive" (2), and the investment boom contradicts prediction from conventional Heckscher-Ohlin models in which an increase in openness of capital-scarce East Asia should reduce the return to capital and as such could not induce an investment boom.[15] In his view, "export orientation in South Korea and Taiwan may have been the product in large part of an increase in propensity to invest, brought about by a rise in profitability of investment" (2). He assigns a dominant role to government interventions in the form of investment subsidies, taking active steps to ensure that private entrepreneurs invested in certain areas and investing in public enterprises that provided key inputs for private producers downstream. Since many other developing countries (e.g., India) intervened in a similar fashion without achieving similar results, the key question is "how successful economies have managed their intervention better than the unsuccessful economies" (Bhagwati 1988, 98).

A part of Rodrik's empirical evidence against conventional wisdom consists of a regression of share of exports (or alternatively share of exports and imports) in GNP, on the logarithm of real effective exchange rates, share of fiscal deficits, and a time trend and finding that *none* of the variables have statistically significant coefficients in the case of Korea and only the time trend has significantly positive coefficient in the case of Taiwan. Since neither the exchange rate nor fiscal deficits is an exogenous variable, this regression suffers from standard simultaneity bias, a criticism that Rodrik (1996) levels against other studies! But if we ignore the endogeneity of these variables and treat the regression as a reduced form, the coefficients cannot be given a structural interpretation, as Rodrik implicitly does. In any case, conventional wisdom is not Rodrik's caricature of it: in conventional analysis, often the comparison is between effective exchange rates for *exportables* and *importables* so that the bias in favor of or against export activities relative to import activities is assessed.[16] Sometimes the comparison is between the *actual real* effective exchange rate, that is, the relative price of tradables to nontradables (and its time path), and its notional *equilibrium* value (and its time path). A lower effective exchange rate for exports clearly biases incentives against them. In the second comparison, it is certainly correct to claim that the tradables sector will be depressed *relative to its equilibrium* path if the actual real effective rate change depresses the path of relative prices of tradables again *relative to its equilibrium.* This statement is not a tautology, and it certainly does not say anything about whether the tradables sector will be growing or declining in equilibrium. It is possible to have constant *equilibrium real exchange rates,* with tradables growing relative to total output in equilibrium, depending in particular on tastes, technology, and the external market developments!

Let me ignore the purely econometric issues relating to Granger causality tests and take Rodrik's results at face value. They show that, in the case of Taiwan, the hypotheses that openness does not cause investment, *as well as* that investment does not cause openness, are *both rejected* at conventional levels of significance although in the case of Korea only the latter hypothesis is rejected. Thus, this evidence is not strong enough to conclude that openness had little to do with investment in these two countries. I am not convinced that his results of causality tests or of the regressions on exports to GNP for Chile and Turkey are particularly informative for analyzing the East Asian experience.

The traditional arguments of development economists in favor of government interventions to provide social overhead capital (i.e., infrastructure) and institutional underpinnings for the market to bring about efficient and rapid development are to be sharply distinguished from the interventions envisaged by industrial and strategic trade policy enthusiasts. The latter presume knowledge and capability on the part of the state to identify in advance the "winners" and provide whatever is needed to ensure they do win. In the case of Korea, Rodrik approvingly quotes Amsden (1989, 80–81) to the effect that the "initiative to enter new manufacturing branches has come primarily from the public sphere. Ignoring the 1950s . . . every major shift in industrial diversification in the decades of the 1960's and 1970's was instigated by the state." Even if indeed the Korean government was the instigator, it is not necessarily the case that its instigation was either appropriate ex ante or proved to have been appropriate ex post.

As Ian Little (1996, 9) points out, "The UK practiced strategic trade policy in these two fields [i.e., passenger aircraft and nuclear reactors] since 1945. . . . the UK was early in the field spending huge sums on the wrong technology to monopolize the world market." The UK failed to become a major actor in either field, let alone monopolize the market. More to the point are his estimates of returns to investment in Korea, which *fell* from an average of 31.1 percent per year during 1963–73 to 13.4 percent in 1974–82.[17] It is well known that, in the period 1974–82, the Korean government actively promoted heavy and chemical industries. Little remarks,

> The figure for the 1974–82 period of 13.4% constitutes a grave lapse into mediocrity. The investment ratio rose and the growth of output slackened. This is the period of the heavy and chemical industries investment drive. Towards the end of the period, in 1980, there was a recession (output fell 1.3%) largely caused by a fall in agricultural output, though probably to some extent the result of fiscal action to cool the overheating of the economy in 1979 that resulted from the investment drive. The recovery of output in 1982 and 1983 was sluggish by Korean standards. Thus the low investment returns in this period were partly caused by macroeconomic disturbance, and are not therefore a fair measure of what the return would otherwise have been. For this reason I have estimated the returns in the period 1974–79 when the economy was booming. The

returns at 18.3% per annum are far below those of the decade 1963–73. (22)

Little also points out that the main Korean state enterprise, the Pohan Steel Company, "has had low financial returns throughout its 20 year life despite heavy subsidisation . . . and protection" (1996, 24). In sum, I find more convincing Little's argument that given the widespread failures of industrial policies elsewhere, it is more plausible that Korea grew fast despite its industrial policies, than Wade's argument (1990, 305–6) as quoted by Little, that "the balance of presumption must be that government industrial policies, including sectoral ones, helped more than hindered. To argue otherwise is to suppose that economic performance would have been still more exceptional with less intervention which is simply less plausible than the converse." (12).[18]

5 Conclusions

The accumulating empirical evidence that countries that have always remained outward oriented and countries that liberalized their trade regimes toward greater openness have a record of better economic growth performance than inward-oriented countries is persuasive. The notion that trade liberalization cannot affect long-run growth but can only have a level effect is not valid in general even in traditional development models, let alone in recent models of endogenous growth in which knowledge spillovers through trade play a major role. An examination of the East Asian success in achieving rapid growth reinforces the conclusion that far from being the result of a wise government picking industrial winners and actively promoting them, their emphasis is on education, enabling government interventions "in fashioning the appropriate organization and institutional infrastructure, [and] reducing transactions costs" (Ranis 1995, 537), and, above all, their outward orientation were the driving forces.[19]

Appendix A

I Consumption Goods Sector

Output of good $i = Q_i^c$ $i = 1, 2$

Domestic use of good $i = c_i^c$ $i = 1, 2$

Stock of capital $= K^c$

Production Frontier $\beta_1 Q_1^c + \beta_2 Q_2^c = K^c$ $\qquad$ (A.1)

Utility function $u = (c_1^c)^\alpha (c_2^c)^{1-\alpha}$ $\qquad$ (A.2)

II Investment Goods Sector

Output of good $i = Q_i^I$

Domestic use of good $i = A_i^I$

Stock of capital $= K^I$

Production Frontier $\gamma_1 Q_1^I + \gamma_2 Q_2^I = K^I$ $\qquad$ (A.3)

Aggregate investment $I = (A_1^I)^\delta (A_2^I)^{1-\delta}$ $\qquad$ (A.4)

III Capital Accumulation

Let λ be the share of investment devoted to accumulation of K^I. Then

$$\dot{K}^I \equiv \frac{dK^I}{dt} = \lambda I \qquad (A.5)$$

$$\dot{K}^c \equiv \frac{dK^c}{dt} = (1 - \lambda) I. \qquad (A.6)$$

IV Autarky

$c_i^c = Q_i^c$ and $A_i^I = Q_i^I$ for $i = 1, 2$.

Maximization of (2) subject to (1) leads to

$$c_1^c = \alpha K^c / \beta_1, \; c_2^c = (1 - \alpha) K^c / \beta_2 \text{ and } U = \left(\frac{\alpha}{\beta_1}\right)^\alpha \left(\frac{1 - \alpha}{\beta_2}\right)^{1-\alpha} K^c. \quad (A.7)$$

Maximization of (A.4) subject to (A.3) leads to

$$A_1^I = \frac{\delta K^I}{\gamma_1}, \ A_2^I = \frac{(1-\delta)K^I}{\gamma_2}.$$ (A.8)

Substituting (A.8) in (A.4) one gets

$$I = \left(\frac{\delta}{\gamma_1}\right)^{\delta}\left(\frac{1-\delta}{\gamma_2}\right)^{1-\delta}K^I$$ (A.9)

$$\equiv \eta K^I \quad \text{where} \quad \eta = \left(\frac{\delta}{\gamma_1}\right)^{\delta}\left(\frac{1-\delta}{\gamma_2}\right)^{1-\delta}.$$ (A.9')

Using (A.9') in (A.5) and (A.6) and solving:

$$K^I = K_0^I e^{\lambda \eta t}$$ (A.10)

$$K^c = K_o^c + \left(\frac{1-\lambda}{\lambda}\right)K_o^I (e^{\lambda \eta t} - 1).$$ (A.11)

Thus the long-run growth rates of K^I, K^c, I, and U are the same and equal $\lambda\eta$.

V Free Trade in Consumer Goods at a Relative Price Π^c of Good 2 in Terms of Good 1 and Autarky in Investment Goods

Without loss of generality assume $\Pi^c > \beta_2/\beta_1$. Then it is optimal to produce only good 2, export part of the output, and import good 1. It is easy to show that

$$Q_1^c = 0, \ Q_2^c = \frac{K^c}{\beta_2}, \ c_1^c = \frac{\alpha\Pi^c K^c}{\beta_2}, \ c_2^c = \frac{(1-\alpha)K^c}{\beta_2} \quad \text{and}$$

$$U = \alpha^{\alpha}(1-\alpha)^{1-\alpha}(\Pi^c)^{\alpha}\frac{K^c}{\beta_2}.$$

It is easy to verify that given $\Pi^c > \beta_2/\beta_1$ welfare U under free trade is higher than under autarky for *any* K^c. Since the investment goods sector is closed to trade, the dynamics of the system are unaffected so that the paths of K^c and K^I continue to be given by (A.10) and (A.11). Hence the long-run growth rates of K^c, K^I, I, and U are still $\lambda\eta$ though the level of U at each t is higher than under autarky.

VI Free Trade in Investment Goods at a Relative Price of Π^I of Good 2 in Terms of Good 1 and Autarky in Consumption Goods

Without loss of generality assume $\Pi^I > \gamma_2/\gamma_1$. Then it is optimal to produce only good 2, export part of the output, and import good 1. It is easy to show that

$$Q_1^I = 0, \ Q_2^I = \frac{K^I}{\gamma_2}, \ A_1^I = \frac{\delta\Pi^I K^I}{\gamma_2}, \ A_2^I = \frac{(1-\delta)K^I}{\gamma_2} \quad \text{and}$$

$$I - \delta^\delta(1-\delta)^{1-\delta}(\Pi^I)^\delta \frac{K^I}{\gamma^2}.$$

It is easy to verify that given $\Pi^I > \gamma_2/\gamma_1$, investment I under free trade is higher than under autarky for any K^I. Now using (A.5) and (A.6) and solving one gets

$$K^I = K_o^I e^{\lambda\mu t} \quad \text{where} \quad \mu = \{\delta^\delta(1-\delta)^{1-\delta}(\Pi^I)^\delta\}/\gamma_2$$

and

$$K^c = K_o^c + \left(\frac{1-\lambda}{\lambda}\right)K_o^I(e^{\lambda\mu t} - 1).$$

Now given $\Pi^I > \gamma_2/\gamma_1$ it follows that $\mu > \eta$. Hence the value of K^I and K^c at each time t under free trade in investment goods is higher than their corresponding values under autarky and the long-run growth rates of K^c, K^I, and I are the same at $\lambda\mu$, which is also higher than its value $\lambda\eta$ under autarky.

Since the consumption goods sector is under autarky given

$$K^c, \ Q_1^c = C_1^c = \frac{\alpha K^c}{\beta^1}, \ Q_2^c = C_2^c = \frac{(1-\alpha)K^c}{\beta_2} \quad \text{and}$$

$$U = \left(\frac{\alpha}{\beta_1}\right)^\alpha \left(\frac{1-\alpha}{\beta_2}\right)^{1-\alpha} K^c.$$

Since K^c is higher at each t under free trade in investment goods than under autarky, U is higher as well. Since K^c grows faster, U grows faster as well.

Appendix B: Transitional Dynamics of Cass-Koopmans Model

Define $x_t \equiv k_t - k^*$, $y_t \equiv \log c_t$ and $z_t \equiv y_t - y^*$.

Linearizing (7) near the steady state,

$$\dot{x}_t = \Pi\alpha\,(k^*)^{\alpha-1}x_t - \Pi c^* z_t - (n + \delta)\,x_t$$

$$= \rho x_t - \rho k^* z_t \tag{B.1}$$

(using (8) and (9) of the text). Linearizing (12) near the steady state

$$\dot{z}_t = \frac{1}{\sigma}\alpha(\alpha - 1)\Pi(k^*)^{\alpha-2}x_t$$

$$= -\frac{(1 - \alpha)}{\sigma k^*}(n + \delta + \rho)\,x_t \tag{B.2}$$

(using (8) of the text)

$$\equiv -\theta x_t \quad \text{where} \quad \theta = \frac{(1 - \alpha)\,(n + \delta + \rho)}{\sigma k^*} > 0. \tag{B.3}$$

Solving (B.1) and (B.3),

$$x_t = Ae^{\eta_1 t} + Be^{\eta_2 t} \tag{B.4}$$

$$z_t = Ce^{\eta_1 t} + De^{\eta_2 t}, \tag{B.5}$$

where η_1 and η_2 are roots of

$$\eta^2 - \rho\eta - \theta\rho k^*. \tag{B.6}$$

Thus

$$\eta_1 - \frac{\rho + (\rho^2 + 4\theta\rho k^*)^{1/2}}{2} > 0 \tag{B.7}$$

$$\eta_2 = \frac{\rho - (\rho^2 + 4\theta\rho k^*)^{1/2}}{2} < 0. \tag{B.8}$$

Since

$$\rho\theta k^* = \frac{\rho(1-\alpha)(\eta + \delta + \rho)}{\sigma},$$

η_1 and η_2 do not involve Π. Now x_t and z_t converge to their steady state values of zero as $t \rightarrow \infty$. As such, the constants A and C corresponding to the positive root η, have to be set at zero. Constants B and D are determined by initial conditions

$$x_0 = k_0 - k^* = B \tag{B.9}$$

$$z_0 = y_0 - y^* = \log c_0 - \log c^* = D. \tag{B.10}$$

Substituting in (B.4) and (B.5):

$$k_t - k^* = (k_0 - k^*)e^{\eta_2 t} \tag{B.11}$$

$$\log\left(\frac{c_t}{c^*}\right) = \left[\log\left(\frac{c_0}{c^*}\right)\right]e^{\eta_2 t}. \tag{B.12}$$

Thus

$$\frac{\dot{k}_t}{k_t} = \frac{\eta_2(k_0 - k^*)\,e^{\eta_2 t}}{k^* + (k_0 - k^*)\,e^{\eta_2 t}}$$

$$-\frac{-\eta_2}{\dfrac{k^*}{(k^* - k_0)}e^{\eta_2 t}} - 1 \tag{B.13}$$

$$\frac{\dot{c}_t}{c_t} = -\eta_2(\log c^* - \log c_0)e^{\eta_2 t}. \tag{B.14}$$

Since $\partial k^*/\partial \Pi > 0$, $\partial c^*/\partial \Pi > 0$ and $\eta_2 < 0$ for initial values $k_0 < k^*$ and $c_0 < c^*$, it follows

$$\frac{\partial}{\partial \Pi}\left(\frac{\dot{k}_t}{k_t}\right) > 0 \quad \text{and} \quad \frac{\partial}{\partial \Pi}\left(\frac{\dot{c}_t}{c_t}\right) > 0.$$

This in turn means that a move to free trade from autarky raises the growth rate of capital (and hence output) and consumption along the transition to steady state.

NOTES

I thank Jagdish Bhagwati, William Nordhaus, Dani Rodrik, Gary Saxonhouse, and Nikola Spatafora for their comments. I thank Nikola also for catching my errors and typos as well as for his editorial suggestions.

1. Since Schumpeter 1961, it has been known that the process of development is different from that of growth. But for the limited purpose of analyzing the dynamic effects of openness, it is not essential to distinguish between the two.

2. Strictly speaking, only Harrod's "warranted equilibrium path," along which available savings are continually absorbed into investment without changing the capital-output ratio, corresponds to this model. The First Five Year Plan (1951–56) of India included projections of income growth based on this model. Recent writers, in apparent ignorance of the earlier literature, have reinvented this model and have christened it the "AK" model since output Y in such a model is the product of capital K and its productivity A!

3. I have drawn extensively from Srinivasan 1993 in writing this section.

4. I thank Gary Saxonhouse for drawing my attention to these two contributions.

5. As is well known, in this model the social planner's optimum is also an intertemporal competitive equilibrium given a complete set of markets.

6. This definition is unsatisfactory. With the tariff barrier set at 40 percent no country is classified on the basis of tariffs alone. Alternative, equally plausible, definitions of nontariff barriers do not often yield mutually consistent results. In addition, some nontariff barriers could be covert and informal, as is alleged to be the case in Japan and some East Asian economies. Besides, the black-market premium is a catchall endogenous variable that reflects both exchange rate and commercial policy distortions. I thank Dani Rodrik for chiding me for ignoring these issues in an earlier draft.

7. Saxonhouse suggested (in correspondence) that once it is recognized that, in a multisector world, domestic and foreign barriers are very likely to apply to different sectors, both could be expected to depress aggregate domestic investment.

8. Knowledge stock for each industrial country is the cumulative real business sector R&D expenditures added to a calculated benchmark and depreciated at the rate of 5 percent a year.

9. Lucas was not the first to call extraordinary economic performance a miracle. Bhagwati (1988, 98), in discussing the role of government in East Asian success, suggests that we are all prey to self-indulgence toward our own economic beliefs and sarcastically asks, "After all, how could an *economic miracle* have

occurred if the policy makers had not followed our preferred policies?" He formulates the law "*Economic miracles* are a public good; each economist sees in them a vindication of his pet theories" (emphasis added). It is possible that others may have used the term *miracle* in this context earlier.

10. Thus, having an educated labor force is not sufficient if the policy framework, in particular orientation toward trade, is not conducive to its most efficient use. For example, India has one of the world's largest concentration of graduates in science. Yet, until recent reforms, the incentive structure did not allow its efficient utilization.

11. Nelson and Pack (1996) argue that conventional growth-accounting exercises such as those of Young and others could be very misleading since they assume that factor shares did not change significantly in a period when massive increases in factor inputs took place and that the elasticity of factor substitution was unity. Even if alternative assumptions were to yield higher shares for TFP growth in total growth, the fact that conventional exercises appear to fit the data just as well suggests that one cannot *reject* the hypothesis that the contribution of TFP growth was modest.

12. Korea's investment in heavy and chemical industries in the late 1970s, an investment that failed to yield adequate returns (Little 1996), is an exception.

13. This is consistent with the view of Nordhaus. He suggested in his comments on this paper that "for all but the largest and technically advanced countries, the level of knowledge is exogenous. There is simply no sense in which Hong Kong is going to grow significantly faster by increasing the general level of technical knowledge. The other two paths to growth are technological convergence and factor accumulation. We know that countries differ tremendously in the extent to which they effectively utilize existing knowledge — in their X-efficiencies. The presumption is that open economies are induced by carrots and sticks to adopt more efficient technologies and procedures more rapidly than those which are closed to international markets. Moreover, given the vast pool of knowledge, most developing countries can grow a very long time before they have exhausted the global pool of knowledge. The technological catchup of Gerschenkron effect is by its nature a level effect, but given the differences in level between poor and rich countries the levels are so different that the growth effect can persist for many decades."

14. According to World Trade Organization 1995, their share in world merchandise trade was 10.4 percent in 1994.

15. This holds in a two-commodity, two-factor model as long as the economy is incompletely specialized before and after trade liberalization (i.e., a rise in the price of labor-intensive goods). Thus a rise in the relative price of the labor-intensive good, following the liberalization of capital-intensive imports by a capital-scarce economy, will lower (resp. raise) the return to capital (resp. labor) in terms of both goods. However, if the economy is completely specialized in the labor-intensive good, a rise in its price will raise the returns to *both* factors in terms of the capital-intensive good, while leaving them unchanged in terms of the labor-intensive good.

16. Rodrik (1995a, 62–63) does consider the relative price of exportables in the case of Korea and argues that in fact it was actually quite a bit higher in the mid-1950s than in the 1960s. However, my reading of his figure 4, there was no trend (up or down) in the relative price over the period 1955–75 but only fluctuations around a constant value. Since theory does not suggest that an upward trend in the relative price of exports is necessary for a rise in the share of exports in GDP, nor is it the only indicator of export orientation, I do not view this constancy as evidence against conventional wisdom.

17. Global shocks (e.g., oil shocks of 1973 and 1979, recession and inflation in industrialized countries) could have adversely affected the returns in the period 1974–82. Still, the extent of the actual fall seems much larger than what could be attributed to external shocks.

18. Saxonhouse, in his comments on this paper, rightly suggests that although the Korean government was heavily involved in the sectoral allocation of resources, its strategy "when successful, usually merely emulated the market outcome of similarly situated economies, past and present."

19. I entirely agree with Bhagwati's (1996) argument that their authoritarianism and cultural attributes (Confucian heritage) also have little to do with their success.

REFERENCES

Amsden, A. 1989. *Asia's New Giant: South Korea and Late Industrialization.* New York: Oxford University Press.
Baldwin, R. E., and E. Seghezza. 1996. "Testing for Trade-Induced Investment Growth." Discussion Paper 1331, Centre for Economic Policy Research, London.
Bayoumi, T., D. Coe, and E. Helpman. 1996. "R&D Spillovers and Global Growth." Discussion Paper 1467, Centre for Economic Policy, London.
Bayoumi, T., D. Hewitt, and S. Symansky. 1995. "MULTIMOD Simulations of the Effect on Developing Countries of Decreasing Military Spending." In *North-South Linkages and International Macroeconomic Policy,* ed. D. Currie and D. Vines. Cambridge: Cambridge University Press.
Ben-David, D. 1996. "Trade and Convergence among Countries." *Journal of International Economics* 40:278–98.
Ben-David, D., and A. K. M. A. Rahman. 1996. "Technological Convergence and International Trade." Discussion Paper 1359, Centre for Economic Policy Research, London.
Bhagwati, J. 1988. *Protection.* Cambridge: MIT Press.
———. 1996. "The 'Miracle' That Did Happen: Understanding East Asia in Comparative Perspective." Keynote Speech delivered on May 3, 1996 at the conference "Government and Market: The Relevance of the Taiwanese Performance to Development Theory and Policy," Cornell University.
Cass, D. T. 1965. "Optimum Growth in an Aggregative Model of Capital Accumulation." *Review of Economic Studies* 32 (July): 233–40.

Coe, D. T., and E. Helpman. 1995. "International R&D Spillovers." *European Economic Review* 39:859–87.

Coe, D. T., E. Helpman, and A. W. Hoffmaister. 1997. "North-South R&D Spillovers." *Economic Journal* 107:134–49.

Domar, E. 1957. *Essays in the Theory of Economic Growth.* London: Oxford University Press.

Edwards, S. 1993. "Openness, Trade Liberalization, and Growth in Developing Countries." *Journal of Economic Literature* 31:1358–1391.

Erutna, Ö. 1972. "Allocation of Investment in an Open Fel'dman Model." *Revista Internazionale di Scienze Economische e Commerciali* 19, no. 10:999–1005.

Fel'dman, G. A. 1928. "K teorii tempov narodnogo dokhoda." *Planovoe Khoziaistvo* 11:146–70 and 12:152–78. This is discussed in Domar 1957, chap. 9.

Harrison, A. 1996. Openness and Growth: A Time Series, Cross-country Analysis for Developing Countries." *Journal of Development Economics* 48:419–47.

Keller, W. Forthcoming. "Are International R&D Spillovers Trade Related? Analyzing Spillovers among Randomly Matched Trade Partners." *European Economic Review.*

Koopmans, T. C. 1965. "On the Concept of Optimal Growth." In *The Econometric Approach to Development Planning.* Amsterdam: North-Holland for Pontificia Acadamia Scientarium.

Kornai, J. 1992. *The Socialist System: The Political Economy of Communism.* Princeton, Princeton University Press.

Kravis, I. 1970. "Trade as a Handmaiden of Growth: Similarities between the Nineteenth and Twentieth Centuries." *Economic Journal* 80:850–72.

Krueger, A. 1987. "The Importance of Economic Policies: Contrasts between Korea and Turkey." in *Protection and Competition in International Trade,* ed. H. Kierzkowski. Oxford: Basil Blackwell.

———. 1990. "Asian Trade and Growth Lessons." *American Economic Review* 80, no. 2:108–12.

Krugman, P. 1994. "The Myth of Asia's Miracle." *Foreign Affairs* 73, no. 6:62–78.

Lau, L. J., and J. Kim. 1994. "The Sources of Economic Growth of the East Asian Newly Industrializing Countries." *Journal of Japanese and International Economies* 8:235–71.

Little, I. M. D. 1996. "Picking Winners: The East Asian Experience." Occasional Paper, Social Market Foundation, London.

Lucas, R. E. 1993. "Making a Miracle." *Econometrica* 61, no. 2:251–72.

Mahalanobis, P. C. 1955. "The Approach of Operational Research to Planning in India." *Sankhya* 16, parts 1–2:3–62.

Nelson, R., and H. Pack. 1996. "Firm Competencies, Technological Catchup, and the Asian Miracle." Paper presented at a conference in honor of Gustav Ranis, Yale University, May 10–11, 1996.

Ranis, G. 1992. "East and South-East Asia: Comparative Development Experience." *Bangladesh Development Studies* 20, nos. 2–3:69–88.

―――. 1995. "Another Look at the East Asian Miracle." *World Bank Economic Review* 9, no. 3:509–34.

Ranis, G., and S. Mahmood. 1992. *The Political Economy of Development Policy.* Oxford: Basil Blackwell.

Robertson, D. 1940. *Essays in Monetary Theory.* London: P. S. King and Son.

Rodrik, D. 1995a. "Getting Interventions Right: How South Korea and Taiwan Grew Rich." *Economic Policy* 20:55–107.

―――. 1995b. "Trade and Industrial Policy Reform." In *Handbook of Development Economics,* vol. 3B, ed. Jere Behrman and T. N. Srinivasan. Amsterdam: Elsevier Science Publishers.

―――. 1996. "Understanding Economic Policy Reform." *Journal of Economic Literature* 34:9–14.

―――. 1997. "Trade Strategy, Investment, and Exports: Another Look at East Asia." *Pacific Economic Review* 2, no. 1:1–24.

Sachs, J. D., and A. Warner. 1995. "Economic Reforms and the Process of Global Integration." *Brookings Papers on Economic Activity* 1–118.

Schumpeter, J. 1961. *The Theory of Economic Development.* New York: Oxford University Press.

Srinivasan, T. N. 1993. "Comment on 'Two Strategies for Economic Development: Using Ideas and Producing Ideas' by Romer." In *Proceedings of the World Bank Annual Conference on Economic Development.* Washington, D.C.: World Bank.

Ünsal, E. 1990. "Allocation of Investment in an Open Fel'dman Model Reconsidered." *Revista Internazionale di Scienze Economische e Commerciale* 37, no. 7:645–54.

Wade, R. 1990. *Governing the Market: Economic Theory and the Role of the Government in East Asian Industrialization.* Princeton: Princeton University Press.

World Bank. 1978, 1983, 1984, 1993a. *World Development Report.* Washington, D.C.: World Bank.

―――. 1993b. *The East Asian Miracle: Economic Growth and Public Policy.* New York: Oxford University Press.

―――. 1996. Press Release: Press/44 of March 22, 1996, World Trade Organization, Geneva.

World Trade Organization. 1995. *International Trade: Trends and Statistics.* Geneva: World Trade Organization.

―――. 1998. *Focus Newsletter,* no. 28 (March). Geneva: Information and Media Relations Division of the WTO.

Young, A. 1995. "The Tyranny of Numbers: Confronting the Statistical Realities of the East Asian Growth Experience." *Quarterly Journal of Economics* 641–80.

CHAPTER 7

Firm Competencies, Technological Catch-up, and the Asian Miracle

Richard R. Nelson and Howard Pack

I Accumulation and Assimilation Theories of the Asian Miracle

Over the past thirty-five years Korea, Taiwan, Singapore, and Hong Kong have transformed themselves from technologically backward and poor to relatively modern and affluent economies. Each has experienced more than a fourfold increase of per capita income. Each now has a significant collection of firms producing technologically complex products competing effectively against rival firms based in the United States, Japan, and Europe. The growth performance of these countries has vastly exceeded those of virtually all other economies that had comparable productivities and income levels in 1960. On these grounds alone the question of "how they did it" obviously is of enormous scientific and policy importance.

It has been less well noted that their growth has been historically unprecedented. The development of Japan in the half century after the Meiji restoration is widely regarded as comparable. However, Japan's growth rate over this period was less than half that of the Asian newly industrialized countries (NICs) since 1960. Of course, growth rates in general were slower during this earlier period. But the rate of catch-up by the NICs still is remarkable. It certainly would seem that there is an "Asian miracle" that cries out for explanation.

Of course, economists have not been blind to or unattracted by the challenge. Over the last decade a number of different theories have been put forth purporting to explain the "Asian miracle" (Amsden 1989; Kim and Lau 1994; Krugman 1994; Pack 1992; Pack and Westphal 1986; Rodrik 1995; Westphal, Kim, and Dahlman 1985; World Bank 1993; Young 1995). There is unanimity among the different theories regarding the identity of some of the key causal factors. All of the Asian NICs

197

have experienced rapid growth of their physical capital stock. All have been marked by very high rates of investment in human capital. Virtually all theories about "how they did it" place these investments center stage in the explanation.

However, there are significant differences in the causal mechanisms stressed. At the risk of doing some violence to the actual diversity, for our purposes we find it useful to divide up theories of the Asian miracle into two groups. One group, which we will call "accumulation" theories, stresses the role of these investments in moving these economies "along their production functions." The other group, which we will call "assimilation" theories, stresses the entrepreneurship, innovation, and learning that these economies had to go through before they could master the new technologies they were adopting from the more advanced industrial nations; it sees investment in human and physical capital as a necessary, but far from sufficient, part of the assimilation process.

The accumulation theory has been pushed hard over the past few years by several economists, in a way clearly designed to strip away most of the "miraculous" from the Asian miracle. What lies behind rapid development is, simply, very high investment rates. Economists who take this point of view do not deny that adoption and mastering new technology and other modern practices was an important part of the story. Rather, the position is that one should try to explain as much as one can in terms of investments that enable movements along a production function, and see if anything much is left over, thus requiring explanation on other grounds. Several economists who have followed this path find that, according to their calculations, the lion's share of increased output per worker can be explained simply by increases in physical and human capital per worker. Thus there is little need to assign much of the credit for the growth "miracle" to entrepreneurship, innovation, or learning, except insofar as these are terms given to the shift to more capital- and education-intensive ways of production (see, e.g., Young 1995; Kim and Lau 1994; Krugman 1994).

To assimilation theorists, this point of view seems odd. The technologies that the NICs came progressively to master during the 1970s and 1980s were ones with which, in 1960, they had no experience at all. To learn to use them effectively required the development of new sets of skills, new ways of organizing economic activity, and familiarity with and competence in new markets. To do this was far from a routine matter but involved risk-taking entrepreneurship as well as good management (see, e.g., Pack and Westphal 1986; Dahlman 1994; Amsden 1989). What makes the Asian miracle miraculous is that these countries did these things so well, while other countries were much less successful. To be sure, adopting the technologies of the advanced countries required, among other things, high rates of investment in physical and human capital, and the NICs achieved these high rates. But to say that these investments simply enabled these economies to "move along their production functions" seems a strange use of language. At the least, it poses the question of just what is meant by "moving along a production function."

Are we drawing a distinction without a real difference? We do not think so. The accumulation account stresses, simply, investments. The message is that other countries could have done as well as the successful NICs if they had made the same investment effort. If the nation makes the investments, marshals the resources, development will follow. In contrast, the assimilation account stresses learning about, risking to operate, and coming to master technologies and other practices that are new to the country, if not to the world. The "marshaling of inputs" is part of the story, but the emphasis is on innovation and learning, rather than on marshaling. Under this view, if one marshals but does not innovate and learn, development does not follow.

A convinced accumulationist might respond by saying that, if one educates the people and provides them with modern equipment to work with, they will learn. An assimilationist might respond that the Soviet Union and the Eastern European Communist economies took exactly that point of view, made the investments, and didn't learn. There is nothing automatic about the learning business. The response of the accumulationist might be that the old Communist countries provided an economic environment where there was no incentive to learn to be efficient, either in a technological or an economic sense, much less to innovate. The assimilation theorist might agree but then propose that it is important to understand, therefore, just how the successful NICs did it. The accumulationist would reply that they got the prices right and made the necessary public investments. Economists who stress entrepreneurship, innovation, and learning would reply that it is not all that simple and point to countries like Chile that have had high investment rates, and have got most of the prices right, but are growing at far lower rates than the Asian NICs.

The difference between the theories shows up strikingly in the way they treat the following four matters: what is involved in entrepreneurial decision making, the nature of technology, the economic capabilities lent by a well-educated workforce, and the role that exporting played in these countries' rapid development.

Accumulationists pay little explicit attention to firms, seeing their behavior as being basically determined by the environment — the incentives and constraints — they face, which determines the actions that are most profitable. Assimilation theorists, on the other hand, see entrepreneurial firms, and their ability to learn rapidly, as a critical factor behind the success of Korea and Taiwan, with their behavior supported by their environments, but only partially determined by external forces (see, e.g., Hobday 1995; and Kim 1997). For an assimilation theorist, at least our brand, when firms contemplate venturing onto ground that is new for them, the profitability of such venturing is highly uncertain, in the sense of Knight. Some firm managers will dare to venture; others will choose to stick close to the familiar. Thus, what firms do is determined by the daring of their decision makers, as well as by their environment. And whether an entrepreneurial venture will succeed or fail also is only partly determined by environmental factors. It depends, as well, on the zeal and smarts and learning abilities of firm management and workers.

Part of the difference here resides in how the different theories see technology. Accumulationists seem to believe that the state of technological knowledge at any time is largely codified in blueprints and associated documents and that for a firm to adopt a technology that is new to it but not to the world primarily involves getting access to those blueprints. In contrast, assimilationists argue that only a small portion of what one needs to know to employ a technology is codified in the form of blueprints; much of it is tacit, and learning is as much by doing and using as by reading and studying (see, e.g., Nelson and Winter 1982; and Rosenberg 1994). More, while many economists believe that technology is defined in terms of engineering and physical science, in fact the lines between the engineering aspects of technology and the organizational aspects are blurry, and controlling a technology often involves knowing how to manage a very complex division of labor as much as it involves knowing the relevant physics and chemistry.

Both of these differences show up in terms of how the two theories go about explaining the fact that the NICs were able to increase greatly and rapidly their capital-labor ratios (by more than fourfold over the thirty-five years in question) without experiencing a significant decline in the rate of return to capital. The accumulationist would tend to invoke the concept of the elasticity of substitution, which refers to innate technological opportunities, and propose that the phenomenon in question indicates that the elasticity of substitution was high. The assimilationist, on the other hand, would argue that there is no such thing as a set of technological possibilities that can be defined independently of decision makers' ability to search and see and effectively take on board new technology. That is, what the accumulationist would explain in terms of the nature of the parameters of a conventionally defined production function, an assimilationist would explain in terms of skillful entrepreneurship and learning.

Along the same lines, the two theories also differ regarding how they see the effects of the rapidly rising education levels in these countries. For the accumulationist, rising human capital is treated simply as an increase in the quality or effectiveness of labor. Assimilationists, on the other hand, tend to see the effects of sharply rising educational attainments, in particular the creation by these countries of a growing cadre of reasonably well trained engineers and applied scientists, in ways similar to that sketched out many years ago by Nelson and Phelps (1966). Well-educated managers, engineers, and workers have a comparative advantage in seeing new opportunities and effectively learning new things. Thus the growing human capital of the NICs was a very important support for successful entrepreneurship.

The difference between the two theories also shows up sharply in how they treat the strong export performance of the NIC manufacturing firms. The accumulationists tend to see the steep rise in manufacturing exports as just what one would expect in economies where the stocks of physical and human capital were rising rapidly and shifting comparative advantage toward the sectors that employed these inputs intensively. From this perspective, there is nothing noteworthy about the surge of manufacturing exports, save that it is evidence that the economic policies of these countries let comparative advantage work its ways. In contrast, the assimilationists, while not denying that the NICs were building a comparative advantage in various fields of manufacturing, tend to highlight the active efforts by government to induce, almost force, firms to try to export, and to highlight the entrepreneurship, innovation, and learning the firms had to do in order to compete effectively in world markets, even with government support.

Several economists of the assimilation school have argued that exporting stimulated and supported strong learning in two ways (see, e.g., Pack and Westphal 1986). First, being forced to compete in world markets made the managers and engineers in the firms pay close attention to world standards. Second, much of the exporting involved contracting with American or Japanese firms who both demanded high performance and provided assistance to achieve it. The story here clearly is different than one that sees the development of these new competencies as, simply, the more or less automatic result of changing factor availabilities that called them into being.

We have noted that the assimilationists' position, at least the one we espouse, sees the high rates of investment by the NICs in physical and human capital as a necessary, if not a sufficient, component of the assimilation process. These high rates themselves are remarkable, even if not miraculous. Under the argument of the assimilationists, these investments were at least partially induced by, and sustained by, the rapid innovation and learning that was going on.

Successful entrepreneurship in the NICs certainly was facilitated by the growing supply of well-trained technical people. On the other hand, it was not automatic that newly trained engineers would find work in entrepreneurial firms. There had to be entrepreneurial firms in which to work, or the opportunity to found new ones. Thus aggressive entrepreneurship supported and encouraged rapidly rising educational attainment.

Successful production of new products almost always required that firms acquire new physical capital. There is no question that policies in these countries encouraged saving. But on the other hand, what made saving and investment profitable was the strong and effective innovative performance of the firms that were entering new lines of business.

We think it apparent that the two broad theories differ both in their causal structures and in the hints they give about "how to do it." The emphasis of the accumulationists is on getting investment rates up and the prices right. The message of the assimilation theorists is that successful industrial development requires innovation and learning to master modern technologies; effective innovation and learning depend on investments and a market environment that presses for efficient allocations, but it involves much more. And, indeed, to a considerable extent, the investments needed are induced by successful entrepreneurship.

Section II considers the argument that careful attention to the numbers and rigorous calculation supports the accumulationist theory, and there is little evidence that innovation and learning played much of a role. We argue that the commonly used calculations do not do what their proponents claim. In section III, we propose a different way for discriminating between a change in output accompanied by changes in inputs that can be considered simply "a movement along the production function," and a change that seems to involve innovation and learning. In the light of the argument we develop there, in section IV we consider the evidence. We propose that that evidence strongly supports the assimilationists' case. Section V considers in what ways the differences between the two theories matter.

II Why the Standard Calculations
in Fact Don't Discriminate

The case put forward by its proponents for the accumulationist theory is based on calculations of two sorts. One is a growth accounting. The other involves fitting a dynamic production function. In both methods the strategy is, basically, to try to calculate the effect of input growth on output growth, holding the "production function" constant, and see (under growth accounting) if anything much is left over as a "residual," or (under production function fitting) whether the passage of time itself seems to contribute to output growth over and above what is explained by input growth over time. We argue here that, contrary to widespread views in economics, neither kind of calculation can separate out growth that "would have occurred without technical advance" from growth that involved technical advance.

It often is not recognized adequately that the simple logic of growth accounting is only applicable to the analysis of *small* changes in inputs and outputs (see, e.g., Nelson 1973). The procedure basically involves making estimates of the marginal productivities (or output partial elasticities) of the various inputs that have changed and, in effect, using these to calculate the contribution of input expansion to output growth by using a first-order Taylor series. However, in the case of the Asian tigers the investments whose contribution to growth is being estimated have been cumulatively very large. While repressed by the format of growth accounting, which usually sets up the calculations in terms of average yearly changes and thus makes the changes *appear* relatively small, in the countries in question capital per worker increased more than four times over the past three decades, and years of average educational attainment also increased greatly.

The calculations in standard growth accounting take marginal productivities as estimated by factor prices (or output elasticities as estimated by factor shares) as exogenous. However, under the assumptions of neoclassical production function theory (which lie behind the growth-accounting logic), large finite changes in inputs can lead to large finite changes in marginal productivities. For that reason, the factor prices (or factor shares) that are treated as exogenous in growth accounting need to be understood as endogenous. Thus a "growth accounting" of the standard sort does not provide a way to calculate growth that would have occurred had there been no technical advance, if input changes are large. Sustained high marginal productivities (output elasticities) of the most rapidly growing factors, which lead a growth accountant to propose that most of growth is explained by their expansion, could be largely the result of the fact that technical advance offset the diminishing returns that otherwise would have set in.

We know that, in the countries in question, despite the large changes in their quantities, the rates of return on physical capital and on education stayed high. We noted earlier that one explanation is that technologically determined elasticities of substitution, in the sense of standard production function theory, were quite high, and thus significant increases in these inputs relative to others had only a modest effect on marginal productivities as the economy moved along its ex ante production function. Under this explanation a good share of output increase indeed would have occurred without any technical advance. This seems to be the implicit argument of the proponents of the accumulation theory. However, another explanation is that the elasticities of substitution, defined in the standard way, were quite low, and that only the rapid taking on board of new technologies prevented the sharp diminishing returns that one would have observed had these economies stayed on the production functions that existed at the start of the development traverse.

Consider the latter explanation, which we believe is the correct one. Under it, innovation and rapid learning are driving growth. However, a growth accounting of a standard sort might show a very small residual, or even a negative one. The factor shares of the more rapidly growing factors — physical and human capital — would be and would remain high, as a consequence of the rapid learning that made their continued expansion productive. These investments themselves would be and would remain high, because rapid technical advance kept their returns high. Thus a growth accounting might "attribute" the lion's share of output growth to input growth. There would be little left to explain in terms of innovation and learning, despite the fact that these are the basic factors driving growth.

The use by some scholars of the Tornqvist index for the weights applied to input increases represents acknowledgment that, if one is interested in the impact on output of finite changes of inputs along a production function, output elasticities can change along the way. But the use of such an index (as by Young 1995) does not deal with the problem highlighted here. The index uses actual shares, at the end as well as the beginning of the period. But the actual shares at the end of the period can be, and in the case in question almost surely were, affected by the technological changes that occurred over the period. In general they are not what the shares would have been at the new input quantities had the production function stayed constant over the traverse. Thus, contrary to widespread belief, the use of the Tornqvist index does not enable the analyst to estimate what would have happened to output had inputs grown (finitely) as they did and the production function remained constant.

We want to underline this point because many economists presume that the absence of a large residual in a growth accounting is strong evidence that the lion's share of growth was due to movements along a

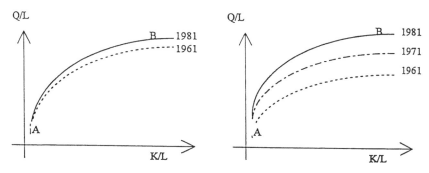

Fig. 7.1. Alternate interpretations of growth

prevailing production function. This is just not so if the input changes involved are large. Growth accounting alone cannot tell whether the relevant elasticities of substitution were large or small and thus cannot distinguish between the two stories sketched above about the sources of growth. There is an "identification" problem.

One might think that the fitting of a dynamic production function can avoid this logical limitation of growth accounting, when input changes are large and finite. However, in practice the identification problem cannot be resolved this way.

Thus, consider the two "explanations," depicted in figure 7.1, for a large increase in output per worker, between time 1 and time 2, associated with a large increase in capital per worker. In the explanation on the left-hand side, much of experienced labor productivity increase would have occurred even had the economy stayed on its production function of period 1 (the dotted curve). The way the production function is drawn depicts only weak diminishing returns to increasing capital intensity. The firm or economy in question is presumed to know, at time 1, how to operate effectively at much higher capital intensities than were employed then but chooses not to do so because prevailing factor prices made it more profitable to operate at low capital intensity. Between time 1 and time 2, factor availabilities changed.

In contrast, in the explanation on the right-hand side, experienced productivity growth is almost totally the result of the establishment of a new production function (the solid curve) in that very little productivity growth would have occurred had the economy remained on its old production function. Under this explanatory story, at time 1 the firm or economy in question knew very little about how to operate effectively at significantly higher capital intensities. To have increased capital per worker without learning about and learning to use new techniques would very quickly have led to low or zero marginal returns. Thus the economy, in order to deal productively with the changed factor price regime of period 2, had to do a lot of "learning," or "innovating," and in fact it did.

In the language of tradition theory, under the first explanation the elasticity of substitution was close to 1, and technological advance was modest and neutral. Under the second the elasticity of substitution was much less than 1 and technological advance was large and labor saving. Both can explain the large increases in output per worker that came with the large increases in capital intensity, and the approximate constancy of capital's share.

That is, both explanations fit the data at time 1 and time 2 reasonably well. The "levels" and the "slopes" of the old production functions at time 1 are approximately the same, and the levels and slopes of the new production functions are approximately the same at time 2. This "identification problem" was highlighted by Diamond, McFadden, and Rodriguez (1978), and Nelson (1973), over twenty years ago. It seems to have been forgotten.

When one "fits" a dynamic production function statistically (through many, not just two, points and slopes), how does one discriminate between these two explanations? Obviously one needs to place some restrictions on the form fitted, for example, that the rate and direction of "technical advance" be constants over the period, or that the underlying production function always have a particular "kind of general shape." Most of the econometric exercises we are concerned with here have imposed relatively loose restrictions, although sufficient to enable a best-fitting equation to be calculated. However, even if an equation that looks like the left-hand side explanation wins the "maximum likelihood" contest (as in Kim and Lau 1994), if the constraints on functional form are relatively loose, it is a good bet that an equation that looks like the right-hand side explanation is not very far behind. Standard regression techniques of the sort that have been employed do not enable confident acceptance of one explanation and rejection of the other.

The graphs drawn in figure 7.1 are in fact regressions estimated from the actual data for Korea's manufacturing sector for the years 1962–81. The dynamic production function fitted to the data is a standard CES, with two inputs — capital and labor — and constant returns to scale. To keep the analysis simple and transparent we constrained technological advance to be neutral and constant over the period in question. The key parameters to be estimated are r, the rate of technological progress, and e, the elasticity of substitution.

In the left-hand figure we forced e to be large, .9. Since growth of K/L

then "explains" a lot of the growth of Q/L, the estimated rate of technological change, r, came out low, .016. (For regression runs in which we set e as greater than 1, the estimated rate of technological change was even smaller, and for large values of e came close to zero.) In the right-hand figure we constrained e to be low, 0.2. Since under this constraint the growth of K/L cannot "explain" much of the growth of Q/L, the estimated rate of technological progress, r, came out high, .045. Both of these regressions, and one in which all parameters were chosen by least squares, yield values of R^2 of .99, leaving little to choose among the regressions on a statistical basis.

Again, we want to underline the point. The fact that the best fit of a dynamic function provides an explanation for growth in which technological advance plays a small role, and input growth accounts for the lion's share of growth, does not itself provide strong evidence against the argument that, in fact, growth would have been far less if there had not been significant technological advance. Only the imposition of particular constraints on the dynamic production function enables econometric technique to choose between the explanation on the left-hand side and the right-hand side of figure 7.1. These constraints are basically arbitrary. And the imposition of somewhat different ones can change radically the estimated contribution of technical advance in the attribution.

The authors in question certainly have been careful with their data and in the use of their methods. The problem is that the methods employed just don't do the job they are thought to do. Nor, at this stage of our argument, are we introducing "new data," although we agree that the issue is an empirical one. Before considering new evidence, it would seem important to do some rethinking of the kind of data that would discriminate between growth where entrepreneurship, innovation, and learning were central, and growth where they were not.

III Back to Basics

How is one to decide between two different explanations, each broadly compatible with the macroeconomic data, when one stresses "movements along a production function" and the other emphasizes "entrepreneurship, innovation, and learning"? We propose that to get an empirical answer requires that one first ask some conceptual questions. What might one *mean* when one says that an observed change in inputs and outputs simply reflected a move along a production function? What might one *mean* if one argued it was not that simple, but that entrepreneurship and innovation in fact were involved? If we agreed on answers to these conceptual questions, we might be able to agree on what kind of empirical evidence would be relevant.

Regarding what we economists seem to mean by "a move along the production function," reflect on the simple treatment in undergraduate microeconomics texts. The production function, there, is said to be the "efficiency frontier" of the "production set" — the set of all input-output combinations a firm can choose among. One way of explaining the set to students is to say that a firm "knows" a certain set of production techniques or activities, and the production set is generated by different levels and mixes of those activities that a firm might choose. In any case, the firm is viewed as both "knowing about" each of the alternatives, and "knowing how" to do whatever is associated with achieving the input-output vector associated with each.

The verbal articulation may admit that there might be modest "setup" costs associated with marshaling and organizing to shift operations to a point within the set that is different from what the firm currently is doing, and that some adjustments (another form of setup cost) might be required to get the new choice operating smoothly, although these shift costs are generally repressed in the formal modeling. However, it seems inconsistent with the "operating within the production set" idea if the setup costs for shifting to a new point involved doing a lot of exploratory "search and study" to identify and get a better feel for alternatives that, up to then, had been unfamiliar to the firm, and the "adjustment" involved a lot of trial-and-error learning by doing and using. At least it would seem inconsistent if the results of searching and learning were highly uncertain, both to the firm ex ante, and to an economist trying to predict what the results would be.

Of course, a plausible interpretation of the production set idea might admit a certain amount of statistical uncertainty regarding inputs and outputs, particularly if there were unknowable outside forces, like the amount of rainfall, that bear on the process. But if the decision maker in question has only very rough ideas about the consequences of trying to do something, and initially about how to do it, that something does not seem to be an activity that can be regarded as within the unit's production choice set. The production set of a firm would appear to be limited at any time to those things the firm knows about and knows how to do, with good confidence and skill. Or at least that is how economists implicitly define the concept.

On the other hand, a move that involves a lot of study of initially hazy alternatives, or research and development where even the nature of the outcome is not clear in advance, would, according to these criteria, be regarded as a "technological" change or "innovation" for the firm in question. We do not see how such a move possibly can be regarded as one "along a prevailing production function," if economists adhere to what they teach about the meaning of choice sets.

We call attention to the fact that, under the way we are proposing the distinction be drawn, a firm's production set in principle could be very extensive. Indeed, much of what some versions of the new neoclassical growth theory treat as "technological advance" would, under the principles suggested here, be regarded as moves along a firm's prevailing production function. In these models (see, e.g., Romer 1990) investments in R&D are strictly up-front costs required to make a product or technique operational. But in these models (if not in fact) R&D is strictly a setup cost to make an activity the firm always knew about available for use. There are no Knightian uncertainties involved.

However, once we get away from particular abstract models, most economists who have studied the processes empirically understand that the introduction to the economy of products or processes significantly different from any employed before does not look like a move "along a prevailing production function." It is well documented empirically that, while theoretical engineering calculations at any time encompass a wide range of techniques not yet brought to practice, the bringing to practice of new technology invariably involves "up front" research and development costs, with Knightian uncertainties at least early in the process (see, e.g., Nelson and Winter 1982; and Rosenberg 1994). While R&D can resolve some of these uncertainties, there are uncertainties in the R&D process itself. Further, even after R&D, there almost always are "bugs" at the start of operation, and it usually takes some time before the operation is really under control. In many cases the attempts at innovating prove unprofitable and need to be abandoned, or radically revised.

Of course, in this essay we are dealing with the adoption of technologies that, while new to the firm or country, are not new to the world. The issue, then, is whether such changes in the behavior and performance of firms in the NICs can meaningfully be explained as changed choices within largely unchanging choice sets.

The accumulationists clearly have in mind that, if a technology is in effective use in one country, there are ways that firms in other countries can use to take aboard that technology at relatively low cost, and without significant uncertainties regarding the outcome of their efforts. Quite often detailed descriptions are available. One can hire consultants who are familiar with the practices involved. In many cases one can get assistance from the firms who are operating the technology, although some license fees may be required.

The assimilationist, in contrast, is skeptical about easy "technology transfer." To be sure, for many of the technologies that the firms in the NICs adopted there were available engineering texts and articles and the like. Blueprints and specific handbooks often could be obtained. There are lots of consultants for hire.

However, the assimilationist would stress that such a move invariably involves not only "up front" costs of identifying, learning about, and learning to master the technique in question, but also significant uncertainties. The range of options is hazy. Things often do not work out as expected. Consultants seldom can guarantee success. Inevitably there is a lot of learning by doing and using. The costs, and the uncertainties, are greater the farther the technique being adopted is from those the firm actually has employed. In many cases major changes in firm organization may be required. The firm may need to learn to sense new markets. Firms attempting these changes can and often do fail. Those that succeed do so because they successfully learn to do things they simply could not do before. That is, they succeed by expanding their production sets.

IV What Does the Evidence Indicate?

We can return now to the question of what kind of evidence one would need to determine whether an observed change was within a prevailing capability or choice set, or required an expansion of the sets of things the organizations in question knew how to do. The prior section argued that the standard data and techniques for deciding simply do not do the job. We propose here that the kind of evidence that is relevant involves examination of process, not simply time paths of inputs and outputs, and that the persuasive data are to be found at a quite low level of aggregation.

A major problem with highly aggregated economic data is that it masks the magnitude and even the nature of the allocational changes going on. Thus, earlier we noted that in the 1990s Korean and Taiwanese manufacturing firms were heavily engaged in producing products that in the 1960s they were not producing at all. This is strikingly illustrated by table 7.1 for Taiwan. In particular, note Taiwan's production of electronic goods, which by the late 1980s were accounting for roughly 21 percent of Taiwanese manufacturing exports. In 1960 virtually no electronics goods were produced in Taiwan.

Such a change in the allocation of activity within the manufacturing sector almost certainly would be associated with considerable turnover of firms, with firms going out of business in the declining sectors, and new firms entering the expanding fields. And within the expanding areas one would expect to see a certain amount of turnover as some firms try and fail while others succeed. Unfortunately, we do not have the firm turnover data that are directly relevant to the phenomena we are characterizing. However, there are data on the number of firms of different sizes in Korea and Taiwan for several years, and a summary of these data is presented in table 7.2. The pattern is roughly what one would expect under the assimilationists' story. There has been a striking decline in the number of very small firms, most of which very likely were locked into old technologies and producing traditional products, and a sharp rise in the number of middle-size or larger firms; we conjecture that a large share of these were new firms entering the new product fields or older firms that succeeded in taking on board modern technology. In the early 1970s the productivity of these larger firms was strikingly higher than that of the small firms that, according to the story we are proposing, they were replacing.

However, to get at the details of what was going on would seem to require studying individual firms. Only by studying firms can one see just what was involved when they came to master new technologies and learn what was needed to operate in new product fields.

Happily, over the last few years several scholars have developed detailed studies of Taiwanese and Korean manufacturing firms, tracing

TABLE 7.1. Changes in Physical Production Levels for Selected Industrial Products, Taiwan, 1960–90

Product	1960	1990
Man-made fibers (millons of tons)	1,762	1,785,731
Polyvinyl chloride (millons of tons)	3,418	920,954
Steel bars (millions of tons)	200,528	11,071,991
Machine tools	0	755,597
Sewing machines	61,817	2,514,727
Electric fans	203,843	15,217,438
Television sets	0	3,703,000
Motorcycles	0	1,055,297
Telephones	0	1,055,297
Radios	0	5,892,881
Tape recorders	0	8,124,253
Electronic calculators	0	44,843,192
Integrated circuits (1,000)	0	2,676,865
Electronic watches	0	5,115,695
Shipbuilding (tons)	27,051	1,211,607

Source: Taiwan Statistical Data Book, 1992, Council for Economic Planning and Development, Republic of China, Taipei, table 5–6c.

the sources of the firms' rapidly growing range of manufacturing competencies. Thus, Alice Amsden has provided a detailed history of a Korean textile firm, which describes what was going on over a period of time when it achieved very significant productivity gains. Table 7.3 shows what happened to machine and labor productivity during the decade after 1977, when it purchased most of its capital equipment. The reduction in worker hours per unit of output was considerable, particu-

TABLE 7.2. Percentage Distribution of Employment by Firm Size

| | Number of Employees | | | | | |
	4–9	10–19	20–49	50–99	100–499	500+
Taiwan						
1954	18	13	14	9	16	31
1961	18	10	14	8	17	34
1971	8	7	11	9	29	37
Index of value added						
per worker, 1971		100	91	100	117	259
Korea						
1958	17	16	21	13	21	12
1963	15	14	16	12	21	22
1975	4	5	8	9	30	44
Index of value added						
per worker, 1971		100	133	193	256	304

Source: Ho 1980, tables 3.1, D2, D3.

TABLE 7.3. Learning in a Korean Textile Factory

	1977	1986	1986 International Best Practice
Labor Productivity			
Kilograms per manhour, ring spinning	52.4	78.5	156.3
Kilograms per manhour, open end spinning[a]	137.1	210.3	324.3
Meters per manhour, weaving	216.2	224.1	360.4
Machine Productivity			
Kilograms per spindle, ring spinning	.20	.23	.21
Kilograms per rotor, open end spinning[a]	.91	1.26	1.11
Meters per loom, weaving	36.1	35.4	39.8

Source: Columns 1 and 2 adapted from Amsden 1989, table 10.4; column 3 calculated from column 2 plus coefficients from Pack 1987, tables 3.1 and 3.2 and calculations underlying those tables.
[a]Initial year is 1979

larly in spinning. Amsden explains the productivity growth in terms of active learning. Early in the period its foreign equipment suppliers provided technical assistance. Later in the period it employed its own engineers to help it increase productivity. Note that in 1986, while it had become much more efficient than it was a decade earlier, its labor productivity still was lower than that in comparable plants in advanced industrial countries, a phenomenon not consistent with a move along a freely available international production function.

For our purposes, one of the most interesting set of firm studies are those undertaken by Michael Hobday of Korean and Taiwanese electronics companies. Hobday describes in detail how these firms started out, usually producing quite simple products, and then progressively moved on to more complex ones. In most of the cases he studied, these new complex products first were made to order for their foreign customers who, in the early stages, provided detailed engineering instructions and assistance. Gradually, however, many of these companies came to be able to do their own design work. In a number of cases, recently they have moved on to sell under their own brand label. Throughout the history of these firms, one can see them actively working to learn to do the things they were doing better, and to be able to do more sophisticated and profitable things. In the early stages, this learning involved reverse engineering. As the companies began to do their own design work, this engineering effort began to be counted as research and development.

Linsu Kim (1997) provides a set of analyses of Korean firms, in several different industries, that show much the same phenomena as does Hobday's study. The firms started out using relatively unsophisticated technologies and learned, over the years, progressively to master more sophisticated ones. By the 1990s many of these firms were approaching the technological frontier. But the paths they took were not simple, and success never was guaranteed.

The story about the development of Korean and Taiwanese firms told by Amsden, Hobday, and Kim is strikingly similar to that told by Odagiri and Goto (1996) in their study of how Japanese industry learned about and learned to master the technologies of the West in the years between the Meiji restoration and the advent of World War II. They find that a major amount of searching, exploring, trying, failing, and learning was required before Japanese firms acquired proficiency in the Western technologies they were adopting and adapting. The decisions of firm managers to get into the new ways involved major uncertainties. Odagiri and Goto stress their "entrepreneurial" nature and the innovation and learning that were involved. Our argument is that Korean and Taiwanese firms went through much the same process, half a century later.

Table 7.4 shows the rise in accounted R and D, and patenting by nationals, in Taiwan. A similar progression from engineering work focused largely on mastering and adapting foreign technology, to work on designs sufficiently new that the effort legitimately could be called R and D, occurred in Korea. And of course the same phenomena occurred in Japan in the early postwar period.

To return to our basic analytic argument, we do not think that the industrial development of Korea and Taiwan since the 1950s, or of Japan a half century earlier (see Saxonhouse 1974; as well as Goto and Odagiri 1997), can be interpreted as "moving along production functions," at least if that term connotes changing choices within a largely unchanging choice set. On the other hand, if the kind of entrepreneurship, innovation, and learning on the part of firms revealed in the case studies is considered as perfectly consistent with the notion of "moving along a production function," we do not know what that concept would exclude, and hence it becomes meaningless.

V Do the Differences Matter, and If So, How?

The differences between the two theories would appear to matter for two different reasons. The first is, simply, regarding how one understands what happened. What lies behind the Asian miracle? The second is that the two theories might imply somewhat different things regarding appropriate economic development policy. What kinds of government policies are helpful, and what are the lessons for other countries?

It is apparent that, for many economists, one of the strongest attractions of the accumulation theory is that it is clean and simple, and its basic outlines conform with the general theory about economic activity that one finds in modern economic textbooks. It is at once delightfully iconoclastic and comfortably conservative to take the miraculous out of

TABLE 7.4.   R&D and Patenting Activity in Taiwan

Year	R&D/GDP	Total Patents	Taiwanese Nationals' Patents	Foreign Patents
1981	.95[a]	6,265	2,897	3,368
1986	.98	10,526	5,800	4,726
1991	1.65[b]	27,281	13,555	13,726

Source: Taiwan Statistical Data Book, 1992, tables 6.7 and 6.8.
[a]1984
[b]1990

the Asian miracle by proposing that it all was a simple matter of moving along a production function. No appeal is needed to the idea of entrepreneurship or innovation, the sources of which might very well lie outside the effective province of neoclassical economics.

It also is clear that a major source of resistance to the assimilation theory is that it seems a complex theory that raises as many questions as it answers. This raises suspicions that the assimilation theory cannot be cleanly formulated. It is a comfort, therefore, that a simpler, more familiar theory seems capable of providing all the explanation that is needed.

And yet, what is at odds intellectually may be only a small part of the corpus of traditional economic theory. More, that particular part, which proposes that production sets can be sharply defined, and that there is a clear distinction between moving along the production function and having the production function shift, came into economics only a relatively short time ago. Perhaps these particular conceptions are not needed for most standard economic arguments, and maybe they have been accepted too uncritically in any case.

A strong argument can be made that the assimilationist perspective is quite consistent with an older set of ideas in economics. The idea that economic growth can be explained by increases in the factors of production, and also by improvements in their productivity, goes back at least as far as John Stuart Mill. However, a striking feature of the earlier analyses of economic growth, as contrasted with the more contemporary treatments, is that there was no compulsion to separate sharply between the contributions of different sources of growth. For Adam Smith, increases in the size of the market, invention of better ways of performing a task, growing mechanization, and changing organization of work all go together. They would seem to also do so in Mill. The early post–World War II growth accountants, in particular Moses Abramowitz, also stressed the interaction of technological advance, growing physical capital intensity of production, increasing exploitation of scale economies, rising educational attainments, and changes in the organization of production, as factors behind experienced economic growth. The question of which of these factors should be interpreted as moving the economy along a production function and which should be regarded as shifting it seems not to have been of major concern to these authors.

In section II we argued that standard techniques do not permit one to separate sharply between movements along and shifts in the production function. Now we would like to argue that the very notion that one can make such sharp splits, even in principle, may not be a useful theoretical premise.

In particular, we would like to argue that "innovation" in practice is a matter of degree, not kind, and that our growth theory ought to recognize this explicitly. For any firm or organization at any time, there are some activities that are under practiced control, some that are not at present but seem easy to learn, others harder, others presently impossible but perhaps with research and experimentation achievable over the long run. The problem with now standard production theory is that it does not recognize these continuities, but rather presumes a sharp cliff between the known and the unknown.

The case studies of firms, briefly discussed in section III, show them moving from the known to the unknown, but cautiously, and drawing from the known as much as they can. Yesterday's unknown becomes today's known, and the firms venture further. An effective theory of what has been happening requires, we believe, abandonment of the notion that production sets at any time are sharply defined, and thus that there is a clear distinction between moving to another perceived point and innovation. Rather, there is a continuum.

If one explicitly recognizes that that distinction is in fact fuzzy, does not that mean one has a fuzzy theory? Not at all. One of the striking features of the various "evolutionary models" of economic growth that has been built over the last decade is that, within them, innovation is treated as a matter of degree, firms move step by step into the unknown, and in so doing seldom move very far from the known.

Abandoning the sharp distinction between moving along a production function and innovation clearly is a big step analytically. Such a step would involve placing learning and adaptation at center stage of the behavioral analysis, and letting go of analytic techniques and arguments that presume that "profit maximization" is something that managers actually are able to achieve, rather than something they strive for intelligently. Yet it is arguable that most of the important and useful propositions about the role of markets and competition depend on the latter, not the former.

The notion that competition tends to force prices down toward costs, and to stimulate reform or elimination of high-cost producers, goes far back in economics. The argument does not depend on the existence of sharply defined production sets, or the achievement by firms of policies that actually maximize profits, given the full set of theoretical alternatives. It is intelligent striving that does the job. Similarly, the argument that a change in factor prices will induce behavior that economizes on the factor whose cost has risen does not require either sharply defined production functions or actual maximization, but only intelligent striving.

What are the policy implications of taking an assimilationist, or evolutionary, view on what happened in the Asian miracle? Are the policy prescriptions fundamentally different under an assimilationist theory than under an accumulationist theory? In many ways the policy prescriptions in fact are quite similar, although the reasons behind the arguments differ somewhat.

Both neoclassical and assimilationist theories put considerable weight on investments in human capital. By stressing the importance of innovation and learning, and the role of an educated workforce in these processes, the assimilationist might push even harder on the education front than would a modern neoclassical economist.

No disagreement either on the importance of investment in physical capital. However, the assimilationist would highlight the role of such investments as a vehicle for taking aboard more modern technologies, and stress that if capital formation is not linked to effective entrepreneurship, the returns to investment almost surely will diminish greatly after a point. On the other hand the assimilationist would point to effective entrepreneurship as a key vehicle for keeping investment rates of return high and would put less emphasis on simply trying to lift up the savings rate.

Both theories stress the importance of exporting. However, here too the reasons for the emphasis are somewhat different. The assimilationist sees exporting as an extremely important vehicle for learning, as well as a way of exploiting evolving comparative advantage. Thus, the assimilation theorist might be even stronger on the importance of exporting, and willing to bias the incentive system to induce firms to try to export.

Both theories stress the essential role of private enterprise, profit incentives, and an environment that stimulates managers to make decisions that enhance economic development. A neoclassicalist would focus on getting the prices right and making necessary public infrastructure investments. The assimilationist would take a somewhat more complex view on both of these matters. In particular, an assimilationist might stress the role of government funding and organization in building up national scientific and technological infrastructure from which firms can draw assistance. But under both theories, it is the energy of private enterprise that is key, and under both there is deep skepticism about the value of detailed government planning.

Both neoclassical and evolutionary theorists stress the great importance of competition. However, here too the reasons differ somewhat, with the proponent of evolutionary theory pushing competition especially in contexts where innovation is both important and risky. From this point of view, competition is valuable largely *because* choice sets are not clear or not clearly defined and it is highly valuable, therefore, to get a lot of things tried.

So, the policy differences between the theories may be significantly smaller than the conceptual or analytic differences. This should not be a surprise. Economists were stressing the importance of profit incentives, and competition, and the dangers of government planning, long before the idea of a sharply defined production set came into vogue. Indeed, one can find these basic arguments in Adam Smith's *Wealth of Nations*.

NOTE

We would like to thank M. Abramovitz, G. Akerlof, M. Gersovitz, K. Pavitt, D. Rodrik, V. Ruttan, G. Saxonhouse, T. N. Srinivasan, L. Westphal, S. Winter, and participants in seminars at the Johns Hopkins University and the Canadian Institute for Advanced Studies for comments on earlier drafts. Mu-Yen Hsu provided excellent research assistance.

REFERENCES

Abramovitz, Moses. 1986. "Catching Up, Forging Ahead, and Falling Behind." *Journal of Economic History* 46, no. 2:385–406.
———. 1989. *Thinking about Growth.* Cambridge: Cambridge University Press.
Amsden, Alice. 1989. *Asia's Next: South Korea and Late Industrialization.* New York: Oxford University Press.
Dahlman, Carl. 1994. "Technology Strategy in East Asian Developing Economies." July. Photocopy.
Dahlman, Carl, Howard Pack, and Lawrence W. Westphal. Forthcoming. *Industrialization in Developing Countries.*
Diamond, Peter, Daniel McFadden, and Michel Rodriguez. 1978. "Identification of the Elasticity of Substitution and the Bias of Technical Change." In *Production Economics: A Dual Approach to Theory and Applications,* ed. Melvin Fuss and Daniel McFadden. Amsterdam: North-Holland.
Goto, Akira, and Hiroyuki Odagiri. 1997. *Innovation in Japan.* New York: Clarendon Press.
Ho, Samuel. 1980. "Small-Scale Enterprises in Korea and Taiwan." World Bank Staff Working Paper No. 384. Washington, D.C.
Hobday, Michael. 1995. *Innovation in East Asia: The Challenge to Japan.* London: Edward Elgar.
Kim J. I., and L. J. Lau. 1994. "The Sources of Economic Growth in the East Asian Newly Industrialized Countries." *Journal of Japanese and International Economics* 8, no. 3:235–71.
Kim, Linsu. 1997. *From Imitation to Innovation: Dynamics of Korea's Technological Learning.* Boston: Harvard Business School Press.
Krugman, Paul. 1994. "The Myth of Asia's Miracle." *Foreign Affairs,* December, 62–78.

Nelson, Richard R. 1968. "A Diffusion Model of International Productivity Differences in Manufacturing Industry." *American Economic Review* 58: 1219–48.

———. 1973. "Recent Exercises in Growth Accounting: New Understanding or Dead End?" *American Economic Review* 73:462–68.

———. 1995. "Recent Evolutionary Theories about Economic Change." *Journal of Economic Literature* (March): 48–90.

Nelson, Richard R., and Edmund Phelps. 1966. "Investment in Humans, Technological Diffusion, and Economic Growth." *American Economic Review* 56:69–75.

Nelson, Richard R., and Sidney Winter. 1982. *An Evolutionary Theory of Economic Change.* Cambridge: Harvard University Press.

Pack, Howard. 1987. *Productivity, Technology, and Industrial Development.* New York: Oxford University Press.

———. 1988. "Trade and Industrialization." In *Handbook of Development Economics,* ed. H. B. Chenery and T. N. Srinivasan. North Holland. Amsterdam:

———. 1992. "Technology Gaps between Industrial and Developing Countries: Are There Dividends for Latecomers." *Proceedings of the World Bank Annual Conference on Development Economics* Washington, D.C.: The World Bank.

Pack, Howard, and Larry E. Westphal. 1986. "Industrial Strategy and Technological Change: Theory vs Reality." *Journal of Development Economics* 22:87–128.

Rodrik, Dani. 1995. "Getting Interventions Right: How South Korea and Taiwan Grew Rich." *Economic Policy* 20:55–107.

Romer, Paul. 1990. "Endogenous Technological Change." *Journal of Political Economy* 71–192.

Rosenberg, Nathan. 1994. "Uncertainty and Technological Advance." Photocopy.

Saxonhouse, Gary. 1974. "A Tale of Japanese Technological Diffusion in the Meiji Period." *Journal of Economic History* (March): 149–65.

Westphal, Lawrence, Linsu Kim, and Carl Dahlman. 1985. "Reflections on Korea's Acquisition of Technological Capability." In *International Technology Transfer,* ed. Nathan Rosenberg and Claudio Frischtak, New York: Praeger.

World Bank. 1993. *The East Asian Miracle: Economic Growth and Public Policy.* Oxford: Oxford University Press.

Young, Alwyn. 1995. "The Tyranny of Numbers: Confronting the Statistical Realities of the East Asian Growth Experience." *Quarterly Journal of Economics* 110:641–80.

CHAPTER 8

Factor Proportions and Industrial Development in China

Keijiro Otsuka

I Introduction

Nowhere in the world has the development of rural industries been more spectacular than in China. While it is true that the production efficiency of state enterprises has greatly improved due to the introduction of profit motives and the expansion of free-market transactions, it is important to recognize that the leading sector of China's economy has been the rural industry consisting of the so-called township-village enterprises, or TVEs, but not the state sector (Chen, Jefferson, and Singh 1992; Jefferson and Rawski 1994; Perkins 1994). In fact, the average annual growth rate of the rural industry exceeded 20 percent since the inception of economic reform in 1978, whereas the growth rate of the state sector fell short of 10 percent for the same period.

During the socialist regime the development of small-scale, labor-intensive rural industrialization was suppressed due to heavy-industry oriented, urban-based development strategies, in which activities of rural industries were restricted to the production of locally consumed commodities (Perkins 1988; Solinger 1991). Economic reform abolished such discriminatory policies and attempted to promote rural industrialization through the development of TVEs, which in fact brought about modern technologies and new products to rural areas, particularly suburban areas of large cities on the coastal areas. Also important to the rural industrialization in China was reform of the farming system from collective to individual farming, known as the household responsibility system reform, implemented from the end of the 1970s to the early 1980s, which released labor and financial resources from agriculture to industrial sectors in rural areas (Lin 1988; Johnson 1988). To use the term of Ranis and Stewart (1993, 81–85), the economic environment facing rural industries changed suddenly from the situation akin to "the unfavorable post-colonial archetype" to the situation resembling to "the favorable post-colonial archetype" for the rural industrialization.

According to Naughton (1992), China's industrial structure had been dominated by the monopolistic state-owned enterprises (SOEs), which had been firmly protected by the government. Once the entry barriers were removed by economic reform, however, TVEs rapidly entered into markets to share monopoly profits. TVEs are financially independent with hard budget constraints and are in principle free to discharge their employees, unlike SOEs, which are subject to soft budget constraints and a variety of regulations, including employment policies. Since TVEs are located in rural areas, they have better access to cheap labor than urban-based SOEs. TVEs, however, did not possess industrial skills and management know-how necessary to launch modern rural industrialization. Thus, it seems reasonable to hypothesize that overwhelmingly successful development of TVEs rests on the effective utilization of cheap labor force by means of adopting labor-using production methods in labor-intensive industrial sectors, while introducing new ideas from outside.[1]

As table 8.1 demonstrates, not only real value added but also the number of employees have grown more rapidly in the TVE sector than in the state sector, even though the growth rate of employment decelerated in the TVE sector in recent years.[2] As a result, TVEs have almost caught up with SOEs in terms of the total value added, total employment, and even labor productivity by 1994. Such remarkable growth

TABLE 8.1.   Growth of State and TVE Sectors, 1978–94

	State Sector			TVE Sector[a]		
	Real Value Added (billion ¥)[b]	Number of Employees (million)	Labor Productivity (thousand ¥)	Real Value Added (billion ¥)[b]	Number of Employees (million)	Labor Productivity (thousand ¥)
1978	329	31	10.5	39	17	2.2
1986	639	40	16.2	175	32	5.5
1994	1,174	44	26.9	989	38	26.3
Average annual growth rate (%):						
1978–86	8.7	2.9	5.6	20.8	7.8	12.1
1986–94	7.9	1.2	6.5	24.2	2.2	21.6

Source: State Statistical Bureau 1989, 1990, 1991, 1995; *China Statistical Yearbook of Industrial Economy.*

[a]Township- and village-run industrial enterprises with exclusion of private enterprises.

[b]Real values at constant 1978 prices by using price index derived from the ratio of nominal to real national outputs in the state industrial sector.

performance of the TVE sector would not have been possible without the choice of appropriate, labor-intensive technologies in appropriate industries. While Ranis (1957) demonstrated the importance of optimal factor utilization for a developing economy based on the historical experience of Japan,[3] this essay is intended to reinforce his argument based on the postreform experience of China.

The organization of this essay is as follows. Section II attempts to show the importance of appropriate factor proportions in achieving efficient production based on the case studies of garment and machine tool industries. Section III intends to generalize the importance of factor proportions in China's industrial development by estimating the profit rate function, which includes the capital-labor ratio as an explanatory variable, while using data of thirty-nine rural industrial sectors. Finally we discuss the implications of this study for rural-based industrialization in developing economies.

II Case Studies

Even though the growth performance of TVEs has been spectacular, there is a mixture of pessimistic and optimistic views about the efficiency and future prospect of TVEs. Some argue that TVEs are profit-seeking, rational production organizations facing fierce market competition under hard budget constraints (Byrd and Gelb 1990; Byrd and Lin 1990; Perkins 1994). Others contend that TVEs are far from maximizing profit because of the unclear ownership rights and the excessive intervention into management by the township and village governments, which are concerned with the welfare of local residents (Du 1990; Song and Du 1990; Nee and Young 1991; Naughton 1994; Rawski 1994; Chang and Wang 1994). Furthermore, it is often argued that TVEs rely on small-scale, excessively obsolete technologies (Wong 1985). If these claims are true, TVEs will not be so efficient and, hence, they may well be outcompeted by state-owned enterprises, once SOEs are sufficiently reformed. These views, however, are based generally on casual empiricism, not on solid empirical evidence.

Hayami's article in this volume emphasizes the importance of the community mechanism of resource allocation and contract enforcement. Although kinship cooperation reemerged in certain areas of China for the management of TVEs (Yang 1994), the use of personal and community ties in China seems rather limited in my observation. It will probably take some time to establish stable contractual relationships among local governments, enterprise managers, and workers. Furthermore, enterprise managers, who now have greater decision making authority, are often retired employees of urban-based, state-owned enterprises, who do not have origins in rural areas. Therefore, they generally do not possess community ties with employees of TVEs.

In order to identify rigorously the production efficiency of TVEs, it is appropriate to compare the production performance of TVEs with other types of enterprises, such as SOEs and joint ventures (JVs), in the same industry by estimating production function. The comparison with JVs is particularly interesting, because the behaviors of JVs are expected to be no different from private enterprises in free-market economies; they are free from government regulations due to the policies to promote JVs in China, and their objectives can be assumed to maximize profits, as their management is supported by profit-seeking foreign enterprises. It is also of interest to undertake case studies in both light industries, where TVEs have already entered and overwhelmed SOEs, and heavy industries, where TVEs have begun to enter and compete with SOEs. In this section, we present major findings of the production function analysis from the case studies of garment and machine tool industries, which are based upon my own surveys conducted in selected locations of China in collaboration with the State Statistical Bureau. Judging from the general consistency of the data with a priori expectations and the absence of abnormal information, the quality of survey data seems reasonably high.

Case Study of the Garment Industry

Undertaking a survey of 111 garment enterprises in Shanghai, Beijing, and Guangzhou, Murakami, Liu, and Otsuka (1994) compare production efficiency of different types of enterprises, which include state enterprises, urban collectives, TVEs, and JVs, with domestic and foreign enterprises mostly from Hong Kong. TVEs are further classified into "ordinary," independent enterprises and "cooperative" enterprises. The latter are "joint ventures" between state enterprises or urban collectives and TVEs, in which managers and engineers are sent from "parent" companies and profits are shared in accordance with the investment shares. Murakami, Liu, and Otsuka argue that cooperative TVEs are new production organizations designed to combine free management environments facing TVEs and potential management ability and technology know-how possessed by the traditional socialist enterprises. Out of nineteen cooperative TVEs, thirteen cases are cooperation between SOEs and TVEs and three between urban collectives and TVEs. In the case of JVs, there are six joint ventures with SOEs, four with urban collectives, and five with TVEs. Three types of JVs, however, are not markedly different in terms of capital-labor ratio, labor productivity, and the size of enterprises.

In terms of the number of employees, the state enterprises are largest, but cooperative TVEs are also relatively large (table 8.2). JVs are small, partly because they were newly established in the late 1980s. Labor productivity, defined as the average value added per employee, is highest in JVs, as they use advanced, relatively capital-intensive production methods to produce high-quality products primarily for exports. Capital-labor ratio is lowest in both independent TVEs and cooperative TVEs. Despite the equal capital-labor ratio, however, labor productivity is much higher in cooperative TVEs than in independent TVEs, suggesting that the production efficiency of cooperative TVEs is much higher due to learning of technical skills and management know-how from SOEs and urban collectives. As a matter of fact, cooperative TVEs employ engineers and old equipment of the parent enterprises, and sell products with the brand names of the parent enterprises through their marketing channels. SOEs and urban collectives have incentives to provide skills and management know-how to TVEs under cooperation, because while their profit-seeking behaviors are constrained by a variety of regulations, including lifetime employment and the provision of housing and other social services, they can earn a share of profits from the operation of TVEs under less regulated conditions.

It is also clear that cooperative TVEs are more efficient than SOEs and urban collectives because TVEs achieve higher labor productivity while employing less capital per worker. The difference in productivity between TVEs and the urban enterprises will be accounted for, in a

TABLE 8.2. Capital-Labor Ratio and Productivity in the Garment Industry by Type of Enterprise, 1990

Type of Enterprise	Number of Sample Enterprises	Number of Employees	Labor Productivity Index[a]	Capital-Labor Ratio Index[b]	TFP Index[c]
State	14	750	100	100	100
Urban collectives	33	300	78	60	116
Independent TVEs	30	364	83	48	141
Cooperative TVEs	19	587	110	48	192
Joint ventures	15	394	147	91	204

Source: Murakami, Liu, and Otsuka 1994.
[a]Index of the ratio of value added to the number of employees with state enterprise = 100.
[b]Index of the ratio of real value of capital stock to the number of employees.
[c]Total factor productivity index.

large measure, by the inefficient management of the latter enterprises. The comparison between cooperative TVEs and JVs is less clear, as both labor productivity and capital-labor ratio are lower in cooperative TVEs. In order to explore the relative production efficiency more rigorously, Murakami, Liu, and Otsuka estimated production function by instrumental variable method to deal with the problems of the measurement errors of capital stock and endogeneity of capital-labor ratio. The relative production efficiency is evaluated from the estimated coefficients of enterprise dummies, which is summarized in the form of the total factor productivity (TFP) index in the last column of table 8.2.[4]

An important result is that the TFP index of cooperative TVEs is twice as large as that of SOEs and urban collectives and almost as large as that of JVs. These observations indicate that by choosing the labor-intensive technology, cooperative TVEs have achieved production efficiency substantially higher than that of the traditional socialist enterprises and comparable to that of modern capitalist-type enterprises. The latter result is remarkable in view of the fact that TVEs rely on technical skills and management know-how of SOEs and urban collectives, whereas JVs must have better access to advanced foreign technology. This indicates that like the historical experience of Japan (Ranis 1957; Otsuka, Ranis, and Saxonhouse 1988), the appropriate technology for rural areas of China characterized by the abundant endowment of labor force is not necessarily the scientifically most advanced capital-intensive technology developed in advanced economies but the more labor-intensive and less modern type, so that JVs do not have a decisive advantage over the locally established enterprises. In China, too, the choice of appropriate technology seems to play a critical role in the development of TVEs.

Case Study of the Machine Tool Industry

While TVEs have actively entered into light industries, such as garment and textiles, there are some that have entered into "heavy" industries dominated by the state sector. Most of them, however, are engaged in the production of parts and intermediate products, and simple equipments. One major exception is machine tool industry. Since the production of machine tools requires precision, experienced, skilled workers as well as expensive capital equipment need to be employed in this industry. Furthermore, like the production of other machineries, a large number of parts and intermediate products are required in the production of such machine tools as lathes and boring machines. Many state enterprises used to produce almost all kinds of parts within huge factories because interenterprise transactions of parts were largely suppressed. Under such situations, the entry of TVEs would not have been possible due to the financial constraints. Recently, however, many small TVEs have entered into the part-supplying industries, like cast metal and gears, for sale to state enterprises and other TVEs. Taking advantage of the new development of market transactions, a few TVEs have entered into the machine tool industry, while specializing in assembly by purchasing used machineries and recruiting retired employees from state and urban collective enterprises. Those TVEs attempt to build and maintain cooperative relations with those urban enterprises formally or informally.

Murakami, Liu, and Otsuka (1996) conducted a survey of enterprises in the machine tool industry located in three cities and their suburbs that have been major centers of the machine tool industry in China, that is, Shenyang, Shanghai, and Wuhan. There were nine SOEs in Shenyang, sixteen in Shanghai, and five in Wuhan, all of which were covered by the survey. In Shanghai three TVEs were also sampled. In addition, various cities in Jiangsu Province located between Shanghai and Wuhan, where a number of TVEs were newly established, were covered. Twelve TVEs were sampled in this province in addition to three traditional socialist enterprises.[5]

For the sake of exposition, SOEs are classified into three size classes: large, medium, and small (table 8.3). The five large enterprises were by far the largest, employing more than five thousand workers, whereas no other enterprises employed more than two thousand. The rest of SOEs are equally divided between medium and small enterprises. TVEs are distinctly smaller, the average number of employees being 219.

TABLE 8.3.   Capital-Labor Ratio and Productivity in the Machine Tool Industry by Size and Type of Enterprise, 1991

Size Class and Type of Enterprise	Number of Sample Enterprises	Number of Employees	Labor Productivity Index[a]	Capital-Labor Ratio Index[b]	Purchased Parts Ratio (%)[c]	TFP Index[d]
Large state	5	6,111	100	100	11	100
Medium state	14	898	99	69	28	104
Small state	14	379	103	58	39	125
TVEs	15	219	104	41	39	146

Source: Murakami, Liu, and Otsuka 1996.
[a]Index of the ratio of value added to the number of employees with state enterprises = 100.
[b]Index of the ratio of real value of capital stock to the number of employees.
[c]The ratio of the value of purchased parts to the total value of purchased inputs.
[d]Total factor productivity index.

It is found that labor productivity in terms of average value added per employee is largely the same across the four enterprise categories. Yet there are enormous differences in capital-labor ratios, the highest being large SOEs and the lowest being TVEs. These observations strongly indicate that the larger the enterprises, the lower the production efficiency. As far as the machine tool industry is concerned, evidence to indicate scale diseconomies is strong, contrary to socialist ideology, which assumes the advantage of large-scale production units. Such divergence in production efficiency between large SOEs and small TVEs has emerged partly because TVEs operate under less regulated conditions and partly because SOEs cannot adjust the size of enterprises downward in response to changing circumstances, due largely to the difficulty of dismissing workers.

It can be also confirmed from table 8.3 that the smaller the enterprise, the larger the dependence on purchased inputs, which is measured by the ratio of the value of purchased parts and intermediate products, such as gears and cast metal frames, to the total value of purchased inputs. The average size of TVEs is smallest, and their reliance on purchased inputs is highest. It may well be that while large enterprises had an advantage over small enterprises when market transactions of parts and intermediate products were suppressed or highly distorted, small enterprises have an advantage over large enterprises when market transactions are liberalized. This is because small enterprises can realize the efficiency gain arising from the division of labor among enterprises specializing in the production of different products, along the arguments advanced by Stigler (1951) and Coase (1937). Indeed, the market transactions lessen the need to coordinate a large number of production processes internally, which also tends to reduce the installation of rarely used capital equipments.

China's machine tool enterprises are markedly large by comparison with neighboring East Asian countries. In Japan, where advanced, numerically controlled machineries by computers are extensively used, the average number of employees of 129 major enterprises was 272 in the late 1980s (Japan Society for the Promotion of Machine Industry 1990). The average number of employees was reported to be only 70 in Taiwan and about 30 in Korea (Japan Society for the Promotion of Machine Industry 1991). The major reason for the difference in the size of enterprises between China and other East Asian countries was found to be the heavy dependence of machine-tool-producing enterprises in the latter countries on subcontracting with a large number of part-supplying companies (Japan Society for the Promotion of Machine Industry 1991; Amsden 1985). More generally, the strength of the Japanese production system is considered to lie in the use of the so-called subcontract system between a large parent company and layers of small-scale part-supplying companies (see, e.g., Aoki 1990). Many machine tool enterprises in China seem excessively large because most enterprises internally produce major parts and intermediate products. Internal production of a large number of parts is costly, because internal coordination of various production processes is difficult, so that various machines tend to be underutilized. This seems true particularly for large SOEs in China. Such underutilization, however, can be prevented if parts and intermediate products can be freely sold or purchased at the markets. In practice, however, spot markets are not well developed, and it takes time and effort to establish stable, long-term contractual relationships with part-supplying enterprises.

According to the estimation results of production function by Murakami, Liu, and Otsuka (1996), neither scale economies nor diseconomies were observed when the purchased-parts ratio was included as a shifter of the production function. The coefficient of the purchased-parts ratio was positive and highly significant. As we observed, this ratio is negatively associated with the size of enterprises. Thus, the scale diseconomies were found to emerge if we omit the purchased-parts ratio from the specification of production function.[6] In consequence, total factor productivity, which essentially reflects the impact of purchasing parts, is highest in TVEs, followed by small SOEs, and lowest in large SOEs (table 8.3).

Considering the fact that most TVEs started their operation in the late 1980s, their achievement is truly remarkable. One of the reasons for the success of TVEs in this industry seems to be the choice of labor-intensive technology and an appropriate mix of products internally produced and procured from other enterprises.

III Factor Proportions and Profitability across Industrial Sectors

The objective of this section is to explore, by using aggregate sectoral data, how far we can generalize the major findings of the two case studies reviewed in the earlier section, that is, the superior production efficiency of TVEs over SOEs with larger employment of labor relative to capital. According to official statistics of the State Statistical Bureau (*China Statistical Yearbook* and *China Statistical Yearbook of Industrial Economy*), the whole industry in China has been classified into forty industrial sectors.[7] Omitting the cigarette industry, we analyze the data of thirty-nine industrial sectors.[8] For expository purposes, these thirty-nine industrial sectors are classified into (1) mining industry, (2) light industry, (3) chemical industry, and (4) heavy industry.[9] Table 8.4 shows the number of industrial sectors classified into the major industrial categories, examines production shares of the four major industries in 1987 and 1992, and compares the growth rates of production of the state and TVE sectors by industrial sector. Only a little change can be observed in the production shares of the major industries over the five years from 1987 to 1992. In fact, the average growth rates of production in the four major industrial groups were similar at around 10 percent per year (see the last column). These observations indicate that the imbalance of the industrial structure in favor of heavy industry, as well as chemical industry, had been largely rectified by the entry of TVEs to formerly depressed sectors before 1987.

There were enormous differences in the growth rates of the value of production between the state and TVE sectors in any major industry. The average annual growth rate of the TVE sector from 1987 to 1992 was 20.8 percent, which was almost four times as fast as the growth rate of the state sector. Thus, there is no question that the TVE sector had greater growth momentum than the state sector in almost any industry.

Somewhat unexpectedly, the lowest growth rate of the TVE sector was recorded in the mining industry and the highest in the chemical industry. These observations, however, do not imply that TVEs have most actively entered into the chemical industry and least actively into the mining industry. On the contrary, the production share of the TVE

TABLE 8.4. Production Shares of Major Industrial Sectors and Average Annual Growth Rates of Real Value of Production by Enterprise Sector from 1987 to 1992 (in percentages)

Major Industrial Sector	Number of Industrial Sectors	Production Share[a] 1987	Production Share[a] 1992	Annual Growth Rate[b] State Sector	Annual Growth Rate[b] TVE Sector	Average[c]
Mining industry	9	8.5	7.9	6.4	16.6	9.5
Light industry	12	29.5	28.5	4.1	20.4	12.3
Chemical industry	9	27.5	28.2	7.5	24.7	11.0
Heavy industry	9	34.6	35.4	5.0	21.6	10.2
Total	39	100.0	100.0	5.6	20.8	10.9

[a]All figures are simple averages of industrial sectors.
[b]Growth rate of the real value of production in terms of 1987 constant prices.
[c]The growth rate of each industrial sector is the weighted average of the growth rates of state and TVE sectors.

sector was second highest in the mining industry and lowest in the chemical industry in 1987, as shown in the fifth column of table 8.5. It appears that TVEs actively entered into the mining industry before 1987, whereas they began to enter into such a knowledge-intensive and capital-intensive industry as the chemical industry mainly after 1987. In terms of changes in the production share in percentage points, light industry achieved the best growth performance. In fact, the TVE share was highest in light industry in 1992 (sixth column in table 8.5). While the TVE share also increased considerably in heavy industry, TVEs seem to have been engaged mainly in the production of simple equipments, parts, and intermediate products at the present stage of their development. It is also likely that even in the same category of industry TVEs were engaged in the production of simpler products or production processes, which require simpler techniques.

Comparison of Profitability between TVEs and SOEs

In order to compare the production and management efficiency across industrial sectors, we computed the profit rate, which is defined as the ratio of gross profit, that is, the sum of tax payments and retained profits, to the real value of capital stock inclusive of fixed and liquid assets.[10] We presume that the profit rate thus defined will reflect the level of technical efficiency, allocative efficiency, and the efficiency of investments in the past. SOEs, however, faced dual prices, in which they had to deliver a certain share of outputs to the government at prices lower than free-market prices. Although the dual pricing system gradually gave away to the market system, it would have reduced the profit

TABLE 8.5.   Profit Rate and TVE Production Share in 1987 and 1992 by Major Industrial and Enterprise Sectors (in percentages)

	Profit Rate of State Sector		Profit Rate of TVE Sector		TVE Production Share	
Major Industrial Sector	1987	1992	1987	1992	1987	1992
Mining industry	7.0	2.8	30.4	19.9	30.2	35.4
Light industry	18.3	6.3	18.4	20.4	42.2	57.1
Chemical industry	22.5	9.1	19.1	15.8	19.8	29.5
Heavy industry	13.5	6.8	18.3	15.8	29.0	40.0
Average	15.6	6.3	21.3	19.2	31.2	41.8

Note: The profit rate is measured by the ratio of gross profit to the value of total capital stock, both of which were deflated into 1987 values. All figures are simple averages.

rates for the state sector to some extent. Also note that the profit rate does not measure the social rate of return, importantly because it does not capture the value of information flow from SOEs to TVEs.

Several important observations can be made from table 8.5, which exhibits the profit rates in 1987 and 1992 by major industry and enterprise sectors. First, the average profit rate in the TVE sector was 21.3 percent in 1987, which was modestly higher than the 15.6 percent profit rate in the state sector in the same year. Second, the profit rates of the state sector in all major industrial sectors significantly declined from 1987 to 1992, whereas the profit rates in the TVE sector largely remained constant during the same period, except in the mining sector. These observations indicate that the profit rate in the state sector generally declined due to increased competition with the TVE sector, as manifested in the increasing production share of TVEs. In contrast, the TVE sector largely maintained the profit rate over time partly because TVEs acquired production skills through experience and learning from SOEs and foreign enterprises. Third, there is no clear association between the profit rates in the TVE sector relative to the state sector in 1987 and the growth rates of the TVE sector from 1987 to 1992. For example, the profit rate of the TVE sector was highest in the mining industry in 1987, but this is the industry in which the growth and expansion of production share of the TVE sector were most sluggish. Conversely, there was no difference in the profit rate in light industry between the state and TVE sectors in 1987, but TVEs actively entered into this industry thereafter. It seems that the expansion of production by the TVE sector was made on the basis of expected returns but not necessarily on the basis of the prevailing returns actually observed. Fourth, the profit rates were always more uniform in the TVE sector than in the state sector, and became less variable in 1992 than in 1987.[11] It appears that as the competition among TVEs has been intensified, the rate of return to capital tended to converge. Thus, the "convergence hypothesis" advanced by Jefferson, Rawski, and Zheng (1992) and Jefferson and Xu 1994 seems to hold at the individual industry level in the TVE sector.

Comparison of Factor Proportions between TVEs and SOEs

In our view, one of the reasons for the lower profitability of the state sector was the adoption of inappropriately capital-intensive production methods. This point is born out by the data on capital-labor ratio shown in table 8.6; the real capital-labor ratio in the state sector was 2.5 to 5 times as high as in the TVE sector. It is also interesting to observe that capital-labor ratios in the TVE sector were particularly low in the mining and light industries, in which both the TVE share and the profit rate of the TVE sector tended to be greater than in the chemical and heavy industries. These observations are clearly consistent with our hypothesis that the comparative advantage of the TVE sector lies in the labor-intensive industries, which is supported by the adoption of labor-intensive technology.

It is highly unlikely for TVEs to enter into knowledge-intensive industries indicated by high R&D intensities. Table 8.6 exhibits the R&D intensity or the ratio of research expenditures incurred by the government to the value of production in the state sector.[12] The R&D intensity was largest in the heavy industry, followed by the chemical industry. It may well be that TVEs do not have comparative advantages in these industries not only because of the high capital intensity but also because of the high requirement of scientific knowledge.

As Perkins (1994) and Naughton (1994) argue, SOEs may continue to dominate TVEs in those industries in which significant scale economies operate. Table 8.7 shows the average size of enterprise in terms of both the real value of production and the number of employees by enterprise type, which are supposed to reflect the scale advantages. There were huge differences in the size of enterprises; on the average, SOEs were 117 times as large as TVEs in 1987 and fifty-two times as large in 1992 in terms of the value of production. The differences were smaller but still sizable in terms of the number of employees. Note that the differences in the size of enterprises were narrowed from 1987 to

TABLE 8.6.   Real Capital-Labor Ratio and R&D Intensity by Major Industrial and Enterprise Sectors (1,000 ¥ /person and in percentages)

Major Industrial Sector	Capital-Labor Ratio in State Sector		Capital-Labor Ratio in TVE Sector		R&D Intensity in State Sector[a]	
	1987	1992	1987	1992	1988	1992
Mining industry	27.6	42.7	4.8	8.0	2.4	0.8
Light industry	16.4	23.4	5.1	8.9	2.9	0.9
Chemical industry	38.3	56.8	9.6	17.8	3.4	1.1
Heavy industry	24.8	34.1	7.5	13.4	7.1	2.1
Average	26.0	38.0	6.6	13.4	3.7	1.2

Note: Real capital-labor ratio is defined as the ratio of the estimated value of real capital stock to the number of employees.
[a]Ratio of R&D expenditure to the value of production in the state sector.

1992 not because the size of SOEs generally shrank but because the size of TVEs increased considerably. Thus, despite declining profitability, SOEs in general neither went bankrupt nor reduced the size of enterprise operation, except for the mining sector. It must be also pointed out that the differences in the size of enterprises between the state and TVE sectors were particularly large in the mining industry and small in the light industry. Yet the TVE production shares were high in both of these industries, which suggests that the large size of enterprises per se will not properly reflect the extent of entry barriers for TVEs, because TVEs can operate small-scale, labor-intensive, and efficient factories.

Factor Proportions and Profitability

It is difficult to identify the impact of appropriate factor proportions on the profit rates by the descriptive analysis because of the multiplicity of factors affecting profitability. Moreover, the factor proportions in the case of the TVE sector are likely to be endogenous choice variables of TVEs, in contrast to the case of SOEs, where the intention of the central and provincial governments is decisive. In this study we regress, first, capital-labor ratio in the TVE sector on capital-labor ratio, R&D intensity, and the average enterprise size in the state sector, while regrading all the variables in the state sector as exogenous. Secondly, the profit rate of the TVE sector is regressed on the predicted capital-labor ratio, among other things, to examine whether and to what extent the factor proportions affect the profitability of enterprise management in the TVE sector.

The estimation results of the capital-labor ratio function for the

TABLE 8.7. Average Size of Enterprises in Terms of Real Value of Production and the Number of Employees in 1987 and 1992 by Enterprise and Major Industrial Sectors

	Real Value of Production (Million ¥)				Number of Employees			
	State Sector		TVE Sector		State Secctor		TVE Sector	
	1987	1992	1987	1992	1987	1992	1987	1992
Mining industry	135	125	0.2	0.3	3,649	3,109	42	42
Light industry	6.5	6.9	0.3	0.8	332	351	42	52
Chemical industry	48.4	58.2	0.6	1.5	861	955	43	61
Heavy industry	25.3	28.5	0.7	1.4	1,012	1,027	52	60
Average	50.2	50.9	0.4	1.0	1,376	1,283	44	54

TVE sector are shown for 1987, 1990, and 1992 in table 8.8. The fit of the regression equation is fairly good, as can be seen from reasonably high values of R^2. As might be expected, the coefficients of capital-labor ratio in the state sector are all positive and significant. The estimated coefficient was 0.96 in 1987, which is not significantly different from unity, but declined to 0.65 in 1992, which is significantly smaller than unity. Thus, other things being the same, capital-labor ratio in the TVE sector increased less than proportionally with increases in capital-labor ratio in the state sector, particularly in recent years. This supports our hypothesis that TVEs adopt more labor-intensive technology than the state sector.

It is interesting to observe that capital-labor ratio in the TVE sector was negatively associated with the size of enterprises in the state sector, measured by the average value of production. We conjecture that, as in the case of the machine tool industry, large enterprises are likely to have idle capital equipments because of the difficulty of coordinating a variety of activities within a self-sufficient, huge factory composed of a number

TABLE 8.8.   Estimation Results of Capital-Labor Ratio Function in the TVE Sector by OLS

	1987	1990	1992
Intercept	0.47	2.36	3.97
	(0.32)	(1.52)	(2.39)
ln (capital/labor) in state sector	0.96[b]	0.78[b]	0.65[b]
	(6.09)	(4.78)	(3.69)
ln (average size) in state sector	−0.17[b]	−0.12[a]	−0.14[a]
	(−2.92)	(−2.00)	(−2.02)
R&D intensity	−0.00	−0.06	−0.12
	(−0.12)	(−0.78)	(−1.18)
Mining industry dummy	−0.73[b]	−0.74[b]	−0.89[b]
	(−3.54)	(−3.95)	(−3.88)
Light industry dummy	−0.23	−0.32	−0.48[a]
	(−1.11)	(−1.66)	(−2.12)
Chemical industry dummy	−0.12	−0.12	−0.10
	(−0.65)	(−0.63)	(−0.49)
R^2	0.683	0.642	0.601

Note: Dependent variable is ln (capital/labor) in the TVE sector. Both dependent and explanatory variables employed pertain to the same years except for R&D intensity in 1987, for which data in 1988 were used because of the lack of data. Numbers in parentheses are t-statistics.
[a]Denotes significance at 5%
[b]Denotes significance at 1%

of plants specializing in the production of parts, intermediate products, and assembly processes. In contrast, TVEs have installed a lesser amount of capital per employee when the size of SOEs was large. While the large size of SOEs may appear to indicate the existence of scale economies, which will act as entry barriers for TVEs, it is, in practice, not the good indicator of scale economies nor the existence of entry barriers. After all, the range of technology choice in terms of capital-labor ratio is considerably wide in China, which is consistent with general observations on the technology choice in developing countries by Ranis (1973).

While the R&D intensity in the state sector did not exert any influence on the capital-labor ratio in the TVE sector, the mining industry dummy has negative and significant coefficients in all three years, indicating that the production methods of mining in the TVE sector were particularly labor-intensive. Note that capital-labor ratio of the mining industry was second highest following the chemical industry in the case of the state sector, whereas it was lowest in the TVE sector. It appears that the elasticity of substitution between capital and labor is particularly large in this industry. Taking advantage of such flexible factor substitutability, TVEs seem to choose highly labor-using methods of production for the higher profits.

The next question is whether the lower capital-labor ratio results in higher profitability of enterprise management in the TVE sector. Thus, we estimated the profit rate function in which the profit rate is explained by capital-labor ratio, the average size of TVEs, R&D intensity represented by that of the state sector, and the three industrial dummy variables.[13] Since capital-labor ratio and the average size of enterprises are regarded as endogenous, we applied the instrumental variable method for estimation. The results are shown in table 8.9.[14]

Consistent with our hypothesis, the estimated coefficients of capital-labor ratio are all negative, and two of them are highly significant. The estimated coefficients range from -0.13 to -0.21, which would imply that when capital-labor ratio declines 10 percent, the profit rate increases 1.3 to 2.1 percentage points. This result is significant, given the substantial differences in capital-labor ratio among industrial sectors, as shown in table 8.6. There seems to be no doubt that the factor proportions had significant impacts on the profitability of enterprise management in the TVE sector.

None of the other variables have significant coefficients. The insignificant effect of the size of enterprises seems to indicate the absence of scale advantages or disadvantages in rural industries in China. The coefficients of R&D intensity in the state sector are consistently negative but insignificant. It may be that this variable pertaining to the state sector has no relevance for the behaviors of the TVE sector, which may be interested in imitation more than innovation requiring formal R&D activities. Nonsignificant coefficients of the three industry dummies is consistent with the hypothesis that TVEs competitively entered into various industries toward the equalization of the rates of return to capital across industrial sectors.

To recapitulate, TVEs adopted technologies more labor-intensive than SOEs and realized higher profitability owing, at least partly, to the adoption of such technologies. Thus, the sectoral analysis supports the results of the case studies of the garment and machine tool industries. There is also indication that the profit rates were equalized among TVEs through competition. In contrast, SOEs did not restructure their organizations nor reduce production despite declining profitability over time. If the current trend continues, TVEs will capture larger market shares in many industrial sectors, and, consequently, many SOEs will suffer from increasing deficits, and most will eventually go bankrupt, unless proper

TABLE 8.9. Estimation Results of Profit Rate Function in the TVE Sector by 2SLS

	1987	1990	1992
Intercept	1.89	1.49	2.57
	(2.57)	(2.23)	(1.79)
ln (capital/labor) in TVE sector	−0.18[b]	−0.13[b]	−0.21[a]
	(−2.76)	(−2.54)	(−1.85)
ln (average size) in TVE sector	−0.01	−0.02	−0.05
	(−0.23)	(−0.44)	(−0.71)
R&D intensity in state sector	−0.64	−2.50	−3.74
	(−0.89)	(−1.41)	(−1.12)
Mining industry dummy	−0.05	−0.07	−0.27
	(−0.42)	(−0.67)	(−1.37)
Light industry dummy	−0.11	−0.08	−0.16
	(−1.34)	(−1.17)	(−1.32)
Chemical industry dummy	0.00	0.00	−0.04
	(0.07)	(0.13)	(−0.75)
Standard error of regression	11.44	6.02	9.36

Note: The results of two-stage least squares regression, in which predicted values of ln (capital/labor) ratio and ln (average size) are used. Dependent variable is the ratio of gross profit to the total value of capital stock. Both dependent and explanatory variables employed pertain to the same years except for R&D intensity in 1987, for which data in 1988 were used because of the lack of data. Numbers in parentheses are *t*-statistics.
[a]Denotes significance at 5%
[b]Denotes significance at 1%

incentives are created in the state sector that induce SOEs to adopt appropriate, labor-intensive technologies. In all likelihood, this will require genuine enterprise reform or de facto privatization.

IV Concluding Remarks

Recent studies in development economics highlight the importance of technology catch-up with developed countries for the development of less developed countries. This point has been long recognized since the seminal work of Gerschenkron (1962). It is also well known that Japan's success in economic development has depended heavily on technology borrowed from abroad, and its subsequent assimilation and adaptation to domestic conditions (e.g., Ohkawa and Rosovsky 1968; Otsuka, Ranis, and Saxonhouse 1988). Essentially the same process of technology transfer seems to have played a major role in the "miraculous" development of other East Asian countries (World Bank 1993). The case of China's economic development in general and rural industrialization in particular is no exception.

Simple theory of technology choice, coupled with the accumulated empirical evidence, points to the importance of labor-intensive technology for the development of LDCs, where labor is abundant relative to capital. If so, appropriate technology transfer from high-income to low-income economies cannot be a simple transfer of capital-intensive technologies widely in use in high-income countries. In other words, the choice of appropriate technology is not simply a choice from the "shelf" of techniques, but it involves a whole series of conscious efforts for adaptation (Evenson and Westphal 1995). Therefore, the process of technology transfer is inherently dynamic. Ranis (1957) was the first study in the economic literature that shed light on the critical role of appropriate factor proportions in the dynamic context. Nonetheless, empirical inquiries into the appropriate technology since then often lost the dynamic perspectives, with the result of failing to establish its critical importance.

The case of China is particularly interesting for the study of the dynamic process of adopting appropriate technology partly because the introduction of modern technology to rural areas took place in such a short period of time and partly because the two structurally different sectors of economy—the state sector subject to government regulations and the TVE sector subject to fierce competition within itself—have evolved and experienced contrasting patterns of technology choice and development. Although there is limited data in China, the available evidence is sufficient to establish that the choice of appropriate technology in appropriate industries plays a critical role in the development of rural industries. Such an interpretation is consistent with the synthesis of the development experience of the high-performance East Asian countries by the World Bank (1993), which identifies the efficient development paths with the development of labor-intensive industries followed by the development of capital-intensive industries before launching industrialization of the knowledge-intensive high-technology sectors.

How far successful experience of rural industrialization in China can be replicated in other developing countries, however, can be questioned on the grounds that the development of TVEs has been prompted by the failure of reforming SOEs. In fact, TVEs often competed with SOEs, whereas rural enterprises in other East Asian countries typically play a role supplementary to modern, large-scale urban enterprises through subcontracting. Good examples are weaving and garment enterprises in rural villages engaged in putting-out contracts with urban enterprises and traders. The size of TVEs is also larger by far than rural enterprises in other countries, which are often family-type operations. Why did the type of rural industrialization observed in other Asian countries not take place in China? Specifically, why are rural enterprises in China so large? Why did SOEs or TVEs not develop subcontracts with another layer of small-scale enterprises in rural areas of China? In order to develop proper perspectives on technology choice and rural industrialization, further research is needed toward filling the gap in our knowledge on the success and failure of rural industrialization.

NOTES

I would like to thank Dwight Perkins, Gary Saxonhouse, and T. N. Srinivasan for helpful comments. I am also heavily indebted to Deqiang Liu and Naoki Murakami, who have jointly carried out a research project on the People's Republic of China from which this essay partly draws.

1. Our hypothesis is consistent with the theory of appropriate technology, which asserts that labor-intensive technology is generally more cost-effective than capital-intensive technology in labor-abundant low-income economies. See White (1978) and Evenson and Westphal (1995) for surveys.

2. Although the term TVEs refers not only to township- and village-run enterprises but also to rural private enterprises, we focus only on the former, because the latter are engaged mainly in services and small-scale traditional industrial activities, such as construction and crafting.

3. The Ranis thesis was supported by the case study of cotton textile industries in Japan by Otsuka, Ranis, and Saxonhouse (1988).

4. Murakami, Liu, and Otsuka (1994) also assess the allocative efficiency by comparing factor share of labor with its production elasticity. Significant allocative inefficiencies are found to exist in the traditional socialist enterprises, that is, SOEs and urban collectives.

5. Strictly speaking, three urban collective enterprises were included in the survey. For simplicity, however, we do not distinguish between SOEs and urban collectives in the discussion.

6. The arguments of Murakami, Liu, and Otsaka can be summarized as follows. They first estimated the following from the Cobb-Douglas production function:

$$\ln (V/L) = C + \alpha \ln (K/L) + (\alpha + \beta - 1) \ln (L) + \gamma (PPR),$$

where V stands for value added, L for labor, K for capital, and PPR for purchased-parts ratio; C is an intercept term, α and β are production elasticities of capital and labor, respectively, and γ measures the effect of purchased parts on production efficiency. In this equation, the coefficient of labor, $(\alpha + \beta - 1)$, is expected to capture the existence of scale effects. It is found that the coefficient of labor is insignificant, whereas the coefficient γ is positive and highly significant. An important point is that PPR is negatively associated with $\ln (L)$, so that if it is omitted from the estimation of production function, the coefficient of $\ln (L)$ captures not only the pure scale economies reflected in $(\alpha + \beta - 1)$ but also the indirect effect of enterprise size on production efficiency through the impact on the purchase of parts.

7. The official statistics do not provide the breakdown of the sectoral data into the state and TVE sectors. In this study, we used unpublished data classified into the two sectors from 1987 to 1992.

8. We deliberately excluded the cigarette industry because of the restriction on the entry of TVEs into this sector. In fact, the production share of the TVE sector has been negligible, and the profitability of the state sector has been exceedingly high compared with other industrial sectors.

9. Following the ordering system of industrial sectors adopted by the State Statistical Bureau *(China Statistical Yearbook)* until 1992, we have classified thirty-nine industrial sectors into four major industrial groups in the following way: (1) mining industry—coal mining and processing, petroleum and natural-gas extraction, ferrous-metal mining and processing, nonferrous-metal mining and processing, nonmetal mineral mining and processing, other mineral mining and processing, salt extraction and processing, logging and transport of timber and bamboo, tapwater production and supply, and electric power, gas, and water production; (2) light industry—food processing, beverages, feed processing, textiles, garments, leather and furs, timber and bamboo processing, furniture, paper, printing, educational and sports articles, and artistic products; (3) chemical industry—petroleum, coking and coal gas, chemical products, medical

and pharmaceutical products, chemical fibers, rubber products, plastic products, and nonmetal mineral products; and (4) heavy industry — smelting and processing of ferrous metals, smelting and processing of nonferrous metals, metal products, machinery manufacturing, transportation equipment, electric equipment and machinery, electronic and telecommunication, instruments and meters, and other manufacturing.

10. Real fixed capital stock in 1992 was estimated by the following procedure: First, we took the differences in nominal values of fixed capital stock between each pair of consecutive years from 1987 to 1992 and regarded them as net investments. Second, we deflated the investments by price index with the base year of 1987, which was obtained by taking the simple average of shipment price indexes of machinery and building materials. Finally, we added the estimated real investments to the nominal stock of fixed capital in 1987. The same deflation procedure was applied to liquid capital.

11. The same tendency is observed for the coefficient of variation of the profit rates (Otsuka, Liu, and Murakami 1998).

12. Care must be taken in interpreting and comparing R&D data in the state sector in 1987 and 1992, because the data in 1987 pertain to planned expenditures, whereas those in 1992 pertain to actual expenses of independent research and development organizations. Data sources are the State Statistical Bureau (*Statistics on Science and Technology in China, 1949–89,* 1990, and *Science and Technology Yearbook of China,* 1993). Also note that data on the R&D intensity in the TVE sector are not available.

13. Considering that the profit rates will be affected by many structural factors, such as the characteristics of market demand, the extent of market imperfection, and the availability of entrepreneurship, Otsuka, Liu, and Murakami (1998) applied the fixed-effect model to the estimation of the profit rate function using the pooled data from 1987 to 1992. Similar to the results shown in table 8.9, their estimation results also show the importance of capital-labor ratio in the determination of the profit rate in the TVE sector.

14. We also estimated the profit rate function for the state sector, but the estimation results are less clear, as the coefficients of capital-labor ratio are significant only at the 10 percent level.

REFERENCES

Amsden, Alice H. 1985. "The Division of Labour Is Limited by the Rate of Growth of the Market: The Taiwan Machine Tool Industry in the 1970s." *Cambridge Journal of Economics* 9 (September): 271–84.
Aoki, Masahiko. 1990. "Toward an Economic Model of the Japanese Firm." *Journal of Economic Literature* 28 (March): 11–27.
Byrd, William A., and Alan Gelb. 1990. "Why Industrialize? The Incentives for Rural Community Government." In *China's Rural Industry: Structure, Development, and Reform,* ed. William A. Byrd and Qinsong Lin. Oxford: Oxford University Press.

Byrd, William A., and Qinsong Lin. 1990. "China's Rural Industry: An Introduction." In *China's Rural Industry: Structure, Development, and Reform,* ed. William A. Byrd and Qinsong Lin. Oxford: Oxford University Press.

Chang, Chun, and Yijiang Wang. 1994. "The Nature of the Township-Village Enterprises." *Journal of Comparative Economics* 19 (December): 434–52.

Chen, Kang, Gary H. Jefferson, and Inderjit Singh. 1992. "Lesson's from China's Economic Reform." *Journal of Comparative Economics* 16 (June): 201–25.

Coase, Ronald H. 1937. "The Nature of the Firm." *Economica* 16 (November): 386–405.

Du, Haiyan. 1990. "Causes of Rapid Rural Development." In *China's Rural Industry: Structure, Development, and Reform,* ed. William A. Byrd and Qinsong Lin. Oxford: Oxford University Press.

Evenson, Robert E., and Larry E. Westphal. 1995. "Technological Change and Technology Strategy." In *Handbook of Development Economics,* vol. 3, ed. Jere Behrman and T.N. Srinivasan. Amsterdam: North-Holland.

Gerschenkron, Alexander. 1962. *Economic Backwardness in Historical Perspective.* Cambridge: Harvard University Press.

Hayami, Yujiro. 1998. "Community Mechanism of Employment and Wage Determination: Classical or Neoclassical." In this volume.

Japan Society for the Promotion of Machine Industry [Kikai Shinko Kyokai Keizai Kenkyusho]. 1990. *Production Capacity of Machine Tool Industry and Structure of Subcontracting* (in Japanese).

———. 1991. *Trend of Supply and Demand of Machine Tools in Asia* (in Japanese). Tokyo.

Jefferson, Gary H., and Thomas G. Rawski. 1994. "Enterprise Reform in Chinese Industry." *Journal of Economic Perspectives* 8 (spring): 47–70.

Jefferson, Gary H., Thomas G. Rawski, and Yuxin Zheng. 1992. "Growth, Efficiency, and Convergence in China's State and Collective Industry." *Economic Development and Cultural Change* 40 (January): 239–66.

Jefferson, Gary H., and Wenyi Xu. 1994. "Assessing Gaines in Efficient Production among China's Industrial Enterprises." *Economic Development and Cultural Change* 42 (March): 597–615.

Johnson, D. Gale. 1988. "Economic Reform in the People's Republic of China." *Economic Development and Cultural Change* 36 (April): 225–45.

Lin, Justin Y. 1998. "Rural Reforms and Agricultural Growth in China." *Economic Development and Cultural Change* 36 (April): 199–224.

Murakami, Naoki, Deqiang Liu, and Keijiro Otsuka. 1994. "Technical and Allocative Efficiency among 'Socialist' Enterprises: The Case of the Garment Industry." *Journal of Comparative Economics* 19 (December): 410–33.

———. 1996. "Market Reform, Division of Labor, and Increasing Advantage of Small-Scale Enterprises: The Case of the Machine Tool Industry in China." *Journal of Comparative Economics* 21 (December): 256–77.

Naughton, Barry. 1992. "Implications of the State Monopoly over Industry and Its Relaxation." *Modern China* 14 (January): 14–41.

———. 1994. "Chinese Institutional Innovation and Privatization from Below." *American Economic Review* 84 (May): 266–70.

Nee, Victor, and Frank W. Young. 1991. "Peasant Entrepreneurs in China's 'Second Economy': An Institutional Analysis." *Economic Development and Cultural Change* 39 (January): 293–310.

Ohkawa, Kazushi, and Henry Rosovsky. 1968. *Economic Growth: The Japanese Experience since the Meiji Era.* Homewood, Ill: Richard D. Irwin.

Otsuka, Keijiro, Dequiang Liu, and Naoki Murakami. 1998. *Industrial Reform in China: Past Performance and Future Prospects.* Oxford: Clarendon Press.

Otsuka, Keijiro, Gustav Ranis, and Gary Saxonhouse. 1988. *Comparative Technology Choice in Development: The Indian and Japanese Cotton Textile Industries.* London: Macmillan.

Perkins, Dwight H. 1988. "Reforming China's Economic System." *Journal of Economic Literature* 26 (June): 601–45.

———. 1994. "Completing China's Move to the Market." *Journal of Economic Perspectives* 8 (spring): 23–46.

Ranis, Gustav. 1957. "Factor Proportions in Japanese Economic Development." *American Economic Review* 47 (September): 594–607.

———. 1973. "Industrial Sector Labor Absorption." *Economic Development and Cultural Change* 21 (April): 387–408.

Ranis, Gustav, and Frances Stewart. 1993. "Rural Nonagricultural Activities in Development: Theory and Application." *Journal of Development Economics* 40 (February): 75–101.

Rawski, Thomas G. 1994. "Chinese Industrial Reform: Accomplishments, Prospects, and Implications." *American Economic Review* 84 (May): 271–75.

Solinger, D. J. 1991. *From Lathe to Looms: China's Industrial Policy in Comparative Perspective, 1979–1982.* Stanford: Stanford University Press.

Song, Lina, and He Du. 1990. "The Role of Township Governments in Rural Industrialization." In *China's Rural Industry: Structure, Development, and Reform,* ed. William A. Byrd and Qinsong Lin. Oxford: Oxford University Press.

State Statistical Bureau. 1990. *Statistics on Science and Technology, 1949–89.* Beijing: China Statistics Publishing House.

———. 1993. *China Science and Technology Yearbook.* Beijing: China Statistics Publishing House.

———. Various years. *China Statistical Yearbook.* Beijing: China Statistics Publishing House.

———. Various years. *China Statistical Yearbook of Industrial Economy.* Beijing: China Statistics Publishing House.

Stigler, George J. 1951. "The Division of Labor Is Limited by the Extent of the Market." *Journal of Political Economy* 59 (June): 185–93.

White, Lawrence J. 1978. "The Evidence of Appropriate Factor Proportions for Manufacturing in Less-Developed Countries: A Survey." *Economic Development and Cultural Change* 27 (October): 27–59.

Wong, Christine P. W. 1985. "Material Allocation and Decentralization: The

Impact of the Local Sector on Industrial Reform." In *The Political Economy of Reform in Post-Mao China,* ed. E. Perry and Christine P. W. Wong. Cambridge: Harvard University Press.

World Bank. 1993. *The East Asian Miracle: Economic Growth and Public Policy.* New York, NY: Oxford University Press.

Yang, M. 1994. "Reshaping Peasant Culture and Community: Rural Industrialization in a Chinese Village." *Modern China* 20 (April): 57–79.

CHAPTER 9

Economic Development and the Art of Maintenance

Mark Gersovitz

Introduction

In one of his first papers (Ranis 1957), Gus addressed the question of factor proportions and factor substitution in Japanese economic development. He provided a pioneering analysis of how labor-intensive production allows poor economies "to squeeze the most out of the fund of savings painfully conserved at each stage of development" (Ranis 1957, 595).

In this chapter, I discuss the maintenance of investments in poor countries, another determinant of how much they can squeeze from savings. Based on project documents of aid agencies and casual observation, there is a widely perceived paradox: Investment funds and capital goods are scarce in these countries, yet investments often deteriorate faster than in rich countries. By contrast, there is another casual, although perhaps less often articulated, perception that some classes of capital equipment are retained in active service far longer in poor than in rich countries. These concerns lead naturally to an investigation of the microfoundations of maintenance, depreciation, and the policy implications of any associated market failures.

Maintenance practices also lead directly to the aggregate analysis of growth and development because they influence the condition of the capital stock and thereby the level of aggregate output. Recent literature on these topics is permeated by controversy over the contribution of capital accumulation to economic growth. In making estimates of the capital stock one is inevitably led to assumptions about the rate of depreciation, and these authors typically assume that it does not vary among countries:

And there is neither any strong reason to expect depreciation rates to vary greatly across countries, nor are there any data that would

244

allow us to estimate country-specific depreciation rates. (Mankiw, Romer, and Weil 1992, 410)

Although in agreement with the second assertion, I hope to show that the first assertion is not at all plausible. Similarly, the finding of King and Levine (1994, 284) that differences in their estimated capital/output ratios are too small to be consistent with the differences in output per person depends on their assumption of a depreciation rate of 7 percent that is invariant among countries (272). Put simply, one reason that differences in estimated capital stocks may not account for differences in per person output is that these capital stocks do not in fact exist in the poorer countries of their sample; they have depreciated rapidly. Conversely, analysts of aggregate growth, for example, De Long and Summers (1991), who argue that investment in equipment is an important source of growth, must worry about whether equipment will be maintained after it is installed in poor countries.

One way that maintenance affects growth is through economies of scale that can be external to the firm. It thus exemplifies an externality that depends on the volume of capital as posited by such endogenous growth theorists as Romer (1986). The stocking of spare parts and learning about the maintenance of specialized equipment may exhibit these types of economies.

Because maintenance in poor countries is a topic on which there is neither systematic statistical information nor theoretical analysis, what follows is unavoidably speculative with the goal of defining issues for future analysis.[1] A source of information, although a necessarily anecdotal rather than systematic one, is the many project documents of aid agencies; a wide-ranging summary of this information is provided by Srinivasan and Srinivasan (1986, chap. 9). And there is a good deal of theoretical work in other fields of economics and in operations research[2] that bears on maintenance in poor countries.

The ultimate goals of future analysis would be to understand (1) whether maintenance practices differ between poor and rich countries and how, and (2) whether maintenance practices in poor countries are the best that can be managed under the circumstances or reflect problems that can be corrected cost-effectively. Answers to these questions may differ according to the type of investment and the type of investor.

Many characteristics of an investment affect how it is maintained and its length of life. Investments in structures (including infrastructure) differ from investments in equipment. Indeed, there are important potential differences within the categories of structures and equipment depending on the sector or the particular job. The maintenance problems of scarce, specialized equipment differ from those of widely available equipment that uses interchangeable parts or for which the labor skills necessary to maintain them are widely available. Who made the initial investment decision and who controls the operation of the investment may make a difference, whether it started as an aid project, or its operation lies in the public sector or in the private sector. Whether spare parts are domestically available or importation is necessary is another consideration. In many cases, safety is intimately tied to maintenance. I now turn to an elaboration of these factors, beginning with maintenance in the private sector.

1 Maintenance in the Private Economy

A simple organizing framework for the study of the economics of maintenance is the following cycle.

specify and purchase $\rightarrow$ operate $\rightarrow$ maintain preventively $\rightarrow$ rehabilitate

This cycle, excluding its first stage, may repeat many times before the end of an investment's life. Decisions at different stages of the cycle combine to determine the life of the investment and its productivity; these decisions are largely interdependent. Equipment in poor shape may equally well reflect initial specification of a relatively fragile design or rough operation as poor maintenance. Conversely, the anticipation of poor maintenance may suggest the desirability of specifying robust equipment. In principle, an enumeration of the options at each stage and how choices among them are made should lead to an understanding of whether and why maintenance practice and the lives of investments differ between poor and rich countries, as well as what can and should be done to affect them.

This description of the maintenance cycle encompasses many situations but lacks precision. An augmented dynamic model of factor usage can help to guide thinking even though it lacks generality. Consider a firm that maximizes the present value of its profits (PDV) discounted at rate r:

$$PDV = \int_0^\infty [p_Q F(K,L) - wL - p_I I - p_m mK] e^{-rt} \, dt \tag{1}$$

where p_Q is the price of its output, p_I is the price of investment goods, p_m is the price of maintenance, w is the wage, L is labor, K is capital, I is investment, and m is the amount of maintenance per unit capital. Maximization is subject to the constraint

$$\dot{K} = I - \delta(m)K, \tag{2}$$

where δ is the rate of depreciation with $\delta' < 0$. The optimal control solution to the intertemporal maximization is given by

$$\frac{\partial H}{\partial L} = (p_Q F_L - w)\, e^{-rt} = 0, \tag{3a}$$

$$\frac{\partial H}{\partial I} = (-p_I + \phi)\, e^{-rt} = 0, \tag{4a}$$

$$\frac{\partial H}{\partial m} = -(p_m + \phi\delta')\, Ke^{-rt} = 0, \tag{5a}$$

and

$$(r\phi - \phi)e^{-rt} = \frac{\partial H}{\partial K} = [p_Q F_K - p_m - \delta\phi]\, e^{-rt}, \tag{6a}$$

where ϕ is the (undiscounted) costate variable and H is the Hamiltonian. These results simplify to

$$p_Q F_L = w, \tag{3b}$$

$$p_I = \phi, \tag{4b}$$

$$p_m + \delta' p_I = 0, \tag{5b}$$

and

$$p_Q F_K = (r + \delta)\, p_I + p_m m. \tag{6b}$$

The first conclusion from these equations is that the amount of maintenance per unit capital, m, and therefore the proportional depreciation rate, δ, and its inverse, the average life of capital, do not depend on the interest rate, r. Instead, they depend only on the marginal effectiveness of maintenance, δ', relative to the ratio of the price of maintenance, p_m, to that of new investment goods, p_I.[3] The intuition behind this perhaps paradoxical result is that maintenance and investment provide two (contemporaneous) substitute ways of increasing the capital stock. This result is important, because it is widely believed that the interest rate is higher in poorer countries, and the interest rate does, of course, influence the capital-labor ratio via equation (4b). When the interest rate is higher in this model, firms conserve capital relative to labor, the result stressed by Gus. They do not, however, maintain their capital relatively more (or less) in this model in contrast to a view that firms should conserve capital through better maintenance when the interest rate is higher. But how general is this result of the invariance of maintenance to the interest rate?

There are other formulations of the maintenance problem that may introduce a role for the interest rate. Some of these formulations seem, however, to do so by implicitly eliminating investment activity as a means of augmenting the capital stock, for instance Hartl 1983 and the references therein. With the elimination of equation (2a), equations (3a) and (4a) then imply a role for the interest rate in determining maintenance because maintenance is the only way to control the level of the capital stock. In the Hartl model, a higher interest rate decreases maintenance because there is an incentive to lesser investment (greater disinvestment).

Other ways in which the interest rate may affect maintenance do not rely on eliminating investment as a means of augmenting the capital stock. Costs of adjustment in investment activity provide a classic formulation that would make the interest rate a determinant of maintenance; in this case, p_I depends on I with $p_I' > 0$ and $p_I'' > 0$. Or, the capital-labor ratio itself may be a (technological) argument of the depreciation function, δ. It is not clear, however, whether more capital-intensive technologies require relatively more or less maintenance per unit capital. Another way the interest rate may affect the desirability of maintenance is by increasing the cost of holding inventories of spare parts and thereby increasing the cost of maintenance, p_m. In this case higher interest rates once again provide incentives for worse maintenance rather than for the conservation of capital. Finally, the costs of maintenance may incorporate a component based on downtime when the equipment is unavailable and when production workers may be idled. In this case the interest rate will affect the valuation of the costs and benefits of shortening the downtime. As with other dimensions of maintenance, however, higher interest rates encourage the firm to choose poorer maintenance, manifested in this instance by longer downtimes (see the appendix). Inventory cost and downtimes bring the discussion around to the costs of maintenance.

In the model of equations (1) through (6), the cost of maintenance,

p_m (relative to p_l), does influence decisions that affect the lifetimes of investments. It is this dimension of the maintenance problem that I believe explains many of the differences between rich and poor countries. In poor countries relative to rich ones, prices of spare parts are often high relative to prices of new machines (e.g., UNIDO 1979, 13). Delays in getting spare parts are also likely to be greater in poor countries. These problems are exacerbated when the equipment is imported. Communication with the manufacturer is likely to be slow and expensive in comparison to the situation in rich countries. The situation tends to be particularly bad outside major cities (e.g., ILO/UNDP 1981). Governments may make things worse by interfering with the timely purchase of spare parts through import controls.

This situation of a relatively high cost of maintenance in poor countries does not necessarily prevail: For instance, artisans can fabricate certain types of spare parts, say by sand casting, that in rich countries would always be factory produced. It may be that such substitute solutions are only justified at the relatively high price of factory parts that prevail in poor countries (i.e., p_m is higher in poor countries if factory- rather than artisan-produced parts are used). Nonetheless, maintenance may be expensive relative to replacement investment (p_m/p_l is higher in poor than in rich countries). By contrast such artisanal parts might also be cheaper relative to replacement investments at the low wages of poor countries so that service lives for these types of equipment in poor countries would exceed those in rich countries (i.e., p_m/p_l is lower in poor than in rich countries). But these conditions are unlikely to be representative of the situation in such sectors as health, where the dictates of mechanical precision and electronics make artisanal spare parts generally infeasible.

In principle, one solution to some of the problems with spare parts is to stockpile them, but it leads to other high costs. In poor countries there are limited numbers of pieces of specialized equipment and an inventory of spare parts is therefore relatively costly. With few pieces of equipment, the demand for spare parts will be relatively variable, so that costs of inventorying parts to ensure a given level of availability may be relatively high; inventories are well known to exhibit economies of scale. Furthermore, with very few pieces of equipment of a particular type, costs of learning how to maintain or repair them per piece of equipment may be relatively high.

Costs of maintenance are therefore high in poor countries to some extent because the user base of equipment is small. Because firms decide about investments that increase a user base, the base is endogenous. Because the size of the user base affects not just the firm that is deciding on an investment but all firms forming part of the user base, there is an externality. This externality arises in the decision to be part of a user base (the form of the investment) and in the amount of the investment because a larger investment increases the user base more. The former externality is the concern of the standardization literature (Dybvig and Spatt 1983; Farrell and Soloner 1985; and Katz and Shapiro, 1985, 1986a, 1986b). The latter externality is an example of the type of externality among users of capital assumed by Romer (1986) and other endogenous-growth theorists. Presumably, however, the marginal benefit from an increase in the user base is falling, so the importance of these externalities should tend to diminish as the economy grows, at least to the extent that new specialized pieces of equipment are not constantly being invented.

While the dependence of costs on the user base involves externalities, it is unclear how the market-determined pattern of user bases differs from the optimal. In general, the gains from increasing one user base come from decreasing another user base and have offsetting costs. If all firms had identical needs and were simultaneously choosing a type of equipment for all time, the optimum would surely involve the same choice of equipment by all of them to minimize costs by maximizing a single user base. It is also hard to see what would stand in the way of private firms somehow coordinating on this single standard; regardless, the conditions of this example are only hypothetical.

In reality there are costs to complete standardization. Different firms find different kinds of equipment to be more or less suitable to their needs given the sizes of the user bases. One could then imagine a set of costs conditional on user bases that leads the market to choose one standard when two would be better; there is overstandardization.[4] More generally, the market-determined and the optimal bases may differ. Furthermore, not all firms adopt at the same time. As time passes, new (and better) equipment that is incompatible with older models becomes available. Late-adopting firms weigh their private gains from adopting the new against their costs of forgoing compatibility with the old without regard to the costs imposed on existing users by their defection from the old standard.

In all these cases, there are externalities in the choices about equipment compatibility by users who have no institutional mechanism for directly and explicitly coordinating their decisions to minimize the total costs of equipment. In principle, there is then a role for government in affecting compatibility depending on the balance of forces just discussed (see section 2). In practice, firms may be left to deal with an environment of costly maintenance arising from a small user base by choosing equipment that is relatively robust.

All these problems with spare parts manifest themselves in the prevalence of the cannibalization of equipment. Cannibalization suggests that spare parts frequently may be the real bottleneck; if workers can cannibalize one piece of equipment for parts for others, then presumably if they had the spare parts they could rehabilitate all the equipment. In other words, cannibalization may be a sort of good news; it may not be necessary to emphasize the training of personnel in these circumstances.

The role of labor in maintenance is, however, more complicated than these considerations suggest. The maintenance process is an inherently difficult one to monitor, and therefore to control for quality of work or effort. It may be difficult to know if either preventive or rehabilitative maintenance has been done to specification.

Other things equal, these difficulties are such that at earlier stages extra effort and expense might be made to postpone or avoid entirely if possible the need for rehabilitation, thereby conserving capital equipment and extending its useful life. But are other things equal in poor countries? Working backward, I turn to the next stages of the sequence, preventive maintenance and operation, activities that are often done by the same workers.

A number of factors arise in connection with production workers. When equipment is inoperative, the associated production workers may be idled. Different manning practices and different wage rates in poor countries affect the costs of downtime relative to the situation in rich countries. The use of relatively low-skilled and badly trained workers in poor countries may lead to a lack of care in doing preventive maintenance. Deficient practices in operating equipment also increase wear and tear on equipment. Such circumstances are illustrated by X-ray equipment; failure to warm up the unit leads to significantly earlier failure of the X-ray tube, a component that can be worth many thousands of dollars. Workers in poor countries have less experience with maintenance of all kinds including consumer durables than their richer counterparts in rich countries. For instance, merely owning a car teaches (most) people some of the consequences of poor preventive maintenance and abusive operation and may develop skills and attitudes that carry over to the workplace. Workers in poor countries may therefore be less experienced in doing simple sorts of preventive maintenance, or avoiding certain types of poor operating practices.

The maintenance question is entangled with the question of safety, either of workers or consumers. To this extent, costs and benefits of maintenance are not measurable directly in financial terms, although in principle there are methods that can value different levels of safety. Here again, however, there is an important distinction between the situation at the time the investment is specified and the situation after the investment is made.

For a particular choice of investment, inadequate maintenance often leads to dangerous situations, either for workers or consumers. In many instances, it is not just a question of something that either works to specification or is entirely unusable; in between these extremes is a range of increasingly dangerous operations. These circumstances certainly obtain if broken parts are safety devices, or if safety devices are ill maintained and therefore operate imperfectly. Catastrophic failure of equipment as a consequence of poor maintenance is also hazardous to operators. To the extent that worker safety is less emphasized in poor countries, there will be a corresponding negative effect on safety-related maintenance and thereby on the operating status of the equipment. One of the benefits of maintenance is the reduction of these dangers; maintenance and safety are complementary goals.

The interaction between maintenance and safety may carry over to situations in which there is a relative disregard of consumer safety. In some service industries the consumer comes into direct contact with equipment. Again drawing an example from health equipment, in some x-ray procedures it is recommended practice to shoot and develop a sequence of brief x-ray exposures to localize the area in a patient that needs further detailed x-ray examination. A poorly trained or supervised operator may, however, leave the unit on for a considerable length of time, observing the patient on a cathode tube to localize the area that requires photos. Such continuous operation exposes the patient to excessive radiation and also radically shortens the life of the x-ray tube.

By contrast, when the investment is initially specified, the goals of maintenance and safety are often in conflict. Many features of an investment that will later require maintenance were devised for safety reasons. For instance, in major pieces of medical equipment such as X rays and anesthesia machines only the absolutely very best of the machines sold in poor countries will even be offered for sale in rich countries. What the less costly models often lack are safety components. Anesthesia can be undertaken by connecting two cylinders of gas to a Y-joint and thence to a simple mask to be placed over the patient's face; such a device needs little maintenance. What distinguishes the more complex anesthesia machines from this "roadside" device are its components designed to modulate the delivery of the anesthetic and monitor its effects on the patient; these devices are for safety purposes. But it is exactly these safety components that require maintenance to ensure operation over the life of the equipment. Specification of safety devices at the time of purchase commits the firm to more complex maintenance requirements subsequently.

Turning to the earliest stage of the sequence with which I began, purchase, one finds many choices that affect the need for, and ease of, maintenance afterward. Technological and environmental factors such as high humidity, heat, or dust may promote wear and tear in the tropics. Such problems suggest the need to pay attention to technological choices at the time investments are made. An example is given by consultants who evaluated a Canadian International Development Agency (CIDA) project that failed to specify heavy-duty options for road maintenance equipment, such as blades for road graders (Hickling 1984, 38).

Finally, a very general notion is that mistakes at the time of purchase for any reason are likely to lead to poor maintenance later as the mistakes are realized. For instance, if demand turns out to be unexpectedly low after the investment has been made, then it will be cost-effective to allow equipment that was bought earlier with more optimistic expectations to deteriorate more rapidly than otherwise. Minimal maintenance may be the quintessential method by which one lets bygones be bygones and avoids throwing good money after bad.

To the extent that future conditions and the future usefulness of particular equipment under particular conditions are more difficult to anticipate in poor countries, maintenance will be worse than in rich countries. Certainly in the case of equipment that is scarce in poor countries but common in the rich, the greater experience in the rich countries will lead to purchase decisions that more often justify maintenance subsequently. For equipment imported from rich countries, it is clearly easier for users in rich countries to get information from suppliers about the suitability of equipment for proposed applications.

All the foregoing considerations are based on the assumption of a rational cost-minimizing firm making optimal choices about maintenance. The evidence on this sort of behavior is limited. Kennet (1993 and 1994) for aircraft engines, Parks (1977) for cars, and Rust (1987) for buses provide some evidence on rational decision-making on maintenance in rich countries.

2 Maintenance in the Public Sector

Governments decide about the maintenance of the capital they own and, less directly, affect the economic environment in which private businesses decide about the maintenance of their capital stock. Maintenance and equipment life in the private sector respond to many government policies, including (1) trade policies that affect the original choice of equipment and the availability of spare parts; (2) educational and training policies that affect the quality of manpower; (3) price controls that affect the desirability of maintenance, most especially of equipment that was installed prior to the imposition (or anticipation) of controls; and (4) the interest rate insofar as it affects variables like the cost of maintaining inventories of spare parts. But it is in their decisions about their own capital stock that governments have the most direct effects.

Much of the capital that governments in poor countries own is in the form of buildings or infrastructure. The maintenance of these investments as well as that of equipment under the authority of large bureaucracies poses special problems for getting the job done. Within these categories of investments there is a wide range in the obstacles faced in organizing maintenance. It is not adequate to summarize all these problems of organization in the ratio of the price of maintenance to the price of new investment, and so I now turn to some of these problems of public management.

School buildings in the rural sector provide one example where the organization of maintenance is relatively easy. Of course, the first requirement is that government budget adequately for maintenance on a regular basis. But funding is only the first step. A work program needs to be established, implemented, and monitored.

In Bangladesh, for instance, a field engineer works with a local school management committee at the thana level to assess annual maintenance needs. Application for funds is then made to the district level. Once expenditures are authorized, specifications are drawn up and put out for competitive bid by private contractors. The engineer and the committee monitor the work to ensure that it meets specification.

A simple system operates well for rural schools because many factors are favorable. First of all, rural schools are simple structures, much simpler than structures elsewhere, such as in the health sector, or highways, or earthen works for water control. This simplicity makes for relatively easy assessment of maintenance needs, specification of tenders, and supervision of work. In particular, simplicity facilitates the participation of laymen such as the school management committee. Another important factor favoring success in school maintenance is that the people who enjoy the bulk of benefits are clearly defined and spatially concentrated, namely the students and their parents. This factor makes it feasible for beneficiaries to participate. For other investments, the beneficiaries are not similarly concentrated, for example for long-haul roads or health facilities in their important public-health attributes. Indeed, in the case of earthen waterworks, local interests diverge so much from project goals that people nearest the investment actually see a benefit from breaching its integrity to flood their own fields or fish ponds.

Despite the apparent success of a simple system for maintenance as in the case of rural schools, this type of system is not entirely satisfactory. Perhaps most importantly, the initial step is not sufficiently anticipatory; it involves drawing up a work program for the coming year. Systematic budgeting, however, requires forecasting maintenance requirements beyond one year. For instance, it should be possible to establish a relationship between the age of an investment, its past maintenance, and its future maintenance, in effect a cohort-based analysis. If, for instance, there has been a rapid expansion of investments, there will be a corresponding expansion in maintenance as the investments age.

Field inspection does not allow the anticipation of bunching, although it has the advantage of reporting actual conditions and is robust to mistaken assumptions about a maintenance schedule. Both field and cohort methods are desirable, but even the simplest cohort-based method requires planning resources at the central level, including an inventory of investments and their status.

As noted for the private sector, another important principle of maintenance is that decisions on the initial specification of investments affect the cost of maintaining them as they age. Almost always there are choices about the initial robustness of investments and their vulnerability to neglect. An extreme example arises in the context of earthen works for water control, where as already mentioned locals may breach them intentionally. This problem, however, could have been mitigated by providing sluice gates that would allow flooding without compromising water control. Other examples include the specification of heavy-duty components or the stocking of spares at the time of initial purchase. By contrast, rural schools are simple structures, and while in principle it should be possible to find examples of specification choices that affect subsequent maintenance even in this sector, the issue is not prominent.

Like private businesses, governments need to attend to standardization, an important example of decisions at the time of investment that affect subsequent maintenance. Of course, governments must also trade off the benefits of standardization from a larger pool of compatible equipment within the government against the costs of forgoing incompatible equipment that is better suited for a particular task.

In general, a government should concern itself with the economy as a whole. It should, therefore, consider the effects of its investments on the user base in the country as a whole as it affects the costs of the private sector. Importantly, for government to increase the economy-wide user base its equipment cannot be compartmentalized from the rest of the economy. Such compartmentalization would occur if governments stockpile spare parts in their own workshops rather than use private repair facilities that can effectively merge the inventory of spare parts for equipment in the private and public sectors. Thus, the need to consider the consequences for the private economy affects the desirability of force-account maintenance versus contracting for maintenance with the private sector.[5]

The issue of standardization arises much more for equipment than for structures and is important in government hospitals, in road maintenance, and wherever the government owns equipment. Standardization of structures where possible should also have the potential for economies in working out design defects that lead to maintenance problems and in familiarizing maintenance staff and supervisors with maintenance problems. The simple nature of rural schools tends to make such issues of secondary importance.

Failure to standardize is widely seen as arising from the policies of bilateral donors who specify equipment from their own national suppliers. The resulting hodgepodge of imported equipment becomes difficult to maintain. An example from the Sudan makes this point. Consultants undertaking an evaluation of a CIDA project dealing with road maintenance equipment concluded:

> Further, consideration should be given to the possibility of standardizing equipment type. It is recognized that this is difficult given the Canadian content rules of CIDA, but the existing approach extracts a tremendous penalty from the recipient country in wasted equipment and ill trained mechanics and operators. (Hickling 1984, iv)

Sometimes these problems may be compounded by the past use of barter agreements that has left behind equipment from the former Soviet bloc. Additionally, the supposed bias of donors for capital over recurrent-cost grants means that they are not around to fund the maintenance of projects. Recipients may find that the original design of the project does not justify their own expenditure on maintenance. Or recipients may feel that they can get new capital funding if they neglect maintenance and wait for the original aid-financed project to collapse. A similar dynamic has been argued to characterize the experience with the government's funding of buses in Canada (Frankena 1987) and the United States (Cromwell 1991).

While the organization of maintenance for rural schools is relatively straightforward (because of the nature of maintenance in the sector) and relatively successful, the situation is often very different in such cases as medical equipment in the public sector. The process of approval for repairs is typically time consuming and troublesome. Many times government rules mandate that work must be done by government workshops rather than by original equipment vendors or third parties. At least part of the reason is that health equipment is complex, and so all sorts of considerations arise leading to a reluctance to decentralize authority.

Too little centralization may lead to decisions being made by people who make them so infrequently as to be unable to assess costs. Decentralized decision makers may also be ill positioned to judge whether equipment should be maintained or scrapped to keep the stock of equipment relatively standardized, thereby lowering its cost of maintenance. Beneficiary participation may be difficult outside certain sectors, either because beneficiaries are dispersed or because they lack essential knowledge. For instance, patients and potential patients, the ultimate beneficiaries of the hospital system, cannot easily participate in the oversight of complex medical equipment the way beneficiaries can for rural schools. Furthermore, safety considerations are of central importance in the health sector but are difficult to quantify. Too much centralization or centralization that is done incorrectly, however, leads to problems, so there may be no really good solution.

3 Conclusions

Theoretical considerations point to the cost of maintenance relative to the cost of new investment as a crucial determinant of maintenance activity and the service life of capital. There may be a role for the rate of interest, in most cases as it works through the cost of maintenance in one way or another. In the models presented, a higher interest rate leads to poorer maintenance of capital because maintenance, by incurring expenses in exchange for future benefits, is similar to investment, which, in turn, is generally discouraged by higher interest rates. This finding provides a possible resolution for the paradox of capital scarcity and neglected maintenance in poor countries. Right now there is no systematic empirical information on maintenance in poor countries, but anecdotal evidence suggests many places to begin a more systematic empirical investigation.

Appendix: Downtimes

In a simple model of downtime the equipment becomes inoperable at time t_1 until time t_2, when it has been restored to full operability; otherwise it neither depreciates nor requires other types of maintenance.

These cycles repeat indefinitely. The firm chooses an initial capital stock (number of pieces of equipment), K, which costs p_K per unit at the time the investment is made and employs labor, L, which it pays a wage, w, only when it is producing output using the production function $F(K,L)$. The output is sold at price p_Q. When production occurs, revenues net of labor costs, R, are

$$R = p_Q F(K,L) - wL. \tag{A.1}$$

The present discounted value, PDV, of the investment is then

$$PDV = \frac{\int_0^{t_1} R\, e^{-rt}\, dt}{(1 - e^{-rt_2})} - C(t_2)K - p_K K, \tag{A.2}$$

in which C is a cost that is paid initially and that determines the length of time equipment is down. This cost is per piece of equipment, with $C' < 0$ and $C'' > 0$. The firm maximizes its present discounted value with respect to its choice of L, K, and t_2. After simplification, the corresponding first order conditions imply:

$$\frac{\partial PDV}{\partial L} : p_Q F_L - w = 0, \tag{A.3}$$

$$\frac{\partial PDV}{\partial K} : \frac{(1 - e^{-rt_1})}{(1 - e^{-rt_2})} p_Q F_K - r[p_K + C(t_2)] = 0, \tag{A.4}$$

and

$$\frac{\partial PDV}{\partial t_2} : \frac{(1 - e^{-rt_1})}{(1 - e^{-rt_2})} \frac{R}{(e^{rt_2} - 1)} + C'K = 0. \tag{A.5}$$

The substitution of equations (A.3) and (A.4) into (A.5) yields an equation for t_2 that is independent of K and L but does depend on r:

$$\frac{r}{(e^{rt_2} - 1)}[p_K + C(t_2)] + C'(t_2) = 0. \tag{A.6}$$

Total differentiation of this equation, along with the first-order conditions, establishes that an increase in r increases t_2.

The cost of decreasing downtime may arise in ways that differ from the one-time expense of C in the preceding model. For instance, payments may be made through each cycle of length $t_2 - t_1$ as inputs are used to rehabilitate the equipment. But I believe that most if not all alternatives will embody the property that higher interest rates imply longer downtimes. Expenditures to shorten downtimes inevitably occur before the equipment is up and running and the benefits from shortening downtime are realized; these expenditures therefore have the nature of an investment and should generally be deterred by higher interest rates.

NOTES

I thank Howard Pack and Matthew D. Shapiro for comments on an earlier version.

1. One exception is Newbery (1988), who looks at the consequences of road user costs for the pricing of road access under different road maintenance rules.

2. Operations research and reliability engineering give detailed attention to the specific technological relations that determine depreciation, failure, and the ameliorative effects of maintenance and their implications for cost-minimization from the perspective of the owner of an investment. Two classic treatments of this sort are Jorgenson, McCall, and Radner (1967) and Jardine (1973). Elsayed (1996) provides a recent textbook treatment of reliability engineering, and Crowder et al. (1991) review strategies for estimating the technological relations that constrain maintenance.

3. This result has been known at least since Schmalensee (1974).

4. For instance, assume $N-1$ of N users prefer type A equipment but only to a small degree over type B equipment, while one user very much prefers type B over A. Assume furthermore that the costs of adopting B when one is the sole user of B are very high, while type A equipment does not exhibit a network externality so that its benefits are independent of the size of its user base. In the competitive equilibrium, all producers choose A: the $N-1$ users because they prefer it and the Nth producer because it is too expensive to go it alone. The social optimum might easily involve some (or all) $N-1$ producers choosing B equipment if their costs are only slightly increased while the costs of the Nth producer are dramatically lowered.

5. As yet there is no theoretical work on optimal policy toward the user base in models of networks, and so the specifics of government policy in this area are matters for conjecture. In deciding on whether to isolate itself from the private economy through force-account maintenance, a government must consider the effect of its equipment base on the size of the different bases in the private economy and on their composition. Once the latter factor is taken into consideration, it is no longer evident that compartmentalization is undesirable because the government by participating in the economy-wide user base could tip the adoption decisions of the private economy into a suboptimal pattern.

Another class of policies that governments might consider is subsidies to bring the market-determined user base into line with the optimal one. But such poli-cies are not easy to implement. In the example of an earlier note, the govern-ment would have to subsidize only switches from type A to type B equipment, and only the right number of them. Such a subsidy policy is difficult to undertake because it must be targeted at individual adopters and in addition must not affect their other decisions, such as on the volume of investment.

REFERENCES

Cromwell, B. A. 1991. "Public Sector Maintenance: The Case of Local Mass-Transit." *National Tax Journal* 54, no. 2:199–212.

Crowder, M. J., A. C. Kimber, R. L. Smith, and T. J. Sweeting. 1991. *Statistical Analysis of Reliability Data.* London: Chapman and Hall.

De Long, J. B., and L. H. Summers. 1991. "Equipment Investment and Eco-nomic Growth." *Quarterly Journal of Economics* 106:445–502.

Dybvig, P. H., and C. S. Spatt. 1983. "Adoption Externalities as Public Goods." *Journal of Public Economics* 20:231–47.

Elsayed, E. A. 1996. *Reliability Engineering.* Reading, Mass.: Addison Wesley Longman.

Farrell, J., and G. Soloner. 1985. "Standardization, Compatibility, and Innova-tion." *Rand Journal of Economics* 16, no. 1:70–82.

Frankena, M. W. 1987. "Capital-Biased Subsidies, Bureaucratic Monitoring, and Bus Scrapping." *Journal of Urban Economics* 21:180–93.

Hartl, R. 1983. "Optimal Maintenance and Production Rates for a Machine." *Journal of Economic Dynamics and Control* 6:281–306.

Hickling, James F. 1984. *Evaluation of the Southern Roads Maintenance Proj-ect, Democratic Republic of Sudan.* Canadian International Development Agency. May.

International Labor Organization/United Nations Development Program. 1981. *Revised and Updated Feasibility Study on Establishing Cooperatively Owned Workshops for Maintenance and Repair of Mechanical Equipment in Sudan.* Khartoum: ILO/UNDP, May.

Jardine, A. K. S. 1973. *Maintenance, Replacement, and Reliability.* New York: Wiley.

Jorgenson, D. W., J. J. McCall, and R. Radner. 1967. *Optimal Replacement Policy.* Amsterdam: North Holland.

Katz, M. L. and C. Shapiro. 1985. "Network Externalities, Competition, and Compatibility." *American Economic Review* 75, no. 3:424–40.

———. 1986a. "Product Compatibility Choice in a Market with Technological Progress." *Oxford Economic Papers* 38:146–65.

———. 1986b. "Technology Adoption in the Presence of Network Exter-nalities." *Journal of Political Economy* 94, no. 4:822–41.

Kennet, D. M. 1993. "Did Deregulation Affect Aircraft Engine Maintenance? An Empirical Policy Analysis." *Rand Journal of Economics* 24:542–58.

————. 1994. "A Structural Model of Aircraft Engine Maintenance." *Journal of Applied Econometrics* 9:351–68.

King, R. G., and R. Levine. 1994. "Capital Fundamentalism, Economic Development, and Economic Growth." *Carnegie-Rochester Conference Series on Public Policy* 40:259–292.

Mankiw, N. G., D. Romer, and D. N. Weil. 1992. "A Contribution to the Empirics of Economic Growth." *Quarterly Journal of Economics* 107:407–37.

Newbery, D. M. G. 1988. "Road Damage Externalities and Road User Charges." *Econometrica* 56:295–316.

Parks, R. W. 1977. "Determinants of Scrapping Rates for Postwar Vintage Automobiles." *Econometrica* 45:1099–1115.

Ranis, G. 1957. "Factor Proportions in Japanese Economic Development." *American Economic Review* 47:594–607.

Romer, P. M. 1986. "Increasing Returns and Long-Run Growth." *Journal of Political Economy* 94, no. 5:1002–37.

Rust, J. 1987. "Optimal Replacement of GMC Bus Engines: An Empirical Model of Harold Zurcher." *Econometrica* 55, no. 5:999–1033.

Schmalensee, R. 1974. "Market Structure, Durability, and Maintenance Effort." *Review of Economic Studies* 41:277–87.

Srinivasan, M. S., and S. Srinivasan. 1986. *Maintenance Standardization for Capital Assets.* New York: Praeger.

United Nations Industrial Development Organization (UNIDO). 1979. *Feasibility Study for a Central Workshop for the Manufacture of Spare Parts for the Sudanese Textile Industry.* Vol. 1 Milan: Borghi e Baldo Ingg, November.

Part 3. The International Economic Regime and Economic Development

CHAPTER 10

The Economic Consequences of a Declining Hegemon

Koichi Hamada

1 Introduction

After World War II, economic activities of the United States occupied a major space within the world's economic activities. A large proportion of output was produced by the United States, and a large proportion of trade originated from or was directed to the United States. In terms of the current account, the United States was among the few major surplus countries in the world. Not only did its magnitude of economic activities excel, but its political leadership also excelled. The United States was the shepherd of international agreements, cooperations, regimes, and international institutions.

The United States has joined military alliances such as the North Atlantic Treaty Organization (NATO) and the Mutual Security Agreements with Japan, Korea, and other countries. Moreover, it has actively supported the General Agreement on Tariffs and Trade (GATT) and has remained a crucial player in the Bretton Woods System. For at least a quarter century after World War II, the United States played the role of a responsible leader of the world that promoted and supported growth of output, international trade and investment, and international monetary stability.

Reflecting on this role of the United States, the concept of hegemonic stability was developed by Kindleberger (1986a, 1986b), Gilpin (1987), and others.[1] This concept rests on the assumption that a responsible leader country of the world behaves in such a way as to realize the desirable state in the world. The leader country, or the hegemon, is supposed to provide a sufficient amount of public goods and to build a proper infrastructure that includes international laws and international organizations. "World economic stability is a public good that has to be provided, if at all, by some country that takes charge, accepts responsibility, acts as a leader" (Kindleberger 1988, ix). Without the leadership of a country in charge, the world is devoid of crisis management capacity.[2]

Beginning in the 1970s, the hegemonic role of the United States was overshadowed. The Bretton Woods regime of fixed exchange rates depending on the dollar standard collapsed in 1971. The U.S. current account started accumulating deficits on a yearly basis, and, consequently, the United States became a large debtor country. The country started being involved in many trade-restricting measures such as voluntary export restraints (VERs) and voluntary import expansions (VIEs) instead of being a guardian of the free-trade regime.

In accordance with the relative decline of the role of the United States in the world economy, academic discussions of hegemony shifted their focus as well. In the 1980s, the main theme was what would stabilize the world system given the fact that the United States was losing some of the prerequisites of a hegemon. Hence came the discussions of what happens *After Hegemony* (Keohane 1984), or how a number of countries can form a privileged group for the supply of public goods (Snidal 1985).

Moreover, reflecting the self-centered U.S. attitude toward trade issues, Bhagwati (1994a, 1994b) argues that a previously altruistic hegemon, the United States, has recently stopped playing its responsible role by often disregarding the due processes required for sustaining international public goods and that it has started playing the role of a selfish hegemon. He focuses on the recent patterns of U.S. trade diplomacy that rely on bilateral negotiations rather than multilateral negotiations through international agreements or organizations.

This essay is an attempt to reexamine the concepts of international public goods and hegemony from the standpoint of an economist. I will focus my attention on the incentive structure that a large country or hegemon as well as other countries face while they make individual or collective decisions. I will ask what are and will be the economic consequences to the world if the United States further loses its position as a leader country.

Kindleberger has a paternalistic, if not benevolent, view of the leadership: "The father of family — usually has important responsibility and is often a leader" (Kindleberger 1988, 154). Accordingly, he does not like the usage of *hegemony,* which has overtones of force, threat, and pressure. He prefers the word *leadership.* This essay, however, will explore the economic implications of a hegemon that cannot be free from selfishness and clout to use for arm-twisting. The reason for this is as follows. To the eyes of economists, who are accustomed to regarding economic behavior as the outcome of rational or individually selfish endeavors, it is strange that a nation, which consists of an aggregate of selfish individuals, would behave altruistically. Thus, the concept of a selfish hegemon (Bhagwati 1994a) is a matter of course. Bhagwati argues that the United States became a selfish hegemon because of the change in its position in the world economy. Instead, I would rather argue that the United States was selfish even when its power dominated the world, but during that time its selfish behavior roughly coincided with the world welfare. Now, however, the coincidence has disappeared, and U.S. conduct reveals obvious selfishness.

In order to illustrate the basic logic of hegemonic stability, let us consider an example of a manor, reminiscent of North and Thomas (1973), where a feudal lord (a hegemon) and many small farmers live. Suppose that manor requires the supply of public goods such as irrigation, roads, and a court system, and that the provision of public goods has the qualities of nonrivalry and nonexclusiveness. The lord occupies a large part of the land and, accordingly, considers the state of affairs on the total manor as if the manor were his own state. Thus the lord can take the total situation of the manor as his own and will provide public goods because doing so is advantageous to him. On the other hand, small farmers can get a free ride on the public goods supplied by their lord.

This story explains the nature of incentive mechanisms concerning the supply of public goods. By getting a free ride, the small can take advantage of the large (Olson 1965; Olson and Zeckhauser 1966). However, if the relative weight of a hegemon declines, the provision of public goods will be increasingly deficient. The lord that has only a relatively small fraction of land will be less eager to provide public goods. Furthermore, in the case of provision of private goods, the large may exploit the small by exercising monopolistic power.

If we leave this hypothetical land and return to the present world economy, the decline in the relative power of the United States, as long as it is a selfish hegemon, will be a negative factor for the provision of international public goods. Is there a self-enforcing mechanism to compel nations to provide international public goods, or to commit to mutually beneficial rules without reneging?

In this way, the logic of collective action (Olson 1965) effectively explains the incentive of a large hegemon to supply an adequate amount of international public goods, and that shows small countries can exploit large ones by free riding on the supply of public goods.

Models of international trade, on the other hand, give different answers. In the case of trade in private goods, monopolistic (monopsonistic) power is relevant (Conybeare 1987), and the large exploit the small. In order to reconcile differences in predictions, we have to specify the situation precisely because the result depends crucially on whether we are talking about public goods or private goods.

To explain the present behavior of the United States and the world system, one needs to appeal to multiple explanations in addition to the two basic paradigms described above, that is, the theory of international public goods and the theory of monopolistic behavior in the private-goods domain. For example, I will appeal to the following explanations: the multiple, political, economic, and military goals of nations (Gowa 1989), the logic of two-level games (Putnam 1988), the analysis of rules and games (Ostrom 1991), and the concept of international organization as an epistemological community (Haas 1992; Keohane and Martin 1994).

In this paper I will develop the following arguments:

1. The negotiations needed for trade restrictions such as tariffs and quotas and those needed to create international public goods such as a security or trade regime are completely different kinds of games. The first is associated with private goods; the second is concerned with public goods. In the latter case, the small exploit the large. In the first case the large may exploit the small. The controversy between Conybeare (1987) and international public goods proponents can be better understood if we are aware of these distinctions. Moreover, the role of regionalism in trade currency and foreign-aid issues can be analyzed only in terms of this distinction between international private and public goods.

2. Using Nash equilibrium terminology, the trade restriction game can be a strategic-complements game, while the supply of public goods is always a strategic-substitutes game. In both cases, the Nash equilibrium outcomes will be worse than the Pareto optimal for negotiating countries.

3. At present, the United States is willing to exploit a part of its monopolistic power in trade even if it gives up its advantages of being a hegemon that supplies international public goods.

4. It is difficult to explain U.S. behavior without referring to domestic conflicts, as the theory of the two-level game emphasizes. It is barely possible to understand VERs and VIEs from merely the aggregate national economy point of view. The behavior of small nations must also be explained, in part, by the motives of vested interest groups, because tariffs and other import restrictions usually hurt overall national welfare.

5. It is misleading to treat many different situations equally with a

simple concept like public goods or hegemony. Agreeing on an environmental treaty, agreeing on regional economic integration, agreeing on a trade or monetary regime, and establishing an international organization to manage a regime all involve different procedures and different degrees of commitment. One has to be careful about what kind of commitment to action or inaction is made, and what kind of incentive mechanism exists to impose sanctions on violators of rules.

6. A dynamic framework is needed to account for the time-related distinctions among a "once and for all" mutual provision of public goods, international agreement or commitment, an emergence of a regime (Krasner 1982), and an establishment of an international organization. Concepts from dynamic and repeated games, such as reputation building and time consistency, help us understand the emergence process of an international regime.

This essay is organized as follows. Section 2 presents a brief account of the extent to which the United States, other advanced countries, and developing countries are either imposers or those being imposed upon. Sections 3 and 4 illustrate, with simple examples, the incentive structures for trade in private goods as well as for the provision of public goods among countries of different sizes in the world economy.

In section 5, I point out that many international conflicts and co-operation that have been analyzed in terms of international public goods, a hegemony, or a regime do differ in the dynamic properties and strategic structures of their political and economic processes. Based on the apparatus and considerations reviewed in these sections, we will discuss, in section 6, the question of how we can explain the recent behavior patterns of the United States as a declining hegemon. The last section discusses the role of regional arrangements that fortify or augment the function of a declining hegemon.

2 The Quantitative Significance of the United States in the World Economy

To begin with, let us briefly review quantitative indicators of the country's relative importance in the world economy. Table 10.1 indicates the share of output, and trade (export and import), for the United States, Japan, and several EC countries in the OECD for the decades since World War II. The shares of the United States in that magnitude de-

TABLE 10.1. Relative Shares of Nations

A. GDP

| | Share (GDP) | | | | |
	1960	1970	1980	1990	1993
U.S.	52.24%	46.02%	33.55%	32.77%	32.73%
Japan	4.51%	9.27%	13.12%	17.50%	22.04%
U.K.	7.35%	5.64%	6.66%	5.82%	4.92%
France	6.18%	6.50%	8.23%	7.14%	6.55%
Germany	7.88%	9.05%	10.81%	9.66%	9.99%
Italy	4.03%	4.89%	5.61%	6.54%	5.18%
OECD	100.00%	100.00%	100.00%	100.00%	100.00%
billion $	985.32	2,197.99	8,072.60	16,753.82	19,123.52

B. Trade

| | Share (export) | | | | | |
	1950	1960	1970	1980	1990	1994
U.S.	18.0%	18.0%	14.5%	11.9%	11.8%	12.2%
Japan	1.4%	3.5%	6.6%	6.9%	8.6%	9.4%
U.K.	11.1%	9.3%	6.6%	5.8%	5.6%	4.9%
France	5.4%	6.0%	6.1%	6.1%	6.5%	5.6%
Germany	3.5%	10.0%	11.7%	10.2%	12.3%	10.0%
Italy	2.1%	3.2%	4.5%	4.5%	5.1%	4.5%
World	100.0%	100.0%	100.0%	100.0%	100.0%	100.0%
(billion $)	57.1	114.6	293.4	1,895.6	3,334.4	4,201.3

| | Share (import) | | | | | |
	1950	1960	1970	1980	1990	1994
U.S.	16.3%	13.6%	13.7%	12.9%	15.0%	15.9%
Japan	1.6%	3.7%	6.1%	7.1%	6.8%	6.4%
U.K.	12.4%	10.8%	7.1%	5.8%	6.5%	5.2%
France	5.2%	5.2%	6.2%	6.8%	6.8%	5.3%
Germany	4.6%	8.5%	9.7%	9.5%	10.0%	8.6%
Italy	2.5%	3.9%	4.8%	5.1%	5.3%	3.9%
World	100.0%	100.0%	100.0%	100.0%	100.0%	100.0%
(billion $)	59.0	120.2	309.7	1,986.3	3,455.4	4,324.9

C. The Balance of Current Account

| | Current Account (in percent of GDP) | | | | |
	1960	1970	1980	1990	1994
U.S.	0.56	0.24	0.10	−1.70	−2.30
Japan	0.32	0.98	−1.00	1.20	2.80
U.K.	−1.00	1.60	1.30	−3.40	−0.10
France	n.a.	0.04	−0.60	−0.80	0.70
Germany	1.53	0.46	−1.60	3.20	−1.20
Italy	0.85	0.90	−2.30	−1.60	1.40

clined slightly, while that of Japan increased very rapidly. The table also indicates that ratio of the current account deficit to GDP.[3]

The degree of trade protection has also changed over time. With the success in trade negotiations, in particular with the Tokyo Round negotiations in GATT, tariff rates in many countries have declined during the postwar period. Tariff rates on trade in manufactures in 1974 averaged 40 percent. The average rate had come down to 7 to 10 percent even before the Tokyo Round multilateral trade negotiations during 1974–79 (World Bank 1987). The Tokyo Round tariff cuts made the average tariff rate on manufactures 6.0 percent in the EC, 5.4 percent in Japan (it made it even lower), and 4.9 percent in the United States (see table 10.2). The Uruguay Round negotiations that started in 1986 reinforced this trend, according to the World Bank (1995). By 1993, industrial countries had agreed on commitments on maximum tariffs for 99 percent of imports of manufactured goods and had rendered 20 to 43 percent of imports duty free. The trade-weighted average tariff for industrialized countries was cut by 40 percent, from 6.2 percent to 3.7 percent. The average tariff rate for developing countries was cut by 30 percent (see fig. 10.1).

In spite of the progress in tariffs that has made it appear that the world is moving in the direction of free trade, various nontariff barriers (NTBs) and "voluntary" restraints on exports have plagued the world economy. Table 10.3 shows the degree to which imports of textiles and

TABLE 10.2. Tariff Averages Before and After the Implementation of the Tokyo Round

Country or Country Group	Tariffs on Total Imports of Finished and Semifinished Manufactures		Tariffs on Imports from Developing Countries of Finished and Semifinished Manufactures	
	Pre-Tokyo	Post-Tokyo	Pre-Tokyo	Post-Tokyo
European community				
Weighted	8.3	6.0	8.9	6.7
Simple	9.4	6.6	8.5	5.8
Japan				
Weighted	10.0	5.4	10.0	6.8
Simple	10.8	6.4	11.0	6.7
United States				
Weighted	7.0	4.9	11.4	8.7
Simple	11.6	6.6	12.0	6.7

Source: Adapted from World Bank 1987.

Note: Weighted: Trade Weighted Average; Simple: Simple Average.

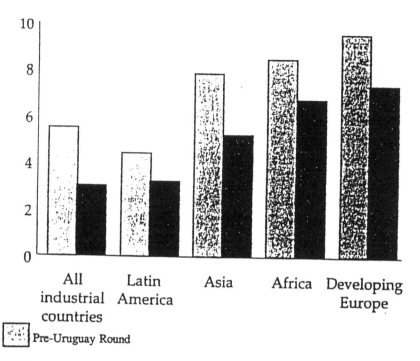

10

8

6

4

2

0

All
industrial
countries

Latin
America

Asia

Africa

Developing
Europe

▓ Pre-Uruguay Round

■ Post-Uruguay Round

Fig. 10.1. Average most-favored-nation tariffs in industrial countries on imports (in percentages)

TABLE 10.3. Imports Subject to Nontariff Barriers, 1983 (%)

| Country or Group | Textile and Clothing | | | Manufacturing | | |
	Total	From Industrial Countries	From Developing Countries	Total	From Industrial Countries	From Developing Countries
United States	57.0	31.1	64.0	17.1	16.5	18.6
European community	52.0	15.6	68.9	18.7	15.2	29.9
Japan	11.8	11.0	13.0	7.7	9.7	4.4

Source: Adapted from Goto 1989

clothing, and, for comparison, manufactured goods, were subject to nontariff barriers in 1983 (Goto 1989). Table 10.4 indicates the prevalence of multifiber arrangements (MFAs) and VERs (later VIEs should be counted), which the World Bank calls the "hard-core" nontrade barrier. Moreover, the degree that the United States relied on the nontariff barriers was increasing (table 10.5). Thus the world's pace toward free trade was substantially disturbed by nontransparent restrictive measures. In fact, a hegemon, the United States, and large advanced coun-

TABLE 10.4. Industrial Country Imports Subject to "Hard-Core" NTBs, 1981 and 1986 (percent)

	Source of Imports			
	Industrial Countries		Developing Countries	
Importer	1981	1986	1981	1986
EC	10	13	22	23
Japan	29	29	22	22
United States	9	15	14	17
All industrial countries	13	16	19	21

Source: Adapted from Goto 1989
Note: "Hard-core" NTBs represent the NTBs that are most likely to have significant restrictive effects. Hard-core NTBs include import prohibitions, quantitative restrictions, voluntary export restraints, variable levies, MFA restrictions, and nonautomatic licensing.

TABLE 10.5. Import Coverage Index of a Subgroup of NTBs Applied by Selected Industrial Market Economies, 1981–86 (1981 = 100)

	NTBs (Hard-Core)				
Importer	1982	1983	1984	1985	1986
Austria	100.0	100.0	100.0	100.0	99.3
Canada	108.6	106.0	108.4	112.1	121.3
EC[a]	105.7	110.9	113.9	120.8	118.3
Finland	102.5	102.5	102.5	101.0	101.0
Japan	99.2	99.2	99.2	99.2	98.6
New Zealand	100.0	100.0	100.0	92.6	86.1
Norway	101.1	96.4	94.4	86.6	85.3
Switzerland	100.4	100.4	100.8	100.8	100.8
United States	105.5	105.6	112.1	119.2	123.0
All	104.6	107.1	110.2	115.3	115.8

Source: Adapted from World Bank 1995
[a]Excluding Portugal and Spain

tries like Japan and the major European countries were often engaged in imposing these types of nontariff trade restrictions on their imports from developing countries. One of the major achievements of the Uruguay Round was to agree to eliminate voluntary export restraints within four years and the MFA within ten (World Bank 1995). This pledge may be too optimistic, but the success or failure in abolishing nontariff barriers is important because large countries exercise their monopoly power in the world market in the form of "sophisticated" or "modern" protectionism. This is the area in which one can observe the monopoly power that large countries have exercised, contrary to the common perception of public economics that large countries will serve the interest of small countries.

3 A Hegemon, Country Sizes, and the Supply of Public Goods

In this section and in the next, I will examine the strategic nature of international interdependence in a world where countries are of different sizes. I will start with the case of public goods, which was the principal theme in the theory of the logic of collective action.

Consider a situation already exemplified by the parable of a manor. A large participant, the lord, is greatly affected by the supply of public goods and, accordingly, motivated to take responsibility of supplying public goods. Even a selfish lord takes care of necessary irrigation or defense. However, it does not always follow that he will be the privileged member (group) who provides a sufficient amount of public goods. Since small farmers are tempted to free ride, the public goods produced are likely to be short of the most desired amount. A similar international situation can be analyzed by the following analytical model. (For a discussion of the calculus of public goods, see Sandler 1992.)

Consider a two-country world in which good 1 is a private good and good 2 is a public good. The public good has, like environment or safety, the nature of nonrivalry and nonexclusiveness. Each citizen and, accordingly, nation contributes a certain amount of income to the supply of international public goods. The hegemon has the population (normalized by the world population) of $1 - p$, and the smaller country, the periphery, has the population of p.

Suppose the utility of a representative individual in the two countries is respectively

$$c_1^{2/3} c_2^{1/3} \quad \text{and} \quad c_1^{2/3} c_2^{1/3}, \tag{1}$$

where c_1, c_2 are respectively consumption of private goods and consumption of public goods by the citizen of the hegemon, and c_1^*, c_2^* are consumption of private goods and consumption of public goods by the citizen of the periphery country.[4]

To each individual, a unit of income is given like manna in the form of private good 1, a part of which she consumes as good 1, and the rest of which she contributes to the world community to provide public goods. (The effect of the difference in wealth, or income, will be discussed later.) Thus,

$$c_1 + x_2 = 1, \qquad c_1^* + x_2^* = 1. \tag{2}$$

Here x_2 and x_2^* are the per capita contributions of citizens in the two countries. The world per capita supply of the public good is assumed to be the weighted sum of these contributions:

$$c_2 = c_2^* = (1 - \varepsilon)x_2 + \varepsilon x_2^*. \tag{3}$$

The governments collect these contributions equally from individuals. They are assumed to play strategically under the assumption that the amount of the contributions of the periphery country is given.

The Nash solution in this public-goods game is given by the interaction of the reaction curves of the two countries. One can derive the reaction curve of each country in terms of the contributions. By maximizing utility (1), given the budget constraint (2) and public goods provision (3), and given the value of x or x^* of the other country, we obtain as country 1's reaction curve and country 2's reaction curve

$$x_2 = \frac{1}{3} - \frac{2\theta}{3} x_2^*, \quad \text{and} \quad x_2^* = \frac{1}{3} - \frac{2}{3\theta} x_2, \tag{4}$$

where θ is defined by $\theta \equiv \varepsilon/(1 - \varepsilon)$, with $\varepsilon < 1$, $0 < \theta < 1$. A smaller value of ε corresponds to a smaller value of θ, that is, a larger relative size of the hegemon.

Figure 10.2 illustrates these reaction curves. If ε and accordingly θ are small, the reaction curve of the hegemon does not diverge from the optimal provision of the public good $x_2 = 1/3$. In fact one can easily ascertain that the contract curve (cooperative solution) lies on a curve that passes through point $(1/3, 1/3)$. On the other hand, when ε and θ are small, the reaction curve of the smaller country diverges much from the optimal provision $x_2^* = 1/3$. The internal solution for the Nash equilibrium is given by $x_2 = (3 - 2\theta)/5$ and $x_2^* = (3 - 2\theta)/5$. When the periphery

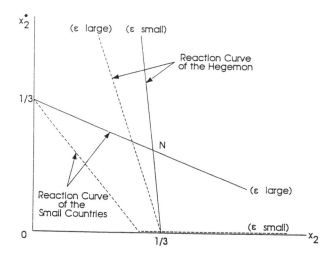

Fig. 10.2.   Reaction curves of the hegemon and a smaller country

country is so small such that $\theta \leqq 2/3$, or $\varepsilon \leqq 2/5$, the equilibrium strategy of the periphery country is $x_2^* = 0$, or to stop contributing completely. As is indicated in the diagram, the small can exploit the large in this analysis of the public goods.

Essentially, this approach was taken by Olson 1965 and in particular by Olson and Zeckhauser 1966, which draws a diagram like figure 10.2. "There is a systematic tendency for 'exploitation' of the great by the small" (Olson 1965, 29). Few seem to be aware of the fact that this exploitation property stems from the nature of public good. The exploitation by the small no longer holds in the case of private goods, as will be shown in the next section.

One can extend this approach to a scenario in which many small countries coexist with a large hegemon. Suppose that a small country occupies a fraction ε of the world economy, but that there are n small countries. Accordingly, the hegemon occupies the proportion $(1 - n\varepsilon)$ of the world. The hegemon's reaction function does not change except that θ is now defined as $n\varepsilon/(1 - n\varepsilon)$. Reaction functions of the hegemon and the smaller countries are modified. That is, in the simplest

$$x_2 = \frac{1}{2n + 1} - \frac{2\theta}{(2n + 1)}\, x_2^*, \qquad x_2^* = \frac{1}{2n + 1} - \frac{2}{(2n + 1)\theta}\, x_2. \qquad (5)$$

The behavior of larger periphery countries will diverge from optimal behavior, and that of smaller countries will diverge even further down-

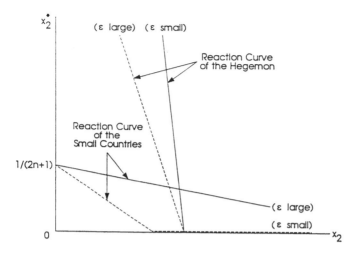

Fig. 10.3. Divergence of the hegemon and small countries reaction curves from optimal behavior

ward (fig. 10.3). The resulting supply of public goods falls short of the optimal, and smaller countries enjoy free-rider positions.

The Nash equilibrium supply of public goods is given by

$$x_2 = \left\{ \frac{1}{2n + 1} - \frac{2\theta}{(2n + 1)^2} \right\} \Big/ \left\{ 1 - \frac{4}{(2n + 1)^2} \right\},$$

$$x_2^* = \left\{ \frac{1}{2n + 1} - \frac{2}{(2n + 1)^2\theta} \right\} \Big/ \left\{ 1 - \frac{4}{(2n + 1)^2} \right\}. \tag{6}$$

One can see that the hegemon increases its contribution as its selective population in the world increases (θ decreases), and that peripheries reduce their contribution as θ decreases. An increase in the number of small countries n increases keeping θ constant; the contribution by the hegemon increases and the contributions by small countries decreases. All are expected from the "exploitation by the small" hypothesis. Incidentally, the per capita public good is expressed as

$$(1 - n\varepsilon)x_2 + n\varepsilon x_2^* = \left\{ \frac{1}{2n + 1} - \frac{2}{(2n + 1)^2} \right\} \Big/ \left\{ 1 - \frac{4}{(2n + 1)^2} \right\} \tag{7}$$

and a decreasing faction of the number of small countries.

I have been concerned thus far with countries of various sizes but have assumed that incomes are identical. The world consists of countries with different income levels among which burden sharing problems can be serious. Thus, let us introduce different levels of income to the case of two countries — extension to a many-country case would be straightforward. Let the hegemon receive per capita income y and the other country receive per capita income y^*. I will assume $y > y^*$ for convenience, but this assumption is not essential. Equation (2) will become

$$c_1 + x_2 = y, \qquad c_1^* + x_2^* = y^*. \tag{2a}$$

The resulting reaction functions are

$$x_2 = \frac{y}{3} - \frac{2\theta}{3} x_2^*, \qquad x_2^* = \frac{y^*}{3} - \frac{2}{3\theta} x_2. \tag{4a}$$

In terms of figures 10.2 and 10.3, in this case the reaction curve of the hegemon starts from $y/3$ instead of $1/3$, and that of the other country starts from $y^*/3$ instead of $1/3$. From this one can conclude that a large country tends to spend a larger proportion of its income for international public goods than does a small country. This justifies the common procedure of testing the Olson-Zeckhauser hypothesis by checking whether a large country spends more proportionately on military expenditures, as with income rises.

4 The Size of Countries in a Model of Tariffs

The story of the last section will be dramatically reversed if one considers the situation associated with trade of private goods (instead of public goods) and tariff wars. The nature of strategic interdependence changes from strategic substitutes to strategic complements (Bulow, Geneakopolos, and Klemperer 1985). Also, the exploitation of the large by the small becomes the exploitation of the small by the large.

Consider the simplest two-country Ricardian model where labor is the only factor of production. In production of two goods, 1 and 2, the larger country (hegemon) has input coefficients a_1, a_2; the smaller country has input coefficients a_1^*, a_2^*. The larger country has a comparative advantage in producing good 1 so that $a_1/a_2 < a_1^*/a_2^*$. The two countries have a labor endowment, L and L^*, and the larger country is large enough to warrant

$$\max \left(\frac{L}{a_1}, \frac{L}{a_2} \right) > \max \left(\frac{L^*}{a_1^*}, \frac{L^*}{a_2^*} \right).$$

(Here L is assumed to be large enough. Instead, one could interpret the first country as being the more productive country, so that either a_1 or a_2 is small enough to satisfy the inequality.) Finally, the utility function of the representative consumer is expressed as an identical function of per capita consumption c_1, c_2, and c_1^*, c_2^*, or $U(c_1,c_2)$ and $U(c_1^*,c_2^*)$. Both governments are assumed to conduct their tariff policies in such a way as to maximize the utility of the representative consumer.[5]

The offer curves for this model are shown in figure 10.4. The case illustrated in figure 10.4 is one in which the hegemon is so large that the smaller country's offer curve intersects with that of the hegemon on the straight line (with slope a_1/a_2) through the origin. The smaller country satisfies the definition of a "small country" and thus cannot take advantage of the elasticity of the hegemon's offer curve. The hegemon can, on the other hand, impose an optimal tariff to exploit its monopolistic power in export, or monopsonistic power in import, in such a way that its trade indifference curve will be tangent to the offer curve of the smaller country, that is, at T.

If the size of the smaller country is very small, the gain accrued to the hegemon from imposing the optimal tariff is also small. The gain in terms of trade does not bring substantial welfare gain because the

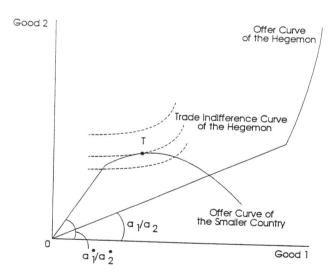

Fig. 10.4.   Offer curves of a large hegemon and smaller countries

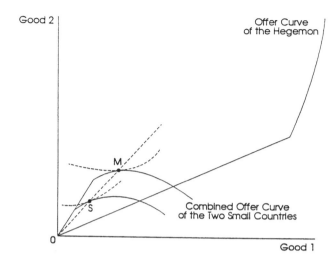

Fig. 10.5. Offer curves of the hegemon when imposing the optimal tariff, compared with those of smaller countries

amount of trade is limited (see point S in fig. 10.5). China would not gain much from imposing tariffs on imports from Monaco. The gain from a tariff is larger if the smaller country has some magnitude in the world economy (see point M).

The two-country assumption can now be relaxed. Suppose there is one hegemon and n smaller countries. Point M of figure 10.5 also illustrates the case in which $n = 2$ with two identical countries whose offer curves go through S. There is no incentive for smaller countries to impose tariffs on imports, since they cannot change the terms of trade offered by the hegemon, and, therefore, the same utility level as point M on the combined offer curve can be enjoyed by the hegemon, while the smaller countries are both left at point S.

The strategic situation can be depicted by reaction curves in the space of the tariff rate of the hegemon t and that of the smaller country (or countries) t^* (fig. 10.6). In this Ricardian situation the reaction curve of the smaller country (or countries) coincides with the horizontal axis. The reaction curve of the hegemon starts upward from the optimal tariff $\hat{t}$. Therefore, the Nash solution N is the combination $(\hat{t}, 0)$, which coincides with the von Stackelberg solution with the hegemon as the leader. The smaller country (or countries) has no incentive to be a leader.

It is well known that when the two (or more than two) countries have similar size, more complex situations emerge in which a tariff by a single country triggers retaliation by the other. Here the reaction curve

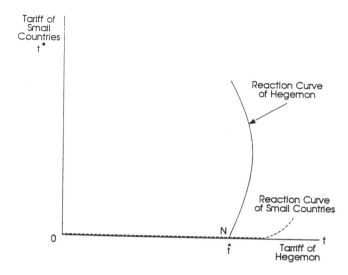

Fig. 10.6.   Reaction curves in the space of the tariff rate of the hegemon
and that of the smaller country

may take the property of strategic complements rather than that of strategic substitutes (Bulow, Geneakopolos, and Klemperer 1985). The case of strategic complements, the case in which both reaction curves are upward sloping, arises when the tariff rate of a foreign country triggers a rise in the tariff in the home country.

In this situation concerning private goods and tariffs, a large country is motivated to be a von Stackelberg leader and to exploit small countries. In a trade of goods situation with tariffs as instruments, the hegemon will thus be able to manipulate the terms of trade to its advantage. Therefore, we may say, contrary to Olson's expression, "The large exploit the small." If this case is generalized to one in which there is a productivity difference such that $a_1 \ll a_1^*$, and/or $a_2 \ll a_2^*$ ($\ll$ indicates a large difference), then it is possible to say, "The rich exploit the poor."

In the Heckscher-Ohlin model with multiple mobile factors of production as well in the Viner model with an immobile factor of production, the offer curve of a large country no longer has an exactly linear segment. Still, a large country has an almost linear segment, and our strategic results will hold without qualitative modifications.

In a more modern version of international trade theory with increasing returns and with the oligopolistic situation, a similar situation will emerge. The only difference is that the case of strategic substitutes usually takes place. As demonstrated by Gros (1987), and developed by Krugman (1991), the reaction function of a large country starts with a certain tariff level and then becomes a declining function of the tariff rates of smaller countries (see also Goto and Hamada 1994).

Conybeare (1987) claims that trade issues are primarily the benefit and cost associated with private goods and relative prices. The logic of collective action ceases to hold there, and the large may exploit the small, as is easily understood from the above discussions. We will discuss later why, in the real world, large countries do not necessarily impose, or do not threaten to impose, high duties on the products of small countries.

On the other hand, agreeing on a rule with spillover clauses such as the most favored nation (MFN) clause, establishing a free-trade regime like the GATT, and building an institution like the WTO is a process of creating public goods. Rules and institutions have externalities and possess the nature of public goods, as will be discussed below. The process for agreeing on a rule of the game is a different kind of game than the game that is played by tariffs, quotas, and nontrade barriers. The controversy between proponents of the hegemonic stability approach and proponents of the trade-taxing game (Conybeare 1987) will be at least clarified, and even resolved, by recognizing the distinction between the creation of public goods and the interplay of strategic instruments in the game that involves private goods.

5 Cooperation, Regimes, International Organizations, and Public Goods

The strategic interaction of nations can have many different patterns from the two simplest abstract examples we have studied above. The first example is extreme in that it is concerned with a pure public good that is completely nonexclusive and nonrival consumption; the second is extreme in that the strategy is limited to tariffs. Many conceptual issues need to be clarified in order to apply these analytical tools to real issues.

In international political economy, the words *international public goods* are used quite ambiguously, resulting in many different meanings. Whenever one hears the words international public goods, their exact meaning should be scrutinized. Often the use of the concept of public goods may be ultimately justified, but it may refer to many varied entities or situations, from concrete goods or environment, to conventions that countries find useful to follow, to agreements with or without sanctions against their breach, or to the functioning of an international institution that manages public goods.

First, it is necessary to distinguish the pure public good, whose consumption is nonexclusive and nonrival, from the "club" good, whose consumption can be exclusive and competitive. The environment is probably an example of the first, and unified currency for a region or a free-trade area are both examples of the second. However, there is always a gray area in this distinction. For example, a unified currency for a region benefits primarily the residents in the region, but it also has positive externalities or spillover effects to people outside the currency union by reducing their calculation and transaction costs. Defense can be considered as a club good for an alliance. However, to the extent that externalities or nonmember nations are substantial, it can assume the nature of an international public good.

The incentive mechanism for a public good studied in section 3 is modified if the good is a "club good." In addition to examining whether a scheme supplies the right amount of public goods, we need to ask whether there is an incentive scheme to keep the number of club members optimal.

Second, it is important to identify how the cost of providing an international public good is shared. In most cases, the cost is paid in terms of private (nonpublic) goods or services. To provide security, countries fund military budgets. To clean the air and produce cars better for the environment, countries add additional materials and labor.

However, in other cases, commitments to actions and, particularly, commitments to inactions constitute the substance of creating public goods. To clean the air, we may reduce the amount of driving; to clean water, we may restrict polluting industrial activities; and to protect the ocean, we may restrict fishing. In the case of the international monetary regime, the commitment to intervene, or the commitment not to intervene, in the exchange market determines the choice of a regime between the fixed and the flexible exchange rate. With respect to the trade regime, the commitment to inactions, that is, not to impose tariffs, is essential to the free-trade regime.[6]

Therefore, international public goods can now be classified into the following categories: (i) pure public goods, like defense and the environment, which are produced by sacrificing some private goods of member nations, and which are nonexclusive and nonrivalry; (ii) club goods, like the monetary benefit of a currency union, which can be enjoyed by participants who pay the cost but cannot be fully exclusive; (iii) unilateral or mutual commitments for certain actions or inactions; (iv) a combination of any of the above three elements that is organized in such a way as can be called a regime or an order; and (v) the services of international institutions that manage regimes.

i Pure Public Goods

Safety from a (possible) common enemy is certainly a public good. In order to attain the service of this public good, nations sacrifice a part of goods and services. The service from defense usually satisfies the nature of inexclusiveness and nonrivalry. Here the logic of collective action (Olson 1965; Olson and Zeckhauser 1966) is applicable. Similarly, environmental activities such as protection against pollution, congestion, or preservation of species should belong in this category. In this case, as is illustrated above, a large country tends to bear more of the burden of producing public goods. The small exploit the large.

ii Club Goods

Regional economic cooperation, regional economic integration, and regional currency integration are typical international club goods. A military alliance in a particular region can partially be a club good. Thus, the distinction between the pure public good and the club good can be subtle. Nevertheless, it seems to be useful to discuss regional trade and monetary cooperations in this category of club goods.

First, a participating country gives up certain private goods in order to participate in regional cooperation or integration. In the case of a regional free-trade area or customs union, a country gives up the right to impose tariffs (often above a certain rate) on the goods from the member of the free-trade area and, in the case of a customs union, in addition the right to choose freely the rate of a tariff to the rest of the world. Once collective actions generate a public benefit, the benefit will be enjoyed mainly by participating members. In the case of the creation of a free-trade area or a custom union, the spillover effects to the rest of the world are negative (e.g., Goto and Hamada 1994). Trade is created within the area, but trade is diverted from the rest of the world according to Viner's "trade diversion effect." This implies that if the decisions are left to the initiative of individual nations, too many, as well as too large, customs unions or free-trade areas will be created (see, e.g., Krugman 1984).

In the case of a monetary unification or close exchange rate coordination, the cost for a country is its sacrifice in stabilization policy. Countries give up the merit of domestic macroeconomic stabilization to attain stability or predictability in exchange rates. The sacrifice is in private goods in terms of the income losses due to restricted macroeconomic policies. The potential gains are public goods because the benefit of unified currencies is common to all the participating nations. Some benefits even extend to the rest of the world. In contrast to customs unions and free-trade areas, the spillover effect is positive in the case of a currency union or currency unification. If European currency is unified, North Americans need not convert money while traveling, nor prepare for the currency risks among European currencies. Therefore, there will be too few currency unions, or currency unions will become too small, if their formation is left to national initiatives. (See, for its political-economy aspect, Hamada 1987; Hamada and Porteous 1992.)

The time profile of benefits and costs has to be considered as well. The economic cost of forgoing stabilization policy is immediate. On the other hand, the benefit from stable or fixed exchange rates, as well as the benefit from a unified currency, will come years after. Therefore, it is difficult to reach an agreement for stable exchange rates and a unified currency. The recent European monetary turmoil, which began in 1992 and occurred just before the planned target date for integration, illustrates the difficulties involved in monetary unification.[7]

iii Commitments of Participants to Actions or Inactions

In many of the above examples, countries do not just provide private goods or public goods for a collective action. They promise or commit themselves to engage in certain actions or to refrain from them. In a free-trade area, member countries commit themselves not to impose tariffs on the goods from member countries; in a customs union, member countries do the same and, in addition, they commit to impose identical rates of tariffs on the goods from nonmember countries.

During the formation of a currency union, countries promise that they will intervene in the exchange rate market to keep their currencies at an agreed-upon exchange rate or within an agreed-upon range. The flexible exchange rate is the regime in which countries promise that they will *not* intervene in the exchange rate market. This is therefore often called a "nonsystem."

In terms of a dynamic game framework, two questions are important. First, is the commitment or promise credible? The Bretton Woods Regime collapsed in 1971 because the credibility of the vehicle currency was in doubt. One of the reasons for the success of the monetary union of East and West Germany was that it was much more credible in advance than in the case of the European union. Second, does the presence of a hegemon help credibility? The answer to this is probably affirmative. Until the middle of the 1960s, the United States was the dominant economic power, and, accordingly, the commitment by the United States was taken with more credibility. It has taken the initiative to commit to free trade and the fixed exchange rate regime, and it seldom showed any sign of reneging on its commitment. Now that the relative importance of the United States has declined in the world, the country may not necessarily have sufficient incentive to play the role of world leader, that is, to provide an adequate amount of international public goods. Nor do other countries trust completely the commitment of the United States to serve as a leader. This leaves the world in an age of uncertainty.

iv International Regimes

The definition of an international regime is frequently debated by political scientists and economists. Cooper 1975 defines a regime as a particular set of rules and conventions governing monetary and financial relations between countries. *Regime* is, in a sense, more general than *system* or *order* because the latter imply systematic and consistent rules and conventions. *Regime* is distinguished from *agreement* because one does not regard a once-and-for-all, ad hoc international agreement as a regime. The words *regime* and *rules* or *conventions* suggest a situation where agents themselves interact with each other repeatedly following specific patterns of behavior.

Some political scientists define a regime in a more strict fashion. Many authors in Krasner 1982a take a consensus view: A regime is "a set of implicit or explicit principles, norms, rules, and decision-making procedures around which actors' expectations converge in a given area of international relations." Here principles are defined as "beliefs of fact, causations, and rectitude," and norms are "specific prescriptions or proscriptions for action." Decision-making procedures are "prevailing practices for making and implementing collective choice" (Krasner 1982a, 2). The role of expectations is emphasized.

To understand the importance of expectations, we should pay attention to the dynamic nature of the role of international agreements, and regimes should be considered.[8] If countries agree on a certain set of rules, it is usually under situations in which economic activities can be repeated following these rules. Commitment to action or inaction already presumes some sequential or repeated behavior, and it is particularly reflected in the definition. In other words, the situation is usually that of a sequential game or repeated game. If nations precommit to their behavior in the future, trust others' commitments, and, in fact, deliver on their commitments, then the world will proceed without serious problems. If a country does renege its commitment, then the situation will become difficult if not more interesting.

In the above definition, the phrase "expectations converge" is an addition to the conventional definition of a regime. To economists, this phrase sounds vague. Do they talk about the convergence of an entity of expectations? Do they converge over time or across countries? If there is no common knowledge among nations, how can they find a way to learn? Agreement is only the first step in the learning process. If I take a position more sympathetic to political science, they probably mean the following. People have expectations about what will be going on, and the expectations are converging. Therefore, the regime, according to this definition, essentially entails a rational-expectations equilibrium. Not only is an agreement made, but agents expect that other parties will follow the rules. A hegemon definitely helps to build a regime. The role of common knowledge is important. If countries share common causal knowledge, they will find it much easier to cooperate or coordinate economic policies (Haas 1992). They will build an epistemic community, "a network of professionals with recognized expertise and competence in a particular domain and authorities claiming policy-relevant knowledge within that domain or issue area" (Haas 1992). If these professionals can help create common knowledge on the economic mechanism, obstacles against coordination will be moderated. (For the obstacles in the world where perception of the model is different, see Frankel and Rockett 1988.) The common expectations on the part of the public, which a regime requires, will emerge more easily.

It is important not to be too optimistic, however. First, in economic issues, specialists do not always agree on what is policy-related knowledge (Frankel and Rockett 1988). Second, if they agree on common knowledge, countries and/or groups within a country may have conflicts of interest among them. Under certain situations, agreement or the understanding of a regime should be left "incomplete" (Keohane and Martin 1994), and the ambiguity from incomplete contracts may help to bind participants in a regime.[9]

The way to sustain the situation of repeated games is the trigger strategy. Sanctioning against the reneging is the means to achieve the mutually beneficial results. The low rate of time discount helps to sustain the equilibrium. In a time of peace, when the discount rate is low, this can be done more easily.

Ostrom (1991) clearly illustrates this for a "common-pool resource" (CPR). CPR is like a lake where the long-run public interest to conserve fish conflicts with the private interest to catch fish now. Most environmental problems belong to this category. Ostrom points out not only the need for coordination, but traces the emergence of coordination. She considers the situation to be the Kreps finitely repeated game in which one of the sequential equilibria is a desirable solution. "It will pay one player to signal to other players an intention to cooperate, in the hope that they will reciprocate for a series of mutually productive plays" (Ostrom 1991, 43). In order for the commitments made by players to be credible, either external coercion is needed, or some self-organized mechanism of mutual monitoring should evolve. Almost all of Ostrom's discussions can be translated to the question of an international regime. General implications would be that the existence of a hegemon helps, but that an appropriate regime may emerge in a synergic manner if agents are patient enough.

In the time of crisis, one becomes impatient. At this time, some political leadership, rather than rules or a regime, is needed for discretion (Jackson 1991). The savior at the crisis stressed by Kindleberger can be interpreted by this need. "Rules are desirable on trend. In crisis the need is for decision" (Kindleberger 1988, 139). Often a crisis leads to a drastic change of the regime (Hamada 1985). Since the present payoffs become intolerable, participants are willing to agree on a new rule that is not completely satisfactory at ordinary times.

When the United States was, by itself, a privileged country that could provide sufficient public goods independently, the United States could enjoy the stability of a free-trade regime. It hardly had any intention to break the rules. The recent selfish or regime-eroding U.S. attitude may be traced to its lack of patience. In other words, its political, if not economic, discount rate might have become higher in the disturbing storm.[10]

v International Organizations

Building an international organization is also a subject of the calculus of participation. Nations agree to build an institution as long as the merit of building the institution exceeds the cost of creating it. The logic of collective action works in this case as well. When the positive spillover or externalities stemming from international organizations exist, as is often the case with the outset of an organization, the pace of formation of international organizations by voluntary national initiatives can be considered to be short of the desirable pace. Through an international organization, monitoring national activities, giving sanctions against internationally illegal activities, and accumulating knowledge for future prospects become easier. In many cases, international organizations will facilitate the creation of an environment in which commitments by nations become more credible.

Keohane and Martin (1994) ask why and under what circumstances countries are willing to delegate their functions to an international organization. Their discussion focuses on information and the distribution of welfare. By establishing an international organization, countries can improve the flow of information and can thus create the critical information required for the coordination of policies. When there are multiple equilibria, the sharing of information is crucially important to choose the best among these equilibria. The international organization is an epistemological community (Haas 1992). Even in an international organization, some agreements have to remain "incomplete contracts." To keep fairness among members in case of an unforeseen contingency, the linkage among many issues is useful (c.f. Gowa 1989). The interaction between delegating issues to an international organization and delegating them to domestic politics is systematically described in Keohane and Martin 1994.

Economists often consider this issue from a somewhat different angle. After an international organization is established, it begins behaving more or less independently.[11] Indeed, some officials of the institution are from member countries and advocate policies of their home countries, but the secretariat of an institution will develop and start developing independent ideas and then preferences. Delegation is considered as a common agency problem, in which many countries, as principals, delegate a task to an international organization. Economists are concerned with the principal-agent relationship in this delegation (Grossman and Helpman 1994). They ask how the contract between countries and the international organization can be written efficiently and how possible conflicts of interest can be resolved among principals who do not necessarily possess a common goal.

In this respect, bureaucracy is a necessary ingredient of an international organization. It is thus quite possible that an international organization may acquire, in time, the rigidity, in addition to the information advantages, of a bureaucracy and, therefore, resist changes in the policy of the institution that become necessary when external conditions change. Bureaucracy may by itself "lock in" activities of the organization. Thus it becomes a serious task to build some possible incentive structure for the institution for participating nations to avoid the incidence of Parkinson's Law, while keeping the useful functions of an international organization. It is difficult as well as important.

6 Can We Explain the Symptoms of a Declining Hegemon?

Sections 3 and 4 have shown two completely different implications for the effects of country size depending on whether the issue involves private goods or public goods. Given these possibly opposing effects, can we explain typical phenomena of the present international order as symptoms of a "selfish" or rational declining hegemon?

First, the logic of collective action seems to explain why the United States recently adopted protectionistic policies by the imposing VERs and VIEs as well as by its threats to impose them. Since the relative economic and political weight of the United States is declining, as shown in section 2, one may argue that U.S. commitment to the responsibility of keeping a regime of free trade, which has the public-good character, has also declined. The "new" protectionism measures are virtually a breach of the international economic order and erode the reputation of the United States. However, the United States seems to prefer reaping the instantaneous gains that accrue in the private-good domain.

According to the model explained in section 4, a large country has, in general, incentives to appeal to the optimal tariff in the trade-negotiating game. But it may have another argument in its utility function. The United States practiced free-trade policy presumably because the merit of providing a free-trade regime and building a regime of *pax americana* was more important to the U.S. government than realizing the fruits of monopolistic tariffs. The benefit from public goods was supposedly more important than the opportunity cost in terms of private goods. Therefore, if the United States has recently shown reluctance to bear the major burden of providing international public goods, this would imply some of the following factors.

The relative economic and political magnitude of the United States has recently declined. The United States no longer serves as the police for the world and, therefore, can hardly be a guardian of world peace or the environment, or be meddlesome in many economic and political conflicts around the world. On the other hand, neither Germany nor Japan is fully ready to assume the leadership role and begin *pax germanica* or *pax japonica*.

Second, after the end of the Cold War, defense has lost some of its importance as an international public good. Therefore, it is no longer of eminent priority for the United States to provide the free-trade regime as a means of sustaining the military stability under U.S. initiative.

Incidentally, there has been a change in the strategic structure of the defense expenditure game since the end of the Cold War. When the Communist bloc was considered to be the threatening enemy of the Western bloc, led by the United States, the public-good nature of defense expenditure could be analyzed by the Olson-Zeckhauser apparatus. Small countries could take advantage of the free-ride possibility, and the United States bore the burden more than proportionately. Defense was certainly public "goods" for the Western bloc.

Since the Cold War ended, defense expenditures are spent in order to defend each country from other countries. The loss to any nation can be considered to depend roughly on the difference between the average holding of weapons of a potential adversary nation and the holding of weapons of the particular nation. Under this situation, instead of trying to free ride, players try to accumulate weapons in order to beat their neighbors. The structure of the Nash game changed from that of strategic substitutes to that of strategic complements after the collapse of the Berlin Wall. (For these concepts, see Bulow, Geneakopolos, and Klemperer 1985; and for the application for strategic structure, see Hamada 1995.) Under the situation of strategic substitutes a country's defense expenditure discourages the other's expenditures; in other words, it creates free-riding incentives. Under strategic complements, a country's defense expenditures escalates the other's—this generates a situation similar to a different type of prisoners' dilemma from that under the Cold War. Here the undesirable situation is excessive armament of countries. Defense loses its public-goods aspect and assumes the public "bads" nature. Not only large countries, but also small countries, attempt to accumulate more weapons than are necessary. In contrast to the Olson-Zeckhauser result, a small country may spend a greater proportion of its income on defense than a large country. Acquisition of munitions in East and Southeast Asia may be seen as an example of the strategic-complements structure.

Third, the role of the discount rate is important. Many interventions by the United States into the rules of free trade make one suspect that the U.S. national discount rate has increased. In the face of many internal problems, Americans no longer seem to be patient enough, at least in the political economic sense, to sacrifice present gains in order to sustain the free-trade regime for the future benefit.

The consideration of the multiplicity of public goods and the linkage of trade issues to political public goods like defense (Gowa 1989; Keohane and Martin 1994) also help to explain the present phenomena. The temporary gain from new protectionism is one dimensional, all measured in present economic gains. However, there are many kinds of public goods that the United States provides as a hegemon: military security, trade regimes, investment regimes, protection of intellectual-property rights, an international monetary system, and so forth. Even though material benefits from each international public good are not substantial, the consideration of a set of public goods, or a particular combination such as trade and security, could have been sufficient to make the United States behave well in trade issues. Now that the relative size of the United States has declined and that the external environment for security issues has changed because of the collapse of the Berlin Wall, then the United States may prefer a present gain.

Basically, however, the above theories can fully explain neither the trade barriers in small countries nor the new protectionism in developed countries including the hegemon, the United States. The theories fail to explain the prevalence of protection in many small developing countries, because, according to trade theory, small countries do not gain by tariffs or quotas (with the possible exception of dynamic infant industry effect). If a country is small in economic scale, it cannot change the world terms of trade, and, accordingly, its national income cannot be increased from trade restrictions. Only when the layers of conflict discussed in two-level games are introduced will it be possible to explain the protectionistic practices of small countries.

The above theories, based on the "Third Image" level (Gowa 1994), fail to explain the prevalence of new protectionism, that is, the prevalence of commodity arrangements like MFAs, VERs, and VIEs by the initiative of advanced countries. The United States is instrumental in pursuing the last two arrangements. These arrangements usually decrease incomes of advanced countries.[12] In the first two cases, exporting countries are asked to limit the amount of export. In contrast to the import restrictions by advanced countries, tariff revenues and the rent from quotas will accrue to self-restricting exporting countries rather than to protectionistic importing countries. The national income as well as the national welfare of the country that requests such restrictive devices will decline.

Therefore, unless one refers to conflict of interest among domestic groups, it is hard to explain the motives for these arrangements of new protectionism. For the case of the VIEs again, the national welfare of the exporting country that requests such an arrangement will decline. In other words, if the United States imposes quotas on Japan's imports of American cars, the loss to American consumers of cars usually exceeds the gain in profits to American automakers.

As figure 10.4 illustrates, in terms of national interest, small countries have little incentive to take the protectionistic policy. In reality, however, many developing countries have high duties. Also, a large country does not impose monopolistic tariffs. The United States as a nation will lose if it asks its trading partners to adopt the VERs. In reality the United States insists that its trading partners agree on the VERs. (The VIEs also distort the offer curve, and national welfare of the partner country deteriorates. VERs make the partner choose a preferable point on the original offer curve, but VIEs force it to choose an inferior point.) These examples show that nations are not negotiating for their well-defined, unique, "national" interest.

To repeat, only by introducing the element of domestic conflict into the analysis of international economic negotiations (Putnam 1988; Evans, Jacobson, and Putnam 1993; Grossman and Helpman 1994), in other words, only by combining the "Second Image" approach with the "Third Image" approach, if we extend Gowa's (1989) theory, can one fully account for the present state of international political economy. Interest groups in a domestic economy can exert influence strong enough to realize an economic outcome unfavorable to the national economy. Of course, if a nation can have a nonmyopic perspective, opposing groups may reach some reconciliation for the benefit of national income. For this purpose as well, a relatively calm economic and political environment that leads to more (time) patient group behavior will be helpful.

The degree to which the two-level approach is indispensable for explaining the conditions of the present world differs from topic to topic. Defense is the area where national interests are more easily, if not completely, defined than in other areas. For issues in which the interests of various groups within a country differ greatly, the layers of interests at the international and at the domestic level are important. First, trade issues and the choice of a trade regime are the most relevant areas for the two-level concept because strong conflicts of interest exist concerning trade liberalization between producers and consumers, and between exporters and importers. Here the interests of groups interact like cross fire over the ocean. For example, Japanese automobile makers have much in common with American consumers, and American farmers have much in common with Japanese consumers. Producers' interests tend to be more than proportionately represented in the political process. This asymmetry drives the world to the protectionistic situation as a prisoners' dilemma outcome. Second, domestic conflicts of interest certainly affect international cooperation in environmental protection, but to a lesser degree. Since environmental protection exhibits external economies, national negotiations may lead to an outcome short of sufficient preservation. Therefore, the existence of environmental pressure groups in each country will help the international Nash equilibrium approach the Pareto optimal situation. Conversely, strong opposition from industrial groups may deter a desirable international environmental agreement.

Third, in international monetary coordination, the effect differences in the interests of the treasury, central bank, and industrial circles (Putnam 1988; Henning 1994) are more subtle than in trade. In this case, the balance of power between the treasury department (ministry of finance in some countries) and the central bank could affect the degree of monetary coordination and the choice of the monetary regimes. Putnam 1988 describes how the balance of influence between the German Finance Ministry and Bundesbank was affected in favor of the ministry's expansionary position when international coordination of macroeconomic policies after the Bonn Summit of 1978, when the "locomotive" theory of international coordination was coined. One of the reasons Japan's economy fell into a prolonged recession could be traced to the continuation of the very low interest rate policy from 1987 to 1989. The policy was taken in order to, or by the excuse to, sustain the dollar to fulfill Japan's commitment to international policy coordination.

To summarize, the domestic political structure in the United States does not seem to allow the attainment of the first best solution for the United States as a nation. Similarly, other countries are bound by internal domestic conflicts. In case of trade, lobbying pressures from import-competing industries, such as the American automobile industries and Japanese farmers, restrict the "win set," that is, the set of negotiation outcomes that sustain the political stability of the incumbent party. Without consideration of these domestic factors, the present situation would be more difficult to interpret. If there is a hegemon that has a transcendent power, it might be capable of mitigating the impasse created by domestic economic conflicts. Thus, political leadership by a hegemon may be a means of widening the "win set" by reducing uncertainty (for the role of uncertainty in the two-level game, see Iida 1993), by changing the perception of pressure groups, or by creating credible threats.[13]

7 The Prospect for the Future

When a hegemon begins to lose its power or its relative scale in the world, what kind of consequences follow? This is our main question.

I have argued that any country, hegemon or not, should be regarded as selfish or rational any time. The consequences of rationality depend on the size of a nation relative to others as well as on its situation. The United States could have been a (partially) altruistic hegemon because its selfish behavior happened to coincide with the adequate supply of international public goods. In any situation we need a careful study of incentive structures for nations and domestic groups in order to explain the course of events in international political economy.

Instead of repeating our main messages that were summarized in the introductory section, let us end this essay by referring to the role of regionalism for the future course of the world political economy. I discuss the two examples, the international monetary regime and the international trade regime. Here again we emphasize the distinction between the strategic interaction with respect to public goods and that with respect to private goods.

When a hegemon begins to lose prominence, what are the adequate mechanisms for the world to supply the adequate amount of international public goods, and under what conditions will the next hegemon emerge? Keohane (1984) proposed an answer to the first question, that a world system or regime may emerge by the combination of rational choices of nations, and, by the inertia from the *pax americana,* the world may continue to be a viable system for some length of time. Snidal (1985) applies a *k*-stability theory to the problem and argues that a group of nations can be motivated to supply an adequate amount of international public goods.

The case of the international regime illustrates the case where the public good that the incumbent hegemon provides may not be the one the next challenger will provide. The choice of the international money, or the existence of the international money, is a public good, though the international money in your wallet is a private good. In other words, money, or more precisely the use of a common money, has a public good character. Like language, money is used because others accept the same money. Here the competition of monies such as the pound sterling, the dollar, the deutsch mark, and the yen is to be analyzed by analogy to the competition between languages or, even better, computer languages. A wider use of a certain computer language has strategic advantage because of the network externalities (e.g., Katz and Shapiro 1985). Monies can then be called "differentiated international public goods." A wider use of a currency facilitates further its international use. As argued by Hayek (1984), a country with a more stable monetary and fiscal policy will be able to provide a desired international money. Currently, the world seems to have developed a doubt whether the U.S. fiscal policy is adequate to encourage foreigners to hold the dollar as an international money.

Because of the public-good character of money, it is hard to take over the incumbent international currency. However, once another currency reaches the stage when its characteristic is attractive enough, the process of money selection may have the nature of a catastrophe in a dynamic nonlinear model (Krugman 1984). The transition to another currency will occur like an avalanche.

The applicability of *k*-stability theory can be tested by the process of the European monetary unification. First, the question remains whether European countries can agree and succeed to achieve a monetary unification as a club good. Second, if the unification is realized, does it provide a public good to the world? The answer is negative except for the spillover effect to travelers and traders living outside Europe. The road from a club good or a regional public good to an international public good is still remote.

Finally, let us now turn to the trade regime. We have already mentioned the changing attitude of the United States evidenced by VERs and VIEs. In addition, we observe the move toward regionalism. The benefit-cost structure in economic integration will be derived from the model discussed in section 4. The European Union, the North American Free Trade Agreement (NAFTA), and a looser union like the Asia Pacific Economic Cooperation (APEC) can be interpreted thus as a move for creating clubs and club goods. These movements are beneficial for those who join the union, because of the trade creation effect, but those outside the union will most likely lose because of the trade diversion effect. In other words, trade will be created within a region with lower internal trade barriers, while trade outside the region will be reduced because nations tend to buy more from nations within the region. The welfare of the world can be affected negatively through trade diversion effect in spite of a clause like GATT article 24, which prohibits the increases in external tariffs of a free-trade area or a custom union.[14]

The public-goods-providing capacity of international organization like the WTO is curtailed by the "selfish" bilateral behavior of a declining hegemon. In this case, the United States erodes the system of international public goods. Or, as in the case of NAFTA and APEC, the hegemon is trying to strengthen its potentially declining position by enlarging the domain of economic activities under its influence. The United States is attempting to forge an "augmented hegemon," or "fortified hegemon." There is a gap between the phenomenon of regional agreements and the argument of *k*-stability. *K*-stability talks about the creation of international public goods, while in the move toward regional integration only a club good is created. Only if these regional movements facilitate the establishment of an overall free-trade regime for the world can they be considered as a step toward the adequate supply of international public goods.

NOTES

I appreciate the thoughtful discussions and continuous encouragement by Jagdish Bhagwati and Mancur Olson on an earlier draft, which was circulated as an IRIS Discussion Paper. I also thank Simon Evenett, Christopher Clague,

Mary Ann Dimand, Jun-ichi Goto, Ann Judd, Yusaku Horiuchi, Frances Rosenbluth, and T. N. Srinivasan for their helpful comments and Sunghyun Kim for his research assistance. Al Fishlow and Gary Saxonhouse gave valuable criticisms at the festschrift conference.

1. *Hegemony* or *hegemon* originated during the Greek era. According to the *Larousse Dictionary*, in 224 B.C., Antigonos II of Macedonia organized the Hellenic Alliance of Greek cities and called the alliance a "hegemon." Kindleberger (1986b) cites the *Columbia Encyclopedia*, which relates this word to the struggles for dominance between Athens and Sparta.

2. For example, the international disaster in the Great Depression is considered to have been aggravated by the lack of a leader country that could serve as a lender of last resort.

3. This is the comparison of macroeconomic variables by exchange rate conversion. I think that this method is relevant as the relative measure of international purchasing power and the index of international influence. If we use the ppp-adjustment by Summers and Heston (1991) for reference, the relative size of U.S. income went down from 44 percent in 1960 to 38 percent in 1990, while that of Japan increased from 7 percent in 1960 to 15 percent in 1990.

4. The same qualitative results can be obtained without assuming specific forms of the utility function, but I rely on (1) for the sake of exposition.

5. This is indeed a strong assumption because the interests of various sectors could be distinctly different.

6. Most of the examples are externalities concerning individual consumption. But these externalities create the question of externalities of national public policies.

7. On the other hand, the German monetary unification seems to imply that unification of currency is perfectly enforceable in the presence of political unity.

8. A popular common discussion in the dynamic theory of trade is that of the infant industry. If the industry to be protected is under increasing returns to scale, external economies, and learning by doing, in such a way that competitive price mechanism cannot capture the total benefit, then there are cases for protection of an infant industry. Then some of the protectionistic attitudes taken by smaller developing countries can become explicable as well.

9. An Asian diplomat coined the phrase *instrumental ambiguity*. According to him, nations cannot agree if everything is expressed clearly. By leaving ambiguity, nations are motivated to participate in a joint action.

10. Talking about fishery, Ostrom (1991) says, "Discount rates are affected by the levels of physical and economic securities faced by appropriators. Appropriators who are uncertain whether or not there will be sufficient food to survive the year will discount future returns heavily."

11. According to conventional view, the IMF is under European control, the World Bank is under American control, and the Asia Development Bank (ADB) is under Japanese control. The nationality of the presidents in these situations supports this view.

12. For the exceptional case of welfare improvement, see Saxonhouse in this volume.

13. If a country is not a democratic country where vested interests compete by means of political or economic (bribery) processes, the nature of a nondemocratic political system, such as dictatorship, may affect the trade policy. According to McGuire and Olson (1995), intensity of trade or openness of the economy may influence the need for and the availability of tariff revenues. The interaction of domestic political system and trade policy would also be modified if a country is ruled by a dictator.

14. GATT 24 forbids that a custom union or free-trade members increase their tariff rates against the rest of the world after integration. For the economic implication of this clause and its insufficiency to sustain the welfare of the rest of the world see Goto and Hamada 1994.

REFERENCES

Bhagwati, J. A. C. 1987. *Trade Wars.* New York: Columbia University Press.
Bhagwati, J. N. 1988. *Protectionism.* Cambridge: MIT Press.
———. 1994a. "Comments." In *The New GATT,* ed. S. M. Collins and B. P. Bosworth. Washington, D.C.: Brookings Institution.
———. 1994b. "Threats to the World Trading System: Income Distribution and the Selfish Hegemon." *Journal of International Affairs* (spring).
Bulow, J. I., J. D. Geneakopolos, and P. D. Klemperer. 1985. "Multimarket Oligopoly: Strategic Substitutes and Complements." *Journal of Political Economy* 93:485–511.
Conybeare, J. A. C. 1987. *Trade Wars: The Theory and Practices of International Commercial Rivalry.* New York: Columbia University Press.
Cooper, R. N. 1975. "Prolegomena to the Choice of an International Monetary System." In *World Politics and International Economics,* ed. C. F. Bergsten and L. B. Krause. Washington, D.C.: Brookings Institution.
Evans, P. B., H. K. Jacobson, and R. D. Putnam, eds. 1993. *Double-Edged Diplomacy: International Bargaining and Domestic Politics.* Berkeley and Los Angeles: University of California Press.
Frankel, J., and K. Rockett. 1988. "International Macroeconomic Policy Coordination When Policy-Makers Do Not Agree on the True Model." *American Economic Review* 78:318–40.
Gilpin, R. 1987. *The Political Economy of International Relations.* Princeton: Princeton University Press.
Goto, J. 1989. "The Multifibre Arrangement and Developing Countries." *World Bank Research Observer,* July.
Goto, J., and K. Hamada. 1994. "Economic Integration and the Welfare of Those Who Are Left Behind: An Asian Perspective." Mimeo.
Gowa, J. 1989. "Rational Hegemons, Excludable Goods, and Small Groups: An Epitaph for Hegemonic Stability Theory?" *World Politics* 41, no. 3:307–24.
———. 1994. *Allies, Adversaries, and International Trade.* Princeton: Princeton University Press.

Gros, D. 1987. "A Note on the Optimal Tariff, Retaliation, and the Welfare Loss from Tariff Wars in a Framework with Intra-industry Trade." *Journal of International Economics.*

Grossman, G. M., and E. Helpman. 1994. "Protection by Sale," *American Economic Review* 84:833–50.

Haas, P. 1992. "Introduction: Epistemic Communities and International Policy Coordination." *International Organization* 46:1–35.

Hamada, K. 1985. *The Political Economy of International Monetary Interdependence.* Cambridge: MIT Press.

———. 1987. "On the Political Economy of Monetary Integration: A Public Economic Approach." In *The Political Economy of International Monetary Interdependence.* Cambridge: MIT Press.

———. 1991. "On the Political Economy of the Regime Choice." *Osaka Economic Papers,* n.s. 40, nos. 3–4:70–85. Reprinted in *Public and International Economics,* ed. Ali M. El-Agraa. (New York: St. Martin's Press, 1993).

———. 1995. "Strategic Structure of Arms Races before and after the End of the Cold War: From Strategic Substitutes to Strategic Complements." December. Mimeo.

Hamada, K., and D. Porteous. 1992. "L'integration monetaire en perspective historique." *Revue d'economie financiere* 22:77–92.

Hayek, F. 1984. Contribution to *Currency Competition and Monetary Union,* ed. Pascal Salin. The Hague: M. Nijhoff Publishers.

Henning, R. C. 1994. *Currencies and Politics in the United States, Germany, and Japan.* Washington, D.C.: Institute for International Economics.

Iida, K. 1993. "When and How Do Domestic Constraints Matter? (Uncertainty in International Relations)." *Journal of Conflict Resolution,* 37, no. 3:403–27.

Jackson, J. H. 1991. *The World Trading System: Law and Policy of International Economic Relations.* Cambridge: MIT Press.

Katz, M., and C. Shapiro. 1985. "Network Externalities, Competition, and Compatibility." *American Economic Review* 75:424–40.

Keohane, R. O. 1984. *After Hegemony: Cooperation and Discord in the World Political Economy.* Princeton: Princeton University Press.

Keohane, R. O., and L. L. Martin. 1994. "Delegation to International Organizations." Harvard University. Mimeo.

Kindleberger, C. P. 1986a. "International Public Goods without International Government." *American Economic Review* 76:1–13.

———. 1986b. Review of *After Hegemony: Cooperation and Discord in the World Political Economy,* by Robert Keohane. *International Organization* 40, 841–47.

———. 1988. *The International Economic Order.* Cambridge: MIT Press.

Krasner, S. D., ed., 1982a. *International Regimes.* Ithaca, N.Y.: Cornell University Press.

———. 1982b. "Structural Causes and Regime Consequences: Regimes as Intervening Variables." In *International Regimes,* ed. S. D. Krasner. Ithaca: Cornell University Press.

Krugman, P. 1984. "The International Role of the Dollar: Theory and Prospect." In *Exchange Rate Theory and Practice,* ed. F. O. Bilson and Richard C. Marston. Chicago: University of Chicago Press for National Bureau of Economic Research.

———. 1991. "Is Bilateralism Bad?" In *International Trade Policy,* ed E. Helpman and A. Razin. Cambridge: MIT Press.

McGuire, M. C., and M. Olson. 1995. "The Economics of Autocracy and Majority Rule: The Invisible Hand and the Use of Force." Mimeo.

Ministry of International Trade and Industry (MITI). 1995. *White Paper on Unfair Trade.* Tokyo: MITI.

North, D.C., and R. P. Thomas. 1973. *The Rise of the Western World: A New Economic History.* Cambridge: Cambridge University Press.

Olson, M., Jr. 1965. *The Logic of Collective Action: Public Goods and Theory of Groups.* Harvard Economic Studies, vol. 124. Cambridge: Harvard University Press.

Olson, M., Jr., and R. Zeckhauser. 1966. "An Economic Theory of Alliance." *Review of Economics and Statistics,* 48 (August): 266–79.

Ostrom, E. 1991. *Governing the Commons: The Evolution of Institutions for Collective Action.* Cambridge: Cambridge University Press.

Putnam, R. D. 1988. "Diplomacy and Domestic Politics: The Logic of Two-Level Games." *International Organization* 42:427–60.

Sandler, T. 1992. *Collective Action: Theory and Applications.* Ann Arbor: University of Michigan Press.

Snidal, D. 1985. "The Limits of Hegemonic Stability." *International Organization* 39.

Summers, R., and A. Heston. 1991. The Penn World Table (Mark 5): An Expanded Set of International Comparisons, 1950–1988." *Quarterly Journal of Economics* 106, no. 2:327–42.

World Bank. 1987, 1995. *The World Development Report.* Washington D.C.: World Bank.

CHAPTER 11

Technological Specialization in
International Patenting

Jonathan Eaton, Robert Evenson, Samuel Kortum,
Poorti Marino, and Jonathan Putnam

1 Introduction

Explaining why poor countries are poor, and how poor countries become
rich, has been a central effort of our profession for over two centuries, and
one to which Gus Ranis has made an enormous contribution. One polar
explanation is that rich countries are rich simply because they have more
capital and a better-educated workforce. Another is that rich countries
are rich because they operate with more advanced technologies.

Mankiw (1995) makes a vehement case that the first pole provides a
good working hypothesis: Since people "can read blueprints anywhere,"
he finds the existence of serious impediments to technology flows implausible. In their classic book on the development of the labor surplus
economy, Fei and Ranis are more skeptical about the ease with which
poor countries can import foreign technology:

> While the availability of potentially useful techniques developed
> abroad certainly represents an asset in terms of the avoidance of
> costly trial and error, and while the advantage of a latecomer status
> should be exploited to the fullest, it is rarely economically sound or
> feasible that such techniques should be transplanted whole to the
> underdeveloped economy without considerable adjustment and ad-
> aptation to the radically different conditions prevailing. (1964, 66)

Ranis elaborates this point:

> It is not our view that there is some vast national and international
> shelf of technology ready to offer just the "right" process or product
> to be plunked down in a particular country and industry context.

While the choice of a technology already in use elsewhere is a critical step—and by no means easy or costless, as we shall see— modifications will almost always have to be made before it can be installed and become fully "appropriate." (1979, 27)

How serious are impediments to technology flows? While, as Mankiw (1995) points out, we do not observe these flows directly, they do leave footprints. Our research is directed toward exploring a particular set of footprints, international patents.

Obtaining patent protection is costly. Many minor innovations are not patented at all, while many others are patented only where they are invented. A decision to patent an invention in a foreign country presumably reflects the inventor's expectation that it might prove useful, and hence have a market there, justifying the cost of patenting.[1] Patent data should tell us something, then, about where inventions will be used, and how often they cross international borders.

Previous studies, including Slama (1981), Bosworth (1984), and Evenson (1984), have exploited the international patenting data for this purpose. Evenson (1984) found that the vast majority of patents originate from inventors in a few industrialized countries and that nearly all the patenting in developing countries is done by foreigners. This pattern suggests an underlying diffusion process from the more to the less advanced economies.[2]

Eaton and Kortum (1996, forthcoming) use aggregate data on international patenting to infer patterns of technology diffusion among industrialized countries. Their estimates imply that research performed abroad is about two-thirds as potent as domestic research for these countries. Putnam (1996) uses microlevel data on the set of countries where inventors sought patent protection for a particular invention to estimate a model of the patent-filing decision. He estimates that over 95 percent of the total value of patent rights worldwide is contained in inventions that are filed in at least one country outside their home country.

These studies have focused on the geographic dimensions of invention and patenting but have ignored the technological dimension.[3] Yet the technological dimension of the patent data is one of its unique and perhaps most interesting features. This dimension arises because patent examiners assign patents to internationally consistent classes of technology defined by the International Patent Classification (IPC) system. In this paper we explore the interaction between the technological and geographical dimensions of the patent data. We examine differences across technologies in terms of where innovations occur, where they are used, and their rate of migration abroad.

In the present study, we extend the aggregate framework of Eaton and Kortum (1996) to allow for differences across classes of patented technology. The Eaton-Kortum model yields a decomposition of the multidimensional international patenting data that illuminates a number of issues about technological mobility: In particular, it allows us to examine (1) which countries are the major sources and destinations of innovation in the world economy; (2) which country pairs tend to share their inventions the most; (3) to what extent countries specialize as sources and destinations for specific classes of technology; and (4) which technologies appear to be most mobile.[4]

Answers to these questions shed light on a number of policy issues. For developing countries an issue of particular interest is the appropriate direction of research and development effort. Our analysis helps to identify (1) the technologies for which research performed abroad is most likely to prove transferable; (2) the countries that provide those technologies; and (3) the technologies for which domestic research is most needed to obtain productivity advances. For example, we provide further evidence that, for a small country, at least, the national payoff to research in agriculture might be particularly high, since innovations in this area appear least able to cross international borders.[5]

By applying some theory, we can infer the size of our quarry from the tracks that it leaves. Section 2 of the essay provides a model of innovation and international diffusion of technology to relate an inventor's patenting decision to the underlying pattern of international technology diffusion. Section 3 describes our data and section 4 our empirical methodology and findings. In section 5 we offer some concluding remarks.

2 A Model of Innovation, Diffusion, and Patenting

Eaton and Kortum (1996) develop a model of international technology diffusion and patenting in which the number of patents filed by inventors from country i in country n, P_{ni}, decomposes into three fundamental factors: (i) *innovation*, a_i, the rate at which country i generates patentable inventions; (ii) *diffusion*, ε_{ni}, the fraction of innovations from country i that find a use in country n; (iii) the *propensity to patent*, f_{ni}, out of those innovations that diffuse, the fractions that are worth trying to patent.[6]

The theory itself is agnostic about the source of randomness in patenting. Since data on patent applications are counts and since they are generated by the individual decisions of many different inventors, we follow Hausman, Hall, and Griliches (1984) and treat them as the realization of a Poisson random variable with mean $\bar{P}_{ni}$ reflecting the combined impact of the three factors identified above,

$$\bar{P}_{ni} = \alpha_i \varepsilon_{ni} f_{ni}.$$

In the present paper, we apply this basic model to an individual technology class rather than to the aggregate. Adding a technological dimension retains the same decomposition into three fundamental factors, so that the number of patents in technology class c applied for by inventors from country i in country n has a Poisson distribution with mean $\bar{P}_{nic}$ given by

$$\bar{P}_{nic} = f_{nic} \varepsilon_{nic} \alpha_{ic}, \; n = 1, \ldots, N; \; i = 1, \ldots, I; \; c = 1, \ldots, C, \quad (1)$$

where N is the number of destination countries, I is the number of source countries (perhaps equal to the number of destinations), and C is the number of classes of technology. Here α_{ic} represents innovation in country i in technology class c, ε_{nic} is the fraction that diffuses to country n, and f_{nic} is the fraction of those inventions that are expected to be worth patenting.

While our theory identifies three factors determining patenting, the patent data themselves naturally have three dimensions as well: their source, their destination, and their technology class. Nonetheless, there is no unique correspondence between innovation, diffusion, and propensity to patent, on the one hand, and the source, destination, and technology class of a patent, on the other. The only implication of the theory so far is that innovative capacity in the source country is independent of the destination of its patents. We can, however, impose some plausible restrictions to tighten this correspondence in order to glean some inferences from the patent data.

To facilitate interpretation, but without imposing additional restrictions, we break country i's innovativeness in technology class c into factors that reflect country i's overall innovativeness, $\tilde{\alpha}_i$, total inventive activity in technology class c, $\tilde{\alpha}_c$, and a term that reflects country i's comparative advantage in producing innovations in technology class c, $\tilde{\alpha}_{ic}$. Thus $\alpha_{ic} = \tilde{\alpha}_i \times \tilde{\alpha}_c \times \tilde{\alpha}_{ic}$. Implicit in this decomposition and the ones that follow is a set of restrictions, in this case

$$\sum_{i=1}^{I} \ln \tilde{\alpha}_{ic} = 0, \; c = 1, \ldots, C \quad \text{and} \quad \sum_{c=1}^{C} \ln \tilde{\alpha}_{ic} = 0 \quad i = 1, \ldots, I.$$

We are more restrictive in how we decompose diffusion and the propensity to patent. We break the diffusion term ε_{nic} into factors reflecting country n's overall ability to absorb technology, $\tilde{\varepsilon}_n$, its relative ability to absorb technologies in class c, $\tilde{\varepsilon}_{nc}$, its relative ability to absorb technologies from country i, $\tilde{\varepsilon}_{ni}$, and other factors that depend on whether country n is the same as country i or not. To denote this last set of factors we introduce a superscript h where $h = 1$ if $n = i$ (as in domestic patents) and $h = 2$ if $n \neq i$ (as in foreign patents). Using this notation, overall differences in diffusion within and between countries are captured by $\tilde{\varepsilon}^h$. To the extent that this home bias differs by technology class it is captured by $\tilde{\varepsilon}_c^h$, and to the extent that it differs by destination country (the relative technological autarky of country n) it is captured by $\tilde{\varepsilon}_n^h$. Hence $\varepsilon_{nic} = \tilde{\varepsilon}_n \times \tilde{\varepsilon}_{ni} \times \tilde{\varepsilon}_{nc} \times \tilde{\varepsilon}^h \times \tilde{\varepsilon}_n^h \times \tilde{\varepsilon}_c^h$. Countries with a low value of $\tilde{\varepsilon}_n^1$ (i.e., high values of $\tilde{\varepsilon}_n^2$) are technologically more open, while technologies with a low value of $\tilde{\varepsilon}_c^1$ (i.e., high values of $\tilde{\varepsilon}_c^2$) are internationally more mobile. Note that we treat diffusion as independent of, among other things, the source country (except as it interacts with the destination). Variation across sources in their ability to diffuse innovations is conceptually indistinguishable, within our model, from variation in their ability to innovate.

Finally, we break the propensity to patent term f_{nic} into factors reflecting country n's overall attractiveness as a place to patent, $\tilde{f}_n$, the overall propensity to patent in technology class c, $\tilde{f}_c$, an overall home bias in patenting, $\tilde{f}^h$, the relative home bias in patenting in country n, f_n^h (possibly reflecting the extent to which country n's patenting system discriminates in favor of domestic inventors), and the home bias in patenting in technology class c, $\tilde{f}_c^h$. Hence $f_{nic} = \tilde{f}_n \times \tilde{f}_c \times \tilde{f}^h \times \tilde{f}_n^h \times \tilde{f}_c^h$. Note that, given our restrictions, the propensity to patent does not depend on the source (except that if the source is domestic, the propensity may be higher).[7] This restriction is valid, for example, if all the costs and benefits of patenting are independent of the nationality of any foreign inventor. Thus we attribute all variation across foreign sources to differences in inventiveness. We also assume that the propensity to patent in a destination country does not vary across particular country-technology pairs (although it may vary by technology).

Under these restrictions the equation for the mean of patenting becomes

$$\bar{P}_{nic} = \tilde{f}_n \times \tilde{f}_c \times \tilde{f}^h \times \tilde{f}_n^h \times \tilde{f}_c^h \times \tilde{\varepsilon}_n \times \tilde{\varepsilon}_{ni} \times \tilde{\varepsilon}_{nc} \times \tilde{\varepsilon}^h \times \tilde{\varepsilon}_n^h$$

$$\times \tilde{\varepsilon}_c^h \times \tilde{\alpha}_i \times \tilde{\alpha}_c \times \tilde{\alpha}_{ic} \tag{2}$$

for $n = 1, \ldots, N$; $i = 1, \ldots, I$; $c = 1, \ldots, C$; and $h = 1$ if $n = i$ ($h = 2$ otherwise). Although the dimension h is determined by the (n, i) pair, it is convenient to treat it as a fourth dimension of the data in what follows. We can group the thirteen terms on the right-hand side of equation

(2) into nine sets of identifiable effects depending on (1) the destination country D_n, (2) the source country S_i, (3) the technology class T_c, (4) the home effect H_h, (5) the interaction of the destination and source $(DS)_{ni}$, (6) the interaction of the destination and technology $(DT)_{nc}$, (7) the interaction of the source and technology $(ST)_{ic}$, (8) the interaction of the destination and the home effect $(DH)_{nh}$, and (9) the interaction of the technology and the home effect $(TH)_{ch}$.

Introducing an overall constant effect A, our equation becomes

$$\bar{P}_{nich} = A \times D_n \times S_i \times T_c \times H_h \times (DS)_{ni} \times (DT)_{nc} \times (ST)_{ic}$$

$$\times (DH)_{nh} \times (TH)_{ch}, \tag{3}$$

for $n = 1, \ldots, N$; $i = 1, \ldots, I$; $c = 1, \ldots, C$; and $h = 1$ if $n = i$ ($h = 2$ otherwise).

These equations are subject to the restrictions

$$\sum_{n=1}^{N} \ln D_n = \ldots = \sum_{h=1}^{2} \ln H_h = 0;$$

$$\sum_{n=1}^{N} \ln(DS)_{ni} = 0, i = 1, \ldots, N, \sum_{i=1}^{N} \ln(DS)_{ni} = 0, n = 1, \ldots, N,$$

$$\ldots \sum_{c=1}^{C} \ln(TH)_{ch} = 0, h = 1, 2, \sum_{h=1}^{2} \ln(TH)_{ch} = 0, c = 1, \ldots, C;$$

and

$$\ln(DS)_{nn} = 0, n = 1, \ldots, N.$$

Table 11.1 indicates the relationship between the parameters of the model, that is, the various effects (by row) and the three fundamental

TABLE 11.1.   Interpretation of the Parameters

	Propensity to Patent	Diffusion	Innovation
D_n	f_n	$\tilde{\varepsilon}_n$	
S_i			$\tilde{\alpha}_i$
T_c	$\tilde{f}_c$		$\tilde{\alpha}_c$
H_h	$\tilde{f}^h$	$\tilde{\varepsilon}^h$	
$(DS)_{ni}$		$\tilde{\varepsilon}_{ni}$	
$(DT)_{nc}$		$\tilde{\varepsilon}_{nc}$	
$(ST)_{ic}$			$\tilde{\alpha}_{ic}$
$(DH)_{nh}$	$\tilde{f}^h_n$	$\tilde{\varepsilon}^h_n$	
$(TH)_{ch}$	$\tilde{f}^h_c$	$\tilde{\varepsilon}^h_c$	

factors determining patenting (by column). Where a row of the table has only one element, the model parameter in that row reflects the indicated factor determining patenting. Hence overall source-country effects S_i reflect sources' importance in generating innovations $\tilde{\alpha}_i$, while source-country effects interacted with technology class $(ST)_{ic}$ reflect comparative advantage in innovating within specific technologies $\tilde{\alpha}_{ic}$. Similarly, destination interacted with source $(DS)_{ni}$ reflects patterns of diffusion $\tilde{\varepsilon}_{ni}$, while destination interacted with technology $(DT)_{nc}$ reflects comparative ability to absorb technology $\tilde{\varepsilon}_{nc}$. However, the overall destination effects D_n confounds destination n's ability to absorb innovation with its desirability as a place to patent, while the overall technology effect T_c confounds the level of innovative activity in a technology with the propensity to take out patents in that technology. Note finally that in order to infer the relative immobility of a technology $\tilde{\varepsilon}_c^h$ from the technology class interacted with the home effect $(TH)_{ch}$ requires the additional restriction that $\tilde{f}_c^h$ is one, that is, that there are no systematic differences across technologies in the extent to which inventors prefer to take out patents at home relative to abroad, given their pattern of diffusion. We now turn to the patent data themselves.

3 International Patenting by Technology

Before introducing our particular dataset, we take a broader look at international patent applications.[8] Table 11.2, based on data from the World Intellectual Property Organization (WIPO 1970, 1977, 1993), shows the top ten industrialized and top four developing countries in terms of foreign patent applications received. Among these countries, the United Kingdom, Germany, France, the United States, and Japan are consistently at the top. The analysis below considers only these five as destinations for patents, although we include applications originating from anywhere in the world. A consequence of this focus is that we ignore applications for patents in developing countries. But, as table 11.2 makes clear, these countries generally receive far fewer applications than developed countries.

In general countries obtain more applications from foreign residents than from their own residents. The extreme example is Belgium, where foreign applications dominate domestic applications by a factor of ten in 1970 and 1977 and by even more in 1993. The anomaly is the Japanese, who seek vast numbers of patents locally. It turns out that these applications contain few claims of invention, and we account for this in all the subsequent analysis by scaling down Japanese domestic applications by a factor of 4.9.[9] The tendency for countries to receive

TABLE 11.2.   Countries Receiving the Most Patent Applications from Abroad

	Applications in 1970		Applications in 1977		Applications in 1993	
Country	Domestic	Foreign	Domestic	Foreign	Domestic	Foreign
Top 10 Countries						
United Kingdom	25,227	36,874	21,114	33,309	24,401	76,841
Germany	32,772	33,360	30,247	30,154	46,865	70,903
France	14,106	33,177	11,811	28,167	16,042	66,099
United States	72,343	30,832	62,863	38,068	102,245	89,141
Japan	100,511	30,318	135,991	25,015	332,460	47,575
Canada	1,986	28,524	1,832	23,337	4,067	43,685
Italy	7,241	24,587	n/a	n/a	9,040	56,130
Netherlands	2,462	16,647	1,960	12,669	3,825	54,997
Belgium	1,339	15,848	1,073	11,453	1,438	45,082
Sweden	4,343	13,515	4,503	10,476	5,417	50,224
Top 4 Developing Countries						
South Africa	2,428	6,316	2,966	4,762	5,347	4,460
Brazil	3,839	5,385	1,645	7,071	2,467	14,477
Argentina	1,982	5,096	1,704	2,800	n/a	n/a
India	1,278	3,864	n/a	n/a	1,209	2,511

Source: WIPO 1970, 1977, 1993. The countries are ordered by the number of foreign patent applications in 1970. A different set of developing countries would top the list if we were to use the 1993 data.

most of their patent applications from abroad has become more pronounced over time. This increased globalization of patenting has occurred mostly after 1977, however. We now turn to our primary interest, which is the technological dimension of the patent data.

We analyze patent counts cross-classified by source country (the country of inventor), destination country (the country where patent protection is sought), and the class of technology patented. The technological dimension comes from a dataset assembled at Yale's Economic Growth Center based on extracts from files of the European Patent Office (EPO). The unique aspect of this dataset is that each patent is assigned to an International Patent Class (IPC).[10] We aggregate the 100,000 IPC classifications into twenty-three groups, as defined in table 11.3.[11]

We focus on a subset of the Yale data covering all patents that were applied for in 1977 (with a comparison made to 1970) and that were eventually published in one of five industrial countries: France, Germany, Japan, the United Kingdom, and the United States.[12] We consider patenting from all source countries, but after aggregating smaller countries we end up with seventeen distinct sources.[13]

One difficulty in using the Yale data for cross-country comparisons is that there is no international standard definition of a published patent.[14] Another difficulty has to do with the definition of the source country. The problem is that the Yale data identify the source as the country where patent protection is first sought, which may differ from the residence of the inventor.[15]

International patent application data from WIPO avoid both of these problems. Patent applications do have an international standard definition, and the applicant's or inventor's country of residence is identified as the source. For this reason, we use WIPO application data by source and destination country as the basis for benchmarking the Yale data.[16] This amounts to scaling the Yale data so that totals by source and destination country match the totals published by WIPO. Tables 11.A.1 and 11.A.2 in the appendix compare (in 1970 and 1977 respectively) the Yale data with WIPO data classified by source and destination country (note the small number of patent applications from the developing-country sources, 17_OT). The scaling factor in 1977 for destination-France by source-

TABLE 11.3. Technology Groupings

	Definition of Grouping	Component Classes of the IPC
Ag	Agriculture	A01 (less A01N)
Fo	Foodstuffs	A21-A24
Pe	Personal or domestic	A41-A47
He	Health and amusement	A61-A63 (less A61K)
Ph	Pharmaceuticals	A61K
Se	Separating and mixing	B01-B09
Sh	Shaping	B21-B32 (less B31)
Pr	Printing	B41-B44
Tr	Transporting	B60-B68
Ch	Chemistry	C01-C14 (plus A01N, less C06)
Me	Metallurgy	C21-C30
Te	Textiles and other	D01-D07
Pa	Paper	D21 (plus B31)
Bu	Building	E01-E06
Dr	Drilling and mining	E21
Pu	Pumps and engines	F01-F04
En	Engineering	F15-F17
Li	Lighting and heating	F21-F28
We	Weapons and blasting	F41-F42 (plus C06)
In	Instruments	G01-G12
Nu	Nucleonics	G21
El	Electricity	H01-H05
XX	Other	Other

France is 0.94, while for destination-France by source-Germany it is 1.05. In the United States many patent applications never make it through the examination process to become published, hence the scaling factor for destination-United States by source-Germany, for example, is 1.52 in 1977. The analysis in the remainder of the essay is based on the Yale data benchmarked in this way.

The benchmarked Yale data contain 1,955 cells (observations) in 1977 (five destination countries by seventeen source countries by twenty-three technologies). The total number of patents across all these observations is 308,501. There are 119 observations with zero patents. This forms our main dataset for analysis. We conclude by comparing the stability of results between 1970 and 1977. To do this we drop Japan as a destination since those data are not available in 1970.

4 A Decomposition of the International Patent Data

We estimate the parameters of equation (3) by maximum likelihood under the assumption that observed patenting, P_{nich}, is the realization of an independently distributed Poisson random variable with mean $\bar{P}_{nich}$.[17] Note that by adding the home dimension h we have a table with $N \times I \times C \times 2$ observations, half of which are structural zeros (i.e., we set $P_{nich} = 0$ in the cases of $n = i$ and $h = 2$ or $n \neq i$ and $h = 1$). The theory of log-linear models for cross-classified categorical data suggests an iterative algorithm for obtaining the maximum likelihood estimates in tables with structural zeros.[18] The theory also provides a framework for testing restrictions of the model and assessing its overall fit.

We begin by estimating the model on the 1977 patent data (with 3,910 observations, 1,955 of which are structural zeros). Before presenting the parameter estimates we provide a brief discussion of how well our basic model fits and the contribution of each set of effects on the margin. We then turn to the parameters themselves, presented in a series of tables. We conclude with tests for differences between the parameters in 1977 and 1970.

4.1 The Fit of the Model

We can test various models *(k)* by evaluating the maximum likelihood estimates, $\hat{P}_{nich}^{(k)}$, of the Poisson means $\bar{P}_{nich}$. An interesting feature of the Poisson assumption is that we can estimate a model with no restrictions whatsoever on $\bar{P}_{nich}$. This is called the saturated model s, and the maximum likelihood estimates of the Poisson means are simply $\hat{P}_{nich} = P_{nich}$.

The likelihood ratio statistic for testing the null hypothesis of model (k) against the alternative of the saturated model is

$$G^2(k) = 2\sum P_{nich} \ln(P_{nich}/\hat{P}_{nich}^{(k)}),$$

where the summation is over all observations that are not structural zeros (note that for the saturated model $G^2(s) = 0$). This statistic has a χ^2 distribution with *df* degrees of freedom under the null hypothesis that model k is correct, where *df* equals the number of observations less the number of structural zeros less the number of parameters in model k (net of the number of restrictions).[19] The likelihood ratio statistic $G^2(k)$ and degrees of freedom *df* for a number of models k are presented in table 11.4 below. The models are identified according to the highest levels of interaction effects that they contain. The first is the saturated model, *s*, which allows for a full set of interactions between destination country, source country, and technology (note that this set of interactions subsumes any interactions with home). The second model, 0, is the most restrictive and allows for only one dimensional effects (Source, Destination, and Technology Class). The third row represents the baseline model (model 1) as in equation (3). Each of the last four models (models 2–5) represents various restrictions on the baseline model (i.e., a different set of effects is removed in each). Normally the destination-country by home effects are subsumed in the destination-country by source-country effects. In model 2, however, where we remove source country effects, we include destination-country by home effects.

The test statistics indicate that any restrictions on the saturated model can be rejected, including the restrictions imposed by our baseline model. This means that there is a statistically significant interaction between technology and destination-country by source-country interac-

TABLE 11.4.   Model Fit

k	Model	Configuration	*df*	$G^2(k)$	$R^2(k)$	$AIC(k) - q$
s	saturated model	[DST]	0	0	1.00	0
0	most restrictive	[D][S][T][H]	1,911	58,719	0.00	54,897
1	baseline model	[DS][DT][ST][TH]	1,385	6,346	0.89	3,576
2	no dest.-source	[DH][DT][ST][TH]	1,445	13,825	0.76	10,935
3	no dest.-tech.	[DS][ST][TH]	1,473	9,835	0.83	6,889
4	no source-tech.	[DS][DT][TH]	1,737	30,641	0.48	27,167
5	no tech.-home	[DS][DT][ST]	1,407	12,919	0.78	10,105

tions that is not completely captured by the technology-home effects. A higher-order interaction of this sort may be statistically significant, even if it has little economic importance, so we investigate further. An analog of the coefficient of determination in a typical regression equation can be calculated by taking the percentage reduction in G^2 relative to a very restrictive model such as model 0. Hence, following Christensen (1990), we define $R^2(k) = [G^2(0) - G^2(k)]/G^2(0)$, hence $R^2(0) = 0$ and $R^2(s) = 1$. The R^2 values are a heuristic device for assessing the fit of the various models. These values are shown in the second-to-last column of table 11.4. The baseline model explains about 90 percent of the variation remaining after all one-dimensional effects have been removed. We also see that model 3 (which excludes destination-country by technology effects) also does quite well. In contrast, the model that excludes source-country by technology effects explains less than half of the residual variation in the data. This suggests that technological specialization in innovation is a more important phenomenon than technological specialization in absorption of technology.

One problem with drawing conclusions from R^2 is that it does not take account of the number of parameters in each model. We therefore turn to Akaike's information criterion (AIC) to compare the statistical information contained in each model. Letting q be the number of observations less the number of structural zeros, Christensen (1990) shows that $AIC(k) - q = G^2(k) - 2(df)$ (with low values preferred and the saturated model having a value of 0). This calculation is performed in the last column of the table. The saturated model is still preferred to our baseline model. Furthermore, of the various restricted versions of the baseline model (none of which are preferred to the baseline model itself) the model without destination-country by technology effects is most preferred and the model without source-country by technology effects is least preferred. Thus, again we conclude that technological specialization in innovation is a particularly important phenomenon. We now turn to the parameters estimated for the baseline model.

4.2 Parameter Estimates

We present the parameter estimates in a series of nine tables. Each table corresponds to one of the nine sets of effects entering equation (3). The parameters are multiplicative effects and should be interpreted relative to a mean of 1. Since the parameter estimates satisfy the identifying restrictions listed beneath equation (3), the geometric means of all rows and column are equal to 1.[20] Note also that the diagonal elements of the destination-country by source-country table are each unity.

The estimation methodology we follow allows for observations with zero patent counts. It does, however, require that any summary table have all strictly positive counts. This was an issue, in our case, only for the summary table of source-country by technology in which we had seven zero entries. We simply added 0.1 patents to each of the thirty-five observations contributing to these seven zero entries. We now turn to estimates of the effects themselves. We begin by discussing overall destination country effects.

4.2.1 Destination-Country Effects

How important were our five countries as destinations for foreign patents in 1977? The first set of effects, reported in table 11.A.3, provides an answer. The D effects are purged of any influences due to the importance of each country as a source. They are also purged of the influence of any bias against patents from abroad, as that bias might vary by country.

Note that in 1977 Japan was relatively small as a destination for foreign patenting, while the United Kingdom was the largest destination. The model attributes the higher number of foreign patents received by the United States to the (DH) effects shown below (indicating that the United States was relatively open to patenting from abroad) rather than to the overall attractiveness of the United States as a destination. The key insight from this table is that differences among the countries along this dimension are surprisingly small, the maximum difference being a factor of two.

4.2.2 Source-Country Effects

How much do countries differ as sources of patents? Table 11.A.4 reports estimates of the S effects. Even among the first five countries the variation by source is substantially greater than the variation by destination. In particular, the United States and Germany stand out as powerful innovators, with the United States leading France by a factor of over four. All other countries are far behind. This result corroborates Evenson's (1984) finding that the sources of world patents are highly concentrated.

4.2.3 Technology Effects

Table 11.A.5 reports differences in overall patenting levels according to technology classes (the T effects). The differences across classes are substantial with chemistry, electricity, instruments, and transporting being the big technologies for patenting.[21] Agriculture is moderately sized with building technologies somewhat bigger. Nucleonics, paper, and weapons are the smallest technologies for patenting. Surprisingly, pharmaceuticals is also small, but this could be because many drug patents are showing up in other categories such as chemicals.

4.2.4 Home Effects

Table 11.A.6 reports the estimates of the overall H effect. Note that home patenting dominates foreign patenting by a factor of over six. As we will see below, this home bias does not vary widely by country, although there is an illuminating pattern in how it varies across technologies.

4.2.5 Destination-Country by Source-Country Effects

Once the vast differences between overall home and foreign patenting are taken into account, source and destination effects alone do a remarkable job in explaining cross-country patterns of patenting. This can be seen in the estimates of the (DS) parameters. The cross-country terms reported in table 11.A.7 cluster quite closely around one.[22] The big exception is the link from Canada to the United States, which is more than three times what would be implied by the null that source and destination effects explain everything. Other links that one would expect to be strong on a priori grounds, such as from Austria to Germany or from Belgium-Luxembourg to France, also stand out. Among our five destination countries, the diffusion link from Japan to France is particularly weak, while the link from Japan to the United States is particularly strong. These diffusion links need not obey symmetry; for example, note the average-sized diffusion link from France back to Japan.

4.2.6 Destination-Country by Technology Effects

Table 11.A.8 reports the parameters of the relative attractiveness of the five destination countries as places to patent different technologies. We interpret these (DT) effects as reflecting the relative abilities of these countries to absorb different types of technology. The major observation is that, in comparison with the source-country by technology effects that we turn to next, there is only modest variation across either rows or columns. Two outliers are Japan, first as a destination for patents in nucleonics, where it is big, and in agriculture, where it is small. As for technologies, the most variable is weapons, which is about three times more popular in the United States than in Japan. But the basic message is that these five countries do not differ that much in terms of their affinity for different technologies.

4.2.7 Source-Country by Technology Effects

In table 11.A.9 we report the parameters that describe the relative inventiveness of different countries in different technologies. These (ST)

effects can be interpreted as indicators of the revealed comparative advantage of different countries in different technologies. We see a considerable degree of specialization. Note for instance the specialization of Japan in instruments, of Belgium-Luxembourg in metals and pharmaceuticals, of Italy and Switzerland in textiles, of the Netherlands and Australia-New Zealand in agriculture, and of Scandinavia in paper. We see that small countries tend to specialize more than large ones, corroborating Archibugi and Pianta's (1992) finding.

How important are different countries absolutely as innovators in different technologies, not correcting for their overall level of patenting? The answer can be found by multiplying the overall source-country effects in table 11.A.4 with the appropriate source-country by technology effects in table 11.A.7. This exercise reveals, for example, that in absolute terms the United States dominates innovations in paper, although Scandinavia's contribution remains significant.

4.2.8 Destination-Country by Home Effects

How much do our five destinations vary in their preference for home patenting? Relative to the extreme preference for patenting at home displayed overall, the variation in this home preference across countries is minor. Table 11.A.10 indicates that Japan is about 30 percent more closed than average, while the United States is about 20 percent more open.

4.2.9 Technology by Home Effects

As discussed above, a technology's home bias provides some insight into its geographical immobility, especially if the home bias in the propensity to patent does not vary across technologies. According to table 11.A.11, chemicals and pharmaceuticals are the most cosmopolitan technology classes, with agriculture and building the most parochial. But, given the vast overall home bias in patenting, the extent of variation in that bias across individual technologies is relatively small: The most local technology has about twice the home bias of the most international technology.

4.2.10 Higher-Level Effects

Since our statistical tests suggest that there may be some higher-level interactions that the model fails to capture, we conclude by examining large values of standardized residuals, defined as $[P_{nich} - \hat{P}^{(1)}_{nich}]/[\hat{P}^{(1)}_{nich}]^{1/2}$. Extreme values of the standardized residuals (the residuals divided by an estimate of their standard errors, according to the model) are likely to be observations that are influenced by higher-order interactions not captured by our baseline model. There are four cases in which the absolute value of the standardized residual exceeds nine (a substantial outlier relative to the model). Interestingly, three of these involve chemicals patents. The model overpredicts chemical patent applications in France by Germans (predicted = 1,356, actual = 1,004), it underpredicts them in France by the Japanese, and it overpredicts them in Japan by the Japanese. The last case involves applications for patents on drilling technology in Japan by Scandinavians (prediction = 0.4, actual = 7).

4.3 Changes over Time

How sensitive are our findings to the choice of year, and which sets of effects change the most over time? Here we compare the parameter estimates in 1970 and 1977, with Japan dropped as a destination. So little changes across these time periods that we can summarize the results quite briefly. The only specific changes worth remarking upon are a noticeable slide in the relative importance of the United States and the United Kingdom as sources and a rise in the importance of Japan. The technology effects are stable except for a big rise in the relative importance of pharmaceuticals.

For each set of effects, we also tested the hypothesis of stability over time, allowing all the other effects to vary with time. We can always reject the hypothesis of stability in a statistical sense even though the changes appear to be trivial in terms of their quantitative importance. Using the AIC criterion, the model with stable technology by home-country effects is second best to the model in which all effects vary with time. This result suggests that our finding about the relative mobility of different technologies is a particularly robust one.

5 Conclusion

We have made use of a new set of data on international patents to study the technological dimension of international patenting. Several results are noteworthy. A major finding is that destination effects are much less important than source effects in explaining patenting in different technologies. While the five destination countries seem to take advantage of the entire spectrum of technologies, technological diffusion allows them to be somewhat specialized in the technologies in which they innovate. Smaller countries are even more specialized in their production of technology.

Another finding is that diffusion links between countries follow a simple pattern. Once the size of the source, the attractiveness of the destination, and the bias toward patenting at home are accounted for, there is little left to be explained. The home-bias itself is substantial, suggesting that many innovations have little effect outside their country of origin. This bias does not differ that much by country, but there is an interesting variation across technologies. Chemical and pharmaceutical technologies appear to be the most mobile, with agriculture and building technologies being the least.

The purpose of our analysis here has been to scrutinize international patent data to see what they have to say about comparative advantage in research and about technological mobility. We have not attempted here to link these numbers to international data on research effort, sectoral productivity, or patterns of trade. To date, these other data have received much greater attention. We think that the patent data provide fresh evidence about the role of technological diffusion in economic growth. As developing countries become increasingly important destinations for patents (WIPO 1993) future work might exploit patent data to discern what types of ideas developing countries make use of and where they are getting them from.

Appendix: The Yale Data on International Patenting

In the Yale data each patent is assigned to an IPC code, a reporting country (i.e., a destination country), a priority country (which proxies for the source country), a year of publication, and a year of first filing. We will discuss the definitions of these concepts and how they relate to their analogs in the data from WIPO.

A.1 Comparability across Countries

The Yale data consist of published patents. The exact meaning of published patents differs across countries. Sticky issues of comparability across countries arise because we do not have data on patent applications that are never published.

Countries generally follow either the European system or the U.S. system of patent examination and publication after application. In the European system, there are two stages of patent publication. The first publication takes place routinely eighteen months after the date of application; at this stage the patent has not been screened in great detail. It is after this stage that patents show up in the Yale data. After the first publication, the inventor has to apply for further examination. If the patent is accepted after the second examination, then it is published for a second time and it can be considered a granted patent. This second publication may occur many years after the date of application. For example, almost 40 percent of patents granted in France in 1992 were applied for prior to 1988 (WIPO 1994).

In the U.S. system a patent is published only after the application has been examined and accepted. A patent is generally granted within two or three years of the date of application. For example, less than 15 percent of patents granted in the United States in 1992 were applied for prior to 1990 (WIPO 1994). The screening before publication in the United States is comparable to the screening before the second publication in the European system.

A.2 Priority Country

The priority country is the country in which the inventor first sought patent protection. If inventors generally choose to protect their innovations first at home, then the priority country is a good indicator of the residence of the inventor. To check this assumption, we compare patenting by priority country with patenting by residence of applicant or inventor (published by WIPO) and find that totals by priority country are similar to totals by country of residence. In Table 11.A.1 one can see the similarity, for example for French-destination patents, between the Yale data (where the source country is the priority country) and the WIPO data (where the source country is the residence of the applicant).

A.3 Priority Year

The priority year of a patent is the year of application in the priority country. There is also a year of publication specified with each patent. We use the priority year to organize and analyze the Yale data because the year of publication must be interpreted in different ways depending on whether a country follows the European or the U.S. system of publication.

A further distinction arises between priority year and year of application. In a given destination country, the year of application for domestic patients is the same as the priority year, whereas the year of application for foreign patents is generally one year after the priority year. After the priority application is filed, the applicant has one year to apply for protection in other countries. Inventors seem to use this one-year grace period rather than filing additional applications immediately. To facilitate comparisons with WIPO data on patent applications by year of application we proxy for year of application by adding one year to the priority year for foreign priority patents.

A.4 Comparisons with Aggregate Data from WIPO

In this section we show how the two datasets line up. Tables 11.A.1 and 11.A.2 compare patent application data by year of application and coun-

TABLE 11.A.1. Comparisons of Patent Counts from WIPO and Yale for 1970

	01_FR Data Source		02_GE Data Source		03_UK Data Source		04_US Data Source		05_JA Data Source	
Source Cty.	WIPO Pat. Ct. 70	Yale Pat. Ct. 70	WIPO Pat. Ct. 70	Yale Pat. Ct. 70	WIPO Pat. Ct. 70	Yale Pat. Ct. 70	WIPO Pat. Ct. 70	Yale Pat. Ct. 70	WIPO Pat. Ct. 70	Yale Pat. Ct. 70
01_FR	14,106	16,275	3,040	3,020	2,546	2,329	2,375	1,670	1,354	
02_GE	8,416	8,319	32,772	31,579	7,761	6,450	6,808	4,369	5,901	
03_UK	3,072	3,370	3,623	3,875	25,227	11,018	4,113	2,489	2,485	
04_US	11,538	9,346	12,618	10,981	14,057	10,815	72,343	54,146	13,805	
05_JA	2,526	2,505	3,838	3,984	3,592	3,287	5,295	4,184	100,511	
06_AT	317	383	638	759	294	273	322	238	233	
07_BE	526	393	407	333	408	210	307	147	226	
08_IT	1,015	1,216	1,064	1,138	958	756	1,017	585	455	
09_NT	1,134	899	1,334	976	819	828	738	568	985	
10_SZ	2,041	1,608	2,890	1,998	2,000	1,225	1,506	1,016	1,744	
11_SC	286	202	520	362	594	270	429	181	225	
12_SW	630	666	971	935	843	700	806	533	592	
13_OE	233	204	188	180	275	121	276	81	87	
14_AU	95	115	138	130	324	187	315	130	154	
15_CA	256	110	318	142	677	173	1,535	237	308	
16_SV	1,563	1,017	1,327	1,771	1,151	474	700	253	866	
17_OT	335	95	398	116	595	133	467	106	642	

Destination Country

TABLE 11.A.2. Comparisons of Patent Counts from WIPO and Yale for 1977

Destination Country

Source Cty.	01_FR Data Source		02_GE Data Source		03_UK Data Source		04_US Data Source		05_JA Data Source	
	WIPO Pat. Ct. 77	Yale Pat. Ct. 77	WIPO Pat. Ct. 77	Yale Pat. Ct. 77	WIPO Pat. Ct. 77	Yale Pat. Ct. 77	WIPO Pat. Ct. 77	Yale Pat. Ct. 77	WIPO Pat. Ct. 77	Yale Pat. Ct. 77
01_FR	11,811	12,614	2,761	2,492	2,467	2,096	3,007	2,051	1,488	875
02_GE	7,420	7,064	30,247	29,272	6,749	5,902	8,903	5,851	5,094	2,926
03_UK	2,159	2,512	2,573	2,726	21,114	12,282	4,533	2,678	1,762	1,002
04_US	8,637	7,050	10,283	8,230	11,580	8,958	62,863	41,667	10,836	5,122
05_JA	2,345	2,285	4,626	4,416	3,601	3,429	9,674	6,810	27,753	27,392
06_AT	287	322	605	600	258	221	402	281	196	79
07_BE	443	341	358	308	347	250	415	251	175	50
08_IT	1,059	1,110	1,106	1,081	855	828	1,224	671	478	335
09_NT	1,097	712	1,190	788	1,104	714	1,026	585	879	317
10_SZ	1,838	1,182	2,611	1,726	1,732	1,002	1,964	1,139	1,433	365
11_SC	363	234	598	393	760	285	618	239	320	95
12_SW	704	646	989	895	846	739	1,253	710	610	176
13_OE	281	186	254	157	361	142	434	139	131	78
14_AU	125	125	165	164	362	275	524	271	173	67
15_CA	198	96	260	102	695	143	2,192	293	259	74
16_SV	871	490	1,388	894	838	403	1,024	309	749	114
17_OT	340	92	387	99	754	117	875	134	432	247

try of residence from WIPO with the Yale patent publication data using our proxy for year of application and using priority country as a proxy for the source. Notice that in each destination country under the European system (France, Germany, and Japan) the Yale totals are only slightly below the WIPO totals. We believe the difference represents those patents that fail the screening that precedes the initial publication. For countries that follow the U.S. system of examination and publication (the United States and the United Kingdom prior to 1978), a much greater fraction of patents have failed the standard for publication.[23]

A.5 Parameter Estimates

TABLE 11.A.3.   1977 Data: Estimates of *D* Parameters

Destination Country	Effect
01_FR	0.9
02_GE	0.9
03_UK	1.3
04_US	1.2
05_JA	0.8

TABLE 11.A.4.   1977 Data: Estimates of *S* Parameters

Source Country	Effect
01_FR	2.5
02_GE	7.2
03_UK	2.8
04_US	11.0
05_JA	3.1
06_AT	0.3
07_BE	0.3
08_IT	0.8
09_NT	0.8
10_SZ	1.7
11_SC	0.5
12_SW	1.0
13_OE	0.3
14_AU	0.3
15_CA	0.5
16_SV	0.8
17_OT	0.5

TABLE 11.A.5. 1977 Data: Estimates of T Parameters

Technology	Effect
Ag_Agricult	1.0
Bu_Building	2.6
Ch_Chemist	5.2
Dr_Drilling	0.3
El_Electric	4.2
En_Engineer	1.7
Fd_Food	0.7
He_Health	1.8
In_Instrum	4.6
Li_Lighting	1.7
Me_Metals	1.2
Nu_Nucleon	0.1
Pa_Paper	0.2
Pe_Personal	1.4
Ph_Pharmac	0.4
Pr_Printing	0.7
Pu_PumpsEng	1.2
Se_Separate	1.6
Sh_Shaping	3.6
Te_Textiles	1.0
Tr_Transpor	4.5
We_Weapons	0.3
XX_Other	0.0

TABLE 11.A.6. 1977 Data: Estimates of H Parameters

Domestic or Foreign	Effect
DO	2.6
FO	0.4

TABLE 11.A.7. 1977 Data: Estimates of *DS* Parameters

Source Country	Destination Country				
	01_FR Effect	02_GE Effect	03_UK Effect	04_US Effect	05_JA Effect
01_FR	1.0	1.2	1.0	0.9	1.0
02_GE	1.3	1.0	0.9	0.8	1.0
03_UK	1.0	0.9	1.0	1.1	0.9
04_US	0.9	0.9	0.9	1.0	1.3
05_JA	0.7	1.1	0.8	1.6	1.0
06_AT	1.1	1.7	0.7	0.8	0.9
07_BE	1.7	1.1	1.0	0.8	0.7
08_IT	1.4	1.2	0.9	0.9	0.8
09_NT	1.3	1.0	1.0	0.6	1.2
10_SZ	1.2	1.3	0.8	0.7	1.1
11_SC	0.8	1.1	1.4	0.8	1.0
12_SW	1.0	1.1	0.9	1.0	1.1
13_OE	1.2	0.9	1.2	1.0	0.8
14_AU	0.6	0.7	1.4	1.5	1.2
15_CA	0.5	0.5	1.4	3.2	0.8
16_SV	1.1	1.4	0.8	0.7	1.1
17_OT	0.8	0.7	1.3	1.1	1.3

TABLE 11.A.8. 1977 Data: Estimates of *DT* Parameters

Technology	Destination Country				
	01_FR Effect	02_GE Effect	03_UK Effect	04_US Effect	01_JA Effect
Ag_Agricult	1.5	1.0	1.0	1.2	0.5
Bu_Building	1.2	1.0	1.0	1.1	0.8
Ch_Chemist	0.9	0.9	0.9	1.0	1.4
Dr_Drilling	0.9	1.1	1.2	1.3	0.6
El_Electric	0.9	1.0	0.9	0.9	1.5
En_Engineer	1.1	1.0	1.1	0.9	1.0
Fd_Food	1.1	0.9	0.9	0.8	1.5
He_Health	1.0	1.0	0.9	1.1	1.0
In_Instrum	0.9	1.0	0.9	1.0	1.3
Li_Lighting	1.1	1.0	0.9	0.9	1.1
Me_Metals	1.0	0.9	0.9	0.9	1.5
Nu_Nucleon	0.9	0.9	0.8	0.7	2.2
Pa_Paper	1.0	0.9	0.8	0.9	1.3
Pe_Personal	1.3	1.0	1.0	1.1	0.7
Ph_Pharmac	0.9	0.8	0.8	0.9	1.9
Pr_Printing	1.1	0.9	1.0	0.8	1.3
Pu_PumpsEng	1.0	1.0	1.0	1.1	0.9
Se_Separate	1.0	1.0	0.9	1.0	1.1
Sh_Shaping	1.0	0.9	0.9	0.9	1.3
Te_Textiles	1.0	1.0	1.0	1.0	1.1
Tr_Transpor	1.1	1.0	1.0	1.0	1.0
We_Weapons	1.1	0.9	1.2	1.5	0.5
XX_Other	0.5	2.6	3.3	1.2	0.2

TABLE 11.A.9. 1977 Data: Estimates of *ST* Parameters

	Source Country																	
Technology	01_FR Eff.	02_GE Eff.	03_UK Eff.	04_US Eff.	05_JA Eff.	06_AT Eff.	07_BE Eff.	08_IT Eff.	09_NT Eff.	10_SZ Eff.	11_SC Eff.	12_SW Eff.	13_OE Eff.	14_AU Eff.	15_CA Eff.	16_SV Eff.	17_OT Eff.
Ag_Agricult	0.7	0.6	0.5	0.5	0.4	1.6	0.3	0.8	6.5	0.4	3.1	1.3	1.7	4.2	0.6	1.3	1.1
Bu_Building	0.7	0.7	0.4	0.4	0.5	2.6	1.2	1.1	1.1	0.7	2.1	1.2	2.2	1.3	1.7	0.4	1.8
Ch_Chemist	0.9	1.1	1.4	1.4	1.2	0.8	3.2	1.3	0.8	1.4	0.6	0.3	1.0	0.4	0.8	1.9	0.9
Dr_Drilling	1.2	1.6	1.6	1.8	0.7	1.7	1.6	0.2	1.2	0.2	0.4	2.7	0.4	0.4	3.1	2.2	3.0
El_Electric	1.3	1.2	1.1	1.5	2.5	0.6	0.4	1.2	3.3	1.0	0.9	0.7	0.5	0.5	1.3	1.2	0.9
En_Engineer	1.4	1.4	1.1	1.1	0.9	0.9	0.4	1.2	1.5	1.1	1.6	1.5	1.0	0.7	0.8	0.9	0.7
Fd_Food	0.8	0.5	0.9	0.9	0.9	0.7	1.1	1.2	1.9	1.4	0.9	0.8	1.1	1.3	1.4	0.9	0.8
He_Health	0.8	0.8	0.8	1.2	0.6	2.5	0.7	0.7	0.9	0.9	1.4	1.2	1.8	1.3	0.8	0.6	1.5
In_Instrum	1.1	1.1	1.1	1.5	3.0	0.6	0.7	1.1	1.7	1.4	0.8	0.8	0.5	0.8	0.7	1.4	0.7
Li_Lighting	0.9	0.8	0.7	0.8	0.8	0.9	1.3	1.4	0.9	1.1	1.8	1.9	1.2	0.5	1.0	0.6	1.6
Me_Metals	0.7	0.6	0.8	0.9	1.6	0.9	4.3	0.7	0.7	0.8	1.3	0.8	0.2	1.2	2.9	1.0	1.5
Nu_Nucleon	3.0	3.4	1.7	2.9	3.0	2.3	0.7	0.0	1.9	0.4	0.1	1.8	0.7	5.3	3.1	1.2	0.1
Pa_Paper	0.8	0.9	1.1	1.0	0.6	0.3	0.1	1.1	1.2	2.1	13.9	4.9	0.4	1.7	0.5	1.0	1.8
Pe_Personal	0.7	0.8	0.5	0.8	0.6	0.8	0.9	2.4	0.6	1.2	1.3	1.1	2.1	1.3	1.6	0.4	2.1
Ph_Pharmac	1.3	0.8	1.7	1.4	1.0	0.3	4.9	1.7	0.9	1.0	0.4	0.4	1.0	1.1	0.6	1.4	1.4
Pr_Printing	0.9	1.2	0.8	1.1	2.4	0.7	1.3	1.4	0.5	1.5	0.5	1.2	1.2	1.3	1.0	2.4	0.2
Pu_PumpsEng	1.3	1.6	1.2	1.1	1.9	1.5	0.6	1.5	0.2	1.1	1.1	1.0	0.8	0.8	0.5	0.8	1.9
Se_Separate	0.8	1.0	1.1	1.1	0.8	1.1	1.1	0.7	1.1	1.0	1.3	1.3	1.3	0.7	1.0	1.3	0.9
Sh_Shaping	0.7	0.9	0.7	0.7	1.0	1.6	1.0	1.5	0.9	1.1	0.7	1.0	0.7	0.5	1.2	1.8	1.8
Te_Textiles	0.7	1.1	1.1	0.8	1.2	1.1	0.6	3.1	0.6	3.3	0.5	0.5	1.3	0.8	0.7	3.3	0.6
Tr_Transpor	1.0	1.1	0.9	0.8	0.8	0.9	0.6	1.5	1.1	1.0	1.8	1.3	1.2	0.8	1.0	0.7	1.3
We_Weapons	1.1	1.1	0.5	0.7	0.2	0.5	2.9	1.0	0.5	2.0	1.3	2.8	1.5	2.2	1.9	0.1	5.3
XX_Other	2.1	0.8	5.0	0.9	1.9	2.4	6.6	2.1	0.3	1.0	0.8	0.1	3.9	0.6	0.1	2.0	0.2

TABLE 11.A.10. 1977 Data: Estimates of *DH* Parameters

Destination Country	Domestic or Foreign	
	DO Effect	FO Effect
01_FR	1.0	1.0
02_GE	0.8	1.2
03_UK	1.1	0.9
04_US	0.8	1.2
05_JA	1.3	0.8

TABLE 11.A.11. 1977 Data: Estimates of *TH* Parameters

Technology	Domestic or Foreign	
	DO Effect	FO Effect
Ag_Agricult	1.4	0.7
Bu_Building	1.4	0.7
Ch_Chemist	0.7	1.4
Dr_Drilling	1.0	1.0
El_Electric	0.9	1.1
En_Engineer	0.9	1.1
Fd_Food	1.0	1.0
He_Health	1.0	1.0
In_Instrum	0.9	1.1
Li_Lighting	1.2	0.8
Me_Metals	0.9	1.1
Nu_Nucleon	0.8	1.2
Pa_Paper	0.9	1.1
Pe_Personal	1.3	0.8
Ph_Pharmac	0.7	1.4
Pr_Printing	1.1	0.9
Pu_PumpsEng	0.9	1.2
Se_Separate	0.9	1.1
Sh_Shaping	1.0	1.0
Te_Textiles	0.9	1.1
Tr_Transpor	1.1	0.9
We_Weapons	1.1	0.9
XX_Other	1.3	0.8

NOTES

This essay has benefited from comments by Phillip Levy and Gary Saxonhouse.

1. A patent right excuses others from making, using, or selling the patented device. Thus, patenting abroad also forecloses manufacturing for export to third markets.

2. This interpretation is also consistent with the concentration of the world's R&D activity in a few industrialized countries and with the direction of high-technology trade.

3. Putnam (1996) does estimate separate models for pharmaceutical inventions and for all inventions. He finds much higher patent values, on average, for pharmaceuticals but does not separately estimate the fraction of total value attributable to international inventions. The study closest to ours is by Archibugi and Pianta (1992), who examine the distribution over technologies of patents received by the European Patent Office and by the U.S. Patent Office. The work of Cantwell (1989) is also related, although he uses U.S. patent data by industry and does not consider the technology classes themselves.

4. One limitation of our data is that, while we have the technological detail, we do not have patent data for developing countries. This limits us somewhat in the answers that we provide to these questions, particularly as they relate to economic development. The data do include, however, patents applied for by inventors from all over the world. As we discuss below, most patent activity occurs in developed countries.

5. See Huffman and Evenson (1993) for a comprehensive survey of the returns to national and international agricultural research and extension expenditures. Dowrick and Gemmell (1991) provide very different evidence that bears on this issue. Using aggregate data, they find evidence of technological catch-up in manufacturing, but not in agriculture.

6. The model implies that the propensity to patent f_{ni} depends on imitation rates (for both patented and unpatented innovations), the cost of patenting, and the size of country n's market. Eaton and Kortum (1996) relate the source country's rate of innovation α_i alternatively to its investment in research and to a country fixed effect. They relate diffusion rates ε_{ni} to the distance between i and n, imports from i to n, and the human capital of the receiving country n.

7. Patenting is likely to be more expensive and inconvenient for inventors from abroad since foreign filing requires engaging local counsel and often translation.

8. The argument for looking at applications rather than grants is made in Griliches (1990). In the international context the case for using applications is even stronger, as we discuss in the appendix.

9. Okada (1992) finds that Japanese domestic patents contain only 1/4.9 or approximately 20 percent as many claims on average as do foreign priority patents in Japan. There is no evidence that Japanese patents abroad are similarly anomalous, probably because patent laws in other countries encourage the bundling of related claims into a single application.

10. The appendix provides details about the Yale data. The Yale-Canada Con-

cordance (Kortum and Putnam 1997) augments these data by assigning patented inventions to their industries of origin and use based on the IPC assignment. Here we analyze the international patent data as they come from the EPO.

11. The composition of each of our technology classes is taken from WIPO (1994) with one additional category created for pharmaceuticals.

12. The appendix describes our proxy for the year of application. We narrow our analysis to the years 1970 and 1977 to avoid complications arising from the introduction of the European Patent in 1978 and because the first year of complete data is 1970. In order to use the data after 1977 we must merge in all patents published by the EPO (by date of application) according to the destination countries designated on each patent. This task is not yet complete.

13. Our source countries (and regions) are 01_FR = France; 02_GE = Germany; 03_UK = United Kingdom; 04_US = United States; 05_JA = Japan; 06_AT = Austria; 07_BE = Belgium and Luxembourg; 08_IT = Italy; 09_NT = the Netherlands; 10_SZ = Switzerland; 11_SC = Scandinavia (excluding Sweden); 12_SW = Sweden; 13_OE = Greece, Ireland, Israel, and Spain; 14_AU = Australia and New Zealand; 15_CA = Canada; 16_SV = Soviet bloc; and 17_OT = Africa, Asia (excluding Japan), and South America. Note that all developing countries are included in 17_OT.

14. In the United States (and prior to 1978 in the United Kingdom as well) it corresponds to a patent application that has survived a lengthy period of examination, while in the other three countries it is essentially a rubber stamp that follows the date of application by eighteen months (see the appendix for details).

15. Putnam (1996) models the choice of first-filing (priority) country, which depends on the relative size of the foreign and domestic fee schedules and markets, and the quality of the patent office's initial signal regarding patentability. In the case of Canadian and Belgian inventors, 75 percent of all patents are filed first outside the inventor's country of residence.

16. In principle one could use the WIPO data disaggregated by technology class. This is not feasible in practice, however, due to a preponderance of missing values.

17. We ignore any correlation induced by the fact that the same invention is often patented in several countries.

18. See, for example, Bishop, Fienberg, and Holland (1975) or Christensen (1990).

19. The test requires nonzero patenting in each cell, so in calculating the test statistics we add 0.1 patents to each observation with no patents.

20. For example, in the case of destination-country effects (where the table is a single column),

$$\prod_{n=1}^{N}(\hat{D}_n)^{1/N} = e^{(1/N)\sum_{n=1}^{N}\ln \hat{D}_n} = e^0 = 1,$$

where $\hat{D}_n$ is the maximum likelihood of D_n.

21. While these patterns generally mirror the allocation of R&D by industry,

differing appropriability and regulatory conditions render this correlation less than unity. For example, the aerospace industry—which comprises parts of electricity, instruments, weapons, and transporting—is highly R&D intensive and highly innovative but has a low propensity to patent. Recall from table 11.1 that we are unable to discriminate between technology-specific propensities to patent and technology-specific innovativeness.

22. This result provides some vindication for the assumption, in Eaton and Kortum (forthcoming), that diffusion effects could be broken down into source, destination, and home effects.

23. Comparing patents published by year of grant from WIPO data, we obtained a very close match in the United States and the United Kingdom. This is consistent with our interpretation of a published patent in the U.S.-system countries.

REFERENCES

Archibugi, Daniele, and Mario Pianta. 1992. "Specialization and Size of Technological Activities in Industrial Countries: The Analysis of Patent Data." *Research Policy* 21:79–93.
Bishop, Yvonne, Stephen Fienberg, and Paul Holland. 1975. *Discrete Multivariate Analysis: Theory and Practice.* Cambridge: MIT Press.
Bosworth, Derrick L. 1984. "Foreign Patent Flows to and from the U.K." *Research Policy* 13:115–24.
Cantwell, John. 1989. *Technological Innovation and Multinational Corporations.* Oxford: Basil Blackwell.
Christensen, Ronald. 1990. *Log-Linear Models.* New York: Springer-Verlag.
Dowrick, Steve, and Norman Gemmell. 1991. "Industrialisation, Catching Up, and Economic Growth." *Economic Journal* 101:263–75.
Eaton, Jonathan, and Samuel Kortum. 1996. "Trade in Ideas: Patenting and Productivity in the OECD." *Journal of International Economics* 40:251–78.
———. Forthcoming. "International Technology Diffusion: Theory and Measurement." *International Economic Review.*
Evenson, Robert E. 1984. "International Invention: Implications for Technology Market Analysis." In *R&D, Patents, and Productivity,* ed. Zvi Griliches. Chicago: University of Chicago Press.
Fei, John C. H,. and Gustav Ranis. 1964. *Development of the Surplus Labor Economy.* Homewood, Ill.: Richard D. Irwin.
Griliches, Zvi. 1990. "Patent Statistics as Economic Indicators: A Survey." *Journal of Economic Literature* 28:1661–1707.
Hausman, Jerry, Bronwyn Hall, and Zvi Griliches. 1984. "Econometric Models for Count Data with an Application to the Patents-R&D Relationship." *Econometrica* 52:909–38.
Huffman, Wallace E., and Robert E. Evenson. 1993. *Science for Agriculture.* Ames: Iowa State University Press.
Kortum, Samuel, and Jonathan Putnam. 1997. "Assigning Patents to Industries:

Test of the Yale Technology Concordance." *Economic Systems Research* 9:161–75.

Mankiw, N. Gregory. 1995. "The Growth of Nations." *Brookings Papers on Economic Activity* 1:275–310.

Okada, Y. 1992. "Tokkyoseido no ho to keizaigaku" (The law and economics of the patent system). Staff Paper, Shinshu University.

Penrose, Edith T. 1951. *The Economics of the International Patent System.* Baltimore: Johns Hopkins University Press.

Putnam, Jonathan. 1996. "The Value of International Patent Rights." Ph.D. diss., Yale University.

Ranis, Gustav. 1979. "Appropriate Technology: Obstacles and Opportunities." In *Technology and Economic Development: A Realistic Perspective,* ed. Samuel M. Rosenblatt. Boulder, Colo.: Westview Press.

Slama, Jiri. 1981. "Analysis by Means of a Gravitational Model of International Flows of Patent Applications in the period 1967–1978." *World Patent Information* 3:1–8.

World Intellectual Property Organization. 1970, 1977, 1993, 1994. *Industrial Property Statistics.* Geneva: World Intellectual Property Organization.

CHAPTER 12

Can Agricultural Genetic Resources Be a Bonanza for the South?

Brian D. Wright

1 Introduction

Over the first few decades of the next century, world food production will have to continue its current historically rapid rate of advance if expanding populations are to be properly fed. Expanded cultivation and irrigation will account for very little of the growth in supply. The world must rely instead on continued high rates of yield increases to prevent food shortages and famines in the near future. These in turn depend on continued success in breeding more productive varieties ("cultivars") of major crops. Access of breeders to the necessary breeding materials is obviously essential for success.

Thus germplasm, the "material that controls heredity" (Witt 1985, 8), has become an essential international resource. Most agricultural germplasm originates in the "South" and is used by the North without compensation to its providers. But the rules of exchange are now changing, and the new regime is the subject of intense discussion in several international fora. Many articulate, interesting, and informative studies have addressed this general issue. But they do not deal explicitly with the balance of interests at stake. They may well leave their readers asking: Have the countries of the South been frittering away their national patrimony by allowing free access to their agricultural germplasm? Can germplasm in the next decade become, like oil in the 1970s, the basis for a sudden surge in wealth for countries of the South?

These questions touch on several topics that have benefited from Gus Ranis's research. These include agriculture, national resources, income distribution, the structural effects of growth, and intellectual property. Though Gus Ranis has emphasized that the earnings from natural-resource endowments do not necessarily translate into long-term development benefits, the prospect of a genetic resource bonanza would surely get the attention of policymakers and others who hope to acquire some of the rent from genetic resources.

At a time when the implications of the Convention on Biodiversity are being worked out, the implementation of Agenda 21 of the United Nations Food and Agriculture Origination is under discussion, and the TRIPS provisions (see below) included in the last GATT round have committed countries of the South to extend intellectual-property protection to genetic materials including plants, it might be useful to address the order of magnitude of the prospective gains from exploitation of these rights for agricultural applications, as well as their distributional potential. Methods currently under discussion for capturing these gains on behalf of "farmers' rights" to germplasm they have developed on their own land threaten to impose new costs on the international agricultural-research system. Are the prospective gains sufficient to justify these costs?

2 Compensation for Germplasm Resources: Northern and Southern Approaches

Discussions of intellectual property rights issues relating to plant breeding have been vigorous and extensive over the last few decades. The legal protection of new plant material has expanded quite rapidly in the North over this period, especially in the United States. The latter insisted in the recent GATT negotiations on the agreement on "Trade-Related Aspects of Intellectual Property Rights, Including Trade in Counterfeit Goods" (TRIPS), which calls for protection of plant varieties worldwide. Article 27, 3(b) includes the provision, "Members shall provide for the protection of plant varieties either by patents or by an effective *sui generis* system or by any combination thereof." There is a novelty requirement in Article 27, 1, consistent with existing patent requirements in developed economies. The force of these provisions with respect to agriculture may well depend on the legal interpretation, of novelty, nonobviousness, and of exclusions in Article 27, 2, which include those necessary to protect "human, animal or plant life or health or to avoid serious prejudice to the environment" (Contracting Parties 1994).

Prior to the GATT agreement, concerns about establishment of germplasm rights had been evolving in less developed countries in the opposite direction, toward freer access to currently proprietary resources. Countries of the South understandably were dissatisfied with the great asymmetry between the free access to farmers' traditional varieties ("landraces") and wild and weedy varieties, mostly from the

South, by plant breeders, mostly in the "North" or in the largely North-sponsored Consultative Group on International Agricultural Research (CGIAR) system, and the assertion of property rights by private breeders over the descendants of this germplasm. Their concerns materialized in the Twenty-second Food and Agriculture Organization of the United Nations (FAO) conference in 1983 as the "International Undertaking on Plant Genetic Resources." Article 1 actually supports the kind of access historically enjoyed by breeders with respect to germplasm found in situ in geographic centers of diversity or in major genebanks:

> The objective of this Undertaking is to ensure that plant genetic resources of economic and/or social interest, particularly for agriculture, will be explored, preserved, evaluated, and made available for plant breeding and scientific purposes. This Undertaking is based on the universally accepted principle that plant genetic resources are a heritage of mankind and consequently should be available without restriction.

Private breeders could not, however, tolerate generalization of this principle to the output of their efforts in Article 2, which states that access should extend to "newly developed varieties and special genetic stocks (including elite and current breeders' lines and mutants)" (see Witt 1985, 107–8). Unrestricted access without compensation would destroy their business.

Though the Undertaking was intended as a moral rather than legal commitment, it did not receive official support even from some of the nations that were its original advocates (Witt 1985, 112). Countries with valuable germplasm resources were, like private breeders, understandably reluctant to relinquish their options for future gains via sale of access to these resources.

A shift in the balance between access and remuneration is implicit in the 1992 Convention on Biodiversity (CBD), which states that each contracting party shall,

> Subject to its national legislation, respect, preserve and maintain knowledge, innovations and practices of indigenous and local communities embodying traditional lifestyles relevant for the conservation and sustainable use of biological diversity and promote their wider application with the approval and involvement of the holders of such knowledge, innovations and practices and encourage the equitable sharing of benefits arising from the utilization of such knowledge, innovations and practices. (UNEP 1992, Article 8(j))

Thus, the CBD implicitly advocates compensation for the use of indigenous knowledge (although exactly who should be paid is left vague). The absence of demands for free access to enhanced germplasm and breeders' proprietary cultivars leaves room for recognition of the legitimacy of private markets in the latter. There is, potentially, something for everyone in a regime in compliance with the CBD. I now consider briefly the means for implementation of TRIPS with respect to agricultural genetic resources.

3 Means of Appropriation of Farmer Rights under TRIPS

3.1 Patents

If TRIPS means patents in their present form, it will offer little to farmers who provide in situ conservation beyond, at best, defense of their continued right to free access to the genetic material in the seeds they use. Patent systems provide for compensation only for individuals as distinct from communities, exclude disembodied knowledge, and impose a novelty requirement that would seem to preclude discoveries that were known by a community years before the patent application.

How would less developed countries fare under TRIPS? First, we should recognize that they have real problems with the current balance of rights. Concern with the operation of the United States patent system is eloquently expressed in Rural Advancement Foundation International (RAFI) 1994, which presents several cases in which indigenous knowledge of the South appears to have been used to obtain patents in the North. Other instances of patents incorporating sweeping claims to plant biotechnology are also discussed.

These concerns encompass several dimensions. One is the apparent relaxation of traditional patenting criteria. The requirements of novelty and workability appear to go by the wayside when genes identified using once-novel but currently routine techniques are patented without specification of their function (see Fowler and Mooney 1990). A second and related issue is that United States patent law has traditionally relied heavily on legal challenges to establish the scope and validity of patents. This judicial role tends to become all the more crucial in technologies on the frontiers of science (which tend to be foci of patenting activity), in which it is difficult to find qualified personnel willing to work as patent examiners.

Recent sweeping claims to whole areas of application of new technology, such as the 1992 Agracetus patent that claimed to cover any genetic manipulation of cotton (RAFI 1994, 8), create uncertainty and suspicion among researchers worldwide, even if they are subsequently rejected via legal challenges. Furthermore, the expense of legal challenges tends to exclude from the process parties who do not themselves seek large profits from their intellectual property. It is little wonder that the tendencies in patenting of life-forms cause concern among third-world advocates.

Leaving the above, essentially administrative, problems aside, farmers' rights to their germplasm and knowledge could not be effectively protected by adoption throughout the South of a conventional patent system. Patents have never applied to pure knowledge of techniques or processes, nor to intellectual property acquired from other parties. The notion of an Amazonian tribe obtaining a patent under existing patent law for their traditional communal knowledge of the insecticidal benefits of a jungle plant is unrealistic.

3.2 Alternatives to Patent Protection

Several modes of compensation for development of intellectual property compensation are worth considering in cases for which patents are unavailable. The best known is the agreement between Merck, the multinational drug corporation, and Instituto Nacional de Biodiversidad (INBIO), an institution set up by the government in Costa Rica to conduct biodiversity prospecting and analysis (Lesser and Krattiger 1994). The terms include a fixed fee and an undisclosed royalty for any successful products. The focus is on pharmaceutical inputs growing in forest environments, rather than on crops growing in farmers' fields. There is no direct compensation of indigenous peoples.

"Debt for nature" swaps as in the Brazilian rain forest also compensate governments rather than individuals for conservation of natural ecosystems. When crops must be cultivated to preserve their gene pool, such a lack of incentive for farmers could be fatal to the conservation effort. Indeed, all the above alternatives to a strong patent system seem to offer little protection to national citizens, farmers included, who seek the market rewards for their conservation and crop-breeding efforts.

In another innovative initiative, Vogel (1995) is working to organize native communities to form units capable of protecting local knowledge as a "trade secret" that can be marketed under the protection of trade secrecy law. Earlier he suggested that farmers be converted to "gene-steaders," who are compensated for genetic conservation activities (Vogel 1994). Farmers can also be compensated individually or as a collective group for innovation as well as conservation via transfers to them directly, or to their government as in the Merck-INBIO agreement and in debt-for-nature swaps, which apply to other aspects of bio-diversity conservation.

There is no doubt that development of effective means of compensating farmers for their germplasm and related knowledge is an unsolved problem. Here we concentrate on a separate but related issue. What could such protection be worth to farmers? Assuming full compensation is feasible, what could less developed countries expect from full remuneration for the value of their germplasm currently accruing to farmers and others outside the local community? As a preliminary, we delineate some important distinctions in the next section.

4 Farmers' Rights: North versus South?

The relationship between modern agriculture and its genetic resources is frequently cast as a North-South issue.[1] But this turns out to be an example of the fallacy of composition. It is true that most of the world's agricultural genetic resources hail from the South. But most of the countries of the South are poor in agricultural genetic resources and rely on germplasm originating elsewhere. The ultimate source of agricultural germplasm is often ambiguous or obscure, as crops evolve in the process of cultivation and geographic dispersion.

Most crop germplasm is the product of the evolution of its ancestors in situ, predominantly in farmers' gardens and fields and their weedy margins, in geographic centers of diversity that are predominantly located in the South. Crops grown in these centers of diversity may derive from ancestors that grew elsewhere, as is the case for Ethiopian wheat. Centers of diversity are not necessarily places of origin. In their centers of diversity, crops benefit from ongoing genetic interactions with their wild and weedy relatives. In Mexico, for example, farmers believe that cross-fertilization of their maize with teosinte, a wild forebear that persists in some locations as a weed, strengthens the corn crop. In Arizona, Native American Pima farmers appreciate the taste benefits of cross-fertilization of chili peppers with piquant wild relatives (Nabhan 1989, chap. 2). Moreover, farmers in centers of diversity often exploit the yield-stabilizing effects of mixing seed from several cultivars in a single field, encouraging cross-fertilization.

Despite the various benefits of farming in a diverse environment, most major crop production takes place as monoculture, far removed from centers of diversity, in relatively gene-poor ecosystems. The exception that proves the rule that gene-poor areas are centers of production is the major rice species *Oryza sativa L.,* which is still predominantly grown near its centers of origin in Asia. But within Asia, major areas of irrigated rice cultivation have environments quite different from the gene-rich natural habitats from which the species evolved.

Wheat production is dominated by production regions in China, the former Soviet countries, India, France, the United States, Canada, Argentina, and Australia, distant from one of wheat's centers of diversity in Ethiopia, and bread wheat's major center of domestication in the Syrian-Mesopotamian plains (Harlan 1970, 21). Corn production in the United States, China, Europe, and Africa is similarly remote from its Latin American origins. Commercial soybean production in the United States and Latin America dominates soy output in Asia, the soybean's center of origin. A similar story holds for potatoes, a predominantly European crop originating in the Andes, as well as sugar cane and sugar beets.

The disjunction between major locations of production and centers of diversity holds also for crops that are grown almost exclusively in the South. Coffee in Latin America, India, Indonesia, and sub-Saharan Africa, rubber and oil palms in Southeast Asia, cocoa in Africa, and bananas in Africa, Latin America, and the Caribbean all tend to flourish away from their genetic origins. (Tea is a mixed case; while still important in its birthplace in India and China, it also flourishes in Sri Lanka, Africa, and New Guinea, for example.)

The Vavilov centers of diversity (which were originally defined in relation to crop resources) are a small portion of the South. As tables 12.1 and 12.2, drawn from Kloppenburg and Kleinman 1987 show, if the world is divided into ten production regions, all the regions that are predominantly North are in a historical sense heavily dependent for food crops on germplasm that originated in other regions. But of the predominantly Southern regions, only three (West Central Asia, Indochina, and Hindustan) acquired a majority of their food crop germplasm from their own regions. Most of the world's germplasm originated in Latin America and West Central Asia.

With respect to industrial crops, only Indo-China acquired less than 70 percent of its germplasm from other regions. Latin America (South) and the Mediterranean (North) are the largest sources for the world as a whole. Dependence at the country (rather than regional) level would be substantially greater for most of the South. Note that for Africa, currently the region with the most severe agricultural challenges, about 80 percent of the germplasm listed originates in other regions (although a recent report indicates that native grains with high potential have been underexploited).

TABLE 12.1. Global Genetic Resource Interdependence in Food Crop Production

Regions of Production	Chino-Japanese	Indo-Chinese	Australian	Hindustanean	West Central Asiatic	Mediterranean	African	Euro-Siberian	Latin American	North American	Sum (%)[a]	Total Dependence
Chino-Japanese	37.2	0.0	0.0	0.0	16.4	2.3	3.1	0.3	40.7	0.0	100	62.8
Indo-Chinese	0.9	66.8	0.0	0.0	0.0	0.0	0.2	0.0	31.9	0.0	100	33.2
Australian	1.7	0.9	0.0	0.5	82.1	0.3	2.9	7.0	4.6	0.0	100	100.0
Hindustanean	0.8	4.5	0.0	51.4	18.8	0.2	12.8	0.0	11.5	0.0	100	48.6
West Central Asiatic	4.9	3.2	0.0	3.0	69.2	0.7	1.2	0.8	17.0	0.0	100	30.8
Mediterranean	8.5	1.4	0.0	0.9	46.4	1.8	0.7	1.2	39.0	0.0	100	98.2
African	2.4	22.3	0.0	1.5	4.9	0.3	12.3	0.1	56.3	0.0	100	87.7
Euro-Siberian	0.4	0.1	0.0	0.1	51.7	2.6	0.4	9.2	35.5	0.0	100	90.8
Latin American	18.7	12.5	0.0	2.3	13.3	0.4	7.8	0.5	44.4	0.0	100	55.6
North American	15.8	0.4	0.0	0.4	36.1	0.5	3.6	2.8	40.3	0.0	100	100.0
World	12.9	7.5	0.0	5.7	30.0	1.4	4.0	2.9	35.6	0.0	100	100.0

Source: Kloppenburg and Kleinman, "The Plant Germplasm Controversy," *Bioscience* 37, no. 3 (1987). Copyright 1987 American Institute of Biological Sciences.

Note: Reading the table horizontally, the figures can be interpreted as measures of the extent to which a given region of production depends upon each of the regions of diversity. The column labeled "Total Dependence" shows the percentage of production for a given region of production that is accounted for by crops associated with non-indigenous regions of diversity.

[a]Because of rounding error, the figures in each row do not always sum exactly to 100.

TABLE 12.2. Global Genetic Resource Interdependence in Industrial Crop Production

Regions of Production					Regions of Diversity							
	Chino-Japanese	Indo-Chinese	Australian	Hindustanean	West Central Asiatic	Mediterranean	African	Euro-Siberian	Latin American	North American	Sum (%)[a]	Total Dependence
Chino-Japanese	8.3	4.7	0.0	1.4	7.4	27.5	0.1	0.0	45.4	5.1	100	91.6
Indo-Chinese	5.0	43.5	0.0	7.1	2.9	0.0	22.6	0.0	18.8	0.0	100	56.4
Australian	0.0	51.2	0.0	0.0	1.8	3.3	0.0	0.0	15.4	28.3	100	100.0
Hindustanean	2.6	14.2	0.0	7.2	20.5	17.2	0.9	0.0	35.2	2.1	100	92.7
West Central Asiatic	1.5	14.7	0.0	0.0	4.5	14.2	0.1	0.0	56.6	8.4	100	95.5
Mediterranean	0.0	3.9	0.0	0.2	2.4	25.3	0.0	0.0	31.8	36.5	100	74.9
African	1.3	16.3	0.0	0.1	10.6	0.4	22.4	0.0	46.0	3.0	100	77.7
Euro-Siberian	0.4	0.0	0.0	0.1	12.8	41.3	0.0	0.0	17.5	27.9	100	100.0
Latin American	0.2	30.4	0.0	0.4	5.9	0.4	25.7	0.0	28.0	9.1	100	72.1
North American	0.0	3.7	0.0	0.0	8.3	33.1	0.0	0.0	39.6	15.3	100	84.7
World	2.1	13.7	0.0	2.0	10.8	18.2	8.3	0.0	34.4	10.5	100	

Source: Kloppenburg and Kleinman, "The Plant Germplasm Controversy," *Bioscience* 37, no. 3 (1987). Copyright 1987 American Institute of Biological Sciences.

Note: Reading the table horizontally, the figures can be interpreted as measures of the extent to which a given region of production depends upon each of the regions of diversity. The column labeled "Total Dependence" shows the percentage of production for a given region of production that is accounted for by crops associated with non-indigenous regions of diversity.

[a]Because of rounding error, the figures in each row do not always sum exactly to 100.

Thus most of the world's agricultural output, North and South, grows in areas far from the historical sources of its germplasm. If producers were required to share the value of their output with countries that provided the landraces that are the ancestors of their crops, working out the details could be tricky where landraces have ancestors elsewhere. But certainly the North would be overwhelmingly a net payer. In fact most countries, North and South, would be net payers, and almost all major producers of a given crop would be net payers of germplasm of that crop.

Speculation on such payments is very likely moot. Recent assignments of rights to germplasm have "grandfathered" access to germplasm currently held in genebanks including those of the international centers of the Consultative Group on International Agricultural Research, under the auspices of the International Plant Genetic Resources Institute (IPGRI). Hence, in assessing the prospective gains from farmers' rights, scenarios of interest include

a. Payment and/or prior approval required by countries in centers of diversity for rights to search for or acquire "new" germplasm in centers of diversity

b. Payment and/or prior approval required by national and/or international genebanks on behalf of depositing countries for access to or use of germplasm, with or without the grandfather provision

We discuss these scenarios below. An essential consideration is the extent of current demand for the germplasm held by farmers in centers of diversity, which is the topic addressed in the next section.

5 The Demand for Continuing Access to Farmers' Landraces

Writers supporting the case for compensation of farmers in centers of diversity dispute the inferences drawn from the figures of Kloppenburg and Kleinman (1987). They argue that the North is especially dependent on access to exotic germplasm. Even if they are located outside centers of diversity, "poor farmers in developing countries are far less dependent upon exotic germplasm since they are surrounded by much greater variability" (Fowler and Mooney 1990, 199). The North has a higher reservation price for access to germplasm: "[T]he political 'pain threshold' for Australia, Europe, and North America—with their highly uniform plant varieties and mechanized food processing—is much lower than the threshold for Africa, Asia, or Latin America" (Fowler and Mooney 1990, 200). Certainly the North, with its greater wealth, has a higher capacity to pay, and a lower elasticity of demand for food as a whole. What these facts do or do not imply for any "pain threshold" at a given level of dependence is an interesting question. But here the discussion focuses on the narrower issue: How dependent is the North on continued access to exotic germplasm?

The argument for continued dependence of the North in particular rests on a set of premises about the major crops:

Major crops are held to be dominated by a small number of cultivars at any one time.

Cultivars are relatively quickly superseded as they fall prey to disease or are supplanted by newly bred cultivars with higher yields.

Output from the set of these cultivars is more variable than from landraces due to the small numbers of cultivars and the high vulnerability of each to stress, pests, and disease.

The flow of new cultivars depends critically on the introduction of new germplasm into the set of elite lines from which they are bred.

Let's consider each of these propositions in turn.

5.1 Dominance of a Small Set of Cultivars

There is no doubt about the high uniformity of cultivars of major crops in the North relative to the centers of diversity. In 1969 the National Research Council (1972) reported that of thirteen major crops (maize, soybeans, wheat, cotton, millet, dry beans, snap beans, peanuts, peas, potatoes, rice, sugar beet, sweet potato), the average number of major varieties was about four, and they accounted for an average of 70 percent of area planted. Though these figures are now out of date, the general continued dominance of a small number of cultivars in the United States is undisputed. In Europe, a narrow set of popular cultivars dominates major crops in many countries (Vellvé 1992, chap. 2), and there is little doubt that a similar situation exists in Canada and Australia.

But the above countries are not unique in their reliance on a narrow base of germplasm. Though this phenomenon is sometimes attributed to capitalist accumulation, it has also arisen in socialist states. The 1971 failure of the Ukrainian wheat crop is attributed to heavy reliance on the high-yielding but cold-sensitive Besostaja cultivar (Fowler and Mooney 1990, x–xi). In China hybrid rice, dependent (like United States corn that succumbed to leaf blight in 1971) on one source of cytoplasmic male sterility, dominates production, in some recent years covering more than half of rice acreage. Away from centers of diversity, output of major crops in other less developed countries is in many cases similarly dominated by a few cultivars. For example, one wheat variety, Sonalika, covered 30 percent and 67 percent of the wheat land in India and Bangladesh, respectively, in 1983 (National Research Council 1993, 70). Tree crops such as coffee, rubber, oil palm, and bananas in many countries reportedly sprang from a handful of clones or closely related seed sources imported directly or indirectly from centers of diversity (see Juma 1989; Fowler and Mooney 1990).

A major reason for the typical dominance of a small number of varieties in production is their superior performance, from the farmer's viewpoint, over a relatively wide range of environmental conditions. The spread of "high-yield varieties" has been a major source of increased cereal production as population has continued to increase while acreage expansion has ceased to be a major means of increasing food supply.

The fact that a small set of cultivars accounts for a large share of production does not necessarily imply a corresponding reduction in the variety of germplasm used by farmers. Farmers may maintain their old cultivars on part of their land, even as they adopt widely marketed high-performance germplasm. (See Brush, Taylor, and Bellon 1992 for a characterization of this phenomenon among Andean potato farmers and Brush 1995 for a broader discussion). But any tendency of farmers to maintain old cultivars can be stifled when market incentives to concentrate on a small set of cultivars are augmented by legal prohibitions on growing and/or marketing other cultivars. In the United States, for example, marketing orders for fruit stipulate size limitations. In California, a "one-variety" cotton law restricted growers to one Acala cultivar each year from 1925 to 1978, and then was modified to allow other Acala cultivars (Constantine, Alston, and Smith 1994). In Canada, wheat varieties have been similarly restricted (Carter, Loyns, and Ahmadi-Esfahani 1986; Ulrich, Furtan, and Schmitz 1987).

5.2 Short Useful Life of High-Yield Cultivars

It is true in general that modern high-yield crop cultivars follow a typical cycle of introduction, diffusion, and obsolescence (Reid and Miller 1989). Duvick conducted a survey of major crops that indicated the typical life span of a cultivar was seven to nine years and falling (Duvick 1984, tables 7 and 8). But high-yield cultivars become obsolete mainly because they are supplanted by cultivars with higher yield potential. They tend to be the victims of progress rather than of genetic vulnerability to evolving diseases.

5.3 Variability of New Cultivars

Though informal discussions in the literature often seem to imply greater variability of elite cultivars relative to landraces, empirical support of this proposition is surprising by its scarcity. Given increasing yields, coefficient of variation (standard deviation divided by mean) is preferable to the variance or raw standard deviation. Change in variability is of course extremely difficult to measure in short time series. Singh and Byerlee (1990) show declining variability in wheat between 1951 and 1986, and they detect no effect of high-yield germplasm on variability. Byerlee and Traxler (1995) show that the coefficients of variation (standard deviation normalized by the mean, to correct for trend increases) of a set of modern wheat varieties released by Centro Internacional de Mejoramiento de Maiz y Trigo (CYMMYT) in Mexico has decreased as yields have risen. But even if given cultivars are no more variable than landraces, their very concentration could add to aggregate variability. Consistent with this hypothesis, Anderson, Hazell, and Evans (1987) and Hazell (1989) do find increased correlations across countries and regions between the 1960s and 1971–83, but their results may be dominated by the unusual crop failures of the 1970s, or they might just reflect progress in world market integration. For storable crops, improvement in market competition might induce variation in planned production in response to changes in marketwide stocks (Williams and Wright 1991).

5.4 Dependence of Breeders on Inflow of New Germplasm

The tables discussed above indicate historical aggregate dependence on germplasm from centers of diversity. And the discussion above confirms the reliance on successive generations of improved seeds, each of short duration and containing a small set of high-yielding cultivars. Contrary to common assertions, the current system does not seem, relative to available historical evidence, especially subject to disruption from pests, diseases, or other causes. But is it beholden to a continued flow of germplasm from centers of diversity? This question is addressed below.

6 Current Introduction of Landrace Germplasm Breeding in High-Yield Cultivars

Some writers, noting the rapid turnover of popular cultivars, have suggested that modern growers substitute temporal for cross-sectional diversity. This might seem consistent with continued reliance on new genetic material from the centers of diversity. But the following discussion of important crops highlights the distinction between sequential diversity of cultivars and the diversity of the germplasm used to generate them.

6.1 Maize (Corn)

The major corn cultivars all trace back to six pure line ancestors in the United States. Though 70 percent of a sample of U.S. corn breeders maintained that their base of germplasm was broader in 1981 than in 1970 (Duvick 1984, table 16, p. 169), Smith (1988) concluded that there was no change in genetic diversity of Corn Belt maize from 1981 to 1986, and Cox, Murphy, and Goodman (1988) found that less than 1 percent of U.S. hybrid corn had non–North American exotic germplasm. Moreover, the National Research Council (1993, 73) notes, "Most surveys have shown that there is little immediate prospect for a large-scale increase in diversity of hybrid maize" in the United States. Apparently, within the germplasm base of U.S. hybrid corn (a small fraction of the total world germplasm), the pool of diversity remains sufficient to provide disease resistance in the high-input U.S. environment and to support a remarkable and as yet undiminished rate of yield increase.

Clearly, genetic resources from the South, made available in recent decades to CIMMYT and other germplasm facilities, have not been of very significant benefit to U.S. corn producers. One implication is that the maximum gain to be had by sources of corn germplasm via effective bargaining with U.S. corn breeders may be modest indeed, if retroactive compensation is ruled out.

High-yield varieties (HYVs) are planted in only about half of all maize land in less developed countries, with the share varying by country. The literature implies that CIMMYT has neither succeeded in incorporating a wide base of germplasm for disease resistance in released HYVs, nor in providing a sufficiently flexible breeding response to disease threats. This may be due to lack of adaptive breeding capacity in many developing countries, which also has hindered the use of local germplasm in breeding. The Latin American Maize Project (Salhuana, Jones, and Sevilla 1991), a multilateral initiative partly funded by Pioneer Hi-Bred to assess crosses of thousands of cultivars under diverse conditions, may lead to greater variety of germplasm used by farmers South and North.

6.2 Wheat

For the United States, of 224 wheat cultivars released before 1975 only 31 percent had any germplasm introduced apart from their foundation germplasm, and none of this was introduced later than 1920 (Cox 1991, table 3-1, p. 26, and p. 28). Of cultivars released subsequently, Cox found 75 percent had some more recently introduced parentage, but usually it constituted only a small part of the cultivar's germplasm, typically introduced for disease resistance via crosses and back-crosses. He noted, "The limited utilization of landraces is most striking" (29).

A recent survey of wheat breeders (Rejesus, van Ginkel, and Smale 1996) indicates wide use of advanced lines and CYMMYT cultivars, in breeders' "crossing blocks," the nurseries that furnish the parental stocks for breeding. But only around 8 percent of the materials are landraces (p. 4, table 1), and these generally are not replaced as frequently as other materials; the inflow is disproportionately low.

6.3 Soybeans

Sprecht and Williams (1984, 65) found that of 136 successful soybean cultivars released by U.S. breeders from 1939 to 1981, 121 had cytoplasm from just five introductions. Only six ancestral strains accounted for nearly 60 percent of the germplasm in these 136 releases and for a similar percentage of germplasm in cultivars released from 1971 to 1981 (Sprecht and Williams 1984, table 3-7, p. 68), even though there was large turnover in the set of leading cultivars between 1970 and 1980 (Duvick 1984, table 4, p. 164).

In a more recent study, Gizlice, Carter, and Burton (1994, 1,143) define the genetic base as the "sets of genotypes that contain 99% of the genes found in modern cultivars." They conclude that "the soybean genetic base was largely formed before 1960. Nearly 75% of the genes in modern soybean cultivars is present in 16 cultivars and a breeding line released before 1960. Breeders have remained dependent on this early genetic core of breeding material and have rarely introduced new germplasm" (1,149).

6.4 Rice

The best documented and probably the most widespread use of landraces, farmers' varieties, and wild species is in the international rice-breeding complex for developing countries. Evenson and Gollin (1997) found that the genealogies of 1,709 rice varieties released since the start of the green revolution include 885 new landraces and several wild species. But even in this impressive breeding record, concentration on a small subset of available materials is still an issue. The dissemination of new germplasm is by no means proportional to the number of International Rice Research Institute (IRRI) releases. Evenson and Gollin (1994) show that the amount of new germplasm introduced in the IRRI releases seems to have declined in recent years, as these releases share much of the germplasm of previous releases. Importantly, all are reported to incorporate the same semidwarfism gene, and the Cina cytoplasm is still pervasive (National Research Council 1993, 76).

Breeders at IRRI and at national programs have effectively incorporated successive genes for pest and disease resistance from exotic germplasm; the complexity of this enterprise is illustrated in the account of Plucknett et al. (1987, chap. 9) of the development of IR-36. The work at IRRI also has been complemented by the widespread crossing with landraces by the National Agricultural Research Systems (NARS), in the International Network for the Genetic Evaluation of Rice (INGER) nurseries (Evenson and Gollin 1994). These crosses are no doubt greatly facilitated by the liquidity provided by IRRI as a germplasm "bank."

Furthermore, rice is not the crop on which to base a case for developed-country dependence on farmers' landraces in the South, for rice production and consumption is predominantly South-centered, and the recent international breeding efforts also are South-centered. The U.S. rice industry, a relatively minor part of United States agribusiness, may have a rather narrow base, but it has used semidwarf germplasm from IRRI, from Taiwan, and more recently from China (Rutger and Bollich 1991, 9). It appears to have gained substantially from acquisition of the same international germplasm for semidwarfism that has proven so effective in raising yields elsewhere, but it does not yet seem to have achieved a very great diversification of germplasm via access to sources from the South. China's hybrid rice program, which has recently covered more than half of China's irrigated rice area (Carl Pray, personal communication), relies on a single cytoplasmic source for male sterility (National Research Council 1993, 76). Is this a potential source of disaster in the world food supply system?

6.5 Edible Beans

The continued narrow genetic base of U.S. soybeans has been noted above. For common beans *(Phaseolus vulgaris L.),* the National Research Council (1972, 225) reported that "for a considerable part of the edible dry bean acreage in the United States, annual production rests upon a dangerously small germplasm base." Adams (1977) refined this report by stating that pinto beans faced the highest risk due to their extreme homogeneity. In 1982 this warning was vindicated by a rust epidemic that caused yield losses of 25 to 50 percent in Colorado and Wyoming and cost $15–20 million (National Research Council 1993, 68).While this experience prompted development of rust-resistant cultivars using the Centro Internacional de Agricultura Tropical (CIAT) gene pool, the susceptible variety is still widely grown (National Research Council 1993, 68). Silbernagel and Hannan (1992, 2) comment that "the need for genetic diversity and enactment of PVPA have not stimulated the utilization of the *Phaseolus* collection of more than 11,000 accessions."

6.6 Novel Industrial Crops

Thus far I have discussed some of the popular crops that have been cultivated for long periods and have extremely large, established, worldwide markets. Perhaps it is not too surprising if breeders of such crops tend to have settled on a rather narrow set of germplasm after centuries of intense selection in different countries. But what is the role of germplasm for crops at the other end of the spectrum, that is, crops under research and development for commercial production?

Thompson, Dierig, and White 1992 reviewed the development of a set of potential industrial crops: guayule (for rubber), kenaf and roselle (for paper pulp), guar (for gum), jojoba (for oil for cosmetics, lubrication, and other uses), meadowfoam, industrial rapeseed, lesquerella (for oils), buffalo and coyote gourd (for high-protein, high-oil seeds, and starchy roots), cuphea (for palm oil substitute), and vernonia and Stokes aster (for coatings, plasticizers, and stabilizers).

Because the development of each of these crops is a highly speculative project, it is not surprising that financing is a major constraint. What is surprising is that 6,481 accessions of these varieties have been identified as available to researchers, and only 2.1 percent of these have been "used in developing new germplasm lines or cultivars" (Thompson, Dierig, and White 1992, 39). If this means that the remainder has never been used in any breeding experiments, it would seem that collection of germplasm has moved ahead of utilization, as is the case for crops with well-established production and experimental programs.

Much of the germplasm of major crops and their wild and weedy relatives already resides in genebanks. But the effect of the vast increase in accessions since the 1970s on germplasm utilized for crop production has thus far been modest.

Allard offers a breeder's view of the need for an inflow of novel genetic material:

> Breeding in barley and corn, as well as in other major crops, has increasingly focused on crosses among elite materials and rates of progress indicate not only that this strategy has been successful but also that there has been little, if any, slowing of progress due to reduction of exploitable genetic material . . . . It consequently seems unlikely that readily exploitable genetic variability will soon be exhausted. (1992, 144–45)

Note that these major crops are precisely the ones with the volume most capable of supporting a competitive private breeding industry. It is sobering that their yields can continue to increase without introduction of new genetic material into their breeding lines.

A frequent rationale offered by breeders for their low rate of introduction of new genetic material is that cultivars in genebanks or in situ are insufficiently described and documented, so their potential contributions as part of a breeding system can be hard to assess. This is not the whole story, however. Common beans, though a "minor crop" in the United States, are a staple for millions of people. Moreover, as noted above, their genetic uniformity has led to some disastrous disruption of production. Nevertheless,

> The gap between identification of useful characters in exotic germplasm and the transfer of these potentially useful characters to cultivars has widened. It is economically prohibitive for private companies to commit the time and expense on cultivar development incorporating exotic germplasm in such a minor crop as common beans, and there is no longer much career incentive for public scientists to perform this work. Therefore, the gap ever widens. (Silbernagel and Hannan 1992, 2–3)

Apparently, the potential prevention of a multimillion dollar disaster offers insufficient incentive for private plant breeders even when well-identified, useful germplasm is available gratis. This gives us some clues to the extent to which breeders believe they can hope to capture the social value of their work. It also gives us a reality check on the scope of concerns about "profiteering" by seed companies using germplasm from the South.

7 The Implications of New Technology

At present, the demand for new crop germplasm from farmers in centers of diversity, and from genebanks, is surprisingly modest. But at present the technology of crop breeding is changing rapidly. Is it possible that in the near future these changes will expand the demand for new germplasm?

The answer depends on the balance between countervailing trends. Advances in conventional breeding have increased the scope for incorporating genes from landraces that are distant relatives. Wide crosses have enabled wheat breeders to incorporate genes from other related species grasses. This should, on the one hand, raise the demand for the germplasm of such grasses. But it might also reduce the demand for germplasm from closer relatives. Advances in genetic engineering are likely to increase the feasibility of such wide crosses, and decrease the time needed to incorporate their effects in new cultivars.

However genetic engineering is also expanding the sources of genetic change for crops much farther afield. Commercial cotton is now being grown incorporating a gene for pest resistance from *Bacillus thuringiensis,* and this gene is also being used by breeders of potatoes, tobacco, and other crops. A fish gene has been transferred to potatoes to induce cold tolerance. Farmers' crops and their wild relatives are no longer the sole source of valuable genetic material for crop breeders. They have competition from genes found in the whole spectrum of terrestrial life-forms. For yield increases and stress tolerance, which often entail combinations of genes, crop breeders are likely to concentrate mainly on their own elite lines of breeding materials, as they have in the past (see Duvick 1984). The continued search for higher yields is unlikely to have a major effect in the near future on the demand for exotic germplasm.

In fact the supply of potentially useful genes is even wider. They can be synthesized via several methods (Orton 1988), including irradiation (which produced new barley cultivars), chemically induced mutation, and somaclonal variation (variation induced via in vitro propagation). In addition, transposable elements, which can relocate genes and alter their expression, are another source of genetic variation that might prove to be a fruitful source of genetic improvements.

How these countervailing effects will balance out is still to be seen. Effects may differ in the short and longer runs. But there seems to be no good reason to expect a dramatic change in the profile of utilization presented in the preceding section.

8 The Implications of TRIPS

The property right regimes created in response to the GATT mandate for gradual compliance with TRIPS are still evolving in many countries. But concerns have been raised that plant patenting could mean that traditional farmers could lose the rights to cultivate their own landraces (see, for example, RAFI 1994). Current CGIAR policy precludes such expropriation of materials in its genebanks, but judicial treatment of the legal claims of private breeding corporations is still evolving. Proponents of farmers' rights to their own germplasm have some cause to worry (see, for example, the panel discussion in Adams et al. 1994, 255–71). Researchers in the public as well as private sectors are naturally concerned if broad rights to biotechnology research in a given crop are claimed by large corporations, even if they realize that there is a high probability that such claims will eventually be denied via legal challenges.

On the other hand there is little evidence that TRIPS will increase genetic diversity significantly via its intended stimulation of private crop-breeding activity. In the absence of incentives for public or private breeders directed specifically at diversity, "Decisions in applied breeding programs are based on breeding progress and not genetic diversity" (Gizlice, Carter, and Burton 1993, 623). TRIPS will probably have at most a modest effect on the demand for genes from farmers' landraces.

9 The Bottom Line: The Financial Potential of Farmers' Rights

Popular discussions of the transfers to be had by enforcement of farmers' rights tend toward overoptimism for several reasons. First, there is a natural tendency to confuse the potential market value of plant genes with the potential value of pharmaceutical products derived from plants in centers of diversity. It is widely known that a single drug can have a multibillion dollar market. Even a typically modest percentage royalty can yield a hefty sum. Recently, Simpson, Sedjo, and Reid (1996) have shown that the pharmaceutical potential of natural plants cannot justify conservation of centers of diversity *at the margin* (i.e., cannot justify cessation of development of a small fraction of the remaining Amazonian rain forest). But nothing in Simpson, Sedjo, and Reid denies that the *total* value of the forest, potentially exploitable via management of access to the pharmaceutical industry, could be huge. In the case of agricultural genetic resources, the private market potential from the genes in traditional farmers' landraces is generally much more modest than for pharmaceuticals. (To put things in perspective, the commercial seed market worldwide is $15 billion per year; the comparable figure for pharmaceuticals is $235 billion.)

Other discussions focus on the profits of seed corporations to fix ideas about the value that might be appropriated by traditional farmers should their rights be fully recognized. As discussed above, the current gene flow from landraces to privately marketed cultivars of major crops is surprisingly modest. To have much force, rights must be retroactive (contrary to current trends), or greater future demand must be anticipated. Even so, this focus is misguided for two opposing reasons. First, the profits of the most successful corporations like Pioneer Hi-Bred (which had an operating profit of $384 million in 1994) are predominantly attributable to United States corn sales and are in some large part due to the firm's investments in research, production, and marketing, and to their managerial expertise. After all, the breeding lines on which their genetic material is based are in general available to competitors who earn far less money in the same market.

10 The True Beneficiaries of New Seeds

To focus on profits from seed sales as the measure of the total value of genetic resources is to miss the forest for the trees. The total benefits derived from use of agricultural genetic resources is far larger than the profits of seed sellers. The major achievement of breeders, using genes generally derived from landraces, has been to increase food supply from available resources, thus reducing food prices, or preventing food price increases, as population has multiplied over the past century.

The evidence on food prices is striking. As figures 12.1 through 12.5 show, real prices of the world's major food sources, wheat, rice, and corn, as well as of soybeans as a protein and oil source, have declined dramatically since World War II, and especially over the last several decades. Though other factors also contributed to this decline, the role of general progress in breeding in producing higher yields is indisputable.

The beneficiaries are principally food consumers in developed *and* developing countries. Some farm owners may gain, others may lose, from particular innovations. (For example, corn innovations may reduce prices of competing grains such as barley or wheat.) Producers of other inputs gain or lose depending on the effects of particular seed innovations on demand. "Green revolution" seeds increase nitrogen demand, but reduce land demand. Crops resistant to a specific herbicide increase

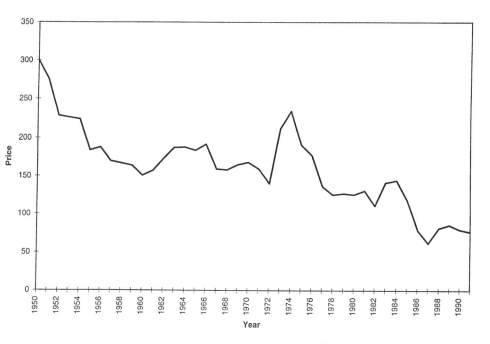

Fig. 12.1.   Corn price (U.S.) (From IBRD 1993.)

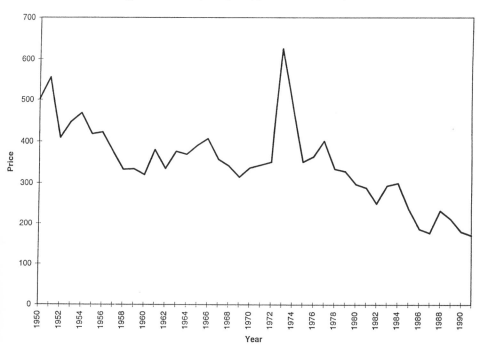

Fig. 12.2.   Soybean price (U.S.) (From IBRD 1993.)

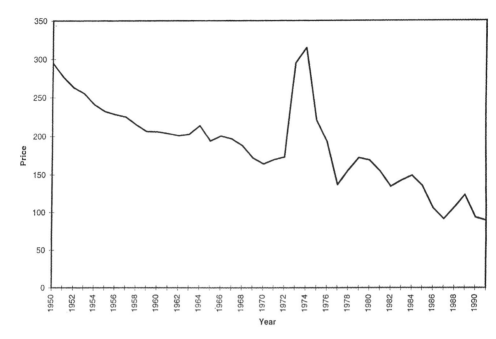

Fig. 12.3.   Wheat price (U.S.) (From IBRD 1993.)

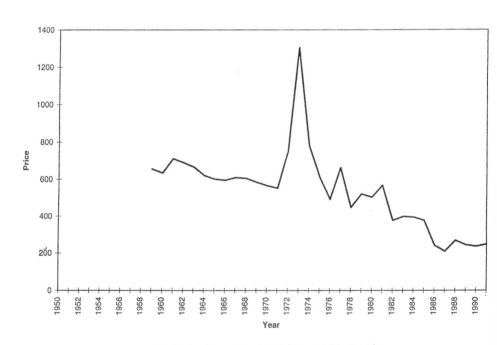

Fig. 12.4.   Rice price (U.S.) (From IBRD 1993.)

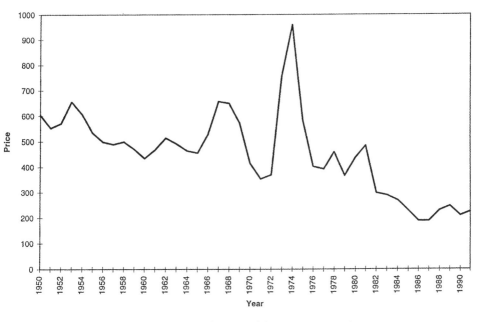

Fig. 12.5.   Rice price (Thailand) (From IBRD 1993.)

the demand for that herbicide at the expense of other herbicides and other weed-control inputs. Crops with pest-resistant genes are likely in many cases to decrease demand for some pesticides.

But it is important to keep the big picture in mind. Consumers North and South are the major beneficiaries of intelligent incorporation of new germplasm in food crops. Apart from the effects of trade barriers and domestic agricultural price policies, the gains accrue roughly in proportion to consumption. Though the rich generally consume more grains, directly and indirectly via animal products, the gains are much more crucial for the larger number of poor consumers in less developed countries.

11 Concluding Remarks

Agricultural genetic resources are crucial for human civilization. The major beneficiaries of the advances in crop production in the present century based on these resources are consumers in all countries, North and South, and the benefits are huge. Once said, this may be obvious. But several of the most informative and interesting recent books on genetic resources do not contain terms such as price, productivity, or food consumption in their indices. The major benefits of genetic resources are surprisingly absent from the discussion.

Despite the high total value of agricultural germplasm, any attempts to earn large rents, akin to those on mineral deposits, from continued supply of agricultural germplasm from the South to breeders in the North will likely fail. Breeders of major crops in the North are not at present highly dependent on flows of new germplasm from developing countries into their breeding stock. Indeed, breeders exploit only a small fraction of the germplasm already available in genebanks in the North or in international centers.

The continued narrowness of the genetic base of crops like hybrid corn and soybeans in the United States is remarkable, given their continuing yield advances. Note that these crops have unusually high income elasticities of demand, due to their use as livestock feed. The crop that has benefited most from the availability of a vast variety of germplasm is rice (in particular tropical rice), a crop that is predominantly produced and consumed in the South. Even if germplasm already stored *ex situ* is not "grandfathered" for free access, significant royalty collection on existing cultivars that can be resown by farmers is unlikely. The chances that any royalties collected will actually benefit farm communities that furnished the landrace ancestors of the cultivar are even more remote.

Unfortunately, there is a real danger that measures intended to capture in the name of farmers' rights some of the rents from the flow of genetic materials to users in developed countries could severely compromise a worldwide breeding enterprise that will be crucial in ensuring that food supplies continue to match population growth, especially in the South. This worldwide enterprise relies on an intensive exchange of germplasm, mostly enhanced materials and released cultivars. (650,000 accessions are reported to be distributed annually by the CGIAR centers, of which 500,000 are "improved material.") Care must be taken that this exchange is not damaged too severely by taxes, fees, monitoring systems, or, worse still, individualized prior-approval requirements. If it is, the current system of predominantly public, decentralized international crop breeding will lose its momentum. Consumers everywhere will lose, and any possible gains to holders of rights to germplasm will be paltry by comparison.

I have argued that the gains to be had from continued supply of new germplasm to crop breeders are more modest than many have expected. This does not mean that the claims are unjustified or that compensation is infeasible. The point is to ensure that any compensation for current or past provision of genetic resources be achieved in a manner that does not unduly hinder the advance of agricultural production in the face of increased demands forecast for the next century.

NOTES

A slightly modified version of this essay was presented at the symposium "The Economics of Conservation and Valuation of Genetic Resources for Agriculture," at Universita di Roma Tor Vergata in Rome, May 14, 1996, under the title "Intellectual Property and Farmers' Rights."

1. For example, "The North's genetic dependence on the South is accelerating for many crops" (Fowler and Mooney 1990, xii).

REFERENCES

Adams, M. W. 1977. "An Estimation of Homogeneity in Crop Plants, with Special Reference to Genetic Vulnerability in the Dry Bean, *Phaseolus vulgaris L.*" *Euphytica* 26:665–79.

Adams, Robert P., et al. 1994. In *Conservation of Plant Genes II: Utilization of Ancient and Modern DNA,*" ed. Robert P. Adams. 181–84, 245–76. St. Louis, Mo.: Missouri Botanical Garden.

Allard, R. W. 1992. "Predictive Methods for Germplasm Identification." In *Plant Breeding in the 1990s,* ed. H. T. Stalker and J. P. Murphy. Wallingford, U.K.: CAB International.

Anderson, Jock R., Peter B. R. Hazell, and Lloyd T. Evans. 1987. "Variability of Cereal Yields: Sources of Change and Implications for Agricultural Research and Policy." *Food Policy,* August, 199–212.

Brush, Stephen B. 1995. "In Situ Conservation of Landraces in Centers of Crop Diversity." *Crop Science* 35:346–54.

Brush, Stephen B., Edward J. Taylor, and Mauricio R. Bellon. 1992. "Technology Adoption and Biological Diversity in Andean Potato Agriculture." *Journal of Development Economics* 39:365–87.

Byerlee, Derek, and Greg Traxler. 1995. "National and International Wheat Improvement Research in the Post–Green Revolution Period: Evolution and Impacts." *American Journal of Agricultural Economics* 77, no. 2:268–78.

Carter, C. A., R. M. A. Loyns, and Z. F. Ahmadi-Esfahani. 1986. "Varietal Licensing Standards and Canadian Wheat Exports." *Canadian Journal of Agricultural Economics* 34 (November): 361–77.

Constantine, John H., Julian M. Alston, and Vincent H. Smith. 1994. "Economic Impacts of the California One-Variety Cotton Law." *Journal of Political Economy* 102:951–974.

Contracting Parties to the General Agreement on Tariffs and Trade, Uruguay Round. 1994. World Trade Agreement. Marrakesh, April 15.

Cox, T. S. 1991. "The Contribution of Introduced Germplasm to the Development of U.S. Wheat Cultivars." In *Use of Plant Introductions in Cultivar Development, Part 1*, ed. Henry L. Shands and Loren E. Wiesner. CSSA Special Publication No. 17. Madison, Wis.: Crop Science Society of America.

Cox, T. S., J. P. Murphy, and M. M. Goodman. 1988. "The Contribution of Exotic Germplasm to American Agriculture." In *Seeds and Sovereignty: The Use and Control of Plant Genetic Resources*, ed. J. R. Kloppenburg Jr. Durham, N.C.: Duke University Press.

Duvick, Donald N. 1984. "Genetic Diversity in Major Farm Crops on the Farm and in Reserve." *Economic Botany* 38, no. 2:161–78.

Evenson, Robert E., and Douglas Gollin. 1994. "Genetic Resources, International Organizations, and Rice Varietal Improvement." Center Discussion Paper 713. Economic Growth Center, Yale University, July.

———. 1997. "Genetic Resources, International Organizations, and Rice Varietal Improvement." *Economic Development and Cultural Change* 45, no. 3:471–500.

Fowler, Cary, and Pat Mooney. 1990. *Shattering: Food, Politics, and the Loss of Genetic Diversity.* Tucson: University of Arizona Press.

Gizlice, Ziya, Thomas E. Carter Jr., and Burton, Joseph W. 1993. "Genetic Diversity in North American Soybean: II. Prediction of Heterosis in F_2 Populations of Southern Founding Stock Using Genetic Similarity Measures." *Crop Science* 33:620–26.

———. 1994. "Crop Breeding, Genetics, and Cytology." *Crop Science* 34: 1143–51.

Harlan, J. R. 1970. "Evolution of Cultivated Plants." In *Genetic Resources in Plants—Their Exploration and Conservation*, ed. O. H. Frankel and E. Bennett. International Biological Programme Handbook No. 11. Oxford: Blackwell Scientific Publications.

Hazell, Peter B. R. 1989. "Changing Patterns of Variability in World Cereal Production." In *Variability in Grain Yields: Implications for Agricultural Research and Policy in Developing Countries*, ed. Jock R. Anderson and Peter B. R. Hazell. Baltimore: Johns Hopkins University Press.

Juma, Calestous. 1989. *The Gene Hunters: Biotechnology and the Scramble for Seeds.* African Centre for Technology Studies Research Series No. 1. Princeton: Princeton University Press.

Kloppenburg, Jack Jr., and Daniel L. Kleinman. 1987. "The Plant Germplasm Controversy." *Bioscience* 37, no. 3:190–98.

Lesser, William H., and Anatole F. Krattiger. 1994. "The Complexities of Negotiating Terms for Germplasm Collection." *Diversity* 10, no. 3:6–10.

Nabhan, Gary Paul. 1989. *Enduring Seeds.* San Francisco: North Point Press.

National Research Council (NRC). Committee on Genetic Vulnerability of Major Crops. 1972. *Genetic Vulnerability of Major Crops.* Washington, D.C.: National Academy of Sciences.

———. Committee on Managing Global Genetic Resources: Agricultural Imperatives. 1993. *Agricultural Crop Issues and Policies: Managing Global Genetic Resources.* Washington, D.C.: National Academy Press.

Orton, Thomas J. 1988. "New Technologies and the Enhancement of Crop Germplasm Diversity." In *Seeds and Sovereignty: The Use and Control of Plant Genetic Resources,* ed. Jack R. Kloppenburg. Durham, N.C.: Duke University Press.

Plucknett, Donald L., et al. 1987. *Gene Banks and the World's Food.* Princeton: Princeton University Press.

Reid, Walter V., and Kenton R. Miller. 1989. *Keeping Options Alive: The Scientific Basis for Conserving Biodiversity.* Washington, D.C.: World Resources Institute.

Rejesus, Roderick, Maarten van Ginkel, and Melinda Smale. 1996. *Wheat Breeders' Perspectives on Genetic Diversity and Germplasm Use: Findings from an International Survey.* Special Report 40. Mexico City: Centro Internacional de Mejoramiento de Maíz y Trigo.

Rural Advancement Foundation International (RAFI). 1994. *Conserving Indigenous Knowledge.* New York: United Nations Development Programme. September 1.

Rutger, J. N., and C. N. Bollich. 1991. "Use of Introduced Germplasm in U.S. Rice Improvement." In *Use of Plant Introductions in Cultivar Development, Part 1,* ed. Henry L. Shands and Loren E. Wiesner. CSSA Special Publication No. 17. Madison, Wis.: Crop Science Society of America.

Salhuana, Wilfredo, Quentin Jones, and Ricardo Sevilla. 1991. "The Latin American Maize Project: Model for Rescue and Use of Irreplaceable Germplasm." *Diversity* 7, nos. 1–2:40–42.

Silbernagel, M. J., and R. M. Hannan. 1992. "Use of Plant Introductions to Develop U.S. Bean Cultivars." In *Use of Plant Introductions in Cultivar Development, Part 2,* ed. Henry L. Shands and Loren E. Weisner. CSSA Special Publication No. 20. Madison, Wis.: Crop Science Society of America.

Simpson, R. David, Roger A. Sedjo, and John W. Reid. 1996. "Valuing Biodiversity for Use in Pharmaceutical Research." *Journal of Political Economy* 104:163–85.

Singh, A. J., and D. Byerlee. 1990. "Relative Variability in Wheat Yields across Countries and Over Time." *Journal of Agricultural Economics* 41, no. 1:21–32.

Smith, J. S. C. 1988. "Diversity of United States Hybrid Maize Germplasm: Isozymic and Chromatographic Evidence." *Crop Science* 28:63–69.

Specht, James E., and James H. Williams. 1984. "Contribution of Genetic Technology to Soybean Productivity: Retrospect and Prospect." In *Genetic Contributions to Yield Gains of Five Major Crop Plants: Proceedings of a Symposium Sponsored by Division C-1 of the Crop Science Society of America, 2 December 1981, in Atlanta, Georgia,* ed. W. R. Fehr. Madison, Wis.: Crop Science Society of America.

Thompson, A. E., D. A. Dierig, and G. A. White. 1992. "Use of Plant Introductions to Develop New Industrial Crop Cultivars." In *Use of Plant Introductions in Cultivar Development, Part 2.* ed. Henry L. Shands and Loren E. Weisner. CSSA Special Publication No. 20. Madison, Wis.: Crop Science Society of America.

Ulrich, Alvin, William H. Furtan, and Andrew Schmitz. 1987. "The Cost of a Licensing System Regulation: An Example from Canadian Prairie Agriculture." *Journal of Political Economy* 95:160–78.

United Nations Environment Program (UNEP). 1992. *Convention on Biological Diversity.* Rio de Janeiro, June 5.

Vellvé, Renée. 1992. *Saving the Seed: Genetic Diversity and European Agriculture.* London: Earthscan Publications.

Vogel, Joseph Henry. 1994. *Genes for Sale: Privatization as a Conservation Policy.* Oxford: Oxford University Press.

———. 1995. "A Market Alternative to the Valuation of Biodiversity: The Case of Ecuador." *Association of Systematics Collection Newsletter,* October, 66–70.

Williams, Jeffrey C., and Brian D. Wright. 1991. *Storage and Commodity Markets.* Cambridge: Cambridge University Press.

Witt, Steven C. 1985. *Briefing Book: Biotechnology and Genetic Diversity.* San Francisco: California Agricultural Lands Project.

World Bank. International Trade Division. International Economics Department. 1993. *Commodity Trade and Price Trends: 1989–91 Edition.* Washington D.C.: International Bank for Reconstruction and Development, World Bank, distributed by Johns Hopkins University Press.

CHAPTER 13

When Are Voluntary Import Expansions Voluntary?

Gary R. Saxonhouse

Gus Ranis's first publication in the *American Economic Review,* "Factor Proportions in Japanese Economic Development," which appeared in September 1957, analyzes how market-driven changes in economic structure were facilitated by the ability of Japanese industry to make use of an abundant underutilized labor force (Ranis 1957; Saxonhouse 1977). The process of reallocation and absorption of resources so well discussed and interpreted by Gus was set in motion by the opening of Japan to foreign trade by the U.S. Navy's Commodore Perry in 1854.

Demands for access to the Japanese market did not end with Commodore Perry. A little over a century later, Japan's trading partners stopped complaining about cheap Japanese labor, shoddy Japanese products, and unfair Japanese competition in overseas markets and began once again to charge that the Japanese market was unfairly closed to foreign products (Saxonhouse 1996). The complaints about market access continue today, not only with Japan but now also with developing economies following in Japan's wake. In the 1990s, rather than simply demanding, as in 1854, that Japan harmonize its border regulations with those of other countries, the U.S. government, in particular, has demanded that, in the absence of some prespecified share of the Japanese market being occupied by foreign products, the presumption must be that Japan is engaging in unfair trading practices (Advisory Committee 1989). Jagdish Bhagwati (1987) has dubbed this form of trade policy *voluntary import expansion,* or VIE.

With the increasing prominence of VIEs as part of American trade policy, there has been greatly increased debate about their welfare consequences. In particular, the architects of the Clinton administration's trade policy—while quick to denounce voluntary export restraints (VERs) as an insidious form of protectionism creating unholy alliances between shielded domestic industries and their foreign competitors, who

359

are suddenly licensed to jack up prices and reap windfall profits — have seen VIEs in a very different light, as a benign tool of trade policy (Tyson 1992; Bergsten 1993; Bergsten and Noland 1993). VIEs, it is claimed, open markets to new competitors, increase international trade, and lower consumer prices in countries on which they are imposed.

The Clinton administration's analysis of VIEs has been widely criticized (Bhagwati 1993; Saxonhouse 1993, 1994a; Passell 1993). Indeed, as they have been applied to Japan, Gus Ranis can be counted among these critics.[1] Why, the critics asked, are the welfare consequences of restraining Japanese firms in their own market different from restraining their sales in the American market?

In fact, public policy discussion of VIEs has been clouded by some suppressed empirical assumptions. The Clinton administration's conclusions regarding the welfare differences between VERs and VIEs rest not on any serious theoretical distinction, but rather on the assumption that VERs normally erect unfair domestic barriers while VIEs normally remove unfair foreign barriers. Indeed, VIEs are thought to be a policy instrument by which what amounts to VERs against American products are removed. Whether the Clinton administration is correct for what is historically true of VERs and VIEs, and for the context of its current proposed uses for VIEs, is itself a matter of considerable controversy (Saxonhouse 1994b; Cline 1994; Irwin 1994). For example, just a decade ago the American automobile industry was arguing that the 1981 American automobile VER imposed on Japan was a necessary measure against unfair foreign competition.

Even if the Clinton administration's assumptions, for example, about the nature and extent of Japan's trade access limitations are correct, it is by no means clear that VIEs are the appropriate instruments to deal with such problems. Theresa Greaney, using a two-country model where a home country firm and a foreign firm produce differentiated, substitutable goods and compete in the home country market, finds that under Bertrand and Cournot competition imposing a market share VIE on a market protected by a tariff-type barrier will make home country consumers and the home country as a whole worse off (Greaney 1993; Irwin 1994). This result apparently holds even when the VIEs are set at the foreign firm–home country firm shares that prevail with free trade. In this world, if it is the objective of the home country government to maximize national welfare, it will resist efforts by its trading partners to impose VIEs.[2]

Japanese government officials will argue that they resist VIEs not simply because VIEs are against the interest of Japanese firms or even the Japanese economy more generally, but because they are against the interest of the international economic system as a whole.[3] Within the context of the models that Greaney explores, the interest of the international economic system is reflected in the welfare measure of total industry surplus (consumer surplus plus the profits of both domestic and foreign firms). Greaney finds that this surplus will decline with the imposition of VIE. This can be true whether or not the VIE replaces some other trade barriers.

Greaney's observation may be too sweeping. Unlike Greaney, consider a traditional model of Cournot oligopoly with homogeneous rather than differentiated goods (Farrell and Shapiro 1990b; Martin 1993; Brander and Spencer 1985).[4] Demand is given by $P(Q)$, where P is price and Q is quantity of the homogeneous good. The absolute value of the elasticity of demand is given by $\varepsilon(Q) \equiv -P(Q)/QP'(Q)$. The industry consists of one foreign firm and n home country firms.[5] Firm i's cost function is given by $c_i(Q_i)$. $C_i \equiv C_i(Q_i)$ is the ith firm's total cost and $C_i' \equiv C_i'(Q_i)$ is the ith firm's marginal cost.

In Cournot equilibrium, each firm i picks its output to maximize its profits given its competitors' output. Firm i's profits are given by

$$\Pi_i(Q_i, q_{-i}) = P(Q_i + q_{-i})Q_i - C_i(Q_i) \qquad i = 1, \ldots, n, \tag{1}$$

where q_{-i} is the output of all firms but the ith firm. The first-order condition for the maximization of Π_i is

$$P(Q) + Q_i P'(Q) - C_i'(Q_i) = 0 \qquad i = 1, \ldots, n, \tag{2}$$

where $Q \equiv Q_i + q_{-i}$. Equation (2) defines firm i's best response function.

Differentiating (2), the slope of firm i's reaction function is given by

$$\frac{dQ_i}{dq_{-i}} = -\frac{P' + Q_i P''}{2P' + Q_i P'' - C_i''} < 0 \qquad i = 1, \ldots, n. \tag{3}$$

The second-order condition for profit maximization requires that the denominator in (3) be negative. The numerator in (3) is the derivative of firm i's marginal revenue with respect to the output of all other firms. Following standard Cournot analysis this is assumed to be negative (Dixit 1986; Shapiro 1989; Farrell and Shapiro 1990b). This guarantees that (3) is negative and that firm i's reaction function slopes downward. If it is also assumed that marginal cost is nondecreasing ($C_i'' \geq 0$), then

$$C_i'' > P'(Q), \qquad i = 1, \ldots, n. \tag{4}$$

This means dQ_i/dq_{-i} is not only less than zero, but it is also greater than -1. This means if its rivals jointly expand production, form i contracts, but by less than its rivals' expansion.

Define

$$\Phi_i \equiv -\frac{dQ_i/dq_{-i}}{dQ/dq_{-i}} = -\frac{P'(Q) + Q_iP''(Q)}{C_i'' - P'(Q)}, \qquad i = 1, \ldots, n. \qquad (5)$$

Φ_i is the decrease (increase) in firm i's output as a fraction of increase (decrease) in total output if all other firms increase (decrease) their output. Given (4) and the downward slope of each firm's reaction schedule, $\Phi_i > 0$ (Gaudet and Salant 1991; Farrell and Shapiro 1990b). Alternatively,

$$\Phi_i = \frac{S_i - S_i^2 E}{S_i + \lambda_i(\varepsilon - S_i)} \qquad i = 1, \ldots, n, \qquad (6)$$

where $E \equiv -QP''(Q)/P'(Q)$ is the elasticity of the slope of the inverse demand curve and where $\lambda_i \equiv Q_iC_i''/C_i'$ is the elasticity of firm i's marginal cost, C_i', with respect to its output Q_i and S_i is the market share of firm i.

With the Φ_i's > 0, consider an exogenous change dQ_j (the consequence of international diplomacy) in the foreign firms' output (subscripted by j) and let the home country firms' outputs adjust to reestablish a Cournot equilibrium among them.[6] Since the firms' reaction curves slope downward and since marginal cost is nondecreasing, as in (4), then total output available for the home country market will move in the same direction as the foreign firm's change, but the absolute value of the change in total output is less than the absolute value of the change in foreign firm's output.[7] This result is enough to show that within this framework, and contrary to Greaney's (1993) finding, any VIE that is imposed will result in an increase in the amount of output available to the home country market.[8] Since demand is $P'(Q) < 0$, this means prices will fall.

That prices fall and available output increases in the home country market as a result of the imposition of VIE means consumer welfare will increase. In analyzing, the welfare consequences of a VIE, however, its impact on the profits of home country and foreign firms as well as its impact on consumer welfare still needs to be examined. Beginning this analysis, first, a small increase in imports as a result of the imposition of a VIE will be examined.

$$dW = PdQ_j - dC_j + \sum_{i \neq j} [P - C_i']dQ_i, \qquad (7)$$

where dW is the change in the welfare of home country consumers and firms and the change in the welfare of foreign firms. The home country firms' output responses are given by (5) ($dQ_i = -\Phi_i dQ$), and their markups are given by (2), ($P - C_i' = -Q_i P'(Q)$). Making these substitutions in (7)

$$dW = (PdQ_j + Q_j dP - dC_j) - Q_j P'(Q)dQ + \sum_{i \neq j} P'(Q)Q_i dQ. \quad (8)$$

In (8), the first three terms constitute the change in the foreign firm's profits, $d\Pi_j$. In the interest of establishing the conditions under which VIEs improve the welfare of the home country and the international economic system as a whole, assume that VIEs increase the foreign firm's profits. Given the diplomatic context within which VIEs are introduced, it is hard to imagine a VIE would exist if this were not the case. Given this assumption, if $dW - d\Pi_j > 0$, this is sufficient to show that VIEs increase both home country welfare and global welfare.
From (8)

$$dW - d\Pi_j = \left(\sum_{i \neq j} \Phi_i Q_i - Q\right)P'(Q)dQ. \quad (9)$$

Defining

$$\beta = \sum_{i \neq j} \Phi_i Q_i - Q, \quad (10)$$

the net change in $dW - d\Pi_j$ from the imposition of a VIE that induces an overall output change dQ is $\beta P'(Q)dQ$, which has the opposite sign from β if $dQ > 0$. (9) and (10) suggest that the direction of the change $dW - d\Pi_j$ depends on S_j, the size of the market share for the foreign firm in the home country market prior to the imposition of a VIE. Converting β into market share terms, a small increase in S_j will mean an increase in $dW - d\Pi_j$ if and only if

$$\sum_{i \neq j} \Phi_i S_i < S_j$$

(Farrell and Shapiro, 1990a, 1990b). If the Φ_i are large, notwithstanding the increase in home country consumer welfare that comes from a decline in prices, Greaney's general result continues to hold, and home country trade officials may legitimately resist VIEs as bad for the interests of the home country as a whole. It is even possible that VIE can be legitimately resisted on the grounds it is bad for the welfare of the international economic system as a whole.

Does the condition

$$\sum_{i \neq j} \Phi_i S_i < S_j$$

also hold for nonmarginal changes? Suppose the imposition of the VIE causes a change from Q_j^{initial} to Q_j^{Final} when Q_j^{Final} is the new equilibrium output for the foreign firm, then

$$\Delta W - \Delta \Pi_j = \int_{Q_j^{\text{initial}}}^{Q_j^{\text{Final}}} \left(\frac{dW}{dQ_j} - \frac{d\Pi}{dQ_j} \right) dQ_j, \tag{11}$$

where for each Q_j^{initial}, the integrand is evaluated assuming a Cournot equilibrium among home country firms given Q_j^{Final}. Using (9) and (10), rewrite (11) as

$$\Delta W - \Delta \Pi j = \int_{Q_j^{\text{initial}}}^{Q_j^{\text{Final}}} \beta(Q)[P'(Q)] \frac{dQ}{dQ_j} dQ_j. \tag{12}$$

This shows that the nonmarginal change $\Delta W - \Pi_j > 0$ is a weighted integral of β. If β can be signed along the path from Q_j^{initial} to Q_j^{Final} then the sign of $\Delta W - \Delta \Pi_j$ will be known. For $\Delta W - \Delta \Pi_j > 0$ with the imposition of a VIE, it is sufficient that (1) $\sum_{i \neq j} \Phi_i S_i < S_j$; (2) $P'' \geq 0$, $P''' \geq 0$ and $C_i'' > 0$; (3) $C_i''' < 0$; and (4) $\Delta P < 0$.[9]

The conditions that allow a nonmarginal change in the VIE to increase $\Delta W - \Delta \Pi_j$ characterize a more than trivial set of cases.[10] All constant elasticity of demand curves, not to mention all linear demand curves, have $P'' \geq 0$. $C'' \geq 0$ is also a familiar condition. For modest change in the size of the foreign firm's market share as a result of the imposition of VIE, P'' and C'' will dominate the calculation of

$$\begin{aligned}
(C'' - P')^2 \frac{d[\Phi_i q_i]}{dQ} = & -(P' + q_i P'')^2 - q_i^2 P'''(C'' - P') \\
& + q_i C'''(P' + q_i P'')^2(C'' - P') \\
& - q_i P_i''[C'' + P' + 2q_i P'']^{11}
\end{aligned} \tag{13}$$

so signs of the third derivatives can be irrelevant. For larger VIEs, however $C''' > 0$ can result in a substantial fall in the Φ_i. Similarly, if $P''' < 0$, foreign firms' response to the size of the VIE diminishes.

If it is assumed that demand curves are linear and that $C' = 0$, this means that $\varphi_i = 1$. With $\varphi_i = 1$, notwithstanding the fall in home country prices the sufficient condition for welfare-improving VIEs,

$$\sum_{i \neq j} \varphi_i S_i < S_j$$

will be satisfied only in the event that the share of imports in the home country market is already over 50 percent. Surprisingly, that the imposition of VIEs is likely to be welfare improving primarily in those cases where home country firms occupy only a small share of their home market does appear to contradict the substance of the Clinton administration's trade policy. The Clinton administration repeatedly points to the very small share foreign manufactures occupy in Japan as justification for the application of special trade measures against Japan (*Economic Report of the President*; Tyson 1992; Bergsten 1993). The very stylized analysis presented here suggests that small foreign market shares may not necessarily be a good justification for not using VIEs. This view, while based on very different grounds, is consistent with the Reagan administration's rejection a dozen years ago of small import shares as a justification for a confrontational bilateral trade policy. The 1984 *Economic Report of the President* argued

> Import barriers in every country protect those sectors that would not have the comparative advantage in a fair fight, at the expense of those sectors that would. In the Japanese case, it is agriculture that is easily the least competitive sector and therefore the most protected. . . . Japan already imports lots of agricultural products indeed it is the largest customer of U.S. agricultural exports. But, in general, a high observed degree of "import penetration" does not preclude the existence of a high degree of protection. In fact, most penetration is often the cause and protection the effect rather than the other way around. (66).

Leaving agriculture aside, perhaps scientific instruments and aircraft, both Japanese industries where foreign penetration is above 50 percent, may be better candidates for welfare-improving VIEs in a Cournot world with linear demand and $C'' = 0$ than the communications industry, where the foreign market share remains under 10 percent.

Are these results robust? Suppose that demand remains linear, but now costs are quadratic. Assume in particular that demand is given by $P(Q) = K - Q$ and costs are given by $C_i(Q_i, h) = Q_i^2/2h$.[12] With these demand and cost conditions $\Phi_i = Q_i/P = S_i/\varepsilon$. The imposition of a VIE will lead to an increase in welfare if

$$S_j > \frac{1}{\varepsilon} \sum_{i \neq j} S_i^2.$$

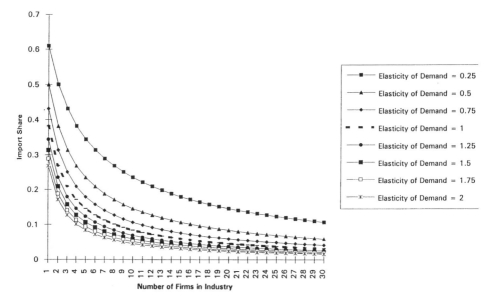

Fig. 13.1.   Welfare, import share, industry concentration, and the elasticity of demand

As before with constant cost, in this case with quadratic costs, the larger the initial share of imports in the home country market, the more likely the imposition of a VIE will be welfare improving. Unlike the case with constant costs, in this case it is not necessary that the initial import share be more than 50 percent. Figure 13.1 presents the results of a simulation where it is assumed that there are $n - 1$ home country firms of equal size with identical quadratic cost functions. As can be seen in this example, the less concentrated the home country industry, the smaller the initial import share need be for the imposition of a VIE to be welfare improving. As long as demand is relatively elastic, even initial market shares far, far below 50 percent are consistent with welfare-improving VIEs.

Why for any given import share are VIEs more likely to be welfare improving when the industry is less concentrated? Given that $\Phi_i = Q_i/P$, the smaller the home country firm, the smaller will be its cutback in output in response to a mandated increase in imports. In this new environment, the increased benefits to home country consumers will be sufficient to balance the loss in home country firm profits. Interestingly, this finding on the relationship between increased imports, concentration, and welfare is at variance with long-term Japanese policy in this area. Throughout the 1960s and 1970s, in the face of impending increase in imports, the

Ministry of International Trade and Industry held that increases in industry concentrations were the key to industrial restructuring.[13]
The condition

$$S_j > \frac{1}{\varepsilon} \sum_{i \neq j} S_i^2$$

and the results presented in figure 13.1 also highlight the relationship between elasticity of demand and the welfare implications of a VIE. With quadratic costs, the more elastic demand, the more likely it is that an increase in imports will increase welfare. The more elastic demand the smaller the markup for home country firms and the less the profit lost by a contraction of their output. With more elastic demand the loss in home country firm profits is too small to overwhelm the benefits that come to home country consumers from lower prices. Once again this is a surprising finding. The Clinton administration has often been admonished to look for high markups when considering where and when it is best to seek a VIE (Bergsten and Noland 1993).
It should be kept in mind that

$$\sum_{i \neq j} \Phi_i S_i < S_j$$

is only a sufficient condition for welfare-improving VIEs. Since the VIE is assumed to result in an increase in the profits of foreign firms, it is possible that

$$\sum_{i \neq j} \Phi_i S_i < S_j$$

even while home country welfare improves, that is, $0 < \Delta W < \Delta \pi_j$. Neither will the condition

$$\sum_{i \neq j} \Phi_i S_i < S_j$$

capture those cases where home country welfare declines, even while the imposition of a VIE on the home country is good for the international economic system as a whole, that is, $\Delta W < 0 < \Delta \pi_j$ and $(\Delta W) < (\Delta \pi_j)$. To deal with these two possible cases, the condition

$$\sum_{i \neq j} \Phi_i S_i < S_j$$

can be supplemented by observing how the foreign firm's stock market valuation changes with news of a proposed VIE.[14]

Finale

Within the context of a very simple market structure framework, the response of home country firms to VIE-induced imports will determine whether or not welfare will increase. Within this simple framework, even while VIEs will always result in a fall in home country prices and an increase in home country consumer surplus, this does not mean that the welfare of the country as a whole will always increase. Under plausible assumptions about the demand and cost conditions, there are many occasions where it may be appropriate for home country officials to resist VIEs regardless of its benign consequences for home country consumers. Even in the case where VIEs are welfare improving for the home country, this does not mean that other policy instruments inducing an increase in imports might not be more efficient. No conjecture is made here about the robustness the results presented for Bertrand competition or for cases where after the imposition of a VIE the character of competition changes. It is also unclear how robust the result here would be in a general equilibrium framework with more than one industry and a foreign market included as part of the analysis. Nor has there been any discussion of the nature of the barriers to the home country market, if any, that foreign firms might be facing. Finally, political-economy considerations have also been largely put aside.

NOTES

1. The *Far Eastern Economic Review* (November 3, 1993) records Gus as being among the opponents of the Clinton administration's policy.

2. See also extensions of Greaney's work in Nakamura 1995.

3. *Nihon keizai shimbun,* June 22, 1995.

4. The analytical framework provided here for the analysis of VIEs follows closely recent developments in the welfare analysis of mergers. See Farrell and Shapiro 1990b; Martin 1993. Important applications of the traditional model of Cournot oligopoly with homogeneous goods to policy issues in international economics were first stimulated by Brander and Spencer 1985. Following Brander and Spencer, Irwin in *Managed Trade* in analyzing VIEs also assumes Cournot behavior and homogeneous goods.

5. It is immaterial for this analysis whether there is one or many foreign firms operating in the home country market.

6. Since dQ_j is the consequence of international diplomacy, the foreign firm is not assumed to have complete Stackelberg power.

7. Since $dQ_i = -\Phi_i dQ$, $dq_{-i} = \Sigma_{j\neq i} dQ_i = -(\Sigma_{j\neq i}\Phi_i) dQ$. Then

$$dQ = dQ_i + dq_{-i} = dQ_i - \left(\sum_{j \neq i} \Phi_i \right)$$

from which

$$dQ = \left(1 + \sum_{j \neq i} \Phi_i \right)^{-1} dQ_i.$$

Since each Φ_i is positive, dQ will have the same sign as dq_i but will be smaller in magnitude. For this result to hold it need not be the case that the domestic firm behave as a Cournot oligopolist. See Dixit 1986 and Farrell and Shapiro 1990b.

8. Greaney's (1993) modeling sets the VIE in market share terms. Here VIE is defined as a mandated increase in imports. Bjorksten 1994 also models VIEs as import increases and finds that within a Cournot framework output available to the home country market will increase.

9. Since the imposition of a VIE involves an increase in Q_j, a small increase in the foreign firm's market share's effect on

$$\beta = \sum_{i \neq j} \Phi_i q_i - Q_j$$

is negative. This means, if a small decrease in imports has a negative effect, further small increases will have still more of a negative impact up to the point where the nonmarginal change in imports is complete. Given that prices are declining over this range, the impact on $\Delta W - \Delta \pi_j$ is positive, but what still needs to be studied here is what happens when the increase in imports Q_j induces changes in Q_i for all $i \neq j$ and hence induces changes in both dQ, the total output available to the home country market and changes $d\phi_i$ in the ϕ's.

$$d[\Phi_i q_i] = \Phi_i dq_i + q_i d\Phi_i \quad \text{and} \quad dq_i = \Phi_i dQ, \text{ so } d[\Phi_i q_i] = -\Phi_i^2 dQ + q_i d\Phi_i$$

$$\Phi_i \equiv -P'(Q) + q_i P''(Q)/C_i'(q_i) - P'(Q)$$

$$\frac{d[\Phi_i q_i]}{dQ} = -\Phi_i^2 + q_i \left(\frac{\partial \Phi_i}{\partial Q} - \Phi_i \frac{\partial \Phi_i}{\partial q_i} \right).$$

Substituting in for Φ_i and its partial derivatives

$$(C'' - P')^2 \frac{d[\Phi_i q_i]}{dQ} = -(P' + q_i P'')^2 = q_i^2 P'''(C'' - P')$$
$$+ q_i C'''(P' + q_i P'')^2 (C'' - P') - q_i P''[C'' + P' + 2q_i P''].$$

See further discussion of this issue in Farrell and Shapiro 1990b.

10. Given that the condition

$$\sum_{i \neq j} \Phi_i S_i < S_j$$

holds for nonmarginal changes in VIEs it follows any time this condition is met, the home country should give the foreign firm complete Stackelberg power.

11. See n. 9.

12. These linear demand and quadratic cost functions are used as examples by Perry and Porter 1985 and by Farrell and Shapiro 1990b.

13. See the discussion in Saxonhouse 1979, and in Nomura sogo kenkyusho, *Kōzō fukyōgyōshu to kabushiki shijō* (Tokyo, 1978). Rather than a quadratic function increasing in costs, the Ministry of International Trade and Industry assumed that costs would decline as a result of industrial restructuring. Even if constant costs are assumed, it is possible to reverse the result of negative relationship between concentration and the welfare impact of VIEs found here.

14. Farrell and Shapiro 1990b. As an example of this analysis, see Ries 1993.

REFERENCES

Advisory Committee on Trade Policy and Negotiations. 1989. *Analysis of the U.S.-Japan Trade Problem.* Washington, D.C.: Office of the United States Trade Representative.

Bhagwati, Jagdish. 1989. "VERs, Quid Pro Quo DFI, and VIES: Political Economy—Theoretical Analyses." *International Economic Journal* 1, no. 1:1–14.

———. 1993. Import Rules Are No Solution." *Financial Times,* August 23.

Bergsten, C. Fred. 1993. "Good and Bad Managed Trade." *Financial Times,* August 18.

Bergsten, C. Fred, and Marcus Noland. 1993. *Reconcilable Differences.* Washington, D.C.: Institute for International Economics.

Bjorksten, Neil. 1994. "Voluntary Import Expansions and Voluntary Export Restraints in an Oligopoly Model with Capacity Constraints." *Canadian Journal of Economics* 27, no. 2:446–57.

Brander, James, and Barbara Spencer. 1985. "Export Subsidies and International Market Share Rivalry." *Journal of International Economics* 18, no. 1:83–100.

Cline, William R. 1994. *International Economic Policy in the 1990s.* Cambridge: MIT Press.

Dick, Andrew. 1995. *Industrial Policy and Semiconductors: Missing the Target.* Washington, D.C.: AEI Press.

Dixit, Avinash. 1986. "Comparative Statistics for Oligopoly." *International Economic Review* 27, no. 1:107–22.

Economic Report of the President. Washington, D.C.: Government Printing Office, 1994.

Farrell, Joseph, and Carl Shapiro. 1990a. "Asset Ownership and Market Structure in Oligopoly." *Rand Journal of Economics* 21, no. 2:275–92.

———. 1990b. "Horizontal Mergers: An Equilibrium Analysis." *American Economic Review* 80, no. 1:107–26.

Gaudet, Gerard, and Stephen W. Salant. 1991. "Increasing the Profits of a Subset of Firms in Oligopoly Models with Strategic Substitutes." *American Economic Review* 81, no. 3:658–65.

Greaney, Theresa. 1993. "Import Now! An Analysis of Voluntary Import Expansions VIEs to Increase U.S. Market Share in Japan." University of Michigan Research Forum on International Economics Discussion Paper No. 343.

Irwin, Douglas. 1994. *Managed Trade: The Case against Import Targets.* Washington, D.C.: AEI Press.

Martin, Stephen. 1993. *Advanced Industrial Economics.* Oxford: Blackwell.

Nakamura, Hiroshi. 1995. "Does Minimum Share Target Really Increase Competition in an Importing Country." Stanford University.

Passell, Peter. 1993. "The Wisdom of Managing Trade Is Coming under Scrutiny." *New York Times,* October 11.

Perry, Martin K., and Robert H. Porter. 1985. "Oligopoly and the Incentive for Horizontal Mergers." *American Economic Review* 86, no. 1:219–28.

Ranis, Gustav. 1957. "Factor Proportions in Japanese Economic Development." *American Economic Review* 47, no. 5:594–14.

Ries, John. 1993. "Windfall Profits and Vertical Relationships: Who Gained in the Japanese Auto Industry from VERs." *Canadian Journal of Economics* 41, no. 3:259–76.

Saxonhouse, Gary. 1977. "Productivity Change and Labor Absorption in Japanese Cotton Spinning, 1891–1935." *Quarterly Journal of Economics* 91, no. 2:195–219.

———. 1979. "Industrial Restructuring in Japan." *Journal of Japanese Studies* 5, no. 2:273–319.

———. 1993. "Managed Trade Called Threat to International Economic System." *Financial Times,* October 22.

———. 1994a. "The Economics of the U.S.-Japan Framework Talks." Hoover Essays in Public Policy No. 53.

———. 1994b. "Japan and the 1994 Economic Report of the President." University of Michigan Research Forum in International Economics Discussion Paper No. 372.

———. 1996. "A Short Summary of the Long History of Unfair Trade Allegations against Japan." In *Fair Trade and Harmonization,* ed. Jagdish N. Bhagwati and Robert E. Hudec. Cambridge: MIT Press.

Shapiro, Carl. 1989. "Theories of Oligopolic Behavior." In *The Handbook of Industrial Organization,* ed. R. Schmalensee and R. Willig. New York: Elsevier North Holland.

Tyson, Laura D. 1992. *Who's Bashing Whom?* Washington, D.C.: Institute for International Economics.

Part 4. Finance and Economic Development

CHAPTER 14

Nominal Anchor Exchange Rate Policies as a Domestic Distortion

Anne O. Krueger

For policymakers confronted with crisis situations involving triple-digit rates of inflation, inability to maintain voluntary debt service, and highly protectionist trade regimes, a frequent policy prescription has been to adjust the underlying fiscal imbalance and to undertake a once-and-for-all devaluation; thereafter, the exchange rate should be used as a "nominal anchor" for slowing down the rate of inflation.[1] This could be achieved by maintaining a fixed nominal exchange rate (despite continuing inflation) or by preannouncing a schedule of minidevaluations at a rate below the rate of inflation.[2]

Simultaneously, other policy reforms would be undertaken or begun in order to alter the structure of the economy.[3] Among these other reforms, an important one would be a realignment of the trade and payment regime in order to move away from restrictive protectionist policies and toward a more outward orientation. This would normally entail the removal of quantitative controls over imports and a reduction, or an announced schedule of reductions, in the rate of protection for import-competing goods.

The nominal anchor exchange rate policy has been advocated primarily by macroeconomists who, on the premise that the demand for real money balances may be unstable or unpredictable in the aftermath of a triple-digit (or more) inflation rate, argue that the predetermined time path of the nominal exchange rate will "anchor" the price level and therefore inflationary expectations.[4]

It is the purpose of this essay to view a nominal anchor exchange rate policy from a different perspective: that of international economics. It will be argued that, just as a tariff creates a distortion and an associated welfare cost by driving a wedge between the domestic and international marginal rates of substitution and transformation, so a nominal anchor exchange rate policy creates a distortion by driving a wedge between the domestic and the international intertemporal rate of substitution. Once the case is made, estimates of the cost of the nominal anchor exchange rate policy in the case of Mexico are presented. Even if there were no welfare costs associated with the distortion created by a nominal anchor exchange rate policy, a number of serious questions arise as to their potential usefulness. The first section reviews some of these issues. The second section then analyzes a nominal anchor exchange rate policy from the perspective of trade theory, in light of the dual objectives of inflation reduction and of restructuring production toward exportables and away from import-competing goods. The third section provides the analysis of nominal anchor exchange rates as a distortion. The final section then applies the analysis to the Mexican experience from the late 1980s until the December 1994 devaluation.

1 Nominal Anchor Exchange Rate Policies in Macroeconomic Perspective

Variants of a nominal anchor exchange rate policy have been used on many occasions. In the late 1970s, the "Southern Cone" countries of Argentina, Chile, and Uruguay adopted tablitas indicating the future paths of the nominal exchange rates, with depreciations at rates less than the prevailing rates of inflation.[5] These policies were undertaken in the hope of bringing the rate of inflation down, on the reasoning that the "law of one price" would prevent the domestic price level from rising as rapidly as it otherwise might.[6]

In the 1980s, additional countries had undertaken these policies. Mexico began a variant of the nominal-anchor policy starting in 1987, after which the maximum rate at which the peso would be permitted to depreciate was negotiated in a pact with the labor unions—the maximum permitted rate of depreciation always being considerably below that warranted by purchasing power parity as determined by the then-prevailing inflation rate differential between Mexico and the rest of the world. Israel relied on a nominal anchor exchange rate policy for the first several years of the stabilization program begun in 1985. And, most recently, Argentina has adopted an extreme form of such a policy, with an absolutely fixed exchange rate,[7] while Brazil is following a much looser version of the same policy.

Since, by definition, a nominal anchor exchange rate policy entails real appreciation of the currency, it is clear that an "exit policy" is necessary if a long-run successful outcome is to be achieved. Following the policy "too long" will clearly result in difficulties as it becomes recognized that increasing currency overvaluation is resulting in depletion of foreign assets; at that point, the bubble will burst, and the results of the anti-inflationary program will be at least partially undermined by the maxidevaluation that must inevitably follow.[8] The difficulties of achieving an appropriate exit are widely recognized, and many economists have questioned the advisability of a nominal anchor exchange rate policy on that ground alone.

A second difficulty arises because it is clear that a nominal anchor exchange rate policy can succeed only if the underlying fiscal-monetary policies of the country are consistent with the eventual reduction in the rate of inflation anticipated by the nominal anchor exchange rate policy. If they are, one can also question whether the nominal-anchor policy itself is necessary, although proponents, as already noted, conclude that the nominal-anchor policy leads to a more rapid deceleration in the rate of inflation than would otherwise occur.

Finally, if the opening of the trade and payments regime is undertaken in order to alter the structure of the economy and induce producers to shift from import competing to exportable production, one has to ask how expectations of the sustainability of the policy will be affected by simultaneous announcement of a policy that entails gradual real appreciation of the currency.

The need for exit, the apparent contradiction between attempting to pull resources into exportable production and real appreciation, and the necessity for fiscal-monetary consistency each raises considerable doubts as to the wisdom of a nominal anchor exchange rate policy.

For purposes of this essay, however, these issues are overlooked, and it will be posited that the nominal exchange rate adjustments over a considerable period fall short of the domestic rate of inflation and that foreign reserves are sufficient during that interval to deter speculation against the currency.[9] Thus, it is assumed that agents are sufficiently myopic, or otherwise convinced (perhaps because they believe that a "rescue" operation may be mounted by international agencies or interested foreign governments) that the exchange rate regime can be maintained for the period of time for which the analysis pertains.[10]

2 Nominal Anchor Exchange Rates and Trade Policies

Calvo, Reinhart, and Vegh (1995) give a good, brief statement of the rationale for use of a nominal anchor exchange rate policy:

In an open economy, either the money supply or the nominal exchange rate can serve as a nominal anchor. Such an anchor is usually viewed as a necessary condition for macroeconomic stability since, at least in the long run, all nominal variables will converge to the pre-set rate of growth of either the money supply or the exchange rate. Assuming that appropriate fiscal and microeconomic policies are in place, the price stability brought about by a nominal anchor should ensure that the economy achieves long-run economic growth. (97–98)

A second argument in support of a nominal anchor exchange rate policy relates to the difficulties that can arise when the authorities attempt to target the "wrong" real exchange rate. Clearly, an inappropriate real target could result in inflation or deflation as the nominal exchange rate was repeatedly altered to maintain an inappropriate real level.

Bruno and Fischer (1990) have also defended the use of a nominal anchor exchange rate policy. They base their argument on the possible existence of multiple equilibria and the need for a nominal anchor in order to avoid a higher equilibrium inflation rate than is necessary, given the underlying fiscal-monetary stance of the economy (Bruno and Fischer 1990, 373).

Other arguments in support of nominal anchor exchange rate policies have been made, but without the same degree of analytical rigor. Chief among these is the "inertial" inflation argument. Some have claimed that there is an inertial component in inflation, and that use of a nominal anchor exchange rate can result in a more rapid convergence of the rate of inflation to the new, underlying rate consistent with fiscal and monetary reforms than would otherwise occur.[11]

Under the nominal anchor exchange rate policy, the rate of nominal devaluation and possibly its timetable is preannounced at a rate below the prevailing rate of inflation.[12] Alternatives traditionally offered to a nominal anchor exchange rate policy include floating, a "crawling peg" where adjustments are undertaken to keep the rate at purchasing power parity with major trading partners, and a currency board.[13]

Under a crawling peg, there would be adjustments in the exchange rate equal to the differential in inflation rates at sufficiently frequent intervals to reduce the profitability of speculation against these changes.[14] Under a currency board, the exchange rate is rigidly fixed and the supply of money is determined by foreign-exchange holdings.[15] Under any of these alternative policies, the nominal money supply would, of necessity, provide the "nominal anchor." As already mentioned, the objection to that policy has been that, in the context of a high inflation, policymakers cannot know what the behavior of the demand for real balances will be once the rate of inflation begins to drop. Hence, so the argument goes, they run the risk either of curtailing the money supply too sharply (thus inducing very high nominal — and real — interest rates) or of permitting too large a money supply (if they overestimate the demand for real balances at lower rates of inflation).

Before turning to the analytics of a nominal anchor exchange rate policy on incentives of trade and capital flows, several aspects of the need for reforms in the trade and payments regime should be noted. As was already pointed out, the impetus to policy reforms usually arises both from the high and usually accelerating rate of inflation *and* difficulties with the trade and payments regime. While symptoms of these difficulties are normally the inability to maintain voluntary debt service and/or increasing restrictiveness of import-licensing regimes, it is now generally recognized that highly restrictive trade and payments regimes are not consistent with satisfactory rates of economic growth over the longer term (World Bank 1993).

The links between the trade regime and growth are many and need not be of concern here, except to note that policy reforms are almost always designed, among other things, to open up the trade regime, reducing the bias against exports.[16] The initial situation before reforms is one in which exports have for years been discouraged by currency overvaluation, high prices for domestically produced intermediate goods relative to the international prices received for exports, and the disincentives arising from protection to import-competing sectors. Moreover, businessmen are accustomed to a sheltered domestic market with the lack of risk, monopoly power, and prospect of assured returns that normally brings.

To achieve a more efficient allocation of resources and basis for growth, therefore, the bias of the trade and payments regime must be reduced and producers must be convinced that the relative profitability of exporting has increased significantly. If they are so convinced, the normal expectation is for *both* exports and imports to grow more rapidly than output as producers respond to the altered incentives.

Thus, at a theoretical level, policy reform should entail a realignment of incentives by undertaking policies that result in a *depreciation* of the real exchange rate to a level that makes exporting considerably more attractive than under the ancien régime.

A realistic real exchange rate is an essential prerequisite for such a strategy to succeed, especially in light of earlier histories of strong discrimination against exports. With those histories, potential entrants to export markets must be convinced that the altered incentive regime will persist before investing the resources and efforts necessary to develop export markets (see, e.g., Krueger 1992 and Edwards 1989). It is certainly evident that a nominal anchor exchange rate policy, leading as it inevitably does while it persists to appreciation of the real exchange rate, provides assurances to potential exporters that, whatever the real return in local currency to exporting might be today, it will be less so in the future. Thus, even if the initial maxidevaluation results in a real exchange rate that would — if maintained — encourage the desired resource reallocation from import competing to exportable activities, doubts about its future path might in themselves dissuade producers from the necessary investments.[17]

3 Analytics of Nominal Anchor Exchange Rate Policies

A nominal anchor exchange rate policy by definition does several things. It alters the relationship between the price of tradables and the price of home goods over time, and it affects relative returns to foreigners and domestic residents on the holding of domestic assets.

By driving a wedge between these returns, it creates a distortion, in exactly the same manner as a tariff or other trade intervention. In this section, the simple analytics of that distortion are set forth. In section 4, the results are then used to estimate the importance of the distortion for the Mexican economy in the years in which a nominal anchor exchange rate policy was, de facto, pursued.

Define the domestic price level as the weighted average of the prices of tradable and nontradable goods:

$$P_d = aP_t + (1 - a)P_h, \tag{1}$$

where P_d represents the domestic price level, P_t is the price of tradable goods, and P_h is the price of home goods. Time subscripts are omitted.

The price of tradable goods can be expected to follow the time path of the exchange rate fairly closely:

$$P_t = EP_w \tag{2}$$

where E is the price of foreign exchange and P_w is the (given and assumed constant) world price of traded goods.

Since a nominal anchor exchange rate policy is, by definition, one of adjusting the nominal exchange rate less rapidly than the rate of increase of domestic prices, it follows that the domestic price of home goods must be rising more rapidly than the nominal exchange rate is depreciating; hence, for the period when a nominal anchor exchange rate policy is in effect, the domestic price of tradable goods is rising at a slower rate than the nominal price of home goods, and thus the relative price of tradables is falling.[18]

Under any specification of production behavior, the supply of tradables will be a function of their relative price;[19] as the relative price of tradables falls over time, domestic output of tradables can be expected to fall, or at least to fail to expand as rapidly as they would at a constant relative price.[20] Of course, it may be that producers anticipate the future path of the real exchange rate and fail to respond to the altered relative prices with which they are temporarily confronted.

When producers and consumers instantaneously adjust to current relative prices, producers will be shifting their production toward home goods while consumers will be shifting their consumption toward tradable goods.[21] Thus, as the real exchange rate appreciates, the current account balance becomes more negative.

It is immediately evident that, regardless of whether adjustment is instantaneous or whether producers fail to respond because they anticipate real exchange rate appreciation, this trajectory is not indefinitely sustainable: increasing domestic consumption of foreign goods must be financed by accumulating liabilities to foreigners, while exportable supply is declining over time. Since the real exchange rate appreciates over time, the magnitude of the current account deficit must also increase over time.

The question immediately arises, then: how can an increasing current account deficit be sustained? Evidently, the increasing current account deficit must be offset by capital inflows. These will be encouraged under a nominal anchor exchange rate policy because the real return to foreigners for holding assets denominated in domestic currency will exceed the real return to domestic residents in the proportion of real appreciation.[22]

Let i be the nominal interest rate paid to holders of assets denominated in domestic currency, p_d be the domestic inflation rate, with p_h being the rate of increase of the price of home goods. From (2), the rate of increase in the domestic price of traded goods, p_t, is

$$p_t = e, \tag{3}$$

where e is the rate of nominal depreciation of the exchange rate. By definition of a nominal anchor exchange rate policy,

$$p_t = e < p_d < p_h. \tag{4}$$

The real rate of interest for domestic residents, r_d, is

$$r_d = i_d - p_d. \tag{5}$$

Since, by construction, the worldwide rate of inflation is zero, a foreigner holding an asset denominated in domestic currency receives a nominal return,

$$i_f = i_d - e, \tag{6}$$

which, in the absence of foreign inflation, equals the real rate of return to foreigners.

By simple algebraic manipulation of these relations, there must be a difference in the real rates of return received by foreigners and domestic residents, equal in amount to the difference between the rate of increase in the domestic price level and the rate of nominal depreciation.

$$r_f = i_d - e; \qquad r_d = i_d - p_d. \tag{7}$$

Therefore, the difference in the real rates of return is

$$r_f - r_d = i_d - e - i_d + p_d = p_d - e, \tag{8}$$

which is the rate at which the currency appreciates in real terms. Since the rate of increase in domestic prices is itself a weighted average of the rate of nominal depreciation of the currency and the rate of increase of home goods prices, foreigners receive a real return on holding local currency denominated assets that is higher than the return accruing to domestic nationals holding domestic assets by the amount of real appreciation entailed in the nominal anchor exchange rate policy (equal to $p_d - e$).

Under a nominal anchor exchange rate policy, there is no way in which foreigners and domestic residents can receive the same real return on holding an asset denominated in domestic currency.[23] Foreigners will earn a higher real return in the amount of the real appreciation of the currency.

If foreigners are willing to hold assets in the country pursuing a nominal anchor exchange rate policy to the point where the expected real rate of return equals that which they can earn elsewhere in the world, then the domestic real rate of return must be *below* the international rate if capital flows are large enough to equate domestic and foreign returns. If foreign investors base their decisions on the real return they can expect to receive in their own currency in the rest of the world, investments will be directed to activities (presumably in the home goods sector) where the real return in domestic currency (or evaluated at an equilibrium exchange rate) is below the real return in the rest of the world.[24]

The distortion, therefore, is the divergence between the real rates paid to domestic and foreign holders of assets denominated in domestic currency. One way of expressing it is that domestic borrowers will maximize subject to their perceived interest obligations, at a real rate below that actually earned by foreign lenders. As such, the real rate of interest actually paid on foreign borrowing may lie above the real rate of return earned by the domestic borrower.

Estimation of the welfare costs of such a distortion can be undertaken in two ways. One can either base the estimate on the excess capital inflow and its costs or on the current-account response to changes in the real exchange rate, following a method suggested by Hause (1966). For a number of reasons, use of estimates based on capital account seems preferable here.[25]

Using the capital account approach, the logic of estimating welfare costs is most evident if one examines two extreme cases: perfectly elastic, and perfectly inelastic, supply of foreign capital to the country in question. Assume first that the foreign supply of capital to a country following a nominal anchor exchange rate policy is perfectly elastic at the world real interest rate.[26] In that event, the domestic real interest rate would lie below the international rate (and might be negative). Domestic residents would save less and invest more (presumably in nontraded goods industries — note that the real return to capital employed in tradable goods would be unaffected except as costs of domestic inputs rose more rapidly than did the price of tradables). The welfare cost of such a policy would, therefore, be the usual area under the triangle, as illustrated in figure 14.1.

The left-hand panel, fig. 14.1a, depicts the domestic supply of savings, S, and demand for funds for investment, D. The world real interest rate is given by r_w, and the domestic real interest rate is below the world rate by the amount of real appreciation of the exchange rate. Figure 14.1b gives the net demand for capital inflows as a function of the real interest rate as perceived by domestic nationals. If domestic nationals correctly perceived the world real interest rate, the inflow would be DC. However, since a lower real interest rate is perceived, investment is greater (OB), domestic saving less (OA), and the capital inflow is $0J$ ($= AB$) in figure 14.1b. The triangle FHC represents the cost of the distorted real interest rate, as producers are borrowing at a true rate greater than their return on capital, while domestic consumers are spend-

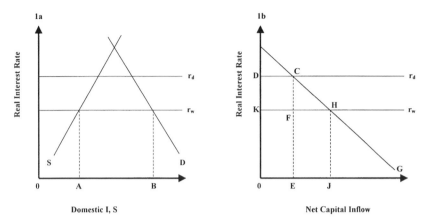

Fig. 14.1.   Welfare cost of nominal anchor exchange rate: perfectly elastic supply of foreign capital

ing more in the current period than they would if they were able to obtain a return equal to the world real rate of interest.

At the opposite extreme, foreigners might allocate their portfolios across countries in fixed proportions, so that the supply of foreign capital to the country were perfectly inelastic. To be sure, in this instance, optimal policy would be to impose a tax on all capital inflows, but for present purposes it suffices to estimate the welfare costs of a nominal anchor exchange rate policy contrasted with laissez-faire at an appropriate real exchange rate. In that extreme case, the entire excess payment to foreigners would represent a loss to the country in question. Figure 14.2 illustrates this case. There is excess demand for capital in the amount AB at the domestic real interest rate, r_d. Given the perfectly inelastic supply of capital, however, the real return to foreigners is augmented by the real appreciation of the currency. Foreign capital, which would otherwise earn the domestic real rate of return, instead earns an increment bc, equal to the rate of real appreciation of the currency. As contrasted with a laissez-faire outcome, the excess costs to domestic residents of the policy are the triangle abc, as there is more domestic investment (yielding a lower real return than the amount paid to the foreign lender) and less domestic saving than there would be if the true real return to foreigners was reflected to them.

Thus, the area under the triangle is the appropriate measure of the welfare cost of the distortion when viewed from the perspective of the capital account. In this case, the distortion in the real interest rate is easily measured by the rate of real appreciation of the exchange rate,

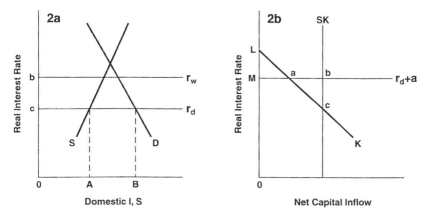

Fig. 14.2. Welfare cost of nominal anchor exchange rate

which corresponds to DK in figure 14.1 and LM in figure 14.2. The base of the triangle is quite clearly the net capital inflow less the "equilibrium rate of capital inflow." Thus, if the annual rate of real appreciation were 10 percent, while the excess capital inflow was 5 percent of GDP, the welfare cost per year of the policy would be 0.25 percent of GDP.

It is therefore evident that one can use an area-under-the-triangle estimate of the welfare cost. This is used in the next section to estimate the loss in Mexican welfare attributable to the use of the nominal anchor exchange rate policy.

4 The Costs of the Mexican Nominal Anchor Exchange Rate Policy

As already stated, Mexico followed a nominal anchor exchange rate policy after undertaking a maxidevaluation in 1987, and maintained that policy until 1994, when large capital outflows were rapidly depleting foreign exchange reserves; an attempt to stem the flow with a devaluation induced even more efforts to move out of pesos and into dollars, and the authorities finally permitted the exchange rate to float.

Table 14.1 gives data on the movement of the nominal and real exchange rate over the period since 1980. As can be seen, the real exchange rate[27] depreciated markedly in the aftermath of the debt crisis in 1982, appreciated during the 1983–85 period, and then once again reached a level almost 50 percent above 1980. It is significant, however, that oil prices declined sharply starting in 1986 (which in itself would

TABLE 14.1.   Mexican Nominal and Real Exchange Rates, 1980–95

	Wholesale Price Index (1990 = 100)	Nominal Exchange Rate per U.S. $	Real Exchange Rate (1980 = 100)	Nominal Interest Rate (%)
1980	0.7	0.0230	100.0	20.63
1981	0.9	0.0245	93.7	29.56
1982	1.4	0.0564	140.8	43.62
1983	2.9	0.1201	146.3	54.70
1984	4.9	0.1678	122.8	43.86
1985	7.6	0.3569	121.9	59.48
1986	14.3	0.6118	149.5	84.68
1987	33.6	1.3782	146.8	97.24
1988	69.8	2.2731	121.1	63.65
1989	81.1	2.4615	118.5	36.29
1990	100.0	2.8126	113.6	31.24
1991	120.5	3.0184	101.4	17.10
1992	136.7	3.0949	92.2	15.68
1993	148.8	3.1156	86.5	15.46
1994	158.9	3.3751	87.8	13.26
1995	221.1	6.4194	124.3	39.18

Source: International Monetary Fund, *International Financial Statistics,* 1995 Yearbook and April 1996.
Note: (1) Nominal exchange rates are new pesos per U.S. dollar for the end-of-period average.
(2) The real exchange rate was calculated between the peso and the U.S. dollar (with whom Mexico does more than 70 percent of trade). The real exchange rate was calculated as the nominal exchange rate times the U.S. producer price index divided by the Mexican wholesale price index.

presumably have called for further depreciation), and quantitative re-strictions were virtually eliminated during the 1985–87 period. The nominal anchor exchange rate policy began in 1987. As can be seen, real appreciation was pronounced in 1988 and 1989. By 1991, the real exchange rate had reattained its 1980 level—despite the fact that the oil price had declined sharply and that imports had been greatly liberalized. By 1993 and 1994, the real exchange rate was more appreciated than it had been at the end of 1981—immediately before the debt crisis.

To be sure, the rate of inflation was decreasing during the years after 1987. As can be seen in column 1 of table 14.1, Mexican wholesale prices more than doubled in both 1987 and 1988; by 1989, the increase was 16 percent, and by 1994 it had fallen to 9 percent. But while the real exchange rate was appreciating at a slower rate, its *level* continued to reduce the relative price of tradables within Mexico.

Table 14.2 gives data on real GDP and on trade for the years since 1980. Real GDP grew only slowly after 1987; one wonders how much of this slow growth was the consequence of declining profitability of produc-

TABLE 14.2.   Mexican Real GDP and Trade Variables (in billions of U.S. dollars)

	Real GDP	Merchandise Exports	Merchandise Imports	Current Account Balance
1980	586.1	15.5	18.9	−10.8
1981	621.6	20.1	23.9	−16.1
1982	629.1	21.2	14.4	−6.3
1983	602.7	22.3	8.6	5.4
1984	624.5	24.1	11.3	4.2
1985	640.7	21.7	13.2	1.1
1986	616.6	16.0	11.4	−1.7
1987	628.1	20.7	12.2	4.0
1988	635.9	20.5	20.3	−2.3
1989	657.2	22.8	25.4	−5.8
1990	686.4	26.8	31.2	−7.4
1991	711.3	26.9	38.2	−14.9
1992	731.3	27.4	48.1	−24.4
1993	735.6	30.0	48.9	−23.4
1994	761.7	34.6	58.9	−29.8

Source: IMF, *International Financial Statistics,* 1995 Yearbook.
Note: Real GDP is in billions of 1990 pesos.

TABLE 14.3.   Structural Changes in the Mexican Economy, 1987–94

	Exports/GDP	Imports/GDP	Net Current Account/GDP (%)	Domestic Savings as % of GDP
1987	.195	.134		22.0
1988	.168	.153		19.3
1989	.160	.162	−2.6	18.8
1990	.158	.169	−2.7	19.2
1991	.138	.170	−4.6	17.8
1992	.126	.181	−6.7	16.1
1993	.124	.167	−6.8	16.7
1994	.131	.189	−7.9	15.8

Source: Banco de Mexico 1994

tion of tradable goods. As can be seen, export earnings continued growing, although the average annual rate of growth of export earnings was 7.5 percent—a relatively slow rate for a country having liberalized its trade regime and counting on an outer-oriented trade strategy as a basis for growth.

Further light on the changes in the Mexican economy is shed by the data in table 14.3. As can be seen, export growth did not keep pace with GDP growth between 1987 and 1994: exports fell from 19.5 percent of

GDP to 12.7 percent. Imports, meanwhile, boomed, rising from 13.4 percent of GDP to 17.8 percent. As a result of these factors, the net current account deficit, which stood at −3.0 percent of GDP in 1989, rose to 7.8 percent in 1994, the year in which the crisis resulted in December. It is significant that the net current account deficit was already over 5 percent of GDP in 1992—which is not consistent with explanations of the Mexican difficulties of 1994 which rely on political events and expenditures surrounding the presidential election.

The final column of table 14.3 provides data on domestic savings, over the period from 1987. As can be seen, savings fell dramatically from the 1987 ratio in later years.[28] The drop after 1987 was more than accounted for by the behavior of private savings: private savings fell to around 7–8 percent of GDP in the early 1990s from a rate of 12 percent in 1989. While public savings rose somewhat, they did not rise sufficiently to offset the entire decline in private savings.[29]

There are alternative explanations of the decline in the savings ratio, although there is as yet no decisive test of their relative importance. One explanation is that the private savings rate fell as Mexicans went on a buying spree for newly available imported consumption goods. This is the explanation given by McKinnon and Pill (1996) more generally for large current account deficits in the aftermath of trade liberalization and would be consistent with the Hause measure of welfare costs. An alternative explanation centers around a declining real rate of return (or profitability of investment) in tradable industries as the real appreciation of the currency continued,[30] and is more consistent with use of the capital account measure of welfare costs.

Regardless of why the domestic savings rate declined, net capital inflows clearly financed the current account deficit until 1994. It is the excess of these flows over the rates that would have taken place if the true interest cost of borrowing had been reflected that constitute the distortion, regardless of whether flows were excessive because of reduced domestic savings or increased investment beyond the point that would have been profitable had the real interest cost been reflected.[31] Tables 14.4 and 14.5 give the real returns to U.S. and Mexican holders of Mexican and U.S. Treasury bills from 1988 to 1994. In table 14.4, the first column gives the Mexican Treasury bill rate.[32] As can be seen, the nominal rates were declining as inflation fell in Mexico. The second column gives the peso depreciation during the year in question. The third column then gives the nominal returns to U.S. nationals from holding either Mexican T-bills (column 3) or U.S. T-bills (column 4). As can be seen, the dollar return realized for holding Mexican T-bills was above that for holding U.S. bills in each year until 1994.

TABLE 14.4.   Nominal and Real Returns to U.S. Holders of U.S. and Mexican T-bills, 1988–94

Year	Mexican T-bill Rate (%)	Peso Depreciation (%)	U.S. Return	U.S. Bill Rate
1988	69.2	3.2	64.0	6.7
1989	45.0	15.8	25.2	8.1
1990	34.8	11.5	20.9	7.5
1991	19.3	4.3	14.4	5.4
1992	15.6	1.4	14.0	3.5
1993	15.0	−0.3	15.3	3.0
1994	14.1	71.4	−33.4	4.3

Source: International Monetary Fund, *International Financial Statistics,* 1994 Yearbook and August 1995, country pages.
Note: U.S. return on holding Mexican T-bills is one plus the nominal rate divided by one plus the rate of depreciation.

TABLE 14.5.   Real Returns to Mexican Nationals from Holding U.S. or Mexican T-bills for One Year (in percentages)

Year	Nominal Returns to Mexicans Holding U.S. T-bills	Nominal Returns to Mexicans Holding Mexican T-bills	Mexican Inflation Rate	Real Returns to Mexicans Holding U.S. T-bills	Real Returns to Mexicans Holding Mexican T-bills
1988	10.1	69.2	20.2	−8.4	40.8
1989	25.2	45.0	26.7	−1.2	14.4
1990	19.9	34.8	22.7	−2.3	9.9
1991	9.9	19.3	15.5	−4.8	3.3
1992	4.9	15.6	9.7	−4.4	5.4
1993	2.7	15.0	6.9	−3.9	7.6
1994	78.8	14.4	35.0	32.4	−15.5

Source: International Monetary Fund and Banco de Mexico.
Note: (1) The Mexican inflation rate is the rate of increase in the consumer price index calculated from *International Financial Statistics.* (2) Nominal returns to Mexican holders of U.S. T-bills were calculated as the nominal interest rate in U.S. dollars adjusted by the rate of peso depreciation. The relevant Mexican inflation rate is taken to be the rate for the year over which the bonds are assumed to be held.

Table 14.5 then gives the nominal and real returns to Mexicans for holding U.S. and Mexican T-bills. As can be seen, the real returns to Mexicans were negative in all years up to 1994, except for 1989, for holding U.S. T-bills; the real return for holding Mexican bills was positive (though declining over time) for holding Mexican T-bills. However, the real returns to U.S. nationals for holding Mexican securities were always above those accruing to Mexicans from holding the same securities.[33]

TABLE 14.6. **Alternative Measures of the Welfare Cost of Nominal Anchors**

Year	(1) U.S. Bank Lending Rates (%)	(2) Peso Real Appreciation (%)	(3) Current Account Deficit (% of GDP)	(4) Welfare Cost (as a % of GDP)
1988	9.32	17.5	−1.4	0.12
1989	10.92	2.1	−2.9	0.03
1990	10.01	4.0	−3.1	0.06
1991	8.46	10.8	−5.2	0.28
1992	6.25	9.0	−7.6	0.34
1993	6.00	6.2	−6.5	0.20
1994	7.14	−2.8	−7.8	N/A

Source: International Monetary Fund, *International Financial Statistics,* 1996 Yearbook; peso real appreciation is calculated from table 1; current account deficit is from table 3; and table 4 is calculated as column (2) × column (3) × 0.5.

The question than is, what was the welfare cost of this distortion to the Mexican economy? Using the capital account measure, table 14.6 provides the calculations. Column 1 gives the U.S. bank lending rate for the year in question, as a standard for comparison. The distortion in the interest rate was presumably the percentage rate of real appreciation, given in column (2) of table 14.6. The difficult question is what the appropriate quantity of capital inflow is, relative to what it would have been. On the one hand, Mexicans were paying the lower interest rate on all their outstanding borrowing; on the other hand, it can be argued that only the current year's current account deficit mattered for purposes of determining any given year's distortion cost. Even then, the question is what the level of capital inflow would have been had a different exchange rate policy been followed. The estimate provided here is, in a sense, a compromise. All of the current account deficit is taken to have resulted from the nominal anchor exchange rate policy, but only each year's current account deficit is counted when estimating the welfare cost.[34]

As can be seen, welfare costs on this basis are estimated at more than a quarter of a percent of GDP for each of the years 1991 to 1994. The estimate is based on the size of the current account deficit,[35] multiplied by one-half times the interest rate distortion. Had U.S. interest rates not declined in the early 1990s, the estimated cost would have increased even more sharply.

Because the estimate is applied only to the year's current account deficit, rather than outstanding foreign-exchange liabilities, it is probably a significant understatement of the true welfare costs of the policy.

Even so, a quarter or a third of a percent of GDP is not a small number, especially when one asks what the benefits of the policy may have been — given the inflation that ensued with the collapse of the peso and the adjustment costs associated with it.

5 Conclusions

A nominal anchor exchange rate policy — for as long as it persists — discriminates against tradables and in favor of production of home goods, while providing incentives for increased domestic consumption of tradables. Simultaneously, a capital inflow induced by the premium earned by foreign investors because of the nominal anchor exchange rate policy can enable the policy to persist. However, the real rate of return paid to foreigners is too high relative to the marginal product of capital in home goods industries (evaluated at constant prices), and a distortion results, with attendant real costs.

Use of a nominal anchor exchange rate policy is fraught with difficulties. Foremost among them is the inevitability of the collapse of the regime when reserves are sufficiently reduced so that agents are no longer willing to bet on the continuation of the regime. On the basis of the data on the Mexican exchange rate, the question should not be why there was a run on the peso at the end of 1994; the more relevant question is how the authorities managed to maintain the policy so long!

Even if an exit from a nominal anchor exchange rate policy can be managed prior to a breakdown of the regime, however, there are serious questions about the policy. Clearly, the realignment of production toward the international economy will be retarded, if not entirely postponed, during the period when a nominal anchor holds sway. As such, the growth objectives of policy reform are certainly to be at least partially thwarted.

In addition, however, there are real costs to the policy. As long as it is in effect, it is equivalent to a subsidy on foreign investments in local assets, in that foreigners are assured a real return above that in domestic currency.

While these considerations are not sufficient to conclude that a nominal anchor exchange rate policy should never be used, they do add to the weight of the evidence in favor of avoiding such a policy if at all possible. In societies where the costs of inflation are sufficiently high, and the domestic currency has lost all credibility, however, it is possible that very large benefits of controlling inflation may outweigh the very high costs of a nominal anchor exchange rate policy. Unless circumstances are truly exceptional, however, it is doubtful whether a nominal anchor exchange rate policy can be warranted.

NOTES

Initial work on this paper was undertaken at Monash University. I benefited greatly from comments of seminar participants there on the literature on nominal anchor exchange rates. I also owe thanks to Rosalinda Quintanilla and Roderick Duncan for helpful discussions and provision of data, and to the participants in the MIT International Workshop — especially Rudiger Dornbusch — and to T. N. Srinivasan for valuable comments and suggestions. None of the above, however, is responsible for the analysis and conclusions. The Smith-Richardson Foundation provided support for the research underlying this paper, for which I am grateful.

1. The anchor could be a fixed exchange rate, or it could function with relatively frequent, but small (relative to the preceding rate of inflation), adjustments, which would then diminish in size as the inflation rate fell.

2. These devaluations would need to be sufficiently small to avoid providing incentives for speculation.

3. In a serious reform program, support is forthcoming from the international financial institutions (IFIs) and debt-servicing obligations are normally rescheduled. Thus, any "balance of payments" or "debt" crisis that triggers policy reform can normally be eased if other policy reforms meet the criteria of the IFIs.

4. This argument presupposes that the announced monetary and fiscal reforms are insufficiently credible by themselves to alter expectations, and that the reforms-cum-nominal-anchor will in fact achieve the result.

5. If one were to follow a purchasing power parity rule, the appropriate rate of depreciation would be the differential between the domestic rate of inflation and the worldwide rate of inflation (with any necessary adjustments for the difference between the world price level and the price index relevant for the country's trade). For a discussion of the Chilean and Mexican experiences with exchange-rate-based stabilizations, see Edwards 1996.

6. In any use of a nominal anchor exchange rate policy, there is an issue as to whether the underlying fiscal-monetary adjustments are sufficient to bring down the rate of inflation. All analysts agree that a nominal anchor exchange rate policy in the absence of a sufficient macroeconomic shift will fail.

7. It may be objected that the Argentine policy is different, because the money supply by law is determined by the supply of foreign exchange. However, the rate of inflation in Argentina has been above the dollar rate of inflation; to date, measures such as tax exemptions and subsidies have offset much of the appreciation of the real exchange rate that would otherwise have occurred.

8. It might be argued that one could start with a devaluation sufficient to *undervalue* the exchange rate initially, and that the nominal anchor policy could be engineered such that it would end with inflation converging to the world rate

and a fixed exchange rate after exactly the right amount of real appreciation had occurred. Many Mexican policymakers did argue that the 1987 devaluation resulted in such an undervalued real exchange rate.

A question of interest, if this policy were deliberately chosen, is the extent to which the initially greater devaluation would lead to a larger increase in the price level than would occur under a policy of shifting to an initially appropriate rate; and whether that once-and-for-all increase in the price level was greater or less than the subsequent reduction that would presumably occur because of the nominal anchor exchange rate policy.

It should also be noted, however, that there is an additional difficulty: just as the demand for real money balances cannot be accurately predicted following a shift in inflationary expectations, so too it is difficult to estimate the appropriate "real exchange rate" if the objective is to alter the restrictionist trade and payments regime. Since, usually, historical evidence covers only a period during which import substitution policies were followed, there is little to guide policymakers as to the appropriate real exchange rate once trade is liberalized. A suggested alternative exchange rate policy focus is given in Krueger (forthcoming).

9. An important question that is not addressed here deals with why individuals would not anticipate the unsustainability of a nominal-anchor policy and hence attempt to sell the local currency, thus bringing about an end to the policy regime. It might be argued that the real puzzle regarding nominal anchor exchange rate policies such as that pursued by Mexico is not why they collapsed, but why they lasted as long as they did.

10. A sufficiently high real return to foreigners generated by the nominal anchor exchange rate policy can provide sufficient inducement to hold local currency provided that reserve levels are adequate to reassure most agents that the nominal anchor policy has a good chance of surviving over the intermediate run. Of course, the inducement to hold is greater, the greater the rate of real appreciation. The greater the (cumulative) real appreciation, however, the larger will be the reduction in the current account balance.

11. This was the rationale for the three Southern Cone "nominal anchor" exchange rate policies in the late 1970s. See Corbo and de Melo 1987 for particulars. It was also the rationale for the "cruzado" plan in Brazil in 1986. Finance Minister Pedro Aspe (1993) also used it in defending Mexican exchange rate policies.

12. The preannounced rate may be a maximal permissible rate (as was the case in Mexico), when the exchange rate is permitted to float within a band. It may instead be a timetable of rates, as was the case in the Southern Cone.

13. Another possibility is to follow a PPP rule with adjustments in the real exchange rate (by smaller or greater nominal exchange rate changes) as the growth of export earnings falls short of or exceeds an estimated target rate. See Krueger (forthcoming) for the argument.

14. The theoretical objection to a crawling peg exchange rate policy is that, if the authorities target the "wrong" real exchange rate, the domestic price level will be destabilized.

15. In most regards, a currency board can be regarded as a nominal anchor exchange rate policy. If it is truly 100 percent backing of the domestic money supply, the policy can become fully credible, although issues regarding the treatment and performance of the tradables sector during the transition may still arise.

16. The bias of a trade regime (in favor of import-competing activities) is normally defined as the difference between the domestic ratio of prices of import-competing to exportable goods and the international ratio of importable to exportable prices. In analysis of actual trade regimes, of course, both the average level of domestic and international prices, and the variance in protective rates, are important.

17. To be sure, there may be "excess capacity" exports that occur in the aftermath of a devaluation, especially when domestic demand falls after the introduction of a stabilization-reform program. Even then, however, resources normally need to be invested in exploring foreign markets, developing the necessary distribution channels, and so on. However, a sustained growth of exports of the kind that will "rebalance" economic activities between exportable and import-competing production requires investment in plant and equipment that is not likely to be forthcoming when the real exchange rate is expected to appreciate.

18. In order for the domestic rate of inflation to exceed the rate of depreciation, there must be some goods in the economy whose prices are not tied to international prices. Whether these prices are nominal wages or the prices of such nontradables as buildings, services, and transport and communications does not significantly affect the argument presented here.

19. A complication is that the price of exportables should rise relative to import-competing and home goods, while the price of import-competing goods should fall relative to exports. However, whether the price of import-competing goods should fall relative to the price of home goods is ambiguous. On this, see Sjaastad 1980.

20. It should be noted that, in countries where import-competing goods have been highly protected and that protection is reduced or removed, real depreciation will be warranted to offset the increased openness of the regime to imports, as well as to reduce the magnitude of imbalances in current account transactions existing at the time of policy reform.

21. A hallmark of episodes in which nominal anchor exchange rate policies were followed has been an inflow of foreign capital. These inflows have appeared to finance "consumption booms" rather than increases in investment. McKinnon and Pill (1996) explain these consumption booms as resulting from the anticipation of future real income increases following policy reform; and alternative explanation, set forth in section 2, has to do with the behavior of the real interest rate confronting domestic residents.

22. It should be recalled that the nominal anchor policy is defined in terms of the exchange rate adjustment being less than the differential in the rate of inflation between the country in question and the rest of the world (or its relevant trading partners). For simplicity, it is being assumed that the rate of inflation in the

rest of the world is zero, so that the excess of the domestic inflation rate over the rate of currency depreciation is the real appreciation of the currency.

23. To be sure, a domestic resident could hold a domestic asset and, upon selling it, convert proceeds into foreign exchange. But that is equivalent to saying that a tariff is not binding because domestic residents could always travel overseas to purchase and consume the good in question.

24. One may also examine the implications of the divergence in real interest rates for producers of tradables and nontradables. Recall that the rate of increase of prices of tradables lies below the rate of increase of the overall domestic price level. For a positive economy-wide real rate of interest, therefore, the same nominal interest rate for producers of home and traded goods must imply a higher real rate of interest (measured in terms of the price of the producer's output) for tradables producers than for producers of home goods. Relative to an optimal allocation of capital (i.e., one with no distortion), too little investment will be undertaken in tradable goods and too much in nontradables. Since the objectives of policy reform programs normally include the expansion of tradables, and especially exportables, output, the resource pulls arising from the differential movements of prices of tradables and nontradables lead to a result opposite from that of expansion.

25. An alternative measure of the welfare cost, examining the behavior of the current account, has been suggested by Hause (1966), who views behavior of an inappropriate real exchange rate as inducing more consumption of tradables during periods of real appreciation (relative to a constant real exchange rate) and less consumption during periods of real depreciation.

Hause shows that, to a first approximation, the welfare cost of an inappropriate real exchange rate, per period of time, is

$$(\eta/2 - \varepsilon) \text{ var } (RER) (P_e T_e),$$

where $\eta/2$ is the negative (price) elasticity of demand for imports and ε the elasticity of supply of exports. RER is the real exchange rate, and $P_e T_e$ is the equilibrium value of trade.

Under that analysis the welfare loss associated with the distortion in the real exchange rate comes about because individuals consume too many home and tradable goods when the real exchange rate is appreciated relative to its equilibrium level and then must curtail their consumption relative to the same equilibrium in periods where the real exchange rate is depreciated. Adjusting the estimate to allow for economic growth would constitute a significant challenge.

In Hause's analysis, excess consumption in some periods is repaid by a reduction of consumption in like amount in later periods, so that the trade balance balances over the period of the analysis (and foreign exchange reserves finance any imbalances). Since the excess interest costs are a focal point of interest in the Mexican case, and since insufficient time has passed for Mexico to repay its excess borrowing in the 1988–94 period, use of the direct capital account approach seems preferable.

26. The analysis would not be affected if the supply of capital were perfectly elastic at the world real interest rate plus a constant.

27. The real exchange rate is calculated using only Mexican and U.S. inflation rates, based on the wholesale price index. Since over 70 percent of Mexican trade is with the United States, this seems reasonable.

28. The ratio of savings to GDP had fluctuated between 21 and 25 percent in the years from 1980 to 1985. See Krueger, forthcoming.

29. Data on public and private savings are from Sachs, Tornell, and Velasco (1995), who cite the Banco de Mexico as their source.

30. Rebelo and Vegh (1995) note that a declining ratio of private (and usually total) savings is an empirical regularity associated with nominal anchor exchange rate regimes.

31. In the aftermath of the Mexican financial difficulties of late 1994, much was made of the bad paper in the portfolios of Mexican banks. It would be of interest to calculate how much of that bad paper was a result of dollar-denominated debts that could have been serviced at the nominal anchor exchange rates but not at a realistic exchange rate.

32. The Mexican government did not permit the sale of Mexican government securities to foreigners until July 6, 1989, when sales of *bondes, tesobonos,* and *adjustabonos* were permitted. In December 1990, restrictions on the sale of CETES were also lifted. One can wonder whether, given the high real rates of return available, foreigners were able to acquire these securities through other means.

33. The total nominal return in dollars to a U.S. national from holding Mexican T-bills from 1988 to the beginning of 1995 (and therefore after the 1994 crash) was 146 percent; holding a U.S. T-bill over the same period provided a total return of 45 percent. Thus, even with the crash of 1994, investors who held Mexican securities throughout the period nonetheless gained contrasted with the U.S. T-bill alternative.

34. If instead it were argued that, for example, half of all borrowing resulted from the perceived lower interest rate, one would multiply the figures in column 2 by half of all outstanding Mexican debt times the ratio of debt to GDP times one-half — a significantly larger number.

35. To the extent that direct foreign investment in home goods industries received excessive returns denominated in dollars, it can be argued that the welfare cost may have been even higher than the use of the U.S. interest rate would indicate.

REFERENCES

Aspe, Pedro. 1993. *Economic Transformation: The Mexican Way.* Cambridge: MIT Press.
Banco de Mexico. 1994. *The Mexican Economy.* Mexico City: Banco de Mexico.
Bruno, Michael, and Fischer, Stanley. 1990. "Seignorage, Operating Rules,

and the High Inflation Trap." *Quarterly Journal of Economics* 105, no. 2:353–74.

Calvo, Guillermo, Carmen M. Reinhart, and Carlos A. Vegh. 1995. "Targeting the Real Exchange Rate: Theory and Evidence." *Journal of Development Economics* 47, no. 1:97–133.

Corbo, Vittorio, and Jaime de Melo. 1987. "Lessons from the Southern Cone Policy Reforms." *World Bank Research Observer,* July, 111–42.

Edwards, Sebastian. 1989. *Real Exchange Rates, Devaluation, and Adjustment.* Cambridge: MIT Press.

———. 1996. "A Tale of Two Crises: Chile and Mexico." NBER Working Paper No. 5794. October.

Hause, John C. 1966. "The Welfare Costs of Disequilibrium Exchange Rates." *Journal of Political Economy* 74:333–52.

Krueger, Anne O. 1992. *Economic Policy Reform in Developing Countries.* Cambridge, Mass.: Basil Blackwell.

———. Forthcoming. "Lessons for Policy Reform in Light of the Mexican Experience." In *Policy Reform and International Trade,* ed. David Greenaway and Christopher Milner. London: Macmillan.

McKinnon, Ronald, and Huw Pill. 1996. "Credible Liberalizations and International Capital Flows: The 'Overborrowing' Syndrome." In *Financial Deregulation and Integration in East Asia,* ed. Takatoshi Ito and Anne O. Krueger. Chicago: University of Chicago Press.

Rebelo, Sergio, and Carlos Vegh. 1995. "Real Effects of Exchange Rate-Based Stabilization: An Analysis of Competing Theories." National Bureau of Economic Research Working Paper no. 5197. July. Sachs, Jeffrey, Aaron Tornell, and Andres Velasco. 1995. "Lessons from Mexico." March. Mimeo.

Sjaastad, Larry A. 1980. "Commercial Policy, True Tariffs, and Relative Prices." In *Current Issues in Commercial Policy and Diplomacy,* ed. John Black and Brian Hindley. London: Macmillan. World Bank. 1993. *East Asian Miracles.* Washington, D.C.: World Bank.

CHAPTER 15

Aspects of Fiscal Performance in Some Transition Economies under Fund-Supported Programs

Willem H. Buiter

I Introduction

I.1 Outline

This essay contains a selective review of some of the key fiscal issues faced by transition economies. The twelve countries that provide the empirical background for this study all have been under International Monetary Fund programs for at least some of the time since they initiated their transitions from plan to market. The subject matter of the paper is vast and complicated. No doubt there are, in the selection of topics covered, both type I and type II errors. The focus of the paper is on medium- and longer-term fiscal issues, such as government solvency and the evaluation of the sustainability of the government's fiscal-financial-monetary program. The purpose of the essay is to assist the design and implementation of future Fund programs and to improve the quality of the debate about the design and conduct of fiscal policy in transition economies generally.

The outline of the essay is as follows. Following the introduction, which contains a brief discussion of the roles of the Fund, section II sets out a framework for evaluating the sustainability of the fiscal-financial-monetary program of the state. Section III contains some numerical material on public debt, deficits (including quasi-fiscal deficits) and monetary financing or seigniorage. Section IV discusses eight specific budgetary issues I consider to be of special relevance to transition economies. Section V concludes by summarizing the lessons from this study in a number of propositions.

I.2 Fiscal Sustainability in Transition Economies

In many transition economies, large fiscal deficits have emerged and persisted. Grave consequences are commonly attributed to "excessive deficits." There is no consensus, however, on when fiscal deficits become excessive, nor is there a generally accepted operational methodology for evaluating the sustainability of alternative fiscal-financial programs. Despite this methodological vacuum, the following qualitative characterization of the consequences of government deficits is likely to be noncontroversial.

Deficits must be financed either by borrowing[1] or by printing money. Compare a fiscal-financial strategy of financing a given spending program by taxing today (using lump-sum taxes) with one of borrowing (that is, postponing taxation) and imposing additional future lump-sum taxes equal in present discounted value to the taxes postponed today. The borrowing strategy will, on balance, redistribute lifetime resources from the young to the old and from generations yet to be born to generations currently alive. Unless generations are linked through operative Ricardian gift and bequest motives, borrowing will therefore reduce national saving and the national financial wealth-income ratio. Whenever domestic and foreign saving are imperfect substitutes (or the world rate of interest is not independent of the government's borrowing program), this will cause *financial "crowding out"* and reduce domestic fixed-capital formation. Government borrowing will likewise raise the cost and/or restrict the availability of working capital for enterprises. This may adversely affect production even in the short run, before any possible adverse effects of lower rates of fixed-capital formation on productive potential have had time to manifest themselves. Calvo and Coricelli (1992) have argued that short-run negative supply-side crowding out may have played a role in Poland during 1990.

When a government reaches the limit of the amount of its debt that the domestic private sector and the rest of the world will absorb voluntarily, monetizing the deficit or default (including arrears) becomes the only financing option if the primary (noninterest) deficit is not adjusted. The real value of the amount of resources the government can extract by issuing additional monetary liabilities (that is, the real value of its seigniorage) is limited by the negative effect of rising nominal interest rates and increasing expected rates of inflation and currency depreciation on the demand for real money balances. When the maximal amount of seigniorage that can be extracted is less than the financing gap faced by the government, hyperinflation and/or default are the only possible outcomes.

While this brief characterization of the consequences of excessive deficits is likely to be noncontroversial, there is no consensus on the key issue of the determinants of the limit on the amount of public debt that would be voluntarily held. In view of the effects of public debt on national saving, financial crowding out and inflation, it is also apparent that public debt can be excessive, even if its quantity is below the maximal amount that would be held voluntarily. Likewise, inflation caused by the monetization of deficits can be excessive even if it falls short of hyperinflation. This essay outlines one simple methodology for quantifying the nexus between public debt, deficits, public spending, taxation, and monetary growth and applies it to twelve transition economies.[2]

I.3 The Roles of the Fund

The Fund performs three distinct roles. The first is its *systemic* role. The second is its *financial* role — the provision, subject to financial and policy conditionality, of short-term financing to individual member countries in balance-of-payments difficulties. The third is its *technical assistance* role. The systemic role — managing the adjustable peg exchange rate system established at Bretton Woods and providing it with sufficient liquidity — effectively came to an end in 1972 with the collapse of the Bretton Woods exchange rate system. Private capital markets increasingly took over the role of the Fund as a provider of global liquidity and a source of short-term financing for the more advanced industrial countries. Exchange rate surveillance is the principal surviving offspring of this systemic role, but it is just a pale reflection of the earlier systemic function, mainly because the Fund has no effective sticks or carrots with which to influence the policies of the leading industrial countries. A second surviving feature of its global or systemic role is the Fund's participation in (and often leadership of) efforts to put together financial rescue packages for countries whose financial troubles are deemed to threaten the stability of financial markets globally.[3] The recent Mexican crisis is a frequently cited example of this function. Effective conditionality tends to be a problem when the client country is significant enough to generate global spillovers.

The Fund's technical-assistance role has gained increasing importance in recent years. Many newly independent countries and countries undergoing profound structural transformations, including those engaged in the transition from central planning to the market economy, did not start off with appropriate institutions for conducting monetary policy, managing the exchange rate, raising revenues, budgeting and controlling public expenditures, and engaging in fiscal and financial policy generally. The Fund has accumulated a vast stock of knowledge and expertise for the creation of the institutions necessary for macroeconomic management in often inhospitable environments.

This essay focuses on the second role of the Fund, that is, its role in assisting individual countries in financial difficulties and with restricted access to the international financial markets. While the resources made available under Fund programs are often characterized as balance-of-payments assistance, that description is not helpful for understanding the causes and consequences of or the solutions to the problems faced by the countries in question. Balance-of-payments crises are symptoms rather than causes of trouble. The causes of persistent and unsustainable balance-of-payments imbalances are almost invariably domestic. So are the remedies. This remains true even when one recognizes that external shocks can be extremely painful and that external assistance, whether in the form of conventional aid or debt forgiveness, can facilitate macroeconomic adjustment and structural reform when the causes of the problem have been properly diagnosed and the appropriate adjustment policies are being pursued.

At the core of virtually any financial crisis, whether it manifests itself as a balance-of-payments crisis or as a crisis of the domestic financial system, lies either an inconsistent and unsustainable fiscal-financial-monetary program or defective financial regulation (or both as in the case of the Russian Federation, among others). This essay will focus on the sustainability of the fiscal-financial-monetary program, although regulatory issues will be referred to where appropriate.

In its individual country assistance role, the Fund has two tasks. The first is to help a government that is insolvent under current and projected future policies to achieve solvency. This involves *diagnosis* (that is, technical assistance) when the cause of the problem is a failure by domestic policymakers to understand macroeconomic causes and consequences and/or *conditionality* capable of inducing the government to pursue policies it would not otherwise have adopted, when political imperatives compel the government to knowingly pursue unsustainable policies. The second task is to ensure that a solvent government is not subject to constraints other than the long-run intertemporal budget constraint; cash-flow, liquidity, or borrowing constraints are examples of such unnecessary and avoidable constraints on a government's freedom to act.

The contribution of the Fund to the achievement of solvency by a prima facie insolvent government is modest, but nevertheless important. Other than expert advice, all it can offer is temporary financing.[4] The Fund cannot itself make a significant permanent resource transfer to countries in financial difficulties. It has neither the authority nor the resources to boost a government's (or nation's) flow of current and future primary surpluses by committing itself to provide a flow of current transfers (aid). Nor can it appreciably reduce a country's indebtedness by making a significant capital transfer out of its own resources. It can be helpful by acting as an honest broker between the debtor government and its creditors and by twisting arms in the right places. For instance, avoiding free-rider problems among creditor countries in the case of a sovereign debtor default is made easier if the Fund and its key member governments can lean on recalcitrant creditors standing in the way of an orderly work-out.

Restoring solvency by boosting primary surpluses is fundamentally the task of the insolvent government itself. The process can benefit from the support of those international agencies and other multilateral and bilateral institutions that provide development assistance, either in the form of explicit foreign aid or through external debt forgiveness. The Fund's role in facilitating an efficient bargain with private external creditors has already been referred to. The Fund's ability to impose effective conditionality of program countries, that is, conditionality capable of altering policies, is as crucial for the success of the program as it is limited, especially in the case of larger and high-profile trouble cases. Mexico and Russia are recent cases in point.

The second task of the Fund when dealing with a country that is in financial difficulties is to ensure that a solvent government is not restricted in the performance of its essential tasks by remediable capital market imperfections. In other words, the Fund should enable a solvent government to act according to the permanent income hypothesis without regard to short-term cash-flow, liquidity, or borrowing constraints.[5] This role is especially important in developing countries undergoing structural change and economic reform and in transition economies. With complete, perfect international and domestic capital markets this function of the Fund would of course not exist. Capital market failure is therefore the essential raison d'être of the Fund.

In the case of the transition economies, the reasons for the failure of private capital markets to generate adequate resource transfers are not difficult to explain. In the early years of the transition, neither the private sector nor the government has much of a track record as borrowers. Creditworthiness, with or without sovereign guarantee, is therefore very difficult to establish. Ambiguous and constantly changing laws, regulations, and legal procedures make contract enforcement problematic and costly for potential private creditors. If it is more costly for a sovereign debtor to repudiate its obligations to the Fund than to private creditors, a special role for the Fund in the international intermediation process for transition economies is easily rationalized.

For overcoming short-term liquidity or cash-flow constraints, even the short-term lending facilities of the Fund can be helpful indeed. In the cases of Mexico and Russia, the magnitudes of the Fund's own credit lines have indeed been significant. Possibly even more important is the "seal of good housekeeping" that the approval by the Fund of a formal Fund program bestows on the program country. This acts as a signal for private lenders and other private sources of funds to revise downward the country risk premium of the program country. The resulting induced inflows of private capital can easily exceed the resources coming from the Fund by an order of magnitude or more. Again the need for (correct) diagnoses of the causes of financial problems to be backed up by effective conditionality on often weak and incompetent governments is paramount.

II Government Solvency and the Sustainability of the Fiscal-Financial-Monetary Program: An Operational Analytical Framework

II.1 The Scope of Government

As emphasized by Tanzi 1993, under central planning, before transition has started, the very concepts of fiscal policy and public finance are nebulous. Public finance exists only if there is private finance, that is, if there exists a significant private sector.

Once transition gets under way and a significant private sector emerges, public finance and public-sector financial deficits become meaningful concepts. For our purposes the relevant definition of the state or the government is that of the *sovereign.* Included are all agencies that can levy taxes or issue legal tender and all agencies engaged in public administration (mainly the provision of intermediate public goods and services, supervision, and regulation). Both the capacity to tax and the ability to issue legal tender are ultimately backed by the state's monopoly of the legitimate use of force. Under normal circumstances these are reinforced by social consensus (or acquiescence) and trust. For practical purposes this means that the government is the consolidated (or combined) general government and central bank. When the term *government* is used without qualification in what follows, it is this combined general government and central-bank sector that we have in mind.

General government includes central, state, provincial, local, and other lower-tier government institutions, as well as off-budget agencies such as the social security funds, privatization funds, etc. It excludes the state enterprise sector. Of course, current and future transfers (subsidies) between the state enterprise sector and the government must all be allowed for in the assessment of the sustainability of the government's fiscal-financial-monetary program.

It is clearly essential that, in addition to the central government, the fiscal role of all lower government tiers be considered. Both expenditure and revenue-raising responsibilities can be shifted between various tiers of government, and lower levels of government often borrow on their own account, but with ultimate recourse to the credit of the central government. By focusing only on one tier, even if this is a key tier like the central government, a very distorted picture of the total financial exposure of the government can emerge.

The need to include all off-budget agencies and units whose liabilities ultimately are the responsibility of the state should be self-evident, as following any other procedure would invite endless window dressing.

II.2 The Central Bank's Quasi-Fiscal Deficit and the Contingent Deferred Fiscal Deficit

The need to include the central bank arises from the ability of the government to shift outlays and receipts from the conventionally measured general government budget to the central bank (giving rise to the *quasi-fiscal deficit of the central bank*) or to the non-central-bank financial sector, giving rise to the *contingent deferred fiscal deficit.* Quasi-fiscal outlays and receipts are operations of the central bank[6] that are functionally equivalent to subsidies and taxes imposed by the general government sector. Some of the most common examples are central-bank credits at subsidized rates of interest (equivalent to interest subsidies), losses associated with the purchase and sale of foreign exchange in a multiple exchange rate system (equivalent to foreign-exchange subsidies or taxes) and the imposition on commercial banks of reserve requirements obliging them to hold central-bank liabilities with below-market rates of interest (equivalent to a tax on deposits). These quasi-fiscal operations should be converted into their subsidy or tax equivalents and added to the conventionally measured primary deficit of the central bank. This *primary deficit of the central bank* then should be consolidated with the primary deficit of the general government sector to obtain what I call the primary deficit of the *government* sector. Likewise the financial deficit of the central bank should be consolidated with the financial deficit of the general government sector to obtain the financial deficit of the *government sector*.[7]

A contingent deferred fiscal deficit arises when the central bank or some other general government agency is known to be willing and able to engage in a future bailout of a state enterprise (or private enterprise with continued political clout) either directly or by bailing out a commercial bank that has made a nonperforming loan to the enterprise in question. Until the bailout transfer from (say) the central bank to (say) the commercial bank actually happens (for instance through a recapitalization of the now bankrupt commercial bank), nothing would be recorded either in the general government financial deficit or in the quasi-fiscal deficit of the central bank, even under the most sophisticated accounting conventions. It is clear, however, that, without its *implicit guarantee* of the commercial-bank loan to the enterprise, the resource transfer from the commercial bank to the enterprise would not have happened. The current resource transfer from the commercial banks to the state enterprise represents a *contingent deferred fiscal deficit.*

The quasi-fiscal deficits and the contingent deferred fiscal deficits matter quantitatively. For instance, Russia's State Savings Bank, Sberbank (as of the end of March 1996) holds about 70 percent of all household savings and has been using these resources to keep other banks and the Russian government afloat. The Russian central bank retains a 51 percent equity stake in Sberbank. The remaining 49 percent is owned by other commercial banks. More than a third of the bank's assets (30 trillion rubles, or $6 billion) are held in Russian Treasury bills (GKO's). This also represents almost a third of the Russian government's Treasury debt. While savings banks in many developed countries hold more than a third of their assets in the form of government securities, there is a sense that Sberbank, acting on the instructions of either the central bank or government or both, accumulated at least some of these GKOs at prices higher than would otherwise have prevailed in the market. In addition, Sberbank appears to have been prodded by the government into keeping the banking industry afloat by lending to several cash-strapped institutions, some of which are its own shareholders. This quasi-official role has been especially prominent since a confidence crisis temporarily paralyzed the interbank market during the autumn of 1995. Even if the government loans were free of default risk (which they are not), the quality of its loan portfolio to the banking sector appears highly dubious, and there is a serious risk of large contingent deferred fiscal deficits, if there are failures among the banks to whom Sberbank has lent and the solvency of Sberbank is thereby threatened. These contingent liabilities either come from the deposit insurance obligations of the state vis-à-vis the depositors (an obligation that is likely to be taken seriously since hyperinflation wiped out the real value of Sberbank deposits during 1992) and from the implicit guarantee given by the state to guarantee the survival of Sberbank as a going concern — the benefit of being an institution too big and too visible to fail.

Conceptually, what one is after is clear. It is the present discounted value of all current and future net resource transfers between the government and any other agent or sector.[8] The present value of these net resource transfers between the government and any other agent can, in principle, be computed in the same way as the *generational accounts* of Auerbach, Gokhale, and Kotlikoff 1991 (see also Buiter 1997), which are accounts, one for each generation, that add up, in present discounted value, the amount of receipts less payments the government can expect to collect from each generation over its remaining lifetime.

The various components of the contingent deferred fiscal deficit accrue in ways that are not recorded in the accounts of any government agency. They ultimately show up as capital transfers (through balance sheet restructuring, through recapitalization of bankrupt commercial banks, through deposit insurance payouts, etc.) often long after the real resource transfers have taken place.

Various coarse practical approximations to these streams of current and future net resource transfers is all that can, in practice, be hoped for. The *conventional fiscal deficit,* the *quasi-fiscal deficit* of the central bank, and the *contingent deferred fiscal deficit* are partial observable proxies for this unobservable sequence of future net resource transfers.

A key lesson for policy reform and "sequencing" is that delayed structural transformation, especially the failure to impose hard budget constraints on (former) state enterprises (or on the agricultural sector) can be a major contributor to all three deficits. Since the quasi-fiscal deficit and the contingent deferred fiscal deficit are much less transparent than the conventional fiscal deficit, a prerequisite for achieving fiscal control in the medium and long term may well be the minimization (and preferably the abolition) of the quasi-fiscal and contingent deferred fiscal deficits. This would be valuable even though it involves, in the first instance, no more than moving the implicit subsidies, grants, and transfers wholesale into the general government budget as explicit budgetary transactions (see Tanzi 1993).

As a simple rule of thumb, one could assume that all credit extended by the central bank to all sectors other than the general government, represents de facto quasi-fiscal grants or subsidies. This may not be totally realistic in the more advanced transition economies, where the central banks probably do extend credit on near-market terms to bona fide, solvent borrowers who service these debts and do not engage in Ponzi finance. The amount of such bona fide central-bank credit is, however, likely to be small.[9] Following the proposed rule of thumb, the *augmented financial deficit* of the central bank would then be the sum of its conventionally measured financial deficit and the net increase in central-bank credit to all nongeneral government sectors.[10] This augmented financial deficit of the central bank could then be added to the financial deficit of the general government sector to get the augmented financial deficit of the consolidated general government and central bank.

Virtually all future outlays and receipts of the government are uncertain. This holds whether or not they derive from formal contractual obligations already entered into (such as interest on floating rate debt or payments due as a result of the exercise of a loan guarantee), from the existing tax-transfer system (or from the tax-transfer system assumed to be operative in the relevant future periods) or from past and present political commitments (which may be more or less credible) to future exhaustive public spending programs. Ideally, such uncertain or contingent future cash flows would be "priced" today, that is, they should be reduced to a current-dated (present value) contingent liability or claim. Conceptually, this is an exercise in option pricing. In practice it often turns out to be an infeasible nightmare. Nevertheless, the ideal should be kept firmly in mind, even in the most practical, applied policy setting, lest grievous errors be committed in the assessment of the viability of the government's budgetary program.

II.3 The Importance of Taking the Long View

The key point for this subsection is to emphasize the need to take a long-term view of the government's fiscal-financial-monetary program. In principle, we should consider all current and anticipated future (uncertain) cash flows between the government sector, the rest of the domestic economy (private sector and state enterprises), and the rest of the world. Failure to do so can lead policy and program evaluation and design to be based on a distorted series of snapshots that can give a wholly inaccurate characterization of the evolution of the underlying fiscal-financial-monetary reality.

One implication of this view is that neither the current value of the financial deficit (even that of the consolidated general government and central bank) nor even the value of the financial deficit over the next two or three years is likely to be an informative indicator of anything that might be of interest to the Fund or anyone else. Specifically it is not a reliable measure of the change in the government's net worth, even if we "correct" for the effects of inflation and exchange rate depreciation on the real value of the outstanding stocks of financial assets and liabilities. Neither is it a reliable indicator of the change in the burden the government is imposing on future generations (and on the generations currently alive during their remaining lifetimes). Neither is it a reliable indicator of the financial crowding-out pressure created by the government budget. The same stricture applies to the change in the current financial deficit, and to any short sequence of such changes. The continuing focus of IMF programs on the conventional general government financial deficit is therefore hard to rationalize.

The same "uninformativeness" attaches to the level of and changes in the current and near-future values of the government's *primary* deficit. The reason is that it is simply too easy to shift cash flows from the present to the future, either by accounting sleight of hand or by economically costly cosmetic (and often unsustainable) changes in expenditures and revenues. The only defense against this is to trace the current and future cash flows of the government far enough into the future to ensure that, with reasonable discount rates, yet later changes in cash flows do not have an appreciable effect on the present discounted value of all current and future cash flows. The myopic financial indicators used by the Fund in the evaluation and design of macroeconomic policy packages are often less than useless (see Kotlikoff 1989 and Tanzi 1993).

II.4 The Government's Solvency Constraint

Central to our evaluation of the medium-term and long-run sustainability of the government's fiscal-financial and monetary program is the government's intertemporal budget constraint or solvency constraint. The starting point is the familiar single-period budget identity of the consolidated general government and central bank (henceforth the *government*), which states that the government's financial deficit is financed by issuing domestic- or foreign-currency-denominated interest-bearing debt, by printing money, or by running down official international foreign-exchange reserves.

With some rearranging and redefinition, the government budget identity yields the two following compact representations of the dynamics of the government debt-GDP ratio: b_t is the ratio of the government debt at the end of period t to period t GDP; r is the real interest rate; g is the growth rate of real GDP; s is the (adjusted)[11] government primary (noninterest) surplus as a fraction of GDP; σ is seigniorage, that is, the increase in the base money stock as a fraction of GDP; π is the inflation rate, d is the (adjusted)[12] government financial deficit as a fraction of GDP, and Δ is the backward difference operator.

$$\Delta b_t \equiv \left(\frac{r_t - g_t}{1 + g_t} \right) b_{t-1} - s_t - \sigma_t \tag{1}$$

and

$$\Delta b_t \equiv -\left(\frac{(1 + \pi_t)(1 + g_t) - 1}{(1 + \pi_\tau)(1 + g_t)} \right) b_{t-1} + d_t - \sigma_t. \tag{2}$$

Equation (1) states that, if the interest rate exceeds the growth rate of GDP, the debt-GDP ratio will be rising unless the sum of the (adjusted) primary surplus and the seigniorage revenue appropriated by the government are sufficient to offset the explosive "intrinsic debt dynamics." Equation (2) states that the rate of decline of the debt-GDP ratio equals (approximately)[13] the growth rate of nominal GDP times the outstanding debt-GDP ratio, plus the (adjusted) government financial deficit (as a fraction of GDP), minus seigniorage (as a fraction of GDP).

Equation (1) is in many ways rather more informative than equation (2), because the financial deficit includes the interest bill of the government, uncorrected for changes in the real value of the government debt or for the effect of real GDP growth on the debt-GDP ratio. The Maastricht fiscal convergence criteria (which are relevant to those transition economies [mainly east European] that have ambitions to join the European Union and are therefore likely to be confronted with the fiscal criteria of the Maastricht Treaty and with the fiscal conditions of the "Stability Pact" likely to succeed it) are specified in terms of a general government debt-GPD ratio ceiling of 60 percent and a general government financial deficit-GDP ratio ceiling of 3 percent. We can reinterpret equation (2) to apply to the debt and deficit of the general government sector by setting seigniorage, σ, equal to zero and reinterpreting b and d as the debt, respectively the financial deficit, of the general government sector, including general government debt held by the central bank. The Maastricht debt and deficit ceilings would be (approximately)[14] consistent with each other at a steady state growth rate of nominal GDP of 5 percent per annum.

The debt-dynamics given in equation (1) imply that at any point in time, the outstanding debt is equal in value to the present discounted value of future primary surpluses and future seigniorage between the current date and some terminal future date, plus the present discounted value of the debt held at that terminal future date. Solving (1) recursively forward in time yields, for $F \geq t$,

$$b_{t-1} \equiv \sum_{j=t}^{F} \prod_{i=t}^{j} \left(\frac{1 + g_i}{1 + r_i}\right)(s_j + \sigma_j) + \prod_{i=t}^{F} \left(\frac{1 + g_i}{1 + r_i}\right) b_F.$$

If the institution of government were known to come to a sudden end at some future date, the natural solvency constraint to impose is that the government cannot leave a positive amount of debt outstanding at the end of the world. If $F \geq t$ is the finite terminal date, the solvency constraint would be $b_F \leq 0$.

It follows that, for any solvent government, the value of its outstanding debt would equal the present discounted value of the future streams of primary surpluses and seigniorage.

$$b_{t-1} \leq \sum_{j=t}^{F} \prod_{i=t}^{j} \left(\frac{1 + g_i}{1 + r_i}\right)(s_j + \sigma_j).$$

While governments have finite horizons, the *institution* of government has no natural terminal date. As long as successive governments honor the debts they inherit, the finite-horizon solvency constraint that any debt be paid off no later than the (finite) terminal date clearly does not apply. Traditionally, it has been replaced by the "No-Ponzi scheme" condition, that, in the long run, the present discounted value of the terminal debt of the government goes to zero, that is,

$$\lim_{F \to \infty} \prod_{i=t}^{F} \left(\frac{1 + g_i}{1 + r_i}\right) b_F \leq 0.$$

Note that this constraint only makes sense in a world where the long-run (after-tax) interest rate on the public debt exceeds the long-run growth rate of GDP. With this constraint, it remains true, even in an economy without a finite terminal date, that the value of the initial stock of debt is equal to the present discounted value of the (infinite) streams of future primary surpluses and seigniorage, that is,

$$\lim_{F \to \infty} b_{t-1} \leq \sum_{j=t}^{F} \prod_{i=t}^{j} \left(\frac{1 + g_i}{1 + r_i}\right)(s_j + \sigma_j).$$

The conventional government solvency constraint or no-Ponzi finance constraint is actually quite weak. In an economy in which the (after-tax) interest rate exceeds the growth rate of GDP each period, it is consistent with the debt-GDP ratio rising without bound, as long as the growth rate of the debt does not equal or exceed the (after-tax) interest rate. The reason why an arbitrarily high (and rising) debt-GDP ratio is not inconsistent with government solvency is that it is assumed implicitly that the outstanding stock of debt is part of the (lump-sum) tax base that permits that same stock of debt to be serviced! The argument assumes that this is possible without the taxes and transfers losing their nondistortionary, lump-sum character. The private sector does not perceive the link between the debt they own and the taxes levied on them to service that debt. If we rule out such fiscal nirvanas, the tighter constraint (if the after-tax interest rate exceeds the growth rate in the long run), that the government debt cannot grow faster than the real resource base of the economy, and that the debt-GDP ratio therefore must remain bounded, must be imposed as a characteristic of any feasible fiscal-financial-monetary program.

When, under current (planned or expected) policies, the government's solvency constraint is violated, a number of policy options exist. The first policy option is to boost current and future primary surpluses, either by cutting public spending or by raising tax and nontax revenues. The second policy option is to increase current and future seigniorage. The scope for seigniorage to close the solvency gap is limited by two considerations. First, as long as we are on the increasing-yield section of the seigniorage Laffer curve, a policy of increasing real seigniorage by raising the growth rate of the nominal stock of base money will, sooner or later, exact the price of higher inflation. Second, even the maximal feasible seigniorage revenue may not be sufficient to close the solvency gap. The third policy option is to default on some or all of the public debt, internal and/or external.

II.5 Primary Gaps

For any initial government debt-GDP ratio at time t, b_{t-1}, and any target future government debt-GDP ratio $N > 0$ periods later, b_{t-1+N}, one can calculate the magnitude of the constant (augmented) primary surplus–GDP ratio that would get the economy from the initial debt-GDP ratio to the target at the required date. Call this the *required* primary surplus–GDP ratio. One can also project the future (augmented) primary surpluses that are likely to materialize under current (or counterfactual) policies and calculate that constant primary surplus whose present discounted value would be the same as the present discounted value of these projected primary surpluses. Call this the *actual* primary surplus–

GDP ratio. The difference between the required and the actual primary surpluses is the *primary gap*[15] (see Blanchard 1990; Blanchard et. al. 1990). The primary gap shows the average correction that will have to be made to the primary surplus-GDP ratio over the N-period time interval starting in period t, in order to achieve the debt-GDP target by the target date.

For instance, the one-period primary gap that just stabilizes the debt-GDP ratio is the excess of the primary surplus that would just stabilize the debt-GDP ratio in period t over the primary surplus planned or expected for period t. This is equal to the difference between, on the one hand, the product of the initial public debt-GDP ratio and the excess of the current period real interest rate over the growth rate of real GDP, and, on the other hand, the sum of the current period's primary surplus-GDP ratio and the current period's seigniorage revenue-GDP ratio.[16]

When the long-run rate of interest exceeds the long-run growth rate of GDP, we can define the permanent primary gap or solvency gap. The *solvency gap* is given by the difference between, on the one hand, the product of the initial public debt-GDP ratio and the excess of the long-run real interest rate over the long-run growth rate of real GDP, and, on the other hand, the sum of the long-run projected primary surplus-GDP ratio and the long-run projected seigniorage revenue-GDP ratio.[17]

The solvency gap is an ex ante measure only. Ex post any positive gap will be closed, through higher future realized primary surpluses or higher future realized seigniorage revenues than were allowed for in the projections, through lower than expected long-run real interest rates or higher than expected long-run real growth rates, or through default. The solvency gap therefore measures the permanent increase in the primary surplus-GDP ratio that will have to be generated in order to avoid a default, given the long-run projected seigniorage revenues and the long-run projected interest rates and growth rates.

While the definition of the solvency gap is simple, its implementation is likely to be something of a nightmare, as it requires the following: (1) the estimation of the long-run real rate of interest and of the long-run real rate of growth, and (2) the prediction of long-run seigniorage-GDP and primary surplus-GDP ratios under some plausible (or benchmark) policy or policies and for some acceptable scenario(s) for the behavior of the external economic environment and other relevant exogenous variables.

A tempting short-cut would be to replace the unobservable permanent expected seigniorage-GDP and primary surplus-GDP ratios by some observable proxies like the recent average behavior of the actual seigniorage-GDP and primary surplus-GDP ratios. An example of such an ad hoc approximation would be to replace the permanent primary surplus and seigniorage ratios by their current values. This would yield the *myopic* solvency gap.[18]

A simple spreadsheet program (see, e.g., Buiter 1993b) can be used to calculate primary gaps for any time horizon given the following inputs: the initial government debt-GDP ratio, projected future real interest rates and real growth rates, projected future (augmented) primary government surpluses, and projected future seigniorage (as fractions of GDP). It is unfortunate that for many of the countries considered in this study (including most of the FSU countries), reliable data on the initial government debt and on current and past government (augmented) primary surpluses are not yet available.

II.6 The Long View Again

The importance of taking the long view can be illustrated by considering the way in which the current (and near-future) values of the government's primary surplus can be doctored to create a mistaken impression of fiscal soundness and sustainability. Similar points can be made about the government's financial deficit or any of its "corrected" measures. The expression for the current value of the primary surplus, $\bar{S}_t$, is given below. T denotes government taxes net of transfer payments and subsidies, N^* is the foreign currency value of net foreign aid inflows, E is the nominal spot exchange rate, C is government consumption spending, F is the gross cash return on the government capital stock, $PRIV$ is privatization proceeds, and A is gross domestic capital formation by the government.

$$\bar{S}_t \equiv T_t + E_t N_t^* - C_t + F_t + PRIV_t - A_t.$$

Failure to pay state pensions on time increases the current value of T (taxes net of transfers and subsidies). If pension arrears have to be made up in due course in present-value terms, the solvency of the government is not improved by such arrears. Bringing forward tax payments from a future fiscal year into the current one also will not improve the government's finances in any fundamental way.

Sequestrations and salary arrears to government employees temporarily depress C (government consumption spending). If, in due course, the sequestrations are reversed and the salary arrears are made good, there is no impact on the present value of current and future government cash flows. This is what seems to have happened in Russia during 1995 and early in 1996, in the run-up to the presidential elections.

Bringing forward privatization (an increase in $PRIV$) also increases the conventionally measured primary surplus. Privatization (the sale of existing government assets) is a financing item that belongs below the line. Since the stock of government assets that can be privatized is given (or rather can only be augmented by government capital formation, A) privatization itself (the asset sale) can only generate a temporary improvement in the government's cash flow. Privatization can have a lasting effect on the public finances only if the privatization proceeds exceed the present discounted value of the future stream of revenues (F) the government would have earned had the assets remained in the public sector. It is of course perfectly possible that the future stream of F (conditional on the asset having remained in the public sector) would have been mainly negative for the privatized assets: the government might have had to make good the losses of the state enterprises it owned. This is not inconsistent with the government getting positive privatization revenues, as the value of the privatized resources under private ownership can exceed their continuation value in the public sector. If preprivatization F is negative and if privatization is not accompanied by an increase in efficiency (or an enhanced capacity to exploit market power), the government may find itself paying future subsidies (smaller future values of T) that match the increase in F produced by privatization. Either way, the link between current $PRIV$ and future F and T must be recognized in assessing the long-run budgetary implications of privatization.

A common tactic by governments faced with an urgent need for budgetary retrenchment is to slash the general government capital formation program, thus reducing A. Infrastructure investment (together with maintenance and repairs, which are part of C) tends to be a soft target for finance ministers looking for blood. To the extent that the spending is merely postponed rather than cut permanently, the improvement in the government's finances is only temporary, and the effect on the present value of present and future cash flows will be small. If additions to the government capital stock yield a positive future cash flow, current cuts in A will be followed by future reductions in F. Even if public-sector capital formation does not yield a *direct* cash return (through user fees, etc.), it may, if it is socially productive, increase the future tax base (for income taxes, VAT, corporate profit taxes, etc.), thus making future values of T larger than they would have been otherwise.

Just as bank regulators are faced with the problem of off-balance sheet assets and liabilities held by the institutions they are supervising, so those charged with the need to supervise government finances are faced with an increasing variety of contingent claims and liabilities held by governments. Loan guarantees, export credit guarantees, deposit insurance, and foreign-exchange guarantees are but some of the more common options owned or written by governments (see, e.g., Mody and Patro 1995). Pricing such contingent claims is a daunting task, but if the scope of these activities continues to increase, there really is no way around it. In New Zealand the government is now legally bound to present a comprehensive public-sector balance sheet that includes explicit valuations of many of the more standard contingent claims and liabilities. These contingent liabilities would be added to the stock of interest-bearing public debt in the calculation of the primary gaps.

Ideally, similar valuations should be made for the nonstandard contingent claims on the government, including its social security health and retirement programs, and government pension schemes. The approach could even be extended to the uncertain future streams of tax receipts, transfer payments, and subsidies. Even crude approximations, like discounting expected future cash flows using risk-free discount rates, would be an improvement over the current practice of throwing in the towel without even putting up a fight.

II.7 Seigniorage

Governments can appropriate real resources by issuing intrinsically valueless (fiat) money, provided private agents believe that fiat money will offer them a competitive rate of return (including saved transactions costs) over the planned holding period. A government can raise the attractiveness to private agents of its fiat money by paying interest on it, by declaring it legal tender, by requiring certain transactions (say tax payments) to be made with it, and by making the use of other transactions media costly or even illegal. Since the private (and social) marginal cost of producing fiat money is (approximately) zero, the government must have some monopoly power over its issuance if it is going to gain command over real resources by varying its quantity.

While the terms *seigniorage* and *inflation tax* are often used interchangeably, this is a dangerous habit, as the two concepts are quite distinct. By *seigniorage* I mean the resources appropriated by the government by expanding the nominal monetary base. This resource measure of seigniorage (as a fraction of GDP), denoted σ, is given by equation (3), where H_t denotes the nominal stock of base money outstanding at the beginning of period $t + 1$, Q is real GDP, and P the GDP deflator.

$$\sigma_t \equiv \frac{\Delta H_t}{P_t Q_t}. \tag{3}$$

In what follows, I treat the monetary base as non–interest bearing. This need not be the case for commercial bank reserves held with the central bank. In Hungary, for instance, near-market interest rates are paid on such reserves. The corrections that must be made to the analysis that follows when commercial bank reserves held with the central bank bear interest are straightforward.

There is a closely related concept, occasionally also referred to in the literature as seigniorage, that defines the interest burden forgone by the government through its ability to issue non-interest-bearing liabilities. This concept of *interest burden forgone* or opportunity cost measure of seigniorage (as a fraction of GDP), denoted ω_t, is given in equation (4); i denotes the domestic short nominal interest rate and $h_t \equiv H_t/(P_tQ_t)$ the base money-GDP ratio, or the inverse of the income velocity of circulation of base money.

$$\omega_t \equiv i_t \frac{H_{t-1}}{P_tQ_t} \equiv \frac{i_t}{(1 + \pi_t)(1 + g_t)} h_{t-1}. \tag{4}$$

The resource measure of seigniorage and the opportunity cost measure are related by the following identity: the present discounted value of current and future seigniorage equals the present discounted value of the current and future interest burden foregone (roughly the operating profits of the central bank), minus the initial stock of base money.

$$\sum_{j=0}^{\infty} \left(\frac{1}{\prod_{k=0}^{j}(1+i_{t+k})} \right) \Delta H_{t+j} \equiv \sum_{j=1}^{\infty} \left(\frac{1}{\prod_{k=0}^{j}(1+i_{t+k})} \right) i_{t+j} H_{t+j-1} - \frac{H_{t-1}}{1 + i_t}.$$

A third notion of seigniorage is the central bank's budgetary contribution to the general government. From the point of view of the approach taken in this essay, the central bank's budgetary contribution to the general government is an *intragovernment* transaction that is of no interest.

The *inflation tax* is generally defined as the reduction in the real value of the outstanding stock of base money due to increases in the general price level. Thus, the inflation tax in period t, as a fraction of GDP, τ_t^π, is given by

$$\tau_t^\pi \equiv \pi_t \frac{H_{t-1}}{P_tQ_t} \equiv \frac{\pi_t}{(1 + \pi_t)(1 + g_t)} h_{t-1}. \tag{5}$$

The inflation tax and seigniorage are related by the identity given in equation (6).

$$\sigma_t \equiv \left(\frac{(1 + \pi_t)(1 + g_t) - 1}{(1 + \pi_t)(1 + g_t)} \right) h_{t-1} + \Delta h_t$$

$$\equiv \tau_t^\pi + \left(\frac{g_t}{1 + g_t} \right) h_{t-1} + \Delta h_t. \tag{6}$$

In the short run, seigniorage can exceed the inflation tax to the extent that there is positive real growth or to the extent that the income velocity of circulation of base money falls.

If there exists a stable base money demand function and if we are able to predict the arguments in the base money demand function for the period of interest, we can provide a map between the seigniorage revenue extracted by the government and the rate of inflation. I illustrate this with an example of a simple small open economy with an ad hoc money demand function. Let real money demand be a negative function of the domestic short nominal interest rate (representing the domestic financial margin of substitution between non-interest-bearing currency and short interest-bearing debt) and the expected rate of depreciation of the currency ε^e (representing the direct international currency substitution margin [see, e.g., van Aarle and Budina 1995]).

$$\ln \left(\frac{H_t}{P_{t+1} Q_{t+1}} \right) \equiv \ln \left(\frac{h_t}{(1 + \pi_{t+1})(1 + g_{t+1})} \right)$$

$$= \alpha - \beta(1 + i_t) - \delta(1 + \varepsilon_t^e). \tag{7}$$

The domestic nominal interest is the domestic real interest rate plus the expected rate of inflation. The rate of nominal exchange rate depreciation is the rate of real exchange rate depreciation plus the domestic-foreign inflation differential. If we can project the real exchange rate, the foreign rate of inflation and the domestic real interest rate, then the monetary base-GDP ratio is uniquely (and negatively) related to the domestic expected rate of inflation.

Consider a steady state, with constant values of the domestic real interest rate, the growth rate of real GDP, the foreign rate of inflation, and the real exchange rate. Expectations are realized. Seigniorage as a function of the rate of inflation exhibits the long-run seigniorage Laffer curve given in equation (8), with seigniorage first rising with inflation and then declining and asymptotically going to zero for very high rates of inflation.[19]

$$\sigma = [(1 + \pi)(1 + g) - 1] e^{\alpha - \beta'(1 + \pi)}. \tag{8}$$

When the demand for money is sensitive to the (expected) rate of inflation, the inflation tax is distortionary, like every other real-world tax, transfer, or subsidy. The normative neoclassical theory of public finance might seem to imply that, in general, a (constrained) optimal design of fiscal policy will require the use of all distortionary tax instruments. Efficiency requires that the excess burdens imposed by the various distortionary taxes be equalized at the margin. This might seem to create a presumption that countries with well-developed direct and indirect tax systems therefore could be expected to make less use of the inflation tax than countries with less efficient revenue administrations and more relaxed public attitudes toward tax evasion. The (constrained) optimal inflation rates might therefore be expected to vary across time and across countries as tax bases, tax administration, and tax ethics vary. This optimal seigniorage argument for differential national inflation rates needs to be qualified, however, even as a purely theoretical proposition, as Friedman's optimal quantity of money result, that the opportunity cost of money should be brought down to zero, turns out to be remarkably robust.[20]

Seigniorage in a Currency Board System
There appears to be quite widespread lack of clarity about how (or in what sense) the government obtains revenues through seigniorage. A frequent comment on earlier versions of this essay was that the definition of seigniorage used in this essay made no sense because under a currency board system the central bank does not extend domestic credit to the (general) government and therefore the (general) government could not be said to get revenues from the issuance of base money under a currency board system.

This argument contains two errors. First, it confuses domestic credit expansion by the central bank (net lending by the central bank to the general government) with the net budgetary transfer from the central bank to the general government sector. Second, it fails to consolidate the central bank with the general government.

As regards the second of these points, the central bank is the monetary agent of the state (and often a key quasi-fiscal agent of the state as well). The central bank's ability to issue non-interest-bearing liabilities *is* the government's ability to issue non-interest-bearing liabilities. If the government (the consolidated general government and central bank) did not have the ability to issue interest-bearing debt, it would have to choose between raising taxes, cutting expenditures, issuing interest-bearing liabilities, and running down foreign-exchange reserves.

As regards the first point, if we look at the balance sheet and budget identity of the central bank in isolation, it soon becomes clear how the government obtains resources when the central bank issues base money, even in the case of a currency board. The stylized balance sheet shown in table 15.1 is self-explanatory. Central-bank net worth equals the value of its assets minus the value of its liabilities. There are non-interest-bearing liabilities (the monetary base) and interest-bearing liabilities, D^{CB}, bearing an interest rate i^{CB}. Assets include domestic assets and official foreign-exchange reserves, R^*. Domestic assets consist of credit to the general government, DC^G, bearing an interest rate i^G and credit to the private sector, DC^P, bearing an interest rate i^P. The interest rate on official foreign-exchange reserves is i^*, and the spot exchange rate is E.

$$\Delta H + \Delta D^{CB} - E\Delta R^* - \Delta DC^G - \Delta DG^P \equiv DEF^{CB} \qquad (9a)$$

$$DEF^{CB} \equiv i^{cb}D^{CB} - i^G DC^G - i^P DC^P - Ei^*R^* + T^{CB} + C^{CB} \qquad (9b)$$

The right-hand side of the central-bank budget identity given in equation (9b), DEF^{CB}, is the financial deficit of the central bank. T^{CB} is the net budgetary contribution of the central bank to the general government, and C^{CB} is the current expenses of running the central bank.

A pure currency board has two defining characteristics: there is an irrevocably fixed exchange rate, and there is no domestic credit expansion, that is, no net lending to the general government sector or to the private sector, so $DC^G = DC^P = \Delta DC^G = \Delta DC^P = 0$, and the monetary base is fully backed by international reserves. The central bank's balance sheet simplifies to the one shown in table 15.2, while its budget identity becomes the one given in equations (10a,b).

TABLE 15.1. Stylized Central Bank Balance Sheet

Assets	Liabilities
DC^G (Domestic credit to the general government)	H (Base money)
DC^P (Domestic credit to the private sector)	D^{CB} (Interest-bearing central bank debt)
ER^* (Official foreign exchange reserves)	NW^{CB} (Central bank net worth)

TABLE 15.2. Stylized Currency Board Balance Sheet

Assets		Liabilities
ER^* (Official foreign exchange reserves)	H	(Base money)
	D^{CB}	(Interest-bearing central bank debt)
	NW^{CB}	(Central bank net worth)

$$\Delta H + \Delta D^{CB} - E\Delta R^* \equiv DEF^{CB} \qquad (10a)$$

$$DEF^{CB} \equiv i^{cb}D^{CB} - Ei^* R^* + T^{CB} + C^{CB} \qquad (10b)$$

On the right-hand side of equation (10b), the interest paid on the central bank's interest-bearing debt and the interest earned on its foreign assets can be taken as given at a point in time. So are the expenses of running the bank. Consider first the case where the central bank has no interest-bearing liabilities ($D^{CB} = \Delta D^{CB} = 0$). If the central bank builds up foreign-exchange reserves, it either issues base money or it reduces its net budgetary transfer to the Treasury. While, by definition, there is no domestic credit expansion under a currency board system, this does not mean that there is no net budgetary transfer (positive or negative) to the Treasury. This argument is not materially affected if the central bank issues interest-bearing liabilities in addition to base money: for the central bank to be solvent, its outstanding net interest-bearing debt[21] must be equal to the present discounted value of its current and future primary surpluses $-(T^{CB} + C^{CB})$ plus the present discounted value of its current and future issues of base money.

A Broader View of the Inflation Tax
The inflation tax of this section is perhaps more accurately referred to as the (narrowly defined) anticipated inflation tax. Anticipated inflation can influence the government's budgetary position through other channels. The most important of these is the Olivera-Tanzi effect through which a higher rate of inflation erodes the real value of taxes subject to a collection lag.[22] The reason is that such deferred tax payments often neither are index-linked nor have a market interest rate reflecting anticipated inflation attached to them.

In addition to using the anticipated-inflation tax (broadly defined), the government can improve its real financial net worth by reducing the real value of its outstanding domestic-currency-denominated fixed interest rate debt through unanticipated inflation. The effect of an unexpected increase in the current and/or future rate of inflation on the market value of the domestic-currency-denominated nonindexed fixed-rate debt increases with the remaining term to maturity of the debt.[23] Even variable-interest-rate, very-short-maturity debt can have its real value eroded by an unanticipated increase in the price *level*. Even if nominal domestic costs are sticky, the CPI will be flexible in an open economy through the import component of the consumption bundle. In a small open economy, a price level jump can be engineered through a discrete (or maxi-) devaluation. The ability to impose unanticipated inflation tax levies on the national debt may be as important as the discretionary use of the anticipated inflation tax for a number of countries with high public debt-GDP ratios and a doubtful capacity for generating significant and sustained primary surpluses. For such countries, the case for a de jure (through a [partial] "consolidation" or default by some other name) or de facto (through an inflation surprise of an unexpected devaluation) capital levy on the public debt may well become irresistible. If a de jure public-debt repudiation turns out to be politically unacceptable, a fierce burst of inflation and a maxidevaluation may well be the only way to reimpose ex post consistency on the public accounts.

III Some Numbers

III.1 Seigniorage

While few people are likely to lie awake about seigniorage for most EU countries (see Buiter 1995a and Grilli 1988), the same cannot be said for some of the transition economies. Of the six East European countries, shown in table 15.3, only Hungary approaches the seigniorage performance of the eleven most advanced EU members. Poland approximates the performance of the least developed EU countries, Portugal and Greece. The Czech Republic and the Slovak Republic raise more than 3 percent of GDP through seigniorage. So does Hungary, if the conventional monetary base measure (domestic currency in circulation plus banks' reserves with the central bank) is used. However, Hungary is the only country in our sample where near-market interest rates are paid on commercial bank reserves with the central bank. This suggests that domestic currency in circulation alone constitutes the base for seigniorage. On this measure, Hungary extracted less than 1 percent of GDP in seigniorage during 1994.

Of the six FSU countries, shown in table 15.4, only Estonia, with its currency board, raises seigniorage comparable to the EU countries. The Ukraine relies most on seigniorage, with a figure of more than 11 percent of GDP for 1994. Kazakhstan, the Kyrgyz Republic, and the Russian Federation all raised more than 5 percent of GDP through seigniorage in 1994.

With conventional tax bases as weak as they are in countries like Kazakhstan, the Kyrgyz Republic, the Russian Federation, and Ukraine, continued reliance on seigniorage as a nontrivial source of revenue seems unavoidable. The question then is what the need to extract, on a continu-

TABLE 15.3.   Seigniorage in Six East-European Countries

	1991	1992	1993	1994	Average
Bulgaria: σ	−1.03	7.81	2.51	5.55	3.71
π	338.8	79.4	63.8	121.9	131.3
h	22.9	14.81	15.19	9.69	15.65
πh	77.59	11.76	9.69	11.81	27.71
Czech Republic: σ			−0.02	3.11	1.55
π			18.75	9.70	14.13
h			11.93	9.94	10.63
πh			2.12	0.96	1.54
Hungary: σ^a	2.26	2.14	1.45	0.91	1.69
	10.70	3.06	3.43	3.67	5.22
π	31.01	24.69	21.13	21.23	24.45
$h*$	9.25	9.77	9.88	9.25	9.54
	21.00	26.91	24.87	23.11	23.97
$\pi h*$	2.87	2.41	2.09	1.96	2.33
	6.51	6.64	5.25	4.91	5.83
Poland: σ	3.12	2.77	1.54	1.70	2.28
π	60.33	44.43	37.69	29.39	42.52
h	9.60	9.02	8.70	7.43	8.69
πh	5.79	4.01	3.28	2.18	3.69
Romania: σ	1.37	4.17	3.49	4.04	3.27
π	222.80	199.21	295.48	61.74	180.35
h	14.69	5.90	3.05	2.67	6.58
πh	32.73	11.75	9.01	1.65	11.87
Slovak Republic: σ			−1.03	3.85	1.41
π			25.00	11.66	18.14
h			9.48	11.95	10.72
πh			2.37	1.39	1.94

Note: I did not include the interest foregone measure, as reliable interest data did not seem to be available. σ: Seigniorage (% of GDP); π: Inflation rate (CPI) (annual percentage rate); h: Money base (bop) (% of GDP); πh: inflation tax (% of GDP). Average is over years for which seigniorage figures are given.

[a]First figure based on domestic currency in circulation only; second figure based on monetary base including bank reserves with the central bank.

ing basis, say 5 percent of GDP through seigniorage implies for the inflation targets that the authorities should set themselves.[24]

Unfortunately, the database at my disposal is not good enough to estimate, with any degree of precision, reasonably robust base money (or domestic currency) demand functions. The time series are too short (and too much affected by parameter instability despite their shortness), and there is too much unobservable cross-sectional heterogeneity to allow for confident time-series, cross-section, or panel data estimation.

An attempt to estimate a long-run seigniorage Laffer curve directly using pooled data for all twelve countries in my sample is re-

TABLE 15.4. Seigniorage in Six FSU Countries

	1991	1992	1993	1994	Average
Estonia: σ			9.38	1.28	5.33
π			35.72	41.58	38.62
h			8.38	11.11	9.75
πh			2.99	4.62	3.76
Kazakhstan: σ				5.95	5.95
π		3050.00	2167.57	1160.26	1160.26
h				0.87	0.87
πh				10.09	10.09
Kyrgyz Republic: σ		15.78	6.45	5.06	9.10
π		1264.00	1366.28	87.15	620.68
h		3.12	2.68	4.84	3.55
πh		39.43	36.62	4.22	22.03
Lithuania: σ			5.80	3.15	4.48
π		1163.50	188.85	44.95	104.61
h			3.40	5.08	4.24
πh			6.42	2.28	4.44
Russian Federation: σ		20.88	11.16	6.14	12.73
π		2501.39	841.62	202.68	805.08
h		1.94	2.63	3.55	2.71
πh		48.53	22.13	7.19	21.82
Ukraine: σ		14.00	17.13	11.03	14.05
π		1860.00	10104.01	408.03	2065.90
h		1.08	0.40	2.37	1.28
πh		20.08	40.42	9.67	26.44

Note: I did not include the interest foregone measure, as reliable interest data did not seem to be available. σ: Seigniorage (% of GDP); π: Inflation rate (CPI) (annual percentage rate); h: Money base (bop) (% of GDP); πh: inflation tax (% of GDP). The average is over years for which seigniorage figures are given.

ported in a longer version of this essay (Buiter 1996). The least objectionable estimates suggests that the long-run seigniorage-maximizing rate of inflation is about 137 percent per annum and that the maximal long-run seigniorage-GDP ratio is about 3.65 percent. Van Aarle and Budina (1995), using longer quarterly time-series, estimate currency and base money demand functions of the semilogarithmic variety (as in equation (7)).[25] Their best equation (currency demand in Poland), has a long-run semielasticity of currency demand with respect to the rate of inflation of -0.21 (with a t-statistic of -3.09) and a long-run semielasticity with respect to the rate of currency depreciation of -0.54 (with a t-statistic of -0.11). These point estimates imply[26] that the long-run seigniorage-maximizing rate of inflation is about 133 percent per annum if (statistically insignificant) international direct currency substitution is taken into account, and about 476 percent per annum if it is not. Maximal seigniorage is about 3.7 percent of GDP if international direct currency substitution is not taken into account and just over 2 percent of GDP if international direct currency substitution is allowed for. It goes without saying that it is very unlikely that the seigniorage-maximizing rate of inflation will ever be the optimal rate.

In view of the importance of seigniorage revenue for countries in the early stages of transition, the estimation of more robust base money and domestic currency demand functions should have high research priority.

III.2 Debts and Deficits

A Quick First Check for Quasi-Fiscal Deficits
In most transition economies, especially in the financially less developed and sophisticated ones, it is safe to interpret any excess of domestic credit expansion (DCE) by the central bank (the increase in the stock of base money minus the official settlements balance, roughly equal to the increase in the central bank's external assets or international reserves) over the financial deficit of the general government to be prima facie evidence of fiscal and/or quasi-fiscal deficits of the central bank. From equations (9a,b) it follows that

$$DCE \equiv \Delta H - E\Delta R^* \equiv \Delta DC^G - \Delta D^{CB} + \Delta DC^P + DEF^{CB}. \quad (11)$$

The last two terms on the right-hand side of equation (11), $\Delta DC^P + DEF^{CB}$, are the *augmented* financial deficit of the central bank, treating all central-bank net credit extended to the nongeneral government sectors, ΔDC^P, as de facto quasi-fiscal transfer payments. This augmented financial deficit of the central bank equals DCE minus credit extended by the central bank to the general government, DC^G, plus the increase in the interest-bearing liabilities of the central bank, D^{CB}. If the data are available to calculate the augmented financial deficit of the central bank directly, either as $\Delta DC^P + DEF^{CB}$ or as $DCE - \Delta DC^G + \Delta D^{CB}$, of course no further approximations are required. If these data are not all available, we can estimate a lower bound on the augmented financial deficit of the central bank if we can assume (1) that the central bank did not issue a significant amount of interest-bearing liabilities ($\Delta D^{CB} \leq 0$), and (2) that the financial deficit of the general government is at least as large as the credit extended by the central bank to the general government. This second assumption would be violated if the general government were retiring domestic or external interest-bearing debt held outside the central bank or if it were selling assets (say through privatization). Retiring public debt does not appear to have been a common occurrence in the transition economies. Privatization has been a source of revenue in many transition economies, but the amounts involved have typically been rather small. If the two assumptions are satisfied, the augmented financial deficit of the central bank is at least as large as the excess of domestic credit expansion by the central bank over the financial deficit of the general government.

In tables 15.5 and 15.6, I check to which extent central bank *DCE* exceeds the reported general government financial deficit figures. For reference, the seigniorage figures are also included.

The figures for the six East European countries are given in table 15.5. On the basis of these figures, only Romania is a clear candidate for sizable quasi-fiscal deficits, given in the fourth row for Romania. Note, however, that the excess of central bank dce over the general govern-

TABLE 15.5.   *DCE* and Financial Deficits in Six East European Countries (% of GDP)

		1991	1992	1993	1994
Bulgaria	σ	−1.03	7. 81	2.51	5.55
	$DCE(1)1$	0.06	2.84	5.39	5.13
	$DCE(2)2$	2.70	4.58	5.45	7.91
	deficit	14.66	15.04	15.72	7.03
Czech Rep.	σ			−0.02	3.11
	DCE			−5.0	−2.5
	deficit			−0.56	1.29
Hungary	σ	10.70	3.06	3.43	3.67
	$DCE(1)3$	2.15	2.17	−2.66	2.72
	$DCE(2)4$	2.54	5.10	−3.42	5.27
	deficit	1.70	5.40	6.80	6.30
Poland	σ	3.12	2.77	1.54	1.70
	$DCE(1)$	4.84	0.85	0.80	−0.98
	$DCE(2)$	4.69	2.20	1.34	0.48
	deficit	6.66	6.63	2.89	2.46
Romania	σ	1.37	4.17	3.49	4.04
	DCE	5.28	6.07	3.69	1.92
	deficit	−0.50	4.60	0.10	1.07
	DCE-deficit	5.78	1.47	3.59	1.85
Slovak Rep.	σ			−1.03	3.85
	DCE			−1.9	−6.0
	deficit			7.60	1.40

Note: σ: seigniorage as a percentage of GDP; *DCE*(i): Domestic credit expansion as a percentage of GDP, based on international reserve accumulation measure *i*, *i* = 1, 2; deficit: general government financial deficit as a percentage of GDP; *DCE*(1) Based on change in NIR; *DCE*(2) Based on change in NFA; *DCE*(3) Based on change in NIR, but including valuation changes due to exchange rate movements.

ment financial deficit only provides a lower bound on the augmented financial deficit of the central bank: it is sufficient, but not necessary, to start worrying about quasi-fiscal deficits.

The figures for the six FSU countries are given in table 15.6. Estonia experienced huge reserve inflows in connection with the creation of its currency board in 1993. Even so, there may be valuation problems associated with its reserve inflows. Kazakhstan, for which only one year (1994) of data is available, passes the plausibility test because of a reported 6.9 percent of GDP quasi-fiscal deficit in 1994 — the only quasi-fiscal deficit reported by the Fund for any year and any country. The Kyrgyz Republic also reports large and wild reserve flows. Reserve valuation problems may again have contributed to some pretty wild

TABLE 15.6. *DCE* and Financial Deficits in Six FSU Countries (% of GDP)

		1991	1992	1993	1994
Estonia	σ			9.38	1.28
	$DCE(1)$			−152.39	−10.11
	$DCE(2)$			NA	NA
	deficit			0.7	1.4
Kazakhstan	σ			NA	5.95
	$DCE(1)$			NA	4.26
	$DCE(2)$			NA	5.17
	deficit			NA	6.55[a]
Kyrgyz Rep.	σ		15.78	6.45	5.06
	$DCE(1)$			27.16	−40.05
	$DCE(2)$			NA	NA
	deficit			13.50	8.40
Lithuania	σ			5.80	3.15
	$DCE(1)$			NA	3.43
	$DCE(2)$			3.98	3.26
	deficit			−0.60	4.40
Russian Fed.	σ		20.88	11.16	6.14
	$DCE(1)$		NA	7.31	6.07
	$DCE(2)$		NA	NA	NA
	deficit		29.36	8.13	11.46
Ukraine	σ		14.00	17.13	11.03
	$DCE(1)$		NA	NA	10.35
	$DCE(2)$		NA	NA	NA
	deficit	14.10	30.40	10.10	8.60

Note: σ: seigniorage as a percentage of GDP; $DCE(i)$: Domestic credit expansion as a percentage of GDP, based on interantional reserve accumulation measure i, $i = 1, 2$; deficit: general government financial deficit as a percentage of GDP.

[a]General government deficit of −0.30 percent of GDP plus quasi-fiscal deficit of 6.90 percent of GDP.

DCE(1) numbers. For Lithuania, *DCE*(2) exceeded the deficit in 1993, and for the Ukraine *DCE*(1) exceeded the deficit in 1994.

Both quasi-fiscal deficits and contingent deferred fiscal deficits are likely to be important in many of the FSU countries, and in Romania and Bulgaria. Even the advanced transition economies (the Baltic republics, the Czech Republic, Hungary, Poland, and the Slovak Republic) are no exception, as the contingent claims on the government represented by likely insolvencies in the financial sector should be allowed for in any medium-term fiscal-financial strategy. The absence of any quantitative information on such current and future contingent claims on the public purse makes it very hard, if not impossible, to perform a meaningful analysis of the sustainability of the fiscal-financial-monetary program. What follows assumes that unreported quasi-fiscal deficits and contingent deferred fiscal deficits are indeed zero. That assumption is likely to be wide off the mark in many cases.

Real Growth Rates and Real Interest Rates
Two key ingredients in the sustainability analysis framework outlined in section II are future growth rates of real GDP and the future real interest rate on domestic government debt. In the hope (but not the expectation) that the past can be a guide to the future, figures on the realized magnitudes of these two variables are presented in table 15.7.

Whatever one may think of the quality of the real growth figures as indicators of the actual behavior of the real economy in the past, it is clear that they are bound to be very poor guides to future real growth. The ex post real interest rates recorded in table 15.7, should also be taken with a pinch of salt, as a guide to either past or future. With the exception of the last year or so for Bulgaria, Hungary, the Czech Republic, Poland, and the Slovak Republic, such nominal interest rates as are reported are unlikely to represent the marginal cost of voluntary domestic lending to the government. More important, the ex post real interest rates recorded in table 15.7 are, again with the five exceptions already mentioned, likely to be extremely poor guides to the ex ante real cost of future voluntary domestic government borrowing in the countries concerned.

Debts, Deficits, and Primary Surpluses
Subject to all the aforementioned qualifications, we can now pull together those key ingredients of a fiscal-sustainability analysis that are available.

I was unable to obtain data on the debt of the consolidated general government and central bank. The data in tables 15.8 and 15.9 refer only to general government debt (even then there are some lacunae). This can clearly lead to distortions from the point of view of the sustainability analysis outlined in section II of the essay. In Hungary, for instance, a large part of the general government debt is owed to the central bank. The debt of the consolidated general government and central bank therefore looks quite different (particularly in terms of the breakdown between domestic and foreign debt) from that of the general government sector. Moreover, while much of the general government debt is at preferential rates, interest rates on the consolidated debt are close to market levels, reflecting the larger share of external debt in the consolidated debt. I recognize the problem, but cannot remedy it with the data available to me.

TABLE 15.7.   Real Growth Rates and Real Interest Rates in Twelve Transition Economies (% per year)

		1991	1992	1993	1994[a]	1995[b]
Bul	g	−11.7	−7.3	−2.4	1.4	2.5
	r	NA	NA	−5.4	−20.7	NA
Cze	g	−14.2	−6.4	−0.9	2.6	4
	r	NA	NA	−6.9	0.4	NA
Hun	g	−11.9	−3.0	−0.9	2	3
	r	1.4	3.2	−0.5	2.2	NA
Pol	g	−7.6	2.6	3.8	5.0	5.5
	r	−1.0	−2.1	−2.1	2.0	NA
Rom	g	−12.9	−10.0	1.3	3.4	4
	r	NA	NA	−47.8	75.5	NA
Slo	g	−14.5	−7.0	−4.1	4.8	5
	r	NA	NA	−7.9	4.2	NA
Est	g	−11	−21.6	−8.4	3	4
	r	NA	NA	−7.7	−16.6	NA
Kaz	g	−13	−12	−12	−25	−12
	r	NA	−95.1	−86.8	−33.8	NA
Kyr	g	−5	−25	−16	−27	−5
	r	NA	NA	NA	NA	NA
Lit	g	−13.1	−33.7	−24.2	1.7	5
	r	NA	NA	−21.5	13.8	NA
Rus	g	−13	−19	−12	−15	−4
	r	NA	NA	NA	NA	NA
Ukr	g	−12	−17	−17	−23	−5
	r	NA	NA	NA	NA	NA

Source: GDP growth rates: Transition Report 1995, EBRD; real interest rates: own calculations based on IMF data.
[a]estimate
[b]projection

Considering first the six East European countries, we find a wide variety of circumstances, as can be seen from table 15.8.

Bulgaria is extremely highly indebted, with a debt-GDP ratio at the end of 1994 of 165 percent, more than two-thirds of which is external debt. During 1994, however, Bulgaria managed a primary surplus of 7.0 percent of GDP. If there are no hidden quasi-fiscal and contingent deferred fiscal deficits, the 7.0 percent of GDP primary surplus would, if maintained indefinitely, be consistent with long-run solvency as long as the long-run real interest rate does not exceed the long-run growth rate of real GDP by more than 4.2 percent per annum. Clearly, a permanent

TABLE 15.8. Debts, Deficits, and Primary Surpluses in Six East-European Countries (% of GDP)

		1991	1992	1993	1994
Bulgaria	debt: tot.	230.9	178.9	172.2	165.9
	dom.	33.5	30.6	35.5	50.2
	ext.	197.4	148.4	136.7	115.7
	deficit	14.7	15.4	15.7	7.0
	prim. sur.	3.2	0.9	−1.5	7.0
Czech Rep.	debt[a]: tot.		20.3	17.4	15.6
	dom.		11.3	9.5	9.1
	ext.		8.9	8.0	6.5
	deficit		2.2	−0.6	1.3
	prim. sur.		−1.2	2.2	0.1
Hungary	debt: tot.	75.9	80.7	91.2	88.4
	dom.	4.8	4.6	5.8	5.6
	ext.	71.1	76.1	85.4	82.8
	deficit	1.7	5.4	6.8	6.3
	prim. sur.	2.1	0.5	−2.0	0.4
Poland	debt: tot.	81.5	85.2	85.8	78.5
	dom.	15.7	21.1	22.9	22.6
	ext.	65.8	64.1	63.0	55.9
	deficit	6.7	6.7	2.9	2.5
	prim. sur.	−5.1	−3.4	0.5	1.5
Romania	debt: tot.	2.9	12.2	23.0	21.1
	dom.	0.0	0.5	12.9	3.6
	ext.	2.9	11.7	10.1	17.53
	deficit	−0.5	4.6	0.1	1.1
	prim. sur.	0.54	4.4	0.9	0.3
Slovak Rep.	debt: tot.		22.7	25.1	36.4
	dom.		2.4	2.7	10.2
	ext.		20.4	22.4	26.2
	deficit		12.8	7.6	1.4
	prim. sur.		−11.6	−4.2	2.9

[a]Central government only

7 percent of GDP primary surplus would be a first in the history of mankind. If Bulgaria could extract 3 percent of GDP in seigniorage in the long run, the picture looks slightly less unrealistic. In addition one could hope for a long-run real growth rate of about 4 to 5 percent per year and an annual long-run real interest rate of no more than 6 to 7 percent. Under these conditions the required primary surplus plus seigniorage would between 1.65 and 4.95 percent of GDP, which may not be infeasible. Finally, on the basis of the data up to the beginning of 1995, Bulgaria looked a likely candidate for some serious external debt

TABLE 15.9. Debts, Deficits, and Primary Surpluses in Six FSU Countries (% of GDP)

		1991		1992	1993	1994
Estonia	debt: tot.		NA	NA	NA	NA
	dom.		NA	NA	NA	NA
	ext.		NA	0.2	0.4	NA
	deficit		−5.2	0.3	0.7	1.4
	prim. sur.		5.2	−0.3	−0.6	−1.1
Kazakhstan	debt[a]: tot.		NA	NA	NA	NA
	dom.		NA	NA	NA	NA
	ext.		NA	NA	36.9	16.3
	deficit[a]		7.9	7.3	3.7	6.6[b]
	prim. sur.		NA	NA	NA	NA
Kyrgyz Rep.	debt: tot.		NA	NA	37.7	NA
	dom.		NA	NA	9.1	NA
	ext.		NA	NA	28.6	NA
	deficit		−4.6	13.5	13.5	8.4
	prim. sur.		4.6	−13.5	−13.1	NA
Lithuania	debt: tot.		NA	NA	NA	NA
	dom.		NA	NA	NA	NA
	ext.		16.6	11.4	9.8	7.9
	deficit		−4.8	−0.7	−0.6	4.4
	prim. sur.		4.8	0.7	0.6	−4.3
Russian Fed.	debt: tot.	84.9	76.9	198.9	74.8	82.3
	dom.		8.0	18.2	10.9	14.78
	ext.			180.7	63.90	67.56
	deficit		NA	29.4	8.1	11.5
	prim. sur.		NA	−18.9	−5.6	−8.21
Ukraine	debt: tot.		NA	NA	NA	NA
	dom.		NA	NA	NA	NA
	ext.		NA	17.2	12.1	28.7
	deficit		NA	NA	NA	NA
	prim. sur.		−14.1	−30.40	−10.1	−8.6

[a]Cash
[b]Including the quasi-fiscal deficit of the central bank

restructuring, which would further improve its medium- and long-term fiscal-financial position. This has indeed happened subsequently.

For the Czech Republic, I only have central-government debt. Unless provincial and local governments and the various off-budget funds greatly inflate the total, Czech government debt is tiny (at 15.6 percent of GDP for the central government in 1994). Its 1994 primary surplus is also tiny (0.1 percent of GDP), but that is hardly worrying. The Czech Republic also satisfies the Maastricht debt and deficit criteria (general government gross debt no more than 60 percent of GDP and the general government financial deficit no more than 3 percent of GDP). In 1995 and 1996, there has been some slippage in Czech fiscal control: despite a booming economy, the general government deficit rose by more than two percentage points of GDP.

With the exception of Bulgaria (prior to its external debt restructuring), Hungary may well be in the worst fiscal shape of any of the six East European countries. With a high debt-to-GDP ratio of 88.4 percent in 1994 and a small primary surplus of 0.4 percent of GDP in that year, it would have to hope for a very favorable constellation of low real interest rates and high growth rates of real GDP to make a continuation of the current primary surplus performance consistent with long-run solvency. Hungary satisfies neither the Maastricht debt criterion nor, with a general government deficit of 6.3 percent of GDP in 1994, the Maastricht deficit criterion.

Poland, with a debt-to-GDP ratio in 1994 of 78.5 percent and a primary surplus of 1.5 percent of GDP, appears to be in better fiscal shape than Hungary. With a deficit of 2.5 percent of GDP it also satisfies the Maastricht deficit criterion. As its debt-GDP ratio appears to be declining quite rapidly, it might be entitled to "Irish" treatment as regards the interpretation of the Maastricht debt criterion.

Romania exited from Communism with a negligible debt-GDP ratio. At the end of 1994 its debt-GDP ratio of 21.1 percent and its primary surplus of 0.3 percent do not suggest any solvency problems. The only qualification has to be the possibility of a hidden quasi-fiscal and contingent deferred fiscal deficit. Romania satisfies both the debt and the deficit criteria of Maastricht.

The Slovak Republic has a low but rapidly rising debt-GDP ratio, which stands at 36.4 percent of GDP at the end of 1994. The primary surplus of 2.9 percent of GDP and the deficit of 1.4 percent of GDP for 1994 suggest the absence of any solvency problems. Both the debt and the deficit criteria of Maastricht were met at the end of 1994.

Turning to the six FSU countries, it is clear from table 15.9 that the only one with a serious debt problem at the end of 1994 is the Russian Federation. The Russian debt is mainly external, much of it accounted for by inherited USSR debt (approximately US$70 billion when the USSR collapsed in 1991). Putting together the figures on the Russian debt with the large primary deficits (8.21 percent of GDP in 1994), it is clear that even if Russia continues to extract as much as 5.0 percent of GDP in seigniorage (which seems unlikely), the country is insolvent without either a significant reduction in the primary deficit or a major write-down in the external debt. The true situation is actually likely to be worse than represented in table 15.9, as it is assumed that there is no quasi-fiscal or contingent deferred fiscal deficit, which is certainly incorrect in the case of the Russian Federation.

Russia's recent successes in rescheduling and renegotiating its external debt have certainly helped improve the rather dismal picture as of the end of 1994, when the total external debt stood at US$119.9 billion. In November 1995, the London Club of commercial bank creditors rescheduled debts totaling US$25.5 billion over twenty-five years. In April 1996, the Paris Club of bilateral creditor nations agreed to reschedule the repayment of $40 billion of debts over twenty-five years. The Paris Club deal involves a six-year grace period on the repayment of principal and is likely to save billions of dollars in debt repayments in the short term. I have not been able to find an estimate of its total effect on the present discounted value of all future debt obligations. Together with the recently signed agreement with the IMF for US$10 billion in loans over three years, the external cash flow constraints on the Russian economy have certainly been relaxed somewhat in the short term.

The Ukraine is the only other FSU country with a non-negligible external debt (at 28.7 percent of GDP in 1994). In view of its large primary deficit, it is clear than only a major reduction in the primary deficit can restore solvency in the Ukraine. It certainly won't be possible to continue to extract the 1994 level of 11 percent of GDP in seigniorage, and even a complete write-down of the external debt would not save much more than 2 percent of GDP in interest payments in the long run. While there ought to be some scope for reducing general government expenditure (at 52.9 percent of GDP in 1994 and estimated to have been around 46 percent of GDP in 1995), it is hard to see how the Ukraine will be able to manage without a sizable inflow of external resources.

As far as I can tell, the internal public debt of the FSU countries was small at the end of 1994, although for most of them the entry under internal debt was "Not Available" rather than "Negligible." In a number of FSU countries, notably Russia, issuance of Treasury bills was growing rapidly. The Russian domestic TB market is segmented from the external one, and considerably higher rates of return are available to domestic TB holders.

Subject to the "quasi-fiscal and contingent deferred fiscal deficit" qualification, the public finances of Estonia look very sound, while one has to withhold judgment on Lithuania until it becomes clear whether its recent primary deficit is likely to be temporary or permanent.

Kazakhstan appears to be in rather bad shape and the Kyrgyz Republic in very bad shape, even if no (further) quasi-fiscal and contingent deferred fiscal horrors are uncovered. Neither of these countries has any sizable external debt to write down or (apparently) any internal debt. Both countries have tax revenue levels that are already dangerously low. Again it is difficult to see a feasible fiscal-financial-monetary program for these two countries that does not involve a large inward transfer of external resources.

IV Some Special Fiscal Issues Encountered by Transition Economies

A closer look at the expenditure and revenue figures for the twelve countries under consideration prompts the following eight reflections.

IV.1 The Collapse of Government Revenues in Some Recent Transition Economies

A startling fact is the collapse of government (especially central government) revenues in some of the countries that have only recently initiated their transitions and that have not yet succeeded in achieving macroeconomic stabilization. Tax revenues as a share of GDP are falling to levels associated with the most underdeveloped countries in the world.

As table 15.10 makes clear, Kazakhstan and the Kyrgyz Republic are firmly in this position. Lithuania too appears to be raising too little gen-

TABLE 15.10.   General Government Revenues in Some Transition Economies (% of GDP)

	1991	1992	1993	1994	1995 estimate[a]
Kazakhstan	25.0	24.6	19.8	17.1	16.0
Kyrgyz Republic	35.7	12.7	23.3	21.6	14.5[b]
Lithuania	41.4	32.1	28.5	24.5	22.4
Russian Federation	NA	41.7	37.8	33.3	
Ukraine	36.5	41.5	41.1	44.3	41.3[c]
Romania	39.3	37.6	33.6	32.5	33.5

[a]From EBRD Transition Report Update, April 1996
[b]Government expenditure and net lending plus government balance
[c]State budget revenue

eral government revenue, and the Russian Federation is also rapidly approaching the danger zone. In October 1996, the IMF threatened to suspend loan disbursements to Russia, because of a spectacular failure to meet the tax revenue conditionality. Surprisingly, if the data are to be believed, general government revenues appear to be holding up rather well in the Ukraine. This may simply reflect the fact that the general government sector still includes much of the state enterprise sector, as privatization has been lagging behind badly in that country. Another candidate explanation is that the figures are wrong. Among the Eastern European countries, only Romania seems to be heading for a dangerously low level of government revenue. Of course, the *structure* of government revenues leaves much to be desired in most transition economies, from the point of view of allocative efficiency, administrative simplicity, and distributive justice.

It seems unlikely that even the barest night watchman duties of the state can be discharged adequately with tax revenues restricted to 17 percent of GDP. The very survival of the state is put at risk by very low tax revenues. In the revenue-deficient countries the first priority of the state should be to strengthen its tax revenue bases and improve the tax collection effort.

The proximate cause of the increase in public-sector financial deficits has been a dramatic decline in public-sector current revenues, especially in the central-government sector. There have also been significant cuts in public spending in most countries (often in consumer subsidies [food, household energy, housing], enterprise subsidies, and in public infrastructure investment), but not by enough to match the decline in revenues and prevent the emergence of unsustainable financial deficits.

The decline in revenues can be attributed in part to a decline in the traditional tax bases and in part to a decline in the government's ability to extract revenue from any given base. The decline in the traditional tax bases, mainly taxes on turnover and enterprise profits, mirrors the sharp decline in output that has occurred, without exception, in the early years of the transition. In several of the East European countries the cumulative (measured) output decline over the period 1990–92 ranged between 20 and 40 percent. Even if the recorded output decline overstates the true decline in real GDP (because of an underrecording of output in the "new private sector," and especially in the private service industries), the GDP of the traditional sectors (largely the [former] state enterprise sector) is a more appropriate indicator of the traditional tax bases, especially for the enterprise profits tax.

Equally important has been the weakening, and in some cases the virtual collapse, of the government's institutional and administrative capacity for collecting such key traditional revenues as the business profits tax. Under central planning, the tax on state enterprise profits was effectively a business withholding tax. With the government setting input and output prices, the tax authorities had direct knowledge of and access to state enterprise profits. Transferring these profits to the center was essentially a simple accounting transaction, effected through the monobank system. With privatization, the breakup of the state mono-bank system, and price liberalization, the information available to the center concerning the profitability of the former state enterprises worsened dramatically and the administrative capacity for transferring profits from the enterprises to the center weakened and in some cases virtually vanished. Much of the new private sector falls outside the net of the enterprise profit tax altogether. Tax compliance is generally poor. Avoidance and evasion are rife.

The common tolerance for poor tax compliance is boosted by the frequently arbitrary nature of assessments and by the many distortions in the tax system that make for inefficiencies and inequities. For instance, high inflation in Poland in 1990 (586 percent per annum) combined with historic cost accounting and the taxation of inventory revaluation profits meant that accounting profits for tax purposes wildly overstated true profits (measured, say, on a cash-flow basis). This provided the government with a (strictly temporary) revenue boost and saddled the enterprise sector with a sometimes crippling tax burden. The next year, inflation declined (to 70 percent at an annual rate), and with it the revenues from the enterprise profit tax disappeared (see Schaffer 1992).

Turnover taxes, too, became harder to collect as wholesale and retail trade were privatized and became more difficult targets for the revenue authorities.

Attempts are being made to enhance the revenue-raising capacity of the transition economies. As regards the enterprise profits taxes, attempts have been made to reestablish fiscal control over the former state enterprises and to bring the new private sector inside the enterprise tax net for the first time. The turnover taxes are being supplemented (or replaced) by value added taxes. With a narrow base and shot through with exemptions and zero ratings, the revenues raised by the value-added tax have frequently been disappointing.

The seriousness of the problems that arise when the central government cannot secure adequate revenues to perform its essential functions becomes apparent when we consider the history of the demise of the former Yugoslav Republic. The refusal of some of the key republics to adequately fund the federal government, and the inability of the federal government to raise revenues in recalcitrant republics without their cooperation, was the death knell of the federal state. While the dynamics of disintegration of public administration and collapse of the capacity to tax are complicated, there can be no doubt that the capacity to tax is a defining characteristic of a viable state.

IV.2 The Premature Adoption of OECD Spending Patterns by the Advanced Transition Economies

A second striking fact is that a number of the more advanced transition economies appear to be settling on a level and composition of public spending that resembles that of the advanced OECD countries. Table 15.11 contains some illustrative figures. The Czech Republic, Hungary, Poland, and the Slovak Republic all appear to be stuck with levels of general government spending that are unsustainably high. This is so even where it is possible to secure noninflationary financing for these expenditures. The distortions and disincentives associated with raising 50 percent or more of GDP in current revenues are bound to be formidable in these still relatively poor and capital-deficient economies. Hungary appears to be in especially bad shape from this point of view, with an almost Swedish-size general government spending program. It is doubtful that with level of productivity and productive efficiency still well below that of the advanced OECD countries, even the advanced transition economies can support an advanced OECD-style welfare state and supply of public goods and services.[27] The fact that these countries also tend to have an OECD-type demographic structure (a rapidly graying population) makes the problem even worse.

Bulgaria too appears to have general government spending at an unsustainably high level. Its spending certainly exceeds its capacity for noninflationary financing. Unlike the other countries included in table 15.11,

TABLE 15.11.   General Government Spending in Some Transition Economies (% of GDP)

	1991	1992	1993	1994	1995 estimate[a]
Bulgaria	55.1	53.4	50.9	45.0	45.3
Czech Republic		49.6	50.1	50.7	NA
Hungary	53.6	60.6	63.3	59.2	56.1
Poland	48.9	50.4	50.5	48.9	NA
Slovak Republic		62.6	55.7	52.8	53
Russian Federation		71.3	45.9	44.7	NA
Ukraine	50.6	71.9	51.2	52.9	45.4[b]

[a]From EBRD Transition Report Update, April 1996
[b]State budget expenditure

however, general government spending in Bulgaria appears to be on a downward path (as a proportion of GDP).

Of the FSU countries, only Russia and (especially) the Ukraine appear to be in need of significant further reductions in the share of general government spending in GDP.

IV.3 Fiscal Federalism

When we consider the transition economies with a federal structure, it often is unclear whether the main problem is the federal (central) government withholding essential (and officially agreed upon) resources from the lower-tier authorities or the lower-tier authorities (ab)using their proximity to the key tax bases to control and appropriate revenue resources that should go to the central authorities. In support of the former view, it is clear that the central authorities have delegated to the lower-tier authorities many functions and spending obligations that were previously centralized. Frequently such mandated tasks and spending obligations have not been adequately funded, either through direct transfers from the center (revenue sharing) or by giving the lower-tier authorities additional revenue bases. In support of the latter view, the experience of the Russian Federation shows that despite the constitutional position of the main tax collection administrations as agents of the federal government, the lower-tier authorities appear to be able to withhold considerable amounts of revenues from reaching the center.

In addition to the official political federal structure of the Russian Federation there appears to be an informal industrial federal structure that allows certain resource-based revenue-rich industries (especially oil and natural gas) to act like states-within-the state. Regaining the ability to enforce constitutionally adopted tax laws, rules, and regulations throughout the entire domain of the state should be a top priority for the federal government.

IV.4 Revenue Tariffs

The revenue implications of trade reform measures should never be ignored. International trade taxes are relatively easy to administer. Replacing nonauctioned quotas by auctioned quotas or preferably by tariffs is always a good idea. While there is no unambiguous theoretical efficiency case for uniformity of tariff rates in traditional international trade theory and public finance, there is a strong case for uniform ad valorem tariff rates without exemptions once we allow for administration, collection, or enforcement costs and for the rent-seeking behavior and corruption encouraged by multiple tariff rates and exemptions. Smuggling of course will always be a problem with any nonzero tariff.

Transition economies should not be encouraged to cut their tariffs to levels below, say, 15 percent, unless adequate alternative revenue sources or additional spending cuts can be identified. Romania appears to be an example of a country in which import tariffs were brought down too rapidly from the point of view of the government's revenue needs.

IV.5 Fiscal Aspects of Privatization

Privatization of state enterprises reduces the information base available to the tax authorities and weakens or eliminates its traditional administrative apparatus for collecting the taxes. When banks have been privatized and bank supervision and regulation have been ineffective, another important source of information for the tax authorities has been lost. This appears to be an especially acute problem in the Russian Federation.

Governments can collect revenues from privatization in two ways. First, they can raise revenues by selling the ownership claims to the state enterprises. Second, they can tax the privatized enterprises after privatization. This can be done even if the enterprises are (partly) foreign owned, if source-based capital income or profits taxes (say in the form of a withholding tax) are imposed.[28] Clearly, the amount of revenue raised from the initial sale of the assets is not independent of the buyers' assessment of what the future tax regime is going to be. Since governments have only a very limited capacity to commit themselves not to impose future taxes, any time-consistent policy will involve lower initial privatization revenues and greater reliance on future taxation than would be optimal if governments could make credible commitments to future tax levels.

Privatization can also affect the expenditure side of the government budget, if privatized enterprises are less effective lobbyists for government subsidies than their state-owned predecessors.

IV.6 The Shifting of Social Expenditures from the Former State Enterprise Sector to the General Government

Under central planning, state enterprises fulfill a number of functions performed by the general government sector in market economies. These include the provision of public consumption goods and services to their employees, public investment, and the provision of part of the social safety net. As the transition proceeds, some of these functions are transferred from the (former) state enterprises to the general government. Others are abandoned by the (former) state enterprises without being taken over by the general government sector.

Transferring social expenditure responsibility from the (former) state enterprises to the general government can create serious revenue problems for the general government: it was considerably easier for the pretransition state enterprises to earmark and mobilize some of their own resources to discharge these social obligations than it is for the posttransition general government sector to raise tax revenues in an efficient and equitable manner to provide an adequate social safety net.

IV.7 Sequestration and "Current Arrears"

Sequestration (the withholding from the spending departments by the ministry of finance of previously authorized funds) should be the means of public expenditure control of last resort, as its occurrence is prima facie evidence that normal budgetary processes and procedures have broken down. Sequestration impacts on government procurement, on government wage and salary payments, and on the transfer payments and benefits side of the budget. Sequestration need not necessarily lead to arrears by the government to nongovernment suppliers of current goods and services and to recipients of government transfer payments, but it will do so if the spending departments had entered into contracts (or other quasi-contractual arrangements) on the basis of their previously authorized budgets. Public-sector wage, salary, and pension arrears (henceforth *current* arrears) have occurred in the Russian Federation, were reduced in the runup to the presidential elections, but appear to have increased again since then. Such current arrears should be viewed as seriously as arrears on the internal or external debt of the government, as they too represent the moral (and sometimes the legal) equivalent of a breach of contract. Furthermore, salary arrears to the armed forces create the risk of mutiny, which does not appear to be good politics.

The Fund has, in my view, taken too relaxed a view of sequestration and current arrears in the past, especially in the Russian Federation. In mitigation, it has to be admitted that, in the case of the Russian Federation, the notion of "previously authorized funds" has often been very ambiguous, with ministries, lower-level government agencies, and high-ranking officials (including the president) claiming the authority to authorize budgetary funds—independent of the Ministry of Finance, or the approved budget (if and when that existed). If such is indeed the case, the rectification of both anomalies (anarchic budgetary appropriation authorization procedures and sequestration/current arrears) should be an essential component of the conditionality attached to any Fund program.

IV.8 The Appreciation of the Real Exchange Rate and the Cost of External Borrowing

The real domestic resource cost of foreign borrowing (that is the real interest cost measured in domestic GDP units), r^f, equals the foreign nominal rate of interest paid on the external debt, $i*$, plus the proportional rate of nominal exchange rate depreciation minus the domestic rate of inflation, that is,

$$r^f \equiv \frac{(1 + i*)(1 + \varepsilon)}{1 + \pi} - 1.$$

Equivalently, the real domestic resource cost of foreign borrowing can be viewed as equalling the foreign real rate of interest (the cost of foreign borrowing in terms of foreign GDP units), $r*$, plus the proportional rate of real exchange rate depreciation, γ, that is,

$$r^f = (1 + r*)(1 + \gamma) - 1.$$

Thus, given the world real rate of interest, real exchange rate appreciation (a decline in γ) reduces the domestic real resource cost of foreign borrowing.[29] Following the massive real depreciations experienced by many of the transition economies in the very early phases of their transition, many are now experiencing a strong (albeit volatile) trend appreciation of their real exchange rates, which reduces the cost of borrowing abroad (see, e.g., Halpern and Wyplosz 1995 and Buiter and Lago 1995).

If there is perfect international financial capital mobility and uncovered nominal interest rate parity prevails, that is, the domestic nominal interest rate equals the foreign nominal interest rate plus the proportional rate of nominal exchange rate depreciation, then the real domestic resource cost of borrowing abroad is equal to the real resource cost of borrowing at home. In a financially small open economy that takes the foreign real interest $r*$ as parametric, an appreciation of the real exchange rate therefore reduces the domestic real rate of interest.

In the reality faced by most transition economies, the domestic currency cost of foreign borrowing differs from the domestic nominal rate of interest not just because of the existence of an exchange risk premium (which can of course be negative) but also because of capital market segmentation due to capital controls, exchange controls, and other administrative and fiscal interventions in the free international flow of financial capital. Nevertheless, unless the domestic financial market is completely cut off from the international financial system, one would expect the expectation of an appreciation of the real exchange rate to lower not just the real cost of foreign borrowing but also the domestic real rate of interest.

V Conclusion: Some General Lessons

I summarize my main conclusions and recommendations as a number of propositions, grouped under three headings: "Data," "Fiscal Policy Design," and "Other." For reasons of space, not all conclusions and recommendations could be developed and motivated in the body of the essay. They are nevertheless presented here both because I consider them important and because they are likely to resonate with those familiar with the area and its circumstances.

V.1 Data

PROPOSITION 1. *For many of the FSU countries and for some of the East European countries, the minimal dataset required to evaluate the sustainability of the fiscal-financial-monetary policy stance is not available. From the officially available data on the general government financial deficit and on the general government primary deficit, it is often virtually impossible to interpret the economic significance of the magnitudes of these financial balances, of variations in them, or of differences (across countries) between them. Under these conditions, policy evaluation and advice can only be based on (informed) guesswork.*

PROPOSITION 2. *The fundamental accounting unit that Fund programs and data collection should focus on is the consolidated general government and central bank. The consolidated balance sheet, (augmented)[30] financial deficit, and (augmented) primary deficit of this sector are the fundamental building block of any medium-term or long-term sustainability analysis. Whatever the formal status of the central bank, it is essential to recognize it and treat it as a key financial and (quasi-)fiscal agent of the government.*

PROPOSITION 3. *All quasi-fiscal activities of the consolidated general government and central-bank sector should be identified as such, and the tax or subsidy equivalents of these activities should be recorded in the accounts. This is essential as much for the proper assessment of the allocative implications of the budget as for a proper interpretation of the financial position of the government.*

PROPOSITION 4. *A practical way of estimating the augmented financial deficit of the consolidated general government and central bank referred to in proposition 2 is to add the conventional financial deficit of the general government, the conventional financial deficit of the central bank, and the net increase in the amount of credit extended by the central bank to all sectors other than the general government. The assumption underlying this, that credit extended by the central bank to all sectors other than the general government is quasi-fiscal in nature, that is, constitutes de facto grants and subsidies, seems reasonable in the context of most transition economies.*

PROPOSITION 5. *In order to adopt a longer-term perspective on the government's finances it is necessary to make explicit estimates of the contingent deferred fiscal deficit of the general government, the (contingent) future claims on the resources of the central bank and the Treasury stored (and often hidden) in the balance sheets of state enterprises and of nongovernment financial and nonfinancial enterprises.*

PROPOSITION 6. *In order to adopt a longer-term perspective on the government's finances, a systematic attempt must be made to identify and value its most important contingent assets and liabilities.*

PROPOSITION 7. *All IMF documents should include only interest rates that are properly compounded. This may seem a trivial point, but the failure to observe this convention invites unnecessary confusion and misinterpretation, especially during episodes of high inflation.*

PROPOSITION 8. *Data on the stocks of internal and external government debt (including arrears) should be collected and published as a matter of routine. This includes information on maturity structure, currency composition, interest rate, grace periods, and other key features of the debt contracts (fixed rate, variable rate, bullet, etc.).*

PROPOSITION 9. *Data on the stocks of external assets and liabilities of the nation as a whole (government, private sector, and state enterprise sector) should be collected and published as a matter of routine. The Fund should make estimates of the external assets of the private sector (including those representing past capital flight) and evaluate the degree to which these assets (or their earnings) are (potentially) part of the tax base. The longer-term fiscal consequences of capital flight are as important as their short-term balance-of-payments and exchange rate implications.*

PROPOSITION 10. *The Fund should maintain a centralized fiscal-financial-monetary database that is updated after every mission and Article 4 consultation. The Fund is the obvious agency to provide this public good. Adequate resources should be allocated to this key activity.*

V.2 Fiscal Policy Design

PROPOSITION 11: *The imposition of hard budget constraints on enterprises is a prerequisite for macroeconomic stabilization. The imposition by the central bank and the ministry of finance of hard budget constraints on the commercial banks is a prerequisite for the imposition of hard budget constraints by banks on nonfinancial enterprises.*

PROPOSITION 12: *In the advanced transition economies (the Czech Republic, Hungary, Poland, and the Slovak Republic), the dominant public-finance problem seems to be the pursuit of a level and structure of public spending more commonly associated with the advanced West European industrial countries. The productivity levels achieved in these four countries would appear to be too low to support a West European–style welfare state.*

PROPOSITION 13: *In early transition economies like Kazakhstan and the Kyrgyz Republic, but also in Lithuania, the primary public-finance problem seems to be a drastic decline in the government's ability to raise tax revenues. The same problem appears to be emerging in the Russian Federation. Surprisingly, the data suggest that this is not (yet) a problem in Ukraine. When a government cannot tax to finance the essential functions of a modern state, not just the survival of the government but that of the state itself is threatened.*

PROPOSITION 14: *No structural-reform measure (such as trade reform and privatization) should ever be implemented without considering its implications for public revenues and expenditures.*

PROPOSITION 15: *Given the limited amount of administrative capacity found in many transition economies, the importance of keeping taxes simple and administratively easy to collect is central. This means, for instance, that a VAT levied and collected at each of the intermediate stages, which brings with it complicated and extensive need for record-keeping by businesses and the need for extensive record-keeping and cross-checking by the tax officials, should not be recommended automatically to any transition economy.[31] If a VAT is deemed desirable, it may be preferable to levy and collect at a single (final) stage, like a retail sales tax on final consumption (see McLure 1992 and Tait 1992).[32]*

PROPOSITION 16. *Tax exemptions undermine revenues, stimulate rent seeking and corruption, and are likely to distort the allocation of resources. The fiscal history of the Russian Federation provides ample confirmation of the truth of this proposition.*

PROPOSITION 17. *Exemptions from import duties (and indeed virtually every deviation from a uniform ad valorem tariff rate on all imports) stimulate rent seeking and corruption and are likely to distort the allocation of resources. The history of customs administration and revenues of the Russian Federation provides ample confirmation of the truth of this proposition.*

PROPOSITION 18. *Sequestration and internal current arrears should be viewed with equal seriousness as arrears on internal and external debt.*

PROPOSITION 19. *If further sustained real exchange rate appreciation can be anticipated for many transition economies, foreign borrowing (denominated in hard currencies) will tend to be cheaper in real terms than domestic borrowing.*

NOTES

This essay is a product of a research project on medium- and long-term aspects of fiscal policy in transition economies I did for the European I and II Departments of the International Monetary Fund. Massimo Russo and John Odling-Smee gave me every assistance I needed, including unrestricted access to Fund documents and departmental staff. Gerard Belanger was especially supportive (and patient). I would like to thank the professional and administrative staffs of both departments for their hospitality and willingness to come up with documents, numbers, and answers at short notice. I would specifically like to mention Michael Deppler, Leslie Lipschitz, Liam Ebrill, Juha Kähkönen, Mark Griffiths, Rachel van Elkan, Emmanuel Zervoudakis, Biswajit Banerjee, Michael Marrese, Russell Kincaid, Craig Beaumont, Max Watson, Reza Moghadam, Daniel Citrin,

Henri Lorie, Ashok Lahiri, Emmanuel van der Mensbrugghe, Piroska Nagy, Peter Keller, Patrick Njoroga, Adalbert Knöbl, and Jonathan Dunn (I hope I did not commit either a type I or a type II error on this list). Finally, I owe a great debt to the splendid work done by Xiaoning Gong, who put together an essential database for the project. Kasper Bartholdy made many useful comments on an earlier version.

The views and opinions expressed in this essay are those of the author only and are not to be taken to represent the views and opinions of the International Monetary Fund.

1. Running down foreign-exchange reserves is counted as a form of foreign borrowing.

2. They are Bulgaria, the Czech Republic, Hungary, Poland, Rumania, and the Slovak Republic (for the European I Department) and Estonia, Kazakhstan, the Kyrgyz Republic, Lithuania, the Russian Federation, and Ukraine (for the European II Department).

3. This function can be viewed alternatively as the application of its second role, that of providing financial assistance to individual countries, when the client country is deemed large enough for its troubles to have systemic externalities.

4. There is a concessional or aid element in most Fund lending, as the rates paid on drawings on the Fund are undoubtedly lower than what the drawing country could have expected to pay in the private loan markets, if it had access to these at all.

5. The national government in turn derives its stabilization role from its ability to remove (or at least minimize the incidence and severity of) liquidity, cash-flow, or borrowing constraints on private-sector spending, through the use of taxes, transfer payments, government borrowing, and monetary financing.

6. And possibly of other public-sector banks and financial institutions (such as general or sectoral development banks).

7. From the point of view of the measurement of the financial deficit of the central bank, the reclassification of quasi-fiscal transactions into their subsidy and tax equivalents will often merely shuffle items from the "net interest paid" column to the "primary deficit" column, without this affecting the magnitude of the financial deficit. This is the case, e.g., when central-bank lending at below-market rates of interest is converted into and recorded as central-bank lending at imputed market interest rates (reducing "net interest paid") combined with an explicit interest subsidy (raising the primary deficit).

8. When markets are incomplete, not only does the present discounted value of these net resource transfers matter, but also their timing.

9. An example in an American context would be "borrowed reserves," which are claims by the central bank on commercial banks.

10. I elaborate on this in section III.2.

11. Let $\bar{s}$ be the conventionally defined primary surplus as a fraction of GDP, then the *adjusted* primary surplus as a fraction of GDP, s, is given by

$$s_t = \bar{s}_t + \left(\frac{1 + i_t - (1 + i_t^*)(1 + \varepsilon_t)}{(1 + \pi_t)(1 + g_t)} \right) b_{t-1}^*,$$

where i is the domestic nominal interest rate, i^* is the foreign nominal interest rate, ε is the proportional rate of depreciation of the nominal exchange rate, and b^* is the stock of net foreign liabilities as a fraction of GDP.

12. Let $\bar{d}$ be the conventionally defined financial deficit as a fraction of GDP, then the adjusted financial deficit, d, is given by

$$d_t = \bar{d}_t + \frac{\varepsilon_t}{(1 + \pi_t)(1 + g_t)} b^*_{t-1}.$$

13. The equality would be exact in a continuous time representation of the debt-GDP dynamics.

14. The equality would be exact in a continuous time representation of the debt-GDP dynamics.

15. Denote the *required* N-period primary surplus–GDP ratio at time t by $s^N_R(b_{t-1} - b_{t-1+N})$ and the *actual* N-period seigniorage-GDP ratio by σ^N_A. Note that

$$\sigma^N_A \equiv \left[\sum_{j=t}^{t-1+N} \prod_{i=t}^{j}\left(\frac{1 + g_i}{1 + r_i}\right) \right]^{-1} \sum_{j=t}^{t-1+N} \prod_{i=t}^{j}\left(\frac{1 + g_i}{1 + r_i}\right) \sigma_j.$$

The required N-period primary surplus–GDP ratio (for $N \geq 1$) is given by

$$s^N_R(b_{t-1} - b_{t-1+N}) \equiv \left[\sum_{j=t}^{t-1+N} \prod_{i=t}^{j}\left(\frac{1 + g_i}{1 + r_i}\right) \right]^{-1}$$

$$\left[b_{t-1} - \prod_{i=t}^{t-1+N}\left(\frac{1 + g_i}{1 + r_i}\right) b_{t-1+N} \right] - \sigma^N_A.$$

Let the *actual N-period primary surplus-GDP ratio* be denoted s^N_A:

$$s^N_A \equiv \left[\sum_{j=t}^{t-1+N} \prod_{i=t}^{j}\left(\frac{1 + g_i}{1 + r_i}\right) \right]^{-1} \sum_{j=t}^{t-1+N} \prod_{i=t}^{j}\left(\frac{1 + g_i}{1 + r_i}\right) s_j.$$

The *N-period primary gap*, denoted GAP^N, is given by

$$GAP^N(b_{t-1} - b_{t-1+N}) \equiv s^N_R(b_{t-1} - b_{t-1+N}) - s^N_A.$$

16. $GAP^1(0)$ is the excess of the primary surplus that would just stabilize the debt-GDP ratio in period t over the primary surplus planned or expected for period t. This is equal to

$$GAP^1(0) \equiv \left(\frac{r_t - g_t}{1 + g_t} \right) b_{t-1} - s^1_A.$$

17. Denoting the long-run real rate of interest by r^∞ and the long-run growth rate of real GDP by g^∞, the solvency gap is formally given by

$$GAP^\infty \equiv \left(\frac{r^\infty - g^\infty}{1 + g^\infty} \right) b_{t-1} - \sigma_A^\infty - s_A^\infty.$$

Here σ_A^∞ denotes the permanent planned or expected seigniorage-GDP ratio and s_A^∞ denotes the permanent planned or expected primary surplus–GDP ratio.

18. The myopic permanent primary gap, $MGAP^\infty$, is defined as follows:

$$MGAP^\infty = \left(\frac{r^\infty - g^\infty}{1 + g^\infty} \right) b_{t-1} - \sigma_t - s_t.$$

19.

$$\beta' = \beta(1 + r) + \delta \left(\frac{1 + \gamma}{1 + \pi^*} \right).$$

The rate of inflation that maximizes steady-state seigniorage is

$$\pi_{max} = \frac{1}{\beta'} - \frac{g}{1 + g}$$

and the maximum level of steady-state seigniorage is

$$\sigma_{max} = \left(\frac{1 + g}{\beta'} \right) e^{\alpha - \beta' \left(\frac{1}{\beta'} + \frac{1}{1 + g} \right)}.$$

20. Recent insights into the optimal use of distortionary taxes on the returns from durable (capital) assets, due to Chamley 1986 (see also Lucas 1990; Zhu 1992; and Roubini and Milesi-Ferretti 1994), imply that, at least in some of the standard neoclassical models, the Friedman rule for the optimal quantity of money (the nominal rate of interest should be zero and satiation with real money balances should occur) still applies despite the fact that there are no non-distortionary tax instruments available for financing public expenditure (see Buiter 1995).

21. Net of the value of its external assets. Obvious corrections must be made if the interest rate on the central bank's interest-bearing liabilities differs from the interest rate on international reserves, when both are expressed in a common currency.

22. The effect applies equally when the delay in payment is limited to the legally permitted grace period and when the tax payments are technically in arrears.

23. To the extent that the Fischer hypothesis does not hold and higher antici-

pated inflation reduces the real rate of interest, the real value of the debt is eroded even by higher *anticipated* inflation.

24. The "need" for seigniorage cannot be inferred accurately from the government deficit–GDP ratio, as this includes nominal interest payments that will be inflated (in every sense of the word) by a high rate of inflation. An inflation- and real growth-corrected deficit-GDP ratio provides a better guide to the magnitude of the seigniorage required in the long run (as a proportion of GDP).

25. Van Aarle and Budina (1995) do not include real output or any other "scale variable" as an argument in their base money demand functions. I interpret their equation as if it had a unitary elasticity of real money demand with respect to real output.

26. I ignore the real growth rate terms in the expressions for long-run seigniorage-maximizing inflation rate and the long-run maximal seigniorage-GDP ratio. Van Aarle and Budina (1995) have the logarithm of real money balances as the dependent variable in their money demand equations and do not include real GDP or some other scale variable as a regressor.

27. When the current advanced OECD countries had the levels of per capita income achieved now by the advanced transition economies, their public-spending shares were considerably below those achieved currently by the advanced transition economies.

28. Taxing the profits of (partly) foreign-owned enterprises will of course be subject to the usual transfer-pricing problems.

29. In this section no attention is paid to the distinction between ex post and ex ante rates of return, as this is not relevant to the point made. I do not recommend this as a general rule of thumb.

30. "Augmented" means inclusive of quasi-fiscal transactions.

31. Indeed the VAT operated in the OECD countries, too, has been shown to have high administrative costs (to the tax department) and high compliance costs for businesses trying to carry out the obligations of calculating and paying the tax (see, e.g., Cnossen 1994).

32. Estonia's tax reform of 1992 and 1993 contained strong elements of tax simplification, by reducing exemptions, and by simplifying rates. In 1994 the personal income tax changed to a flat rate of 26 percent (the same as the corporate income tax rate), with an exemption (or allowance) at the lower end.

REFERENCES

Abel, Andrew, N. Gregory Mankiw, Lawrence H. Summers, and Richard J. Zeckhauser. 1989. "Assessing Dynamic Efficiency: Theory and Evidence." *Review of Economic Studies* 56 (January): 1–20.
Anand, Ritu, and Sweder van Wijnbergen. 1989. "Inflation and the Financing of Government Expenditure: An Introductory Analysis with an Application to Turkey." *World Bank Economic Review* 3, no. 1:17–38.
Auerbach, Alan J., Jagadeesh Gokhale, and Laurence J. Kotlikoff. 1991. "Gen-

erational Accounts: A Meaningful Alternative to Deficit Accounting." In *Tax Policy and the Economy,* ed. David Bradford, vol. 5. Cambridge: MIT Press.

Balcerowicz, Leszek, and Alan Gleb. 1994. "Macropolicies in Transition to a Market Economy: A Three-Year Perspective." *Proceedings of the World Bank Annual Conference on Development Economics, 1994.* Washington, D.C.: The World Bank.

Blanchard, Olivier. 1990. "Suggestions for a New Set of Fiscal Indicators." OECD Department of Economics and Statistics Working Papers, No. 79. April.

Blanchard, Olivier, Jean-Claude Chouraqui, Robert P. Hageman, and Nicola Sortor. 1990. "The Sustainability of Fiscal Policy: New Answers to an Old Question." *OECD Economic Studies* 15 (autumn).

Buiter, Willem H. 1983. "The Theory of Optimum Deficits and Debt." In Federal Reserve Bank of Boston, *The Economics of Large Government Deficits,* Conference Series No. 27. October.

———. 1985. "A Guide of Public Sector Debt and Deficits." *Economic Policy* (October): 14–79.

———. 1993a. "Consistency Checks for Fiscal, Financial, and Monetary Policy Evaluation and Design." World Bank. October. Mimeo.

———. 1993b. "QPFISMO: A Spreadsheet for Checking the Internal Consistency of Fiscal, Financial, and Monetary Policy Programs." World Bank. November. Mimeo.

———. 1995. "Politique macroéconomique dans la période de transition vers l'union monétaire." *Revue d'Economie Politique* 105, no. 5:897–946.

———. 1996. "Aspects of Fiscal Performance in Some Transition Economies under Fund-Supported Programs." University of Cambridge. March. Mimeo.

———. 1997. "Generational Accounts, Aggregate Saving, and Intergenerational Distribution." *Economica* 64:605–26.

Buiter, Willem H., and Kenneth M. Kletzer. 1994. "Government Solvency, Ponzi Finance, and the Redundancy and Usefulness of Public Debt." University of Santa Cruz Working Paper No. 292.

Buiter, Willem H., and Ricardo Lago. 1995. "Enterprises in Transition: Macroeconomic Influences on Enterprise Decision-Making and Performance." European Bank for Reconstruction and Development (EBRD). November. Mimeo.

Buiter, Willem H., Ricardo Lago, and Nicholas Stern. 1995. "Enterprise Performance and Macroeconomic Control." May. Mimeo.

Calvo, Guillermo A., and Fabrizio Coricelli. 1992. "Stabilizing a Previously Centrally Planned Economy: Poland 1990." *Economic Policy* (April): 176–226.

Calvo, Guillermo A., and Manmohan S. Kumar. 1994. "Money Demand, Bank Credit, and Economic Performance in Former Socialist Economies." *IMF Staff Papers* 41, no. 2:314–49.

Chadha, Bankim, and Fabrizio Coricelli. 1994. "Fiscal Constraints and the Speed of Transition." CEPR Discussion Paper No. 993. July.

Chamley, Christophe. 1986. "Optimal Taxation of Capital Income in General Equilibrium with Infinite Lives." *Econometrica* 54 (May): 607–22.

Cnossen, Sijbren. 1994. "Administrative and Compliance Costs of the VAT." Research Memorandum 9402, Research Centre for Economic Policy, Erasmus University Rotterdam.

Dittus, Peter. 1994. "Corporate Governance in Central Europe: The Role of Banks." BIS Economic Papers No. 42, Monetary and Economic Department. Bank for International Settlements. August.

Easterly, William, and Paulo Vieira da Cunha. 1994. "Financing the Storm: Macroeconomic Crisis in Russia." *Economics of Transition* 2, no. 4:443–65.

Grilli, Vittorio U. 1980. "Seigniorage in Europe." National Bureau of Economic Research Working Paper 2778, November.

Halpern, László, and Charles Wyplosz. 1995. "Equilibrium Real Exchange Rates in Transition." Centre for Economic Policy Research (CEPR) Discussion paper No. 1145. April.

Hernández-Catá, Ernesto. 1995. "Russia and the IMF: The Political Economy of Macro-Stabilization." *Problems of Post-Communism* (May–June): 19–26.

International Monetary Fund. 1994. "Eastern Europe—Factors Underlying the Weakening Performance of Tax Revenues." IMF Working Paper, WP/94, European I Department. August.

———. 1995. "Quasi-Fiscal Operations of Public Financial Institutions," IMF Working Paper SM/95/65, Fiscal Affairs Department, April 3.

Koen, Vincent, and Michael Marres. 1995. "Stabilization and Structural Change in Russia, 1992–94." IMF Working Paper WP/95/13, European II Department. January.

Kotlikoff, Laurence J. 1989. "From Deficit Delusion to the Fiscal Balance Rule: Looking for an Economically Meaningful Way to Assess Fiscal Policy." NBER Working Paper No. 2841. February.

Lucas, Robert E., Jr. 1990. "Supply-Side Economics: An Analytical Review." *Oxford Economic Papers* 42:293–316.

McLure, Charles E., Jr. 1992. "A Simpler Consumption-Based Alternative to the Income Tax for Socialist Economies in Transition." *World Bank Research Observer* 7, no. 2:221–37.

Melo, Martha de, Cevdet Denizer, and Alan Gelb. 1995. "From Plan to Market: Patterns of Transition." World Bank. March. Mimeo.

Mody, Ashoka, and Dilip Patro. 1995. "Methods of Loan Guarantee Valuation and Accounting." World Bank. March. Mimeo.

Roubini, Nouriel, and Gian Maria Milesi-Ferretti. 1994. "Optimal Taxation of Human and Physical Capital in Endogenous Growth Models." NBER Working Paper No. 4882. October.

Sachs, Jeffrey D. 1994. "Russia's Struggle with Stabilization: Conceptual Issues and Evidence." *Proceedings of the World Bank Annual Conference on Development Economics, 1994.* Washington, D.C.: The World Bank.

Schaffer, Mark E. 1992. "The Enterprise Sector and Emergence of the Polish Fiscal Crisis, 1990–91." LSE, CEP Working Paper No. 280, London School of Economics. September.

Tait, Alan A. 1992. "A Not-So-Simple Alternative to the Income Tax for Socialist Economies in Transition: A Comment on McLure." *World Bank Research Observer* 7, no. 2:239–48.

Tanzi, Vito. 1993. "The Budget Deficit in Transition. *IMF Staff Papers* 40, no. 3:697–707.

van Aarle, Bas, and Nina Budina. 1995. "Currency Substitution in Eastern Europe." Center for Economic Research Discussion Paper No. 9502, Tilburg University. January.

Zhu, Xiadong. 1992. "Optimal Fiscal Policy in a Stochastic Growth Model." *Journal of Economic Theory* 58 (December): 250–89.

CHAPTER 16

Foreign Aid and Fiscal Stress

Howard Pack and Janet Rothenberg Pack

I Introduction

In this essay we analyze whether foreign aid designated for specific purposes was reallocated among them in Sri Lanka during the period 1960–86, years largely before the civil war exerted a major effect on public spending. It has been widely believed for many years, on a priori grounds, that foreign aid designed to encourage specific categories of expenditure is fungible. In this view the intentions of aid donors are subordinated to the preferences of local policymakers (Singer 1965; Bauer 1972).[1] Despite the prominence of this view in the literature, there was until very recently no direct empirical evidence to support it. In contrast to the small number of studies of the allocation of foreign aid, there is a voluminous empirical literature concerning the similar questions about fungibility of grant-in-aid programs from higher- to lower-level jurisdictions in federal systems like the United States. These studies generally support the proposition that aid is reallocated among expenditure categories, although the results vary from state to state — and from program to program (Gramlich 1977; Luce and Pack 1984; Craig and Inman 1986).

A few have explored the extent of aid diversion across sectors, utilizing cross-country evidence for limited time periods (Cashel-Cordo and Craig 1990) or a limited disaggregation, largely military versus nonmilitary (Gang and Khan 1991). Although an important departure, cross-section research necessarily assumes similar policymaker preferences across countries and weakens the conclusiveness of the empirical results. Although policymakers' preferences within a country may also vary over time, the swings in policy are likely to be more limited than those distinguishing, say, post-1973 Chile and Nigeria. To benefit from the potential insights provided by individual country experiences, Pack and Pack

452

(1990, 1993) utilized time series for Indonesia and the Dominican Republic to analyze the extent of fungibility.[2]

Most of the empirical foreign-aid literature has been characterized by a more macroeconomic orientation. In the 1960s the discussion was dominated by the two-gap model (Chenery and Strout 1966), which argued that foreign aid could relieve either of two ex ante constraints on growth in developing countries—a shortage of domestic saving or of foreign exchange—and empirical research was devoted to determining the relative importance of the two. Interest in this issue declined as a result of several critiques that questioned the usefulness of the two-gap approach (Bruton 1969; Fei and Ranis 1970). A second strand in the literature analyzed whether foreign aid reduced domestic saving (Weisskopf 1972; Papanek 1972, 1973). Finally, the question of whether or not foreign aid has contributed to growth has received intermittent attention. The principal conclusion of this empirical literature has been negative (Mosely, Hudson, and Horrell 1987; Boone 1995).[3]

Fungibility arises when a dollar of foreign aid that donors intend should be spent for a specified purpose leads to less than a dollar spent on that purpose. Fungibility is related to some of the macroeconomic concerns, though it was not raised in the various debates. For example, if aid given to augment investment is diverted to increasing current expenditures or allows governments to reduce tax effort, the addition to saving, and hence to investment, is likely to be less than dollar for dollar. If aid is shifted from potentially high- to low-productivity investments, it may have little or no positive effect on economic growth. Concerns such as these, though never demonstrated to have been quantitatively important, constituted one of the reasons for the increased emphasis on program loans, including structural-adjustment lending, in the 1970s.

The issues involved in the fungibility discussion may be illustrated by referring to figure 16.1, which shows various budget lines and some indifference curves (assumed to be homothetic) of policymakers choosing between expenditures for two public sectors, industry (I) and transportation (T). Given a democratic political system with alternating parties vying for control, the policymakers' preferences are assumed to reflect voter preferences. The country is initially at point A on budget line $T_0 I_0$ spending I_A and T_A (the relevant indifference curve, not shown, is tangent at point A). Two changes occur to alter the initial choice. GDP increases, shifting the budget line to $T_1 I_1$, which would result in a new equilibrium at B. Simultaneously, the country becomes the recipient of sectorally targeted foreign aid in the amounts of $I_B I_{C'}$, and $T_B T_{C'}$, for investments in industry and transportation, respectively. If donors' preferences were shared by recipients, then the aid would be

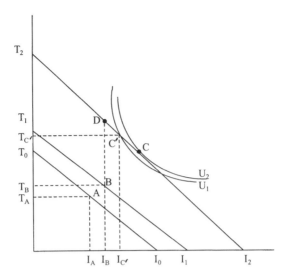

Fig. 16.1. The fungibility of foreign aid

spent as donors intend; investment on I would increase by $I_B I_{C'}$, and on T by $T_B T_{C'}$, with the new division of total expenditures represented by point C'.

If donors and recipients have different preferences concerning how the aid should be spent and donors have imperfect monitoring capacities, then this intended pattern of spending on development projects could be altered. The recipient country could simply add foreign aid to its own revenues and choose a point such as C anywhere along the new budget line $T_2 I_2$. Compared with point A, investment in T and in I have each increased by more than the foreign aid given for those purposes. Part of the increase, however, would have occurred as a result of the change in GDP. The intended increase in investment, above that which the country would have undertaken without aid, $T_B T_{C'}$, in transportation, is not realized while the increase in industrial investment exceeds $I_B I_{C'}$. The divergence between C and C' represents a diversion to the industrial sector of part of the aid intended for transportation. The difficulty facing donors is that the move from A to C consists of two components and it is difficult to determine what the outcome would have been, on the margin, without aid. If there are many donors giving aid for many different purposes, monitoring shifts such as those depicted in figure 16.1 becomes difficult and such diversions become more likely.

Several aspects of this analysis are important for interpreting the empirical results reported below. First, the larger the aid is, $T_B T_{C'}$

$(I_B I_{C'})$, relative to the initial expenditure T_A (I_A), the easier it will be for donors to monitor the use of their aid. Thus, starting at B, if BD of aid were given to be used for road construction, it would be easier for donors to identify the discrepancy in transportation expenditures between D and C than between C' and C. Second, the larger the difference in preferences, the greater the increase in utility to be derived from diverting funds, that is, $U_2 - U_1$ increases with the amount diverted from transportation.

The cost to donors of monitoring adherence to their investment intentions and the strength of incentives to evade it are important elements in determining the extent of fungibility and can be represented as

$$M = m(FA_i/D_i, FAT/G, N, W, I), \tag{1}$$

where M is monitoring cost, FA_i is aid targeted to sector i; D_i is development expenditure in category i; FAT is total foreign aid, the sum of all sectoral aid plus any nonsectoral aid; G is total government expenditure including ordinary government consumption C_g, or $G = C_g + \Sigma_i D_i$; N is the number of donors; W is the extent of coordination among donors; and I is the total number of sectors targeted by donors.

It seems plausible to assume (1) that as FA_i/D_i increases, monitoring costs decrease;[4] (2) as FAT/G increases, monitoring costs decrease; (3) that an increase in the number of donors, a decrease in their coordination, and an increase in the number of sectors receiving aid will increase monitoring costs. Finally, the difference in recipient and donor preferences provides a measure of the incentive for governments to attempt the shifting of funds toward locally desired programs. Equation (1) should be viewed as suggestive — reflecting the monitoring difficulties of donors which are not, however, reflected in figure 16.1.

In section II some of the history of Sri Lanka for the period considered is presented. In section III, the model developed to estimate fungibility is described, and the results are reported in section IV. The magnitude of fungibility is taken up in section V, and in section VI the differences among Sri Lanka, Indonesia, and the Dominican Republic with respect to the fungibility of foreign aid are described and related to characteristics of the three economies. Section VII provides conclusions.

II Sri Lanka: Politics, Economics, and Foreign Aid

Sri Lanka is one of only a few developing countries in which political regimes have regularly alternated as a result of a democratic electoral process. During the years covered by this study, 1960 to 1986, the party in power shifted four times. At the beginning of the period, the Freedom Party, advocate of strong state control of the economy, had been in office since 1956; the United National Party, with its more market-oriented economic policies, was elected in 1965 and served until 1970, when it was replaced by the Freedom Party. Seven years later, the United National Party was returned to power and was still in office in 1986.

Although the alternations of parties with very different orientations to economic policy resulted in policy reversals with respect to the expansion of the state enterprise sector and to shifting priorities concerning social-welfare expenditures and land reform, the most dramatic policy changes occurred after 1977.[5] The United National Party came to power after years of relatively slow overall growth of the economy. Its growth-oriented strategy emphasized liberalization of the heavily controlled domestic economy and international trade regime. A substantial devaluation of the currency and the abolition of most import controls were among the early changes. The responses to these policies included a large increase in foreign aid, in particular by the World Bank, which had little involvement in Sri Lanka during the years of the Freedom Party's tenure.

Over the period 1960–86, foreign aid averaged about 5 percent of GDP, more than 6 percent after 1977. It was an important component of government financing, equal to 26 percent of all domestically raised public revenues and covered 55 percent of the budget deficit, on average, over the period. Moreover, the concentration of economic activity in state enterprises and the extensive nationalizations of private firms carried out under the Freedom Party, which led to capital flight and very low levels of private investment, made government the principal source of investment. In turn foreign aid has been a major source of its investment funds. Therefore, we would expect to find that foreign aid played an important role in the determination of the size and distribution of public expenditures. Whether the aid-related patterns of public expenditures were consistent with donors' priorities or were substantially reoriented to fit different Sri Lankan preferences is the question we investigate.

III Estimating Equations

Irrespective of regime, the central government has been the initiator and implementer of public programs.[6] Given democratic choice of representatives, the government represents individuals choosing among private consumption and a variety of publicly provided goods. Yeitch argues that the budget division of the government is perceived as imposing "its wishes upon individual ministries, with few prospects of negotiation on their part. They regard the whole procedure more as an imposition by the budget division, providing little room for manouevre" (1987, 37).

Estimating equations of the determinants of government spending and taxing decisions that roughly reflect the depiction of the process in figure 16.1 are the following:

$$D_{it} = \beta_0 + \beta_1 GDP_t + \beta_2 FA_{it} + \beta_3 OFA_{it} + \beta_4 DUM + u_1 \qquad (2)$$

$$C_{gt} = \beta_5 + \beta_6 GDP_t + \beta_7 FAT_t + \beta_8 DUM + u_2 \qquad (3)$$

$$R_t = \beta_9 + \beta_{10} GDP_t + \beta_{11} FAT_t + \beta_{12} DUM + u_3. \qquad (4)$$

The variables thus generated must satisfy the government budget constraint,[7]

$$\Sigma_i D_{it} + C_{gt} + DS_t = R_t + FAT_t + DEF_t. \qquad (5)$$

The variable definitions are[8]

D_{it}: development investment expenditures, in category i, year t. The sectors are (1) agriculture; (2) transportation and communications; (3) health, education, and social services; (4) industry and energy; (5) other.

C_{gt}: current government expenditures, year t, including defense and administrative expenditures.

R_t: revenues raised from domestic sources, year t.

GDP_t: gross domestic product, year t.

FA_{it}: foreign aid actually disbursed by donors for expenditures category i, year t. For the period considered, almost all foreign aid was targeted to specific sectors. For agriculture, it is possible to disaggregate aid into grants and loans, and the equation for agricultural investment includes these as separate variables.

FAT_t: total foreign aid, year t ($= \Sigma FA_{i,t}$).

OFA_{it}: other foreign aid, year t (total foreign aid minus aid to expenditure category i).

DUM: takes the value 0 through 1977 and 1 thereafter.

DS_t: debt service, year t.

DEF_t: the budget deficit (or surplus) in year t.

All variables are per capita. The dummy reflects the transfer of power to the United National Party, with its market orientation as contrasted with the state control orientation of the Freedom Party which had controlled the economy for all of the period under study before 1977 with the exception of 1965–70,[9] and reflects a very large aggregate increase in expenditures after 1978–79.

Current expenditures, C_{gt}, and domestic revenues, R_t, are a function of GDP, total foreign aid, and the dummy variable. If categorical aid is spent on the purposes for which it is intended, we should find no significant relationships between total aid, FAT_t, on the one hand, and current expenditures. C_{gt}, or revenues, R_t, on the other. However, if aid is fungible, it may well be used to increase C_{gt} and/or decrease R_t.

These equations assume that the relative price of private and public goods is constant, that relative prices among government investment categories, D_i, remained constant, and that government officials choose a desired mix of public and private expenditures by determining revenue (and implicitly) disposable income. It is possible that both expenditure and revenue decisions represent the outcome of an intertemporal optimization policy and hence should include variables on the right-hand side that are not simultaneous with the dependent variables. However, given the country's major fiscal difficulties,[10] policymakers probably were not able to design an optimal path of expenditure or taxation. Initial efforts at estimation, using plausible lag structures, support this view.

There is also a possibility that equations (2)–(4) are subject to simultaneous equation bias. For example, a shock to C_{gt} will, via the national income identity, increase GDP and lead to a biased estimate of β_6 in (3). Since it is clear that the economy was primarily supply constrained during this period and the major determinant of GDP was production capacity, any Keynesian aspect to the determination of GDP in Sri Lanka would be small. As will be seen below, aid does affect investment and hence eventually increases the capital stock. Thus, in the long run GDP will be affected by aid. But it is likely that investment has an impact only with a lag. Thus, plausible specifications of the production function do not involve any of the dependent investment variables in equations (2)–(4) as independent variables. The production function would not require simultaneous estimation along with equations (2)–(4) but would stand on its own as part of a block recursive system.

Equations (2)–(4) have been estimated using a systems estimation procedure, seemingly unrelated regressions, SUR (Zellner 1962). SUR is employed as the error terms across equations (2)–(4), given (5), will be related, given that $n - 1$ of the equations imply the nth. The efficiency of the parameter estimates is improved by taking account of the correlation in the error terms across equations. DS_t is exogenous, depending on the borrowing pattern of earlier periods. DEF is endogenous, and the equation explaining it is the omitted equation.[11]

IV Empirical Results

A The Estimated Model

The model estimated for 1960 to 1986 is summarized in table 16.1. (The data sources and construction of variables are described in the data appendix). FA_i and OFA coefficients are generally significant at better than 5 percent; GDP has the correct sign and is significant for five of the seven equations. The dummy variable is significant in four of the seven equations and shows large positive shifts to investment in agriculture, in industry and energy, and in transportation and communications, as well as a substantial decrease in current expenditures. These shifts are consis-

TABLE 16.1. The Estimated Model (rupees per capita)

Expenditure Category	Const.	GDP	FA_i[a]	OFA_i	DUM	R^2	DW
Current expenditure	65.38*	.1904*	.3218**		−172.21*	.99	1.38
	(17.40)	(.0104)	(.1596)		(59.00)		
Agriculture	−.6786	.0215*		.2752***	74.88**	.98	2.07
	(9.72)	(.0060)		(.1544)	(36.99)		
Grants			1.7286*				
			(.1841)				
Loans			.2723**				
			(.1476)				
Industry and energy	6.36	.0041	.5390*	−.0902**	46.85*	.81	2.93
	(4.62)	(.0027)	(.2025)	(.0416)	(16.88)		
Transportation	6.78*	.0004	−1.9113*	.2374*	59.28*	.98	2.40
Communications	(1.75)	(.3372)	(.1752)	(.0241)	(5.98)		
Health, education,	−5.72*	.0096*	1.0328*	−.0838*	−.3834	.96	2.68
social services	(1.87)	(.0011)	(.1120)	(.0173)	(6.29)		
Other	−70.75*	.1089*	3.6284*	−1.1237*	86.55	.98	2.58
	(17.88)	(.0116)	(.6959)	(.1699)	(58.09)		
Own-source revenue	−22.28	.2284*	−.1484		−95.28	.98	1.16
	(27.26)	(.0163)	(.2499)		(92.53)		

Note: Standard errors are in parentheses. Significance levels: * $= 1\%$; ** $= 5\%$; *** $= 10\%$
[a]FAT for the current expenditure and own revenue equations

tent with announced government policy favoring investments in agriculture and infrastructure.[12] The adjusted R^2 is above .90 in all but the industry and energy equation. Durbin-Watson statistics permit us to assume there is no autoregression in the error term for five of the equations; in two cases, the value falls in the inconclusive range, but correction for autocorrelation in these equations does not lead to significantly different results.

B Direct and Indirect Effects of Foreign Aid

Foreign aid affects the various categories of investment expenditure in two ways. The *direct* effect is the change, ceteris paribus, in investment expenditure in a particular category that results from a change in own-category foreign aid, and is equal to the value of the regression coefficient of FA_i. Considerable variation in the direct effects of categorical aid is apparent in table 16.1. The direct impact of one rupee of categorical aid to health, education, and social services is about one rupee of additional investment expenditure, whereas aid to "other" investment increases such expenditures by 3.6 rupees. In contrast, a rupee of aid to industry and energy induces only .5 of a rupee of additional expenditure, implying a diversion of the remaining .5 to other purposes. Still more extreme is the result for the transportation and communications sector, where the coefficient on FA_i is negative, a result discussed below.

The effect of foreign aid to agriculture on own-investment depends upon whether the aid is a grant or a loan. Grant aid is quite stimulating — about 1.7 rupees of additional investment expenditure for every rupee of grant aid — whereas loans induce a small expenditure increase, presumably reflecting the smaller grant equivalent of a loan.[13]

Indirect effects arise as foreign aid for other purposes influences expenditures on category i and are reflected in the coefficients of OFA_i. It can be seen from table 16.1 that agricultural investment and transportation and communications respond positively to general aid increases, whereas the other investment groups — industry and energy, health and education, and the aggregated "other" group — experience a reduction in investment. Indirect effects may be explained by several general factors and one quite specific to Sri Lanka. The former include: (1) donors' local matching requirements that differ among categories of aid that are paid for by diverting expenditures from other categories; (2) the initiation of additional complementary investment projects in an expenditure category in which aid-related activity has been stimulated might be financed by a diversion from other sectors' foreign aid; agricultural-irrigation investments (the direct effect) might also lead to increased investment in other agricultural infrastructure, financed by funds shifted from other aid categories (the indirect effect). This mechanism could explain the positive indirect effect of aid on agricultural expenditure in table 16.2.

The negative FA_i coefficient in the transportation and communications equation noted earlier can be explained by the sharp fall in foreign aid to transportation and communications to nearly zero for a ten-year interval between 1967 and 1977. During this time the level of investment in the sector was maintained and even increased somewhat. Thus, the negative coefficient on the FA variable is not due to falling investment as aid increased but rather to the long period of declining aid but increasing investment. The positive coefficient of OFA_i in the transportation and communications investment equation suggests this expenditure was maintained by diverting the aid from other categories, thus accounting for some of the other negative coefficients on OFA_i.

Donors providing categorical aid do not intend to support increases in current expenditures or decreases in tax effort. Nevertheless, the results reported in table 16.1 indicate that Rs. 1 of aid in Sri Lanka increases current expenditure by Rs. .3. Higher levels of public consumption may accurately reflect preferences of Sri Lankan citizens. Aid may also have decreased the tax effort, although this relationship is not statistically significant.

The coefficients of the dummy variable are consistent with the pol-

TABLE 16.2. Foreign Aid Induced Changes in Expenditure (change in expenditure associated with one rupee of total foreign aid, prorated in proportion of average categorical aid)

	Associated Expenditure Changes			
	(1) Aid Share (FA_i/FAT)	(2) Direct $(\beta_i dFA_i)$	(3) Indirect $(\beta_i dOFA_i)$	(4) Total $(2 + 3)$
Current expenditure	0			.3218**
Agriculture	.547		.1247	.4745
Loans	(.138)	.2385		
Grants	(.409)	.1113		
Industry and energy	.139	.0749	−.0777	.0028**
Transportation and communications	.094	−.1120	.2151	.1031
Health, education, social services	.058	.0599	−.0789	−.0190*
Other	.160	.5805	−.9439	−.3634**
Own-source revenue				−.1484

Note: * and ** indicate significant difference from value in first column using a "*t*" test at .01, .05 significance level.

icy changes announced after the election of the United Freedom Party in 1977, namely, a shift to investment expenditures, with an emphasis on infrastructure, agriculture, and industry and energy, and a shift away from current expenditures.

V Is Foreign Aid Fungible?

A The Pattern of Expenditure Shifts

Fungibility, defined here as a statistically significant difference between the sectoral pattern of donor lending and recipient expenditures, depends on the sum of the direct and indirect effects. For example, one rupee of categorical aid to health, education, and social services (HES) stimulates an additional rupee of investment in HES. However, because there is an indirect effect of the change in aggregate foreign aid (comprised of aid to other categories of expenditures) as estimated by the OFA_i coefficient, the effect on D_{HES} of a change of *total* foreign aid by one rupee will differ from the direct effect. Indeed it will be shown that the indirect effect of foreign aid to Sri Lanka on investment in health, education, and social services more than offsets the direct effect.

To calculate the existence and extent of fungibility among expenditure categories, we consider the simultaneous direct and indirect effects of aid on expenditures in each category by calculating the impact of an additional rupee of total aid, divided among categories according to their historic average fraction of total aid.[14] The change in development expenditure, D_i, induced by an aid package consisting of aid to all categories is

$$dD_i = \beta_1 dFA_i + \beta_2 dOFA_i, \tag{6}$$

where $dFA_i = (\overline{FA_i/FAT})dFAT$ and $dOFA_i = (1 - \overline{FA_i/FAT})dFAT$, a bar indicating the average value over the period. The simplest case of nondiversion results if $\beta_1 = 1$ and $\beta_2 = 0$, that is, all of its own aid is spent on investment. We choose, however, to define nondiversion more broadly, namely, that the entire aid program, directly targeted plus all other aid, increases spending in i by the amount of aid to category i. This can be seen in figure 16.2. Aid of I_1I_2 and T_1T_2 constitute the package. If $\beta_{1T} < 1$, the direct impact is a move from the initial level of spending, E, to F. Since $\beta_{2T} > 0$, there is an additional move to F'. At F', $\Delta T = T_1T_2$, the case of no diversion according to (6).

The results of this calculation are shown in table 16.2. The first

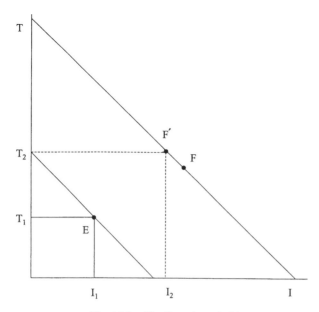

Fig. 16.2. No diversion of aid

column shows the prorated aid shares, (FA_i/FAT). Agriculture, for example, received on average .55 rupees per rupee of total aid. The second column shows the direct effect of aid, $\beta_i dFA_i$, the change that results from the increase in its own aid. The third column shows indirect aid effects, $\beta_i dOFA_i$, that is, the result of aid to other categories, OFA_i, having increased simultaneously by the amounts shown in column 1. Column 4 is the sum of direct and indirect expenditure changes, dD_i. If the change in total expenditure indicated in column 4 exceeds the prorated share of aid (in column 1), then aid has been diverted to the category. Conversely, if the change in expenditure falls short of the prorated share of categorical aid, then aid has been diverted from the category. A t-test is performed to determine whether the calculated divergence is significant.

On average, over the entire period, the direct and indirect effects of foreign aid shown in table 16.2 indicate that aid to agriculture and to transportation and communications increased investment for these purposes by an amount not significantly different from the goals of donors. In industry and energy and in health, education, and social services, foreign aid appears to have been largely diverted to other purposes — it had little net effect on investment. In the "other" investment group, the effect of aid is even more extreme, actually resulting in a decrease in investment. And, of course, the increase in current expenditures that appears to have been stimulated by increased foreign aid was not intended by donors.[15]

Thus, fungibility was very substantial (and statistically significant) in three development expenditure categories. Despite the fact that on the average .14 of each rupee of foreign aid is given for industry and energy, investment in this category hardly increased as a result; for health, education, and social services the picture is very similar; aid of about Rs. .06 per Rs. 1 of total aid leads to a slight decrease. Aid of Rs. .16 for "other" investments contrasts with a decrease in "other" investment expenditure of Rs. .36.

B Explanation of the Pattern of Fungibility

Is the ability to divert aid related to the cost of monitoring as described in equation (1)? Table 16.3 shows the ratio of FA_i/D_i for each of the expenditure categories and the absolute magnitude of diversion from table 16.2. Clearly there is no systematic relationship, although the fact that "other" registers the largest absolute displacement and is the sector in which FA_i/D_i is lowest is suggestive. Examining other variables in equation (1) explains this general lack of association. First, there were twenty-eight donors during the period being examined, many of them participating in aid in some years, dropping out in others (table 16.4). As can be seen from the list of countries within the "aid group" in table 16.4, they would not necessarily have gotten along well with the nations in the "nonaid group." Moreover, even within the consortium, coordina-

TABLE 16.3. Aid, Expenditures, and Aid Diversion

Sector	(1) Average Annual Aid (rupees)	(2) Average Annual Total Expenditures (rupees)	(3) (1)/(2)	(4) Diversion[a]
Agriculture				
Grants	23.21			
Loans	68.72			
Total	91.93	175.13	.52	−.07
Industry and energy	23.41	35.65	.66	−.101**
Transportation and communications	15.85	34.49	.46	.009
Health, education, social services	9.83	22.18	.44	−.077*
Other-source revenue	26.95	251.77	.09	−.54*

Note: * significant at .01, ** significant at .05 (see table 16.2).
[a]Diversion is measured as column (1) − column (4) in table 16.2.

tion among members was limited, and they appear to have engaged in little effective monitoring of the activities of the Sri Lankan government. The Operations Evaluation Department of the World Bank, the group in change of ex post evaluation of World Bank efforts, in a remarkably candid analysis of World Bank efforts in Sri Lanka, wrote the following:

> In general, the Government (of Sri Lanka) appears to prefer minimal coordination among donors, appearing to prefer one-to-one dealings. One view is that this approach enhances its negotiating position. In addition, donors differ in the extent of their interest in enhanced coordination, and in some cases view other donors as competitors. Several bilateral donors specifically mentioned their interest in financing projects that are likely to be successful, not sensitive politically at home or in Sri Lanka, visible, relatively easy to implement and attractive to their commercial interests. Coordination and division of labor, therefore, may be more attractive in theory than in practice. The Bank too is regarded by some donors as just another, and occasionally competing, player. . . . the Bank accepted the role as coordinator (of the aid consortium) only after it was understood and agreed among all participants that the Bank would not interfere with individual bilateral discussions, but would only attempt to ensure that in those discussions no elements of the program were left uncovered. (World Bank 1987, 27–28, 59)

The rest of the document from which this quotation is taken, as well as analysis of the aid process in Sri Lanka by Levy (1989) and Yeitch (1987) provides further confirmation of the disinterest of donors in coordinating their efforts.

In the major recipient sector, donors and Sri Lankan policymakers appear to have had similar preferences, and the absence of aid diversion from agriculture is not surprising in the context of Sri Lanka's history. One of the recurring themes, across the alternating governments, is the preoccupation with agriculture, particularly as a potential generator of jobs with low marginal capital-labor ratios. Each of the governments tried to enlarge the amount of agricultural land available through irrigation projects. The Mahaweli-Ganga program, a thirty-year development project designed to add nine hundred thousand acres of irrigable land and 500 MW of hydropower, was begun in 1970 under the aegis of the Freedom Party. After a change in name to the Accelerated Mahaweli Development Project, it became the major investment of the United

TABLE 16.4. Aid Disbursements 1977-87

	1970	1971	1972	1973	1974	1975	1976
AID GROUP							
Australia	0.9	1.0	1.1	2.2	4.2	8.3	2.0
Belgium	—	—	—	—	—	—	—
Canada	8.4	5.5	5.6	3.7	5.1	11.5	11.5
Denmark	1.2	0.4	0.2	2.1	0.7	0.2	0.6
EEC	1.2	—	—	1.4	2.2	13.1	0.6
Finland	—	—	—	—	—	—	—
France	4.6	2.9	5.6	5.3	3.2	7.1	11.2
Germany	3.3	2.3	4.3	9.3	17.7	12.3	8.7
India	4.8	2.9	2.4	2.3	3.9	2.4	4.7
Italy	1.7	0.9	1.8	0.3	0.3	1.3	—
Japan	5.1	7.6	5.5	9.2	9.2	18.1	11.3
Netherlands	—	—	—	—	—	3.3	4.3
Norway	—	—	—	—	—	—	—
Sweden[a]	—	1.6	—	2.4	3.5	8.6	6.8
Switzerland	—	—	—	—	—	—	—
United Kingdom[b]	10.3	16.1	7.4	4.6	3.0	4.7	7.4
United States	9.9	10.9	25.6	8.5	8.4	26.6	32.7
of which: CARE	(1.3)	(1.8)	(1.5)	(1.1)	(3.2)	(4.9)	(5.5)
Asian Development Bank	1.5	2.8	4.0	3.8	3.0	5.0	8.2
UN Group	0.3	2.3	0.9	0.6	2.6	19.1	16.6
of which: WFP	(0.2)	(1.7)	(0.6)	(0.4)	(1.5)	(6.9)	(13.3)
FAO	(—)	(—)	(—)	(—)	(—)	(—)	(1.9)
World Bank group	1.9	7.5	5.8	10.5	15.6	18.7	6.4
Subtotal aid group	55.1	64.7	70.2	66.2	82.6	160.3	133.0
NON-AID GROUP							
Centrally planned economies	8.8	35.0	13.2	1.2	29.1	3.9	14.9
IFAD	—	—	—	—	—	—	—
Kuwait Fund	—	—	—	—	—	—	9.6
OPEC Fund	—	—	—	—	—	—	—
Saudi Fund	—	—	—	—	—	6.7	—
Others[e]	—	—	—	—	—	34.5[f]	12.6[g]
Subtotal non-aid group	8.8	35.0	13.2	1.2	29.1	45.1	37.1
Total Disbursements	63.9	99.7	83.4	67.4	111.7	205.4	170.1

Source: World Bank 1987

Note: There are no changes in the disbursement figures provided for the period 1970–85. In the 1986 disbursements, upward revisions have been made in respect of aid received from Australia, NORAD, Switzerland and USAID.

[a]Excludes US$2.92, 11.8 and 11.2 million disbursed under Swedish Export Credit for Kotmale Project, respectively in 1982, 1983, and 1984.

[b]Excludes US$10.1 million in 1983 and $15.0 million in 1984 disbursed under Manufacturer's Hanover Trust Company (UK) Loan for Victoria Project.

[e]Excludes US$14.43 million disbursed under Salomon Brothers Incorporation (USA) loan for low cost Housing Programme.

1977	1978	1979	1980	1981	1982	1983	1984	1985	1986	1987
1.7	1.7	2.9	4.2	6.6	9.3	4.5	7.8	0.7	0.8	—
—	—	—	—	—	—	0.2	0.9	0.9	0.1	—
14.7	14.0	16.6	27.8	28.9	28.7	34.5	31.2	22.8	19.6	18.0
0.3	0.9	0.5	3.5	2.5	2.9	1.1	0.2	0.4	0.8	4.1
6.2	3.0	4.4	0.3	16.0	11.4	11.3	14.4	12.1	5.6	6.5
—	—	—	0.6	2.4	4.4	5.5	5.3	5.9	13.4	15.3
3.4	4.5	7.1	5.3	18.5	10.7	13.9	8.6	12.4	9.4	16.3
11.5	28.2	24.2	13.4	5.8	18.5	49.0	44.0	47.3	63.5	27.1
6.2	13.0	9.5	9.1	1.5	3.1	6.6	0.4	0.1	0.2	1.4
0.7	—	—	—	—	—	1.1	—	—	—	3.0
17.2	38.1	37.9	37.7	49.9	50.1	54.2	61.9	86.2	118.7	101.2
9.6	28.3	19.8	11.3	42.4	15.5	13.9	23.9	15.7	10.3	12.7
1.1	5.5	8.3	12.3	16.7	11.8	4.7	11.2	8.7	10.3	12.6
9.4	7.4	34.4	22.8	22.1	21.1	26.4	31.3	34.2	23.8	18.3
—	—	—	0.1	0.6	—	6.9	4.2	4.6	6.2	0.1
2.7	8.9	19.1	63.0	43.6	52.6	36.5	28.7	6.3	15.3	7.3
40.6	39.9	46.2	61.2	37.8	61.7[c]	66.6[d]	88.2	95.7	61.7	44.2
(5.0)	(5.5)	(5.4)	(7.8)	(6.1)	(5.9)	(5.4)	(7.0)	(5.6)	(3.3)	(6.2)
7.7	28.2	10.3	5.3	10.2	18.0	18.8	37.1	30.9	41.9	48.5
15.1	6.4	12.0	13.4	12.2	12.8	16.7	11.8	24.1	21.8	27.1
(8.9)	(0.8)	(2.7)	(1.6)	(1.5)	(2.8)	(4.0)	(2.5)	(8.7)	(6.9)	(12.0)
(2.2)	(0.8)	(3.3)	(−)	(−)	(−)	(−)	(−)	(1.1)	(1.0)	(0.3)
13.9	12.8	12.2	20.2	28.0	59.9	74.7	107.3	73.3	88.9	84.6
162.0	240.8	265.4	311.5	335.7	392.5	447.1	518.4	482.3	513.1	448.3
12.3	5.4	0.8	0.1	16.8	5.4	1.0	1.8	1.7	—	9.8
—	—	—	2.7	3.4	2.0	1.6	3.2	5.1	5.8	2.7
5.3	3.9	1.7	4.7	3.1	1.2	—	—	1.2	10.1	3.8
8.0	1.0	—	1.4	9.6	5.5	3.0	4.0	3.1	2.1	3.1
—	—	—	—	—	—	3.0	7.7	7.9	15.5	2.6
16.1[h]	0.1	0.2	5.5[i]	1.1	1.6	0.7	0.3	0.2	0.3	1.6
41.7	10.4	2.7	14.4	34.0	15.7	9.3	18.0	19.2	33.8	23.6
203.7	251.2	268.1	325.9	369.7	408.2	456.4	536.4	501.5	546.9	471.9

Notes (cont.)

[d]Excludes US$6.18 million disbursed under Salomon Brothers Incorporation (USA) loan for low cost Housing Programme.

[e]Excludes the following loans: Euro-currency loan of US$50 million disbursed in 1980; Euro-currency loan of US$75 million disbursed in 1981; Euro-currency loan of US$100 million of which US$40, 25, and 35 million was disbursed, respectively in 1982, 1983, and 1984; and Japanese Yen Bonds of Yen 3,000 million ($2.14 million) disbursed in December 1982.

[f]Includes Iran loan of US$32.0 million.

[g]Includes UAE convertible currency loan of US$12.0 million.

[h]Includes Libyan loan of US$15.0 million.

[i]Represents the Iraq loan for oil subsidy.

National Party after 1977 and absorbed a large fraction of the increase in foreign aid in the ensuing years.

It has been argued that the Mahaweli project diverted substantial resources from investment in other areas to meet its cost overruns and associated expenditures (World Bank 1987, 28ff.). The model estimated here certainly supports the proposition that agricultural investment took precedence over other developmental investments. The GDP coefficient in the agricultural-investment equation is larger than in all but the "other" category. In addition, the largest significant DUM coefficient is in agriculture, reflecting the large increases in public investment after the 1977 election and the reorientation of government priorities among sectors. However, since a rupee of foreign aid to agriculture has stimulated investment expenditure increases of equal magnitude (table 16.2), the data do not support the proposition that the estimated aid diversions from other sectors' investments were allocated to agricultural investment. The overall picture, however, is that an additional rupee of foreign aid increases total development expenditures, net, by only Rs. .20; increases current expenditures by Rs. .32; and decreases own-source revenues by about Rs. .15 (the latter statistically insignificant). Thus, by the budget constraint of equation (5), about Rs. .33 per rupee of foreign aid is utilized for debt service and deficit reduction.

Thus, foreign aid to Sri Lanka appears to have been extremely fungible and to have had many of the negative aspects identified by skeptics. Diversion of aid initially appears paradoxical if Yeitch's (1987) description of the budget process is correct, namely, that the Sri Lankan government decided on its sectoral priorities and asked aid donors to finance those projects that were most intensely desired. Seemingly, this would lead to a congruence between the objectives of donors and recipient. Nevertheless, ministries whose programs were not financed by aid will have had some of their projects adopted and financed by domestic resources, hence the finding of fungibility in our calculations.

VI Sri Lanka, the Dominican Republic, and Indonesia Compared

We began the empirical investigation of fungibility assuming that the response of recipients to foreign aid would vary and that characteristics of individual countries would influence the extent and pattern of fungibility. While cross-country studies of fungibility are possible, many issues of interest can be addressed only by detailed analysis of the historical experience of individual countries. Analysis across countries may obscure important differences in the economies and in the political environments of countries receiving foreign aid, and these differences may be reflected in the ways in which foreign aid was used by them.

The two countries considered in our earlier studies, Indonesia and the Dominican Republic, provide polar examples of the fungibility of foreign aid (Pack and Pack 1990, 1993). They were not selected to represent extremes — the result emerged from the analysis summarized in table 16.5, panel A. In Indonesia, no diversion was found from development investment to current government expenditures or to tax reduction; all aid was used to increase investment, largely for the purposes for which it was given. In contrast, in the Dominican Republic nearly total shifting occurred — aid did not increase investment in the development expenditure categories. Foreign aid was largely used to finance budget deficits. The preceding results in this paper show that in Sri Lanka, about 20 percent of each rupee of aid is devoted to investment expenditures, 15 percent to reducing own source revenue, 32 percent to increasing current expenditures, and 33 percent to financing the deficit and debt service. More disaggregated results, not shown in table 16.5, reinforce the aggregate findings. In the Dominican Republic there was no development expenditure category that escaped almost total diversion

TABLE 16.5. Comparisons of Sri Lanka, Indonesia, and the Dominican Republic

	Sri Lanka	Indonesia	Dominican Republic
A. Percentage of Aid Spent on:			
Development expenditures	20	100	−5
Indirect investments	NA	NA	−30
Current expenditures	32	0	8
Own-source revenue	−15	0	−39
Financing of government deficit	33	0	88
B. Determinants of Monitoring Costs			
FAT/G (total aid/government spending)	14	19	8
N (number of donors)	29	23	23
W (Hirfindahl index of weighted aid)	.09	.19	.36
C. Structural Comparisons			
Aid/GDP	5	4	1
Deficit/own-source revenue	47	10	12

Note: NA = not applicable. Source of data on number of donors and their aid commitments is OECD, *Geographic Distribution of financial flows to developing countries,* various issues, OECD, Paris.

of foreign aid, whereas in Indonesia there is no category in which there was any diversion of aid at all.

We argued above that one determinant of the extent of diversion was monitoring costs as described in equation (1). Values of some of these variables are presented in panel B in table 16.5. Rather than employing the number of donors alone, a Hirfindahl index of weighted aid, $w = \Sigma_i S_i^2$, is employed where S_i is the share in total aid of each donor.

Of the variables indicating monitoring costs, FAT/G might explain some of the large fungibility measured for the Dominican Republic and the low fungibility in Indonesia. Effective monitoring was more likely in Indonesia, where aid was on average about 19 percent of public expenditures, compared with 8 percent in the Dominican Republic and 14 percent in Sri Lanka. There are few significant differences in monitoring costs that would otherwise explain the major differences in behavior between Sri Lanka and Indonesia. In individual categories of development expenditures, the value of FA_i/D_i in Indonesia, not shown in table 16.5 but corresponding to the third column of table 16.3, was not significantly greater than in Sri Lanka.[16] There were large numbers of aid donors, and the concentration of aid among donors as measured by the Hirfindahl index was greater in Indonesia, which suggests a greater possibility of monitoring. However, it was still greater in the Dominican Republic, which exhibited almost complete diversion of aid. Given commercial interests and Indonesia's attractiveness as a potential market, interest in striking bilateral agreements was also great. How then can the difference in outcomes be explained?

Our conjecture is that the difference may be related to the incentive of each country to diverge from donors' preferences. Sri Lanka exhibited a much larger public-sector deficit relative to internally raised revenues. The greater deficit relative to own-source revenues provided a temptation to utilize aid to finance it and avoid inflationary issuance of money. In the period studied, Sri Lanka's deficit was 47 percent of its domestically raised revenue, providing a strong incentive to finance part of the deficit by utilizing some of the aid inflow for this purpose. In contrast, in Indonesia, deficits relative to tax collections were relatively small, 10 percent, and there was little need to utilize aid to cover budgetary deficits (table 16.5). While it is possible that the deficit/own-revenue figure is partly endogenous, the government's tax-raising efforts depending on how much aid inflow it anticipates, the estimated equations do not reveal a significant relation between revenues and the inflow of aid.

In the Dominican Republic the deficit averaged about 12 percent of own-source revenues, compared with 10 percent in Indonesia. The small difference in the averages masks a major divergence between the two countries, namely that deficits were increasing over the period in the Dominican Republic and declining in Indonesia. In the Dominican Republic, the deficit had been about 1–10 percent before 1978 but ranged between 5 and 42 percent of own-source revenues after that. In Indonesia, the deficit averaged about 10 percent of own-source revenues, but the trend was the reverse of that in the Dominican Republic; about 8–22 percent before 1976 and between 2 and 10 percent thereafter. Thus, deficit pressures were greatest in the Dominican Republic when aid was substantial, with the reverse the case in Indonesia.

VII Conclusions

The results of this essay suggest a number of conclusions. The evidence indicates that in Sri Lanka categorical aid is fungible. Aid intended by donors for development was converted into unconstrained income used for purposes more consistent with Sri Lanka's policymakers' preferences than with donor intentions. Aid was diverted not only among development categories but from development spending to current spending, revenue reduction, and deficit finance. Given that diversion occurred in two of the three countries across the five or six categories that we have examined, it is likely to be an even more severe problem among finer expenditure categories. The micromanagement of aid allocations does not appear to be an easily obtainable objective. The existence and extent of fungibility will vary with local circumstances. The outcomes in the three countries analyzed are very different: no fungibility in Indonesia, total fungibility in the Dominican Republic, and partial fungibility in Sri Lanka. Explanations of these differences may lie in the relative importance of foreign aid to the local economy and its effect on the cost of donor monitoring and the extent to which fiscal stringency in a country increases the incentives for diversion of aid. On the basis of our limited investigation in only three countries, the most important variable appears to be the health of the fiscal system.

We have eschewed normative questions. Aid diversion presumably increases the utility of beneficiaries, as they could have complied with donor intentions. The objective of the recipient governments may not include rapid growth but benefits for a specific region or sector, choices that raise problems for donors unless their objectives with respect to desirable beneficiaries are congruent with that of the government. Equally problematic in the presence of fungibility is the evaluation of the benefits of specific projects or sectoral loans, an issue of increasing importance to donors. In the aggregate, cross-country studies (Mosely, Hudson, and Horrell 1987) demonstrate that aid is not related to growth. Aid advocates in the donor community have argued, nevertheless, that individual projects have significant benefits (Cassen and Associates 1994) and a substantial effort has been made to retrospectively assess the benefits and costs of projects, most notably by the Operations Evaluation Department of the World Bank (World Bank 1994). Nevertheless, however careful the ex ante planning of a project in terms of social cost-benefit analysis and regardless of the measured ex post rate of return, the presence of fungibility indicates that the project or program that requires measurement is the alternative one facilitated by aid. In the case of Sri Lanka, a donor's "successful" industrial project as measured by social cost-benefit analysis may have in fact largely permitted the government to devote its own revenue to an increase in government consumption. Or it may have enabled the government to undertake its preferred domestically financed project that exhibits a negative rate of return. Such issues have yet to be confronted by the donor community.

Finally, the results in this essay and our previous analysis of the Dominican Republic imply that aid givers can be fooled for long periods of time. An alternate interpretation, whose implications would be very difficult to test, is that the aid agencies were aware, at least roughly, that aid recipients were not adhering to the intentions of donors to raise investment in targeted sectors. The failure of the consortium to enforce outcomes (see the quotation above from World Bank 1987) and the implicit approval of LDC budget policies by bilateral donors suggests a number of possibilities: (1) the legislative bodies enacting foreign aid use project aid to mollify antiaid sentiments among voters but are well aware of the possibility that funds will be shifted or used improperly; (2) the national aid agencies responsible for administering the aid programs are anxious to transfer resources to recipients even where parliaments are not so disposed and disregard such violations — the principals, parliaments voting these expenditures, did not adequately monitor their own agents, the aid officials; (3) even if the aid officials were aware of the shifting of funds, they perceived no easy remedy. The experience of the IMF with redressing the violation of conditionality agreements suggests remedies are not easily designed, even for a major lender whose macroeconomic benchmarks are much easier to monitor. Each of these possibilities raises questions about the motivations for aid that are beyond the purview of this essay.

Data Appendix

The foreign aid and expenditure data have been compiled from the Ministry of the Treasury's *Estimates of the Revenue and Expenditure of the Government of the Democratic Socialist Republic of Sri Lanka,* Department of Government Printing, Sri Lanka, various years. The data are disaggregated to nearly two hundred heads (various government agencies). The expenditure data are listed by ministry, but the same head may appear under different ministries in different years. The heads have been reaggregated for each year to form a consistent time series, by category of expenditure. The foreign-aid data are listed by head and are aggregated to the same category as the expenditure head.

The data on own-source revenues and the budget deficit have been taken from various issues of the International Monetary Fund's *Government Financial Statistics Yearbook* and the World Bank's *World Tables.* Population and GDP data also come from the latter and from the International Monetary Fund's *International Financial Statistics.*

NOTES

We received many useful comments while preparing this essay. Those of R. S. Eckaus and T. N. Srinivasan were particularly helpful. Part of this research was financed by a grant from the University of Pennsylvania Research Foundation. Excellent research assistance was provided by Arvid Lukauskas and Adam Rosen.

1. Srinivasan (1989) analyzes fungibility and its implications for food aid.

2. One reason for the small number of studies of individual countries is the difficulty of constructing time series that match donors' intended spending categories with the actual spending categories of recipients. Such series must be constructed from the often not very tidy government accounts of each country.

3. Cassen and Associates 1994 examines the qualitative effects of aid in many dimensions but does not address in a quantitative manner its effect on economic growth or its fungibility.

4. This is certainly the case if the object of monitoring is aggregate government spending in individual sectors. It might be argued that if there were a small number of projects, then site visits by donors could insure these were being implemented. However, there is no way of insuring, *for the sector as a whole,* that the funds financing these monitored projects have been additive rather than replacing the government's own funds, thus allowing expenditures on the margin to be reallocated to other sectors.

5. For example, when the United National Party came to power in 1965, it "recognized the need for fundamental restructuring of the economy. . . . [Nonetheless], the government had only limited success in restraining the growth of

expenditures on politically sensitive social welfare programs" (World Bank 1987, 6–7).

6. Yeitch 1987 has a good discussion of the budgeting process in Sri Lanka.

7. Virtually all aid to Sri Lanka in this period was project aid; hence it is not necessary to have an auxiliary budget constraint on the composition of foreign aid.

8. The data aggregation from the government accounts is complex and is briefly described in the appendix.

9. A dummy variable of zero versus one for party, for the entire period, would be the same as the dummy used here with the exception of the five intermediate years. In looking at the raw data, it is clear that no major systematic changes occurred during that short interim period. However, the major policy changes adopted subsequent to the 1977 change of government are obvious in the data — in the enormous increases in several categories of investment expenditures and in the increase in investment relative to current expenditures.

10. The budget deficit during the period covered averaged about 10 percent of GDP. Although it was only 6 percent in 1977, by 1980 it had reached 23 percent of GDP. As a proportion of domestic revenue the magnitude of the deficit was very large — nearly 50 percent on average over the period.

11. The results reported also suggest the possibility that the underlying data are generated by nonstationary time series and this may introduce further problems. The methods currently available for dealing with nonstationary time series in simultaneous-equation models are not sufficiently well developed to allow us to address the issues of concern.

12. For the net effect on agricultural spending see the discussion in sec. V.A.

13. It may also be that loans are sought for the investment purposes for which they are available, although the intention is in fact to use them for other purposes.

14. Average aid distributions are used in the simulation since the OFA variable is a composite of aid to each of the other categories. Therefore, we cannot separately estimate the indirect effects of each of the categories of aid on each of the other expenditure categories.

15. The sign of the total impact on current expenditures is consistent with the analysis of government preferences described by Yeitch 1987 and World Bank 1987.

16. The values of the FA_i/D_i for the five sectors in Indonesia were .23, .69, .47, .17, and .18.

REFERENCES

Bauer, Peter. 1972. *Dissent on Development.* Cambridge: Harvard University Press.
Boone, Peter. 1995. "Politics and the Effectiveness of Foreign Aid." National Bureau of Economics Working Paper 5308, Cambridge, Mass.
Bruton, Henry. 1969. "The Two Gap Approach to Aid and Development: Comment." *American Economic Review* 59:439–46.

Cashel-Cordo, Peter, and Steven G. Craig. 1990. "The Public Sector Impact of International Resource Transfers." *Journal of Development Economics* 32:17–42.

Cassen, Robert, and Associates. 1994. *Does Aid Work?* Oxford: Clarendon Press.

Chenery, Hollis, and Alan Strout. 1966. "Foreign Assistance and Economic Development." *American Economic Review* 56:679–733.

Craig, S. G., and R. P. Inman. 1986. "Education, Welfare, and the 'New' Federalism: State Budgeting in a Federalist Public Economy." In *Studies in State and Local Public Finance,* ed. H. Rosen. Chicago: University of Chicago Press.

Fei, John C. H., and Gustav Ranis. 1968. "Foreign Assistance and Economic Development: Comment." *American Economic Review* 58:897–912.

Gang, Ira N., and Haider Ali Khan. 1991. "Foreign Aid, Taxes, and Public Investment: The Case of India." *Journal of Development Economics* 34: 355–69.

Gramlich, Edward. 1977. "The Effects of Federal Grants on State-Local Expenditures: A Review of the Empirical Evidence." In *The Political Economy of Fiscal Federalism,* ed. W. Oates. Lexington, Mass.: Lexington Books.

Levy, Brian. 1989. "Foreign Aid in the Making of Economic Policy in Sri Lanka." *Policy Sciences* 22:437–61.

Luce, Thomas, and Janet Rothenberg Pack. 1984. "State Support under the New Federalism." *Journal of Policy Analysis and Management* 3:339–58.

Mosley, P., J. Hudson, and S. Horrell. 1987. "Aid, the Public Sector, and the Market in Less Developed Countries." *Economic Journal* 97:616–41.

Pack, Howard, and Janet Rothenberg Pack. 1990. "Is Foreign Aid Fungible: The Case of Indonesia." *Economic Journal* 100:188–94.

———. 1993. "Foreign Aid and the Question of Fungibility." *Review of Economics and Statistics* 75:258–65.

Papanek, Gustav. 1972. "The Effect of Aid and other Resource Transfers on Savings and Growth in Less Developed Countries." *Economic Journal* 82:934–50.

———. 1973. "Aid, Foreign Private Investment, Savings, and Growth in Less Developed Countries." *Journal of Political Economy* 81:120–30.

Singer, H. W. 1965. "External Aid: For Plans or Projects." *Economic Journal* 75:539–45.

Srinivasan, T. N. 1989. "Food Aid: A Cause of Development Failure or an Instrument for Success?" *World Bank Economic Review* 3:39–65.

Weisskopf, Thomas. 1972. "The Impact of Foreign Capital Inflow on Domestic Savings in Underdeveloped Countries." *Journal of International Economics* 2:25–38.

World Bank. 1987. *Sri Lanka and the World Bank: A Review of a Relationship.* A World Bank Operations Evaluation Study. Washington, D.C.: World Bank.

———. 1994. *Assessing Development Effectiveness: Evaluation in the World*

Bank and the International Finance Corporation. Washington D.C.: World Bank.

Yeitch, Michael D. 1987. "Resource Allocation among Competing Projects: Budgetary Procedures in Sri Lanka." *Manchester Papers on Development* 3:22–44.

Zellner, A. 1962. "An Efficient Method of Estimating Seemingly Unrelated Regressions and Tests for Aggregation Bias." *Journal of the American Statistical Association* 57:348–68.

Contributors

Albert Berry — Department of Economics, University of Toronto

Willem H. Buiter — Faculty of Economics, University of Cambridge

Jonathan Eaton — Department of Economics, Boston University

Robert Evenson — Economic Growth Center, Yale University

Gary S. Fields — School of Industrial and Labor Relations, Cornell University

Mark Gersovitz — Department of Economics, The Johns Hopkins University

Koichi Hamada — Economic Growth Center, Yale University

Yujiro Hayami — Aoyama Gakuin University

Samuel Kortum — Department of Economics, Boston University

Anne O. Krueger — Department of Economics, Stanford University

Poorti Marino — Department of Economics, Boston University

Jennifer C. O'Hara Mitchell — Cornell University

Richard R. Nelson — School of International and Public Affairs, Columbia University

Keijiro Otsuka — Faculty of Economics, Tokyo Metropolitan University

Howard Pack — Wharton Center, University of Pennsylvania

Janet Rothenberg Pack	Wharton Center, University of Pennsylvania
Jonathan Putnam	Charles River Associates
Mark R. Rosenzweig	Department of Economics, University of Pennsylvania
Gary R. Saxonhouse	Department of Economics, University of Michigan
T. N. Srinivasan	Economic Growth Center, Yale University
Frances Stewart	Department of Economics, Oxford University
Joseph E. Stiglitz	The World Bank
Brian D. Wright	Department of Agricultural Economics, University of California, Berkeley

Index